THE VAJRABHAIRAVA TANTRA

Studies in Indian and Tibetan Buddhism

This series was conceived to provide a forum for publishing outstanding new contributions to scholarship on Indian and Tibetan Buddhism and also to make accessible seminal research not widely known outside a narrow specialist audience, including translations of appropriate monographs and collections of articles from other languages. The series strives to shed light on the Indic Buddhist traditions by exposing them to historical-critical inquiry, illuminating through contextualization and analysis these traditions' unique heritage and the significance of their contribution to the world's religious and philosophical achievements.

Members of the Editorial Board
Tom Tillemans (co-chair), Emeritus, University of Lausanne
Leonard van der Kuijp (co-chair), Harvard University
Shrikant Bahulkar, Bhandarkar Oriental Research Institute
José Cabezón, University of California, Santa Barbara
Georges Dreyfus, Williams College, Massachusetts
Vincent Eltschinger, École Pratique des Hautes Études
Janet Gyatso, Harvard University
Paul Harrison, Stanford University
Toni Huber, Humboldt University, Berlin
Pascale Hugon, Austrian Academy of the Sciences
Shoryu Katsura, Ryukoku University, Kyoto
Kataoka Kei, Kyushu University, Fukuoka
Thupten Jinpa Langri, Institute of Tibetan Classics, Montreal
Chenkuo Lin, National Chengchi University, Taipei
Hong Luo, Peking University
Cristina Scherrer-Schaub, University of Lausanne
Ernst Steinkellner, Emeritus, University of Vienna
Jan Westerhoff, Oxford University
Jeson Woo, Dongguk University, Seoul
Shaoyong Ye, Peking University
Chizuko Yoshimizu, Tsukuba University

STUDIES IN INDIAN AND TIBETAN BUDDHISM

The Vajrabhairava Tantra

A Study and Annotated Translation

Aleksandra Wenta

Wisdom

Wisdom Publications, Inc.
132 Perry Street
New York, NY 10014 USA
wisdom.org

Library of Congress Cataloging-in-Publication Data
Names: Wenta, Aleksandra, author.
Title: The Vajrabhairava Tantra: a study and annotated translation / Aleksandra Wenta.
Other titles: Tripiṭaka. Sūtrapiṭaka. Tantra. Vajrabhairavatantra. English.
Description: New York, NY, USA: Wisdom, [2025] | Series: Studies in Indian and Tibetan Buddhism | Includes bibliographical references and index.
Identifiers: LCCN 2024047608 (print) | LCCN 2024047609 (ebook) | ISBN 9781614298472 (hardcover) | ISBN 9781614298694 (ebook)
Subjects: LCSH: Tripiṭaka. Sūtrapiṭaka. Tantra. Vajrabhairavatantra.—Criticism, interpretation, etc. | Vajrabhairava (Buddhist deity)
Classification: LCC BQ2180.V347 W46 2025 (print) | LCC BQ2180.V347 (ebook) | DDC 294.382—dc23/eng/20250304
LC record available at https://lccn.loc.gov/2024047608
LC ebook record available at https://lccn.loc.gov/2024047609

ISBN 978-1-61429-847-2 ebook ISBN 978-1-61429-869-4

29 28 27 26 25
5 4 3 2 1

Cover and interior design by Gopa & Ted2, Inc.

Printed on acid-free paper that meets the guidelines for permanence and durability of the Production Guidelines for Book Longevity of the Council on Library Resources.

Printed in Canada.

Dedicated to the memory of
Kazimierz Wenta (1937–2017).

"Solitary Hero" Vajrabhairava, fifteenth century, Tibet.
The Metropolitan Museum of Art, New York.

Contents

Preface ix

Abbreviations xiii

Introduction 1

Part I. Study

1. An Introduction to the *Vajrabhairava Tantra* 13
2. Vajrabhairava in India 59
3. Tibetan Accounts of Vajrabhairava's Origins 69
4. Lalitavajra's Rediscovery of the *Vajrabhairava Tantra* 81
5. Tantric Sādhana 95
6. The Influence of Nondual Śaiva-Śākta Traditions 153
7. Early Tantric Magic 171
8. Conclusion and Prospects for Future Research 191

Part II. Annotated Translation

Notes on the Translation 197

1. Explanation of the Maṇḍala 201
2. Accomplishment of All Magical Recipes 223
3. Extraction of the Mantra 243
4. Visualization 255
5. The Ritual of Painting the *Paṭa* 277

Preface

It was a sunny day at the Thiksey Monastery in Ladakh when I first encountered Vajrabhairava. My friend Jaiwanti and I were exploring the monastery, marveling at its ancient architecture and serene ambiance. As we wandered through the labyrinthine corridors, we stumbled upon a shrine. Its doors were secured with a lock, but two panels stood slightly ajar. Drawn by an inexplicable magnetism and the darkness peeping from within, I couldn't resist sneaking through the wooden doors. There he was: a four-meter-tall black statue of Vajrabhairava, commanding the room with an awe-inspiring presence. The atmosphere was eerie, the space pervaded with the smell of burned oil and alcohol. It was unsettling yet strangely familiar. Little did I know then that Vajrabhairava would become the topic of this book.

The importance of the *Vajrabhairava Tantra* and lack of a proper Sanskrit edition was first brought to my attention by Péter-Dániel Szántó, who was then supervising my MPhil thesis at Oxford. Upon consulting with Prof. Alexis Sanderson, who confirmed the *Vajrabhairava Tantra*'s significance for understanding the formative phase of tantric Buddhism, I decided to focus my doctoral research on editing this text and understanding its contents. My academic journey at Oxford University, coupled with the privilege of studying Śaivism under the esteemed guidance of Alexis Sanderson, profoundly shaped my understanding of tantric Buddhism. That formative experience instilled in me a deep appreciation for the broader tantric milieu, leading me to perceive tantric Buddhism as a dynamic and interconnected tradition rather than an isolated sectarian practice. This approach allows us to recognize the themes, practices, and philosophical underpinnings that unite these various tantric traditions.

In this study, I aim to explore the *Vajrabhairava Tantra* as a product of this broader tantric milieu. By examining its relationship to Śaivism and Śāktism, we can gain a deeper understanding of the text's significance and see more clearly its particular contributions to the development of tantric thought and practice. By adopting a comparative approach, this study endeavors to reposition the *Vajrabhairava Tantra* within the dynamic landscape of medieval Indian tantra—a space that transcended established sectarian identities. This book examines the *Vajrabhairava Tantra*'s alignment with key tenets of both Śaivism and Buddhism. It investigates the text's engagement with concepts common to the tantric milieu, such as the tantric path, initiations, and the ultimate goal of liberation. Ultimately, this study aspires to contribute to a more inclusive comprehension of tantric Buddhism by acknowledging the fluidity of sectarian boundaries within the medieval Indian context. By highlighting commonalities and differences between the *Vajrabhairava Tantra* and tantric texts from other traditions, I hope to offer a more comprehensive and nuanced interpretation of this enigmatic scripture.

Acknowledgments

This book owes a great debt of gratitude to Péter-Dániel Szántó and Alexis Sanderson. I am deeply grateful to these outstanding scholars and kind mentors for their vast knowledge, invaluable guidance, generous allocation of time, and personal encourgement. Their support has been instrumental both in embarking on this work and in bringing it to fruition. This book is an adaptation of my doctoral thesis carried out at the University of Oxford under the supervision of professors Ulrike Roesler and Diwakar Acharya. To my esteemed teachers, I extend heartfelt thanks. Their emphasis on rigorous inquiry and critical thinking has been pivotal in the realization of this work. Among other teachers who contributed to this project was the late Gen-la Tsering Gonkatsang, who taught me Tibetan. At the final stage, the work benefited greatly from feedback by John Newman, Francesco Sferra, and Robert Mayer that substiantially enriched the contents. I am very grateful to Shaoyong Ye for giving me access to the previously unknown Sanskrit manuscripts of the *Vajrabhairava Tantra* and Kumāracandra's *pañjikā* held at the Peking University. The writing-up phase of this research was financially supported by a Robert H. N. Ho Dissertation Fellowship in Buddhist Studies. I would like to thank Wisdom for providing me with a platform to share this work with the world, and to my editor, David Kittelstrom, whose keen eye and dedication have been instrumental in bringing this book to life.

I am grateful to my former students at Nālandā University for being the source of inspiration and for (unknowingly to them) giving me the strength to presevere through some of the darkest hours of my life. Among them, I am especially grateful to my "tantric" group—that is, Sourajit Ghosh, Sanjivani Dwivedi, Fernando José Benetti, Aditya Jha, Andrei-Valentin Bacrău, Inder Chaudhary, Kristina Ovcharenko, Shubham Arora, Aditya Chaturvedi, Nguyen Trinh, Yenten Thinley, and others, who enthusiastically endured our class readings of the *Vajrabhairava Tantra* and other "bizarre" texts. The legacy of Lalitavajra was once gain brought to light at Nālandā through our readings, discussions, and analyses.

At least, but not last, I must acknowledge the enduring support of my loving family, my mother Bożena and my sister Kasia. I am grateful to my husband, Andrea Acri, for insightful conversations, thoughtful feedback, and partnership in both life and academia.

As I embarked on the journey of writing this book, I faced an unexpected and profound loss. My father, Kazimierz, passed away shortly after I began this project. His absence has been deeply felt throughout this process, and his memory has been a guiding light for me. I dedicate this book to him, with gratitude for all the ways he shaped my life. *To dla Ciebie, Tato!*

Abbreviations

add.	addition
*Akṣobhya	*Śrīvajrabhairavatantraṭīkā*
BDRC	Buddhist Digital Resource Center (bdrc.io)
BY	*Picumata-Brahmayāmala*
Ch.	Chinese
cod.	codices
conj.	conjecture
corr.	correction
del.	deleted
ed.	edition
em.	emendation
fol.	folio
GS	*Guhyasamāja Tantra*
JIABS	*Journal of the International Association of Buddhist Studies*
JIATS	*Journal of the International Association of Tibetan Studies*
*Kṛṣṇācārya	*Vajrabhairavatantrapañjikāratnamālā*
Kumāracandra	*Vajrabhairavatantrapañjikā*
Lalitavajra	*Vajrabhairavatantravṛttyalaṃkāropadeśanāma*
MMK	*Mañjuśriyamūlakalpa*
MNS	*Mañjuśrīnāmasaṅgīti*
ms.	manuscript
mss.	manuscripts
NAK	National Archives Kathmandu
NGMPP	Nepal-German Manuscript Preservation Project
NMAA	*Nāmamantrārthāvalokinī* of Vilāsavajra
NTGS	*Niśvāsatattvasaṃhitā Guhyasūtra*
om.	omitted
r.	recto
SOAS	School of Oriental and African Studies, University of London
*Śoṇaśrī	*Śrīvajrabhairavatantrasūtraṭippaṇīnāma*

STTS	*Sarvatathāgatatattvasaṃgraha*
Toh.	Tōhoku catalog of the Sde dge Bka' 'gyur and Bstan 'gyur
v	verse
vv.	verses
*Vajrasiddha	*Śrīvajrabhairavatantrasūtraṭippaṇīnāma*
VBhT	*Vajrabhairava Tantra*
VS	*Vīṇāśikha Tantra*

Introduction

THIS BOOK is a study and translation of the *Vajrabhairava Tantra* (henceforth, VBhT), a Buddhist tantric text in seven chapters that focuses on the means of attainment (*sādhana*) centered upon the wrathful tantric deity Vajrabhairava. The VBhT, composed in India in the eighth century and written in Sanskrit, is attributed to Lalitavajra (a.k.a. Līlāvajra), a Buddhist master (*ācārya*) at Nālandā Monastery, who is said to have retrieved it from the land of Oḍḍiyāna. It is a work of great importance to the development of tantric Buddhism in India as well as to the understanding of Tibetan Buddhist history more generally. Like most tantras, it is a ritual text, dedicated in all of its seven chapters to the description of rites, such as the drawing of the sacred diagram (*maṇḍala*), the ceremonies performed within it, as well as the performance of various rituals, such as magical rituals (*karmas*), fire offerings (*homa*), recitation of sacred spells (*mantras*), and so on. The VBhT deals with what might have been the earliest form of Vajrabhairava, the Solitary Hero (*ekavīra*), in the charnel ground surrounded by various mortuary objects, weapons, and eight zombies. All of these gruesome symbols clearly reflect the transgressive character of the tantra, associated with the tantric cult of the cremation ground and antinomian practices involving contact with impure places and substances as a means of attaining power. In the subsequent centuries, the pantheon of the Vajrabhairava maṇḍala grew, giving rise to the Seventeen- and the Thirteen-Deity maṇḍalas. The latter was directly influenced by the pantheon of the *Guhyasamāja Tantra*, and could be seen as its direct evolution (Tanaka 2018, 323). Indeed, Thirteen-Deity Vajrabhairava gained widespread popularity also outside India—in Tibet, Mongolia, and China.

The transmission of the VBhT from India to Tibet took place during the Later Dissemination (*phyi dar*), when it was classified as a scripture belonging to the highest unexcelled (*yoganiruttara*) class. The tantra was translated into Tibetan by Rwa lo tsā ba Rdo rje grags (b. 1016), the famous Vajrabhairava sorcerer who used this text to set the record straight with his enemies and rivals. Several Vajrabhairava lineages emerged in Tibet, where the cycle became part of the practice in all the prominent traditions of Tibetan Buddhism, especially in the Sa skya, Jo nang, and Dge lugs. Within several decades of its emergence in the eighth century, Vajrabhairava became one of the most revered deities of Tibetan Buddhism and a pan-Asian phenomenon. The cult of this deity was adopted by the Newar Buddhists in Nepal, where it continues to the present day, and instantiations are attested in Mongolia and China.

But despite Vajrabhairava's popularity, global reach, and considerable impact on the formation of religious praxis in the medieval Buddhist world, the cult of Vajrabhairava has still not received sufficient scholarly attention. While some research has been done on comparatively late milieus, such as the Chinese (Bianchi 2005; Bianchi 2006; Bianchi 2008), Tibetan (Siklós 1996; Cuevas 2021), and Mongolian (Ujeed 2009) instantiations, the early Indian cradle has been neglected. This book intends to fill this gap.

Who Is Vajrabhairava?

In the introductory verse of the VBhT, Vajrabhairava is paid homage to as a form of Mañjuśrī, but unlike his benign predecessor, he is described as being "very fierce" (*atyugra*) and "terrifying" (*bhayānaka*) to all the gods. Indian exegetical commentaries understand these two adjectives as referring to Vajrabhairava's inner and outer natures. He causes terror externally because of his inner wrathful state of mind. Tibetan Buddhists consider Vajrabhairava to be an emanation body (*nirmāṇakāya*) of the bodhisattva Mañjuśrī. Vajrabhairava is said to have emerged from Mañjuśrī's heart to tame those trainees (*'dul bya*) who are difficult to discipline, among whom Yama and Bhairava Maheśvara feature prominently. Prior to the VBhT, various Buddhist tantras made references to Vajrabhairava, although none of them considered him a central deity. The earliest among these textual sources is the seventh-century *Sarvatathāgatatattvasaṃgraha* (STTS), where Vajrabhairava—not yet a god, but a mere messenger (*dūta*)—is accompanied by the mantra:

> *Oṃ Vajrabhairava vajradūta bhakṣaya sarvaduṣṭān mahāyakṣa hūṃ phaṭ.*
>
> *Oṃ* Vajrabhairava, *vajra* messenger, *yakṣa* chief, devour all the wicked ones *hūṃ phaṭ.*

In this mantra, Vajrabhairava is petitioned to destroy (literally, "devour") all the wicked ones (*sarvaduṣṭān*). This early reference given in the STTS may be regarded as the gist of Vajrabhairava's ritual function. Vajrabhairava is requested to engage in retributive action against morally degenerate beings that will bring them into line and into the pursuit of (Buddhist) virtue. This directive seems to be motivated by a sense of responsibility, a need to reform those who have fallen from the path of righteousness. The project of moral reform requires adequate means, for as it is repeatedly said, wicked beings are extremely hard to tame, and the mere exercise of peaceful measures is not enough to uproot the ultimate evil.

The Development of the Vajrabhairava Tantra

The textual configuration of the VBhT suggests that it was written at a time of an important transition in the development of tantric Buddhism. For it was at this time when the earliest class of Buddhist scriptures, the *action tantras* (*kriyātantras*)—focusing on the outer rituals, non-soteriological powers, and techniques of invoking and controlling the deity through mantras—were superseded by the emergence of a new class of tantric Buddhist scriptures, the *yoga tantras* (*yogatantras*), which were more concerned with soteriological goals and meditative union with the deity. This gradual transition is reflected in the textual layers of the VBhT that are by no means uniform. The first three chapters display specific features of the kriyā tantras and might have in fact been the earliest textual stratum that was later enlarged by another four chapters more consistent with the practices of the yoga tantras. This peculiar blend of features created controversy with regard to the tantra's classification in both India and Tibet, a topic that will be discussed further in this work.

The VBhT also reflects another point of transition in the development of tantric Buddhism—namely, the influence of non-Buddhist, particularly Śaiva, traditions. Witness, for instance, the adoption of Śaiva practice of mad laughter (*aṭṭahāsa*) or the ritual consumption of impure substances called the five nectars (*pañcāmṛta*). This reveals the complex origins of the tantra, stemming from the complicated social dynamics between Śaivism and Buddhism in medieval India, which mutually influenced one another and thus owed their shared elements to a process of mutual appropriation and adaptation. Despite diverse academic theories examining the issue of directionality in the much-debated subject of the (mutual) influence and dialectical relationship between tantric forms of Śaivism and Buddhism, the practices discussed in the VBhT, as well as those given in the commentarial literature, are certainly drawing upon the practices of the Śaivas. One example is the consumption of fluids discharged during the sexual intercourse, which is typical of the Kaula strand of Śaivism. Although the VBhT does not possess the markedly Kāpālika elements that are characteristic of the later yoginī tantras, centered upon such deities as Cakrasaṃvara or Vajrayoginī, those few Śaiva elements still point to the fact that the process of appropriation of Śaiva practices was already underway during the emergence of the yoga tantras. Śaiva elements are also visible in Vajrabhairava iconography, a topic discussed further below.

The Vajrabhairava Tantra *and Its Practice*

The VBhT is clearly a practice-oriented text, almost bereft of doctrinal framework. The better part of the VBhT contains magical rituals (*karmas*). This use of the word *karma*, which appears already in the *Atharva Veda* (ca. 1200–900 BCE) to describe magical procedures of a similar kind, is also attested in early tantric Buddhist texts such as the *Siddhaikavīra*, the *Mañjuśriyamūlakalpa* (MMK), and the early Śaiva *Guhyasūtra* of the *Niśvāsatattvasaṃhitā* (NTGS). The magical rituals belong to the repertoire of the advanced practitioner, one who has already mastered the power of the mantra (*mantrasiddhi*), which he can now apply for gaining worldly powers (*siddhi*). The VBhT not only describes what kinds of magic rituals are to be done, it also explains how to do them. Therefore the prescriptive core of "magical know-how" is deeply ingrained in the text's textual fabric. The majority of the karmas described in the VBhT deal specifically with aggressive rites, called *abhicāra*, sometimes also termed "fierce" (*ghora*), directed against the enemies. The *abhicāra* category includes such rites as attracting (*ākarṣaṇa*), subjecting under one's will (*vaśīkaraṇa*), paralyzing (*stambhana*), killing (*māraṇa*), creating dissent (*vidveṣaṇa*), and driving away (*uccāṭana*). These six karmas constitute the so-called six acts (*ṣaṭkarmāṇi*) of tantric sorcery (Goudriaan 1978). Despite the aggressive nature of these karmas, it is mandatory that the adept does not perform these rituals for a wrong purpose or with a wrong intention. If he does, the magic ritual set up by him can rebound on him. To expound this concept, the VBhT uses the important term *pratyaṅgirā*, which betrays an *Atharva Veda* influence. Bloomfield (1899, 66) argues that the term *pratyaṅgirā*, employed in the *Ṛgvidhāna* (4.6.4; 8.3) with the meaning of counteractive sorcery, is a later systematization of the Atharvavedic concept of *pratyabhicaraṇa*, *pratisara*, or *pratīvrata* as retaliative magic.

The VBhT is distinctively practice-oriented also in another sense: following the directive of the yoga tantras, it is grounded in the practice of *yoga*. That means that the adept performing these magic rituals must be in union with the deity. The adept has to dissolve his own individuality, becoming the deity through the meditative stabilization. Therefore the VBhT can be understood as expounding a transformative praxis or a technique of experience that instructs how to realize one's own identity with Vajrabhairava himself. The adept takes on a role of Vajrabhairava trying to emulate his wrathful conduct. With every magic ritual employed to destroy the enemy, the adept ritually reproduces the primordial act of violence of the subjugation of Śiva Maheśvara, returning, as it were, to the mythic origins of the tradition.

The Vajrabhairava Tantra *and Tantric Buddhist Ethics*

The rituals discussed in the VBhT, although somewhat violent and cruel in practice, had to fit into an overall ethical framework of Buddhism. After all, the first of the five ethical rules (*pañcaśīla*) of Buddhism is abstinence from harming living beings. The tantric Buddhist ethics has resolved this conundrum by postulating the double moral standard for the tantric practitioners exemplified by the principle of "compassionate violence" (Gray 2007b) or "ruthless compassion" (Linrothe 1999). Tantric masters harm the evil ones through the use of aggressive magic and thus do them a service. They do not act out of anger; they exercise compassion to liberate those beings from the torments of hell that would otherwise surely await them for their evil deeds. The VBhT clarifies that the aggressive magic can be performed only with "the mind that is moist with compassion." The misuse of the VBhT can be potentially fatal, and wrathful magic performed with intention of harming others rebounds on a doer. Among the most common consequences of this misuse is rebirth as a hell being. The moral lesson intended here is that the retributive punishment for the employment of aggressive magic against those who perform wrathful actions without compassion is severe and entails dire consequences. Thus the ethical core of the VBhT is firmly rooted in the intention to help sentient beings.

Here, the philosophical problem of intention (*cetanā*) and action (*karma*) comes to the forefront. This age-old interplay widely attested in early Buddhism was based on the idea that intention is an integral part of any action. The Buddha explicitly says, "It is intention that I call *kamma*" (Gombrich 1996, 50). As a result, *karma* (Pāli: *kamma*) came to refer to intentional action. Moreover, it is precisely the intention behind the act that is the causal factor animating transmigration in *saṃsāra*. Intention can be either wholesome or wicked, and hence "the ethic of intention" that became the greatest innovation of early Buddhism (Gombrich 2006, 68) placed an obligation to examine one's own motivations. The VBhT seems to follow this line of reasoning when it distinguishes right and wrong intentions. The leading premise of the VBhT's argument in support of aggressive magic as an action motivated by compassion is based on the assertion that intention wholly determines normative principles of tantric practice. Thus violent action motivated by compassion and with the intention of helping sentient beings is considered "right," but violent action motivated by anger and with the intention of harming others is "wrong."

Along with compassion and the intention of helping others, there was a third motivation that ethically informed any violent act—the wish to liberate. This decidedly soteriological drive often appears in Tibetan Buddhist narratives associated with the Vajrabhairava cult, like the one narrated by the seventeenth-century Tibetan historian A mes zhabs, who gives the following account from the life of the tantric sorcerer Rwa lo tsā ba (eleventh century):

> Another time, in the Yar lung Valley, a minister of the king called Rtsa lde stole the horse of Rwa lo tsā ba's attendant while Rwa lo was lecturing on Vajrabhairava. The minister beat up the attendant. [On learning this] Rwa lo began to summon his magical power, but others intervened, offering to get the horse back. He was requested not to use his power, and he promised not to use it. One day later, the king together with the evil people of Gyor po came to that place where Rwa lo was giving lectures on Vajrabhairava and robbed him. Rwa lo's disciples, rising in anger, said: "Because the king and his subjects have harmed us repeatedly, we must unleash our power." Having said that, hail descended over the entire land of the king and the evil people of Gyor po, bringing total destruction. In short, through Rwa lo's magical power and abilities, a great many malicious people were liberated.

Overview of Contents

The first part of this book consists of a study of the VBhT, its historical significance, commentarial literature, provenance, tantric practice (*sādhana*), and relationship with non-Buddhist traditions. My textual and comparative study provides an analysis of Sanskrit and Tibetan sources, mostly unpublished, which paves the way for a better understanding of the Indo-Tibetan context in which the emergence of the Vajrabhairava cult took place. This book studies the contents of the VBhT in the light of relevant sources outside the corpus, such as early tantras like the *Guhyasūtra* of the *Niśvāsatattvasaṃhitā* (NTGS), the *Mañjuśriyamūlakalpa* (MMK), the *Jayadrathayāmala* (JY), and the *Brahmayāmala* (BY), but also of sources within the corpus, like the six canonical commentaries on the VBhT.

Chapter 1 introduces the VBhT by examining its placement within the tantric Buddhist systems in India and Tibet and discusses some pertinent questions regarding the text's dating and problems in identifying the identity of the tantra's alleged revealer, Lalitavajra. My discussion shows that confusion about the real identity of Lalitavajra in Tibet was mainly due to the erroneous translation of his name into Tibetan that resulted in the situation in which the identity of Rol pa'i rdo rje (Lalitavajra) and Sgeg pa'i rdo rje (Vilāsavajra) became conflated. This chapter also provides an overview of the six commentaries on the VBhT, focusing on the issue of chronology and doctrinal leanings, which help us trace the development of the Vajrabhairava cult in India. The earlier commentaries of *Akṣobhya and Lalitavajra are clearly distinguished from the later ones by their focus on the mortuary magic and Śaiva practices. The later commentaries, on the other hand, are more concerned with Buddhist "encoding"—that is, to provide a Buddhist doctrinal and metaphysical framework to the contents, which were almost completely devoid of any Buddhist context. The second part of chapter 1 investigates the history of the Vajrabhairava cult in Tibet and its adoption by the Sa skya and Dge lugs schools. This part is key to tracing the lineages of the Buddhist masters who initiated rulers of China into the Vajrabhairava cult, possibly through 'Phags pa Blo gros rgyal mtshan (1235–80), the nephew of Sa skya Paṇḍita, or his disciples. The exploration of the main Tibetan transmission lineages is important for understanding the adoption of the Vajrabhairava cult on the Tibetan plateau, as well as the history of Tibetan Buddhism more generally. The last part of chapter 1 provides a brief overview of the practices of the Vajrabhairava-Yamāntaka cult in Mongolia, Japan, and Nepal that consolidated this deity as a pan-Asian phenomenon.

Chapter 2 examines the origins of Vajrabhairava in India, concentrating on Vajrabhairava iconography and ritual epithets. This chapter examines the evolutionary theory advocated by some scholars that promotes the clear-cut development of Vajrabhairava from the cult of Yama-Yamāntaka, and points out some of the shortcomings this theory involves. First, the evolutionary theory does not explain all the iconographic features of Vajrabhairava as a simple evolution of Yama/Yamāntaka. For example, its ithyphallic aspect has not yet been satisfactorily explained; while it is a widespread symbol of fertility, in the specific context of Vajrabhairava, it is a sign of iconographic appropriation of attributes belonging to Śiva, pointing also to the yogic practice of semen retention that is typical of the Śaiva tradition. Second, the evolutionary theory does not explain the discrepancy between iconographical representations and ritual epithets. For example, the epithet *vikṛtānana*, or "deformed face," does not point to any specific feature in the iconography of Yama/Yamāntaka or Vajrabhairava. Nevertheless, this appellation is indicative of an established iconographic code through which demonic, dangerous, and highly transgressive beings have been textually represented in the early tantric milieu. Thus I argue that, rather than a straightforward evolution, the iconography of Vajrabhairava must be considered the product of a long process of syncretism and synthesis of Hindu-Brahmanical, Buddhist, Śaiva, and tantric concepts of divinity.

Chapter 3 examines the origins of Vajrabhairava in Tibet. The current conceptual framework in which Vajrabhairava's origins in Tibetan Buddhist tradition is formulated focuses on his role as Yama's destroyer narrated in the so-called Yamarāja Myth. This chapter explores another contextual layer in Vajrabhairava's birth that specifically links him to the Śiva complex and in a distinctive way recapitulates an earlier myth of the subjugation of Maheśvara, in which Vajrabhairava subsumes the role of Trailokyavijaya of the STTS. Interestingly, the ithyphallic attribute becomes enveloped here with the important ritual function of the conversion of Yama and Bhairava Maheśvara. In this regard, the connection between iconography and ritual function is easier to establish through the medium of the mythic narrative, for myth often serves to create a coherent explanation of iconography. The association of Vajrabhairava with the Śiva complex is also visible in the adaptation of the Purāṇic trope of the war between the gods and the demons, in which Vajrabhairava assumes the role of the buffalo Mahiṣa and slays the non-Buddhist gods, as reflected in the Rwa lo tradition as rendered by Tāranātha.

Chapter 4 examines the topic of the tantra's "rediscovery" in the land of Oḍḍiyāna by Lalitavajra, preserved in Tibetan historiographical sources. This account suggests that Lalitavajra was initiated into the tantric path of the **Vajramāyājāla Tantra* cycle, praised Ārya Mañjuśrī for twenty years, and was engaged in the recitation of the *Mañjuśrīnāmasaṅgīti* (MNS) when one of Mañjuśrī's "names" given in this text—"Vajrabhairava who creates fear"—caught his attention. This single moniker together with a prophetic dream was the impetus that prompted Lalitavajra to travel to Oḍḍiyāna and eventually establish a new tantric tradition dedicated solely to Mañjuśrī's wrathful form of Vajrabhairava. This chapter argues that this story contains some important insights that might in fact be true. The comparative analysis of textual layer of chapter 4 of the VBhT dedicated to the process of generating oneself as Vajrabhairava by means of seed syllables closely resembles the generation of oneself as Mahāvairocana in chapter 4 of Vilāsavajra's commentary on the MNS—namely, the *Nāmamantrārthāvalokinī* (NMAA). The similarity between the NMAA and the VBhT with regard to this specific sādhana, and also the outmost importance given to Mañjuśrīkumārabhūta/Ādibuddha, may indicate that the two texts were drawing upon an earlier source—the **Vajramāyājāla Tantra* (as the NMAA itself confirms), a popular yoga tantra available in eighth-century Nālandā that appears to be no longer extant. The comparison of the sādhana passages given in the VBhT and NMAA provides us with an insight into the general development of the praxis concerning the "generation of oneself as a deity" existing in the early yoga tantras. The similarity of those passages with regard to their basic structure and subsequent stages of the sādhana together with the identical seed syllables through which the sādhana is enacted seems to indicate that it was a type of "template" that circulated in tantric circles at that time. It does not seem to be a coincidence that both Lalitavajra and Vilāsavajra were among the residents of Nālandā Monastery, where the tantricized cult of Mañjuśrī had flourished.

Chapter 5 examines the VBhT through the lenses of its tantric sādhana and analyzes the use of tantric technology—mantras, maṇḍalas, yantras, and so on. This chapter presents the material in a manner that is more descriptive than interpretative. It reconstructs the tantric sādhana of Vajrabhairava in the light of the text's canonical commentaries, and thus presents what is hopefully an accurate account of the early cult of Vajrabhairava in India in its various manifestations.

Chapter 6 shows the influence of the Śaiva-Śākta traditions on the development of Vajrabhairava's sādhana by examining some important practices, such as the Śaiva entry into the cremation ground with mad laughter and the ritual consumption of impure substances. Tantrism propagated an ideological shift that affected the way in which ritual practices involving impure substances shaped the religious experience. In this context, impurity emerged not as an entity to be resisted but as a site of knowledge that had, as its important goal, triumph over dualistic thinking and over the horror of death. The logic of such an approach impacted the way in which ritual practices involving impurity were conceived, leading to the integration of impurity into spiritual praxis.

The development of this new cultural trend, which is also visible in the commentarial literature of the VBhT, was ideologically grounded in the concept of nonduality, which in the Buddhist context was the underlying theme of the Mahāyāna doctrine of emptiness stating that impurity is just a concept and not a thing in itself. Impurity does not possess an independent reality and is, like everything else, empty in itself. From an absolute point of view, there are no objects that are "pure" or "impure." Impurity and purity are mere concepts derived from the subject-object dichotomy, which clouds the essential purity (*prabhāsvara*) of the mind. Since purity and impurity depend on the mind, it is only in the mind where they can be broken. In the soteriological context, impurity was recognized as a powerful tool that could be used to help one realize the nonduality and emptiness of everything. The *Prajñopāyaviniścayasiddhi* says, "Both impurity and saṃsāra are the mind endowed with conceptual constructs, whereas nirvāṇa is the mind devoid of these."

Chapter 7 places the VBhT in a wider framework of early tantric magic. In large part, the magical technology of early tantric magic relies on the manipulation of a wide range of material objects or substances—grains, minerals, chemicals, plants, sweets, effigies, animals, items retrieved from the cremation ground, and so forth. My aim in this chapter is to examine the available evidence for the recourse to different magical technologies in the early tantric milieu, and classify them on the basis of the various material objects they use. The early tantras shared a very similar understanding of the magical categories and manipulation of objects that were believed to bring about magical results. This common understanding transcended sectarian boundaries of "Buddhist" and "Śaiva" religious discourses. The existence of such broad similarities across Śaiva and Buddhist tantras may point to an underlying "culture of magic" that may have predated the earliest known textual evidence as part of a religious substratum. Though this substratum cannot be known but only assumed, it can cast some light on the issue of directionality in the much-debated subject of the dialectical relationship between tantric Śaivism and tantric Buddhism. Rather than supporting a monothetic paradigm of one-way influence of Śaivism on Buddhism or vice versa, a shared culture of magic would point to a common phenomenon that crossed sectarian boundaries as well as linguistic, geographical, and sociocultural milieus.

Part II of this book provides the first-ever English translation of the VBhT based on a critical edition of the Sanskrit prepared by me from the following manuscripts: NAK A994/3, NAK B112/16, and Beijing 107, which is forthcoming in another publication. To date, the only available study on the VBhT, presenting the Tibetan and Mongolian editions of the text as well as an English translation and introduction, was published by Siklós in 1996. In spite of its merits, Siklós's study is of limited value since at that time, the original Sanskrit manuscripts of the tantra had not yet been discovered. Moreover, Siklós includes only three out of six canonical commentaries on the VBhT and uses them very selectively to elucidate some aspects of the root text. He passes over in silence the more important and difficult commentaries penned by *Akṣobhya and *Kṛṣṇācārya, which are of great value for understanding the Vajrabhairava cult. This book intends to fill these lacunae by providing the complete testimony of the Indian exegetical tradition that (except for Kumāracandra's *Vajrabhairavatantrapañjikā*) is currently only known to exist through the Tibetan translations in the Tibetan canon, the Bstan 'gyur.

Part I
Study

1. An Introduction to the *Vajrabhairava Tantra*

The Vajrabhairava Tantra *and the Buddhist Tantric Systems*

WITHIN THE SCOPE of the general, ex-post-facto classification of the Buddhist tantric systems in India into *kriyā*, *caryā*, *yoga*, and *yoginī* tantras (Isaacson and Sferra 2015), the VBhT has been classified under the yoga tantras. As the name of this class suggests, *yoga*—understood as "the paradigmatic practice of deity yoga in which practitioners create themselves as enlightened Buddha figures through a series of contemplations and visualizations, each accompanied by repetition of a specific mantra" (Weinberger 2003, 177)—was a prevalent feature of the yoga tantras. Alongside the marked shift in emphasis on the method that stressed the inner yoga over the outer ritual characteristic of the kriyā tantras, the yoga tantras were more interested in the soteriological goals that became as important as the procurement of magical powers (*siddhi*). The classification of the VBhT under the yoga tantras was controversial. In this regard, *Akṣobhya, one of the earliest commentators of the VBhT, outlines the main points of the disputed issue together with the reasoned arguments against those who objected such categorization. He provides the following justification:

> [The VBhT] is called a *yoga tantra* because in this tantra there are many external ritual applications (*prayogas*). But if this is the case, then someone might say that this is a kriyā tantra. [To this I reply:] It is not a kriyā tantra because there is an occurrence of the seventh chapter, which teaches only things to be done by meditation (*yoga*). Moreover, because [the VBhT] teaches internal yoga as essential in every external ritual application, we have the teaching "[He should] be well concentrated (*samāhita*)," and this is an internal aspect of yoga. This is not a kriyā tantra but a yoga that teaches great external ritual applications. Others say that in this tantra, *yoga* cannot be derived from the stem *yuji*, but it can only mean *yoniśas* [i.e., *yoniśo manasikāra*, "right mental attention"], but it is not true. In this tantra, it is the stem *yuji*, and it is, for the most part, *yoniśas* not only in

> the case of the seventh chapter and achieving the body of the deity [but also in case of other chapters]. Even in the kriyā tantras, we have *yoniśas*, and that's why it is not true.[1]

*Akṣobhya tries to refute the first objection of the opponent (*pūrvapakṣa*) that the VBhT should be classified under the "action" or *kriyā* category because of the predominace of outer rituals on the basis of two facts. First, the very existence of the seventh chapter, which relies solely upon rituals conducted through meditation. Second, there is the inner *yoga* component in every outer ritual, conveyed by the phrase *susamāhita/samāhita* in a meaning of "[being] well concentrated," which is to be understood as an inner meditative state characterized as the union with the deity Vajrabhairava that any practitioner (*sādhaka*) performing rituals delineated in the VBhT must assume prior to the engagement in the rituals. According to *Akṣobhya, these aspects alone qualify the VBhT as a yoga tantra.

The second debatable issue brought forth by *Akṣobhya in the above passage revolves around the class of the verbal stem (*dhātu*) from which the term *yoga* was derived. In this regard, the *Dhātupāṭha* distinguishes two classes: (1) the fourth class (IV.68), where *yoga* is derived from the root *yuj-* in the sense of concentration, *yuja samādhau*, and (2) the seventh class (VII.7), where *yoga* is derived from the root *yuj-* in the sense of conjunction, *yuji yoge* (Staal 1997, 122). It was a common practice in Sanskrit exegetical writings to engage in a discussion on the issue of the two aforementioned derivations whenever the topic of *yoga* was considered. For example, the exegetical commentary on the *Yogasūtra*, the *Yogasūtrabhāṣya*—forming together with it the *Pātañjalayogaśāstra* (probably early to mid-fifth century)—gives the following explanation of *yoga*:

> Doubt as to the actual thing (*yoga*) is occasioned by doubt as to the meaning of the word. This doubt is removed by stating that in the language of the sūtra, *yoga* is etymologically derived from the root

1. *Akṣobhya's *ṭīkā*, 373: *sbyor ba'i rgyud ces bya ba ni rgyud 'dir phyi rol gyi sbyor ba rab tu mang bas na'o/ de ltar na 'di bya ba'i rgyud ces brjod do zhe na/ bsam gtan 'ba' zhig gi bya ba ston pa'i le'u bdun pa 'byung ba dang/ phyi rol gyi sbyor ba'i bya ba thams cad la yang shin tu mnyam par gzhag pas bya'o/ zhes nang gi rnal 'byor rab tu yang gces par ston pas na/ bya ba'i rgyud ni min te/ 'on kyang phyi rol gyi sbyor ba chen po'i rnal 'byor gyi rgyud do/ gzhan dag ni 'dir yo ga zhes bya ba yu dzir mi 'dren te/ yo ni sha nyid du 'dren na/de ni ma yin te/ 'dir yu dzir nyid shas che ba'i yo ni sha ni le'u bdun pa tsam las med cing/ lha'i sku bsgrub pa la ni bya ba'i rgyud las yang yo ni sha yod pa'i phyir ro/.*

> *yuja* in the sense of concentration and not from the root *yuji* in the sense of conjunction. (trans. Staal 1997, 122.)

In making a distinction between the two derivations of the word *yoga*, *Akṣobhya goes against the objection of the opponent that denies the possibility of the word *yoga* to be derived from the stem *yuja*, "yoga as concentration," and favors the derivation from the *dhātu yuji*, "yoga as union," expressed through the Buddhist idiom of *yoniśas manaskāra*—"right mental attention." In order to understand *Akṣobhya's reasons for putting forward such an explanation, we have to look at the definition of *yoga* in the *Sgra sbyor bam po gnyis pa*, a commentary on the early ninth-century *Mahāvyutpatti*:

> What is called *yoga* is so called [because of the root, *dhātu*] *yuji*, ["to unite"]. *Yoga* means meditation (*dhyāna*), which unites tranquility (*śamatha*) and insight (*vipaśyanā*). *Yoniśas manaskāra* means the following: *yoni* is *upāya*, the method or tantra, [the affix] *śa*[*s*] means "it teaches" (*śasati*);[2] [this refers to the act of] following and teaching that very same method and means. In general, through meditation on the repulsive (*aśubhabhāvanā*), one eliminates desire, through meditation on the dependent origination, one eliminates ignorance, and so on. Because it is the name for meditation (*dhyāna*) according to the [right] method and means, it is called *yoniśas manaskāra* accordingly.[3]

There are two aspects of the above definition of *yoga* that could throw some light on *Akṣobhya's earlier explanation. First, *yoga* is derived from the Sanskrit root (*dhātu*) *yuji* (that is, "yoga as union"), and it denotes a meditation (*dhyāna*) that is understood in terms of the union of calm abiding and special insight (*śamathavipaśyanā*). Those two technical terms Wayman (1973, 110) defines as the "backbone of tantric practice" insofar that they relate to the development of the one-pointed concentration on tantric Buddhist deities, mantras, and so on, during *śamatha* and the realization of emptiness (*śūnyatā*)

2. I thank Francesco Sferra for suggesting this emendation to the text.

3. *Sgra sbyor bam po gnyis pa* (Mie 1990, 137): *yo ga zhes bya ba* {148b3} *yu dzir yo ga zhes bya ste/ zhi gnas dang lhag mthong zung du 'brel pa'i bsam gtan gyi ming ste rnal 'byor zhes bya/ yo ni sha ma na sk'a ra zhes bya ba yo ni au p'a y'a ste thabs sam rgyud la bya/ sha ni sha* [del. *na* ed.] *sa ti zhes bya ste/ thabs dang tshul de nyid la spyod cing ston pa la bya ste/ spyir na mi* {148b4} *sdug pa sgom pas 'dod chags gzhil ba dang/ rten cing 'brel bar 'byung ba sgom pas gti mug spangs pa la sogs pa ste/ thabs tshul bzhin du sgom pa'i ming yin pas na tshul bzhin yid la byed pa zhes bya/*

in *vipaśyanā*, respectively (Sarbacker 2005, 116). Second, *dhyāna* is also defined through the *yoniśas manaskāra*[4] terminology because of its proximity to skillful means (*upāya*), or the method of meditation that brings specific results—for example, elimination of desire and so on. If we take this explanation as an interpretative tool for understanding *Akṣobhya's definition, we may conclude that in the VBhT, "yoga as union" is considered a skillful means for eliminating all kinds of obstacles through meditation (*dhyāna*), which comes about through concentration and realization of emptiness.

Yet another attempt at classifying the VBhT within the scheme of Buddhist tantras in India came with Vilāsavajra, who placed it within the great yoga (*mahāyoga*) or highest yoga (*yogottara*) category,[5] alongside the *Guhyasamāja Tantra* (GS) and the *Māyājāla Tantra* (Tribe 1994, 5). It is difficult to understand what the basis for Vilāsavajra's classification was. Scholars usually point to several distinctive features of yogottara tantras not found in other classes. For example, an oft-repeated statement is that one of the yogottara tantras' features was a sudden proliferation of wrathful deities of Akṣobhya's vajra family, whose status rose to prominence in that genre of texts (Tribe 1994, 5; English 2002, 4). While this statement may be correct in the case of the *Guhyasamāja* and *Māyājāla*, it cannot be confirmed with regard to the VBhT, where no mention of Akṣobhya is to be found. Similarly, scholars (see, e.g., English 2002, 4; Williams and Tribe 2000, 151–64; Harvey 2013, 182) unanimously maintain that the yogottara tantras are distinguished from the tantras of other classes by their marked emphasis on sexuality, especially initiation involving sexual intercourse as well as the depiction of deities in sexual embrace. While sexuality becomes an important aspect of the *Guhyasamāja* and *Māyājāla*, it is entirely absent in the VBhT. The only feature that the text seems to be sharing with the tantras of the yogottara class is the ritual use of body products. The VBhT employs the ritual consumption of the five nectars (*pañcāmṛta*),[6] and

4. The explanation of the *yoniśo/yoniśas manaskāra/manasikāra* is beyond the scope of this book. For some important implications of this term in the Mahāyāna Buddhism, see Pagel 1995, 169.

5. According to Isaacson (1998), *yogottara* appears to be a later designation invented as it were for the mahāyoga category, while English (2002, 5) points out that Vilāsavajra is not aware of such a category.

6. The VBhT does refer to the consumption of the five nectars (*amṛtas*) in chapter 4, but neither the root text nor the commentaries provide any specific list of the nectars included in this category. Nevertheless, the text habitually refers to urine, excrement, blood, human flesh, and different types of animal meat used in the worship of Vajrabhairava. For the discussion on the five nectars in the VBhT, see chapter 6 below.

thus it follows the "transgressive paradigm" initiated in Buddhist tantras by the *Guhyasamāja*.

Now, let us examine the placement of the VBhT in Tibet. The classification of Buddhist tantras in Tibet went through various stages of development and only in the twelfth century was codified into the well-known fourfold division mentioned above, mainly thanks to the legitimizing efforts of the members of the new schools (*gsar ma*) such as the Sa skya pas (Dalton 2005, 159). The "fourfold" system closely followed the classifications of tantras current in India at that time into "action" or *kriyā* (*bya ba'i rgyud*), "performance" or *caryā* (*spyod pa'i rgyud*), *yoga* (*rnal 'byor gyi rgyud*), and "unexcelled yoga" or *yoganiruttara* (*rnal 'byor bla na med pa'i rgyud*),[7] the last one grouped together the yogottara and yoginī tantras. The yoganiruttara class was further divided into father (*pha rgyud*), mother (*ma rgyud*), and nondual tantras (*gnyis med rgyud*) (English 2002, 6). With regard to this system, the VBhT was categorized under the father tantras of the unexcelled yoga (*yoganiruttara*) class (*anuttarayoga*, Siklós 1996, 4). The father tantras were further organized in accordance with the predominance of afflictive emotions (*kleśa*) present in the trainees—namely hatred, desire, and ignorance. In accordance with this classification, the VBhT—as well as the *Yamāntaka*—were suitable for those trainees who had mainly hatred, while the *Guhyasamāja* and **Vairocanamāyājāla* were appropriate to those who had desire and ignorance, respectively.[8] It is reasonable to assume that the grouping of these three tantras together may have been influenced by Vilāsavajra's model attesting to the inclusion of the same texts under the yogottara category. The father tantras were also distinguished from the mother tantras for its emphasis on the cultivation of the illusory body (*sgyu lus*), which is *upāya* / the material cause of the material body (*gzugs sku*). The mother tantras, on the other hand, emphasize luminosity (*'od gsal*), which is *prajñā* / the material cause of the truth body (*dharmakāya*).[9]

7. Sanderson (1993) pointed out that the term *anuttarayoga*, which is a false modern etic translation from Tibetan into Sanskrit often used in secondary sources, is not attested in Sanskrit sources, and it was probably a mistranslation of the term *yoganiruttara* (lit. "tantras of the highest [*niruttara*] division of the yoga [class]," Sanderson 1994, 98n1, quoted in English 2002, 5). The term *yoganiruttara* is indeed attested in the *Sekanirdeśapañjikā* by Rāmapāla (ed. p. 165.8–9: *kriyācaryāyogayogottarayoganiruttaratantreṣu*) and in the *Muktāvalī* by Ratnākaraśānti (ed. p. 233). I thank Francesco Sferra for this information.

8. A mes zhabs, *Gshin rje chos 'byung* (pp. 8–9): *gdul bya 'dod chags can gtso por 'dul ba'i ched du gsungs pa gsang ba 'dus pa'i skor/ gdul bya zhe sdang can gtso bor 'dul ba'i ched du gsungs pa gshin rje gshed skor/ gdul bya gti mug can gtso bor 'dul ba'i ched du gsungs pa rnam snang sgyu 'phrul dra ba'i skor rnams su yod pa yin no/.*

9. Mkhas grub rje, in Lessing and Wayman 1978, 265. I thank John Newman for this clarification.

The grouping of the VBhT under the unexcelled yoga (*yoganiruttara*) category in Tibet was controversial. The tantras of the yoganiruttara class are qualified as the highest of all tantra classes for one particular reason—they are regarded as a tool for reaching awakening in this lifetime. The dispute revolved around the suitability of classifying the VBhT as a text for attaining liberation in view of its (mostly low-level) magical content designated to harm some target. The ramifications of this controversy were extensive, and it is useful to present the whole argument summarized in Tāranātha's *History of the Yamāntaka Tradition* (*Gshin rje chos 'byung*). Tāranātha was dissatisfied with the perspective of elimination (*rnam bcad*) that viewed the VBhT, in accord with the description of the father tantras, merely as the means (*upāya*) of removing obstacles leading to awakening. He stated that there are various obstacles such as disease or poverty that can also be removed by other things, such as medicine and so on. Their removal, however, does necessarily guarantee awakening (*byang chub*). He writes thus:

> If one cannot attain awakening through the path of [the VBhT in] seven chapters, it would be inappropriate for you [the opponent] to hold that the explanations of the seven chapters of the Skyo and Mal lineages is the supreme dharma, because even though it [the seven chapters] would enable one to accomplish some minor rituals, it would be comparable to the dharma of the non-Buddhists. Again, if one were to examine the position that says "[The VBhT] dispels obstacles to attain awakening," [one may conclude the following]: if all the obstacles can be removed in that way, then [the VBhT] would be the unexcelled (*niruttara*) means of awakening. Because once all the obstacles are removed, it is impossible not to attain awakening. Now, if [the VBhT] only removes disease, harm, poverty, it would be impossible to establish it as [the means of] removing obstacles [leading] to awakening. And if it *can* do it, then, since the knowledge of medicine, substances, magical formulas, methods against the enemy, and so on have the same ability, [the VBhT] would be comparable to the method of village people. In that case, how would you justify [the VBhT] as a valid means of annihilating, protecting [against evil], and destroying [the obstacles]? If you were to argue that [the VBhT] removes the suffering for one or two lifetimes, that too would make it similar to the methods of non-Buddhists.[10]

10. Tāranātha, *Gshin rje chos 'byung*, 5–7: *gal te rtog pa bdun pa'i lam gyis byang chub mi*

On that basis, Tāranātha argued in support of the positive inclusion (*yongs gcod*) that would subsume the VBhT under the unexcelled (*niruttara*) category by associating it with skillful means (*upāya*) as well as with wisdom (*prajñā*). In this regard, *prajñā*—understood as "knowledge of indissolubility of Beatitude and Void on the side of void" (Lessing and Wayman 1978, 265)—precedes the elimination of obstacles. If we take it in a metaphysical sense, as Tāranātha does, we may say that the main "obstacle" the VBhT tries to eliminate—Māra or Yama—requires a skillful means (*upāya*), but this "means" can only be generated from the transcendental wisdom (*prajñā*).

> If you were to argue that [the VBhT] counteracts Māra or Yama, then transcendental wisdom must be generated [for that]. On that basis, one must understand [the VBhT] as referring to the "means (*thabs*) of attaining awakening." From the elimination point of view, it is the case of giving up faults, such as obstacles and so on. From the perspective of inclusion, it may be possible that good qualities may not actually be obtained. The following exemplifies this dharma explanation: Imagine a dirty copper vessel that you wash out and then pour a liquid into; it is like this. Without the stages of knowledge, neither the understanding of the stages of the path nor the giving up of the undesirable can arise here. Therefore, without generating the antidote to the evil one, one will be unable to eliminate the object of elimination.[11]

---

thob na/ rtog bdun gyi bshad pa skyo lug dang/ mal lugs ni mchog tu gyur ba'i chos su khyed rang 'dod pa yang mi 'thad de/ las phran tshogs tsam 'grub du zin yang mu stegs kyi chos dang mtshungs bar thal ba'i phyir ro/ yang byang chub sgrub pa'i bar chad sel zhes zer ba la yang brtags na/ 'di ltar bar chad thams cad sel ba yin no ni/ byang chub sgrub byed bla na med par 'gyur te/ bar chad thams cad spangs nas/ byang chub ma thob pa mi srid pa'i phyir ro/ tshe 'di nad dang gnod byed dang/ 'phongs pa sel ba tsam la byed na ni/ de tsam gyis byang chub kyi bar chad sel byed du 'jog mi thub cing/ de 'dra ni sman dang rdzas dang/ rig pa dang/ dgra thabs la sogs pa'i blo grogs kyis kyang nus pas na/ grong pa'i skye bo rnams dang thun mong du 'gyur bas/ 'dir khyad par chad srung ba dang 'joms pa'i tshad gang la 'jog/ skye ba phyi ma gcig gam gnyis su sdug bsngal sel ba la 'jog na yang/ mu stegs dang thun mongs su 'gyur la/

11. Tāranātha, *Gshin rje chos 'byung*, 5–7: *bdud dang gshin rje thub pa la 'jog na ni/ de la ni 'jig rten las 'das pa'i ye shes skye dgos pas/ de ka la byang chub thob pa'i thabs zhes zer ba go dgos so/ khyed kyi go yul na rnam bcad kyi cha nas/ bar chad la sogs pa'i skyon spangs pa yin pa la/ yongs gcod kyi cha nas yon tan mngon par ma bsgrub pa cig srid/ mtshan gzhi chos skor 'di rnams yin/ dpe zangs gzhong gi dri ma bkrus* [del. *nam*, ed.] *bcud blug pa dang 'dra snyam pa cig 'dug ste/ rig gras tsam ma gtogs lam gyi rim pa dang/ spang gnyen sogs kyi go ba phyogs re tsam yang ma shar ba der 'dug/ des nag nyen po ma skyes par spangs bya spongs mi thub/.*

Tāranātha supports his argument by referring to the well-established Mahāyāna categories of the two accumulations that need to be accomplished during the bodhisattva's ascent through the ten bodhisattva levels. It is only upon the accumulation of merit (*puṇyasaṃbhāra*) associated with *upāya* and of wisdom (*prajñāsaṃbhāra*) associated with *prajñā* that the eradication of the emotional and cognitive obscurations (the *kleśa-* and *jñeya-āvaraṇa*s) is possible.[12] This eradication, in turn, is concomitant with the attainment of awakening.

> Similarly, if the two accumulations of merit and wisdom are incomplete, the two obscurations [emotional and cognitive] will not be cleared, just like you cannot remove darkness without light. Therefore, according to the perspective of inclusion, one generates good qualities and eliminates faults of obstacles; [thus, generation of good qualities] and removal of faults run in tandem. Because this is the way of highest comparability [between the two methods], when one eliminates obstacles, one achieves the unexcelled [realization of awakening], and when one generates good qualities, one also achieves the unexcelled [realization of awakening].[13]

Tāranātha's explanation comes very close to the exposition given by *Kṛṣṇācārya and Kumāracandra in their commentaries on the VBhT, who also understand the purpose of the sādhana delineated in the VBhT as the means of attaining awakening through the eradication of the two obscurations (see pp. 37, 39 below). Tāranātha concludes his defense of the VBhT as the "unexcelled yoga" (*yoganiruttara*) by showing that the generation of the transcendental wisdom is a prerequisite that must necessarily precede the skillful means, and thus that the position that the VBhT is the "tantra of method" (*upāyatantra*) because it merely removes hindrances is untenable.

12. In this regard, the realization of emptiness generated through the meditation on the emptiness mantra (see p. 128 below) is often concomitant in the early sādhanas with the accumulation of *prajñā* wisdom (Tribe 2016, 61–62). The accumulation of wisdom (*prajñāsaṃbhāra*), in turn, preceeds the stage of the generation of oneself as a deity.

13. Tāranātha, *Gshin rje chos 'byung*, 6: *tshogs gnyis ma rdzogs na sgrib gnyis mi dag ste/ dper na snang ba ma byung na mun pa mi sel ba bzhin no/ des na yongs gcod du yon tan skyes pa dang/ rnam bcad du bar chad nyes skyon sel ba bang mnyam mchog* [em.; *mchod* ed.] *mnyam gyi tshul yin pas/ bar chad sel byed mchog tu grub na yon tan skyed byed kyang mchog tu 'grub po/*.

Dating the Vajrabhairava Tantra

Dating the VBhT is somewhat problematic. Based on the evidence presented below, it is currently plausible to date the text to the mid- to late eighth century. The VBhT is mentioned in Vilāsavajra's NMAA, which means it was composed prior to it. The dating of the NMAA ranges between the late eighth and the early to mid-ninth centuries (Tribe 2016, 6),[14] which therefore provides the *terminus ante quem* for the VBhT. The reason for placing the VBhT in the eighth rather than the ninth century is based on the fact that Vilāsavajra grouped the VBhT among other eighth-century tantras, such as the *Guhyasamāja* (GS)[15] and the *Māyājāla*, which may indicate that the connection among these three texts was based on their relative chronology. However, taking into account the evidence of quotations included in the VBhT, it is certain that the VBhT must have been composed after the GS, since it cites, albeit without attribution, a passage from that text's characterization of the enemy (14.47ad), defined as those people who "blame the teacher" (*ācāryanindana*) and "speak ill of the Mahāyāna" (*mahāyānāgranindakāḥ*), and who—as part of retributive punishment—must be killed or else relocated. The existence of an isolated, unattributed quotation from the GS establishes the *terminus ante quem* for the composition of the VBhT. The VBhT is also mentioned in chapter 3 of the *Cakrasaṃvara Tantra* together with other early Buddhist tantras, such as the STTS, GS, and *Sarvabuddhasamāyogaḍākinījālasaṃvarakalpa* (Gray 2007a, 177). Since the *Cakrasaṃvara* is most probably dated to the ninth century (Gray 2012, 6–8),[16] the VBhT must have been written before that time, which in turn could possibly support the dating to the mid- rather than the late eighth century. There is, however, another important piece of evidence that suggests a slightly later date for the composition of the VBhT. Unlike the GS, STTS, and the *Sarvabuddhasamāyogaḍākinījālasaṃvara*, the VBhT is not mentioned in Amoghavajra's *Index of the Vajraśekhara Yoga Sūtra*

14. Davidson (1981, 7) dates Vilāsavajra's NMAA to the mid- to late eighth century.

15. The GS was compiled in India in the early eighth century. The earliest reference to it is found in a Chinese text attributed to the Buddhist monk Amoghavajra, the *Index of the Vajraśekhara Yoga Sūtra in Eighteen Sections*, dated to the mid-eighth century (Gray 2005, 3708–9). For a discussion of the various stages in the development of GS, see Tanemura 2015, 327–28. Matsunaga (1978, xxvi) suggested that the first half of the eighth century "was a formative period of the *Guhyasamāja-tantra*" but concluded that the text was completed later, in the mid- to late eighth century. For the critique of this dating, see Newman 1987, 59–60.

16. On the dating of the *Cakrasaṃvara*, see Gray 2012, 6–8. Newman (personal communication) disagrees with this dating.

in Eighteen Sections,[17] penned after Amoghavajra's return to China in 746.[18] This fact could push the date for the production of the VBhT to the later half of the eighth century.

Lalitavajra: The Revealer of the Vajrabhairava Tantra

The colophons in the Sanskrit and Tibetan versions of the VBhT state that the text was brought from Oḍḍiyāna by a master of the infinitely great maṇḍala (*paramamahāmaṇḍalācārya*), Śrī Lalitavajra. On the basis of this as well as historiographical information included in Tāranātha's *History of Buddhism in India* (*Rgya gar chos 'byung*), it has been accepted that Lalitavajra is the revealer of the VBhT. The identity of Lalitavajra and his whereabouts in the Buddhist world are, however, highly problematic. Tibetan Buddhist historiography gives witness to several individuals who share this or a similar name, and Tāranātha himself acknowledges the mix-up that left the Tibetan lineages that took part in the transmission of the VBhT confused about Lalitavajra's identity. The main problem concerning the identity of Lalitavajra revolves around the erroneous translation of the word *lalita* into Tibetan as *sgeg pa*, while the proper translation should be *rol pa*. Tāranātha thinks that the wrong translation created confusion between Rol pa'i rdo rje (Lalitavajra) and Sgeg pa'i rdo rje (Vilāsavajra), whose separate identities were sometimes conflated into one. Tāranātha refers to this mix-up as follows:

> Thinking that *rol pa* and *sgeg pa* are synonyms, it appears that *lalita* was translated as *sgeg pa*. Thus, *ācārya sgeg pa'i rdo rje* became the ground for confusing him with another person. The translation as *sgeg pa'i rdo rje* is not good; furthermore, *lalita* is mainly expressed through [the Tib.] *rol pa*. The etymology of *sgeg pa* is principally *lāsya* or *vilāsya*, and the meaning of *rol pa* is "play," "frolic," the purpose of which is to be relaxed in one's own nature and behave in whatever manner one wants. Since the term *sgeg pa* connotes "exuding a sense of grandeur," the meaning of the two words [i.e., *rol pa* and *sgeg pa*] is slightly different.[19]

17. For an English translation of Amoghavajra's *Index of the Vajraśekhara Yoga Sūtra in Eighteen Sections* from Chinese, see Giebel 1995.

18. Chou 1945, 292, also quoted in Gray 2007a, 13.

19. Tāranātha, *Gshin rje chos 'byung*, 67–68: *rol pa dang sgeg pa don gcig par bsams nas la li ta sgeg par bsgyur snang yang/ slob dpon sgeg pa'i rdo rje zhes bya ba gzhan 'khrul gzhi'i byung bas/ sgeg pa'i rdo rjer bsgyur ba mi legs shing/ der ma zad la li ta rol pa la gtso bor 'jug*

That Sgeg pa'i rdo rje (Vilāsavajra) and Rol pa'i rdo rje (Lalitavajra) are two different persons has been established by Tribe (1994, 10–11). Sgeg pa'i rdo rje, born in Nor bu gling (Ratnadvīpa)[20] but a resident of Oḍḍiyāna, was a teacher of *Buddhajñānapāda, the founder of the Jñānapāda school of GS exegesis, and "taught him many kriyā and yoga tantras."[21] Tāranātha and 'Gos lo tsā ba make the distinction between the two masters clear when they refer to them by different names: Rol pa'i rdo rje for Lalitavajra and Sgeg pa'i rdo rje for Vilāsavajra/Līlāvajra.[22] They are also consistent in portraying them via different storylines.[23] More importantly, the works attributed to Sgeg pa'i rdo rje in the Bstan 'gyur differ in nature from those assigned to Rol pa'i rdo rje: the former is associated with the authorship of the commentary on the MNS—that is, the NMAA—while the latter being exclusive to titles bearing the names Vajrabhairava, Bhairava, and Kṛṣṇayamāri (Tribe 1994, 11). Although Tāranātha and 'Gos lo tsā ba are most of the time careful[24] in using Rol pa'i rdo rje for Lalitavajra in order to distinguish him from Sgeg pa'i rdo rje, the Tibetan lineages that took part in the transmission of Vajrabhairava cycle had not been as careful. The confusion between the equivalent forms *rol pa* and *sgeg pa* has been indeed transferred to the narratives dealing with Lalitavajra's life. For example, the followers of Bari lo tsā ba Rin chen grags (1040–1111/12) refer to Lalitavajra as Sgeg pa'i- and not Rol pa'i rdo rje. Moreover, in the Bari lineage, Sgeg pa'i rdo rje is succeeded by the line of masters associated

---

cing/ sgeg pa'i skad dod gtso bor la syā 'am/ bi la sya yin pa dang/ rol pa'i don rtsed mo 'am/ gang 'dod dang ci gar rang nyams su lod pa'i don yin/ sgeg pa ni cha byad spros pa bskyed pa'i don yin pas tshig don gnyis gar nas cung zad mi 'dra'o/.

20. 'Gos lo, *Deb ther sngon po*, 446 (trans. Roerich 1949, 1:367), mentions Maṇidvīpa for Nor bu gling, but Tribe points out (1994, 13) that it is most probably Ratnadvīpa, for the Sanskrit colophon of the NMAA indicates this connection (*kṛtir ācāryavilāsavajrasya ratnadvīpanivāsinaḥ*).

21. 'Gos lo, *Deb ther sngon po*, 446 (trans. Roerich 1949, 1:367).

22. 'Gos lo, *Deb ther sngon po*, 255 (trans. Roerich 1949, 1:204), refers to Sgeg pa'i rdo rje (Līlāvajra) as the exegete of the *Mañjuśrīnāmasaṅgīti.*

23. For the storyline associated with Vilāsavajra in Tāranātha's *Rgya gar chos 'byung*, see Chattopadhyaya 1990, 271–72; for Lalitavajra, see Chattopadhyaya 1990, 242–44.

24. 'Gos lo tsā ba refers to Rol pa'i rdo rje (transcribed as Lalitavajra) only once ('Gos lo, *Deb ther sngon po*, 1200; Roerich 1949, 2:1030) when he is described as a direct disciple of Tilopā and a teacher of Mitrayogin (see below). Sgeg pa'i rdo rje is referred to twice, first (transcribed as Lalitavajra) as a tantric teacher of Dam pa sangs rgyas (eleventh century), also known as Black Ācārya (*Ātsāra nag po*) ('Gos lo, *Deb ther sngon po*, 1117; Roerich 1949, 2:869), and second (without transcription) as the author of the commentary on the MNS ('Gos lo, *Deb ther sngon po*, 255; Roerich 1949, 1:204)—i.e., the NMAA.

with the commentarial tradition of the *Nāmasaṅgīti*, which indicates that the Sgeg pa'i rdo rje whom they thought was Lalitavajra was in fact Vilāsavajra (see diagram 1).

Another confusion that contributed to conflating the identity of Lalitavajra with Vilāsavajra was created by the linguistic problem of using the words *lalita* and *līlā* as synonyms. The Skyo lineage accepted the name Līlāvajra (and not Lalitavajra) for the revealer of the VBhT, and in so doing they seemingly confused him with Sgeg pa'i rdo rje (whose name sometimes appears in Sanskrit transcription as Līlāvajra),[25] whom they believed was also the author of the *Gsang ldan* (**Guhyāpanna*).[26] Sgeg pa'i rdo rje, the author of the **Guhyāpanna*, again suggests Vilāsavajra—the late eighth- to early ninth-century author of the NMAA. He is known as the founder of the 'Jam dpal gsang ldan (Mañjuśrī **Guhyāpanna*) school, which was named after Agrabodhi's sādhana to the **Guhyāpanna* (*Mañjuśrīnāmasaṅgītisādhana*, Toh. 2579; see Tribe 1994, 20). Agrabodhi, which is the ordination name of Vilāsavajra, is considered by Tāranātha and Bu ston as one[27] and the same person[28] (Tribe 1994, 19).[29]

The juxtaposition of Vilāsavajra/Agrabodhi with Līlāvajra suggested by Skyo lineage is understandable, especially since those masters share the same interest in the MNS and *Māyājāla Tantra* traditions,[30] and both resided at

25. Tāranātha's *Rgya gar chos 'byung* refers to Līlāvajra (Chattopadhyaya 1990, 271–71) implying Vilāsavajra. In the *Gshin rje chos 'byung* (p. 67), Tāranātha states that using Līlāvajra for Lalitavajra is slightly inappropriate (*li la vajras zhes 'bod pa cung zad mi legs so*).

26. *Skyo lugs gyi brgyud pa'i dbang du byas na/ la li ta vajra dang/ gsang ldan mdzad mkhan kyi sgeg pa'i rdo rje gcig pa ltar gyi bshad pa byed te/*. Tāranātha, *Gshin rje chos 'byung*, 116.

27. Sakurai (1987, 88) agrees with this view and explains that the identification of Agrabodhi with Vilāsavajra is because Agrabodhi's work expounds the *Māyājālasaṃbodhikrama*, also dealt with in chapter 4 of the NMAA, although the exposition follows categories that are not extant in the NMAA. Davidson (1981, 8) and Tribe (1994, 20) disagree with Sakurai, suggesting that Vilāsavajra and Agrabodhi are two different persons who adopted a very similar ritual system.

28. Tribe (1994, 19) suggests that identification of Vilāsavajra with Agrabodhi is based on the mistranslation into Tibetan of the Sanskrit compound *bhāgineyasya* in the colophon of NMAA as two words—*bhāgine* and *yasya* (*skal ba dang ldan pa gang gi*)—and the understanding of Śrīmadagrabodhibhāgin as "to be in apposition to Sgeg pa'i rdo rje."

29. Davidson (1981, 8) thinks that Agrabodhi flourished later than Vilāsavajra, but Tribe (1994, 20), based on the analysis of the compound *bhāgineyasya*, states the opposite, suggesting that Vilāsavajra was drawing upon the earlier work of Agrabodhi, who was his maternal uncle.

30. For the discussion on Lalitavajra's interest in the MNS and *Māyājālatantra*, see chapter 4 below.

Nālandā Monastery. Nevertheless, it is more probable that the Skyo lineage attributed the stories of Vilāsavajra, whom they thought to be the same as Agrabodhi, to Līlāvajra (see diagram 2). This is supported by another piece of evidence: according to the Skyo lineage, Līlāvajra met Mañjuśrīmitra.[31] But as the two Tibetan historiographers confirm, Mañjuśrīmitra was a teacher of both *Buddhajñānapāda ('Gos lo, *Deb ther sngon po*, 449; Roerich 1949, 1:369–70) and Sgeg pa'i rdo rje[32] (Vilāsavajra), and not Līlāvajra.

The real identity of "our" Lalitavajra is difficult to establish. Unfortunately, most of the information about him comes from Tāranātha's *Rgya gar chos 'byung* and *Gshin rje 'chos byung*, whose historical accuracy has often been questioned (Templeman 1981). Tāranātha depicts Lalitavajra, the revealer of the VBhT, as one of the *siddhayogi*s and great masters (*mahācārya*s), contemporary of other great tenth-century siddhas, such as Luipa (also known as Lūyīpā, Lvāvapā, and Kaṃbalapāda), Indrabhūti the Middle, Kukkurāja, and Saroruhavajra (Chattopadhyaya 1990, 240–41). According to the *Rgya gar chos 'byung*, Lalitavajra (whose real name was *Mañjuśastra) was a teacher (*ācārya*) at Nālandā Monastery who did not have a mortal guru but was initiated by Vajrayoginī/Vajraḍākinī when he went to U rgyan (Oḍḍiyāna) to retrieve the three cycles of Vajrabhairava-Yamāntaka, which also featured the VBhT in seven chapters. Tāranātha depicts Lalitavajra's life through the narratives of magical feats, acts of religious conversion of the non-Buddhists, and victorious struggles with natural and supernatural adversaries (Wenta 2021), all of which he employed to emulate a certain siddha ideal.[33] Although Lalitavajra was probably a historical figure, in Tāranātha's work he underwent a kind of canonization, and the gaps in his real life story were filled with wonders and marvelous deeds so that they could become a firm basis for embodying the magical paradigm of the siddha milieu. The fact that Lalitavajra is depicted in the company of other famous siddhas, such as Luipa and Indrabhūti the Middle,[34] who act as direct witnesses of Lalitavajra's display of siddhis, is deliberately designed to consolidate Lalitavajra's status as the accomplished siddha and the founder of a new tantric tradition.

31. Tāranātha, *Gshin rje chos 'byung*, 117: *slob dpon la la li ta de la 'jam dpal bshes gnyen gyis thug*/.

32. Bu ston as reported by Davidson 1981, 6.

33. Lalitavajra's life stories are discussed in chapter 4 of this book.

34. The stories about Lalitavajra's meeting with Indrabhūti the Middle and Luipa are given in Tāranātha's *Rgya gar chos 'byung* (Chattopadhyaya 1990, 244–45) and *Gshin rje chos 'byung*, 61–62.

In the *Gshin rje chos 'byung*, Tāranātha provides us with yet another chronology of Lalitavajra's period of activity, for he places him approximately one hundred years before the great master *Buddhajñānapāda (*slob dpon chen po sangs rgyas ye shes zhabs*) (ca. 770–820).[35] Based on this information, it can be inferred that Lalitavajra would have been active between the second half of the seventh and the first half of the eighth century. Tāranātha says that for about one hundred years after Lalitavajra's discovery of the VBhT, the cycle did not flourish much. After a gap of approximately a hundred years—that is, around the middle of the eighth century—the Vajrabhairava cycle was picked up by *Buddhajñānapāda, who inherited the succession of Lalitavajra and taught the Vajrabhairava-Yamāntaka cycle.[36] The Tibetan lineages that took part in the transmission of Vajrabhairava-Yamāntaka tantras perceive the relationship between the two masters slightly differently, for they consider Lalitavajra to be a disciple of the great vajra-master (*mahāvajrācārya*) of the maṇḍala *Devabuddhajñānapāda (*dkyil 'khor chen po'i rdo rje slob dpon lha sangs rgyas ye shes zhabs*), who "has achieved realization equal to the state of nonduality of Mañjuśrī in peaceful and wrathful forms," and not his teacher.[37] In this regard, both the Zhang and Gnyos lineages (see diagrams 3 and 4) consider *Buddhajñānapāda to be the first actual lineage holder of

35. For the biography of Jñānapāda/*Buddhajñānapāda, see Dalton and Szántó 2019, 264–68.

36. Tāranātha, *Gshin rje chos 'byung*, 68: *slob dpon 'di'i rjes su lo brgya lhag tsam gshin rje gshed kyi chos skor ha cang mang por mched pa med/ de nas rdo rje slob dpon chen po sangs rgyas ye shes zhabs kyis kyang ci rigs par gsungs shing/ la li ta'i rgyud 'dzin dang/ ye shes zhabs kyi rgyud 'dzin rnams gcig tu 'dres te shin tu dar bar gyur to/ de dag ni gtso bar nag po'i skor byung tshul yin la/*. "A little more than a hundred years after the *ācārya* (Lalitavajra), the teachings of Yamāntaka did not spread much. Then the great vajra-master *Buddhajñānapāda again taught the cycle as suitable, and in due order, the holders of Lalita's lineage and Jñānapāda's lineage became mixed together. The cycle came to be widely disseminated. This is the principal way the Black Cycle (Vajrabhairava-Yamāntaka) originated."

37. Tāranātha, *Gshin rje chos 'byung*, 82–83: *srol btod* [em. *brtod* ed.] *mkhan zhang lugs par grags par rnams lo rgyus 'di skad ces 'chad de/ dkyil 'khor chen po'i rdo rje slob dpon lha sangs rgyas ye shes zhabs de/ 'jam dpal zhi khro dang gnyis su med pa'i go 'phang brnyes pa lta bu yin/ des mar me mdzad bzang po la gnang/ 'di dang la li ta chen po gnyis kyi lo rgyus 'khrul gzhi cung zad byung/*. "As for the initiator of the tradition known as those of the Zhang lineage, the story goes like this: The *mahāvajrācārya* of the maṇḍala *Devabuddhajñānapāda has achieved realization equal to the state of nonduality of Mañjuśrī in peaceful and wrathful forms. He gave the teaching to *Dīpaṅkarabhadra. A little confusion has arisen with regard to the lineage of the two great Lalitas."

Vajrabhairava-Yamāntaka cycle, and Lalitavajra to be his disciple.[38] According to the Zhang lineage (see diagram 3), Lalitavajra belonged to a direct transmission lineage of *Buddhajñānapāda through another vajra-master of Vikramaśīla, Dīpaṅkarabhadra, who bestowed upon him the Vajrabhairava-Yamāntaka tradition.[39] Tāranātha tried to resolve this chronological conundrum by stating that there existed two Lalitavajras: Lalitavajra Senior, who brought the VBhT from Oḍḍiyāna, and Lalitavajra Junior, who was a direct disciple of Dīpaṅkarabhadra in the lineage of *Buddhajñānapāda.[40] Lalitavajra

38. See Tāranātha, *Gshin rje chos 'byung*, 82–83, for Zhang lineage, and page 125 for Gnyos lineage: *gnyos kyis ba ling acarya gsan pa yin/ rtsa ba la li ta la thug dgos pa gzhir bcas kyang/ slob dpon sangs rgyas ye shes zhabs kyi man ngag kho na la brten pa'i phyir/ dngos su brgyud pa'i 'go yang de nas 'dren/*. "Gnyos has received the teaching from *Baliṅgācārya. But even though, without any doubt, the root [guru] can be traced to Lalita, since the explanation (of the Vajrabhairava-Yamāntaka tradition) relies exclusively on the master *Buddhajñānapāda, he is at the head of the actual lineage, and one therefore has to quote [him as the first in the lineage]."

39. According to the *Blue Annals* ('Gos lo, *Deb ther sngon po*, 451; Roerich 1949, 1:371), *Dīpaṅkarabhadra was one of the eighteen excellent disciples of Buddhaśrījñāna (Jñānapāda), and among these, four attained the status of great vajra-holder (*rdo rje 'phang chen po*). According to the *Rgya gar chos 'byung* (Chattopadhyaya 1990, 18), he was one of the twelve *vajrācāryas* of Vikramaśīla (to which Buddhajñānapāda, Śrīdhara, Lalitavajra Junior, and Tathāgatarakṣita—who wrote a commentary on the VBhT—also belonged) during the reign of the king Devapāla, just after *Buddhajñānapāda. The scriptures attributed to him in the Bstan 'gyur include the work on Kṛṣṇa and Rakta Yamāris—namely, sorcery via natural forces (*char 'bebs cho ga*), aversion of spirits, exorcism (*klu chog*), destruction (*bsad mnan*), one work on Vajrabhairava, and the explanatory tantras of the GS, such as the *Guhyasamājamaṇḍalavidhiṭīkā*.

40. Tāranātha, *Gshin rje chos 'byung*, 83: *'di dang la li ta chen po gnyis kyi lo rgyus 'khrul gzhi cung zad byung/ de la li ta vajra ma mtshan gzhan li la vajra gyis zhus/ 'dis rgyud rdo rje 'chang zhal gzigs/ nus pa thogs pa med/ dgra nag gi rgyud kyi don 'grel du gshin rje gshed 'byung pa'i bstan bcos mdzad/ zhang pa rnams slob dpon 'dis nag 'jigs skor gsum gyi rgyud rnams spyan drangs par 'dod mod/ slob dpon 'di ni sangs rgyas ye shes zhabs kyi yang slob tu zhang lugs pa rang 'dod pa bzhin du/ don la 'ang gnas par mngon pas/ la li ta chung ba rang yin zhing/ rgyud spyan 'dren pa po ni la li ta chen po yin pas/*. "This, together with the story of the two great Lalitas, became the cause of a little confusion. In this regard, Lalitavajra was called by another name—i.e., Līlāvajra. Through this [VBhT] tantra, he was graced with the vision of Vajradhara, and his powers became unhindered. He completed the treatise on the genesis of Yamāntaka as the commentary on the tantric cycle of the Black Enemy [of Death]. Even though Zhang followers believe that he was the master (*ācārya*) who brought the three cycles of Black Bhairava, according to the vested interest of the Zhang tradition this *ācārya* was also a disciple of *Buddhajñānāpāda, and this seems to be a historical fact too. It must be the junior Lalita, and the one who brought the [VBhT] tantra must be Lalita Senior."

In the *Gshin rje chos 'byung*, Lalitavajra Junior is mentioned as a direct disciple of

Junior was committed to reviving the legacy of Lalitavajra Senior through dissemination of Lalitavajra Senior's earlier works,[41] and he also composed his own treatises (see diagram 5). Since the two Lalitavajras bear the same name, their distinct identities became conflated.

Tāranātha's solution to this chronological problem is to postulate the existence of the two Lalitavajras separated in time and space. His explanation of a revival of Vajrabhairava-Yamāntaka tradition initiated by *Buddhajñānapāda and implemented by Lalitavajra Junior seems viable. Our current knowledge about the scholarly interests of the Vikramaśīla *vajrācārya*s allows for the existence of a strong Vajrabhairava-Yamāntaka tradition at Vikramaśīla Monastery, as suggested by the type of works the tantric masters at Vikramaśīla engaged with. Beginning with *Buddhajñānapāda, who allegedly composed three texts on the Raktayamāri (Toh. 2086, 2084, 2085), through Śrīdhara, the first lineage holder of the Raktayamāri tradition, to Dīpaṅkarabhadra, Lalitavajra Junior, Tathāgatarakṣita, Kamalarakṣita, Kṛṣṇācārya Junior, and so forth, we notice a continuous effort to grant visibility to the Vajrabhairava-Yamāntaka cults in the tantric world.

Six Canonical Commentaries on the Vajrabhairava Tantra

As noted above, there are six known commentaries on the VBhT originally composed in Sanskrit by various Indian authors. These commentaries were written to clarify more obscure or difficult portions of the root tantra (*mūlatantra*), following a word-by-word exegesis. All six of them have been included in the Bstan 'gyur portion of the Tibetan canon, and they are referenced in my annotated translation of the VBhT in part II. Only one of these commentaries[42] has come down to us in the original Sanskrit; the others can

---

Dīpaṅkarabhadra, but in the *Rgya gar chos 'byung* (Chattopadhyaya 1990, 325–29), he is listed as one of the twelve *vajrācārya*s of Vikramaśīla, headed by Jñānapāda and followed by Dīpaṅkarabhadra, Laṅkajayabhadra, Śrīdhara, Bhavabhadra, Bhavyakīrti, Līlāvajra (Lalitavajra Junior), Durjayacandra, Samayavajra, Tathāgatarakṣita, Bodhibhadra, and finally Kamalarakṣita.

41. In the *Rgya gar chos 'byung* (Chattopadhayaya 1990, 224), Lalitavajra Junior is mentioned as a disciple of Lalitavajra Senior: "Līlāvajra committed to writing the works of the *ācārya*. But the *Yamāntakodaya*, the *Śāntikrodhavikrīḍita*, and so on were composed by Līlāvajra the Great." It thus appears that most of the works attributed to Lalitavajra were penned by his disciple on the basis of Lalitavajra Senior's earlier works. These works are listed under the name Lalitavajra in the appendix of the *Rgya gar chos 'byung* (see Chattopadhyaya 1990, 411–12).

42. Siklós (1996, 225) reported the existence of a Sanskrit manuscript of Kumāracandra's

Diagram 1. Vajrabhairava Transmission in the Lineage of Ba ri lo tsā ba

Lalitavajra (Sgeg pa'i rdo rje)

⇩

*Mañjuśrīkīrti ('Jam dpal grags pa)

⇩

*Mañjuśrīkīrti Junior ('Jam dpal grags pa chung ba)

⇩

*Mañjuśrīmitra ('Jam dpal bshes gnyen)

⇩

Amoghavajra Senior

⇩

Amoghavajra Junior

⇩

Ba ri lo tsā ba

Diagram 2. Vajrabhairava Transmission in the Skyo Tradition

Līlāvajra/Vilāsavajra/Agrabodhi

⇩

Mañjuśrīmitra

⇩

⇩	⇩	⇩	⇩
Devākaracandra	Nag po pa	Vīryacandra	Amoghavajra Junior
			⇩
			Skyo ston 'Od 'byung

Diagram 3. Vajrabhairava Transmission in the Zhang Tradition

*Buddhajñānapāda

⇩

Dīpaṅkarabhadra

⇩	⇩
Devākaracandra	Lalitavajra
⇩	
Cog gru Shes rab bla ma	

Diagram 4. Vajrabhairava-Yamāntaka Transmission in the Gnyos Tradition

*Buddhajñānapāda

⇩

Lalitavajra

⇩

Bālyācārya/Baliṅgācārya

⇩

Gnyos lo Yon tan grags (b. 973)

Diagram 5. Vajrabhairava Transmission according to Tāranātha

Lalitavajra Senior (seventh–eighth century)

⇩

*Buddhajñānapāda

⇩

Dīpaṅkarabhadra

⇩

Lalitavajra Junior

only be accessed in Tibetan translation. The history of the VBhT's exegetical writers is even more obscure than the history of its alleged revealer, Lalitavajra. Almost nothing is known about their lives, and any shred of information that can be gathered on some of them, for example from xylographs' colophons, does not throw any light on their affiliation or the lineages they belonged to. Tāranātha does not have much to say about the commentaries either. His brief note contains the following:

> Concerning the dharma cycle of the *Śrīvajramahābhairava* [*Tantra*]: the commentary by Kumāracandra (*Vajrabhairavatantra-pañjikā*) is very limited and appears to be merely fulfilling the oath. [The commentary] by *Vajrasiddha (*Śrīvajrabhairavatantra-ṭippaṇīnāma*) is said to be [the one] by *Śoṇaśrī; despite some differences in their translations, their basic content is the same. There is also a commentary by the so-called Lalitavajra (i.e., the *Vajrabhairavatantravṛttyalaṃkāraupadeśanāma*). The commentary that is said to be written by the *ācārya* *Akṣobhya (*Śrīvajra-bhairavatantraṭīkā*) was composed by Lo tsā ba Cog gru Shes rab.[43] Although later commentaries are more exhaustive than the [commentary] by Kumāracandra, I do not find them clear enough to convey the meaning of the [*Vajrabhairava*] *Tantra*.[44]

Tāranātha's statement that it was Cog gru Shes rab, and not *Akṣobhya, who wrote the commentary on the VBhT is somewhat unusual. Cog gru Shes rab bla ma (tenth–eleventh centuries), also known as Zhang Cog gru lo tsā ba Shes rab, established the earliest of the Vajrabhairava transmission lineages in

---

pañjikā and numbered the manuscript SPMT 276 and 300. The Sanskrit manuscripts of Kumāracandra's *pañjikā* are currently held at the University of Beijing (ms. no. 107, ms. no. 23). I thank F. Sferra and Shaoyong Ye for helping me to gain access to those manuscripts. My critical edition of this text is forthcoming.

43. As discussed below, it is unclear why Tāranātha would make such a statement. The commentary by *Akṣobhya was translated by the Indian paṇḍita Vinayacandra and the lo tsā ba Go rub chos shes, which could be a mistake for Cog gru Shes rab.

44. Tāranātha, *Gshin rje chos 'byung*, 134: *dpal rdo rje 'jigs byed chen po'i chos skor la/ gzhon nu zla bas mdzad pa'i 'grel pa ni/ bshad pa shin tu cha chung ba mna' skyel* [em. *sel*, ed.] *lta bur snang/ rdo rje grub pas mdzad pa dang/ so na sris mdzad ces pa gnyis ni 'gyur khyad tsam ma gtogs ngo bo gcig yin cing/ rol pa'i rdo rje zhes bya ba cig gis mdzad pa'i 'grel pa 'ang yod/ slob dpon mi skyod pas mdzad zer ba'i 'grel pa 'di ni/ lo tsa ba cog gru shes rab* [em. *go rub chos shes*, ed.] *byas pa yin/ 'grel pa phyi ma de rnams gzhon nu zla ba las ni cung zad rgyas kyang/ rgyud don gsal bar rtogs nus pa'i bshad pa mi snang ngo/.*

Tibet, the so-called Zhang lineage (*zhang lugs*). This lineage is traced back to the Indian, or perhaps Newar, paṇḍita Devākaracandra (ca. 1030–1130), who is regarded as the Zhang lineage's root guru (*rtsa ba'i bla ma*),[45] and who is identified by Tāranātha as Bla ma Mgos khub, the "scholar-monk who had a consort" (*mkhas btsun mo can*). Scant biographical information places Cog gru in Nepal and Magadha, where he met Devākaracandra (probably at Vikramaśīla) and received from him the teachings on the *Guhyasamāja*, the *Kālacakra*, and three cycles of Vajrabhairava-Yamāntaka. It is said that Cog gru was empowered into all types of Yamāntaka, particularly Black Yamāntaka.[46] Cog gru's contribution to the dissemination of the Vajrabhairava-Yamāntaka tradition in Tibet is attested in his translation work. The Bstan 'gyur mentions Cog gru's name in the context of several texts that he translated alone or in collaboration with the Indian paṇḍitas,[47] including Prajñāśrīdeva and Amoghavajra Junior. Apart from the translation work, the Zhang lugs's greatest contribution to the development of Vajrabhairava teachings in Tibet was the establishment of a unique tradition of the Forty-Nine-Deity Vajrabhairava system (*dpal rdo rje 'jigs byed zhang lugs lha zhe dgu ma*) (see plate 1). The tradition of the Forty-Nine-Deity Vajrabhairava maṇḍala appears to have been known at the Yuan court and was certainly practiced at the Qing court.

*Akṣobhya

There is some evidence suggesting that *Akṣobhya's (Mi skyod pa) commentary,[48] entitled the *Śrīvajrabhairavatantraṭīkā* (=*Dpal rdo rje 'jigs byed kyi rgyud kyi dka' 'grel*, Toh. 1970),[49] is also one of the earliest commentaries on the VBhT among all those included in the Bstan 'gyur. *Akṣobhya, who in the colophon of his treatise refers to himself as vajra-master (*rdo rje slob dpon*), was probably

45. Tāranātha, *Gshin rje chos 'byung*, 117.

46. See Tāranātha, *Gshin rje chos 'byung*, 84.

47. For the full list of translations attributed to Cog gru, see *Gangs ljongs skad gnyis smra ba du ma'i 'gyur byang bla gsal dga' skyed* (BDRC W24697), 267–68, and Tāranātha, *Gshin rje chos 'byung*, 76.

48. In the introduction to chapter 4, *Akṣobhya refers to the well-established Abhidharma categories of composing scholarly treatises saying that the VBhT as a root tantra (*mūlatantra*) is the goal (*uddeśa*), his commentary as a whole is an instruction (*nirdeśa*), and the exposition of the most difficult parts, such as a detailed description of the deity's iconographical features, is the cross-reference (*pratinirdeśa*).

49. The Tibetan text of *Akṣobhya's *ṭīkā* (*Dpal rdo rje 'jigs byed kyi rgyud kyi dka' 'grel*) is included in all the five editions of the Bstan 'gyur—i.e., Co ne, Beijing, Gser bris ma, Sde dge, and Dpe bsdur ma; see bibliography.

active in the early ninth century. This date is established on the basis of several references included in his work that are uniquely associated with an early tantric milieu. For example, *Akṣobhya quotes a passage on the mantra recitation[50] that also appears at the end of the *Rahasyānandatilaka*, a text attributed to Mahāmati, where it is listed as a quotation from the *Sarvakalpasamuccaya*,[51] one of the earliest supplementary commentaries (*uttaratantra*) on the proto-yoginī tantra *Sarvabuddhasamāyoga* (Sanderson 2009, 154–55). The same passage quoted by *Akṣobhya also appears in the *Susiddhikara Sūtra*, an early kriyā tantra and the only surviving text of the *Susiddhi* cycle that has been translated into Chinese by Śubhākarasiṃha in 724 (Giebel 2001). Another piece of evidence in support of *Akṣobhya's early date is a gloss on the three worlds (*triloka*)[52] explained by him (in chapter 4 of his commentary) through the example of the three brothers, namely, Jayakāra, Madhukāra,[53] and Sarvārthasiddhikāra. The same gloss appears in the NMAA (Tribe 2016, 104), where Vilāsavajra glosses *trailokya* "[with *loka* meaning 'people' rather than 'worlds'] as the three brothers, namely, Jayakāra, Madhukāra, and Sarvārthasiddhikāra." According to P. D. Szántó (in private conversation), the early commentators use the concept of the "three brothers" to refer to the three worlds, but this semantic gloss must have disappeared sometime in the ninth century.

Apart from its value as one of the earliest commentaries on the VBhT, *Akṣobhya's exposition offers a comprehensive and detailed account of magical technologies, especially with regard to the performance of magical procedures in chapter 2 and fire offerings in chapter 6, which (except for Lalitavajra's work) are absent in the later commentaries. The close attention paid to the ritual details[54] throughout his work suggests that at the time when *Akṣobhya was composing the *Śrīvajrabhairavatantraṭīkā*, the cult of Vajrabhairava was

50. For the discussion on this passage, see page 275 below.

51. I thank P. D. Szántó for this information.

52. *Akṣobhya's *ṭīkā*, 381: "Three worlds [means] he is the lord of these [three worlds]: Jayakāra, Madhukāra, Sarvārthasiddhikāra" (*'jig rten gsum zhes bya ba ni de'i bdag po ste/ rgyal bar byed pa dang/ sbrang rtsir byed pa dang/ don kun 'grub pa'o*).

53. Jayakāra, Madhukāra, Vasanta, and Balabhadra come under the Balabhadra group in the Dharmadhātuvāgīśvara maṇḍala of the *Niṣpannayogāvalī* (Bhattacharyya 1958, 378). A reference to Jayakāra and Madhukāra appears also in the *Śūraṅgama* mantra (v. 103), the central mantra of the *Śūraṅgamasamādhisūtra* (Lamotte 2003), when their names are followed by the words: *sarvārthasādhakakṛtaṃ vidyāṃ chedayāmi kīlayāmi*.

54. Indeed, in the colophon *Akṣobhya acknowledges the fact that his knowledge of intricate particulars is based on the teachings of his guru: "This work contains extensive *prayogas*, which accord with the instructions (*upadeśa*) taught by my guru" (*sbyor ba rgya chen ji skad bla mas smras pa bzhin*).

still flourishing. Another feature that sets *Akṣobhya's commentary apart from other exegetical works and also supports the text's early date is a reference to Vajrabhairava as a solitary hero (*ekavīra*) that aligns with both the exposition of the root text and Lalitavajra's commentary, and differs from the later commentaries, which focus on Vajrabhairava in the company of the maṇḍala consisting of thirteen or seventeen deities (see p. 113 below). Moreover, *Akṣobhya makes an attempt to present an integrated ritual system in bringing the Vajrabhairava and Kṛṣṇayamāri traditions together. Insofar as *Akṣobhya's scholarly background is concerned, the commentary does not reveal any dogmatic features that could give an indication of the author's scholarly orientation or doctrinal leanings. In the discussion of the mantra recitation, *Akṣobhya refers to the concept of one's own mantra (*svamantra*/*nijamantra*), and thus he exhibits a distinctive feature of the Jñānapāda school of exegesis (see p. 274), but in other places he quotes a passage from Nāgārjuna's *Pañcakrama*, a text associated with the Ārya school (see p. 162).

Lalitavajra

The commentary on the VBhT entitled *Vajrabhairavatantravṛttyalaṃkāropadeśanāma* (=*Dpal rdo rje 'jigs byed kyi rgyud kyi 'grel pa man ngag dang ldan pa'i rgyan zhes bya ba*)[55] attributed to Lalitavajra (Rol pa'i rdo rje) is an uneven work, which may indicate that it was composed by more than one author. On the one hand, some features of the commentary seem to point to a relatively early date. In this regard, the text stands out for its strong mortuary magic content that is bereft of any attempts at Buddhist "encoding," as is characteristic of later commentaries. Lalitavajra's commentary aligns with the precepts of the root text insofar as it closely follows the original stratum of Vajrabhairava cult in its connection to Yamarāja's mantra as the thirty-two-syllable root-mantra of Vajrabhairava. At the same time, it is strongly reminiscent of an earlier cult of Mañjuśrī as the antecedent to Vajrabhairava cult (see p. 86 below). In this regard, Lalitavajra is the only commentator who refers to Mañjuśrī's root mantra, and unlike other commentators, he is also aware of the symbolism of the letter *a* as the source of Mañjuśrī that is also found in the MNS (see p. 123). Another early feature is the fact that in the visualization procedure, Vajrabhairava is summoned with the mudrā of *vajragraha* that goes back to the STTS (see p. 131). Moreover, Lalitavajra's text contains extensive instruc-

55. The incipit title mentions the Indian paṇḍita Lalitavajra (*rol pa'i rdo rje*) as the author, while the colophons mention the paṇḍita *Las kyi rdo rje* and a monk named Kumāraśīla as translators.

tions on fire offerings (see p. 149) and various magical rituals that are not only very detailed but also distinguished by a strong transgressive and antinomian content. Witness, for instance, the instructions on sexual magic and the consumption of sexual fluids that are characteristsic of the Kaula tradition (see p. 158) and which are not found in other VBhT commentaries. Lalitavajra's text is also the only commentary that begins with the visualization praxis (*dhyāna*) of Vajrabhairava, otherwise mentioned only in chapter 4. On the other hand, this commentary exhibits some features that would suggest later influences. For example, the visualization process (*dhyāna*) includes the generation of Mañjuśrī as the knowledge being (*jñānasattva*) in the heart of Vajrabhairava (see p. 130), which resembles the Mañjuśrī-related sādhanas of the *Sādhanamālā*, where the concept of the knowledge being becomes more and more associated with "the yogic practices based on the deity in the heart" (English 2002, 471). This apparent combination of early and later features included in one text may point to the scenario in which a later author was redacting the writings of an earlier master, as suggested by Tāranātha (see p. 27 above).

*Śoṇaśrī/*Vajrasiddha

The next two works in the exegetical tradition of the VBhT are the commentaries on the difficult points bearing the same title—namely, the *Śrīvajrabhairavatantraṭippaṇīnāma* (=*Dpal rdo rje 'jigs byed kyi rgyud kyi mdor bshad pa zhes bya ba*, Toh. 1971 and 1972) by *Śoṇaśrī[56] and *Vajrasiddha, respectively. These two texts are almost identical in content apart from a very few, mostly stylistic, differences. It is likely that *Vajrasiddha's commentary is an updated version of *Śoṇaśrī's work and may be the result of a scenario in which a diligent disciple updated the text of the master. This suggestion, although nothing more than a hypothesis, is supported by the fact that *Vajrasiddha's text is written in a more elegant and lucid language. Several features identify this commentary as belonging to the later commentarial tradition, perhaps in existence sometime in the tenth or eleventh century. First, Vajrabhairava appears in the company of the maṇḍala of deities. Second, the thirty-two-syllable mantra of Yamarāja that was part of the original stratum of the root text loses its ritual

56. The name *Śoṇaśrī (although given in Sanskrit transcription as Sonaśrī) is not attested in Sanskrit. Prof. Diwakar Acharya has suggested to me that Sonaśrī is a corruption of *Śoṇaśrī (the word *śoṇa* in Sanskrit is the name of a river and it also denotes the color red or crimson). The variant *soṇā* is also attested in Sanskrit with the meaning of "gold." P. D. Szántó has proposed that Sonaśrī is the Middle Indic form of the Sanskrit *suvarṇa*, meaning "gold," "red," or "crimson." Both explanations are viable, and on this basis I have emended the name Sonaśrī to *Śoṇaśrī.

function. Third, the commentary is much less detailed and less comprehensive than those by *Akṣobhya and Lalitavajra, for it does not provide any specifics regarding the performance of the rituals and fire offerings or the explanation of the mantra. Thus the dimension of material culture that plays an important role in the magical technology in the earlier commentarial tradition is almost completely absent here, while the aspects of Vajrabhairava practice associated with visualization (*dhyāna*) receive extensive exegetical analysis.

*Kṛṣṇācārya

Another commentary on the VBhT that belongs to the later exegetical tradition is the *Vajrabhairavatantrapañjikā Ratnamālā* (=*Rdo rje 'jigs byed kyi rgyud kyi 'grel pa rin po che'i phreng ba zhes bya ba*, Toh. 1974) by *Kṛṣṇācārya. *Kṛṣṇācārya certainly belongs to the same oral tradition as *Śoṇaśrī and *Vajrasiddha, for all the three commentaries exhibit very similar exegetical features. Whether this *Kṛṣṇācārya is the same Kṛṣṇācārya who composed the *Yogaratnamālā*, a commentary on the *Hevajra Tantra*, is not a question I attempt to answer here. Both Kṛṣṇācāryas incorporate the threefold division of the tantra into the causal tantra (*hetutantra*), the resultant tantra (*phalatantra*), and the method tantra (*upāyatantra*),[57] and in so doing, they follow the standard hermeneutical method for tantric exegesis prevalent in the tenth–eleventh centuries, adopted also by Ratnākaraśānti.[58] "Our" *Kṛṣṇācārya integrates the method of the threefold division of tantra with another commentarial method: the connections (*anubandhas*) popular in the Yogācāra-Madhyamaka tradition.[59] At the outset of his com-

57. The threefold division of the tantra generally understands *hetutantra* to mean the sādhaka, *phalatantra* to mean the fruit of the sādhana (for example, union with the deity), and *upāyatantra* to mean the method of accomplishing the fruit, or the sādhana itself.

58. Ratnākaraśānti was especially fond of this threefold division. In the *Guṇavatī* commentary on the *Mahāmāyā Tantra* (1.3, Samdhong and Dwivedi 1992, accessible online on http://www.dsbcproject.org/canon-text/book/347), he glosses the word *tantra* as *prabandha* "continuum" of the three aspects: *hetutantra* ("cause tantra"), *phalatantra* ("result tantra"), and *upāyatantra* ("method tantra") (*tantram iti prabandham. trividhaṃ tantram, hetutantraṃ phalatantram upāyatantraṃ ca*). The same system was adopted by Kṛṣṇācārya in his *Yogaratnamālā*, a commentary on the *Hevajra Tantra: tantram iti prabandhaḥ/ tac ca tridhā hetutantraṃ phalatantraṃ upāyatantrañ ca/ tad atra hetur vajrakulīnāḥ sattvāḥ pariṇiṣpannā hevajramūrtiḥ phalaṃ/ upāyo vakṣyamāṇaḥ saparikaro mārgaḥ.* (*Yogaratnamālā* I.1 [4–10], ed. Snellgrove 1959, 105). For the translation, see Snellgrove 1959, 138.

59. The first manual that contained theoretical foundation for writing the commentary for the Mahāyāna tradition was the *Vyākhyāyukti* ("Principles of Exegesis"), the text attrib-

mentary, *Kṛṣṇācārya mentions the five *anubandhas*[60] to introduce his discussion of the text: (1) *prayojana-prayojana*, "the purpose of the purpose," (2) *prayojana*, "the purpose," (3) *abhidhāna*, "the text," (4) *abhidheya*, "the subject matter," and (5) *sambandha*, "the connection." *Kṛṣṇācārya explains the meaning of the *anubandhas*[61] in the context of their application in the *Vajrabhairavatantrapañjikā Ratnamālā* and couples them with the twofold division of the tantra. He is mainly interested in interpreting the *prayojana-prayojana* in terms of resultant tantra (*phalatantra*) and *prayojana* in terms of method tantra (*upāyatantra*). He does not discuss the category of causal tantra (*hetutantra*). With regard to the *prayojana-prayojana* category, he says:

> The Lord Vajradhara himself is the goal to be accomplished through this resultant tantra (*phalatantra*). The sādhana is the path because it is realized through practice; for the yogin, the purpose of the purpose is the accomplishment (*siddhi*).[62]

After that, *Kṛṣṇācārya goes on to explain the purpose (*prayojana*) as well as the purpose of the purpose (*prayojana-prayojana*) categories that become conjoined with the Mahāyāna doctrine of personal benefit (*svārtha-saṃpad*) and benefit for others (*parārtha-saṃpad*). The altruistic context of the Mahāyāna tradition is paired with the classic description of the Mahāyāna praxis predicated upon the distinction between what is to be avoided (*heya*) and what is to be obtained (*upādeya*). *Kṛṣṇācārya offers the following explanation:

> As for the *svārtha-saṃpad*, it is of two kinds: to give up without remainder (*heya-saṃpad*) the two obscurations (*āvaraṇa*), that of afflictive emotions (*kleśa-āvaraṇa*) and that of cognitive obscurations (*jñeya-āvaraṇa*). As for that, this is obtained by *upādeya-saṃpad*, which is obtaining awakening by obtaining

---

uted to Vasubandhu (fourth–fifth centuries CE), which followed the fivefold model (see Cabezón 1991, 233). Tantric Buddhist exegetical writers adopted this system as the commentarial method for explaining the tantras.

60. The list of *anubandhas* varies. The longest list contains six *anubandhas*, the shortest four. For a discussion on the different lists of *anubandhas* in the commentaries on the Mahāyāna sūtras, see Schoening 1995 and Broido 1983.

61. *Kṛṣṇācārya does not use the word *anubandhas* for the description of these categories.

62. *Kṛṣṇācārya's *pañjikā*, p. 443: *bcom ldan 'das rdo rje 'chang de nyid bsgrub bya 'bras bu'i rgyud 'dis bsgrub par byas pas lam sgrub byed do/ rnal 'byor pa la dngos grub dgos pa'i* [em. *dgos pas*, ed.] *dgos pa'o/*.

> awakening. Purpose (*prayojana*) is the sādhana itself, which comes from method tantra (*upāyatantra*). *Prayojana* of that *prayojana* is bringing about benefit for others by overcoming through this tantra demons, non-Buddhists, serpents, *yakṣa*s, wrathful *caṇḍī*s, wrathful *bhairava*s, and so on, those who turn on the teachings and who are intent on hurting sentient beings in general and the teacher (*ācārya*) in particular.[63]

Next, *Kṛṣṇācārya turns to a brief exposition of his understanding of the text, subject matter, and connection, which are also explained in terms of personal benefit and benefit for others:

> The yogin who accomplishes benefit for himself and for others amounts to the text (*abhidhāna*) and the subject matter (*abhidheya*), which have both a causal and an identity relationship because they are mutually related.[64]

After explaining the general meaning of *anubandha*s, *Kṛṣṇācārya then proceeds to show in the commentary itself how these categories can be applied and gives several examples pertaining to the beginning of chapter 1 of the VBhT.[65]

63. *Kṛṣṇācārya's *pañjikā*, p. 443: *de yang rang gi don phun sum tshogs pa gnyis te spangs pa phun sum tshogs pa nyon mongs pa dang shes bya'i sgrib pa ma lus pa spong ba'o/ de yang thob bya phun sum tshogs pa thob pa las te/ mngon par byang chub pas mngon par byang chub pa'o/ dgos pa de yang thabs rgyud las byung ba nyid sgrub thabs so/ dgos pa de'i dgos pa ni gzhan gyi don phun sum tshogs pa ste/ bdud dang mu stegs dang/ klu dang/ gnod sbyin dang/ drag po dang candi dang/ 'jigs byed drag po la sogs pa bstan pa la gnod pa dang/ sems can dang slob dpon la gnod pa la rgyud 'dis bsgrubs pas phan 'dogs pa'o/*.

64. *Kṛṣṇācārya's *pañjikā*, p. 443: *rnal 'byor pas bsgrubs pas bdag dang gzhan gyi don thob pa dang/ brjod par bya ba dang rjod par byed pa de phan tshun 'brel bas de dang de las byung ba dang/ bdag nyid gcig par 'brel pa bstan pa'o/*. I thank John Newman for clarifying this translation.

65. In this regard: *iti*, or the word identifying the lemma of the root text, is the subject matter (*abhidheya*), etc. (*de la zhes bya ba ni brjod bya la sogs pa*). "First" is a part of the purpose (*prayojana*), "first" [meaning] "before undertaking the sādhana" (*dang po zhes pa ni dgos pa de bsgrub pa rtsom pa'i sngon du'o*). "The mantra master" [means] "a yogin who has received initiation, who has performed *pūrvasevā* of the mantra, and who knows various subjects, such as maṇḍala, etc."—this constitutes part of *abhidhāna* (*sngags pa zhes pa ni dbang thob cing sngags kyi bsnyen pa dang dkyil 'khor la sogs pa shes pa'i rnal 'byor pa* [em. *rnal 'byor pas*, ed.] *brjod pa'o*). "Pleasing to the mind" [means] "one should seat himself in an isolated place pleasing to the mind such as a cremation ground; moreover, this should be understood to include his assistant, [as well as] substances, and articles for worship"—

Tendencies of the later commentarial tradition are also reflected in *Kṛṣṇācārya's discussion of the four gateways to liberation while commenting on the chapter 1 of the VBhT. *Kṛṣṇācārya shows the influence of the post-tenth-century Hevajra tradition when he incorporates into his discussion of the gateway to liberation of wishlessness (*apraṇihitadvāra*, see p. 211) that system's description of the four energetic circles (*cakras*) constituting the yogin's subtle body—those located in the navel, in the throat, in the heart, and in the head[66]—but with the mantras typical of the Yamāri tradition. This passage is also important for another reason: it demonstrates a commentarial attempt to reformulate the concept of *apraṇihitadvāra* under the generation stage (*utpattikrama*) category. For what in *Kṛṣṇācārya's commentary is described as manipulation of the energetic centers (*cakras*) located in the subtle body that produces great bliss (*mahāsukham*) and, in turn, releases nectar, corresponds to Ratnākaraśānti's exposition of the completion stage (*utpannakrama*), which rests upon the cultivation of great bliss (*mahāsukham*) "that spreads throughout the sādhaka's body."[67]

Another sign that *Kṛṣṇācārya's commentary reflects a later exegetical tradition is his reference to the practice of identifying as the deity (*devatāhaṃkāra*) during all the activities a practitioner undertakes: when eating, when being initiated into the maṇḍala, when performing rituals, and so on. In this regard, *Kṛṣṇācārya instructs as follows: "One should give offerings to himself after having assumed the identity of Vajrabhairava." This statement correlates with the *devatāhaṃkāra* concept found pervasively in the yoginī tantras (English 2002, 166).

Kumāracandra

The commentary by Kumāracandra[68] (Gzhon nu zla ba), entitled the *Vajrabhairavatantrapañjikā* (=*Rdo rje 'jigs byed kyi rgyud kyi dka' 'grel*, Toh. 1973), also belongs to the later exegetical tradition. This commentary is limited in its

this is filled under *prayojana* because it includes the benefit for oneself (*svārtha*) and the benefit for others (*parārtha*)" (*yid du 'ong zhes pa dur khrod la sogs pa yid dang mthun pa spro ba'i gnas gcig tu gnas par bya'o/ yang grogs dang rdzas dang ldan par byas la sdud* [em. *sdod*, ed.] *par shes par bya'o/ dgos pa zhes pa bdag dang gzhan gyi don*).

66. For a discussion on the four *cakras* and the physiology of the yogin's subtle body in the *Hevajra Tantra*, see Snellgrove 1959, 35–39.

67. See Ratnākaraśānti's commentary on the *Hevajra Tantra* 1.8.24cd–24ab in Isaacson 1999, 470–71, quoted in English 2002, 172–73.

68. Kumāracandra's is also the author of the commentary on the *Kṛṣṇayamāri Tantra*. The relationship between these two texts remains a desideratum.

exposition, for it devotes only one sentence each to chapters 4, 6, and 7 of the VBhT. The beginning of the text and most of the glosses seem to be drawing on either *Kṛṣṇācārya's or *Śoṇaśrī/*Vajrasiddha's exposition. Kumāracandra gives a description of Vajrabhairava almost identical to the one in *Kṛṣṇācārya's commentary (see p. 202), and he also follows *Kṛṣṇācārya's division of the resultant tantra (*phalatantra*) and the method tantra (*upāyatantra*).[69] He also adopts the exegetical method of the connections (*anubandhas*)[70] that closely resembles that of *Kṛṣṇācārya. Moreover, in line with *Kṛṣṇācārya's exposition, Kumāracandra defines the sādhana of the VBhT as the means (*upāya*) for accomplishing a personal benefit (*svārtha-saṃpad*) and a benefit for others (*parārtha-saṃpad*). The personal benefit is of two kinds—the understanding of perfect accomplishments and giving up the perfect accomplishments. The first one is as great as the awakening that leads to the perfect buddhahood; the second one is complete abandonment of the latent traces (*vāsanās*) of emotional and cognitive obscurations (*kleśa-* and *jñeya-āvaraṇas*). The benefit for others, on the other hand, is to instill fear in all wicked beings.[71] Unlike other commentators, Kumāracandra gives a complete extraction of the mantras delineated in chapter 3, which appears to be his only "original" contribution.

The History of Vajrabhairava in Tibet and China

The transmission of the VBhT from India to Tibet took place through the Indian or Newar masters and the Tibetan translators during the later dissemi-

69. Kumāracandra (ms. 106 f1v-1r) gives the following definition of *accomplishment* (*siddhi*), adopting the *upāya-* and *phala-* categories: "As for the *accomplishment*, it is a sādhana, which accomplishes a result (*phala*), and a path is that by which [that result is accomplished]. The path of that sādhana is the method (*upāya*)."

70. Kumāracandra (ms. 106 f1v-1r) adopts the method of the *anubandhas* and shows how these categories can be applied in his commentary—for example, in a gloss to the VBhT that says, "'Bhairava' [means] *abhidheya*. 'Teaching' [means] *abhidhāna*. Their relation (*sambandha*) to each other is that of the named and the name." Kumāracandra defines *siddhi* as the *prayojana* and employs the category *prayojana-prayojana* to explain that the siddhi of the Vajrabhairava sādhana is to generate fear in all wrathful deities.

71. Kumāracandra's *pañjikā*, p. 288: *rang gi don phun sum tshogs pa'o/ de yang gnyis te/ rtog pa phun sum tshogs pa dang/ spangs pa phun sum tshogs pa dang spangs pa phun sum tshogs pa'o/ dang po ni ji snyed mngon par byang chub par bya ba byang chub pa'o/ gnyis pa yang nyon mongs pa dang shes bya'i sgrib pa'i bag chags ma lus pa spangs pa'o/ de'i thabs ni sgrub pa'i thabs kyi lam mo/ de'i yang thabs ni gsung rab bo/ gzhan gyi don phun sum tshogs pa ni gdug pa can 'jigs par byed pa'o/ de'i thabs ni sgrub thabs so/.*

nation (*phyir dar*) of Buddhism in Tibet.[72] As indicated in diagrams 1–5 above and plates 1–5 below, there were five distinct Vajrabhairava transmissions (*lugs*), named after the Tibetan masters who brought the VBhT to Tibet: (1) Zhang, established in the tenth–eleventh centuries[73] by Cog gru Shes rab bla ma (a.k.a. Zhang Cog gru lo tsā ba Shes rab), (2) Skyo, named after Skyo ston 'Od 'byung gnas (a.k.a. Skyo nag 'brom ston, 1126–1200), (3) Gnyos, named after Gnyos lo tsā ba Yon tan grags (b. 973), (4) Mal, established by Mal lo tsā ba Blo gros grags pa (eleventh century), and (5) Rwa, named after Rwa lo tsā ba Rdo rje grags,[74] (b. 1016). These different transmissions introduced Vajrabhairava in a wide variety of forms or manifestations. In this regard, the collection of Ngor maṇḍalas (*Rgyud sde kun btus*)[75] distinguishes the following variations of Vajrabhairava systematized according to their respective lineages:

1. Forty-Nine-Deity Vajrabhairava (Zhang)[76]
2. Nine- and Seventeen-Deity Vajrabhairava (Skyo)[77]

72. According to Tāranātha, a small number of Vajrabhairava sādhanas entered Tibet with the advent of Buddhism (*snga dar*), when its practice was adopted by the first dharma king, Srong btsan sgam po (sixth–seventh centuries).

73. Tāranātha says that Zhang Cog gru lo tsā ba founded the Zhang lineage one generation after the establishment of Bsam yas Monastery (779 CE), which would place him in the ninth century. However, Tāranātha also says that Cog gru lo tsā ba was a contemporary of two lo tsā bas, Leng and 'Brogs, whom the *Blue Annals* ('Gos lo, *Deb ther sngon po*, 320; Roerich 1949, 1:260) identifies as pupils of *Atiśa Dīpaṃkaraśrījñāna (980–1054): "The lo tsā bas Leng and 'Brogs from Lower Gtsang were great disciples of *Atiśa." This would place Cog gru lo tsā ba around the tenth–eleventh centuries as well.

74. For different sources of Rwa lo's biography, see Cuevas 2015. For Cuevas's translation of Rwa lo's *rnam thar* written by Ye shes seng ge, see Ra Yeshé Sengé 2015.

75. *Rgyud sde kun btus* is a collection of Sa skya materials containing initiations, empowerments, and other explanatory texts for the tantric practice of 139 maṇḍalas that have been compiled and painted in the ninteenth century by 'Jam dbyangs blo gter dbang po (1847–1914). The Tibetan edition containing thirty-two volumes of Sde dge blockprints was published in 2004 in Kathmandu by Sachen International and is available on the BDRC website (W27883). In addition, two English translations have been published: Tachikawa 1989 and Lokesh Chandra et al. 2006.

76. For the Forty-Nine-Deity Vajrabhairava tradition according to the Zhang lineage, see, for example, *Zhe dgu ma'i sgrub thabs zhi khro rnam rol bzhugs* of 'Phags pa Blo gros rgyal mtshan or *Dpal rdo rje 'jigs byed zhang lugs lha zhe dgu ma'i dkyil 'khor* by 'Jam dbyangs blo gter dbang po. See plate 1.

77. See *Skyo 'Od 'byung nas brgyud pa'i rdo rje 'jigs byed lha dgu 'am lha bcu bdun dkyil 'khor* (56), pp. 7–50, volume 10 of the *Rgyud sde kun btus*. See plate 2.

3. Thirteen-Deity Vajrabhairava (Rwa)
4. Ekavīra "Solitary Hero" Vajrabhairava (Rwa)
5. Vajrabhairava with eight zombies (*ro langs brgyad*) and thirty-two weapons (*phyag mtshan*) (Mal and Rwa)[78]

The source text for all the above-mentioned Vajrabhairava forms was the VBhT in seven chapters. The tantra was expensive: to have a single manuscript copy made, one had to pay no less than ten *srang* of gold.[79] Moreover, in Tibet, the cult of Vajrabhairava (*rdo rje 'jigs byed*) flourished alongside the similar cult of Kṛṣṇayamāri (*dgra nag po*), which during the time of Abhayākaragupta (d. 1125) surpassed the popularity of Vajrabhairava.[80] Another tantra that appeared in that period was the Tantra of the Six-Faced (*gdong drug gi rgyud*),[81] probably dedicated to the Six-Faced Yamāntaka (*gdong drug*); the text seems not to have gained currency and was used mainly to supplement existing teachings.[82] In Tibetan Buddhism, these three separate cults were

78. This form of Vajrabhairava transmitted by Rwa lo tsā ba was adopted by Sa skya through the lineage of Mal lo tsā ba. See plates 4 and 5.

79. Tāranātha, *Gshin rje chos 'byung*, 74, reports thus: *glegs bam tshar re 'bri ba la yar gser srang bcu'i yon du tshad byad skad.* 'Gos lo tsā ba acknowledges the fact that Rwa lo tsā ba fixed a donation for the instruction of the VBhT, which was one golden *srang*, thus he caused the tantra to become known as a "golden book" ('Gos lo, *Deb ther sngon po*, 457; Roerich 1949, 1:377).

80. Tāranātha, *Gshin rje chos 'byung*, 74: *de rjes slob dpon a bha yā ka ra'i dus tsam na/ dgra nag dar bar yod/ 'jigs mdzad kyi chos skor rnams btsal rnyed tsam las med/.* "Later, during the time of Abhayākara, the Kṛṣṇayamāri became more popular. The cycles of Vajrabhairava were no longer present, and one had to search for it."

81. The identity of the Six-Faced tantra is difficult to establish. Kuranishi (2013, 268) pointed out that the text may be either the *Gshin rje gshed nag po'i 'khor lo las thams cad grub par byed pa* (*Yamārikṛṣṇakarmasarvacakrasiddhikara Tantra*, "Black Yamāri: The Tantra that Accomplishes All by Means of the Wheel of the Black Enemy," Toh. 473) or, following Nishioka 1983, 164, the *Dpal rdo rje 'jigs byed kyi rtog pa'i rgyud* (i.e., the VBhT in seven chapters). Based on Bu ston's classification of tantras given in his *chos 'byung*, the Six-Faced tantra may also refer to the *Gzhon nu gdong drug gi rgyud*, which is listed separately from the *Gshin rje gshed nag po'i 'khor lo las thams cad grub par byed pa* (Nishioka 1983, 66–67). It is, however, unlikely that the Six-Faced tantra is the same as the VBhT in seven chapters. The deity referred to in Tibetan as Gdong drug is the Ṣaṇmukha form of Yamāntaka, and this deity served as an antecedent to the development of Vajrabhairava, as reported in Lalitavajra's legends (see chapter 4). Walter Eugene Clark (1965 part 2, 69, quoted in Decleer 1998, 299n8) has identified this deity as Ṣaṇmukha-Bhairavavajra, ref. 2B30/71. The icon identified by Clark resembles the earliest form of Yamāntaka (see p. 57 below).

82. Tāranātha, *Gshin rje chos 'byung*, 74: *gdong drug gi rgyud ni zhar byung tsam ma gtogs*

initially categorized together as the Triple Cycle of Black Bhairava (*nag 'jigs skor gsum*) or simply the Triple Cycle of the Black One[83] (*nag po skor gsum*), and they were also referred to through their abbreviated names as Dgra/Gdong/'Jigs.[84] The masters who appeared in the Vajrabhairava transmission lineages had often received the empowerment of Dgra and Gdong, but they considered them merely as a "backup" or supporting ritual (*rgyab rten*) for the initiation into Vajrabhairava.

Among the most popular transmissions of Vajrabhairava in Tibet were the Thirteen-Deity Vajrabhairava and the Solitary Hero Vajrabhairava surrounded by eight zombies (*vetāla*s) and thirty-two weapons according to the Rwa lugs that were transmitted through various teachers in the Tibetan Sa skya and Dge lugs schools.

Vajrabhairava in the Sa skya tradition

The earliest transmission received by the Sa skya pas in the twelfth century was the Rwa lugs form of Vajrabhairava surrounded by eight zombies (*rdo rje 'jigs byed ro langs brgyad skor*) that was passed down from Rwa 'Bum seng ge of the [Western] Rwa lugs to the famous Klog skya Dbang phyug grags pa (twelfth century), a student of Btsum rin po che Grags pa rgyal mtshan, the

de'i snga rol nas kyang ha cang dar ba ma byung ba 'dra'o. "As for the tantra of the Six-Faced One, it was not other than a mere ancillary; it had not really spread very much from the beginning."

83. This tripartite division evolved around the time of Ba ri lo tsā ba, who, according to Tāranātha, supplemented those three with the *Yamāntakakrodhavijayatantra* ("Victorious Wrathful Yamāntaka Tantra"); thus the Triple Black Cycle became the Quadruple Black Cycle (*nag po skor bzhi*). See Tāranātha, *Gshin rje chos 'byung*, 20: *ba ri lo tsa ba ni de'i steng du gshin rje gshed rnam par rgyal pa'i rgyud bsnan nas/ nag po skor bzhi zhes tha snyad mdzad*. Tāranātha (*Gshin rje chos 'byung*, 75) also says that the *Yamāntakakrodhavijayatantra* and the *Mañjuśrī-Vajrabhairava[tantra]* are the best antitode (*gnyen po mchog*) against barbarians (*kla klo*) and demons (*lha min*).

84. The classification changed when the translation of the *Raktayamāri* cycle by Dpyal lo tsā ba, Chag lo tsā ba, G.yag sde lo tsā ba, Glo bo lo tsā ba, and Shong lo tsā ba Blo gros brtan pa had begun. These five lo tsā bas gave rise to the five traditions of the Raktayamāri in Tibet; see Wenta 2022. From that time onward, the Dgra and Gdong drug were combined as the Black Cycle (*nag po*). The newly established convention was to refer to the "Three" as "Red, Black, and Terrifying" (*dmar nag 'jigs gsum*)," derived from Raktayamāri (Red Enemy of Death), Kṛṣṇayamāri (Black Enemy of Death), and Vajrabhairava. See Tāranātha, *Gshin rje chos 'byung*, 20: *phyis gshed dmar gyi skor 'gyur ba nas gzung ste/ dgra nag gdong drug gnyis la nag po zhes gcig tu sdoms te/ dmar nag 'jigs gsum zhes tha snyad 'dogs*.

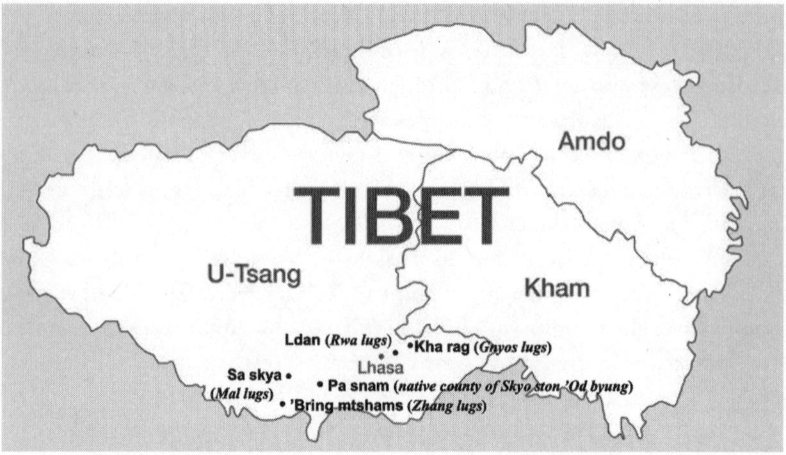

Map. The original clan sites of Vajrabhairava transmission lineages in Tibet

third patriarch of the Sa skya tradition.[85] This particular Klog skya transmission lineage, characterized as descending from master to disciple in an uninterrupted line of succession, has continued through various generations of Sa skya patriarchs.[86]

The Thirteen-Deity Vajrabhairava according to the Rwa lugs was received by the Sa skya pas in the thirteenth century. This particular transmission was passed down through Rong pa Rgwa lo of Dben dmar Monastery[87] and Rong

85. See A mes zhabs, *Sa skya'i gdung rabs ngo mtshar bang mdzod*, 76.

86. The names of the masters from Rwa 'Bum seng up to Ngor chen Kun dga' bzang po given in Ngor chen's *Thob yig* and A mes zhabs's *Gshin rje chos 'byung* are identical, and both sources list the following transmission lineage: Rwa 'Bum seng, Klog skya Dbang phyug grags pa, Ldong ston Shes rab dpal (thirteenth century), 'Phags pa rin po che, Zhang Dkon mchog dpal (thirteenth century), Na bza' brag phug pa Bsod nams dpal (thirteenth–fourteenth centuries), Bla ma dam pa Bsod nams rgyal mtshan (1312–75), who was the fourteenth abbot of the Sa skya Monastery, Mkhan chen Byang chub bzang po, who was the thirteenth-century founder of the Rgyal gling tshogs pa Monastery, Chos rje Ye shes rgyal mtshan (1359–1406), Ngor chen Kun dga' bzang po. While the list of masters in the *Thob yig* ends with Ngor chen, A mes zhabs reports that the lineage until the seventeenth century passed down from Ngor chen further to Kun dga' bkra shis (1558–1603), the fourteenth abbot of Ngor.

87. Rnam rgyal rdo rje (1203–1282), a student of Rwa 'bum seng who became identified as the incarnation of Khams pa Rgwa lo, was also given the name [Rong pa] Rgwa lo (*khams pa rgwa lo'i skye ba yin pas mtshan yang rgwa lor btags*; A mes zhabs, *Gshin rje chos 'byung*, 125). Rong pa Rgwa lo was one of the most important figures in the transmission of the Vajrabhairava-Yamāntaka cycle in Tibet and appears to be a member of a power-

pa Shes rab seng ge,[88] and then through Sa bzang ma ti paṇ chen Blo gros rgyal mtshan (1294–1376) and Sa bzang 'phags pa Gzhon nu blo gros (1358–1412/24), reaching Ngor chen Kun 'dga bzang po (1382–1456), the founder of Ngor evaṃ chos ldan Monastery.

Even though the Sa skya masters were loyal to the original teachings handed down in the Rwa transmission, they also introduced important changes. In this regard, Thar rtse Nam mkha' dpal bzang (1532–1602), the thirteenth abbot of Ngor, and his direct disciple Shar chen Kun dga' bkra shis (1558–1603), the fourteenth abbot of Ngor, introduced "the permission to practice the death rituals" (*las gshin gyi rjes gnang*), and the "instructions on the *utpanna-krama* according to the systems of Rwa and Skyo." Another transmission that became a part of Ngor's Vajrabhairava legacy was a reading transmission (*lung*) of pith instructions on the Nine-Deity maṇḍala practice of Vajrabhairava, *Rdo rje 'jigs byed kyi man ngag phyogs sdeb*,[89] written by Dpal 'dzin grags pa (fourteenth–fifteenth century), known as 'Bri gung pa Dpal 'dzin. The Sa skya pas had also adopted a practice centered on focusing the mind on the horn tips of [Vajra]bhairava that was based on the manual of the Skyo 'Od 'byung tradition.[90]

One of the most important masters in the Sa skya Vajrabhairava lineage was 'Phags pa Blo gros rgyal mtshan (1235–80), also known as Chos rgyal 'Phags

ful family with strong political associations, including a paternal ancestor named Gzhon nu snying po who belonged to one of the eight lineages of Chinese priests of Mi nyag that settled in Yar 'brog in Central Tibet. He was invited by Sam shi—the minister of the king Khri srong lde btsan—to become the officiating priest (*mchod gnas*) of the king himself. See also *Blue Annals* ('Gos lo, *Deb ther sngon po*, 924–26; Roerich 1996, 2:789–90). Rgwa lo attended several famous masters, such as Kashmiri paṇḍita Śākyaśrī, Dpyal lo tsā ba, Sa skya Paṇḍita, and paṇḍita Vibhūticandra. Rgwa lo invited Vibhūticandra to his monastery, Rong Dben dmar, in Gtsang and to Kyog po and Sham bhar monasteries, where he requested from him all the empowerments and pith instructions of the Kālacakra ('Gos lo, *Deb ther sngon po*, 987; Roerich 1996, 796; Stearns 1996, 146). Rgwa lo's perilous ordeals with the wrathful *rgyal po* spirits that were jeopardizing his efforts of receiving the transmission of Yamāntaka from Dpyal lo are recorded in his biography (see the *Dpal chen rgwa lo'i rnam thar*).

88. Rong pa Shes rab seng ge was the second son of Rong pa Rgwa lo, and like his father, he spent the larger part of his life in the monastery of Dben dmar in Rong (Gtsang province). He traveled extensively, teaching various tantric texts and philosophical doctrines ('Gos lo, *Deb ther sngon po*, 926–27; Roerich 1996, 2:791–92).

89. The BDRC (W3CN2615) has a scanned copy of this text, which consists of a handwritten manuscript by 'Bri gung pa Dpal 'dzin himself, but access to this text is restricted.

90. Dhongthog 2016, 175. See, for example, Kun dga' bzang po, *'Jigs byed kyi rwa rtse sems 'dzin skyo lugs kyi brgyud 'debs*.

pa,[91] the seventh patriarch of Sa skya Monastery and a powerful member of the 'Khon family. He earned his fame in the Tibeto-Mongolian Buddhist history as a national preceptor (*guoshi*) and then as imperial preceptor (*dishi*)[92] of the Mongol emperor Kublai Khan (1215–94), founder of the Yuan dynasty. 'Phags pa—whose relationship with Kublai was modeled on the patron-lama (*yon mchod*)[93] association—acted as the Mongols' proxy in Tibet and was in charge of religious institutions throughout the Mongol empire. More importantly, he occupied the office of royal religious officiant (*mchod gnas*) and was responsible for granting the emperor tantric initiations (*dbang*). 'Phags pa seemed to have had a determining influence on Kublai and the religious practices in his court, despite some scholars claiming otherwise.[94] The *Tibetan Script Edict* (*'Ja sa bod yig ma*)—one of the two edicts concerned with the status of monks issued by Kublai—records that 'Phags pa granted three tantric initiations to Kublai in 1253.[95] Kublai was considered an incarnation of the bodhisattva Mañjuśrī,[96] through which his spiritual and political authority

91. For the biographies of 'Phags pa, see *Lam 'bras bla ma brgyud pa'i rnam thar* by Sher chen Ye shes rgyal mtshan in volume *kha* of the *Sa skya pa'i chos kyi snying po bi ru pa'i gsung ngag lam 'bras rin po che*. Another *rnam thar* dealing with 'Phags pa's biography is the *Sa skya gdung rabs chen po rin chen bang mdzod* by A mes zhabs.

92. According to Petech (1990, 36–37), 'Phags pa received the office of national preceptor in 1261 and imperial preceptor in 1269/70.

93. For the *mchod yon* relationship, see Seyfort Ruegg 1997 and 2003.

94. Petech (1993, 651) states that 'Phags pa was "just a tool utilized by Qubilai to implement a policy of control without conquest." Similarly, Wylie (1977, 331) argues that Kublai had chosen 'Phags pa from "a centralized form of hierocratic government in Tibet." Shen Weirong (2004, 196) says that "control of Tibet" was the main objective of Kublai's association with 'Phags pa. For the opposite view supporting 'Phags pa's influential position at the Yuan court, see Franke 1978, Franke 1981 and Smith 2009.

95. A mes zhabs (*Sa gsum*, 124) mentions the receipt of tantric initiation by Kublai in the female water-ox year when 'Phags pa was nineteen but gives no details. Stag tshang lo tsā ba verifies that information and adds that it was a Hevajra initiation (Stag tshang lo tsā ba, *Dpal ldan sa skya'i gdung rabs 'dod dgu'i rgya mtsho*, 20).

96. Various sources validate the claim that Kublai was regarded as an incarnation of Mañjuśrī. The most important is the inscription attributed to Tugh Temür and engraved on the Juyongguan gate, north of the Yuan capital of Dadu (modern Beijing), which states that Kublai fulfilled a prophecy that predicted that Mañjuśrī would incarnate on Mount Wutai in China (see Berger 1994, 106). Another textual genre that attests to this attribution is Tibetan historiographical sources. In the *rnam thar* of U rgyan pa Rin chen dpal (1229–1309), written by Bsod nams 'od zer (thirteenth century), U rgyan pa states that Kublai was an incarnation of Mañjuśrī (p. 176). In Tshal pa's biography of Smon lam rdo rje (1284–1346/47), we find a description of Kublai as a "wondorous manifestation of Mañjuśrī" (see Debreczeny 2011, 22–23, quoting van der Kuijp 2010, n89). For a discus-

was consolidated in accord with the Buddhist ideology of "bodhisattva-cracy" (Seyfort Ruegg 2004, 2). The cult of Vajrabhairava, a wrathful form of Mañjuśrī, was certainly popularized in the Mongolian court of Kublai during the Yuan period, and it is reasonable to believe it was 'Phags pa or his direct disciples who introduced this cult there.[97]

'Phags pa was a lineage holder of the [Western] Rwa lugs transmission of Vajrabhairava through Rong po Rgwa lo and his son, Rong pa Shes rab seng ge. According to A mes zhabs, Rgwa lo remained in a close educational relationship with 'Phags pa for about two decades,[98] but it was Ldong ston Shes rab dpal (thirteenth century),[99] the teacher in the lineage of Rwa 'Bum seng and Klog skya Dbang phyug grags pa, who bestowed on 'Phags pa the Rwa transmission of Vajrabhairava.[100] 'Phags pa composed at least one sādhana of Vajrabhairava based on the teachings of Rwa lo tsā ba,[101] dealing with the generation of oneself in the Solitary Hero form of Vajrabhairava. 'Phags pa was

sion of the theory that only the sixteenth-century sources describe Kublai as the incarnation of Mañjuśrī, see Tuttle 2011, 163–214.

97. According to the *Fozu lidai tongzai*, 49:729–30, the cult of Yamāntaka was introduced to China in the early Yuan dynasty by a disciple of 'Phags pa whose transliterated name reads Ji-ning Sha-luo-ba-guan zhao (see Watt and Wardwell 1997, 95).

98. *'Phags pa rin po che sogs bla ma* [i.e., Rgwa lo] *bcu phrag gnyis tsam zhig bsten nas/*. A mes zhabs, *Gshin rje chos 'byung*, 125.

99. Ldong ston Shes rab dpal, also called the "blind master," met 'Phags pa when he was twenty-three years old. 'Phags pa arrived at Ldong ston's invitation when he was residing at Mount Wutai in China and received Yamāri teachings from him (Dhongthog 2016, 67). Ldong ston Shes rab dpal is better known as a scholar who had contributed to the development of Sa skya epistemology; see van der Kuijp 1986, 51–64.

100. A mes zhabs, *Gshin rje chos 'byung*, 126: *yang rwa 'bum seng nas glog skya dbang phyug grags/ des rwa rgya ldong gsum grub mtha' gcig ces grags pa'i nang tshan ldong ston shes rab dpal la gnang/ de la bla chen 'phags pas 'jigs byed rwa lugs gsan nas/*.

101. The information that 'Phags pa composed a sādhana of Vajrabhairava based on the teachings of Rwa lo tsā ba is given in the colophon of the text entitled *The Light That Destroys Māra, the Sādhana of the Rwa Tradition of Śrī Vajrabhairava* (*Dpal rdo rje 'jigs byed rwa lugs kyi sgrub thabs bdud 'joms snang ba zhes bya ba bzhugs so*), written by Dkon mchog lhun grub (1497–1557). The *Light That Destroys Māra* identifies itself as a text based on the Vajrabhairava sādhana composed earlier by Chos rgyal 'Phags pa (*chos rgyal 'phags pa mdzad pa'i sgrub thabs la gzhi byas*) with reference to the works of Rwa lo tsā ba (*rje btsun rwa lo tsā ba chen po'i gsung rab la yang gtugs shin tu dag par*). The Tibetan text has been published in 1978 as *Dpal rdo rje 'jigs byed rwa lugs kyi sgrub thabs bdud 'joms snang ba* (*A sādhana practice focusing upon Vajrabhairava according to the Rwa tradition transmitted among the Ngor pa by Ngor chen Dkon mchog lhun grub*). The preface to the modern edition says that this particular practice is widely spread among the Sa skya. The same text has been published in English translation in Migmar Tseten 2018.

also a recipient of the Raktayamāri cult of the mahāsiddha Virūpa in the lineage of Glo bo lo tsā ba Shes rab rin chen,[102] the thirteenth-century translator from the Mustang area (*glo bo*) who appears to have granted him the Yamāntaka initiation.[103]

Although there is no evidence that 'Phags pa ever conferred a Vajrabhairava initiation on Kublai, we know that such initiations were conducted for the Yuan dynasty by the imperial preceptors in later years. The first Taidung emperor, Yesün Temür, was granted the Vajrabhairava-Yamāntaka initiation by the imperial preceptor in 1324, and his wife in 1326.[104] It is plausible that the same preceptor performed a Vajrabhairava-Yamāntaka *abhiṣeka* on Tugh Temür (great-great grandson of Kublai Khan and the emperor of the Yuan dynasty from 1328–32) and his wife Budhashiri in 1329, for it is also known that Tugh Temür was bestowed two tantric initiations as an emperor; however, no details of those have been given (Watt and Wardwell 1997, 98). The evidence in support of the theory that it was the Vajrabhairava initiation that was conferred on Tugh Temür, and possibly on Kublai as well, is the existence of the *kesi*-silk tapestry *thang ka* (now at the Metropolitan Museum of Art in New York) designed in the fourteenth-century Sa skya style,[105] usually com-

102. The *Blue Annals* ('Gos lo, *Deb ther sngon po*, 460; Roerich 1996, 1:379) is quite explicit in stating that Glo bo lo tsā ba received teachings on Red Yamāntaka of the Virūpa lineage from Darpaṇācārya and Bharendra and spread them in Central Tibet. According to A mes zhabs, Glo bo lo tsā ba was a prolific translator of the Red Yamāntaka tantras attributed to Śrīdhara, Virūpa, and a certain Yogeśvara. He also translated and disseminated thirteen works of Śrīdhara dealing with the ritual practices of Red Yamāntaka. All of these texts were translated in collaboration with Darpaṇācārya. However, only seven works attributed to Śrīdhara and translated by Glo bo in collaboration with Darpaṇācārya have been identified so far. These are: (1) **Caturyogatattvanāmasvādhiṣṭh ānopadeśa* (*Rnal 'byor bzhi'i de kho na nyid ces bya ba rang byin gyis brlab pa'i man ngag*, Toh. 2025); (2) *Raktayamāryādhiṣṭhānādeśana* (*Gshin rje mthar byed dmar po'i byin gyis brlab pa'i rim pa*, Toh. 2038); (3) *Rakṣacakrādhiṣṭhānapṛṣṭyopadeśa* (*Srung ba'i 'khor lo'i byin brlab dang phyir bzlog pa'i man ngag*, Toh. 2045); (4) *Svacittordhvasaṃkrāntyupade śādhiṣṭhānasaṃyuktā* (*Rang gi sems gong du 'pho ba'i man ngag byin brlab dang bcas pa*, Toh. 2041); (5) *Agnidevapūjā* (*Me'i lha mchod pa*, Toh. 2043); (6) *Adhiṣṭhānakrama* (*Byin gyis brlab pa'i rim pa*, Toh. 2042); (7) *Śrīraktayamārimantrasiddhisādhana* (*Dpal gshin rje gshed dmar po'i sngags kyi dngos grub sgrub pa'i thabs*).

103. A mes zhabs, *Gshin rje chos 'byung*, 134: *'phags pa rin po che'i bla ma yang yin pa glo bo lo tsa ba shes rab rin chen gyis/ 'gro mgon sa pa la gnang ba sogs nas 'phel ba yin te/.*

104. For the details of these initiations described in the *Yuanshi*, see Watt and Wardwell 1997, 99n15.

105. For the Sa skya-style *thang kas*, see Pal 1984.

missioned for imperial initiation rituals[106] (see plate 6). The *kesi* features a nine-headed, thirty-four-armed and sixteen-legged Vajrabhairava as the central figure of the maṇḍala, surrounded by forty-eight attendant deities. This configuration suggests the Forty-Nine-Deity form of Vajrabhairava according to the Zhang lugs (see plate 1).

Vajrabhairava in the Dge lugs tradition

Vajrabhairava is equally important in the Dge lugs tradition. The founder of the reformist Dge lugs school, Tsong kha pa Blo bzang grags pa (1357–1419), popularized the cult of Vajrabhairava in fifteenth-century Tibet and institutionalized Vajrabhairava, the wrathful form of Mañjuśrī, as one of the three main practices in the Dge lugs tradition.[107] Moreover, the form of Yama Dharmarāja, known also as Kālarūpa, is one of the three protective deities (*dharmapālas*) within the Dge lugs tradition, along with Six-Armed Mahākāla and Vaiśravaṇa riding a lion.

Tsong kha pa belonged to the [Western] Rwa tradition of Vajrabhairava[108] through his Bka' gdams pa master Chos rje Don grub rin chen (1309–85), who received the Vajrabhairava transmission from Sman dge Ye shes dpal ba, known also as Bla ma Ye shes dpal. Chos rje Don grub rin chen was the founder and the first abbot of the Bya khyung theg chen yon tan dar rgyas gling Monastery. According to hagiographies of Tsong kha pa composed by his disciples, Don grub rin chen was visited by the deity Vajrabhairava, who

106. Watt and Wardwell 1997, 98.

107. The other two being the GS and Cakrasaṃvara. Tsong kha pa commissioned the construction of three-dimensional maṇḍalas of the GS, Vajrabhairava, and Cakrasaṃvara in the principal Dge lugs Monastery, Dga' ldan, which were installed in 1417. This has been regarded by the tradition as Tsong kha pa's fourth of four great deeds (Repo 2011). Note that Jinpa (2019, 296) says that these were the maṇḍalas of Vajradhātu, Akṣobhya, and Cakrasaṃvara. Jinpa (2019, 294) also identifies the institution of the annual rites and practice of nine tantric deities at Dga' ldan as the fourth great deed.

108. The Vajrabhairava lineage recorded in Tsong kha pa's *Jewel Casket* gives the following transmission sequence: (1) Vajrabhairava, (2) Jñānaḍākinī, (3) Lalitavajra, (4) Amoghavajra, (5) Jñānākaragupta, (6) Padmavajra, (7) Dīpaṅkararakṣita, (8) Rwa lo tsā ba Rdo rje grags, (9) Rwa Chos rab, (10) Rwa Ye shes seng ge, (11) Rwa 'Bum seng ge, (12) Rgwa lo tsā ba Rnam rgyal rdo rje, (13) Rong pa Shes rab seng ge, (14) Bla ma Ye shes dpal, (15) Chos rje Don grub rin chen, (16) Rje Tsong kha pa. After Tsong kha pa, the lineage continued to (17) Mkhas grub Dge legs dpal bzang, (18) Ba so Chos kyi rgyal mtshan, (19) Grub chen Chos kyi rdo rje, (20) Dben sa pa Blo bzang don grub, (21) Mkhas grub Sangs rgyas ye shes, and (22) Paṇ chen Blo bzang chos kyi rgyal mtshan. See Sopa and Patt 2004, 523.

commanded him to take care of a child named Kun dga' snying po (who later became known as Tsong kha pa).[109]

The practice of Vajrabhairava has been an important part of Tsong kha pa's tantric sādhana since his initation by Don grub rin chen (Jinpa 2019, 304). The *Very Secret Biography of Tsongkhapa* composed by Mkhas grub rje Dge legs dpal bzang (1385–1438), one of Tsong kha pa's closest disciples, who was bestowed Vajrabhairava initiation by Tsong kha pa,[110] reports that his teacher had a vision of Vajrabhairava in the year 1394. This incident triggered him to enact a daily practice focused on the generation stage of the deity Vajrabhairava.[111] When Tsong kha pa was residing in retreat on the slopes of the Mount 'Od lde gung rgyal in the 'Ol kha Valley, he composed a sādhana of the Solitary Hero Vajrabhairava,[112] entitled *Complete Victory over the Demons* (*'Jigs byed kyi sgrub thabs bdud las rnam rgyal*). To this day this treatise serves as the basis for many sādhanas dedicated to the Solitary Hero form of Vajrabhairava within the Dge lugs tradition,[113] including the empowerments conducted for the public by H. H. the Fourteenth Dalai Lama.[114] The Solitary Hero Vajrabhairava gained special prominence in the Dge lugs funerary rites

109. Ary 2015, 24.

110. This information is given in an inscription of a painting held in the collection of Shelley and Donald Rubin (HAR 56) depicting Mkhas grub's vision of Tsong kha pa after his death, which reads: *rje btsun chos kyi rgyal po tsong kha pas/ rdo rje 'jigs byed dbang dang gdams pa gnang/ phyag drug mgon po bsnyen bsgrub be bum la/ lhad zhugs bsal mdzad mkhas grub dge legs dpal//* (Debreczeny 2011, 68). For Mkhas grub's five visions of Tsong kha pa after his death, see Charleux 2011.

111. See Mkhas grub rje, *Dad pa'i 'jug ngogs*, 179.2–180.2. On the motif of Vajrabhairava intervening on Tsong kha pa's behalf in Tsong kha pa's biography, see Ary 2015, 113.

112. Jinpa 2019, 305. See the colophon of Tsong kha pa, *'Jigs byed kyi sgrub thabs bdud las rnam rgyal*.

113. For example, the Seventh Dalai Lama composed *The Self-Initiation Portion of the Ekavīra Vajrabhairava Maṇḍalavidhi Called "Triumph Over Māra"* (*Rgyal ba bskal bzang rgya mtsho'i gsung rdo rje 'jigs byed dpa' bo gcig pa bdud las rnam rgyal gyi dkyil chog la bdag 'jug bya tshul 'don sgrigs nag po*), which was based on Tsong kha pa's *Victory over All Demons.* For more contemporary treatises, see, for example, *The Sadhana of Bhagavan Glorious Solitary Hero Vajrabhairava Entitled "Victory over Demons"* by Pha bong kha pa Bde chen snying po (1978–1941), a Dge lugs pa bla ma of the modern era, translated in Gonsalez 2021, 249–94. One of the most influential contemporary propagators of the Solitary Vajrabhairava practice was Skyabs rje Dge legs Rin po che (1939–2017), who frequently taught this practice around the world.

114. On January 21, 2018, H. H. the Fourteenth Dalai Lama conferred the Solitary Hero Vajrabhairava empowerment to a public audience in Bodhgayā, India, where he stressed that this particular sādhana is derived from Rje Tsong kha pa's personal expe-

of cremation. An example of such a crematory manual is the *'Jigs byed dpa' bo gcig pa la brten pa'i sku gdung sreg chog* written for the cremation of Khri chen mchog sprul Blo bzang 'phrin las rgya mtsho.[115]

In the year 1418, Tsong kha pa composed the *Jewel Casket: The Sādhana of the Thirteen-Deity Vajrabhairava*[116] based on the methods of the Rwa and Gnyos traditions. The arrangement of the twelve deities in the maṇḍala around the central figure of Vajrabhairava along with the deities' respective names closely resembles the exposition of the Indian exegetical tradition, especially those of *Śoṇaśrī/*Vajrasiddha and *Kṛṣṇācārya, the recipients of the same oral transmission (see p. 114 of this book). One element that differs in Tsong kha pa's version is the depiction of Vajrabhairava in union (*yab yum*) with a consort, Vajravetālī (see plate 8).

Both the Solitary Hero and the Thirteen-Deity forms of Vajrabhairava became important parts of tantric practice for monastics following Tsong kha pa's tradition. In the principal Dge lugs monastery, Dga' ldan, Tsong kha pa erected a large statue of Vajrabhairava and introduced a mandatory practice of the Thirteen-Deity Vajrabhairava for all adult monks residing there.[117] Tsong kha pa seems to have also systematized Vajrabhairava's iconography with some heads positioned at the back. This iconographic variant, although not found uniformily in all the Dge lugs forms of Vajrabhairava, was reportedly based on Tsong kha pa's meditative vision.

Vajrabhairava also played an important part in the foundation of 'Bras spungs, another principal Dge lugs monastery. According to the *Gshin rje chos 'byung* of Tāranātha, the relics of Rwa lo tsā ba were brought from Ldan (where Rwa lo died) to 'Brag spungs in the year 1416 (the founding year of 'Bras spungs), where they were used as an inner support (*nang rten*) for the statue of Vajrabhairava known as Dharmarāja with the Iron Chain (Chos rgyal lcags

---

rience of Mañjuśrī-Vajrabhairava. See https://www.dalailama.com/news/2018/solitary-hero-Vajrabhairava-empowerment.

115. See A khu ching Shes rab rgya mtsho, *'Jigs byed dpa' bo gcig pa la brten pa'i sku gdung sreg chog*, 179.

116. *Rdo rje 'jigs byed lha bcu gsum ma'i sgrub thabs rin po che'i za ma tog bkod pa*. This text has been partly translated into English as *A Casket of Jewels: Meditation on the Thirteen Deity Glorious Vajrabhairava by Je Tsongkhapa* (San Jose: Gyuto Vajrayana Center, 2009).

117. Jinpa 2019, 298–99. The ritual manual used by all adult monks in the Dga' ldan chos 'phel gling and in majority of Dge lugs pa monasteries is Tsong kha pa's *Jewel Casket*. The version of this text used in the Dga' ldan Monastery is included in the collected rituals of Stag lung brag bsam gtan gling Monastery, entitled *Dpal rdo rje 'jigs byed lha bcu gsum ma'i bdag bskyed bum pa dbang chog smon shis dang bcas pa* (Bentor 1996, 97–98).

thag ma gshin rje gshed).[118] The person who initiated this transfer was Phag gru sne'u rdzong pa Drung chen Nam mkha' bzang po, the patron of Tsong kha pa and the early Dge lugs pas (Hazod 2004, 36).

In the fifteenth century, the cult of Vajrabhairava reached the Qing court of China through the Dge lugs pa masters. The Yongle emperor (r. 1402–24), following in the footsteps of Kublai Khan, commenced the practice of inviting important religious dignitaries to his court. In both 1408 and 1413, Tsong kha pa was invited to the Qing court but refused to undertake the trip himself. Instead, he sent his close disciple Byams chen chos rje Shākya ye shes (1354–1435), the future founder of Se ra Monastery, who conducted tantric rituals of Guhyasamāja, Cakrasaṃvara, and the Forty-Nine-Deity Vajrabhairava (*'jigs byed zhe dgu ma*)[119] at the Qing court in the years 1415–16. Śākya ye shes was probably responsible for introducing the practice of the Solitary Hero Vajrabhairava at the Qing court. The evidence of this tradition being current during the reign of the Yongle emperor is a Chinese silk embroidery *thang ka* of the deity now at the Metropolitan Museum of Art (see plate 9). The figure in the upper right corner has been identified as Śākya Ye shes.[120] The *thang ka* was probably commissioned by the Yongle emperor as a gift for Śākya ye shes to commemorate the introduction of the Solitary Hero Vajrabhairava to his court.[121]

During the reign of the Manchu ruler Qianlong (r. 1735–96), the cult of Vajrabhairava was systematically integrated into the state religion as a symbolic source of legitimization of the Qing emperors through the construction of a spatial symbolism that relied upon the establishment of correspondences between the segments of the capital city of Beijing and the threefold Vajrabhairava maṇḍala.[122] Lessing (1976) identifies the statue of the Solitary Hero Vajrabhairava in Beihai Park as the presiding deity of the first maṇḍala and

118. Sørensen and Hazod 2007, 1:51; Hazod 2004, 44, following Mkhyen brtse's guide, for which see Ferrari 1958, 41n76, 41n97.

119. Mdzad pa po mi gsal, *Byams chen chos rje'i rnam thar,* 4A, l.2. I thank Sonam Tsering Ngulphu for this reference.

120. See www.metmuseum.org/art/collection/search/39742.

121. This argument is supported by another very similar embroidery *thang ka* featuring Hevajra as Kapāladhara accompanied by a long inscription mentioning the Dge lugs lineage of Hevajra ending with Śākya ye shes, who is paid homage to by the Yongle emperor and is given the *thang ka* as a gift; see Heller, "Homage by an Emperor."

122. Lessing (1976, 89–90), referring to an oral tradition still validated by the contemporary Buddhist masters in Beijing (Bianchi 2008, 331), identifies the sector of the Forbidden City as the first maṇḍala symbolizing "wisdom" (*prajñā*), the Imperial City as the second maṇḍala symbolizing "compassion" (*karuṇā*), and the Outer City as the third

the protector of Beijing. He further suggests that the Taihedian, or the great "Audience Hall" located in the Forbidden City, was the center of the maṇḍala, and that its architectural composition replicated Vajrabhairava's palace.[123] The emperor's throne situated in the middle of the Audience Hall would correspond to the seat of Vajrabhairava at the center of the maṇḍala; thus the sovereign would symbolically integrate the deity's protective and wrathful aspects.

Qianlong was an especially avid patron of the Dge lugs cult of Vajrabhairava through his association with the Dge lugs pa master Lcang skya Rol pa'i rdo rje (1717–86; Ch. Zhangjia Ruobi duoji),[124] a follower of Tsong kha pa's tradition.[125] The master acted as Qianlong's main advisor in Buddhist matters and later also as his imperial preceptor (*guoshi*), the tile previously bestowed on 'Phags pa during the Yuan dynasty. Like 'Phags pa before him, Lcang skya was responsible for conducting initiation rituals and transmitting various tantric practices to the emperor, palace officials, and monks,[126] for which he was named Qianlong's root guru (Berger 2013, 60). He reportedly transmitted the initiation manual of Thirteen-Deity Vajrabhairava to an audience of Manchus and Chinese.[127] Qianlong's devotion to the Dge lugs tradition of Vajrabhairava is attested in many temples in the Beijing area erected during his reign.[128] Some of them, such as the Yuhuage (Pavillion of Raining Flowers) established by Qianlong in 1750,[129] housed three Dge lugs deities, including Vajrabhairava,

maṇḍala representing charnel grounds. The walls of the Foribidden City represent the maṇḍala's vajra fence.

123. Bianchi (2008, 333–34) points out the discrepancy in the number of the deities surrounding the central deity Vajrabhairava in his maṇḍala. According to oral tradition, Vajrabhairava is accompanied by a retinue of twelve deities, suggesting the Thirteen-Deity form of Vajrabhairava (Ch. *shisan zun tancheng*), but the ceiling of the Taihedian in the Forbidden City contains only nine niches, which would house only nine out of thirteen deities.

124. For the biography of Lcang skya Rol pa'i rdo rje, see Wang 1995; Wang 2000; Illich 2006; Yongzhang 2008.

125. See Berger 2013, 60; Charleux 2011, 185.

126. For the rituals conducted by Rol pa'i rdo rje in the context of the politics of power, see Hevia 1993.

127. Chen and Ma 2007, 186, and Wang 1995, 126, citing Thu'u bkwan Blo bzang chos kyi nyi ma; see Bianchi 2008, 338.

128. Bianchi (2008, 340–42) reports the existence of a Yamāntaka Hall (Ch. *Yamendaga dian*), also known as Shanyin dian (Good Causes Hall), located in Beihai that housed the statue of Vajrabhairava. In Chanfusi (Confering Blessing Monastery), Vajrabhairava was celebrated during the last month every year by 108 lamas.

129. Wang Jiapeng 1991, 270. For an overview of the main altar, holding a statue and a *thang ka* of each deity, see Yang Xin et al. 1998, 260.

intended for the private worship of the emperor and his court (Bianchi 2008, 339). An annual recitation of the text *Mahāvajrabhairavamaṇḍala* (Ch. *Dabuwei tancheng jing*) was conducted at this site on the eighth day of the fourth month. Other Vajrabhairava statues erected in that area include one in the Fanzonglou ("Hall of Buddhism") established by Qianlong in 1768 (Bianchi 2008, 340).

One of the most important Tibetan Buddhist temples established by Qianlong in Beijing was the Yonghegong,[130] also known as the Lama Temple, which housed a bronze statue of the Solitary Hero Vajrabhairava in its Mizong dian ("Vajrayāna Hall"). The shrine also contained a statue of Tsong kha pa, as well as Vajrabhairava in the *yab yum* position (Bianchi 2008, 344). The Eastern Side Hall, also known as the Hall of the Five Mahāvajras, was a shrine dedicated to the protective deities of the Dge lugs pantheon, which also featured Vajrabhairava with his consort, Vajravetālī. One of the Vajrabhairava statues originally housed in the Lama Temple and currently in the collection at the British Museum, London (see plate 10), has an inscription identifying the donor as the Qing emperor Jiaqing (r. 1796–1820), the beloved son of Qianlong, for whom Qianlong abdicated the throne. At the back of the Yonghegong was the Yamāntaka Tower (Ch. *Yamandaga lou*) located close to the Hall of the War God dedicated to the Chinese god of war, Guanyu. The physical proximity of these two deities points to their martial function.[131] The Yamandaga lou was a martial tower, and it was used to store Qianlong's own weapons and was where he officiated rituals at the time of war (Berger 2003, 118). Stylistic features of Vajrabhairava prominent in that period (see plate 11) are formalized to resemble a warrior-like figure.[132]

The rituals dedicated to Vajrabhairava continue at Yonghegong to this day. Especially worth mentioning is the Festival of Vajrabhairava's Maṇḍala (Ch. *Daweide Jingang tancheng fahui*), which takes place annually in the autumn. According to Bianchi (2008, 345), the festival lasts for three days and involves

130. For a recent study of Yonghegong, see Greenwood 2013. For the description of iconography, see Lessing 1942.

131. On the special days consecrated to Guanyu, a recitation of the sādhana dedicated to the Solitary Hero Vajrabhairava as well as a text praising Guanyu were conducted in the Falun dian ("Dharmacakra Hall"), emphasizing the two deities' symbolic link; see Niu Song 2001, 546–47, cited in Bianchi 2008, 345.

132. The martial aspect of Yamāntaka has been adopted among the Mongols—i.e., the spells invoking Yamāntaka are used for adjusting one's gun, making it shoot straight (*buu-yin tarni*), and for gun incense offerings (*buu-yin sang*); see Rinchen 1959, 38–40, quoted in Siklós 2012, 187.

the preparation of the Vajrabhairava sand maṇḍala, the recitation of sādhana texts, and fire offerings (Ch. *huogong*).

Vajrabhairava-Yamāntaka in other parts of Asia

A wealth of sources testifies to the spread of Vajrabhairava cult throughout the area outside India and Tibet, from the Himalayan region of Nepal to Mongolia and Japan. Unfortunately, a thorough examination of this topic is beyond the scope of this book. Below I briefly mention three instances of this tradition in other parts of Asia.

The cult of Vajrabhairava was popular in the eastern region of Inner Mongolia due to the successful proselytizing efforts[133] of Neichi Toin (1557–1653), a missionary lama and "a theological disciple of Paṇ chen Lama" (Heissig 2010, 591) who effectively promoted the Tsong kha pa tradition of Vajrabhairava-Yamāntaka. The form of Vajrabhairava most widely disseminated in eastern Mongolia was Thirteen-Deity Vajrabhairava, with the Solitary Hero somewhat less common (Heissig 2010, 591). The tradition of Vajrabhairava continued through Neichi's disciple, the First Mergen Gegen, who consolidated the tantric practice of the Mergen tradition of Vajrabhairava based on eleven works, the majority of them dedicated to Thirteen-Deity Vajrabhairava.[134] The three lineage transmissions[135] of the Mergen tradition of Vajrabhairava list Tsong kha pa and Mkhas grub rje at the very top of the Tibetan lineage, with Neichi assuming the position of root guru of the Mongolian Vajrabhairava lineage.

The cult of Yamāntaka was also present in the first half of the seventeenth century in northern Mongolia,[136] where it became enmeshed with the indig-

133. Neichi's method for converting the Mongols to Buddhism was based on substituting the shamanistic pantheon of the Mongolian tribes with tantric Buddhist deities, especially Vajrabhairava-Yamāntaka and (Akṣobhyavajra) Guhyasamāja. Neichi has found the "material" argument an especially effective method of conversion: anybody who recited by heart the mantra of Yamāntaka was promised one ounce of gold. This approach was met with disapproval by the Fifth Dalai Lama (1617–1682), who banished Neichi and his disciples from eastern Mongolia (see Heissig 2010, 587–96). For Neichi's activities in eastern Mongolia, see also Siklós 1996, 12–14, and Kollmar-Paulenz 2012, 241–243.

134. For a detailed list of Mergen's works on Vajrabhairava, see Ujeed 2009, 179–81.

135. Ujeed 2009, 181, reports the existence of the three Mergen Gegen Vajrabhairava lineages as follows: (1) the lineage of Paṇ chen Bla ma, (2) the lineage of the Second Dalai Lama, (3) the lineage of Brtson grus 'Phags pa.

136. The cult of Yamāntaka might have arrived in the northern parts of Mongolia during the reign of Altan Khan of the Tümed (1507–82), who is particularly remembered for his alliance to the First Dalai Lama (Bsod nams rgya mtsho), then abbot of the Dge lugs

enous cult of incense offering of the white and black war standard (*sülde*)[137] of Genghis Khan, who was venerated as a powerful ancestor deity of the Mongol nation (Kollmar-Paulenz 2012, 249). Worship of the war standard took place during war campaigns, and various sacrifices, including human ones, were offered to the standard to appease the ancestor spirit (Ibid.). The "Hymn to Yamāntaka" discovered in the Xarbuxyn Balgas collection (no. 65) shows striking similarity with the ritual texts dedicated to the worship of *sülde* of Genghis not only in terms of analogous textual features, but more importantly in the way in which "the representation of Yamāntaka and the *sülde* of Cinngis coincide" (Chiodo 2000, 146).[138] Both descriptions clearly point to a context of warfare where Yamāntaka and the *sülde*[139] are propitiated to destroy "countless armies" (see note 138 below).

The martial aspect of Yamāntaka, known in Japan as Daiitoku myōō (大威德明王), is also preserved in Kūkai's Shingon and Saichō's Tendai sects of Japanese tantric Buddhism (*mikkyō*), where he became one of the Five Great Wisdom Kings (*godai myōō*). Daiitoku is identified with the righteous wrath of Amida nyorai (Amitābha) of the western quarter (Covaci 2016, 14). Like Vajrabhairava, he is also regarded as the wrathful form of Mañjuśrī (*monju*).[140] The iconography of Daiitoku (see plate 12) resembles the earlier phase in the development[141] of the Vajrabhairava figure, built upon the iconography

---

pa 'Bras spungs Monastery. According to the *Altan erike*, Altan Khan built a temple dedicated to Yamāntaka in Cabciyal, which was the same place where Altan Khan initially met with Bsod nams rgya mtsho; this event marked the beginning of their long term association. See Chiodo 2000, 145n53.

137. For the different meanings of *sülde* as "virtue," "power," and also "soul" that could return after death, see Kollmar-Paulenz 2012, 248–49.

138. The Hymn to Yamāntaka (3r8–3v3) gives the following description of the deity: "Holy Yamāntaka, because you have a fierce mind, you hold a chopper and a skull-bowl. You cut off the heads of countless armies of demons and wear them as a garland (around the neck)." In the *Cayan sülde-yin sang* (3r7–12), we find the following depiction of the *sülde* of Genghis: "Making an offering I bow to you, holy White Standard. Because you are fierce and powerful, angrily you a hold a chopper and spear. You cut off the heads of countless armies and wear them as a garland (around the neck)" (Chiodo 2000, 146).

139. It is interesting to notice that in later times, the *sülde* of Genghis embodied the war deity known as *sülde tenggeri* depicted as a warrior (Kollmar-Paulenz 2012, 249).

140. Paine and Soper 1981, 91.

141. In this regard, White (2000, 21) has also noticed that Kūkai's Shingon follows an earlier "seventh-century Indian paradigm" and that developments in Indian tantra that took place in the eighth century did not exert much impact on Shingon (Matsunaga 1987, 50–52; Yamasaki 1988, 3–12, 9–20).

of the Six-Faced Yamāntaka (see p. 42) rather than Vajrabhairava, insofar as Daiitoku is six-headed, six-armed, six-legged, and riding on a water buffalo. His main face is fierce and often shows fangs. He carries various weapons in his hands, including a club (sometimes represented as the *daṇḍamudrā*), a sword, a trident, and a noose (Covaci 2016, 14). He is always depicted with flames around his head. Another name used in reference to Daiitoku is Goem-mason (Destroyer of Death) because he destroyed the king of the underworld (Emma-O);[142] thus Daiitoku shares the same mythology with the narrative plot of Vajrabhairava-Yamāntaka destroying Yama (see p. 70). The cult of Dai-itoku was linked to the subjugation of enemies both in the court and on the battlefield, and also to the removal of poisons and pain (Fowler 2016, 157). Daiitoku rituals for military victory were conducted for the overthrow of the Taira forces in 1152, 1157, and 1183 (Covaci 2016, 14). The only notable temple dedicated to Daiitokuji established near Osaka during the Heian period, called the Mountain of the Buffalo's Waterfall (*ushinotakiyama*), was a place of pilgrimage at the time of war (Duquenne 1983, 659). The cult of Daiitoku was also involved in the black-magic rites meant to cause harm to some target. These rites were usually comprised of fire oblations and made use of transgressive substances such as animal bones and excrement (Duquenne 1983, 660).

The cult of Vajrabhairava is also found in Nepal. According to Decleer (1998, 296), a textual tradition of the VBhT dedicated to the worship of Vajrabhairava under the name Mahiṣa-Saṃvara continues to be practiced to this day in the temples of Patan and Kathmandu. Furthermore, on the authority of the oral tradition of Newar *vajrācāryas*, Decleer states that one of the *yi dam* deities in the temple's shrines is thought to be Vajrabhairava. More research is needed to establish whether the Newar Mahiṣa-Saṃvara currently propitiated in Nepal could be an example of a syncretic cult combining the worship of the Buffalo-Faced One (Vajrabhairava) and Heruka (Cakrasaṃvara).

142. Coulter and Turner 2000, 140.

2. Vajrabhairava in India

CHAPTER 1 demonstrated that the cult of Vajrabhairava was a pan-Asian phenomenon adopted also by political elites to further their expansionist aims. While the appropriation of Vajrabhairava's cult and his career as a martial and protective Buddhist deity in comparatively late millieus have been well explored by scholars, less attention has been paid to the origins of this deity. This chapter will analyze the main academic theories on the development of Vajrabhairava in India and point at some directions for future research. I argue that the iconography of Vajrabhairava, rather than a result of the straightforward evolution, must be considered the product of a long process of syncretism and synthesis of Hindu/Brahmanical, Buddhist, Śaiva, and tantric concepts of divinity.

Yama/Yamāntaka

Scholars generally agree that the emergence of Vajrabhairava as a fully fledged tantric Buddhist deity has to encompass influences outside the specifically Buddhist context and may include borrowings of the cultic forms from the common Indic culture (Siklós 2012, Linrothe 1999), Indo-Iranian exchanges (Siklós 2012), or an impact of Śaiva-Śākta traditions (Siklós 1996).[143] Despite the claims of many heterogeneous elements that went into the "making" of Vajrabhairava, scholarly pursuits dealing with the deity's origins have so far focused almost exclusively on demonstrating Vajrabhairava's evolution from

143. Siklós (1996, 7) claims that Śaiva influence from Kashmir was probably responsible for the adoption of Śaiva-Bhairava elements into the cult of Vajrabhairava, especially since the cycle connects itself with Oḍḍiyāna. Siklós (1996, 9) writes: "It is then possible that Lalitavajra, given the 'heretic' (i.e., Śaivite) environment, could locate merely non-Buddhist Bhairava treatises in Oḍḍiyāna. The refusal of the ḍākinī to allow him to take the texts necessitating memorizing and subsequent writing down would have provided an opportunity for Buddhicizing the texts." For the legends about Lalitavajra's retrieval of the VBhT, see pages 82–94 below.

the Hindu-Buddhist god of death, Yama, and its tantric Buddhist avatar, Yamāntaka ("Ender of Yama/Death").[144]

In this regard, Siklós (2012, 165–89) has presented consistent evidence for an "evolutionary" model that seeks to establish the historical origins of Vajrabhairava in the Indo-Iranian cult of the deity Yama/Yima. The association of Yama with death and the underworld is present already in the tenth book of the *Ṛg Veda* (10.14), where Yama, still a minor god, is linked to funerary rites in honor of the ancestors (*pitṛ*s). Yama is the first human being to have died, and thus he presides over the Vedic "land of the fathers" (*Atharva Veda* 4.11, in Bhattacharji 1970, 50). In the *Maitrāyanīsaṃhitā* (4.9.8) of the *Yajur Veda*, Yama is accompanied by the Aṅgirases, who are his followers (Bhattacharji 1970, 65). In the Brāhmaṇas, the role of Yama gains new importance as he becomes indistinguishable from the god of death (*mṛtyu*) (Bhattacharji 1970, 50). In this period, a number of epithets began to be employed to describe Yama in his role as the judge of men, such as King of the Law (*dharmarāja*), King of Death (*yamarāja*), and Ender [of Life] (*antaka*),[145] and these appellations for Yama would also later enter the Buddhist lexicon (Wayman 1959a, 44–45). Already in the Vedic period, Yama presides over the system of hells and assumes the position of the directional regent (*dikpāla*) of the southern direction (Bhattacharji 1970, 59). He is called *daṇḍadhara* (Club Holder), and he wields a noose (*pāśa*) with which he captures souls at the time of death. In the *Mahābhārata* and the Purāṇas, Yama became increasingly associated with a Śaiva mythological complex, in two different ways. In the *Mahābhārata* (see Thomas 1994), Yama as *kālāntakayama* or *yamakālāntaka* subsumes the role of Antaka or Kāla[146]—Time as the destroyer (the role later linked to Śiva as Mahākāla and Kālāntaka in the Purāṇas).[147] This is also visible in the STTS, where the Hindu deity Yama becomes Vajrakāla in the tantric Buddhist maṇḍala. Thus he is not only linked to the death of the individuals—

144. Siklós (1996, 8) does acknowledge the influence of the cult of Mañjuśrī in the MNS (which I refer to below, p. 86) on the development of the figure of Vajrabhairava and the possible link between Vajrabhairava and Vajrahūṃkāra/Trailokyavijaya, but he does not explore this topic at all.

145. In the *Garuḍa Purāṇa* (2.8.28–29), Yama is described by a series of seven epithets, i.e., Yama, Dharmarāja, Mṛtyu, Antaka, Vaivasvata (Belonging to the Sun), Kāla (Time), Sarvaprāṇahara (Thief of All Breaths).

146. In the *Śatapatha Brāhmaṇa* (10.3:1–9), Kāla is painted black with red eyes and holding a staff in his hand (Bhattacharji 1970, 55)

147. For the transfer of the Kālāntaka aspect from Yama to Śiva, see O'Flaherty 1976, 233, where she examines examples from the *Matsya Purāṇa* (102.21), *Mārkaṇḍeya Purāṇa* (10.78), and *Liṅga Purāṇa* (1.30.1-25); see Thomas 1994, 271.

although Yama's aspect of a harbinger of individual death is still retained in the *Mahābhārata*—but also to the periodic cosmic destruction of the universe (*pralaya*).[148] Thomas (1994, 267) argues that Yama's role as the cosmic destroyer belongs to an earlier stage of the figure's mythology, which was later "overshadowed by Śiva, and to some extent subsumed by him."[149] In the Purāṇas, the relationship between Yama and Śiva is expressed through the trope of conflict when Śiva rescues his devotees from the clutches of death personified by Yama (e.g., *Mārkaṇḍeya Purāṇa*, chap. 10). Śiva kills Yama, for which he is called Kālāntaka or Mṛtyuñjaya, and thus Yama becomes relegated to a secondary position as a deity subordinate to Śiva, and he remains so indefinitely. The association of Yama with this Śaiva mythological complex seems to be attested also in Old Javanese literature.[150]

For the most part, the concept of Yama in Buddhism was modeled on its Indian antecedents. In this regard, Wayman (1959a) has demonstrated that the cluster of concepts linked to the Buddhist Yama follows the trajectory found in Hindu mythology. Siklós (2012, 180) also shows that the aspects of Yama as *dharmarāja* and the ruler of the hells (*niraya*) are still preserved in Buddhism. The marked difference is the Buddhist association of Yama with Māra that would also influence the wider Indian understanding of Kāma as evil (Bhattacharji 1970, 107). Already in the *Mahāvastu* (compiled between the second century BCE and fourth century CE), we find the four aspects of Māra: (1) *devaputramāra* (sensual pleasure, which tries to obstruct Siddhārtha Gautama from the aim of awakening), (2) *kleśamāra* (afflictive emotions), (3) *skandhamāra* (the five aggregates), and (4) *maraṇamāra/mṛtyumāra* (death itself) (Lamotte 2001, 277). In the Buddhist concept of Māra (whose name is derived from the Sanskrit root *mṛ* "to hurt," "to injure," "to kill") as the personification of evil, the functions of Yama as death and the afflictive emotions that prevent people from achieving nirvāṇa coalesce. In tantric and Tibetan

148. The concept of Yama as *antaka*—destroyer—is reflected in its iconography, where he is depicted with a gaping mouth (see *Rāmāyaṇa* 3.68.49, quoted in Bhattacharji 1970, 56).

149. Thomas (1994, 267) draws upon the earlier argument about the transference of certain aspects of Yama to Śiva made by Keith (1925), Bhattacharji (1970), and O'Flaherty (1976).

150. In the *Śivarātrikalpa*, a fifteenth-century Old Javanese poem by Mpu Tanakuṅ (trans. Teeuw et al. 1969), we find the motif of a war between Śiva's *gaṇa*s and Yama's army when the hunter Lubdhaka dies and his body is taken by Yama. Since at one point in his life Lubdhaka stayed vigilant during the Śivarātri festival and thus performed the highest vow, Śiva thinks that his death was premature. A terrible fight ensues between Śiva and Yama, who disagrees with Śiva's view. Eventually, the army of Yama withdraws, and Yama has to pay homage to Śiva.

Buddhism, this fusion is well attested. The tantric form of Vajrabhairava-Yamāntaka (including Rakta- and Kṛṣṇa-yamāri) is principally the "ender of Yama"—the principle of death itself and the afflictive emotions he embodies. For example, in the exegetical literature of the Mongolian Dge lugs master Dza ya Paṇḍita (1642–1715), *yama* is clearly the principle of death in the body as well as the afflictive emotions (*kleśamāra*), which are in the mind.[151] The same goes with Māra, the principle of evil, who also embodies *kleśamāra* and is represented by the *trimūrti*—namely, Brahmā, Viṣṇu, and Maheśvara—who are often glossed in tantric exegetical literature as the three *kleśa*s,[152] or the three poisons, which Vajrabhairava-Yamāntaka has to vanquish. In his study of the concept of Buddhist Yama, Siklós (2012, 182) simply subsumes Vajrabhairava under Yamāntaka and portrays him only as the destroyer of Yama (the function borrowed from the Indian models of Śiva vanquishing Yama). He does not acknowledge the role Vajrabhairava plays in the wider framework of the Śaiva mythological complex preserved in the Tibetan Buddhist origins' stories, examined below.

An "evolutionary theory" about the origin of Vajrabhairava is also advocated by Linrothe (1999), who studied the progressive development of tantric Buddhist deities mainly through the analysis of visual iconography. Linrothe proposed a three-phased chronology. According to this classification, in phase 1, Yama is a subsidiary attendant of the bodhisattva Mañjuśrī in his function of the *krodha-vighnāntaka*, Fiercesome Ender of the Obstacles; as such, he is usually found in the left corner of statues of Mañjuśrī and carries the characteristic implements of the post-Vedic Yama—namely, a club in his left hand and a noose in his right hand. In phase 2, we encounter the Ender of Death, or Yamāntaka as an independent deity, standing upon a buffalo—the traditional

151. See the Peking edition of his *Thob yig*, 1:272a2–276a3; for the full translation, see Wayman 1959b, 125–30.

152. In *Akṣobhya's *ṭīkā* on chapter 4 of the VBhT, we find an unidentified quote that makes this connotation explicit: "For that reason it is said, 'By overcoming desire (*rāga*), [wrong] view (*dṛṣṭi*), and hatred (*dveṣa*), one tames Mahādeva, Brahmā, and Viṣṇu'" (*de bas na chags dang lta ba zhe sdang bsngo/ lha chen tshangs pa khyab 'jug 'dul zhes bshad do*). In *Guhyasamājasādhanamālā* 35, studied by English (2002, 465n389), we find the prescription of visualization in which Brahmā, Indra, Viṣṇu, and Śiva have to be visualized as being trampled upon by a sādhaka and symbolize the four afflictive emotions or *kleśa*s (*ālīḍhacaraṇākrāntacatuḥkleśaviśuddhabrahmendraharibarām*), meaning the four aspects of Māra. The same is attested in the Tibetan Buddhist story of Vajrabhairava's origins; see below. Note that in the *Vajrāmṛtatantra* (Sferra 2017, 423), the trinity of the Hindu pantheon is treated as the preliminary practice in the meditation of the nectar—i.e., the supreme reality.

mount of Yama—three- four- or five-faced, six-footed and six-armed, black, with fat belly and red eyes, wrathful, and carrying various weapons, including a club. In phase 3, we encounter Vajrabhairava as an "enhanced" version of Yamāntaka of phase 2.[153] He is not riding a buffalo but has a buffalo as his main face (*mahiṣamukha*), he has sixteen legs instead of six, thirty-four arms instead of six, and nine faces stacked up one upon the other. He carries various weapons in his hands, including a club in his right hand and a noose in his left hand.

Such clear-cut continuities may be difficult to demonstrate textually, and the evolutionary model does not explain all the iconographic features that Vajrabhairava—as a simple extension of the cult of Yama/Yamāntaka—possesses. In the following section, I want to concentrate on two aspects that effectively defy the evolutionary paradigm.

Vikṛtānana: *The Bad and the Ugly*

The first aspect concerns Vajrabhairava and Yamāntaka's appellation as the "hideous one" (*vikṛtānana*),[154] which is absent in the list of Yama's titles researched by Wayman (1959a). The leading hypothesis of the discussion that follows is that Vajrabhairava/Yamāntaka's trait as *vikṛtānana* was derived from the attributes of bodily deformity associated with demonic and hostile beings in general that became appropriated in the ritual framework of transgressive tantric sādhanas performed in the cremation grounds. Before examining this issue in a more detailed manner, however, let us first look at the definitions of *vikṛta* to determine which one applies in this context. According to Monier-Williams' *Sanskrit-English Dictionary* (p. 543) and Böhtlingk's *Sanskrit Wörterbuch* (6:78), the adjective *vikṛta* in a sense of "deformed," "changed," "ugly (as a face)," or "mutilated" points to bodily disfiguration of some sort that could be a result of a disease. Therefore *vikṛta* can also mean "diseased" or "sick"; compare the cognate form *vikāra*, meaning "bodily or mental condition, disease, sickness, hurt, injury." Among secondary connotations, we find *vikṛta* conveying the state of "disgust" or "repulsion," as well as antagonistic behavior (namely, *vikṛta* as "hostile" or "rebellious"). In line with this semantic range, the word *vikṛta* is often used to describe the dreadful physique of wrathful or demonic beings. Evidence of this can be found in the twenty-fifth

153. Robert Linrothe, personal communication, October 2018.

154. This appellation is used in the *yama* mantra as a synonym of the ten-syllabled action-mantra of Vajrabhairava: *hrīḥ ṣṭrīḥ vikṛtānana oṃ hūṃ phaṭ*, which is the mantra of Yamāntaka, but it is also identified (with slight variants) in some late Śaiva tantras as the mantra of Yama. For a discussion on Vajrabhairava's ten-syllable mantra, see below, p. 117.

chapter of the *Bālakāṇḍa* of Vālmīki's *Rāmāyaṇa*, in the story of the beautiful *yakṣī* Tāṭakā, who becomes cursed by the sage Agastya, causing her body to transform into a monstrous, deformed shape: "Oh, great *yakṣī*, deprived of your beautiful female body, you will become a man eater, with your face distorted, hideous (*vikṛtānanā*), and your shape that of a monster."[155] In this context, the curse of disfiguration connotes the moral characteristics of being "marked" as evil ("one with horrific behavior," *durvṛttā*; "highly atrocious one," *paramadāruṇā*) and as a person whose power is perverse (*duṣṭaparākramā*).[156] This meaning will also find its way into criminal law of *dharmaśāstra*, where the term *vikṛta* appears in the context of the criminals that have been executed via mutilation—having their heads severed and impaled on a stake or having their fingers, legs, or hands cut off.[157]

The use of *vikṛtānana* becomes constant in the Śaiva-Śākta tantric texts, such as the *Picumata-Brahmayāmala*, where it continues to be applied in a similar sense found in the earlier textual sources as referring to the highly transgressive, hideous, and inherently dangerous nature of demonic entities, such as *śākinī*s (lit. "enablers"), zombies (*vetāla*s), and ghosts of a deceased person (*bhūta*s) often residing in the cremation ground where the sādhaka undertakes his sādhana. For example, in the *Brahmayāmala*, in the course of a sādhana performed in the cremation ground that involves the ritual use of corpses, the sādhaka should meditate on the sacred spell (*vidyā*) with one-pointed awareness and well-maintained senses until the *śākinī*s with hideous faces arrive (*śākinyo vikṛtānanā*) on all sides. These figures are classified as impediments (*vighna*s) who may hinder the success of the sādhana if the sādhaka succumbs to the fear associated with their dreadful looks. If the practitioner is able to retain his composure and honors them with a guest offering (*argha*), they will be mastered and will bestow various boons on him.[158] Elsewhere in

155. Vālmīki's *Rāmāyaṇa*, *Bālakāṇḍa* (25.12b–13): *agastyaḥ parama amarṣaḥ tāṭakām api śaptavān// puruṣādī mahāyakṣī virūpā vikṛtānanā/ idaṃ rūpam vihāyāśu dāruṇam rūpam astu te//*. Trans. Rao 1998; https://www.valmikiramayan.net/utf8/baala/sarga25/bala_5F25_frame.htm.

156. Vālmīki's *Rāmāyaṇa*, *Bālakāṇḍa* 25.14–15.

157. As Olivelle (2005, 334) has pointed out, in *Manusmṛti* 9.279, the term *vikṛta* appears in the context of criminals executed with mutilation, while in the *Arthaśāstra*, the term *vikṛta* seems to be a synonym of "different" (*citra*) and "affliction" (*kleśa*). All of this indicates that the execution of the criminal is preceded by torture and mutilation.

158. BY 46.19–21ab: *smare tad yāvad yuktātmā sarvvā dikṣu samantataḥ/ āgacchanti mahābhāgā śākinyo vikṛtānanā// na bhetavyaṃ tu vai tena arghapātraṃ* [em. *arghapātan*; mss.] *tu pūrvvavat/ arghe datte prasidhyanti varadāś ca bhavanti hi// pūrvoktāni tu vighnāni pūrvvoktena prabhedayet/*. "He should meditate upon it until on all sides illustri-

the *Brahmayāmala* is a similar description, where female deities (oddly called *bhūtāni*) with distorted faces (*vikṛtānanāḥ*) acting as the attendants of the goddess Aghorī arrive on the ninth day of the sādhana, a thousand in number, in order to grant the hero (*vīra*) the boons he desires.[159] Related to the context of terrifying *vighnas* and the praxis of the "heroic sādhana" (*vīrasādhana*) characterized by fearlessness is a passage of the *Brahmayāmala* where we find the description of the zombies (*vetālas*) with hideous faces (*vetālāṃ vikṛtānanā*[*ṃ*]) and enormous fangs (*daṃṣṭrotkaṭa*) who arrive in front of the sādhaka. The practitioner is instructed to neither say nor offer anything but to hurl his sacred spell (*vidyā*), in the form of a weapon, at the zombies and thereby destroy them.[160] Another passage of the *Brahmayāmala* mentions terrible *bhūtas* with distorted faces (*mahāghorā bhūtās tu vikṛtānanā*), who are referred to as *īti* "calamity" or "infectious disease," arising in front of the sādhaka in order to obstruct his sādhana. When they are given a guest offering and see his sword, they bow down to him.[161]

The context in which the word *vikṛtānana* appears in the *Brahmayāmala*

---

ous *śākinīs* with distorted faces arrive. He who has composed mind should not be afraid. [Since he prepared] the vessel for the guest offering as before, having given them the offering, they will be mastered and bestow favors on him. All aforesaid obstacles, he should break through those by this [means] previously stated." For a very similar passage of the impediments that arise during the Vajrabhairava sādhana in chapter 1 of the VBhT, see below, p. 220.

159. BY 47.28–30ab: *āgacchanti mahābhāgā bhūtāni vikṛtānanāḥ/ pratyakṣadarśanībhūtvā sādhakaṃ cābhibhāṣate// mātṝṇāṃ bhaktakas tvaṃ hi tvam eko sādhakottamaḥ/ vatsa vatsa mahāvīra sādhakendra mahātapaḥ// varaṃ vṛṇīṣva me rudraḥ siddho tvan nātra saṃśayaḥ/*, "[At first light the next morning], illustrious *bhūtas* arrive with distorted faces. Having manifested to him, they say to the sādhaka: 'You are a true devotee of the mothers. You alone are the greatest of the sādhakas great ascetic. My dear, great hero, best of sādhakas, choose a boon! You are a *rudra*, you are a siddha, without any doubt.'"

160. BY 46.29ab: *daṃṣṭrotkaṭamahā[--?yo] vetālāṃ vikṛtānanā[ṃ]// āgacchanti mahāvīrā bhairavārūpadhāriṇī// na teṣāṃ vacanaṃ kuryān na cārghaṃ na ca mantrayet/ piṇḍīkṛtvā tato vidyām astrarūpāṃ vinikṣipet// praṇasyanti kṣipeṇaiva bhairavasya vaco yathā/*. "The *vetālas* with hideous faces, most terrible, with huge fangs, fearless, and having the form of Bhairava will approach. He should not say anything and he should not offer them anything, nor should he recite any mantras. Then he should take his *vidyā*, which is in form of the weapon and having made it into a bowl, he should hurl it at them. They are destroyed by that. That is true as Bhairava is true."

161. BY 46.73cd–74: *uttiṣṭanti mahāghorā bhūtās tu vikṛtānanā[ḥ]// arghaṃ* [em. *arghan*, mss.] *datvā tu vai tāsāṃ khaḍgahasto vicakṣaṇaḥ// praṇamanti ca sarvvāṇi khaḍgaṃ* [em. *khaḍgan*, mss.] *dṛṣṭvā tu ītayaḥ/*. "Also, there will arise terrible *bhūtas* with distorted faces; the wise one, with sword in hand, should give them a guest offering; when all these infectious diseases see the sword, they bow down."

is anchored in the metaphysical correspondence between the hideousness of demonic beings and the danger inherent in meeting them. Owing to the unorthodox and transgressive power of the encounter with hideous beings, the tantric sādhana integrates a larger symbolic order. The evil, ugly, and demonic forces, and the power they exude, are controlled through the tantric sādhana. The appearance of the name *vikṛtānana* in the mantra of Yamāntaka and Vajrabhairava suggests that both were perceived through the prism of their association with the ugly, dangerous, and transgressive power of the demonic entities residing in the cremation grounds, power that could be invoked and harnessed during the tantric sādhana to realize the desired aims.[162]

Another connotation of the term *vikṛta* as "transformed, altered, changed, strange, extraordinary" may be also at play here. In this sense, *vikṛta* would relate to the soteriological dimension of the VBhT when Mañjuśrī's peaceful face becomes transformed into the monstrous face of Vajrabhairava. This transformation may be analogous to the transformation of practitioner's "face"—that is, identity—from the misconception of the self (*ātmagraha*, the death that is "self-clinging") to the gnostic realization of emptiness (*yamāntaka*, "destroyer of death").[163] This connotation is indeed implied in the story of the siddha Śrīdhara, associated with the Raktayamāri tradition, who cuts off his own head and puts a buffalo head in its place, thus becoming known as Buffalo-Headed Śrīdhara.[164]

Ūrdhvaliṅga: *A Śaiva Bhairava?*

Another problem with the evolutionary model proposed by scholars to explain the origin of Vajrabhairava is that some iconographical features of Vajrabhairava cannot be traced back to Yama and, therefore, they must have arisen through a different trajectory. This is the case of the depiction of Vajrabhairava as ithyphallic, a characteristic absent from Yama/Yamāntaka's iconography. A likely explanation would be the influence of early Śaiva iconography on Vajrabhairava's depiction. The ithyphallic feature of Śiva and the groups of deities closely related to Śiva, such as Caṇḍeśvara/Caṇḍeśa (Acharya 2006, 216) or Bhairava, who are often represented with the erect phallus (*ūrdhvaliṅga*), is a recurrent feature of early Śaiva iconography. The same symbolism is attested in the case of Lakulīśa, the revivalist of Pāśupata Śaivism, whose recognizable ico-

162. See, for example, chapter 1 of the VBhT, where the success in sādhana is indicated when Vajrabhairava appears to the sādhaka and asks which boons he desires.

163. I thank John Newman for this explanation.

164. A mes zhabs, *Gshin rje chos 'byung*, 70–71.

nography of the erect phallus (*ūrdhvaliṅga/ūrdhvaretas*) has been traced back to the sixth century (Cecil 2014, 146). The Buddhist adaptation of an earlier Śaiva-Śākta iconography belonging to the cults of Bhairava of the *vidyāpīṭha* into the "new" tantric deity Heruka has been attested in Cakrasaṃvara literature, as pointed out by Sanderson (2009, 169–72). Thus Vajrabhairava's ithyphallic iconography could be regarded as another instance of Buddhist appropriation of iconographic attributes of Śaiva deities and reconceptualization of them to evoke the conquest of the non-Buddhist "other."

Such a link is made explicitly in *Akṣobhya's commentary, where the following explanation of Vajrabhairava's *ūrdhvaliṅga* is given:

> By "ithyphallic" it shows that he [Vajrabhairava] is similar to Mahādeva because [Vajrabhairava] has tamed him. It is said that 'because [Mahādeva] was so extremely full of passion after ceasing three years of asceticism, he was not sated with the pleasure of sexual union with Umā, and his *liṅgam* was constantly ready for action. For that reason it is said: "By overcoming desire, [wrong] view, and hatred, one tames Mahādeva, Brahmā, and Viṣṇu."[165]

For *Akṣobhya, Mahādeva is equated with *rāga*—passion, or desire—and this is symbolized by his erect phallus. By appropriating Śiva's *ūrdhvaliṅga*, Vajrabhairava portrays the conquest of that deity and, by extension, the afflictive emotion that it represents. As we will see below in the origin story recounted in Tibetan Buddhist narratives, Vajrabhairava's *liṅga*, recast in the yoga-tantra terminology as the *liṅga* of *jñānavajra*, becomes the weapon of conversion, through which Vajrabhairava tames and subjugates either Yama or Bhairava Maheśvara.

Another important dimension of the *ūrdhvaliṅga* symbolism relates to the yogic practice of semen retention. The epithets *ūrdhvaretas* and *ūrdhvaliṅga*, "he whose seed is raised, he whose *liṅga* is raised," are often employed to emphasize Śiva's status as a great yogin. His ability to reverse the flow of semen is concomitant with stopping the aging process and attaining immortality. The references to the ascetic tradition of *ūrdhvaretāḥ tapasvī*, "the ascetics whose semen is [turned] upward"—precursors of later *haṭha* yogic and

165. *Akṣobhya's *ṭīkā*, 381–82: *mtshan 'greng zhes bya ba ni 'di lha chen po dang 'dra ba bstan pas de 'dul ba'i phyir te/ de ni lhag par chags pa can yin pas/ lo gsum du dka' thub bzlog pa* [em. *ma*, ed.] *dang gnyis kyi gnyis su bde bas bde ba u ma* (em. Newman *ma*, ed.) *tshim zhing rtag tu mtshan pa las su rung ba'o zhes grag go/ de bas na chags dang lta ba zhe sdang bsngo// lha chen tshangs pa khyab 'jug 'dul// zhes bshad do/.*

tantric practices focused on the retention of semen—are found already in the *Mahābhārata*.[166] One such practice especially popular in tantric scriptures is the famous *vajrolīmudrā* (lit. "the seal of *vajra* lineage"), the purpose of which is to enable the yogin to reabsorb the ejaculated semen back into the penis or to somehow absorb partners' sexual fluids after intercourse.[167] That sexual practices resembling the *vajrolīmudrā* had been a part of Vajrabhairava sādhana is attested in Lalitavajra's commentary on the VBhT,[168] where, to prevent the semen from falling into a woman's vagina, the yogin is instructed to collect it through a tube inserted in the urethra.[169] The goal of this practice is to prolong life.

This chapter has argued that the development of Vajrabhairava's iconography cannot be reduced to a simple evolution from the Hindu-Buddhist deity Yama but must be seen as sustained processes of synthesis and syncretism. The synthesis aspect is visible in the adoption of the epithet "hideous face," which like other ferocious beings of early tantra, was meant to consolidate Vajrabhairava's identity as a transgressive deity. The latter aspect, syncretism, is discernible in Vajrabhairava's ithyphallic aspect, which allowed him to adopt a prominent iconographic feature of Śiva, which, in the Buddhist context, comes to exemplify the conquest of the afflictive emotion passion as represented by Śiva.

166. Mallinson and Singleton 2017, 280.

167. Mallinson 2018, 181–222.

168. See below.

169. See Mallinson 2018, 185.

3. Tibetan Accounts of Vajrabhairava's Origins

THE MYTHIC STORY associated with the origins of the deity Vajrabhairava, preserved in Tibetan sources, has two versions. The first, which I call the Yamarāja Myth, is the most popular. It is principally the Tibetan Buddhist rendering of the subjugation of Maheśvara myth appearing for the first time in chapter 6 of the *Sarvatathāgatatattvasaṃgraha* (STTS).[170] The second version, which comes from the oral tradition of Rwa lo tsā ba, narrates the origins of Vajrabhairava in the context of the Purāṇic battle between the gods (*suras*) and the demons (*asuras*). Both versions incorporate several major themes: the subjugation of the non-Buddhist gods through the theoretical model of conversion (*vinaya*; *'dul ba*), the explanation of Vajrabhairava's wrathful iconography as part of the mechanism of subjugation, and the depiction of Vajrabhairava's *liṅga* as a weapon of conversion. Moreover, the narrative of Rwa lo tsā ba reflects an example of Tibetan Buddhist borrowing of the well-known Indian myth of the subjugation of the demon Mahiṣā (*mahiṣāsura*).

The Yamarāja Myth

According to Tāranātha, the Yamarāja Myth is narrated in the seven-chapter VBhT, but in fact, the text as we know it today does not contain this myth. There is however a short separate text containing the Yamarāja Myth preserved in the Bka' 'gyur and translated into English by Siklós (1996, 64). This text does not have a Sanskrit title, and the descriptive Tibetan title *gtam rgyud*, or "story," seems to be a later addition (Siklós 1996, 18). A full retelling of the Yamarāja Myth (with the exception of the Yamāntaka mantra), said to be quoted from the VBhT, is given in Tāranātha's *chos 'byung*:

170. Two doctoral dissertations have been written on the STTS; one dealing with its general structure (Kwon 2002) and the other with its placement in the classification of Buddhist tantras (Weinberger 2003).

> From the seven-chapter *Vajramahābhairava Tantra* of Mañjuśrī: "Now the Bhagavān, the emanation of body, speech, and mind of Vajramahābhairava manifesting on the peak of the Mount Meru, realized that the time had come to tame those who were to be tamed—namely, Yamarāja and his retinue. [Vajrabhairava] crossed the southern ocean and destroyed the seats of Yamarāja, sixteen iron fortresses, with his sixteen feet. He tore down the central iron fortress with the *liṅga* of knowledge vajra (*jñānavajra*), and Yamarāja was subdued. Having conquered all other groups of demons, he obliterated them. The eight classes [of violent deities] offered their life-essence and took a vow to serve him. Yamas and the "mothers" (*ma mos*) were liberated and blessed [to become] male and female servants (*kiṅkaras*). They were ordered to protect the teaching." This much comes [from the VBhT].[171]

The Yamarāja Myth narrated above, which closely resembles the *gtam rgyud* from the Tibetan canon translated by Siklós, is part of a larger mythic story that I was able to trace in A mes zhabs's *Gshin rje chos 'byung* (1633). Given the fundamental importance of this account for the understanding of the origins of the deity Vajrabhairava in the Tibetan tradition, I recount it here in full.

The extended version of the myth begins with the description of Rudra-Karmayama, "Terrible Yama with dominion over those born from karma" (*drag po las kyi gshin rje*), who, having built Mount Meru out of skeletons on a base of human flesh surrounded by an ocean of blood, began to incite violence and oppression among all the sentient beings in the three realms.[172] At that time, all the buddhas in the pure land of Akaniṣṭha (*'og min*) single-mindedly brought forth from the heart of peaceful Mañjuśrī's enjoyment body (*saṃbhogakāya*) the emanation body (*nirmāṇakāya*) of Vajrabhairava (with nine heads, thirty-four arms, and sixteen feet).[173] The purpose of bringing Vajra-

171. Tāranātha's *Gshin rje 'chos byung*, p.41.

172. The image of the Meru-sized mountain of skeletons surrounded by the ocean of blood bears a striking resemblance to the story of Heruka appearing on Mount Meru found in the eighth-century **Guhyagarbha Tantra*; see Davidson 1991, 205.

173. A mes zhabs, *Gshin rje chos 'byung*, 13: *drag po las kyi gshin rje de nyid sha chen gyis gzhi/ khrag gi rgya mtsho/ keng rus kyi ri rab brtsigs nas khams gsum gyi sems can thams cad la 'tshe ba dang 'joms par byed cing gnas pa las/ de'i tshe 'og min du sangs rgyas thams cad kyi dgongs pa gcig pas/ longs sku zhi ba'i 'jam dpal gyi thugs ka nas sprul sku rdo rje 'jigs byed dbu dgu phyag so bzhi zhabs bcu drug pa zhig sprul te/.*

bhairava into the world was to tame the Terrible Yama who has a dominion over those born from karma.[174]

Yama is depicted as the personification of evil, so mighty in power that a collective effort of all the buddhas is required to find a means to defeat him. Vajrabhairava, functioning as Yama's assassin, is brought forth to combat the forces of evil, but en route to Yama's fortress, he visits the three realms of Buddhist cosmology—the desire, form, and formless realms—and by means of the four magical activities (*'phrin las bzhi*) of pacifying, increasing, subduing, and destroying, he disciplines (*btul*) various gods and deities residing in those realms.[175] The narrative of Vajrabhairava's visit to the desire realm builds up around the introductory lemma from the root text describing Vajrabhairava as "very fierce and terrifying to all the gods" (*de yi lha rnams thams cad la drag shul che zhing 'jigs par byed; sarveṣām eva devānām atyugraṃ hi bhayānakam*) and offers the following explanation:

> Then [Vajrabhairava], having gone to the heaven of the Thirty-Three,[176] disciplined all the gods who abide on Mount Meru with four furies—the fury of body, the fury of speech, the fury of mind, and the fury of action. These are the four furies of the magical rituals (*karmas*). Among these, the *fury of body* [means] they are converted with his hands, feet, face and eyes, and so on. With the first pair of hands, through conversion or wrathful action, he subjugated Indra and Indrāṇī. With the remaining thirty-two hands, he disciplined the thirty-two Viṣṇus and bound them under oath. With his three eyes, he disciplined the three [gods] Brahmā, Rudra, and Viṣṇu.
>
> Then, having arrived at the heaven of the Four Great Kings,[177]

174. A mes zhabs, *Gshin rje chos 'byung*, 13: *drag po 'jigs byed las kyi gshin rje ste/ de 'dul ba'i ched du rdo rje 'jigs byed dbu dgu phyag gsum cu so bzhi zhabs bcu drug pa ma he'i zhal can nyid sprul pa yin pas so/.*

175. See A mes zhabs, *Gshin rje chos 'byung*, 13–14.

176. The heaven of Thirty-Three, Trayastriṃśa, is situated atop the world axis Mount Meru. It is the second lowest of the six heavens of the realm of desire (*kāmadhātu*). Trayastriṃśa is inhabited by thirty-three gods of the Hindu pantheon, presided over by Indra, whom the mythic story portrays as the first god subjected to Vajrabhairava's taming fury. Scholars have noticed that the number thirty-three parallels the original number of the Indian gods in the *Ṛg Veda* and may therefore suggest a deliberate attempt to absorb the ancient Indian pantheon into the Buddhist cosmological structure (Buswell and Lopez 2014, 921–22).

177. The heaven of the Four Great Kings or *Cāturmahārājika* is situated on the slopes

he bound under oath the gods that dwelled there. They offered him [their] life-essence mantra, and because it was inserted between the seed syllables *hūṃ phaṭ oṃ*, it became the root mantra of the Lord [Vajrabhairava] himself. Moreover, because they offered the ten-letter life-essence [mantra] of the guardians of the ten directions, they were blessed by the Lord, and it became the heart mantra (*hṛdayamantra*) of the Lord.

Then again, with eight faces, he disciplined the eight classes of gods and demons[178] and bound them under oath. When he wished to discipline the eight great common gods—Indra, Brahmā, Maheśvara, Viṣṇu, the Six-Faced Kumāra, Vināyaka, Gaṇapati, and Rāvaṇa—with his main face, he bit off the heads of those eight and devoured them. He appeared with blood, fat, marrow, and so on dripping from his mouth. Then he also disciplined the sun and the moon, the sons of the gods, with the sun disc, which is at the heart of the wrathfulness of the mind. Then he blessed them with the [*liṅga* of] knowledge vajra (*jñānavajra*) of the Lord.

How he generated magical creations for the benefit of others: from his body gathered terrifying clouds and pitch-black darkness; from his tongue, he released terrifying flashes of lightning; he bellowed violent terrifying roars of thunder; his hand(s) arrayed innumerable terrifying weapons such as vajras. He rendered the wrathful

---

of Mount Meru. It is the lowest heaven of the desire-realm gods, and the four kings who rule there generally serve as protectors of dharma (*dharmapālas*). They are typically called Virūḍhaka, Dhṛtarāṣṭra, Virūpākṣa, and Vaiśravaṇa (the last being their leader), and their respective retinues consist of: (1) in the south *kumbhāṇḍas*, sometimes regarded as minions of Māra who are listed together with evil beings such as *rākṣasas*, *bhūtas*, and *piśācas*; (2) in the east *gandharvas*, celestial musicians who subsist on smells; (3) in the west *nāgas*, serpents usually associated with underwater kingdoms and the roots of trees; and (4) in the north *yakṣas*. Buswell and Lopez 2014, 171.

178. The first appearance of the eight classes of gods and demons (*lha srin sde brgyad*)—traditionally connected to Padmasambhava's taming of local Tibetan deities under oath and assisting him with the building of Bsam yas Monastery—is traced back to the eighth century (see Yeshe Tsogyal 2004, 72). These eight classes of gods and demons subdued by Padmasambhava became the first *dharmapālas* in Tibet (Buswell and Lopez 2014, 249–50). Another common list considers the eight to be a combination of local Tibetan spirit-deities and Buddhist semidivine beings, such as *gshin rje* (*yama*), *ma mo* (ferocious female beings, closely connected to the *mātṛkās*), *bdud* (*māra*), *btsan* (red, male spirits of monks who rejected their vows), *rgyal po* (king spirits or spirits of high lamas who failed to uphold their vows), *klu* (*nāgas*), *gnod sbyin* (*yakṣa*), and *gza'* (planet seizers) (see Samuel 1993, 162–63).

Bhairava unconscious. Then the Lord [Vajrabhairava] installed Bhairava as his main face. Having swallowed him into his body, he purified all of Bhairava's afflictive emotions in the clear light. He [Bhairava], having regained his senses, generated the enlightened mind (*bodhicitta*). Having burnt [Bhairava's] body generated from karma and afflictive emotions with the fire of clear light, he [Vajrabhairava] created ashes, which he expelled through his anus. He initiated his [main] face with the mudrās. Thus it was predicted that [Bhairava] in the future would become the buddha Lord of Ashes (Bhasmeśvara). The offspring of Bhairava's ignorance is Kāla; the offspring of Bhairava's hatred is Mahākāla; the offspring of Bhairava's desire is young Kārttikeya; those three offered [themselves] dutifully. Moreover, those who were extremely angry due to hatred, including the eight male mounts, offered themselves as cushions for his [eight] right feet. Those who were extremely angry due to desire, including the eight female mounts, offered themselves as cushions for his [eight] left feet. Moreover, all of them were recollected and included in the maṇḍala as emissaries; they were allowed to hear the speech of the Lord.

Then, again, having crossed the southern sea, he arrived at the sixteen barred iron gates, the house of Yama, the Lord of Death. With sixteen feet, he kicked upon the sixteen iron gates. Having crushed the great iron house at the center with his one-pointed *liṅga*, symbolizing the one-pointed wisdom of the enlightened mind, he bound Yama Dharmarāja under oath.

Again, he arrived at the fourteen places,[179] such as a solitary tree, a cremation ground, and so forth, ferociously uttering the syllables *ha ha* and *hūṃ hūṃ phaṭ phaṭ*. Because he shouted these words, all fierce female spirits (*ma mo*), *ḍāka*s, *bhūta*s, *vetāla*s, *rākṣasa*s, *preta*s, *garuḍa*s, *mahoraga*s (great-bellied pythons), *piśācī*s, and so on were disciplined and bound under oath. At that time, the oath-bound protectors, such as Dharmarāja and so on, who were crushed in the same way, requested: "I will accomplish your purpose, Great Hero, and because we have properly offered the essence of our life, we ask to be accepted by the Great Hero." The offering of the life essence of eight classes of gods and spirits is as follows: YA of Yama, MA of *ma*

179. The "fourteen places" probably refer to the suitable places for undertaking the Vajrabhairava sādhana specified in the root text (see p. 203), however, it is difficult to count more than thirteen.

> *mo*, RA of *rākṣasa*, KṢE of *yakṣa*, NA of *nara*, SA of *sa bdag*, CCA of *tsan*, DA of *dānava*. Having offered this, they all promised to be [his] servants.[180]

This extended version of the Yamarāja Myth has several functions. It explains the iconographic features of Vajrabhairava framed within the standard model of taming and binding under oath, which can be traced back to Padmasambhava's legend of the tantric conversion of Tibet and the subjugation of demons (Guenther 1996; Dalton 2004). However, in this specific context of Vajrabhairava's journey through the heavens of gods in the realm of desire, the above narrative emulates the myth of the subjugation of Maheśvara of the STTS[181] that was used to legitimize the authenticity of the emergent tantric Buddhist scriptures (Davidson 1991, 198) and that also provided a rationale for the appearance in the world of wrathful tantric Buddhist deities, such as Trailokyavijaya/Vajrahūṃkāra, Vajrabhairava, Heruka, and Cakrasaṃvara, as part of their mythogenesis (Davidson 1991; Gray 2007a).

The myth of the subjugation of Maheśvara was also popular on the Tibetan plateau. Davidson (1991, 203–14) explores the different versions that existed in fifteenth-century Tibetan Buddhist textual sources, especially among the Sa skya pas, who adopted this myth to explain the birth of the deity Heruka. A mes zhabs, one of the most prolific Sa skya pa patriarchs, must have been similarly influenced by the subjugation of Maheśvara myth and therefore could have adopted it in the above narrative to rationalize the origins of Vajrabhairava.

What narrative frameworks and literary tropes does A mes zhabs adopt in the narrative above? First, we can discern the common trope of the conversion of Hindu gods and their integration into the tantric Buddhist maṇḍala as *dūta*s (emissaries). Second, Vajrabhairava converts the deities by means of four magical actions that are modeled on the four magic acts performed by Vajrahūṃkāra in the STTS.[182] Third, Vajrabhairava's journey through the three

180. A mes zhabs, *Gshin rje chos 'byung*, 14–16.

181. The myth was translated into English by Davidson 1995a, 547–55, and partially by Snellgrove 1981. Iyanaga 1985, Davidson 1991, Stein 1995, Linrothe 1999, Mayer 1996, and Mayer 1998 give detailed analyses of it.

182. In the STTS, chapter 6, Vajrapāṇi in the form of Vajrahūṃkāra, also performs the four magical *karma*s of summoning (*ākarṣaṇa*), drawing in (*praveśana*), binding (*bandhana*), and subjecting under one's own will (*vaśīkaraṇa*), all the deities such as Maheśvara, together with humbling them (*huṃkāreṇa ca mahādevādisarvadevākarṣaṇapraveśanabandhanavaśīkaraṇapātanakṣamo bhavati*).

realms, where he binds under oath the gods that dwell there, is modeled upon the Trailokyavijaya (Conqueror of the Three Realms), and thus Vajrabhairava subsumes the function of Trailokyavijaya of the STTS. In line with the concept of defilements (*kleśa*s) found in the STTS, the theme of the conversion of non-Buddhist deities by Vajrabhairava in the extended Yamarāja Myth is portrayed through the allegory of the purification of the desire-realm beings' base inclinations and *kleśa*s in the fire of dharma. According to Buddhist cosmology, *deva*s in the desire (*kāma*) realm are attached to sense objects and sensual pleasures because desire is the predominant affliction (*kleśa*) for them. Because this afflictive power of desire holds them in its grip, desire-realm *deva*s are regarded by Buddhists as mundane (*laukika*) gods, and therefore they are contrasted to the transmundane (*lokottara*) buddhas and bodhisattvas, who are free of such binding *kleśa*s. In this regard, the act of taming (*'dul ba*) is understood as an exercise of compassion, since it benefits the mundane gods, ultimately transporting them to the transmundane level of existence, where they assume a higher position as the protectors of the dharma.

The distinction between the *laukika* and *lokottara* spheres with reference to the categorization of non-Buddhist and Buddhist deities and enlightened beings in the context of *'dul ba* has been discussed by Seyfort Ruegg (2008). Seyfort Ruegg highlights this soteriological function of *'dul ba*, motivated by the bodhisattvas' compassionate intention. This model can also be applied to the extended Yamarāja Myth and can be used as a theoretical framework to explain the passage narrating Vajrabhairava's purification of Bhairava's body "generated from karma and afflictive emotions in the fire of clear light." The myth is influenced by the STTS's depiction of Maheśvara-Bhairava as the hypostasis of evil, a feature he shares with Māra. According to Davidson (1991, 202), "It is clear that Maheśvara became the 'Māra' of the Vehicle of Spells, and the similarities between the Buddha's conduct of Māra and the treatment of Maheśvara, were quite explicit." The aspect of *kleśamāra* embodying "evil" afflictive emotions became a potent concept that found its way to the tantric exegetical literature, where the Hindu trinity (*trimūrti*)—Brahmā, Viṣṇu, and Maheśvara—is often glossed as the three *kleśa*s.[183]

In the story above, we also find the common association of Bhairava (the wrathful form of Śiva) and his "sons" (Kāla, Mahākāla, and Kārttikeya) with the "evil" afflictive emotions. Vajrabhairava installs Bhairava as his main face and purifies all afflictive emotions inside his body in the fire of clear light; then he creates ashes, which he expels through his anus. He initiates his new Bhairava face with *mudrā* gestures. The text ends with the prophetic line: "Thus it

183. See note 152 above.

was predicted that [Bhairava] in the future would become the buddha Lord of Ashes (Bhasmeśvara)."

The reference to Bhairava-Bhasmeśvara appears for the first time in the "Maheśvara episode" of the *Kāraṇḍavyūha*,[184] one of the Mahāyāna sūtras composed sometime in the fourth or fifth century CE.[185] In it, the bodhisattva Avalokiteśvara prophesizes that in the future Maheśvara will become the buddha Bhasmeśvara. The same Bhasmeśvara story was adopted in esoteric Buddhism in the seventh century when it became a part of the core narrative of the subjugation of Maheśvara first attested in the STTS. In the STTS, the bodhisattva Vajrapāṇi in his wrathful form of Trailokyavijaya first annihilates Śiva Maheśvara with his vajra and then resuscitates him into the Vajradhātu maṇḍala as the tathāgata Bhasmeśvaranirghoṣa, "Silent Lord of Ashes," in the Ash Parasol (*bhasmacchatrā*) world system.[186] The story of Bhasmeśvara as a future buddha had a formative influence on the development of the origin myths of all major tantric Buddhist deities, such as Heruka and Cakrasaṃvara,[187] which points to its great popularity in tantric Buddhist circles. However, in addition to the subjugation and conversion context in which the Bhasmeśvara story commonly appears, the extended Yamarāja Myth also indirectly hints at the role of the Buddhist appropriation of the Śaiva/Bhairava cult in the making of Vajrabhairava. This is conveyed through the idiom of tantric initiation, which passes through several stages: (1) the installation of Bhairava as Vajrabhairava's main face, (2) the generation of Bhairava's enlightened mind (*bodhicitta*), and (3) the initiation of Bhairava's face with mudrās. Thus, alongside the recy-

184. For the general introduction to the history of the *Kāraṇḍavyūha* in Tibetan Buddhism, see Roberts 2012. For the Śaiva-Buddhist encounters in the *Kāraṇḍavyūha* and its connection to the Śivadharma corpus, see Sinclair 2015 and Bisschop 2018.

185. The *Kāraṇḍavyūha* is perhaps the earliest appearance of the Maheśvara as Bhasmeśvara, the future Buddha. In the text, Maheśvara requests the bodhisattva Avalokiteśvara to give him a prophecy of this "true unsurpassable enlightenment." Avalokiteśvara replies by listing the ten famous epithets of the Buddha: "Noble son, in the world named Vivṛta, you will be the Tathāgata, the arhat, the *samyaksaṃbuddha*, perfect in wisdom and conduct, the sugata, the knower of the world, the unsurpassable guide who tames beings, the teacher of gods and humans, the buddha, the Bhagavat Bhasmeśvara" (*Kāraṇḍavyūha* 2.94, trans. by Roberts).

186. The tathāgata Bhasmeśvaranirghoṣa of the Bhasmacchatrā realm enters the body of Maheśvara and revives him in this form. Thus Maheśvara becomes a crown prince for the benefit of all sentient beings and for converting those who are evil (Snellgrove and Chandra 1981, 47).

187. For the same Bhasmeśvara episode recycled in the mythological account of the birth of the deity Heruka, see Gray 2007a, 48.

cled context of Bhairava becoming a future buddha, the extended Yamarāja Myth casts Bhairava as the Śaiva deity who is being ritually appropriated as the main aspect of Vajrabhairava. The same influence and incorporation of Śaiva elements is seen in Vajrabhairava's ithyphallic iconography. As we saw attested above in *Akṣobhya's commentary (see p. 67), the appropriation of iconographic attributes formerly belonging to Śaiva deities and their reconceptualization is an evocative expression of the conquest of the non-Buddhist religious other.

The Oral Tradition of Rwa lo tsā ba

The second version of Vajrabhairava's mythic origins, preserved in Tāranātha's *chos 'byung*, goes back (as Tāranātha tells us) to the oral tradition of Rwa lo tsā ba.[188] Tāranātha provides the following account:

> Once upon a time, in the incalculable past, a son of Maheśvara was the general of the gods, Six-Faced Kumāra, and he disagreed with a fierce *asura*, the Outcaste (*caṇḍāla*), as to who should be the master of the world. They fought for a long time. When Six-Faced Kumāra gained command over the world, Maheśvara was residing deep within Mount Meru and realized this. [Maheśvara] recruited to arms the Thirty-Three gods and so on, who move in the sky, the eight diseases, and the eight gods and demons and so on, all the spirits who are above ground, and the *asuras*, *nāgas*, and so on, all those who move around below ground. [Then] the wrathful Maheśvara and all those wrathful ones arrived, and the fierce Outcaste became frightened, for he had no protector.
>
> Then he remembered the *bhagavān* Mañjughoṣa. Raising his face to the sky, he cried out the name [of Mañjuśrī] with a loud voice and prayed. To that place came Mañjuśrī in the flesh, manifesting in the wrathful body [of Vajrabhairava] to tame the evil ones. He devoured the eight Bhairavas of the cardinal directions with his eight different mouths. With his main face and *liṅga*, he wrathfully tamed Bhairava Maheśvara. With his two buffalo horns, he destroyed the cavalry of *asuras*. With his two hands holding aloft

188. Taranātha, *Gshin rje chos 'byung*, 41: *_yang grub thob brgyud pa'i bla ma rnams kyi snyan du brgyud pa'i gtam rwa lo chen po'i gsung rgyun las byung ba ni/*. "The story from the oral transmission of the lamas of the siddha lineage is recounted by Rwa lo tsā ba in the following way...."

an elephant skin, [he destroyed] Indra; with his other thirty-two hands, he destroyed the thirty-two Viṣṇus. With his eight right feet, [he destroyed] the eight evil spirits, and with his eight left feet, he pressed down the eight diseases. He strung up the *nāgas* as ornaments, and furthermore, some of the evil gods and demons he ate, and some he flattened under his feet.

This is how it happened, and through the power of this, he moreover tamed the nine planets with nine faces, the nine guardians of the directions, and the eight or nine Bhairavas, and with twenty-seven eyes, he tamed the stellar constellations. With this, the purpose was achieved. In the same way, all the black poisons, *devas*, *nāgas*, *asuras*, *bhūtas*, *dāhas*, and nonhumans, he first annihilated and then liberated them. First he displayed fearful acts, such as eating their heart and blood and so on, and afterward he revived and supported them, and initiated them into the wisdom maṇḍala.[189]

This narrative reflects a marked Purāṇic influence, not only in its adaptation of the classic mythologeme of the Purāṇic battle between the gods and the demons who fight over claim to the universe, but also in its appropriation of the trope of a "good" demon-devotee—commonly also an outcaste—popular in *bhakti* mythologies found in Indic Sanskrit and vernacular traditions.[190] The beginning of the narrative above reflects the first verses of the second subdivision of the Purāṇic text the *Devīmāhātmya*, dated to the fifth or sixth century (Kinsley 1978, 490), where the gods led by Indra battle the *asura* demons led by Mahiṣa.[191] In the *Devīmāhātmya*, the gods lose the battle, and Mahiṣa becomes their chief. As he takes over the territories of the Vedic gods Sūrya,

189. Tāranātha, *Gshin rje chos 'byed*, 41–43.

190. Especially in South India, but also in the ninth-century iconographic examples of the goddess Mahiṣāsuramardinī from Java, the demon assumes the form of a devotee (*bhakta*) (Rodrigues 2009, 542). One telling example of this kind is the myth of the demon Prahlāda, a son of Hiraṇyakaśipu (king of the Daitya *asuras*), whose ardent devotion to Viṣṇu brought the Man-Lion (*narasiṃha*) manifestation of Viṣṇu to save him from the demonic assaults of his father. For vernacular examples of the demon-devotee trope, see chapter 5 in Shulman 1980 (317–45). For localized versions of demon-devotee legends in contemporary Hinduism, see various ethnographic studies in Hiltebeitel 1989.

191. The second subdivision of the *Devīmāhātmya* (2.1–2) begins: "Once upon a time, a battle between the gods (*devas*) and *asuras* raged for a full hundred years, when [the buffalo demon] Mahiṣa was leader of the *asuras* and Indra was leader of the gods. The gods' army was conquered there by the mighty *asuras*, and having conquered all the gods, the *asura* Mahiṣa became lord [literally Mahiṣa became Indra]"; in Coburn 1998, 36.

Indra, Agni, Vāyu, Candra, Varuṇa, and Yama, the conquered gods approach Śiva and Viṣṇu to assist them in combating Mahiṣa. The gods emanate the goddess Caṇḍikā, also called Bhadrakālī or Ambikā, from the fiery effulgence (*tejas*) of their faces and bodies.[192] The gods arm her with their weapons, and she takes up the battle with the *asura* and his troops. Eventually, the goddess captures the buffalo demon (*mahiṣāsura*) with a noose and tramples his throat beneath her foot.[193] Thus she is known as "the one who slayed the buffalo demon" (*mahiṣāsuramardinī*).[194]

The narrative of Rwa lo tsā ba distinctively draws upon an earlier version of this story, based on the mythology of Kumāra Skanda,[195] also known as Six-Faced Kārttikeya (the son of Śiva and Umā), who was begotten to destroy the demon Tāraka. This episode of Kumāra's mythology is narrated already in the *Mahābhārata*.[196] The selection of the Purāṇic trope, which seems to have been quoted virtually verbatim (see note 191 above), is constructed with a purpose, there being a thoroughly Buddhist agenda behind the choice of this particular narrative and the moulding of the story in a way that changes its earlier meaning. Rwa lo tsā ba's manner of adapting the main storyline conveys the

192. The goddess is also called *mahāsurī* ("great demoness") due to her transgressive behavior, such as drinking wine, which highlights her fierce or *raudra* nature existing alongside her benevolent or *saumya* nature.

193. Hiltebeitel (1978, 786) argues that by overcoming the buffalo, Durgā (Caṇḍikā) overwhelms Yama (Mahiṣa) as death symbolized by the buffalo.

194. The appropriation of Purāṇic tropes, especially that of Durgā or Mahiṣāsuramardinī vanquishing the demon, had a great impact on conceptualization of evil in tantric Buddhist contexts. Iyanaga (1985) was the first to suggest that the STTS adopted the names of the two demons Śumbha and Niśumbha from the *Devīmāhātmya*'s second main episode, where Trailokyavijaya's secret *dhāraṇī* reads: *oṃ śumbha niśumbha hūṃ gṛhṇa gṛhṇa hūṃ gṛhṇāpaya hūṃ ānaya ho bhagavan vajra hūṃ phaṭ* (STTS, 159, lines 6–10; for a translation of this mantra, see Linrothe 1999, 182). The powerful depiction of the conquest of evil expressed by the act of trampling of the *mahiṣāsura* by Durgā in a warrior pose (*pratyālīḍha*) harmonized easily with the moral prerogative held by the Buddhists, who seem to have adopted this dramatic expression to convey the same message. The mythologeme of destroying evil by trampling them underfoot, adopted for the first time in the STTS, soon became a central motif in many depictions of tantric Buddhist deities, where trampling upon the Hindu gods relegates the non-Buddhist deities to the role of demons. In one of the stone Trailokyavijaya images from Bodhgayā analyzed by Linrothe (1999, 199), a short inscription beneath Maheśvara reads *bhūta*, "demon," and under Umādevī, *bhūtī*, "demoness."

195. For a detailed account of Kumāra Skanda mythology, see Mann 2012.

196. Although his mythologies vary, from the second century onward, Kumāra Skanda subsumes the role of Senāpati, the war god (Mann 2012, 12).

antagonism between the two classes of beings, which is further reinforced by their sectarian identities as a Śaiva god and a Buddhist demon. In addition, the Buddhist demon is named Caṇḍāla, "outcaste," which emphasizes his low social status within the Brahmanical caste system. Not only is Caṇḍāla a low-caste demon at the opposite end of the social scale as Kumāra, the son of the chief god Śiva, he also has no powerful protector to aid him in combatting the forces of Śiva's approaching army. Fearful of looming defeat, Caṇḍāla assumes the form of a demon-devotee and calls out in prayer to Mañjuśrī, who promptly arrives in his wrathful form to "discipline the evil ones."

Rwa lo tsā ba picks up the story of the demon Mahiṣa, archenemy of the gods, and develops it in a new direction that creates a vaguely ironic representation of the original. The depiction of Vajrabhairava is largely implied, in that the Vajrabhairava character appears in the shape of the demon Mahiṣa through his feature of the buffalo face (*mahiṣamukha*). By creating this subtext, Rwa lo tsā ba gives a new context to the original storyline to make the Purāṇic battle serve the Buddhist purpose. The original meaning of the conquest of evil in which the demons are vanquished is still recognizable, but it is turned on its head: Vajrabhairava takes the place of Caṇḍikā or Skanda as the slayer of the demonic gods, and the *asuras* triumph.

4. Lalitavajra's Rediscovery of the *Vajrabhairava Tantra*

THIS CHAPTER analyzes the origin story of the VBhT itself. This narrative is contained in the biography of the siddha Lalitavajra, who retrieves the Vajrabhairava-Yamāntaka tantras guarded by the ḍākinīs, thereby reintroducing the textual tradition of Vajrabhairava in the world. Here, the motif of origins serves the purpose of consolidating the tradition's authenticity by legitimizing the authority of its revealer, around whom the identity of the tradition can crystallize.

According to Tāranātha, the VBhT is a timeless revelation that had been controlled by the siddhas since beginningless times, but at some point the tantra was sealed because it could no longer benefit people.[197] The tantra's concealment in Oḍḍiyāna becomes imagined in many ways in parallel to the Tibetan treasure tradition (*gter ma*),[198] where important scriptural revelations and other artifacts are hidden only to be rediscovered in future times. For Tāranātha, the "hidden text" has ramifications for the narrative of the siddha Lalitavajra, who, in a manner of the treasure revealer (*gter ston*), resuscitates what had become a forgotten tradition. Tāranātha relates several narratives associated with the rediscovery of the Vajrabhairava-Yamāntaka corpus. All of

197. "Then, after some time, having realized that the tantra can no longer benefit people, the tantra was sealed and stayed in the land of O rgyan in the place called Treasury of Dharma (*dharmagañja*), it is said. Thus this tantra was controlled from the beginning by the siddhas." (*de nas bar skabs su mi rnams kyi don du mi 'gyur par mkhyen nas/ o rgyan gyi gnas dharma gany+dza chos kyi mdzod du rgyas btab nas bzhugs ces 'gyur na/ rgyud 'di gdod nas grub pa'i dbang du byas te*). The term *dharmagañja* is a Persian loanword, not attested in Pāli and Prakrit but found also in Kharoṣṭhī documents, where it means "treasury" or "treasure-store" (Edgerton 1953, 207). *Gañja* alone also means a "tavern" or the abode of low people (Monier-Williams 1899, 278).

198. With regard to the traditional division of *gter ma*, a "hidden" *text* would belong to the category of earth treasures (*sa gter*), concealed in a physical location, as opposed to a mind treasure or a pure-vision teaching; see Doctor 2005, 27.

them revolve around the figure of Lalitavajra, a.k.a Līlāvajra,[199] and the legend of his journey to Oḍḍiyāna.

Oḍḍiyāna was the kingdom known to the Tibetans as U rgyan or O rgyan, said to be located northwest of Kashmir in the Swat Valley, in present-day Pakistan.[200] Its high status as a special place for a tantric sādhana is attested by the various designations by which it is referred to. In the early Śākta tradition of the Krama, dedicated to the worship of the tantric goddess Kālī and her emanations, Oḍḍiyāna is often referred to as the "primordial sacred seat" (*ādipīṭha*) or *oṃkārapīṭha*. It is also often identified as the "northern seat" (*uttarapīṭha*).[201] Several accounts attest to various Hindu and Buddhist tantric traditions, masters, and texts originating from Oḍḍiyāna.[202] According to traditional Tibetan accounts, the "lotus-born" progenitor of Buddhism in Tibet, Padmasambhava, was born in Oḍḍiyāna, and so was Dga' rab rdo rje (*Prahevajra), the human originator of Great Perfection (*rdzogs chen*) teachings. The colophon of the manuscript containing the Sanskrit version of the VBhT describes the tantra as a text that was brought down from Oḍḍiyāna.[203] The high status of Oḍḍiyāṇa as the sacred seat (*pīṭha*) of esoteric knowledge is further attested by the fact that masters from India and Tibet typically went there in search of lost scriptures containing esoteric knowledge.

199. The problem of Lalitavajra *versus* Līlāvajra is discussed in chapter 1; see page 22 above.

200. In fact, the location of Oḍḍiyāna (variously spelled Uḍḍiyāna, U/Oḍiyāna, U/Oḍyāna, and U/Oḍḍayāna) used to be a matter of controversy. Tucci 1940, Sircar 1948, Davidson 2002, and, based on inscriptional evidence, Kuwayama 1991, 281–86, locate Oḍḍiyāna in the Swat Valley, while Lokesh Chandra 1980 puts it in Kāñcī. Donaldson 2001 places it in Odisha (Orissa).

201. The reference to the Krama teachings is not out of place in this context insofar that it is generally believed that the Krama "may have been influenced by Buddhist ideas" (Sferra 2003, 64). *Pīṭhas* or *siddhapīṭhas* are especially powerful places where particular yogins or ascetics meditated for attaining siddhis (Sircar 1948, 3). The *pīṭha* motif was appropriated by both Buddhist and non-Buddhist tantric traditions, and it conveyed the transformation of ordinary places into sacred topography, as abodes for the powers and deities dwelling in them (Beane 1977, 247).

202. Bhattacharyya 1999; Bharati 1993; Sircar 1948; Shaw 1998; Simmer-Brown 2001.

203. See VBhT ms. A, fol. 16v. Similarly, the excipits of manuscripts containing the earliest Śākta texts of the Krama tradition—namely, the *Kramasadbhāva* and *Devīpañcaśatikā*, dated to the seventh century—state that they were brought down by [the master] Śrīnātha from the sacred northern seat, which as noted is a synonym for Oḍḍiyāna: *iti śrīmaduttarapīṭhavinirgate śrīnāthapādāvatārite śrīkālikrame śrīkramasadbhāve* (*Kramasadbhāva* 1.1).

One of the masters who undertook such a journey was Tāranātha's own guru, *Buddhaguptanātha.[204]

Oḍḍiyāna was famous also as the seat inhabited by the mistresses of yoga—yoginīs or ḍākinīs. The Sanskrit version of the VBhT designates Oḍḍiyāna as the *yoginīpīṭha*, "the sacred seat of the yoginīs," which clearly indicates this connection. This is also attested in the early Śākta texts of the Krama tradition. For example, the *Khacakrapañcakastotra*, by Jñānanetra, begins with a salutation to the yoginīs who have assembled in the sacred northern seat, the seat of the lotus (*abjapīṭha*).[205] Oḍḍiyāna as the coveted home of the yoginīs and ḍākinīs is also attested by U rgyan pa Rin chen dpal (1230–1309), who visited Oḍḍiyāna. The description of his visit is reported in his *Guide to Oḍḍiyāna* (*O rgyan lam yig*), where "All the women know the art of miraculous transformation. If you ask them who they are, they say that they are yoginīs" (Tucci 1940, 54). The same text describes ḍākinīs as shapeshifters assuming the forms of "wild boars, poisonous snakes, vultures, crows, jackals, and the like" (56). Tāranātha's guru *Buddhaguptanātha also attests to this perception when he says, "All women [of U rgyan] are of ḍākinī family; they are accomplished and powerful, and they adopt various forms and display magical abilities."[206]

Not only do yoginīs and ḍākinīs bestow coveted siddhis on tantric practitioners, they also act as guardians of the tantric texts and pledges (*samayas*).[207] In the Tibetan tradition, meetings with the yoginīs or ḍākinīs[208] became a core narrative element in the massive corpus of *gter ma* revelations. On the one hand, ḍākinīs act as the treasure protectors (*gter srung*) and create obstacles to prevent the treasure revealer from finding the hidden text (Gyatso 1993, 118–19); on the other, they play a critical role in locating the treasure site and bringing it to the attention of the retriever (225). This twofold role of the ḍākinī figure as both the agent creating impediments and the guide pointing the way to the hidden text is also highlighted in Lalitavajra's life story. In setting out for the journey to Oḍḍiyāna and in his encounters with the yoginīs and ḍākinīs, Lalitavajra emulates the trope of recovering hidden texts as the

204. See Tāranātha, *Buddha gupta'i rnam thar*, 539.

205. *Khacakrapañcakastotra*, v. 7cd; see Dyczkowski 2018, 82.

206. See *Buddha gupta'i rnam thar*, 540.

207. In the narrative of the siddha Kṛṣṇācārya, ḍākinī Bhadrī of Pretapuri is in the possession of the *Saṃpuṭatilaka Tantra*; see Tāranātha's *Life of Kāṇha* (Templeman 1989, 10). The mahāsiddha Tilopa is instructed by the ḍākinī to go to Oḍḍiyāna to meet Jñānaḍākinī, who guards the entrance to the temple containing prophecies and commitments (*samaya*); see Mar pa Chos kyi blo gros 2003, 35.

208. On the role of ḍākinīs in the *gter ma* tradition, see Gyatso 1998, 243–64.

source validating the inception of a new scriptural tradition. The impulse to proceed to Oḍḍiyāna is triggered by a prophecy. According to Gyatso (1991, 152), prophecy as a visionary instruction that propels the discoverer to find the hidden treasure is an important element of the *gter ma* paradigm. The act of prophesy implies two interrelated notions: first, that the proper time has finally come to unearth the revelation; second, that the discoverer is a person predetermined to receive the treasure. What is striking, however, in the context of Lalitavajra's narrative is the rationale for this rediscovery, which points to the strains and tensions in the social dynamics existing on the human level between Buddhists and non-Buddhists (*tīrthikas*).

Tāranātha's *Gshin rje chos 'byung* provides three different versions of the narrative recounting Lalitavajra's trip to Oḍḍiyāna. The first narrative, as Tāranātha tells us, is popular in India, and since it comes from a historical account (*lo rgyus*), it is not distorted.[209] This narrative is also repeated in a shorter version in Tāranātha's *Rgya gar chos 'byung*.[210] The second narrative, according to Tāranātha, is widespread among the Skyo lugs; in this version, Lalitavajra is referred to as Līlāvajra (see p. 23). The third narrative comes from the oral tradition of Ba ri lo tsā ba and features a Sgeg pa'i rdo rje, whom the followers of Ba ri lo tsā ba consider to be Lalitavajra (see p. 23 above).

Narrative 1

> Once there was the master Lalitavajra, who was born in Orissa. Tibetans have explained his caste as brahman. After going to the glorious Nālandā, he became a master of the five sciences and received many Vajrayāna teachings. He received the empowerment of the Māyājāla [system] from a tantric master. Because the flower fell on Mañjuśrī[211] [during his initiation], Mañjuśrī proved to be his tutelary deity. His secret name was Lalitavajra, and his actual name was *Mañjuśastra. After meditating on Ārya Mañjuśrī for about

209. Tāranātha, *Gshin rje chos 'byung*, 58: *'phags yul rang du grags pa ltar yin cing/ lo rgyus kyi yi ger yang bkod pa yin pas 'khrul pa med do*. "Because [the first account] is well known in the Land of the Āryas [India] itself, and because it is set forth in a written historical account, it is without error."

210. Chattopadhyaya 1990, 242.

211. This refers to the ritual of *puṣpapātaḥ* ("casting of a flower") during standard tantric initiation, in which the flower cast by a novice determines the family (*kula*) of buddhas to which he belongs. The ritual of intiation is completed when the new "tantric" name is granted to the novice. Wayman (1974) cites various sources about the casting of the flower and the implication of where it falls, as well as about attendant symbolism.

twenty years, [Lalitavajra] had a vision of him and achieved a few common siddhis.

According to Tibetan legends, the master [Lalitavajra] asked paṇḍitas of the time who were experts in mantras about the passage in the *Mañjuśrīnāmasaṅgīti* "He is Vajrabhairava, the frightening one, the terrifying six-faced wrathful king who has six eyes and six arms and is endowed with power." He also asked the paṇḍitas: "What is the mantra, tantra, maṇḍala, and so on of this deity?" They said that these were different forms of Mañjuśrī. When he asked about each of his [Mañjuśrī's] subdivisions, the paṇḍitas could not give him any specific answer. When Lalitavajra asked his own teacher or paṇḍita, who was very old, he was told: "The tantras for each of these [subdivisions] are in the hands of *ḍāka*s and ḍākinīs, and because they are unavailable in the human world at present, to [receive them you must] meditate on Ārya Mañjuśrī!" [Lalitavajra] said: "I shall meditate [on him]." Then the master stabilized the generation stage, and he attained a little bit of power.

He received the prophecy that he should also retrieve the tantra for subduing the "haughty ones" from the glorious land of Oḍḍiyāna. He gradually proceeded north and competed with the non-Buddhists (*tīrthika*s) all around the vicinity of Oḍḍiyāna and prevailed over everyone. However, on one occasion, a non-Buddhist *tīrthika* yoginī gave him a fierce gaze, and Lalitavajra fell unconscious for a while.[212] When the hex subsided, he prayed fervently to the vajra yoginīs. Bhagavatī Vajravetālī (*ro langs ma*) appeared in person in the form of a human woman and initiated him into the maṇḍala of the emanations of Yamāntaka. In the master's mental stream arose the correct wisdom of the empowerment.

Lalitavajra meditated in the same place for two and a half months. Stabilizing the wisdom of the generation and completion stage, he reached the stage of *heat* (*drod*). He summoned a wild buffalo from the forest and rode it, behaving like a crazy person for six months. Afterward, he went to cities such as Jalapatan and Talapatan, and stopping at a crossroads, he asked the beer-selling women for beer, drinking all they had in one gulp. The next day, all the pots of the beer-selling women from which they served him beer were filled with gold, silver, jewels, and other precious substances, and they were overjoyed.

212. *Yug cig = skabs shig.*

> On another occasion, he practiced the meditation of drawing the blood of humans and cattle of the city, when a huge cauldron appeared in front of him, filled with blood, and [the goddess] Vajracarcikā showed herself face to face. Because he had propitiated her, his power became immeasurable. He was able to hold down elephants with one finger and uproot a large *śālmalī* tree trunk with one hand. All the people and cattle in the city became emaciated. When they all became scared and worried, those who had become emaciated (*nang bar bkug pa*) became inflated [with blood] again, and by that, all the humans and cattle of the city became strong. He also composed a sādhana of Vajracarcikā.
>
> Having done some service for the benefit of sentient beings through practices (*vidyāvrata*s) such as these, he arrived at Treasury of Dharma, Dharmagañja, in the glorious Oḍḍiyāna. There he received counsel from the vajra ḍākinīs and retrieved the three cycles of Kṛṣṇayamāri, Yamāntaka, and Vajrabhairava.[213]

The above narrative is important because it provides a clear trajectory for the development of the cult of Vajrabhairava in general and the production of the VBhT in particular. The passage claims that an early tantric Buddhist text of the *saṅgīti* genre—namely, the MNS (or simply *Nāmasaṅgīti*)[214]—directly influenced the VBhT. This short text (167 verses) praises the "names" of Mañjuśrī embodying the principle of the perfection of wisdom (*prajñāpāramitā*), on the one hand, and the primordial buddha (*ādibuddha*), on the other. Composed around the seventh and eighth centuries (Davidson 1995b, 104),[215] the MNS played a formative role in the development of early tantric Buddhism in India, as can be attested from its extensive commentarial literature.[216] The

213. Tāranātha, *Gshin rje chos 'byung*, 55–58.

214. The MNS has been translated into English in Wayman 1985 and Davidson 1995b.

215. Wayman (1985, 5–6) proposed to date the MNS to between the sixth and the seventh centuries, which appears to be too early.

216. Among the tantric commentaries that have survived to us in Sanskrit is the *Nāmamantrārthāvalokinī* (NMAA) by Vilāsavajra, researched in detail by Tribe (1994; 2016), the *Amṛtakaṇikā* by Raviśrījñāna (Lal 1994), the *Gūḍhapadā* by Advayavakra (probably a typo for Advayavajra; Sferra 2019, 885). For a small fragment of another Sanskrit commentary on the MNS found in the University Library of Cambridge, see Sferra 2019. As for the commentaries preserved in the Bstan 'gyur, these have been grouped as yoga tantra and anuttarayoga commentaries (Wayman 1985, 6–7). The yoga tantra commentaries on the MNS are represented by the work of Smṛtijñānakīrti, who belonged to the Vilāsavajra lineage, and Candrabhadrakīrti, who belonged the Mañjuśrīmitra lineage

MNS is conscious of itself as being a part of the larger tantra (16,000 verses) that is the *Māyājāla Tantra* (or *Śrīmāyājāla Tantra*),[217] but Tribe (2016, 116) concludes that the relation between those two texts is not apparent and may be merely an example of tantric strategy to legitimize the MNS's authority by associating itself with a more esteemed scripture.

Especially important for the purpose of determining the origins of Vajrabhairava is chapter 7 of the MNS, called "Mirror-Like Awareness" (*ādarśajñāna*),[218] which begins with the quarter-verse (66d–67ab) "Vajrabhairava who creates fear" (*vajrabhairavābhīkaraḥ*)[219] and ends with "the best of those with a voice—that is, the Gentle-Voiced, Mañjughoṣa." This chapter of ten and a quarter verses focuses on the wrathful form of Mañjuśrī, who, after the initial quarter-verse cited above, is praised as:

> Six-faced, fearful ruler of the wrathful ones,
> six-eyed, six-armed powerful one,

(Wayman 1985, 6–7). The anuttarayoga commentaries are interpreted from the Kālacakra perspective and include, for example, commentaries by Raviśrījñāna or Narendrakīrti (Wayman 1985, 6–7; Tribe 1994, 113–14). Narendrakīrti's commentary may be a Tibetan pseudoepigraphon attributed to Kalkin Yaśas (*mi'i dbang po grags pa*), wrongly Sanskritized as *narendrakīrti*. See Newman 2021. Nāropā's commentary on the *Hevajra Tantra* contains a great numer of stanzas derived from the *Mañjuśrīnāmasaṅgīti*. For the Kālacakra's dependence on the MNS, see Newman 1987 and Newman 2021.

217. See, for example, v. 1.13 in Wayman 1985, 61.

218. The commentators of the MNS associate the Mirror-Like Awareness chapter with the family of Akṣobhya, who presides over the vajra family (*vajrakula*), in which one thinks, "I shall destroy." Mañjuśrī's name linked to Akṣobhya is Duḥkhaccheda, "one who destroys suffering" (Wayman 1985, 25). Thus Vajrabhairava subsumes the role of Akṣobhya of the wrathful deities of the *vajrakula*, whose role rose to prominence in the *yogottara* tantras, especially the GS.

219. There is a difficulty in establishing where the Mirror-Like Awareness chapter exactly begins. According to the commentaries of Narendrakīrti, Smṛti (Wayman 1985, 31), and Vilāsavajra (Tribe 2016, 35), it begins with the word "Vajrabhairava" insomuch as the chapter is dedicated to the sādhana of Vajrabhairava. Davidson (1995b, 23) follows the same structure. Nevertheless, according to the commentary by Candrabhadrakīrti (Wayman 1985, 31), the chapter begins with *kulatrayadharo mantrī*, 6.24 in Wayman's division of the text (Wayman 1985, 81), which amounts to the total of twelve (and not the usual ten) verses of the Mirror-Like Awareness chapter. This means that Vajrabhairava is associated with the functions of vajra noose (*vajrapāśa*) and vajra goad (*vajrāṅkuśa*), thus subsuming the role of Trailokyavijaya of the STTS, which indeed he does, since in MNS 7.5 he is referred to as Vajrahūṃkāra—that is, the aspect of Trailokyavijaya that has arisen to subdue and convert Maheśvara and Umā in the *Trailokyavijayamahāmaṇḍala* of the STTS.

skeleton with terrible fangs,
the hundred faces of Halāhala.[220]

According to the above narrative, repeated in a shorter version in Tāranātha's *Rgya gar chos 'byung*, this verse along with Mañjuśrī's "name" Vajrabhairava inspired Lalitavajra, the retriever of the VBhT, to look for a guru who could explain to him the tantric tradition of this wrathful deity. Lalitavajra's endeavors failed since neither the paṇḍitas nor his own guru had any knowledge of it. The passage seems to suggest that Lalitavajra[221] was part of the tantric community that promoted Mañjuśrī as a tantric deity: not only was he initiated into the tantric path of the *Māyājāla Tantra* cycle (the same text that the MNS claims to be a part of), but he also had Mañjuśrī as his tutelary deity (*kuladevatā*), as it was determined during the tantric ritual of initiation of "casting the flower" (*puṣpapātaḥ*).[222] Moreover, Lalitavajra is said to have meditated on Ārya Mañjuśrī for twenty years, and, no doubt, he praised the "names" of Mañjuśrī through the recitation of the MNS, since Vajrabhairava, being one of Mañjuśrī's names celebrated in this text, caught his attention. This single name became the impetus for the creation of a totally new tantric tradition dedicated solely to Mañjuśrī's wrathful form of Vajrabhairava.

The above narrative tracing the origins of Vajrabhairava to the names of Mañjuśrī in the MNS can be further compared to chapter 4 of the VBhT, dedicated to the exposition of a sādhana by means of which one transforms oneself into Vajrabhairava.[223] The process of generation is explained in terms of turning oneself into the deity by means of seed syllables. The stages of visualization, starting with Mañjuśrī, along with the specific seed syllables through which this transformation is enacted, closely resemble the generation of oneself as Mahāvairocana described in chapter 4 of the NMAA (Vilāsavajra's commentary on the MNS), entitled "On the Method of Awakening according to *Māyājāla*." Tribe (1994, 6) has suggested that chapter 4 of the NMAA might be the earliest exposition of the sādhana genre in yoga tantra texts extant in Sanskrit.[224] The similarity between the NMAA and the VBhT with regard to

220. Sanskrit text and translation by Wayman (1985, 83, slightly modified): *krodharāṭ ṣaṇmukho bhīmaḥ ṣaḍnetraḥ ṣaḍbhujo balī/ daṃṣṭrākarālakaṅkālo halāhalaśatānanaḥ//*.

221. Lalitavajra was the name given to him during tantric initiation, and was possibly based on the STTS, since the conferral of the vajra names during an introduction of the initiand into the maṇḍala during initiation is attested there (STTS 1:6–18).

222. See note 211 above.

223. See translation notes 729, 731, 733, and 738 below.

224. Tribe (1994, 6) points out that the two yoga tantras STTS and *Sarvadurgatipari-*

this specific sādhana may indicate that the two texts were drawing upon an earlier source—in all likelihood the *Māyājāla Tantra*, which, as the NMAA itself confirms, was a popular yoga tantra extant in Nālandā by the eighth century but of which no Sanskrit versions have been identified to date.[225] Thus, at the very least, both texts represent an early example of the sādhana genre current in the yoga tantras.[226]

Narrative 2

> Now we consider the master named Līlāvajra. He was an expert in tantras and had many disciples. One day a yogin came to him and performed various acts of sorcery—killing, expelling, causing dissent, and paralyzing. Līlāvajra's disciples were so impressed by him that the master thought, "We could use occult powers to protect the Buddhadharma. First, I will teach them which uses of sorcery are inappropriate; later, I will need a dharma that accomplishes the supreme [siddhi]." With this thought in mind, he left in search [of the teaching].
>
> He met a woman carrying water whose feet did not touch the ground. She asked, "Where are you going?"
>
> He replied, "I am traveling in search of the dharma of such-and-such kind."
>
> She said, "And have you found it?" Realizing she was a ḍākinī, he prostrated before her and circumambulated and made prayers

---

śodhana, which have been preserved in Sanskrit, do not contain accounts of sādhanas but only give the descriptions of the production of the maṇḍalas and of tantric initiation (*abhiṣeka*).

225. No passage containing features of the sādhana given in the VBhT and NMAA could be identified in the *Māyājāla Tantra* preserved in the Tibetan canon as *Sgyu 'phrul dra ba* (Toh. 466). Interestingly, in the Bka' 'gyur, the *Sgyu 'phrul dra ba* is followed by the two scriptures of the Black Cycle—i.e., *Kṛṣṇayamāri Tantra* and VBhT. Their position in the canon indicates that these texts are affiliated to the *Māyājāla* cycle. According to Szántó 2013, 359, a fragment of five folios from the now-lost Sanskrit *Māyājāla* has been found, but the location of the fragment is unknown.

226. When compared with the NMAA, the VBhT's account certainly looks much less elaborate and somewhat primitive; nevertheless, both descriptions of the generation process follow the same stages: (1) generation of the syllable *a* and a moon disc, (2) generation of Mañjuśrī from the syllable *dhīḥ*, (3) generation of Vairocana from the syllable *āḥ*, and (4) transformation of the syllable *hūṃ* into a vajra. For the explanation, see translation notes 729, 731, 733, and 738.

to her. She led him to the Cool Grove cremation ground [near Bodhgayā] and delivered him to another ḍākinī of the *mamo*[227] class. She led him to Oḍḍiyāna in the west and escorted him to the great Vajra Cave. There, he beheld the Terrifying Blessed One, Yamāntaka with a laughing face and palpitating eyes. Vajra ḍākinīs gave him instructions. They said that from among the collection of tantric books, he should take out as much as could be removed with a golden ladle four inches wide. He took them out accordingly, and the tantra of the three Black Cycles emerged: that is to say, (1) the Black Enemy, the wrathful Vajradhara, [the tantra] for taming Devaputramāra, (2) the Six-Faced One (Yamāntaka), the wrathful Vajrapāṇi, [the tantra] said to be for taming the Lord of Death (Yamarāja), and (3) Vajrabhairava, the wrathful Mañjuśrī, [the tantra] said to be for taming Īśvara (=Śiva).

It is said that even though all three are similar in character to mahāyoga, [Vajra]bhairava is compatible with kriyā; it teaches principally the practice of painting the image. The Six-Faced One is compatible with yoga; it seals the four mudrās.[228] The Black Enemy is intended to have the same basis as mahāyoga. There [in the cave], he copied two other tantras. As for the volume on Vajrabhairava, he took the original and carried it away with him.

The large bell of a stūpa rang spontaneously. Birds and dogs ran into the east. All the trees bowed their crowns down to the east, it is said. And the ḍākinīs returned in [his] dream visions and so on; they pursued him, but the master could not be seen. [In his dream] he saw the volume placed in front of the statue of Bhagavān Vajrabhairava. The ḍākinīs took the volume and went away. Upon waking, thinking that even if he could retrieve the volume, it would not be especially useful, he again went to stay in Oḍḍiyāna for some time. After memorizing the tantra, he left, and later he brought it forth from his mind and wrote it down. Thus it is explained.[229]

227. *Ma mo* are mostly wrathful female deities who create obstacles and inflict disease. In the Tibetan tradition, *ma mo* are believed to inhabit cremation grounds and often form the entourage of a central deity such as Ekajātī. See Hatley 2012.

228. Thupten Jinpa (2022, 760n87) says that the *Caturmudrāviniścaya*, attributed to Nāgārjuna, identifies the four sequentially as (1) *karmamudrā*, a consort, (2) *dharmamudrā*, wisdom perceiving the dharmadhātu, (3) *mahāmudrā*, the gnosis of bliss-emptiness, and (4) *samayamudrā*, embodiments of the enlightened mind.

229. Tāranātha, *Gshin rje chos 'byung*, 65–67.

Narrative 3

> The followers of Bari lo tsā ba explain [the story of Lalitavajra] in these words:
>
> The master Lalitavajra (*sgeg pa'i rdo rje*) achieved a little bit of power because he meditated on Black Yamāntaka. In the southern region, he performed ascetic observances (*vrata*). When he competed with a non-Buddhist (*tīrthika*), even though [the *tīrthika*] could not withstand him, the men and women in his [Lalitavajra's] retinue were turned into goats and sheep.
>
> Thinking that it was premature for him to practice [Black Yamāntaka], he prayed to Khasarpāṇi [a form of Avalokiteśvara]. In a dream, he received a prophecy, and in accordance with the prophecy, he traveled to the sacred Oḍḍiyāna, where he met a *yoginī*. He acted as her servant for three years, performing austerities. After that, she said, "What do you want?"
>
> He replied, "I do not want anything. I serve you out of devotion, madam."
>
> It was the same at the end of six and nine years. At the end of twelve years, she said to him, "What siddhi do you wish for?"
>
> He made a request: "I wish for a method to instantly annihilate *māra*s and *tīrthika*s without violating the Buddha's teachings." She conferred on him the tantric initiation of Bhagavān Vajrabhairava and gave him the [*Vajrabhairava*] *Tantra* in seven chapters. The name of that *yoginī* was Sukhacakṣuḥ. After that, he wrote down the seven chapters [of the *Vajrabhairava Tantra*] on a white silk cloth using goat's milk and took it with him. Even though the ḍākinīs wanted to suck the blood from his heart, they could not catch him, since the master had obtained the siddhi of swift-footedness and had already arrived back at his own place. He annihilated all those *tīrthika*s from the past. So it is said.[230]

The three narratives quoted above, describing Lalitavajra's rediscovery of the Vajrabhairava-Yamāntaka corpus in Oḍḍiyāna, seek to explain the reasons for the emergence of the cycle specializing in wrathful rituals at that particular point in time. The rationale given for its appearance indeed points to the historical context of interreligious struggle between the Buddhists and the

230. Tāranātha, *Gshin rje chos 'byung*, 67.

tīrthikas[231] (non-Buddhists). The enemy, depicted above as a religious "other," is regarded as a threat that needs to be eradicated or at least tamed for the sake of collective welfare.

The process of othering and stigmatizing the non-Buddhists demonizes the religious other through the concept of Māra (*bdud*), a common way of representing evil in Buddhism in general (Boyd 1971). In narrative 3, Lalitavajra asks for the method to "instantly annihilate *māras* and *tīrthikas*," as a result of which, he is given the VBhT in seven chapters. In narrative 2, we learn that the wrathful *abhicāra* rites are employed to "protect the Buddhadharma," which implies that malevolent external forces threaten the Buddhist teachings.

One of the critical issues that emerges from scholarly deliberations on the origins of tantric Buddhism in general is the extent to which the employment of a "violent dharma" against the religious other reflects Hindu-Buddhist dynamics in the actual social reality. There are scholars who think that accounts of the violent subjugation of *tīrthikas* and their gods should be read allegorically and had little to do with actual hostility between Śaivas and Buddhists.[232] Another opinion is advocated by those who adhere to the "agonistic view," stating that textual and iconographical representations of interreligious violence reflect a Śaiva-Buddhist hostility in real life.[233] One of the most vocal proponents of the agonistic view is Giovanni Verardi, whose recent publications (2011; revised 2018) claim that the main historical force behind the emergence of tantric Buddhism was the desire to subdue the non-Buddhists. Verardi theorizes a long-standing social crisis caused by Brahmanical hatred

231. The word *tīrthika*—whose semantic range is not well understood—and the problems associated with its translation as "heretic" have been investigated by Christopher V. Jones in a recent article (Jones 2021), where he points out that the English term *heretic* refers to someone within one's own tradition, whereas a *tīrthika* is someone outside of one's system. Scherrer-Schaub (1999, 71) and Eltschinger (2013, 12n38) translate *tīrthika* as "allodox."

232. In this regard, Iyanaga 1985, Linrothe 1990, and Seyfort Ruegg 2008 adhere to the allegorical explanation and consider the theme of violence not as "expression of (sectarian and secular) antagonism between two great religions of India but, rather, a structured opposition between two levels, namely the worldly/mundane (*laukika*) and the supramundane/trans-mundane (*lokottara*)" (Seyfort Ruegg 2008). Linrothe (1990, 20) perceives Maheśvara to be the symbolic representation of the "Indestructible Person" (*akṣarapuruṣa*), who stands in opposition to the Buddhist notion of the illusory self, and the act of violence inflicted upon Maheśvara by Trailokyavijaya as an allegory for the Buddhist doctrine of emptiness and the absence of self in all dharmas (*sarvadharmanairātmya*).

233. Davidson (1991, 215), one exponent of the agonistic view, says that the myth of Maheśvara's subjugation indicates real tensions between Buddhist and Śaiva factions, in particular the Kāpālikas.

and persecution of "heretical" (*pāṣaṇḍinaḥ*) Buddhists,[234] which intensified during the Gupta period and which was the main reason for the emergence of tantric Buddhist ritual. According to Verardi, *abhicāra* technologies propounded by Buddhist tantras during the Pāla period were directed against two enemies: Brāhmaṇas/Śaivas (*tīrthikas*) and Muslim invaders, who from the eleventh century onward began to raid the Indian subcontinent.[235] It is not impossible that the narratives of growing influence of the *tīrthikas* threatening Buddhist survival may reflect a period of "Buddhist hiatus" caused by the decline of the Pāla empire from approximately 850 to 977, which could have had a negative effect on the royal support for the monasteries (*mahāvihāras*) at Nālandā and Vikramaśīla (Sanderson 2009, 96–97; Acri 2016a, 19). There is also a possibility that these narratives merely emulate common literary tropes found in Buddhist literature at large. If we, therefore, suspend historical frames and examine these narratives only through their value as literature (Flores 2008), we notice that the theme of the fight against adversary forces assuming the garb of the *tīrthikas* and *māras* was inspired by a widespread narrative of the conquest of Māra (*māravijaya*) that proliferated in different versions in many Indian and Chinese sources (Anderl and Pons forthcoming).

The placement of the *tīrthikas* on equal footing with Māra is a common literary trope of Buddhist literature, among the earliest instances of which is the *Mahāparinirvāṇa Mahāsūtra*, where the arrival of the Mahāyāna is depicted as the Buddha's act of saving countless beings from Māra and his followers, the *tīrthikas*.[236] In the same sūtra, the Buddha tells Kāśyapa that "seven hundred years after my death, the devil Māra Pāpīyas will gradually destroy my true dharma" (Chappell 1980, 139; Nattier 2011, 38). The appearance of Māra[237] in

234. Verardi's interpretation of *pāṣaṇḍa*—referring to those outside of the Vedic fold, primarily Buddhists and Jainas—has been criticized by Sanderson (2015), who demonstrated that in fifth-century India, *pāṣaṇḍa* had a wider application that also included Śaiva sects and Pāñcarātra Vaiṣṇavas.

235. Sanderson, on the other hand, maintains that Śaiva-Buddhist interactions during the Pālas were characterized by symbiosis and that through their acts of generous endowments and royal support of Buddhist institutions, the Pālas made sure that Buddhism "was in no position to oust or diminish Śaivism" (Sanderson 2009, 116). Inscriptional evidence and manuscript colophons demonstrate a strong Pāla patronage of Śaivism, despite the fact that some among these rulers are identified as *paramasaugataḥ*, "a devotee of the Sugata (i.e., the Buddha)"; see also Sanderson 2010.

236. The *Prajñāpāramitā Sūtra* was preached by the Buddha on the Gṛdhrakūṭa in Magadha, where he "destroyed Māra and his people, the *tīrthikas*, and saved innumerable beings" (Lamotte 2001, 43ff.).

237. On the plurality of *māras*, see Boyd 1971. For an overview of the *māravijaya* as a

the garb of the non-Buddhist other is often conceptualized within the Buddhist prophecy of a gradual decline of the "true dharma" (*saddharma*) and the strengthening of the "counterfeit dharma"—that is, the false non-Buddhist paths (Schmidt-Leukel 2022). In the *Gaṇḍī Sūtra*, the decline of the dharma is conterminous with the appearance of discordant monks, who fall ill, while the non-Buddhists and *māra*s are empowered and come to the fore.[238] The same trope of the damaging effects of the Kaliyuga bringing to the forefront the false dharma of the *tīrthika*s (who, as the followers of Śiva, are labeled "the perpetrators of the conduct of Māra," *māracaryāsamāratāḥ*) is found in the *Guṇakāraṇḍavyūha Sūtra* (4.79ab),[239] an expanded version of the *Kāraṇḍavyūha Sūtra* composed by the Buddhist Newars in the fifteenth century (Douglas 1998; Sinclair 2015).

The literary trope of *māra*s and *tīrthika*s threatening the survival of the true dharma is posed as a point of reference indicating that fight against evil is believed by the tradition to be an important part of the Buddhist struggle in the quest for spiritual perfection. Lalitavajra's journey to Oḍḍiyāna to retrieve the tantras capable of destroying *māra*s and *tīrthika*s replicates the archetype of the Buddha's victory over Māra. And within the tantric context, as investigated above, it also mirrors Vajrabhairava's subjugation of the non-Buddhist deities, especially Śiva Maheśvara.

---

widespread Buddhist narrative, see Schmidt-Leukel 2022; cf. Nichols 2019.

238. *Gaṇḍīsūtra* (Toh. 298), see trans. in Bien 2020, 1.13–14; https://read.84000.co/translation/toh298.html.

239. See Sinclair 2015, 467.

5. Tantric Sādhana

THE BACKBONE of any tantric system is its sādhana. The Sanskrit word *sādhana* is often translated into English as "a practice," however, the etymology of this term, derived from the verbal root √*sādh*, means "to accomplish," "to bring about," or "to perform." In this regard, *sādhana* is better translated as a "means of mastering." Indeed, *Śoṇaśrī and *Vajrasiddha provide a linguistic gloss of the Vajrabhairava sādhana, saying that "it is a method by which one accomplishes (*sādh*) Vajrabhairava" (*rdo rje 'jigs byed du thabs gang gis sgrub par byed*). That is followed by a semantic gloss: "That which causes one to become [Vajrabhairava] himself is his sādhana" (*bdag nyid du 'gyur bar byed pa ni de'i sgrub thabs so*). This definition has two implications. First, a sādhana always consists of a set of methods or ritual and meditative techniques including the use of maṇḍala, mantra, and so on. Second, this set of methods is purported to bring about either the identification or union (that is, *yoga*) of the practitioner with the deity (especially in the yoga tantras), or some non-soteriological accomplishment or siddhi (especially in the kriyā tantras). Like any tantric system, the Vajrabhairava sādhana has its own tantric technology, which consists of a ritual diagram (*maṇḍala*), ritual device (*yantra*), sacred spells (*mantra*), visualization (*dhyāna*), image of the deity (*paṭa*), and fire offerings (*homa*). This chapter examines each of these items in the light of the text's canonical commentaries. What I hope to achieve through this presentation is an accurate account of an early cult of the Vajrabhairava sādhana in India in its myriad manifestations.

Maṇḍala

In tantric traditions, a *maṇḍala*, sometimes translated as a "circle," is a geometric design that delineates the space inhabited by a deity or a group of deities, who are invoked by means of mantras (Bühnemann 2003, 13). While usually a circle, maṇḍalas may also assume other shapes, like a square or a triangle. Bühnemann (2003, 14) outlines three important referents of the word *maṇḍala* in tantric traditions. According to her classification, *maṇḍala* may refer to (1) the pantheon of the deity in a specific system or school, (2) a place where the sādhaka can invoke and behold the deities, or (3) a ritual device that can be used for the attainment of supernatural powers (*siddhi*). Moreover, viewing the maṇḍala diagram is an important part of tantric initiation (*dīkṣā*, *abhiṣeka*).[240]

Among the most common types of maṇḍalas in tantric traditions are the powder (*rajo*) maṇḍalas, and this type is also used in the VBhT. The *rajo*

240. The VBhT's commentators disagree as to whether the maṇḍala drawing is suitable for initiation. *Kṛṣṇācārya says that the maṇḍala should only be drawn during sādhana and not during initiation (see note 487), but *Akṣobhya endorses its use as an instrument for initiation, whether for initiation of a disciple or for self-initiation. As noted above, in Buddhist tantra, initiation of a disciple employs the ritual casting of a flower (*puṣpapātaḥ*) onto the maṇḍala to determine one's Buddha family. From the *Mahāvairocanābhisaṃbodhi* onward, this is followed by the four *abhiṣeka*s (Sanderson 2009, 209), and it is these that distinguish Buddhist initiation from the Śaiva and Śākta ones. In those non-Buddhist initiations, the blindfolded disciple, under the influence of power (*śakti*) activated in him by the gaze or touch of a powerful guru, casts a flower into the maṇḍala to determine which Śaiva deity or family of the mother goddesses (*mātṛkula*) he will belong to (*tataḥ prakṣepayet puṣpaṃ sā śaktis tatkarasthitā/ yatra tat patate puṣpaṃ tatkulaṃ tasya lakṣayet*: *Mālinīvijayottaratantra* 11.20, quoted in Wallis 2008, 263).

The section on the initiation of a disciple in the *Cakrasaṃvara Tantra* (1.15–4.1) is seemingly based on the *Yoginīsaṃcāra* section of the *Jayadrathayāmala* (8.3–28), which includes the same *puṣpapātaḥ* ritual but omits any mention of the four *abhiṣeka*s. Sanderson (2009, 203) takes this to be an example of redacting Śaiva tantras to produce the Buddhist ones. Similarly, *Akṣobhya, in his discussion of initiation in the VBhT, passes over in silence the four *abhiṣeka*s and refers only to the *puṣpapātaḥ*. Thus, he says, the *puṣpapātaḥ* ritual determines what type of rituals an initiand is meant to accomplish. If a flower falls onto any of the nine core places of the innermost circle where the nine mortuary symbols are placed, a disciple will achieve the supreme siddhi. *Akṣobhya justifies his argument quoting from the *Sarvamaṇḍalasāmānyavidhiguhyatantra*: "If a flower falls on the core, he will never be without a purpose (*anartha*)." He says further: "If a flower falls on the sign of the outermost edge in the north, he will achieve pacifying rituals; in the south, annihilating activities; in the west, attracting and summoning; and in the east, augmentation. If a flower falls outside the [maṇḍala] line or in between the two symbols three times, a disciple should not be bestowed initiation." Following that are the instructions for the ritual of self-initiation: "The sādhaka should place the body of the lord [Vajrabhairava]—which is either cast [in metal], drawn, or sculpted—on the corpse [in the center of the maṇḍala]. He should then throw a flower and proceed with self-initiation. If he wishes to accomplish some kind of boon, as described in the *Vajrabhairava Tantra*, that is achieved while sitting on the radiant seat of the deity in the center of the maṇḍala." *Akṣobhya's *ṭīkā*, 370–71.

In any case, initiation is considered mandatory: without it, one should not perform any rituals given in the VBhT; indeed one should not even be allowed to see the text. As *Śoṇaśrī (p. 396) puts it: "Rituals mentioned in the tantra should not be performed without initiation, and also the tantra should not be seen. To understand what has been said, it

maṇḍalas are drawn during the ritual with the use of three, four, or five colors. These are classified in the tantras as the guidelines regarding the color of the powders (*rajaḥvidhi*).[241] The *rajo* maṇḍalas act as a support for the deity, which is invited to take a temporary residence there for the duration of the ritual. At the end of the ritual, the deity is invited to depart, the *rajo* maṇḍala is wiped out, and the space is deconsecrated.

The original pantheon of the Vajrabhairava maṇḍala, described in the root text, depicts him as a solitary hero (*ekavīra*) in the cremation ground surrounded by the thirty-two weapons he holds in his hands and attended by eight *vetāla* zombies in the eight corners of the maṇḍala. Vajrabhairava is ritually invoked and takes up his residence in the center of the maṇḍala atop a corpse.[242] The commentarial tradition on the VBhT demonstrates that two decades after the "birth" of Vajrabhairava, there was a transition from a solitary hero to a fully-fledged deity hosted in a maṇḍala with other deities, and that this gave rise to the two maṇḍala traditions—that is, the Thirteen-Deity and Seventeen-Deity traditions. Since these are closely related to the seed syllables of the mantra system, the discussion of these maṇḍala traditions is found in the section on mantras below.

Yantra

A *yantra*,[243] also called a *cakra*, is an instrument or a magical device, etymologically derived from the Sanskrit root √*yam*, meaning "to control." A *yantra* is a

is logical to teach the maṇḍala of powders first" (*dbang ma bskur bar rgyud du gsungs pa'i las mi bya ba dang/ rgyud kyang blta bar mi bya'o zhes rtogs par bya ba'i phyir dang po nyid du rdul tshon gyi dkyil 'khor bstan par rigs so*).

241. The *rajaḥvidhi*s for drawing the Vajrabhairava maṇḍala were not uniform but, as different commentaries indicate, varied. *Śoṇaśrī and *Vajrasiddha instruct that the maṇḍala should be drawn with powders of five colors—white, black, yellow, red, and green—to include the five tathāgata families commonly found in the scriptures of the yoga class of tantras. They also specify how to acquire these colored powders: white from cremation-ground ash, black from the charcoal of a cremated corpse, yellow from orpiment, red from cremation-ground brick, and green from the leaves of mangrove trees. *Akṣobhya, however, insists on drawing the maṇḍala with a single line, using only the ash of the cremation ground. He justifies his choice by saying, "Here [in the VBhT], because the chief topic is wrathful rites, [the Lord] teaches ash instead of divine colors. For the same reason, make only one line instead of five."

242. Both *Akṣobhya and *Kṛṣṇācārya make this connotation clear: the former glosses the corpse as the seat (*āsana*), the latter as the *pīṭha*—the throne of the deity.

243. Among the most compelling scholarship on yantras in tantric traditions we find Bühnemann 2003; Rastelli 2003 and Brunner 2003, who discuss yantras in Pāñcarātra

small, usually geometric, diagram[244] inscribed with seed syllables and mantras. Bühnemann (2003, 3) glosses *yantra* as a "magic diagram" and distinguishes three roles played by these magical devices in tantric traditions. According to her classification, yantras can (1) establish a foundation for a temple or a deity, (2) be used for worship, or (3) be employed in desire-oriented rituals performed on special occasions. In this taxonomy, the yantras employed in the VBhT fall into the third category. As Kiss (2014, 152) points outs, in the Śākta tantra the *Picumata-Brahmayāmala* (fifth *paṭala*), yantras seem to refer to magical rituals in general, and they are mainly used for accomplishing black magic, such as the death of an enemy. This function of yantras certainly captures the essence played by yantras in the VBhT. Not invariably, however, yantras facilitate the performance of aggressive magic. Bühnemann (2003, 28) shows that in Kaula texts, yantras can also have protective function.[245]

The VBhT employs only one sixteen-segmented yantra for all aggressive rites (§13). Unlike the maṇḍala, the yantra is mobile, and depending on the nature of the ritual (*karma*), it is employed in various ways by being buried in the cremation ground, under the threshold of the target's house, under the fire hearth, near a solitary *liṅga*, and so on for such purposes as seizing the enemy with fever, killing the enemy, causing dissension, and so on. The substances as well as the substratum on which the yantra is drawn vary, but these variations do not depend on the nature of the rite. For example, for the rite of killing (*māraṇa*), two different procedures are given, which employ different substances and bases. The most common substances for drawing the yantra are poison (*viṣa*), blood (*rudhira*), salt (*lavaṇa*), black mustard seed (*rājikā*), neem (*nimba*), juice of thorn apple (*dhatura*), and charcoal of the cremation ground (*cityaṅgāra*). Among the less common substances are saffron (*kuṅkuma*), bovine concretion (*gorocanā*), blood from a ring finger (*anāmikārakta*), yellow orpiment (*haritāla*), and turmeric (*haridrā*). Concerning the substratum, the root text says that the yantra should be drawn on a rag of the cremation ground (*śmaśānakarpaṭa*) or on a banner cloth (*dhvajakarpaṭa*), a strip of

---

and Śaivasiddhānta; Kiss 2014 for yantras in early Śaiva tantras; and Kuranishi 2013 for yantras in Yamāri tantras. For yantras as war machines, see Brockington 1998 and Raghavan 1952.

244. Kiss (2014, 54) shows that in the BY (*paṭala*s 5 and 45), yantras are mostly devoid of geometric designs.

245. *Kulārṇavatantra* 17.61 (quoted in Bühnemann 2003, 28): *yamabhūtādisavebhyo bhayebhyo 'pi kuleśvari/ trāyate satatam caiva tasmād yantram itīritam//*. "O mistress of the Kula, because it protects always from absolutely all dangers, such as Yama and evil spirits, therefore it is called *yantra*."

any cloth (*karpaṭa*), a slab of a stone (*śilāpaṭṭa*), a birch bark (*bhūrja*), or—somewhat less commonly—a skull (*kapāla*). Some of the commentators develop this topic further by giving a sophisticated list of yantra bases specific to the nature of the intended rite. According to *Śoṇaśrī and *Vajrasiddha:

> For killing (*māraṇa*), one should draw the yantra on the fire disc in the belly of Yama.
> For driving away (*uccāṭana*), [one draws the yantra] on a wind disc placed on camel's back.
> For paralysis (*stambhana*), one should place the yantra in the middle of Mount Meru adorned with eight peaks.[246]
> For subjecting to one's own will (*vaśīkaraṇa*), one should draw a *dharmodayā*,[247] the inverted triangle of a woman [i.e., the vagina].
> For summoning (*ākarṣaṇa*), one draws the yantra on the back of the eight-footed lion [the mythical *śarabhā*].
> For pacification (*śāntika*), [one draws the yantra] into the moon.
> For increase (*pauṣṭika*), [one draws the yantra] into a yellow moon.
> For separation (*vidveṣaṇa*), [one draws the yantra] onto the heart of a fighting water buffalo and a horse.
> For stupefaction, [one draws the yantra] onto the heart of a goat.[248]

*Kṛṣṇācārya discusses only a few yantra bases and says that in case of killing (*māraṇa*), one should draw a cremation ground; for driving away (*uccāṭana*), one should draw a *cakra* on the back of a camel and also a wind circle under the

246. For the explanation of Mount Meru with eight peaks in tantric Buddhist sādhana literature, see English 2002, 146–47.

247. For the vagina drawings that summon a person from a long distance in the NTGS, see note 447 below. A similar recipe is given in the *Saṃvarodaya* (19.13): "[The practiser,] drawing a *bhaga* with red chalk of golden color and putting the left hand on it, should recite [the mantra] eight hundred times. The man, whose name [the practiser] pronounces while reciting the mantra, will arrive at the very moment" (trans. Tsuda 1970, 302).

248. *Śoṇaśrī's *pañjikā*, 397–98: *bsad pa la gshin rje'i lto bar gnas pa'i me'i dkyil 'khor du 'khor lo bri'o/ dgar ba la ni rnga mo'i rgyab tu gnas pa'i rlung gi dkyil 'khor la'o/ rengs pa la ri rab zur brgyad pas nye bar mdzes pa'i dbus so/ dbang du bya ba la bud med kyi chos kyi 'byung gnas kyi nang du'o/ dgug pa la rkang pa brgyad pa'i seng ge'i rgyab tu'o/ zhi ba la zla ba'o/ rgyas pa la zla ba ser po'o/ dbye ba la ma he dang rta'i snying gar ro/ lkugs par bya ba la ra'i snying gar ro/.* *Kṛṣṇācārya's *pañjikā*, 450: *de yang gsad pa ni dur khrod nyid/ bskrad pa ni rnga mo'i gzugs rgyab tu 'khor lo can bris pa la rlung gi 'khor lo dang 'og gi bya ba dang ldan par skrod par 'gyur ro/.* *Kṛṣṇācārya's *pañjikā*, 451: *gzhung man ngag gis zhi ba la/ dbus kyi ya dbyi ba dang/ zla ba'i dkyil 'khor la bsgrub bya gzhag par bya'o/ rgyas pa la zla ba ser po la bzhag pa dang 'khor lo la rab gnas bya ba'o/.*

camel. Furthermore, *Kṛṣṇācārya recalls the authority of the oral traditions saying that in case of rites of pacification (*śāntikarma*), one should erase the central *ya* (in the yantra drawing) and place the target (*sādhya*) on the moon disc. In case of reinvigoration/increase (*puṣṭi*), however, one should place the target on the yellow moon, and one should perform the ritual installation (*pratiṣṭhā*) ceremony for the yantra/*cakra*.

As for the writing instruments by which the yantra is drawn, the root text mentions a quill from a big crow or, alternatively, a pen. Since the root text and all the commentaries, except for *Akṣobhya's, do not give any instructions regarding the drawing of the sixteen-segmented yantra, my reconstruction of the Vajrabhairava yantra that follows is based entirely on *Akṣobhya's *ṭīkā* commentary.

Drawing the yantra

The drawing of the Vajrabhairava yantra (fig. 1) begins with outlining the three perimeters placed one inside the other. The outer perimeter has sixteen compartments, and that is the reason why the root text calls the Vajrabhairava yantra "the sixteen-segmented" (*ṣoḍaśakoṣṭhaka*, *ṣoḍaśacakra*). The intermediate perimeter has twelve compartments; the central one has eight, with the ninth in the center, which is not counted. The drawing of the yantra begins with the central perimeter in accordance with the scriptural injunctions: "Beginning with the southern direction, outline the perimeter with eight boxes."[249] Each compartment is allotted a specific mantra syllable or syllables.

In the outer perimeter with sixteen compartments, the ten-syllable mantra of Yamāntaka, beginning with *oṃ hrīḥ*, should be deposited into eight compartments, leaving every second box empty.[250] Since the mantra has ten syllables and only eight compartments are to be used, the last three syllables (*tā*, *na*, *na*) of the five-syllable *vikṛtānana* ("hideous one") are deposited into one box. In the eight remaining compartments, one has to deposit all the *hūṃ* and *phaṭ* syllables again according to the aforementioned procedure.

249. *Akṣobhya's *ṭīkā*, 374: *'di skad bstan te/ lho nas brtsam pa'i re'u mig brgyad bar du dor ba la/.*

250. *Akṣobhya seems to refer to the more common version of the Yamāntaka mantra, *oṃ hrīḥ ṣṭrīḥ vikṛtānana hūṃ phaṭ*, while the extraction of the mantra procedure (*mantroddhāra*) given in chapter 3 gives a variant of this mantra as *hrīḥ ṣṭrīḥ vikṛtānana oṃ hūṃ phaṭ*. For the discussion of the different variants of this mantra, see below.

FIGURE 1. SIXTEEN-SEGMENTED YANTRA ACCORDING TO *AKṢOBHYA'S *ṬĪKĀ*[251]

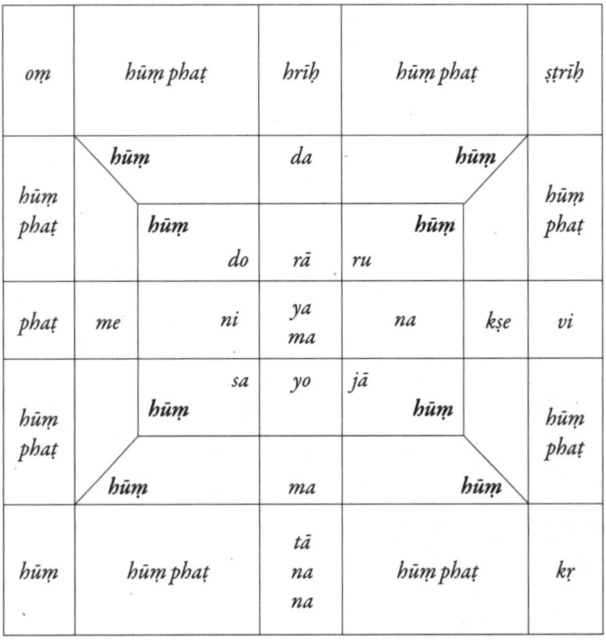
oṃ
hūṃ phaṭ
hrīḥ
hūṃ phaṭ
ṣṭrīḥ
hūṃ
da
hūṃ
hūṃ phaṭ
hūṃ
hūṃ
hūṃ phaṭ
do
rā
ru
phaṭ
me
ni
ya ma
na
kṣe
vi
sa
yo
jā
hūṃ phaṭ
hūṃ
hūṃ
hūṃ phaṭ
hūṃ
ma
hūṃ
hūṃ
hūṃ phaṭ
tā na na
hūṃ phaṭ
kṛ

In the intermediate perimeter with twelve compartments, one should deposit five syllables: *ya* in the center, *ma* in the south, *me* in the west, *da* in the north, and *kṣe* in the east. Each of these syllables symbolizes an afflictive emotion that is represented by a corresponding deity. The syllable *ya* in the middle stands for hatred (*dveṣa*) and Vajrabhairava.[252] *Ma* in the south stands for slander (*piśuna*) and Yama. *Me* in the west stands for attachment (*rāga*), represented by Rāga-Yamāntaka. *Da* in the north stands for envy (*īrṣyā*), represented by Īrṣyā-Yamāntaka; and *kṣe* in the east stands for ignorance (*moha*), represented by Moha-Yamāntaka. These five[253] have to be imagined as conjoined with the syllable *ma* in the central perimeter.

Besides the syllable *ma*, the twelve syllables *rā jā sa do ru na yo ni rā ya cca ni*

251. Note the absence of the syllables *rā ya cca ni*, which cannot be fitted in the central perimeter because there are only eight compartments (*koṣṭhas*) whereas we need to place twelve syllables.

252. For the explanation, see page 114 below.

253. These five letters are the seed syllables of the five main Yamāris installed in the *Kṛṣṇayamāri* maṇḍala (Kuranishi 2013, 273).

of the root mantra seem to be deposited in the central perimeter with eight compartments.[254] However, no instructions are given about how to do it.[255] They represent the four Yamāntaka gatekeepers stationed at the eastern, southern, western, and northern gates and holding a hammer, a stick, a lotus, a sword. Then we have the four goddesses and the four skulls (*kapālas*).[256] Then the syllable *hūṃ* has to be placed in the four corners of the central and intermediate perimeters (see fig. 1).[257]

Even though the seed syllables and the correspondence of the seed syllables with the deities in the Vajrabhairava yantra to some extent match[258] the classification of the Kṛṣṇayamāri yantra delineated in the *Ratnāvalīpañjikā* and *Sahajālokapañjikā* (Kuranishi 2013, 272–75), there are discrepancies, not only with regard to the placement of the syllables within the compartments but also with the arrangement of the syllables, which do not exactly match. It is impossible to determine whether the discrepancies occur due to corruption of the Tibetan translation of *Akṣobhya's *ṭīkā*, or whether these two yantras represent distinct, albeit similar, traditions. *Kṛṣṇācārya, the latest of all the commentators, seems to believe that the Vajrabhairava yantra is based on the Kṛṣṇayamāri tradition. As he explains:

254. *Akṣobhya's *ṭīkā*, 374–75.

255. I have reconstructed the locations of the twelve syllables in the yantra drawing based on the exegetical literature (see p. 114).

256. These are also the seed syllables of the yoginīs, the four *kapālas*, and the gatekeepers of the Kṛṣṇayamāri system (see Kuranishi 2013, 273).

257. *Akṣobhya's *ṭīkā*, 375: *de ltar dbus su re'u mig cha bzhi mtshams su gnas pa de dag la ci zhig bri bar bya zhe na/ de'i phyir yi ge hūṃ brgyad bri'o/ zhes bya ba gsungs te/ 'di ltar mtshams re rer/.*

258. In the *Ratnāvalīpañjikā* (ed. pp. 46–47, see Kuranishi 2013, 273n34), we find the same five seed syllables—*ya*, *me*, *kṣe*, *ma*, and *da*—along with the identical locations and corresponding emotions they embody as those attested in the exegetical literature of VBhT, but these five are not called the five main Yamāris in the VBhT. The twelve syllables of the Kṛṣṇayamāri yantra also match those in the VBhT, but the sequence is somewhat different: in the Kṛṣṇayamāri yantra the sequence begins with the three syllables *ya cca ni*, and these appear last in the Vajrabhairava yantra. Nevertheless, the correspondence between the twelve seed syllables and the respective deities again match those given in the Kṛṣṇayamāri tradition (see Kuranishi 2013, 273). Also, the root mantra of the Kṛṣṇayamāri system, *oṃ hrīḥ ṣṭrīḥ vikṛtānana hūṃ hūṃ phaṭ phaṭ svāhā* (Kuranishi 2013, 274), is actually called the *action mantra* in the VBhT's mantra system. The above mantra slightly differs from the ten-syllable action mantra extracted from chapter 3 of the VBhT (see below) and in *Akṣobhya's version of the same (see p. 100) in that it has fourteen and not ten syllables.

> "Sixteen-segmented [yantra]" [means]: just like in the *Kṛṣṇayamāri Tantra*, on the outer perimeter, one should place the action mantra (*karmamantra*); in the cardinal and intermediate directions and in between them, one should put the name of the target; in the twelve [intermediate] compartments, in the four cardinal compartments and the middle, one should place the syllables of the root mantra, which are seventeen; and in the middle, one should include the name of the target (*sādhya*) with four *me* syllables. And with the action mantra, in such places as the head, heart, and so on, one should also deposit eight *hūṃ*s and *phaṭ*s beginning with the head, placing them in the south and in the intermediate directions. According to the oral instruction, the yantra into which this is inscribed is blazing together with all the cakra points of the deities.[259]

Despite what *Kṛṣṇācārya claims, the Vajrabhairava yantra he describes (see fig. 2) bears little resemblance to the standard Kṛṣṇayamāri yantra discussed by Kuranishi (2013, 276). Thus, despite the shared ritual system unified by aspects of what appears to be the older religious substratum that goes back to the *yamarājaśloka* (see below), the Vajrabhairava and Kṛṣṇayamāri traditions maintain distinctive and separate identities. Furthermore, the yantra described by *Kṛṣṇācārya also differs in significant ways from the yantra drawing elaborated by *Akṣobhya (see fig. 1). These variations indicate that despite the employment of the same ritual "software"—the same mantras inscribed onto the yantra—their customization,[260] their particular arrangement inside the yantra perimeters, was far from formalized.

259. *Kṛṣṇācārya's *pañjikā*, 449.

260. In this regard, *Kṛṣṇācārya explains that *customization* (*vidarbhaṇa*) refers to a threefold process—namely, customization of (1) the seventeen-syllable mantra in the yantra drawing, (2) the order of mantra recitation, and (3) the name of the target (see below). "*Vidarbhya* [Tib. *spel te*, with "te" reproducing Sanskrit absolutive], 'customizing,' [means] one should take the previously taught seventeen-syllable mantra and customize it, this is how it should be written; [*vidarbhya*] also means [customizing the name of the target] by writing *māraya phaṭ* and *uccāṭaya* and *vidveṣaya*. Also [customization] applies to the recitation [of the mantra], which will be taught later" (*spel te sngags yi ge rnams dgod par bya zhes pa ni/ sngon du bstan pa'i bcu bdun po de yang mā ra ya phat dang ucca ta ya dang/ vi dve sha ya dang spel te bri ba dang/ phyis bzlas pa dang yang 'brel to*), *Kṛṣṇācārya's *pañjikā*, 450.

Customizing (*vidarbhaṇa*) the yantra

The concept of *vidarbhaṇa* refers to the particular rule of customizing the mantra that appears both in Śaiva and Buddhist traditions. For example, the Śaiva *Svacchandatantra* (9.62ab) gives the following definition of this term: *śikhyāhvena tu deveśi sādhyanāma vidarbhayet* ("One should customize the name of the target, O empress of the gods, with the mantra called *flame*"). Kṣemarāja's commentary glosses "one should customize" (*vidarbhayet*) as follows: *vidarbhayed iti abhidheyaṃ bhavet pūrvaṃ tato mantraṃ sakṛt bhavet*, "'One should customize [the name of the target]' [means, following the rule stated in another tantra,] 'first the name, then the mantra.'" Kṣemarāja's commentary on the *Netratantra* quotes the same definition of *customization* (*vidarbhaṇa*).[261] In the VBhT, the base of the yantra has to be customized with the name of the target (*sādhya*). However, here, unlike in the Śaiva *Svacchandatantra*, the name of the target has to be placed not after the mantra but in between the two fire syllables. In this regard, the definition of what constitutes the two fire syllables, mentioned in the root text, varies across the commentators. For *Śoṇaśrī, it means between the two syllables *ra*, while for *Akṣobhya, it means between the two syllables *phaṭ*.[262] Taking the example of the killing (*māraṇa*), *Akṣobhya specifies: "If someone asks how to customize the name of the target, it is said *phaṭ amukaṃ* [so-and-so] *māraya* [kill!] *phaṭ*."[263] This particular procedure of customization does not seem to be consistent across Buddhist tantras. *Akṣobhya refers to the fact that some other tantras teach that the name of the target (*amukaṃ*) should be placed in between the syllables *ṭa* and *pha*.[264]

261. The *Netratantra* (18.10–11) lists eleven modes of mantra, one of whose *mantravāda* system is *vidarbhaṇa*. This is further explained in Kṣemarāja's commentary on the *Netratantra*.

262. *Śoṇaśrī (p. 396) says that the name of the target (*sādhya*) should be put between the two fire letters—i.e., *ra* (*me gnyis kyi dbus su zhes bya ba ni me ni ra yig go*). *Akṣobhya ascribes to the same tradition as *Śoṇaśrī, in which the name of the target should be put in between the two fire letters, but says that the fire letter is the *phaṭ*, because it is similar to fire (see above).

263. *Akṣobhya's *ṭīkā*, 374: *me gnyis kyi dbus su bsgrub bya'i ming smos shing zhes bya ba la/ me ni yi ge phaṭ yin te/ me dang 'dra ba'i phyir ni sreg pa mthar ni gzhan zhes gzhan las bstan to/ ji ltar smos she na phaṭ a mu kam mā ra ya phaṭ ces so/.*

264. *Akṣobhya's *ṭīkā*, 374: *rgyud gzhan las ṭa dang pha'i bar du ming bcug ste zhes gsungs pa nyid 'dir me gnyis kyi dbus su bsgrub bya'i ming smos pa'o zhes gzhan kha cig 'dod do/.*

FIGURE 2. CUSTOMIZED YANTRA ACCORDING TO *KṚṢṆĀCĀRYA'S *PAÑJIKĀ*

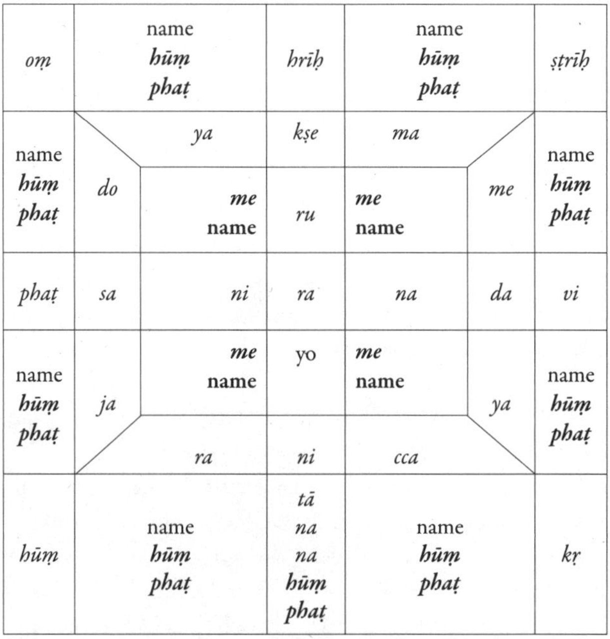
oṃ
name hūṃ phaṭ
hrīḥ
name hūṃ phaṭ
ṣṭrīḥ
name hūṃ phaṭ
ya
kṣe
ma
name hūṃ phaṭ
do
me name
ru
me name
me
phaṭ
sa
ni
ra
na
da
vi
name hūṃ phaṭ
me name
yo
me name
ja
ya
name hūṃ phaṭ
ra
ni
cca
hūṃ
name hūṃ phaṭ
tā na na hūṃ phaṭ
name hūṃ phaṭ
kṛ

In the second type of customization, one places the name of the target in between the two *hūṃ*s: *hūṃ amukaṃ* [so-and-so] *māraya* [kill!] *hūṃ*, such that the eight *hūṃ*s at the corners of the central and intermediate perimeters enclose the name of the target (see fig. 2). These two techniques of *vidarbhaṇa* are used for all aggressive rites.[265] The difference lies only in the imperative form of the verb denoting the nature of the rite. For example, if the mantrin wants to drive a person away, he substitutes the imperative *māraya* ("kill!") with the imperative *uccāṭaya* ("scatter!"), and so on. As for the rules for erasing the yantra, *Śoṇaśrī seems to be quoting, without attribution, the passage from Śrīdhara's *Sahajālokapañjikā* (Kuranishi 2013, 275) "To achieve pacification when it comes to erasing the yantra, first erase the final *ya*, then the two *ni*, and after that, the central *ya*. For the remaining syllables, [proceed] as you wish."[266]

265. In increase (*pauṣṭika*), or reinvigoration, the two *hūṃ*s are used instead of eight.

266. *Śoṇaśrī's *pañjikā*, 398: *zhi bar bya ba'i phyir 'khor lo dbyi ba la dang por mtha'i yi ge ya/ dbyi byin dang ni gnyi ga dang/ phyis nas dbus kyi yi ge ya/ yi ge lhag ma ci bde bar/*.

Mantra

The mantra system expounded in the VBhT (§38–41) consists of three different mantras: (1) the thirty-two-syllable root mantra (*mūlamantra*); (2) the ten-syllable action mantra (*karmamantra*), and (3) the heart mantra (*hṛdayamantra*). All these mantras are encrypted in the root text, and in order to decode them, one has to follow the Śaiva method of encrypting the mantras known as *mantroddhāra*.

The earliest instance of the *mantroddhāra* procedure adopted by the Buddhist tantras appears in the *Sarvakalpasamuccaya*, the supplementary proto-yoginī tantra of the *Sarvabuddhasamāyogaḍākinījālasaṃvara* (Sanderson 2009, 154). According to the Śaiva understanding of the rite of *mantroddhāra*, each mantra must ritually come forth from the sonic matrix of all the letters, the *mātṛkā* (Padoux 1992).

In the VBhT, the *mantroddhāra* takes place in a purified place, which *Akṣobhya glosses as "a solitary place" (see p. 243 below). First of all, the mantra master has to draw the forty-nine letters of the Sanskrit syllabary on a solid, mud floor, which is smooth and previously anointed with fragrance.[267] *Kṛṣṇācārya (see p. 243) also mentions the performance of worship (*pūjā*) prior to the commencement of a drawing. Then one can begin to draw the syllabary using a piece of chalk (*khaṭikā*).[268] The letters have to be drawn in the following order: gutturals and palatals, cerebrals and dentals, labials and semivowels, followed by sibilants and the aspirate *ha*. When the letters assigned to each section are clearly drawn, one adds the vowels. Then the mantra master extracts the specific mantra from the "body" of the *mātṛkā*, letter by letter, either by writing the mantra letters down or by reciting them.

The *mantroddhāra* has to be performed by a mantrin with a fully concentrated mind (*susamāhita*); otherwise, the mantra will be ineffective or will cause an evil outcome. *Akṣobhya comments on the concentrated mind imperative with the following words:

> "Just like people who hold a sword, if they do not hold it properly, their hand will be cut off, in the same way, if one does not recite the mantra properly, there will be no [desired] result, and indeed, the outcome will be misfortune." In order to eliminate the situation taught in this verse, when one performs the extraction of the man-

267. See note 643.

268. See note 645.

tra, at that time, it is very bad to have the mind on something else, just like it is forbidden to defecate and urinate while bathing.[269]

The logic of this passage is reminiscent of Nāgārjuna's *Mūlamadhyamaka-kārikā* 24.11,[270] where both a wrongly recited mantra and a snake being seized incorrectly are said to bring destruction to the person concerned.

The thirty-two-syllable root mantra (vv.1–13)

The first mantra extracted through the *mantroddhāra* procedure is the thirty-two-syllable root mantra of Vajrabhairava, known as the *all-purpose mantra* (*sarvakarmakaraḥ*). The mantra reads:

yamarājā sadomeya yamedoru ṇayodaya
yadayonī[271] *ra yakṣe-ya yakṣe-ya cca nirāmaya*

The above thirty-two syllables are followed by the three seed syllables, or *bīja* mantras:

oṃ or *hūṃ*[272] *phaṭ phaṭ*

The first thirty-two syllables, with different variants, are accepted as a more-or-less standard mantra of Yama-Yamāntaka, referred to as such in various Hindu and Buddhist tantras in the context of aggressive rites (*abhicāra*).[273] The mantra

269. For the Tibetan text, see note 715.

270. *Vināśayati durdṛṣṭā śūnyatā mandamedhasam/ sarpo yathā durgṛhīto vidyā vā duṣprasādhitā//.* "Emptiness misunderstood destroys the slow-witted, like a serpent wrongly held or a spell wrongly executed" (trans. Siderits and Katsura 2013, 274). I thank P. D. Szántó for alerting me to this passage.

271. The Tibetan text (Siklós 1996, 38) has here "connecting it with the third vowel," which would give *ni*. This indeed seems to be the correct reading insofar that it is attested in other examples of the same mantra. However, the original Sanskrit reading with *na* may in fact be correct because *yadayona* forms an inverted pair with the preceeding *nayo-daya*, except for the dental and not retroflex "ṇa." For the explanation of this principle, see below.

272. For the explanation of this discrepancy, see notes 681 and 682 below.

273. Bühnemann (1991, 314–20) refers to the different variants of this mantra appearing in various Buddhist and Hindu tantras. For example, she refers to the Mantrapāda section (47.11) of the *Īśānaśivagurudevapaddhati* (*Tantrapaddhati*), composed around the eleventh or twelfth century, as citing the Yamāntaka mantra, which Dwivedi believes to have

is referred to in the Rāghavabhaṭṭa's commentary on the twelfth-century *Śāradātilaka* (v. 18, p. 866, in Bühnemann 1991, 315) as *yamarājaśloka*, and it is also found (in various variants) in the Buddhist collection of hymns from Bali (thirteenth–sixteenth centuries), which the editors called *yamarājastavas* (Goudriaan and Hooykaas 1971; Hooykaas 1973, in Bühnemann 1991, 317). The first thirty-two syllables extracted from chapter 3 of the VBhT[274] almost exactly match the mantra of Yamāntaka referred to in the *Kṛṣṇayamāri Tantra* 1.6–13 (see Bühnemann 1991, 316), with the variants *ni* (for *na*) in *yadayoni*[275] and the second *kṣa* (for *kṣe*) in *yakṣa*. Thus the same mantra seems to have been appropriated into the Vajrabhairava-Yamāntaka traditions.

There are various interpretations regarding the alleged meaning of this mantra. Goudriaan and Hooykaas (1971, 544, mentioned in Bühnemann 1991, 318) think that the expression *yamarājasadomeya* refers to Yama's dog Sadomeya, which is an alternative of Sārameya (the name of Yama's dog in Indian mythology), since one version of the mantra appearing in no. 942 of the Balinese hymns reads *yamarājasārameya*. Hooykaas (1964, 67, mentioned in Bühnemann 1991, 318) also suggested that the *sadomeya* comes from *sadodyama*, "one who perpetually exerts himself," which seems unlikely. The most characteristic feature of the mantra is that some of the syllables are inverted, forming pairs; for example, *sadomeya* is the inverted *yamedoru* (the letters *sa* and *ra* look very similar in the *devanāgarī* script, thus the corruption may have easily occurred), *ṇayodaya* is the inverted *yadayona* (except for the dental "na"), and the last word in the mantra, *niramāya*, is the female inversion (*yamarāni=yamarāṇī*) of the first word in the mantra, *yamarājā* (also mentioned by Hooykaas 1964, 67, referred to in Bühnemann 1991, 318). This practice of inverted syllables is known as *pratilomayamaka* in Indian poetics, and following this scheme, Bühnemann (1991, 319–20) has reconstructed the verse of the mantra and suggested an intelligent translation of it.

According to Bühnemann (1991, 315), the thirty-two-syllable Yamāntaka mantra adopted by the cult of Vajrabhairava is an example of Hindu borrowing of mantras from Buddhist sources. But the appropriation of this mantra by different sectarian traditions, including Śaiva sects, is also attested. The evidence

---

been borrowed from the *Kṛṣṇayamāri Tantra*. This mantra is also found in the fifteenth-century *Tantrasārasaṃgraha* (17.9cd–10ab) and in Lakṣmaṇadeśika's *Śāradātilaka* (24.18), where it is employed in the yantra of Pretarāja—i.e., Yama—and in the texts citing the *Śāradātilaka*, such as the *Śrīvidyārṇava Tantra*.

274. Siklós (1996, 38–39) did not attempt to extract the mantra.

275. As mentioned above, *yadayoni* seems to be also attested in the Tibetan witness of the VBhT; see note 271 above.

for that is found in an Old Javanese text from West Java that contains a fragment of a narrative called the *Bhīmasvarga* (ca. fifteenth century), where the *yamarāja* mantra appears to be linked to the early Śaiva sect of the Pāśupatas.[276] In that narrative, Śiva, referred to as Bhaṭāra Guru, reproaches Bhīma (the wrathful version of himself, forming a coalition between the epic hero Bhīma and Bhairava), who defeated Yama and destroyed the abode of gods ("heavens," *kadevātan*). Bhaṭara Guru thinks that Bhīma wants to become his equal and decides to teach him a lesson. After a lengthy dialogue, Bhaṭāra Guru recites a verse (*śloka*) called the "enigma to appease Kāla" (*cacaṅkriman panulak bhaṭāra kāla*), because Bhīma Bhairava is Kāla. Bhaṭara Guru asks Bhīma about Bhaṭara Guru's names linked to the cardinal directions, their colors, and their mantras. In his reply, Bhīma answers, "You are in the east as Kuśika, in the south as Garga, in the west as Maitri, in the north as Kuruṣya, and in the center as Yamarāja."[277] Bhīma then recites the *yamārajastava* (Gunawan 2019, 234):

> *Oṃ yamarāja jaramaya, yamarāṇi niramaya,*
> *yamedoro rodomeya, yamedosa sadomeya,*
> *yadayoda dayodaya, yadayoṇi niyodaya,*
> *ya sirasih ya yasiha, yasi jaya jaya śiva.*
> *Oṃ ya namo namaḥ svāha*

When Bhīma answers all the names correctly, Bhaṭara Guru merges with Bhīma, and the text ends with a series of verses devoted to the five faces of Śiva and their respective mantras, known as the *pañcabrahmā* mantras. Therefore, in the mantra recited by Bhīma, there are the names of the manifestations belonging to the category of the five Kuśikas: Kuśika in the east, Garga in the south, Maitri in the west, and Kuruṣya in the north, but the customary Pātañjala in the center is substituted by Yamarāja. This suggests that the *yamarājaśloka* may be linked to a Pāśupata myth, because Kuśika, Garga, Maitri, and Kuruṣya are the four disciples of Lakulīśa, which in Old Javanese sources is substituted by Pātañjala (see Acri 2014). Yamarāja is the most important part of this cycle, as he is substituting Pātañjala, and the mantra is linked to the appeasement of Kāla, which is used to exorcise Bhīma from his demon-like nature to make him realize his divine nature. In the Sanskrit *stuti* from Bali no. 815 (Goudriaan and Hooykaas 1971, 491–93; see also Hooykaas 1964,

276. I thank Andrea Acri for alerting me to this source. An edition and Indonesian translation of the text has been published in Aditia Gunawan 2019.

277. The names of the five Kuśikas and corresponding faces of Śiva have been reconstructed by Aditia Gunawan (2019, 233).

60–67), we find a separate instance of the *pāśupata* mantra ending with the *yamārajastava: oṃ yama-rāja sado-meya, yame dorodayodaya, yada-yoni ra yakṣi-ya yakṣi, sañca niramaya.* In a version of the mantra, *sañca* is substituted by *pañca,*[278] and this could possibly refer to the number five, which could originally represent the *pañcabrahmā* mantras, and the five Kuśikas.

As to the usage of this root mantra in the VBhT, according to *Akṣobhya, it is to be used only for the yantra rituals.[279] When we look at the syllables with which the Vajrabhairava yantra needs to be customized (see p. 101 above), we immediately recognize the seventeen syllables of the root mantra given above (table 1). The letters in bold indicate the seventeen syllables of the root mantra that match the seventeen syllables to be inscribed into the Vajrabhairava yantra.

TABLE 1. VAJRABHAIRAVA YANTRA AND THE ROOT MANTRA

The seventeen syllables to be inscribed in the Vajrabhairava yantra	The root mantra of Vajrabhairava
rājā sado runa yoni *rāya cca ni*	*yama**rājā** **sado**meya* *yamedo**ru** **ṇa**yodaya* *yada**yoni***[280] ***ra** yakṣe-**ya*** *yakṣe-ya **cca nirāmaya***
ya in the middle	***ya**marājā*
ma in the south	*ya**ma**rāja*
me in the west	*ya**me**doru*
da in the north	*nayo**da**ya*
kṣe in the east	*ya**kṣe**-ya*

278. For the alternative reading of the *yamarājastava* with *pañca* instead of *sañca,* see Hooykaas 1964, 63, 66; Hooykaas 1973, 210; and Goudriaan and Hooykaas 1971, *stutis* 815 and 941. *Stuti* 941 reads: *yamarāja sadomeya, yame rodo dayodaya, yadayoni sirapiya, yakṣi pañca nirāmaya/ yame dosa yame-doro, yada yoda yada yoni, yura kṣiya yakṣi yakṣi, yamarāja yamarāṇi.*

279. For *Akṣobhya's explanation of this, see note 684.

280. For the discussion on *yadayona* vis-à-vis *yadayoni,* see note 271.

*Śoṇaśrī and *Vajrasiddha give almost identical lists of the seventeen syllables (with the exception of one letter—i.e., *ra* for *me*) while discussing the root mantra of Vajrabhairava and refer to them as the seventeen-syllable mantra and not as the thirty-two-syllable mantra given above, which Siklós (1996, 36) finds unclear. Siklós (1996, 52ff.) further reinforces this confusion when he says that *Vajrasiddha gives an explanation of the seventeen syllables making up the root mantra of Vajrabhairava, when obviously he is not. *Śoṇaśrī and *Vajrasiddha select only seventeen syllables from the root mantra and refer to them as the innate nature (*svabhāvaḥ*) of the seventeen deities in the wisdom maṇḍala of Yamāntaka. They explain those seventeen syllables as follows:

> [The yogin] should meditate on the seventeen syllables [*ya, kṣe, ma, ra, da, ya, cca, ni, ra, ja, sa, do, ru, na, yo, ni, ra*] as having the innate nature of the seventeen deities. With the rays of light issuing from his heart, he invites the real wisdom maṇḍala consisting of Yamāri and the seventeen deities, and he beseeches them to be seated in front of him. He gives them a guest offering (*arghya*) and so on, and with the employment (*prayoga*) of the hammer and so on, he introduces them into the *cakra* that has been previously drawn. Then, in the sequence that is taught in accordance with the [specific] ritual, he visualizes himself [as the deity], and having completed the mantra repetition, he accomplishes the ritual (*karma*).[281]

*Kṛṣṇācārya follows in the footsteps of *Śoṇaśrī and *Vajrasiddha, glossing the same seventeen syllables as those given in the Vajrabhairava yantra, but he interprets them as referring to the Thirteen-Deity maṇḍala of Yamāntaka. The incorporation of the same seventeen syllables in the Vajrabhairava yantra and the Thirteen-Deity maṇḍala of Kṛṣṇācārya is illustrated in table 2. The letters in bold indicate the syllables in the Vajrabhairava yantra that correspond to the letters representing the thirteen deities in the maṇḍala mentioned by *Kṛṣṇācārya.

281. *Śoṇaśrī's *pañjikā*, 398–99: *yi ge bcu bdun gyis de dag/ lha bcu bdun gyi rang bzhin du rnam par bsgoms la/ rang gi snying ga'i sa bon gyi 'od zer rnams kyis gshin rje dgra lha bcu bdun gyi bdag nyid kyi ye shes kyi dkyil 'khor spyan drangs la mdun du rnam par bzhugs su gsol la/ mchod yon la sogs pa phul nas sngar bris pa'i 'khor lo la tho ba la sogs pa'i rab tu sbyor bas bcug la/ de nas las dang rjes su mthun par gsungs pa'i rim pas bdag nyid rnam par bsgoms la/ sngags yongs su bzlas te las rab tu bsgrub par bya'o/.*

Table 2. Vajrabhairava yantra and Thirteen-Deity maṇḍala (*Kṛṣṇācārya)

The seventeen syllables to be inscribed onto the Vajrabhairava yantra	Thirteen-Deity maṇḍala according to *Kṛṣṇācārya
ya in the middle	1. *ya*: hatred
ma in the south	2. *kṣe*: ignorance
me in the west	3. *ma*: slander
da in the north	4. *me*: attachment-Yamāntaka
kṣe in the east	5. *da*: makes everybody envious
ra ja sa do ru na yo ni ra ***ya*** *cca ni*	6. *ya*: hammer
ra ja sa do ru na yo ni ra ya ***cca*** *ni*	7. *cca*: stick
ra ja sa do ru na yo ni ra ya cca ***ni***	8. *ni*: lotus
ra *ja sa do ru na yo ni ra ya cca ni*	9. *ra*: sword of death
ra ***ja*** *sa do ru na yo ni ra ya cca ni*	10. *ja*: Carcikā
ra ja ***sa*** *do ru na yo ni ra ya cca ni*	11. *sa*: *mātṛkā* Vārāhī
ra ja sa ***do*** *ru na yo ni ra ya cca ni*	12. *do*: Sarasvatī
ra ja sa do ***ru*** *na yo ni ra ya cca ni*	13. *ru*: Gaurī
ra ja sa do ru ***na yo ni ra*** *ya cca ni*	*na yo ni ra*: four Kapālas deposited in the corners that are not counted as part of the Thirteen-Deity maṇḍala[282]

282. *Kṛṣṇācārya's *pañjikā*, 452: *de yang ya yig zhe sdang nyid du 'gyur/ kshe yi yi ge gti mug brjod/ ma yig phra ma nyid du 'gyur/ me ni 'dod chags gshin rje 'joms/ da yig phrag dog las kun byed/ ya cca tho ba dbyug pa dang/ ni ra padma ral gri gshed/ dza yig lha mo tsā rci kā/ phag mo yum gyi sa nyid do/ do* [em. *de*, ed.] *las dbyangs can yum du grub/ ru ni gau ri'i rang bzhin no/ na yo ni ra thod pa bzhi/*.

*Kṛṣṇācārya gives the following explanation:

> "These seventeen syllables make up the seventeen deities; one achieves all rituals by means of those." By the teaching of this verse, the Thirteen-Deity initiation maṇḍala, prior service (*pūrvasevā*) and sādhana [is taught]. Moreover, by means of these thirteen deities, thirteen buddha wheels, thirteen deities of the colored-powder maṇḍala, and the thirteen-deity yantra, the yogin should summon and so on, kill, and purify.[283]

The above quote and *Kṛṣṇācārya's interpretation acknowledge the existence of the two traditions: the Thirteen-Deity and the Seventeen-Deity maṇḍala of Vajrabhairava. The only difference between the two is that in the Thirteen-Deity maṇḍala, the four Kapālabhairavas deposited at the corners outside the main maṇḍala are not counted as part of the maṇḍala retinue, thus giving thirteen rather than seventeen deities. Although the commentaries do not provide any information about the deities' location in the maṇḍala, this detail is included in Tsong kha pa's Thirteen-Deity sādhana, the *Jewel Casket*. The Thirteen-Deity maṇḍala features Vajrabhairava (with a consort, Vajravetālī) in the center surrounded by the eight Yamāntaka deities situated in the eight directions of the maṇḍala and the four goddesses in the southeast, southwest, northeast, and northwest directions. The *Jewel Casket* does not give the syllables of the deities but only their descriptions—that is, the afflictive emotions (*kleśa*s) and signs (*cihna*s) they symbolize—and these match the ones given by *Śoṇaśrī, *Vajrasiddha, and *Kṛṣṇācārya. This is summarized in table 3. In the Indian exegetical tradition, the first syllable *ya*, symbolizing hatred, stands for Vajrabhairava himself.

283. *Kṛṣṇācārya's *pañjikā*, 452: *yi ge bcu bdun lha bcu bdun/ las kun de yis byed par 'gyur/ zhes pas dbang bskur ba'i dkyil 'khor dang/ bsnyen sgrub la lha bcu gsum sgrub cing bskul ba'o/ de yang rnal 'byor pa lha bcu gsum dang/ sangs rgyas kyi 'khor lo bcu gsum dang/ rdul tshon gyi dkyil 'khor lha bcu gsum dang 'khrul 'khor lha bcu gsum gyis dgug pa sogs dang/ bsad sbyang bya ba'o/.*

Table 3. Thirteen- and Seventeen-Deity maṇḍalas

Sādhana of the Thirteen-Deity Vajrabhairava (Tsong kha pa)	Seventeen-Deity maṇḍala according to *Śoṇaśrī and *Vajrasiddha	Thirteen-Deity maṇḍala according to *Kṛṣṇācārya
1. center: Vajrabhairava and Vajravetālī	1. *ya*: hatred (Vajrabhairava)	1. *ya*: hatred (Vajrabhairava)
2. east: ignorance Yamāntaka	2. *kṣe*: ignorance	2. *kṣe*: ignorance
3. south: miserliness Yamāntaka	3. *ma*: slander	3. *ma*: slander
4. west: desire Yamāntaka	4. *me*: attachment	4. *me*: attachment (Yamāntaka)
5. north: jealousy Yamāntaka	5. *da*: makes everybody envious	5. *da*: makes everybody envious
6. eastern portal: hammer Yamānatka	6. *ya*: hammer	6. *ya*: hammer
7. southern portal: club Yamāntaka	7. *cca*: stick	7. *cca*: stick
8. western portal: lotus Yamāntaka	8. *ni*: lotus	8. *ni*: lotus
9. northern portal: sword Yamāntaka	9. *ra*: raised sword	9. *ra*: sword of death
10. southeast: Carcikā	10. *ja*: Carcikā	10. *ja*: Carcikā
11. southwest: Vārāhī	11. *sa*: Vārāhī	11. *sa*: Vārāhī
12. northwest: Sarasvatī	12. *do*: Sarasvatī	12. *do*: Sarasvatī
13. northeast: Gaurī	13. *ru*: Gaurī	13. *ru*: Gaurī

At the four corners outside the main maṇḍala are four skullcaps (*kapāla*) filled with nectar.[284]	14–17. *na yo ni ra*: Kapālabhairavas/ Kapālayamāntakas[285]	*na yo ni ra*: four Kapālas deposited in the corners that are not counted as among the main deities of the maṇḍala[286]

The four goddesses and the four Kapālabhairavas represent the Vajrabhairava maṇḍala's iconographical inclusivism in the sense that the goddesses represent the four major Indian religions: Carcikā (Durgā) represents the cult of the mother goddess; Vārāhī, as the wife of Vāraha—an incarnation of Viṣṇu—represents Vaiṣṇavism; Sarasvatī, as the wife of Brahmā, stands for Brahmanism; and Gaurī, known also as Parvatī, the wife of Śiva, represents Śaivism.[287] The tendency to include the pantheon of non-Buddhist deities into Buddhist maṇḍalas has been a standard practice in the esoteric Buddhist texts since the dissemination of the STTS. The inclusion of wives, in particular, usually features in the context of subjugation of non-Buddhist deities; thus, for example, in the eighth-century *Sarvabuddhasamāyogaḍākinījālasaṃvara*, Heruka subdues Brahmanical gods and takes their wives as consorts (Sanderson 2009, 150–56). The four Kapālabhairavas may represent the cult of Bhairavas of *vidyāpīṭha* Śaivism, but at this early stage of research on the early tantric traditions, that is impossible to establish conclusively.

284. See Tsong kha pa's *Rdo rje 'jigs byed lha bcu gsum ma'i sgrub pa'i thabs rin po che'i za ma tog ces sogs*, 34–39. Scanned manuscript originally from the National Library of Mongolia, digitally available at BDRC (W1NLM97).

285. *Śoṇaśrī's *pañjikā*, 398: *ya yig phra ma zhes byar 'gyur* (*zhe sdang nyid du 'gyur*, *Vajrasiddha)/ *kshe yig gti mug tu brjod do/ yi ge ma ni phra mar grags/ me ni 'dod chags dgra gsod pa'o/ phrag dog ngo bo da yig 'gyur/ yacca tho ba dbyug pa nyid/ ni yig lag ni pad ma ste/ ra yig ral gri bsgreng ba'o/ dza yig lha mo tsā rci kā/ phag mo yang ni sa yig nyid/ do yig dbyangs can ma ru grags/ ru yig rang bzhin gau ri nyid/ na yo ni ra'i rang bzhin yang/ thod pa'i* [om. *dus*, ed.] *ni 'jigs byed rnams* (*thod pa gshin rje 'joms pa'o*, *Vajrasiddha).

286. See page 113 above.

287. According to the Kṛṣṇayamāri tradition, the names of the four goddesses are preceded by the word *vajra*, but this is absent in the VBhT. For other examples of Vajrayāna transformation of the deities belonging to the Hindu pantheon through the addition of the prefix *vajra* to their names, see, for example, *Vajrajvālodayā*, 176v: *Huṃ Vajranārāyaṇi jhir; Oṃ Vajramāheśvari haṃ haṃ haṃ* [. . .], etc., quoted in Sanderson 2009, 156. The same is attested in the yoga tantra *Paramādya*, where the consorts of Viṣṇu and Rudra become Vajraśrī, Vajragaurī, etc., and form the retinue of Vajrasattva (Tomabechi 2007, 904; Sanderson 2009, 151).

The reason why the Thirteen-Deity maṇḍala of Vajrabhairava became more popular than the Seventeen-Deity one is because the former was consistent with the Guhyasamāja system (Tanaka 2018, 323). The deites located in the four cardinal directions, beginning with the ignorance-Yamāntaka, correspond to the four buddhas of Guhyasamāja: Vairocana, Ratnaketu, Amitābha, and Amoghasiddhi (Tanaka 2018, 322). The four goddesses in the four intermediate directions correspond to the four buddha mothers presiding over the four elements. Similarly, the Yamāntakas stationed at the gates, holding characteristic implements, correspond to the four wrathful gatekeepers of the Guhyasamāja maṇḍala. On the basis of this evidence, Tanaka (2018, 323) concluded that the Thirteen-Deity maṇḍala of Vajrabhairava could be seen as a direct evolution of the earlier Guhyasamāja system.

The above discussion has also shown that the thirty-two-syllable root mantra of Vajrabhairava mentioned in the root text became the basis for various interpretations in the exegetical literature where the seventeen or thirteen syllables, extracted from the root mantra, represent the seventeen or thirteen deities of Vajrabhairava's retinue. These variations have developed in conjunction with, and as an expression of, the development within the Vajrabhairava tradition, which went through several stages. In the first stage, the thirty-two-syllable root mantra reflects an appropriation of the ancient *yamarājaśloka* and constitutes the original substratum of the Vajrabhairava tradition, which features Vajrabhairava as a solitary hero (*ekavīra*) attended by the zombies (*vetālas*) in the maṇḍala drawing. In the second stage, Vajrabhairava appears in the company of the retinue of the deities in the wisdom maṇḍala. The thirty-two-syllable root mantra still exists but only as a relic of the past, for the ritual function of the root mantra is now carried forward by the seventeen or thirteen syllables, and the rest of the letters become a superfluous addition devoid of any ritual function. In the third stage, Vajrabhairava becomes styled on the prototypical model of the deities in the yoginī tantras and is given a consort, Vajravetālī. Thus the first two centuries after the birth of Vajrabhairava in the eighth century saw his transition from a solitary hero to a full-fledged deity accompanied by a maṇḍala with other deities and in sexual union with a consort. The fact that the explanation of Vajrabhairava's retinue is only mentioned in the commentaries written by *Śoṇaśrī, *Vajrasiddha, and *Kṛṣṇācārya (tenth–eleventh centuries) indicates that these exegetical traditions represent a later development, perhaps influenced by the Guhyasamāja, thereby establishing a relative dating for the earlier ninth-century commentaries by *Akṣobhya and Lalitavajra.

The ten-syllable action mantra (vv.14–19ab)

The next mantra extracted from chapter 3 of the VBhT is the ten-syllable action mantra, suitable for all the rituals: *hrīḥ stṛīḥ vikṛtānana oṃ hūṃ phaṭ*. Just like the root mantra, this mantra also has various forms in different Hindu and Buddhist tantras, the most commonly found being the variants in twelve and fourteen syllables. According to the *mantrapāda* section of the *Īśānaśivagurudevapaddhati* (47.12ab), the twelve syllables *oṃ hrīṃ vikṛtānanāya hūṃ phaṭ svāhā* is the mantra of Yama (Bühnemann 1991, 321). The same, or variants thereof, are attested in other late Hindu tantras (see Bühnemann 1991). Various versions of this mantra are also found in the exegetical tradition of the VBhT. The mantra extracted from the root text of the VBhT[288] has *stṛīḥ* as the *bīja* mantra, unlike canonical commentaries, which has *ṣṭrīḥ*. That variant of the mantra resembles the Kṛṣṇayamāri tradition, where the fourteen-syllable mantra of Yamāri is given as *oṃ hrīḥ ṣṭrīḥ vikṛtānana hūṃ hūṃ phaṭ phaṭ svāhā* (Bühnemann 1991, 321). Bühnemann (323) points out that in the Hindu versions of the mantra, the *bīja*s often end in the nasal (*hṛīṃ ṣṭrīṃ*), while in the Buddhist tantras those same seed syllables end in *visarga* (*hrīḥ ṣṭrīḥ*).[289]

*Kṛṣṇācārya is the only author who comments on this mantra, quoting from some unidentified text:

> From the same text: "*Oṃ* is Indra, *hrīḥ* is Yama, *ṣṭrīḥ* is the protectors of the directions. The yogin should employ these in the ritual. By visualizing himself as Yamāntaka, he should do the **pratyātmavedana* [that is, he should have a perception of himself as Yamāntaka]." What is spoken by this is that *oṃ* is for impelling the deities, *hrīḥ* is to teach the dharma by impelling the protectors of dharma (*dharmapālas*), *ṣṭrīḥ* and so on is to bestow wealth and to convert the wicked by means of visualization (*dhyāna*); this is the explanation.[290]

288. Bühnemann (1991, 322) encodes this mantra from chapter 3 of the VBhT slightly incorrectly as *hrīḥ ṣṭrīḥ vikṛtānana hūṃ hūṃ phaṭ* on the basis of Siklós 1996, 37, 92–93. Siklós wrongly identifies *vairocana* here as the syllable *hūṃ*; however, Lalitavajra and Kumāracandra confirm that it is *oṃ* (see notes 701 and 711 below). Therefore the last three *bīja* mantras in this mantra are *oṃ hūṃ phaṭ*, and not *hūṃ hūṃ phaṭ*, as recorded by Bühnemann.

289. For the exception to this rule, see Bühnemann 1994, 323.

290. *Kṛṣṇācārya's *pañjikā*, 452: *de nyid nas oṃ ni brgya byin/ hrīḥ gshin rje/ ṣṭrīḥ la sogs*

The heart mantra (vv.20–23ab)

The third mantra extracted from chapter 3 of the VBhT is the heart mantra (*hṛdayamantra*): *yamāntaka oṃ hūṃ phaṭ*. According to *Akṣobhya, this mantra is used merely for inviting the deity during the ritual. He also says that the heart mantra is generally taught for those who find visualization difficult:

> The heart mantra is prescribed for those yogins who, for the most part, find it difficult to visualize [the mantra]. This is called *heart* because the reciter is to definitely meditate upon it in his heart. Although it is possible for mantras generally to achieve their effect merely by recitation, when it comes to heart mantras, they surely achieve their effects through visualization. Therefore it is said, "What is known as *samādhi* is the heart; it is where the mind is endowed with equipoise."[291]

Dhyāna

Like other yoga tantras that focus on union (*yoga*) with the deity, the core practice of the VBhT is to realize one's own nature as the deity Vajrabhairava through the practice of visualization, or *dhyāna* (§42). The basic *dhyāna* delineated in the root text[292] deals with the generation (*utpatti*) of the deity Vajrabhairava in stages from the heart of Mañjuśrī through the transformation of the seed syllables. The commentators of the VBhT give different explanations of the *dhyāna* procedure presented in the root text, and they assign different meanings to its constituent parts. In this regard, *Akṣobhya's commentary stands for its unique description in which one is instructed to visualize the peaceful form of Ārya Mañjuśrī, seated on a moon disc, who in the subsequent stages of visualization[293] becomes more and more wrathful, eventu-

---

phyogs skyong yin/ rnal 'byor pa yis las bcol lo/ ya man ta kas rang rig byed/ ces pas lha la bskul zhing/ chos skyong bskul ba'i bya bas chos bshad/ nor byin bsdigs pa dngos dang bsam gtan gyis gdug pa can la bya ba man ngag go/.

291. For the Tibetan text, see note 714 below.

292. The *dhyāna* explanation given in the VBhT may be one of the earliest examples of the sādhana genre current in the yoga tantras and, in its basic features, the procedure in the VBhT closely resembles the *dhyāna* description contained in the NMAA (see pp. 259–62 below).

293. *Akṣobhya's *ṭīkā*, 380–81, "However, having seen that those very hostile beings have not been tamed, again one empowers oneself together with the sun [disc] as a blazing vajra. Then emanations [of oneself and the sun disc as a blazing vajra] become situ-

ally assuming the form of Vajrabhairava himself. This progressive transition from a peaceful to a wrathful form of Mañjuśrī is explained by *Akṣobhya as the method of taming the three classes of beings: hostile, very hostile, and extremely hostile. The extremely hostile ones are classified as the deities of the Hindu pantheon (namely, Brahmā, Indra, Śiva, and Kumāra) and their retinue. *Akṣobhya is clear that the reason for generating oneself as Vajrabhairava is to uproot the ultimate evil.[294] The mantra master thus embodies "wrath," and he meditatively reproduces the general pattern of taming (Skt. *vinaya*, Tib. *'dul ba*) of the Hindu deities, returning, as it were, to the mythic origins of the tradition.[295]

The later commentaries on the *dhyāna* procedure by *Śoṇaśrī/*Vajrasiddha and *Kṛṣṇācārya are similar in the general outlook of the sādhana—namely, with regard to the stages of visualization and the specific practices they are correlated with—but they sometimes differ in their respective explanations. Unlike *Akṣobhya, they also follow the more common pattern of the meditation practice that is correlated with the stages of the Mahāyāna type of supreme worship (*anuttarapūjā*).[296] Below is a translation of the sādhana as it appears in the commentaries by *Śoṇaśrī and *Vajrasiddha, which I correlate with *Kṛṣṇācārya's and Lalitavajra's exegesis in the annotation.

> **Next** (*athātaḥ*) [means] immediately after the [chapter on the] extraction of the mantra; **I will duly explain** [means] the correct

ated upon the heads of those to be tamed. And even though that has intimidated them, the extremely hostile ones are [still] not tamed. Then again, having taken on the body of Mahābhairava, one annihilates them." *'on kyang rab tu sdang ba dag mi 'dul bar gzigs nas/ yang bdag nyid dang nyi mar bcas pa/ rdo rje 'bar bar byin gyis brlabs shing de'i sprul pa rnams 'dul ba de dag gi spyi bo'i steng du/ gnas te bsdigs pa na yang shin tu rab tu sdang ba rnams 'dul ba ma yin no/ de nas ni yang 'jigs byed chen po'i sku 'dzin par gyur pas/ de dag tshar bcad de/.* *Akṣobhya's *ṭīkā*, 380–81.

294. "The yogin [who visualizes himself as Vajrabhairava] also tames the retinue deities (*saṃgrahadevatā*), because they are merely servants. As for those extremely hostile ones, these are Brahmā, Indra, Īśvara (=Śiva), Kumāra. They are said to be devoured, as will be explained below." *de dag rnal 'byor pa des rkang* [em. *kyang*, ed.] *rjes su spyod pa tsam yin pas na/ bsdu ba'i lha rnams kyang 'dul ba yin la/ shin tu rab tu sdang ba de rnams ni/ tshangs pa dang/ brgya byin dang/ dbang phyug dang/ gzhon nu rnams gsol bar mdzad pa zhes 'chad par 'gyur ba'o/.* *Akṣobhya's *ṭīkā*, 381.

295. See the mythic stories of Vajrabhairava's birth preserved in the Tibetan Buddhist tradition, especially among the Sa skya pa (see p. 71 above).

296. For the explanation of the sevenfold *anuttarapūjā* in the Mahāyāna sources with the corresponding phases of the tantric Buddhist sādhana dedicated to Vajravārāhi based on the *Sādhanamālā* and *Guhyasamayasādhanamālā*, see English 2002, 124.

meaning here will be explained through the oral instruction of the guru; **the sādhana of Vajrabhairava** [means] the method by which one achieves Vajrabhairava. Concerning this, the instruction is as follows. **First of all (*purvakaṃ*)**, the mantra master, relying on some special person, should sit on a comfortable seat. He should place in his mouth a pellet (*guṭikā*) made of five nectars. The yogin should be naked, with hair disheveled, and facing south.[297] Then he visualizes that from his heart, rays of light of the seed syllables abiding in the sun pervade the ten directions. He invites the buddhas, bodhisattvas, and the deities, starting with furies (*krodha*).[298] He asks them to hover in the air in front of him, and he propitiates them with [the help of] the four goddesses—Vajracarcikā and so

297. The beginning of *Kṛṣṇācārya's description (p. 453) is similar to that of *Śoṇaśrī and *Vajrasiddha, but it diverges from them in introducing protection of the vajra net and of the practitioner himself: "**First of all** [means] first, at that time, in those places [i.e., suitable places previously described (see chapter 1)], he should take a comfortable seat, and he should purify his mouth with the five nectars (*amṛtas*). Naked, his hair disheveled, facing south, with the letter *ma* in the heart and the seed syllable, he performs the protection of the lattice tent (**jālapañjara*), both the sides and the top. He protects the place and the deity with compassion, and with the meditation on emptiness, he protects himself, the yogin." (*dang po kho nar zhes pa ni de'i tshe dang po ste gnas der stan bde ba la 'dug ste/ bdud rtsi lnga yis kha dag par byas la/ gcer bu skra grol ba lhor mngon par phyogs par bya ste/ snying ga'i ma dang sa bon gyis dr[w]a gur gyi bsrung bas/ gnas dang snying rje chen pos* [em. *po*, ed.] *dang lha dang stong pa nyid kyi ting nge 'dzin bsrung bas rnal 'byor pa yang bsrung bar 'gyur ro*). Meditation on emptiness as the supreme protection is an idiomatic expression, and when it is mentioned in tantric sādhanas, it is given as an alternative to *prajñārakṣitā*. In Lūyipāda's commentary on the Heruka sādhana (*Cakrasaṃvarābhisamaya*, quoted in the *Guhyasamayasādhanamālā*, ed., p. 132; see also English 2002, 448, and Sakurai 1998), we find the following passage: "One should not object, asking why there is meditation on emptiness after setting up the protection tent (*pañjara*). He explains: because this is *adhimātraprajñā*, the supreme *prajñā*, for such a person, emptiness is the supreme protection" (*rakṣāpañjarāder anantaraṃ śūnyatābhāvanoktā tad adhimātraprajñādhikārāt. tasya śūnyataiva parā rakṣeti*). I thank P. D. Szántó for this reference. Other instances of the same idea are found in the *Yogimanohārapañcakramaṭippaṇī*, 23:13): *tad anu paramārthe śūnyataiva paramā rakṣeti* (quoted by English 2002, 448), and in Ratnākaraśānti's *Muktāvalī* on *Hevajra Tantra* 1.3.3. The *Abhisamayamañjarī* quotes Lūyipāda's *Cakrasaṃvarābhisamaya*'s passage (above), saying that to consider emptiness as the supreme protection is not only meant for advanced practitioners with "exceptional insight" but also for ordinary practitioners. The vajra tent is required to effect protection, and it is taught immediately after meditation on emptiness. The passage from the *Abhisamayamañjarī* is translated in English 2002, 136.

298. These are typically the ten *krodha* deities found widely in the Jñānapāda school of the GS, forming a protection wheel (*rakṣācakraṃ*) around the sādhaka (Tanaka 2018, 292).

on—who arise from the light of the seed at [his] heart. They [the four goddesses=*pūjādevīs*] present offerings in front of the buddhas, holding sacrificial implements for worship, such as a lotus, in their hand. He confesses his sins and so on and dismisses them.[299]

What is expressed by the phrase **selfless nature of all dharmas** (***sarvadharmanairātmya***) is the meditation on the four sublime states (*brahmavihāras*). In this regard, love (*maitrī*) has the characteristic of love for all sentient beings as though they were your own son; compassion (*karuṇā*) is the desire to completely liberate [sentient beings] from suffering and the cause of suffering;[300] joy (*muditā*) [means] stabilizing contentment by means of firm bliss; and equanimity (*upekṣā*) is to be even-minded, disregarding all thought constructs related to perception (*grāhyaṃ*) and perceiver (*grāhakaḥ*).[301]

Then, he [should contemplate the emptiness by] perceiving the dependent origination of all and by being devoid of

299. *Kṛṣṇācārya (pp. 453–44) has a corresponding passage that reads: "With that light endowed with five rays in the seed syllable of his heart, pervading all the world systems in the ten directions, he impels all the five lineages of the buddhas. Having purified the five classes of beings, he visualizes in the space in front of him all the buddhas, bodhisattvas, wrathful ones, and [his] gurus. From the seed syllable in his heart, he emits the *pūjādevīs* and, with Vajracarcikā and so on, he correctly offers the outer (*bāhya*), inner (*antara*) and real (*tattva*) forms of worship" (*snying ga'i sa bon gyi 'od zer lnga dang ldan pa'i 'od de nyid kyis phyogs bcu'i 'jig rten gyi khams thams cad du khyab pas sangs rgyas thams cad rigs lnga bskul/ 'gro ba'i rgyud lnga sbyangs nas/ sangs rgyas dang byang chub sems dpa' dang khro bo dang bla ma thams cad mdun gyi nam mkha' la dmigs la/ rang gi snying ga'i sa bon las mchod pa'i lha mo spros la rdo rje tsā rci kā la sogs kyis phyi dang nang dang de kho na nyid kyi mchod pas yang dag par mchod pa dang*).

300. Here I adopt *Vajrasiddha's reading (p. 419): *snying rje ni sdug bsngal dang sdug bsngal gyi rgyu las yang dag par sgrol bar 'dod pa'o,* which is more elegant. *Śoṇaśrī's reading (p. 400) is *sdug bsngal dang sdug bsngal gyi rgyu las yang dag par 'don pa'i snying rje,* "Compassion is what completely extracts sentient beings from suffering and the cause of suffering."

301. *Kṛṣṇācārya has a corresponding passage: "He confesses his sins and so on, and he meditates on the four *brahmavihāras*; one knows them [as follows]: (1) *maitrī-lakṣaṇa,* 'love,' is defined as that which is never forsaken and graciously extends to all the beings; (2) *karuṇā-lakṣaṇa,* 'compassion,' is defined as that which desires to protect all sentient beings from suffering; (3) *muditā-lakṣaṇa,* 'joy,' is defined as a desire to rescue the beings from saṃsāra [this normally features in the *karuṇā-lakṣaṇa*] and place them in contentment and a desire to not to be dissociated from them; (4) *upekṣā* is defined as that which understands 'equanimity,' freedom from the divisiveness of a biased mind, and freedom from the eight worldly dharmas" (for the Tibetan text, see note 726 below).

the four alternatives (*catuṣkoṭi*), and he should both recite and realize the meaning of the mantra: "*Oṃ* I have as my nature the nondual (lit. 'adamantine') gnosis of emptiness" (*oṃ śūnyatājñānavajrasvabhāvātmako 'ham*); he should strip the appearance ([*an*]*ābhāsa*) of both himself and the three realms.[302] And then, from the power of aspiration, the letter *āḥ*, red in color, appears and then turns into a sun disc. Atop the sun disc appears the letter *hūṃ*, emitting five-colored light that changes into a crossed vajra (*viśvavajra*) and that turns into a vajra fence (*vajraprākāra*), a vajra tent (*vajrapañjara*), and the vajra ground (*vajrabhūmi*).[303]

302. *Kṛṣṇācārya repeats the same instruction on the meditation on the four alternatives (*catuṣkoṭi*), suggesting a Madhyamaka orientation, as follows: "Then, realizing that nothing is established as existing innately (*svabhāvaḥ*) [and that they are instead] empty of one and many, free of four points or *koṭi*s [i.e., existence, nonexistence, both existence and nonexistence, and neither existence nor nonexistence], and arise in the dependent origination (*pratītyasamutpāda*), [in order to seal this realization], he recites the mantra *oṃ śūnyatājñānavajrasvabhāvātmako 'ham*. The purpose of that mantra is to place his mind in a "no focus on anything" state, pervading the entirety of space, having the knowledge of the immutable gnosis of emptiness." For the Tibetan text, see note 726.

303. Insofar as the building of the base for the generation of the deity is concerned, *Kṛṣṇācārya's commentary (p. 454) differs from that of *Vajrasiddha and *Śoṇaśrī in substantial ways: "From the letter *yaṃ* in the space disc [means:] from the collection of the previous suchness (*dharmatā*) and by the force of aspiration (*praṇidhāna*) [the yogin starts generating the base for the deity, as follows]: from the sequence of *yaṃ*, *raṃ*, *vaṃ*, *laṃ*, *suṃ*, there arise the four elements of blue, red, white, and yellow colors, which constitute the four continents of the maṇḍala. On the top of [that maṇḍala] with four continents arises Mount Meru, the king of mountains, in a form of a 'peak' (*śṛṅga*), transformed from the syllable *suṃ* in the *rāga* maṇḍala; atop the sun maṇḍala [transformed] from the [letter] *ma*, he should visualize the vajra ground, a fence, and a tent transformed from the crossed *vajra* (*viśvavajra*), which [arises] from the syllable *hūṃ*. Inside this, a palace comes from the transformation of Mañjuśrī-*jñānasattva*; he should generate, as before, the maṇḍala with corners, four gates, and cremation grounds" (*nam mkha'i dkyil du yaṃ yig las/ zhes pa ni chos nyid las sngon du tshogs dang smon lam song ba'i mthus/ yaṃ raṃ vaṃ laṃ suṃ gyi rim pa las sngo ba dang dmar po dang dkar po dang ser po'i kha dog can gyi 'byung ba bzhi'i dkyil 'khor gling bzhir chags pa'i dkyil du sum ri rab ri'i rgyal por gyur pa lcog bzhi dang bcas pa'i steng du/ ma las nyi ma'i dkyil 'khor dang de'i steng du hūṃ las sna tshogs rdo rjer gyur nas rdo rje'i sa gzhi dang/ ra ba dang gur dang/ bla re dag bsgom mo/ de'i nang du gzhal yas khang 'jam dpal ye shes sems dpar gyur pa las/ gru bzhi sgo bzhi dur khrod dang bcas pa sngon bzhin bskyed la*).

Lalitavajra (p. 322) has a corresponding passage: "Then, in the space that appears, he meditates on emptiness; this is the meaning of 'he should visualize that which arises from the [syllable] *yaṃ*.' On top of that, he should visualize that which manifests by itself as the center of a crossed vajra, which itself comes from the [transformation of the syllable] *hūṃ*. Reciting the mantra with four *hūṃ*s, he visualizes the [vajra] fence and tent with the

After he has visualized all of this, he should visualize the **wind disc [transformed] from the letter *yaṃ***, [which means] through the connection with a nasal sound (*anusvāra*). **From the syllable *dhīḥ***, [which means] from the yellow *dhīḥ*, [he should visualize] **Mañjuvajra**,[304] [which means] the protector with one face and two arms, holding a sword and a book [in his hands]. [Mañjuvajra should be visualized] sitting in the crossed-legged vajra posture (*vajraparyaṅka*) and as being of the nature of the causal vajra-holder (*hetuvajradhara*). Then he [Mañjuvajra] should be generated as adorned with the eight cremation grounds [around him], which symbolize that he has the nature of the resultant vajra-holder (*phalavajradhara*) as taught in various tantras. That means that he is free of egoism (*nirahaṃkāra*), nondual with regard to existence (*bhāva*) and cessation (*nirvāṇa*).[305] At this point, he [the yogin]

---

light of that [mantra]. Inside that, in the center of space, he visualizes the maṇḍala, which arises from the four [seed syllables] beginning with *yaṃ*. On the top of that there is Mount Meru. On top of [Meru] transformed from [the syllable] *bhrūṃ* is a body vajra [. . .]. This is the meaning of 'He should visualize a palace endowed with the eight cremation grounds that comes from the transformation of that [body vajra].' With regard to 'First, he should generate the [first] vowel [*a*] on top of that,' [it means:] on top, in the center of palace. 'First' [means:] the moon that comes from the [vowel] *a*. As for 'on the top of that,' [it means:] *dhīḥ* on the top of the moon. As for the sword that is generated from that [*dhīḥ*], it manifests by itself. Therefore this is the meaning of generating the body of Mañjuśrī. By 'he should place in the heart,' [it means:] the sun in the heart of Mañjuśrī" (*de nas bar snang gi nam mkha' ste stong pa nyid bsgoms pa de nyid la/ yam las byung ba bsam par bya zhes pa'i don to/ de'i steng du hūṃ las byung ba'i sna tshogs rdo rje'i lte ba la de nyid kyis mtshan pa bsams la hūṃ bzhi pa'i sngags brjod pas/ de'i 'od kyis ra ba dang bla re bsgoms la/ de'i nang du nam mkha'i dbus su yam la sogs pa bzhi las 'byung ba'i dkyil 'khor ro/ de'i steng du ri rab tu grub ba'o/ de'i steng du bhrum las byung ba'i de las sku'i rdo rje* [lacuna] *lte ba la de nyid kyis/ de gyur pa las gzhal yas khang dur khrod brgyad dang bcas pa bsams la/ zhes bya ba'i don to/ de steng dbyangs yig dang pos bskyed zhes bya ba la/ de steng gzhal yas khang gi dbus su'o/ dang po ni a las byung ba'i zla ba'o/ de'i steng ni zla ba'i steng du dhīḥ'o/ de las bskyed pa'i ral gri la de nyid kyis mtshan pa'o/ de nas 'jam dpal gyi skur bskyed pa'i don to/ de'i snying khar bya ba ni 'jam dpal gyi snying khar nyi ma'o*).

304. The Sanskrit has Mañjuśrī, but in *Śoṇaśrī's lemma, there seems to be Mañjuvajra (*jam pa'i rdo rje zhes bya ba ni*), while *Vajrasiddha retains the Sanskrit Mañjuśrī (*'jam dpal zhes bya ba ni*). The iconographical description of Mañjuśrī/Mañjuvajra that follows is identical in both commentaries. Lalitavajra (p. 24) understands Mañjuśrī as a knowledge being (*jñānasattva*) and describes him as having one face, two arms, and a yellow complexion (*'jam dpal ye shes sems dpa' zhal gcig phyag gnyis sku mdog ser por ru'o*).

305. Sitting in a crossed-legged vajra posture, he is existence (*bhāva*), and as adorned with the eight cremation grounds, he is cessation (*nirvāṇa*), but in fact he is neither, hence "nondual."

should recite the mantra: "*Oṃ* all phenomena are empty of intrinsic nature; I am empty."[306]

Then he empowers his eyes and so on. After consecration (*abhiṣeka*), he visualizes [himself] as being initiated by Akṣobhya on his head. "He is endowed with all the aesthetic sentiments (*rasas*) beginning with erotic (*śṛṅgāra*), but from the outside, it looks as if he has a wrathful form."[307] The buddhas with their sons are invited, and then he sees them in front of him, emitting light. The four goddesses beginning with Carcikā hold pots completely filled with the five nectars and so on. The pots are like the moon. The yogin visualizes that the goddesses, preceded by benedictory verses, initiate him.[308] With the rays of the seed syllable from his own heart, he invites knowledge being (*jñānasattva*), offering water to drink (*arghya*) and water to wash feet (*pādya*). With the mantra *oṃ mudgara jaḥ*, he attracts them; with [the mantra] *oṃ daṇḍa hūṃ*, he introduces them; with [the mantra] *oṃ padma vaṃ*, he binds them; with [the mantra] *oṃ khaḍga hoḥ*, he makes them abide in his

306. *Śoṇaśrī and *Akṣobhya quote the mantra: *oṃ svabhāvaśūnyatāḥ* [corr. *shu nya*, ed.] *sarvadharmāḥ* [corr. *sar wa dhar ma*, ed.] *svabhāvaśūnyo 'ham*, thus substituting the word *śuddha*, which commonly appears in this mantra (i.e., *oṃ svabhāvaśuddhāḥ sarvadharmāḥ svabhāvaśuddho 'ham*), with the word *śūnya*. This is either a mistake or an attempt to conflate the purity mantra and the emptiness mantra. I thank John Newman for bringing this issue to my attention.

307. The Tibetan translation is corrupted. The idea behind this passage is that the deity should embody all the aesthetic sentiments (*rasas*). The oldest reference to this idea appears already in the *Sarvabuddhasamāyoga* 5.48ab (*raudrādirasasaṃyogavicitramukhavibhramaiḥ*). This is certainly worth taking into consideration in the context of the above passage, which discusses the homologization of the senses as the deities. This concept could have been influenced by Śāktism, especially by the Krama tradition, where one frequently encounters references to the divinization of the senses; see, for example, *Mahānayaprakāśa* 12.4–6 and *Tantrāloka* 3.262–64. Erotic sentiment (*śṛṅgārarasa*) usually appears in the description of the yoginī-tantra deities, such as Hālāhala Lokeśvara in *Sādhanamālā* 27 (p. 65: *śṛṅgārarasasundara*), and of tantric forms of Mañjuśrī in NMAA chapter 4 (Tribe 1995, 106): *saśṛṅgāra*, translated by Tribe as "possessing the erotic sentiment," and in the *Sādhanamālā* 59, 60 (p. 124): *mahāśṛṅgāramūrti* (see English 2002, 463n383). Heruka, too, is described as possessing all the nine *rasas*—for example, in the *Bhramaharanāma Hevajrasādhana* (p. 7), clearly influenced by the *rasa* theory of Indian aesthetics, cited in English 2002, 464. See also Newman 1990.

308. The idea is that the goddesses pour whatever is in their pots on him. Even though here the literal meaning of sprinkling is certainly intended, it is uncertain whether we should understand this ritual as a part of initiation (*abhiṣeka*).

will.[309] Then, with Vajracarcikā, and so on, who arises from the seed syllable of his heart, the wise one should perform worship with various offerings. Then he should consume nectars (*aṃrtāsvādanam*)[310] that have been prepared with the ritual instruction that begins with heating them up. Thus he applies himself; it is neither real

309. The mantra *jaḥ hūṃ vaṃ hoḥ* is connected to the four actions of introducing the deities into the maṇḍala. Snellgrove (1987, 222–23) shows that these four actions appear in the Trailokyavijaya passage of the STTS in the context of the four guardians of the maṇḍala through which "the great beings, the Buddhas and others are summoned, drawn in, bound, so entering his power." Thus *jaḥ* stands for Vajrāṅkuśa and the east, whose function is to summon (*ākarṣa*); *hūṃ* stands for Vajrapāśa and the south, whose function is to draw them in (*praveśa*); *vaṃ* stands for Vajrasphoṭa and the west, whose function is to bind (*bandha*); and *hoḥ* stands for Vajrāveśa/Vajraghaṇṭā and the north, whose function is to draw within one's power (*āveśa/vaśīkaraṇa*). Discussing the *jaḥ hūṃ vaṃ hoḥ* sequence in the context of the Ṭakkirāja mantra recovered from Old Javanese and Indo-Tibetan sources, Acri (2016b, 334) has pointed out that these four actions are also hinted at in the *Sarvavajrodaya* (section 56) as *vajrāṅkuśādibhir ākṛṣya praveśya baddhvā vaśikṛtya* in the context of the four actions performed by Vajrahūṃkāra. The appearance of this sequence with minor variants is also attested, as Acri (2016b, 334–35) points out, in the *Sarvadurgatipariśodhana* (Skorupski 1983, 103) and in the *Vajraśekhara* (Nihom 1998, 248; 253n16–17). See also Ratnākaraśānti's *Bhramaharanāma Hevajrasādhana* (p. 10): *jaḥ hūṃ vaṃ hoḥ ity ebhir yathākramaṃ ākarṣaṇapraveśanabandhavaśikaraṇāni kṛtvā*, and *Sādhanamālā* 226 (p. 441): *jaḥ hūṃ vaṃ hoḥ vajrāṅkuśādiyogena ākṛṣya praveśya baddhvā vaśan nayet* (quoted in English 2002, 470n410). In some texts, however, such as the *Sādhanamālā* 251 or the *Herukasādhana* of Huṅkāravajra, 204r5–7 (Sanderson 2009, 153n349), the sequence bears the feminine names of the goddesses, and the last *bīja hoḥ* stands for "pleasing" (*toṣaṇa*). See, for example, *Hevajrasekaprakriyā* (p. 8): *jaḥ hūṃ vaṃ hoḥ yathākramaṃ gaurīcaurīvattālighasmarībhī rajomaṇḍale ākarṣaṇaṃ praveśanaṃ bandhanaṃ toṣaṇaṃ cakṣurādyadhiṣṭhānaṃ kuryāt* (quoted in English 2002, 469n406). The sequence referred to by *Śoṇaśrī/*Vajrasiddha refers to the earlier version of the mantra sequence that goes back to the STTS and the yoga tantras in general. The sādhaka assumes the functions of the four Yamāntaka gatekeepers, as can be evinced from the fact that the four actions are facilitated by the weapons held by the Yamāntakas and not by the typical weapons of the four guardians holding a hook, noose, chain/fetter, and bell.

310. This is a reference to the ritual of tasting nectar (*amṛtāsvādanam*) that appears in sādhana texts, such as the *Abhisamayamañjarī*, the *Cakrasaṃvarabalividhi*, or the *Guhyasamayasādhanamālā*. The nectars constitute the typical transgressive substances—the five "nectars" (*amṛtas*) and the five meats (of a cow, dog, horse, elephant, and man). The heating begins with the preparation of the hearth, which is fashioned from the three heads (*trimuṇḍacullikā*), the top skull acting as the cauldron. The fire heats up the ingredients; these are called the *knowledge nectars* and should be offered to the *ḍākas* and *ḍākinīs* in the ten directions. For the whole description of *amṛtāsvādanam* based on the *Cakrasaṃvarabalividhi*, see English 2002, 210–11.

nor unreal. He should mediate on the aspect of the deity; then he should remember those aspects.[311]

1. The preliminary practice requires the Vajrabhairava sādhaka to be naked, with disheveled hair, to face the inauspicious southern direction, and to ingest the five "nectars" (*amṛtas*). This description is a part of the Vajrabhairava sādhana's tantric antinomianism.
2. Then follows the rite of protection—that is, setting up the vajra tent (*vajrapañjara*), which appears only in *Kṛṣṇācārya's commentary. Especially notable in this regard is the protection of the yogin through meditation on emptiness, which some sādhana authors, such as Lūyipāda (eleventh century), consider the supreme protection (see note 297).
3. The next stage of the sādhana includes the visualization of the rays of light emitted from the seed syllable from the yogin's heart that go out in the ten directions of space and invite the buddhas, the bodhisattvas, the wisdom goddesses, the *krodha* deities, and sometimes also the teachers in the space in front of him in order to offer worship with the help of the four *pūjādevīs*, who act as the intermediaries of worship. This phase corresponds to the first stage of the Mahāyāna type of supreme worship (*anuttarapūjā*), where the worship is offered to the deities and other beings invited specifically for that purpose. The rays of light[312] are a common instrument in the visualization practice in both Mahāyāna and tantric forms of Buddhism. They are conceived as the energy of the deity that pervades space in all directions and reaches beings everywhere. The summoned deities and beings are requested to "hover in space" in front of a sādhaka—an image that is commonly found also in the Mahāyāna sūtras. The *pūjādevīs* emitted from the mantra master's heart are allocated different names in different sādhana texts,[313] but

311. *Śoṇaśrī's *pañjikā*, 399–401.

312. The verb used in reference to the rays of light that appears in the Skt. and Tib. recensions of the VBhT as well as in the VBhT's commentaries is *saṃcodya* (Tib. *bskul ba*), meaning "impel," "incite," or "excite." This is a common expression in the sādhana texts (English 2002, 120) that is sometimes coupled with the image of a hook (*aṅkuśa*) through which the rays of light draw in the deities and other celestial beings in order to impel them to take part in the ritual. For the syllable *dhīḥ*, which assumes the form of rays as hooks, see *Sādhanamālā* 58 (1:121) . . . *dhīḥkārabījavinirgatāṅkuśakāraraśmyākṛṣṭārapacana-*; for the rays as hooks, see also *Ḍākinījālasaṃvara* (Sanderson 1994, n10, fol. 3r–v). In the VBhT, the rays take on a form of the deity Vairocana. They can also assume the colors of the five buddhas in the Mañjuśrī sādhana; see *Sādhanamālā* 52 (1:109), English 2002, 433n252.

313. For the names of the four *pūjādevīs* in the NMAA, see Tribe 2006, 54. Sometimes the *pūjādevīs* are sixteen in number but also divided into four sets; see *Abhisamayamañjarī*.

the VBhT's commentaries mention only two names—namely, Vajracarcikā and Vajracaṇḍikā. *Kṛṣṇācārya specifies the three forms of worshiping the *pūjādevīs*, offering *pūjā* as outer (*bāhya*), inner (*antara*), and real (*tattva*).[314]

4. In the VBhT commentaries, worship concludes with the confession of sins; this represents the third stage in the sevenfold Mahāyāna *anuttarapūjā*. As the above section indicates, the first three stages of the Mahāyāna version of worship—namely, invitation of the deities, worship *per se*, and confession of sins—have been appropriated into the exegetical tradition of the VBhT.
5. The next step in the sādhana practice is meditation on the four *brahmavihāras*. This too follows the appropriation trajectory from the Mahāyāna model of worship, which similarly prescribes the meditation on the four *brahmavihāras*[315] immediately following the sevenfold *pūjā*. The *brahmavihāra* meditations are typically understood as fulfilling the sādhaka's accumulation of merit (English 2002, 123).
6. The next stage of the sādhana is the meditation on emptiness as constituting the inherent nature of all reality. The sādhaka is instructed to contemplate emptiness (*śūnyatā*) by perceiving the dependent origination of all and by seeing everything as devoid of Nāgārjuna's tetralemma[316] (*catuṣkoṭivinirmukta*),[317] which is done through the realization and recitation

314. The commentators do not give any explanation of the *pūjā* items offered, but these generally consist of *arghya* (water for drinking) and *pādya* (water for washing the feet), and offerings such as the seven precious things (*saptaratna*) and the eight auspicious symbols (*aṣṭamaṅgala*) in *bāhyapūjā*; the offerings of the five sense organs (*kāmaguṇas*) represented by sense objects—e.g., incense for smell, bell for sound, and so on in *antarapūjā* (English 2002, 121), and sexual intercourse with a consort in *tattvapūjā* (Sinclair 2014, 221–22).

315. The *brahmavihāra* meditations are already found in the Nikāyas and Mahāyāna sūtras, and later in tantric Buddhism. The explanation given by the VBhT's commentators (see note 726 below) represents a standard feature found also in other tantric Buddhist sādhanas, with the exception of *upekṣā*, commented upon by *Śoṇaśrī and *Vajrasiddha in untypical fashion—possibly influenced by the Yogācāra-Vijñānavāda school—as: "Equanimity (*upekṣā*) is to be even-minded, disregarding all thought constructs related to perception (*grāhyaṃ*) and perceiver (*grāhakaḥ*)." If so, this example demonstrates how a popular Buddhist concept became updated to a newer version in accordance with the system of thought current in the era in which these commentators were composing their exegesis.

316. The employment of the Nāgārjunian model in the exegetical tradition of the VBhT is somewhat unusual, and shows the influence of the Madhyamaka school on the VBhT's commentators. On the other hand, the recitation of the emptiness mantra is a common feature in the tantric sādhana texts.

317. The application of the "tetralemma" in the context of Madhyamaka's logical discourse has been generally interpreted as the need to ascertain conceptual flows in all

of the emptiness mantra: *oṃ śūnyatājñānavajrasvabhāvātmako 'ham* ("I am identical with the inherent nature of vajra knowledge of emptiness"). *Kṛṣṇācārya explains the purpose of reciting the emptiness mantra as follows: "The purpose of that mantra is to place his mind in a 'no focus on anything' state, pervading the entirety of space, having the knowledge of the immutable gnosis of emptiness."[318] The technical term used by *Kṛṣṇācārya is *anupalabdhamānasa* (Tib. *blo mi dmigs par bzhag go*), which connotes the Madhyamaka concept of meditative absorbtion in emptiness where phenomenal things are not observed.[319] This concept puts forward the idea that no object or experience of an object should be "observed" by the mind—that is, conceived as something with an inherent existence—including the experience of emptiness as nonduality. The purpose of its application in the sādhana practice is to assign a merely provisional role to the experience of emptiness arising from the meditation on emptiness (English 2002, 129). With the state of non-observation, the yogin has to realize that the subsequent stages of his visualization practice are as real or illusory as anything else, and that the gnosis of emptiness is like all-pervasive space, with no boundaries of subject-object duality.

7. The next stage of the sādhana commences with building an abode suitable for the deity, which means creating a cosmos, sometimes a maṇḍala, and always a palace for the deity.[320] Lalitavajra and *Kṛṣṇācārya conform their exegesis to a more traditional Abhidharmic universe, in which the yogin visualizes a cosmos with four continents produced from the respective seed syllables: *yaṃ*, *raṃ*, *vaṃ*, and *laṃ*,[321] endowed with specific colors and the

---

definitive philosophical positions in order to conclude that the only defendable position is that "cause and effect are empty" and thus demonstrate that all things are unoriginated (*anutpāda*) and devoid of inherent existence (*niḥsvabhāvaḥ*). See Buswell and Lopez 2014, 745–47, and Seyfort Ruegg 1977.

318. For the Tibetan text, see note 726.

319. I thank John Newman for this explanation.

320. This part of the sādhana differs in each of the commentaries by *Kṛṣṇācārya and *Śoṇaśrī/*Vajrasiddha; this is also the case when Lalitavajra's exegesis can play a role in our comparative analysis insofar that his sādhana description begins with the creation of a cosmos. I have tabulated these differences in table 4.

321. Sanderson (1994, n35) shows that the *bījas yaṃ*, *raṃ*, *vaṃ*, and *laṃ* in Buddhist sādhanas correspond to those found in Vaiṣṇava and Śaiva tantric traditions. He further argues that these are Brahmanical in origin. Heilijgers-Seelen (1994, 20) demonstrates that the four syllables are indeed attested in the *Yogatattva-Upaniṣad* (84ff.), where earth is square and yellow and represented by the syllable *la*, presided over by Brahmā; water symbolized by a crescent moon is white and represented by the syllable *va*, presided over

mountain-axis Meru (*suṃ*) in the center in the form of a peak. On the top of Meru is a palace (or a maṇḍala and a palace) with the eight cremation grounds (which is the abode of the tantric forms of deity influenced by the Kāpālika culture of the cremation grounds), which comes from the transformation of the vajra ground that has arisen from the transformation of the seed syllable *bhrūṃ*. Lalitavajra and *Kṛṣṇācārya use the basic template of the traditional Abhidharmic concept of the cosmos and augment it with the elements proper to the tantras, such as the eight cremation grounds and with the aspects of the generation of the deity found in the yoga tantras (i.e., the seed syllables *āḥ*, *hūṃ*, *dhīḥ*, etc.). *Śoṇaśrī and *Vajrasiddha are more restricted in their exegesis and merely follow the stages delineated in the root text, which makes their commentaries more aligned with the sādhana genre current in the yoga tantras.

8. When the cosmos and the palace as the abode for the deity are visually created by a yogin, the next stage of the sādhana begins—the generation of oneself as a deity. Before the generation of oneself as Vajrabhairava *samayasattva*[322] can start, the commentaries instruct about the generation of Mañjuśrī as "knowledge being" (Mañjuśrī Jñānasattva, also called Mañjuvajra) as a preliminary practice. The commentaries generally conform with the same iconographical description of Mañjuśrī Jñānasattva that occurs in the NMAA—that is, he is described as arising from the transformation of the seed syllable *dhīḥ* seated on a moon disc, one faced, two-armed, often yellow in color, holding a sword and a book in his hands, and sitting in the heroic (*vajraparyaṅka*) cross-legged vajra position. *Śoṇaśrī and *Vajrasiddha provide an account of the consecration (*abhiṣeka*) of a yogin with the five nectars and worship in which Mañjuśrī Jñānasattva is invited by means of the four mudrās and which is followed again by consuming the five nectars (*amṛtas*). Interestingly, Lalitavajra gives a very similar description of the whole process; however, the main deity invited and worshiped in this scenario is not Mañjuśrī Jñānasattva but Vajrabhairava as a pledge being (a *samayasattva*, or as Lalitavajra calls him, *rang bzhin gyi*

---

by Viṣṇu/Nārāyaṇa; fire is triangular, red, and represented by the syllable *ra*, presided over by Rudra; and air is hexagonal, black, represented by the syllable *ya*, and presided over by Īśvara. Finally, there is ether, represented by the syllable *ha*, which does not feature in the Buddhist sādhanas.

322. Buddhaguhya in his *Tantrārthāvatāra* (Toh. 2501, see Lessing and Wayman 1978) makes a distinction between the *samayasattva* ("symbolic being," Lessing and Wayman 1978, 235n30; "pledge-being," English 2002, 469n405) and the *jñānasattva*, or "knowledge being." The *samayasattva* is a deity the yogin meditatively generates himself into, while the *jñānasattva* is the actual manifestation of the buddhas or the bodhisattvas.

rdo rje 'jigs byed, "innate-Vajrabhairava"), which has arisen from the seed syllable *hūṃ* in Mañjuśrī's heart.[323]

9. The final stage of the sādhana is a detailed visualization of the deity Vajrabhairava. *Śoṇaśrī and *Vajrasiddha use the expression "applying oneself," which in this context refers to visualizing the shape of the deity with all his implements, "which is neither true nor false, in order to purify it." The aspects of the deity Vajrabhairava undergo the process of purification

323. Lalitavajra gives two descriptions of the sādhana practice: first at the beginning of chapter 1 and then again as an exegesis of chapter 4. These two descriptions are not identical, although they align on some crucial points. In the exegesis on chapter 4, Lalitavajra (p. 323) begins with the visualization of the seed syllable *hūṃ* in the sun in Mañjuśrī's heart: "If someone asks how it is that the innate Vajrabhairava [comes] from the light of that [*hūṃ* in the sun of Mañjuśrī's heart], that innate nature itself is visualized just like the Buffalo-Faced One of the conventional maṇḍala (*sāmānyamaṇḍala*). It is explained like this: with the light of *hūṃ*, he should be invited by means of mantras and the mudrā of *vajragraha*. In front [of him], he should place as offerings the guest water and the preliminary offerings with the five mantras. Then he should summon and so on with the four mudrās, and having done that, he should remain. This is the meaning of "he should visualize that innate-nature (*svabhāvaḥ*) Vajrabhairava." "He sits in the place of Vajrabhairava" [means] by abiding in the pride of the deity in the six—that is, eye, ear, nose, tongue, body, and mind—he should generate the sequence from the letters of the names. In other words, Vajradhara, the heart of earth; Avalokiteśvara, the heart of space; and Samantabhadra, the removal of obstacles. Moreover, he should also affix the three syllables in three places. With the light of the *hūṃ* in the heart, he should invite the buddhas and so on; they are worshiped, and prayers are made. He should visualize them holding a jar with five nectars (*amṛtas*). With *hūṃ*, he purifies; with *a*, he examines; with *oṃ*, he blazes. Because he is in union with the vajra tongue, he makes the body maṇḍala pleased. Because he has gathered all in the [body] maṇḍala, he makes a eulogy; this is the meaning of "he should make them pleased."

Chapter 1 of Lalitavajra's *pañjikā* (p. 303) gives the following description of the generation of Vajrabhairava: first the yogin is to visualize the vajra fence (*vajraprākāra*), etc., and the maṇḍala with Meru arising in the center of space, the lineages of the gurus, and the eight cremation grounds. In the middle of that, he should visualize the moon born out of a lotus. In the center of that, he should visualize a sword arising from the seed syllable. That sword transforms into a red form of Mañjuśrī bearing a yellow sword and a lotus and having five locks of hair. In Mañjuśrī's heart arise five lights, and with this intense light, the buddhas and their sons are summoned. They dissolve into that light, and from the transformation of that light arises a mass of fire. From that fire arises *hūṃ*, and he visualizes a wrathful black vajra. With the light of that vajra, he visualizes the sugatas and their sons abiding in the sun. With that sentient beings are purified and then again reenter the vajra; because of that, the vajra is great. From that vajra, he generates the Buffalo-Faced One with the characteristics of the four eons. In this heart, he visualizes the knowledge being (*jñānasattva*), whose body is yellow, with one face and two arms, together with *hūṃ* on

(*viśuddhi*)[324] understood both as a "pureness of Buddha's nature itself" and as a "process or means" (Sferra 1999, 85), and they are matched with corresponding ideas from the Mahāyāna tradition. The concept of *viśuddhi* integrated into exegetical tradition of VBhT represents an attempt of tantric exegesis to enlist those foreign elements coming from the Śaiva tantric ritual and pair them with the well-known concepts from the Mahāyāna world.

---

the top of the sun. He utters: *oṃ ehyehi bhagavān yamāntaka āgaccha āgaccha oṃ saṃjñā hūṃ*. [The yogin] invites him with the mudrā of *vajragraha*. Placing him in front, the yogin should offer water (*arghya*), the preliminary offerings, etc. Then the yogin assumes the pride of Yamāntaka, which means that the six senses—the eyes and so on—are generated as vajra seats (*vajrāsanas*). Then, with the light from his own heart, he invites the buddhas, because he worships them with the vase of five nectars (*amṛtas*); they are poured on the top of his head, and he receives consecration (*abhiṣeka*).

The mudrā of *vajragraha* can be traced back to the STTS, where Vajrabhairava is mentioned in the context of the pledge *mudrā* and utters the mantra *oṃ vajragrahe hūṃ*. Lalitavajra's commentary is interesting because it shows that Vajrabhairava has Mañjuśrī Jñānasattva in his heart. English (2002, 470n411) points out that Mañjuśrī-related texts were probably influential in the development of the concept of the knowledge being (*jñānasattva*), which is still poorly understood. English brings attention to the Mañjuśrī *sādhanas* of the *Sādhanamālā*, where the concept of *jñānasattva* becomes more and more associated with "the yogic practices based on the deity in the heart" (English 2002, 471). In those sādhanas, the *jñānasattva* seems to be unified with the self-generated deity, just like in the above passage, where Mañjuśrī as *jñānasattva* abides in the heart of the self-generated Vajrabhairava.

324. Sferra (1999, 85–86) explains the meaning of purification (*viśuddhi*) in tantric sādhana texts as a hermeneutical device that "deals with the crucial theme of the essential nature of things, not merely as aiming at theoretical definitions, but also as a starting point of the practice that leads to awakening. In this second context, we see the term 'purification' is used in two different ways. On the one hand it indicates pureness, Buddha's nature itself, the ever shining and pure condition that is always present in all things. This pureness represents one of the foundations on which the practice and doctrine of the Buddhist Tantras is based and which can be exemplified by the formulas *viśuddhis tathatā* and *tathātmikā śuddhiḥ*. On the other hand, the term indicates 'purification' and therefore a process or a means: *yayā sarvabhāvā nirdoṣā bhavanti sā viśuddhiḥ*." One may also add that *viśuddhi* connotes the meaning of "rectification, removal of error," in the sense that although all phenomena are primordially pure, ignorance superimposes intrinsic nature upon them, so that they, and we ourselves, must be purified/corrected through the purification/correction of our mind. I thank John Newman for this explanation.

TABLE 4. VISUALIZING THE COSMOS, THE PALACE, AND MAÑJUŚRĪ JÑĀNASATTVA

*Śoṇaśrī/*Vajrasiddha	*Kṛṣṇācārya	Lalitavajra
āḥ (red)~sun	*yaṃ* (blue), *raṃ* (red), *vaṃ* (white), *laṃ* (yellow): four continents	space and *yaṃ*
hūṃ (light with five colors)~*viśvavajra*	*suṃ* (Mount Meru), center	*hūṃ~viśvavajra*
viśvavajra~vajraprākāra~vajrapañjara~vajrabhūmi	*ma~sūrya* maṇḍala	*viśvavajra~vajrabhūmi, etc.*~maṇḍala
yaṃ~vāyu maṇḍala	*hūṃ~viśvavajra*	On the top of maṇḍala Mount Meru
dhīḥ (yellow)~Mañjuvajra	*viśvavajra~vajrabhūmi~vajrapañjara~vajraprākāra*	atop Meru, *vajrabhūmi*~ from *bhrūṃ*
	Mañjuśrī Jñānasattva~palace~maṇḍala with four corners, eight cremation grounds, etc.	*vajrabhūmi*~palace with eight cremation grounds
		atop palace, *a*~moon
		atop the moon, *dhīḥ*~sword~Mañjuśrī

Paṭa

One of the popular elements of tantric Buddhist technology was drawing the *paṭa*,[325] a term given to traditional cloth-based scroll painting of the deity. The origins of the cult of *paṭa* in tantric Buddhist traditions has been traced to Pāla Buddhism (Kapstein 1995) and, more specifically, to the early kriyā tantra the *Mañjuśriyamūlakalpa* (MMK). The tantra provides examples of paint-

325. For the etymology of the word *paṭa* and its synonyms in other languages, see Wallis 2002, 87–88.

ing preparation (*paṭavidhāna*) for the worship of the deity Mañjuśrī, and given its date of composition—the seventh or even the late sixth century[326]—these descriptions may be considered antecedents to painting instructions for the later tantric Buddhist deities. Kapstein (1995, 253) argues that Tibetan *thang kas* can be thought of as a direct offshoot of the esoteric traditions of Pāla Buddhism. Among important early tantric Buddhist sources that provide detailed procedures of painting the *paṭa* of wrathful tantric deities is the VBhT and the so-called "Yamāntaka Chapter" of the MMK. While the MMK employs the painted image of Yamāntaka for the enemy-destroying magic rites (*abhicārahoma*),[327] the VBhT makes use of the painting (*paṭa*) featuring Vajrabhairava for the purpose of accomplishing the unspecified accomplishments (*siddhi*). The descriptions included in these two tantras are important not only for providing various ritual ramifications of the painting preparation but also for the broader understanding of social transactions that underlay this particular cultic practice.

Hero's fee (*vīramūlya/vīrakraya*) and painter (*citrakara*) (§48)

Both texts suggest it was a custom to commission a craftsman (*śilpin*) or a professional painter (*citrakara*) to paint the image of the deity. The commission of the painting operated on a fee-for-services basis (rather than by free-will offerings), and the amount is specified in both texts as "the hero's fee" (Skt. *vīramūlya/vīrakraya*,[328] Tib. *dpa' po'i yon*). A definition of the *hero's fee*[329] is given in the MMK (4.11–12ab): "Having given the price the craftsman asks, the mantra master should give the craftsman the price at his first word, quickly, without hesitation; this is called the *hero's fee* (*vīrakraya*)."[330]

326. On the date of the MMK, see Sanderson 2009, 129.

327. In this regard, the MMK (51.23, p. 432) says: "Having himself made the painting complete and full in all details, or having seen that it accords with his desire (as painted by a professional painter), he may do any ritual, any fierce, enemy-destroying procedure" *parisphuṭaṃ tu paṭaṃ kṛtvā dṛṣṭvā vā manasepsitam/ sarvāṃ ca* [= *sarvāṃś ca*] *kārayet karmāṃ* [= *karmān*] *raudrāṃ* [= *raudrān*] *śatrūpaghātakān* [em. *śatrūpaghātakām*, ed.]//.

328. Tanemura (2004, 237–238n52) discusses the usage of the term *vīrakraya* in some Buddhist tantras. Goodall and Isaacson (2016, 36) identify *vīrakraya* as a feature of the shared syntax of early tantric ritual.

329. The word *vīrakraya* occurs also in the *Jayadrathayamāla* 3.14.1.5cd, in the context of buying a fish, and in the *Jayadrathayāmala* 3.14.2.37c–2.38, in the context of buying a pot of wine from a wine merchant and setting it up in front of the goddess. I thank Alexis Sanderson for these references.

330. MMK 4.11–12ab, p. 40: *yathāmūlyaṃ tato datvā yathā vadati śilpinaḥ/ prathame*

The basic meaning implied by the verse is that the first price the craftsman requests should be supplied without bargaining. Another passage in the MMK says the hero's fee (*vīramūlya*) is a substantial fee that makes the craftsman always pleased[331] and that it should reflect the client's generosity: "In brief, he should give the hero's fee as [the craftsman] himself desires. The ritual performed in dependence on the craftman's work will achieve success if [the yogin] gives him as much as his wealth allows. He must transact in such a way that the craftsman is satisfied."[332] This definition conforms to the gloss given by *Vajrasiddha, who says, "In some scriptures, the word for this is *hero's fee*, and it [means] that he gives to the painter [the fee] he desires."[333] *Akṣobhya glosses *hero's fee* as "a special price," which is "a price that is superior to the normal price of a painter."[334] Apparently, paying a hero's fee was considered a good investment, according to the MMK: "He should recite the mantra a hundred thousand times in front of the painting, then he should offer into the fire a hundred flowers bought through the hero's fee (*vīrakraya*) smeared with ghee, honey, and yogurt. Whatever price [the yogin] bought it for will be returned to him [through this magical procedure] a hundred times."[335] The VBhT (§49) refers to the hero's fee in the context of accomplishing siddhi, which the painting of the image of the deity may bring, when it says, "If he wishes the *siddhi*, he should offer a hero's fee with his hand."

Not unrelated to the success of the ritual painting of the image of the deity are the painter's qualities. According to the VBhT (§49), a person must possess a whole set of character traits to qualify as a suitable painter (*citrakara*) for this task. He must be pure, clever, skillful, endowed with faith, compassionate, free from thought constructs, without anger, and so on. On the contrary, the MMK prefers a painter who is fierce, angry, and scary, therefore resem-

vāksamutthāne śilpinasya sa mantravit// dadyāt puṇyaṃ tataḥ kṣipraṃ vīrakrayeti sa ucyate/.

331. MMK 51.19, p. 432: *dattvā tu śilpine prabhūtaṃ cāpi mūlyaṃ vai yena vā tuṣyate sadā/.*

332. MMK 51.20–21ab, p. 432: *yathepsitaṃ tasya kurvīta vīramūlyaṃ samāsataḥ/ saphalaṃ śilpinaḥ* [em. *śilpine*, ed.] *karma nirāmiṣaṃ cāpi varjayet// tathā tathā prayuñjīta yathāsau sampratuṣyate/.*

333. For the Tibetan text, see note 834.

334. Ibid.

335. MMK chap. 55, 540–41: *paṭasyāgrato lakṣaṃ japet/ tataḥ śatapuṣpāyā vīrakraye krītvā dadhimadhughṛtāktānāṃ juhuyāt/ yāvantakena mūlyena krītāni bhavanti; tacchataguṇamūlaṃ bhavati/.*

bling the wrathful qualities of the deity he is painting.[336] Alternatively, and this option is attested in both texts, the mantra master may do the painting himself if he is oppressed by suffering and fear caused by his enemies. In that case, the painting must be done with calm mind, preceded by a mantric self-protection[337] (possibly with the *niśumbhana* mantra; see note 543), while the sādhaka is seated on a human skull.[338] Lalitavajra (see note 824), while conforming with the description of the two types of people eligible to draw the painting, maintains that the painter has to be also formally initiated: "[It can be painted by] a painter who has the above qualities and who has been initiated, [or it can be painted] by a sādhaka—that is, a hero[339]—who makes an effort to attain siddhis." A reference to the painter as a *samayin* (lit. "one who relies on a vow") is also attested in the *Saṃpuṭodbhava* 9.3.5.

Canvases, pigments, and brushes

The VBhT (§48) lists the following canvases suitable for painting the *paṭa*: a piece of cloth from the garment of a hero fallen in battle (*vīrakarpaṭa*), a cloth used to cover a dead body (*śavapracchāditakarpaṭa*), the cloth of a menstruating woman (*strīpuṣpa*), or a cloth on which a child was born (*prasūtakarpaṭa*). If these are not available, any cloth can act as a canvas.[340] The MMK adds to the above list of suitable canvases a corpse in the cremation ground and the garment of a brahman obtained on the fourteenth or the eighth day of the lunar month, or at night, during the dark fortnight, which should be then covered with blood, washed with water, and made thoroughly dry.[341] The

336. MMK 51.4ab, 431: *krūraṃ citrakaraṃ kruddhaṃ bhīṣaṇe cāpi lekhayet/.*

337. The MMK (51.21cd–22, 431) says: "He must perform a major rite of protection, otherwise he will die; the performer of the rite will die along with his own household. And he should also protect himself. He should do it after he has recited the *vidyā*; the procedure is not said to be done otherwise" (*mahārakṣā ca kartavyā anyathā mṛyate* [= *mriyate*] *hy asau// sakuṭumbo naśyate karmī ātmanaṃ cāpi* [em. *ātmanaś cāpi*, ed.] *rakṣayet/ japtavidyena karttavyaṃ nanyātha* [em. *nānyeṣāṃ*, ed.] *vidhir ucyate*).

338. MMK 51.6, 432: *kapāle mānuṣāsīne* [em. *mānuṣākapāle āsīnaḥ*, ed.] *kṛtarakṣaḥ samāhite/ svayaṃ vā ālikhen mantrī ariduḥkhabhayārditaḥ //.*

339. Kṣemarāja's commentary on the Śaiva *Svacchandatantra*, the *Svacchandoddyota* (3.212, p. 252 of vol. 1 of the *paṭala* 3), provides the following definition of the hero (*vīra*): "A *hero* is a fearless person who abandoned the demons of castes and others" (*vīra iti tyaktajātyādigraho niṣkampaḥ*). In the *Svacchandoddyota* (5.46), heroes are "those devoted to secret practice" (*vīrā rahasyacaryāniṣṭhāḥ*).

340. See note 822 below.

341. MMK 51.2ab–3, 431: *gṛhya kṛṣṇe niśāpakṣe caturdaśyāṣṭau* [em. *āṣṭam*, ed] *tithau/*

painting should be drawn with bright colors with pigments drawn from the painter's own blood, mixed with human fat and butter. Bowls of human skulls serve as receptacles.[342] The brush for mixing the pigments is made of hair from the crown of the head.[343] All this gruesome paraphernalia reflects the influence of the tantric culture of the cremation grounds embodying the Kāpālika style.

A key step in drawing the *paṭa* is painting the cremation grounds beneath Vajrabhairava (§51). The cremation grounds must evoke fear and should be populated with semidivine and demonic beings such as nature spirits (*yakṣa*s), demons (*rākṣasa*s), zombies (*vetāla*s), and site guardians (*kṣetrapāla*s). Cremation grounds are typically home to inauspicious and impure animals such as crows, vultures, dogs, and jackals, which should also be represented in the painting along with the gruesome depictions of people dying a violent death—being burned (*dahyamāna*), hung from a banyan tree (*vaṭavṛkṣasya udbaddhā*), impaled on a stake (*śūlabhinna*), or run through with a spear (*kuntabhinna*).

Depiction of the corpses in the maṇḍalas of tantric Buddhist deities is a persistent feature of esoteric Buddhism, and such corpses play an important role in tantric sādhanas in both Śaiva-Śākta[344] and Buddhist traditions. For example, in the beginning of chapter 46 (vv. 1–6) of the *Picumata-Brahmayāmala*, we come across a description of a heroic sādhaka who enters a cremation ground, having let loose the jackal cry. Facing Bhairava and surrounded by excellent companions, he performs the sacrifice (*yāga*), having first made a small pavilion (*maṇḍapikā*) with various corpses. As that text describes, "He should make a frightening pavilion with various corpses hanging on the southern entrance of the maṇḍala. He should make it as he desires, with decapitated corpses (*kabandha*),[345] corpses impaled on a stake (*śūlaprota*),[346] and corpses hung

śmaśāne mṛtakaṃ prāpya brāhmaṇasya ambaraṃ tam// gṛhya tato rātrau asṛjāṃ [em. *asṛṇāṃ*, ed.] *raṅgayet tataḥ/ bhūyo jalaśaucaṃ tu suśuṣkaṃ kārayet tataḥ//*.

342. MMK 51.15cd–17ab, 432: *etat kruddhavaraṃ likhya ātmaśoṇitavarṇakaiḥ// vyatimiśram ujjvalair lekhya mahāvasāgavyamiśritaiḥ/ kapālabhājanaiś cāpi mānuṣāsthisusambhavaiḥ// kūrcakair varkikair yukto* [em. *mukto*, ed.] *mṛtakeśasusambhavaiḥ/*.

343. See note 839.

344. In the *Svacchandoddyota* by Kṣemarāja (vol. 4, *paṭala* 8, p. 8), a suitable offering is said to be human meat from a person hanged to death (*udbaddhā nāramāṃsa*) and a person impaled on a stake (*dhvaja*) (i.e., *śūlāropita*) offered in a fire offering (*homa*).

345. According to the *Manusmṛti* (9.237), an image of a headless corpse (*kabandha*) should be branded with a hot iron onto the forehead of a person who kills a brahman.

346. According to the *Manusmṛti* (9.276), robbers who break into houses at night should be impaled on a pointed stake. In the *Arthaśāstra* (14.3.4), the skulls of a person impaled on a stake and a person killed by a weapon have special magical properties: "If a person

from a tree (*udbaddhā*). Having done that, the great hero should begin the great sādhana."[347] The *Sārasvata*, a text linked to the *Picumata-Brahmayāmala* cycle and quoted in the *Nityādisaṃgrahapaddhati* by Rājānaka Takṣakavarta, gives the following list of corpses that bestow the hero's accomplishment (*vīrasiddhi*): *dhvajahata* ("impaled"), *rājeṇa hata* ("killed by a king" or "executed"), *udbaddhā* ("hung on a tree"), and *haṭhasādita* ("violently killed").[348] In the commentary on the *Kṛṣṇayamāri Tantra* (p. 68), we find a list of desirable corpses for a sādhana that include the already mentioned impaled on a stake (*śūlaprota*) and hung from a tree (*udbaddhā*), followed by the corpses of the *akṣata* type ("uninjured," i.e., with all the limbs) and the *nirvraṇa* type, which here means "undamaged by weapons" (*śastreṇa nākṣataṃ*).

Despite the fact that the portrayal of the cremation grounds as inhabited by terrifying corpses and demonic beings appears to have been originally an important element in the painting of the image of Vajrabhairava, later commentaries indicate that this particular detail could be substituted with depictions of the vajra ground, vajra roof, and vajra walls around the deity. This is confirmed by *Akṣobhya's commentary: "As for this [cremation ground], it should be surrounded by the host of nonhumans. Or if the basis is not drawn in the style of the maṇḍala, install the vajra ground, and so on [that is, a vajra fence and tent]."[349] These three vajras traditionally constitute the circle of protection (*rakṣācakra*).[350] The fact that they are given here as an alternative may indicate that the nonhumans populating cremation grounds were originally conceived as the protectors of the Vajrabhairava maṇḍala.

---

wants to become invisible, he must plant barley seeds (*yāvan*) in soil placed 'in the skull of a man who has been either killed by a weapon or impaled on a stake' (*śastrahatasya śūla protasya vā puṃsaḥ śiraḥkapāle*) and sprinkle it with sheep's milk."

347. BY 46.6–7: *purasya dakṣiṇe dvāre śavair nānāvidhais tathā/ kuryān maṇḍapikāṃ ghorāṃ kabandhānāṃ vilambināṃ// śūlaprotāṃ svam udbaddhāṃ tatra kuryān manepsitāṃ/ evaṃ kṛtvā mahāvīro mahāsādhanam ārabhet//*. In the next verse of the same text, we learn that the corpses must be bathed with water and smeared with ashes imbued with the power of the mantras (*mantrabhasmāmbusuṣnātā*), and they must be purified by the installation of the three *tattvas* (*tritattvapariśodhitāḥ*).

348. I thank Prof. Alexis Sanderson for this reference. A copy of a single manuscript of this text originally from Pune is kept at the Bodleian Library, University of Oxford (acc. no. MS Stein Or. d. 43).

349. For *Akṣobhya's commentary and the context in which this passage appears, see note 850.

350. For the description of *rakṣācakra* in the yoginī tantras, see English 2002, 131.

Homa

A considerable number of magical recipes found in tantras belong to the category of invocatory fire offerings, or *homa*, a type of magical technology that seems to have developed from the Vedic *homa* and the Indo-Iranian cult of fire (Payne 2016). The archaic ritual syntax—that is, the use of verb *juhuyāt* for the performance of fire offerings, as well as the technical vocabulary used to denote firepits, firewood, ladles, and so on—bears this out (Goodall and Isaacson 2016, 20–22). Even though the *homa* recipes form a distinct category of tantric magical procedures and are often treated separately (see, for example, chapter 6 of the VBhT, entitled "The Prescriptions for the Rule of Homa"), they can also be adopted for a wide range of other aggressive (*abhicāra*) technologies, for the gain of magical siddhis, and even for initiation. It is certainly not unusual to find individual recipes for the *abhicāra*-related purposes containing *homa* components and existing alongside other "magical" technologies, such as the manipulation of material objects, or the specifically tantric technologies of yantra, mantra, and so on.

Chapter 6 of the VBhT gives instructions for the *homa* recipes for ten different purposes. Among them, killing (*māraṇa*) receives two recipes, creating dissent (*vidveṣaṇa*) two, driving away (*uccāṭana*) four, paralyzing (*stambhana*) two, recuperating after an illness or effecting prosperity (*puṣṭi*) one, pacifying (*śānti*) one, subjugating under one's will (*vaśya*) seven, attracting (*ākarṣaṇa*) two, "becoming the ruler of the whole world" one, "inducing madness" one, "turning wealth into poverty" one. The largest number of recipes are for subjugation under one's will and not, as one might expect, for killing.

Table 5 summarizes all the *homa* rituals described in chapter 6 of the VBhT. It is easy to discern a pattern based on the types of firewood and the oblations prescribed for each specific *homa* rite. That is, killing, creating dissent, and driving away seem to belong to the same category insofar that they use the same type of firewood—wood collected from the funeral pyre, or wood that is thorny or bitter—and similar transgressive substances are offered as oblations. Indeed, *Śoṇaśrī classifies all three under the aggressive/fierce (*abhicāra*/*krūra*) rites. The rites of attracting and subjugating under one's will also share similar features: these are the only two types of *homa* that make use of *acacia* wood and the five nectars (urine, feces, semen, blood, and phlegm) that play an important role in both Śaiva and Buddhist tantric ritual (see p. 154). In *Śoṇaśrī's classification, attracting (*ākarṣaṇa*) comes under the subjugation, or *vaśya*, category. Recuperating after an illness or effecting prosperity (*puṣṭi*) and pacifying (*śānti*) are categories on their own, and it is interesting to find the three "sweets"[351] (*madhus*) popular in both Śaiva and Buddhist tantric texts as the oblations required for the *śāntihoma*. Paralysis (*stambhana*) appears to have been left out of the classification. In light of the type of wood used and the impure substances to be offered as oblations, it is tempting to include it under the aggressive *abhicāra*. However, *Śoṇaśrī does not incorporate it under *abhicāra* or under any other of the three categories. The second *stambhana* recipe atypically makes use of the magical substances (*siddhadravyas*), which constitute the distinguishing feature of the "ritual syntax" of early tantras (see Goodall and Isaacson 2016, 25).

TABLE 5. SUMMARY OF THE *HOMA* RITUALS IN THE ROOT TEXT OF THE VBHT

Killing / Māraṇa	
Firewood	From a cremation ground, from an outcaste (*caṇḍāla*)
Offerings	Human bone, feces, donkey dung, thorns, hair, fingernail clippings, pungent mustard-seed oil (*kaṭutaila*)
Target	Any person

Table continues overleaf

351. The commentary *Uddyota* by Kṣemarāja to the Śaiva *Netratantra* (6.17b) uses the phrase *trimadhvāktaṃ*, "anointed with the three sweets"—namely, milk, ghee, and honey. The context of the verse is the rite of invigoration (*puṣṭi*), which occurs by doing *homa* with pills of *gugullu* incense smeared with three *madhus*: butter, milk, and sugar (*gugulludupagolikabhir ajakṣīrakṣaudraṃ*). The *Svacchandatantroddyota* (vol. 3, *paṭala* 6, p. 158), by the same author, refers to the three sweets as *kṣīraśarkaraghṛtam*, "milk, sugar, and ghee." Buddhist tantric texts are also aware of the existence of the three *madhus* but sometimes present them in different combinations. In the *Cakrasaṃvaravivṛtti* of Bhavabhaṭṭa (verse 14), we read that the three *madhus* are molasses, honey, and sugar (*trimadhuraṃ guḍa madhu śarkāra*). The standard three *madhus* are also attested in the *homa* for averting evil (*śānti*) in the VBhT. In the MMK, milk (*dadhi*), honey (*madhu*), and ghee (*ghṛta*) occur very often, and they are used for different magical purposes and siddhis. See, for example, MMK chap. 55, p. 556: *vaikaṅkatasamidhānāṃ dadhimadhughṛtāktānāṃ palāśakāṣṭhair agniṃ prajvālya juhuyāt, suvarṇasahasraṃ labhati*, "Having lit the fire with *palāśa* wood, he should sacrifice the fuel sticks of *vaikaṅkata* smeared with milk, honey, and ghee; he will [then] obtain a thousand pieces of gold." In the NTGS, sesame seed (*tila*) is often said to be smeared with the three *madhus*—e.g., in NTGS 10.114: *tryaktaṃ caiva tilāṃ* [corr. *tilān*, ms.] *hutvā yāmenākarṣaye drutam*, "Having offered sesame seed anointed with the three, he will be able to attract quickly, in a single watch."

Creating Dissent / Vidveṣaṇa	
Firewood	From a cremation ground
Offerings	Crow, owl, feathers, peacock, snakeskin, hair, unhusked rice, buffalo flesh, horse flesh
Target	Any person
Driving Away / Uccāṭana	
Firewood	From a cremation ground, neem tree, thorn apple
Offerings	Crow flesh, dog flesh, hen flesh, camel dung, dog dung, wine, cat blood, crow's nest, unhusked rice
Target	Any person, or specifically an entire city or Vajradhara, i.e., Indra
Paralyzing / Stambhana	
Firewood	N/A
Offerings	The *siddhadravyas*: yellow orpiment, turmeric, realgar, and bovine concretion; thorns, poison, mustard seed, human blood
Target	Any person, or specifically a woman
Recuperating after an illness or effecting prosperity / Puṣṭi	
Firewood	*Uḍumbara*
Offerings	Sesame, unhusked rice, barley, ghee
Target	N/A
Pacifying / Śānti	
Firewood	*Palāśa*
Offerings	The three "sweets" (*madhus*)—ghee, honey, and milk—and bermuda grass
Target	Country [at war]

Attracting / Ākarṣaṇa	
Firewood	*Khadira*, acacia
Offerings	Image in mustard seed, five nectars, ghee
Target	Any person
Subjugating under one's will / Vaśya	
Firewood	Acacia
Offerings	Beef, blood, dog flesh, urine, horse flesh, excrement, elephant flesh and semen, fish, wine, sesame, rice, menstrual blood
Target	Any person together with his wealth, the king and his army, any kind of people, all women

Homa rituals in the commentaries of the VBhT

The commentaries provide detailed prescriptions for the ritual firepits (*agnikuṇḍa*) and the altars (*vedī*); the suitable time and place for the performance of the *homa*; the emotional state of the sādhaka; the colors associated with the *homa* rites; the directions in which the sādhaka is facing while performing *homa*; and the ritual sequence of *homa*. I have tabulated these details below. Table 6 summarizes the prescriptions concerning the firepits in *Śoṇaśrī's *pañjikā* (pp. 406–7). The numbers in the left-hand column represent: (1) the shape of the firepit and the altar, (2) the color connected with the rite, (3) the width of the firepit, (4) the depth of the firepit, and (5) the color of the vajra garland (*vajrāvalī*):

TABLE 6. DETAILS OF THE *HOMA* FIREPITS (*AGNIKUṆḌA*) ACCORDING TO *ŚOṆAŚRĪ

	Abhicāra	*Śānti*	*Puṣṭi*	*Vaśya*	*Ākarṣaṇa* (belonging to *vaśya*)	*Māraṇa/Uccāṭana/Vidveṣaṇa* (belonging to *abhicāra/krūra*)	*Vidveṣaṇa* (alternative)
1	triangle	—	square	square	square	triangle	—
2	red	—	yellow	—	—	red	—
3	20 *aṅgulas* on each side	1 cubit	2 cubits	2 cubits[352]	2 cubits	20 *aṅgulas* on each side	2 cubits
4	10 *aṅgulas*	1/2 cubit	15 inches	—	—	10 *aṅgulas*	15 inches
5	red	white	—[353]	—	—	red	indigo

In *Śoṇaśrī's classification, killing (*māraṇa*), driving away (*uccāṭana*), and creating dissent (*vidveṣaṇa*) come under aggressive (*abhicāra*) or fierce (*krūra*) rites. The firepit type for all the aggressive *abhicāra* rites is the same, with an additional alternative hearth for creating dissent (*vidveṣaṇa*). The firepit type for subjugating under one's will (*vaśya*) and attracting (*ākarṣaṇa*) is the same. Lalitavajra, who often refers to the firepit as a *maṇḍala*, discusses only the hearth types for aggressive rites (*abhicāra*) and pacification (*śānti*), which conforms exactly with the instructions delineated by *Śoṇaśrī. But he adds that in case of the hearth for fire offerings intended to bring peace (*śāntihoma*), the firepit should have a raised platform of four fingers and be smeared with incense and white earth.[354] Lalitavajra and *Akṣobhya also say the firepit for paralyzing, or *stambhana* (which *Śoṇaśrī omits), should be square, which

352. The description (p. 407) reads, "He construes the firepit for eight exactly like before" (*brgyad la sngar bzhin du thab kh*ung byas), which probably means that it is square, 2 cubits per side, giving a total of 8.

353. In case of *puṣṭi*, one should encircle the firepit with a row of jewels (*ratnāvalī*).

354. See note 906.

Lalitavajra glosses as "wide hearth" and *Akṣobhya as "similar to the earth maṇḍala and yellow in color."[355]

Table 7 summarizes the prescriptions for firepits (*agnikuṇḍa*) according to *Kṛṣṇācārya (pp. 460–61). The numbers in the left-hand column represent: (1) the shape of the firepits, (2) the color connected with the rite, (3) the width of the firepit, (4) the depth of the firepit, (5) the symbols surrounding the firepit, and (6) the number of oblations:

TABLE 7. DETAILS OF THE *HOMA* FIREPITS (*AGNIKUṆḌA*) ACCORDING TO *KṚṢṆĀCĀRYA

	Abhicāra	*Vidveṣaṇa*	*Uccāṭana*	*Śānti*	*Puṣṭi*
1	triangle	—‖—	bow	round	—
2	black	—‖—	blue	white	—
3	20 *aṅgulas*	—‖—	1 cubit	—[356]	1 cubit
4	10 *aṅgulas*	—‖—	1 cubit	—	2 cubits
5	*vajrāvalī*, seed syllables *raṃ* and *vaṃ*	—‖—	hammer, vajra, stick, rosary	—	—
6	29	—‖—	8 and 14	—	15

Table 8 summarizes the regulations for the four main types of *homa* according to *Śoṇaśrī concerning the following: (1) the time of the performance of the rite, (2) the emotional state of the practitioner, (3) the color of the form of Vajrabhairava with whom the practitioner has to unite meditatively, and (4) the direction the practitioner faces:

355. See note 899.

356. *Kṛṣṇācārya says that the measurement of the firepit for *śāntihoma* should be the same as in other cases, possibly one cubit deep; see note 906.

Table 8. Regulations of the four main types of *homa* according to *Śoṇaśrī

Table 9	*Abhicāra*	*Śānti*	*Puṣṭi*	*Vaśya*
(1)	14th dark fortnight	the first bright fortnight	full moon	—
(2)	hateful	peaceful	—	passionate
(3)	black	white	yellow	red
(4)	—	—	north	east

Table 9 gives a general typology of *homa* rites according to *Akṣobhya (pp. 384–86) concerning: (1) the phase of the moon for the performance of *homa* or the color of the sky, (2) the direction the practitioner faces, (3) the color associated with the rite, (4) the emotional state of the practitioner, and (5) the time of the day suitable for the performance of rites:

TABLE 9. GENERAL TYPOLOGY OF *HOMA* ACCORDING TO *AKṢOBHYA

	Abhicāra	*Śānti*	*Puṣṭi*	*Vaśya*	*Ākarṣaṇa*	*Māraṇa*	*Vidveṣaṇa*	*Uccāṭana*	*Stambhana*
1	waning moon	waxing moon	waxing moon	waning moon	when the sky is red				
2	south	north	east	west		southeast	southwest	northwest	northeast
3	black	white	——	red					
4	angry	loving	joyous	passionate					
5	midnight	daybreak (*pradoṣa*)	daybreak (*pradoṣa*)	sunset					

Prescriptions for the ritual sequence of *homa*

The commentaries by *Śoṇaśrī/*Vajrasiddha and *Kṛṣṇācārya provide very similar accounts of the ritual sequence of *homa*—that is, the generation of the fierce or *krodha* type of fire deity (*agnideva*) followed by generation of the deity Vajrabhairava. The ideal place to perform *homa* is either a cremation ground or an isolated place, which commentators gloss as one's own house and sometimes as the outskirts of the city.[357] This differs from the list of ideal *homa* sites enumerated in chapter 13 of the MMK, where we find:

> [The site for *homa* should ideally be] pure, swept clean, on the bank of the river, in the place where there is a single tree (*ekasthāvara=ekavṛkṣa*), in the cremation ground, in an empty house, on a mountaintop, in an empty temple, in the great forest; all those places for sādhana, which have been told by the āryas, the buddhas and bodhisattvas, are prescribed for the fire rituals (*homakarma*).[358]

Before beginning the ritual of *homa*, the sādhaka has to meditatively unite with Vajrabhairava. The *homa* is described as oblations of various substances into the mouth of the fire divinity (*agnideva*). The fire used for the aggressive (*abhicāra*) rites is either a fire taken from a cremation pyre or acquired from an outcaste (*caṇḍāla*), a cobbler, or a butcher. For pacification (*śānti*), fire acquired from monks is recommended, and for the fire offering for recuperation after an illness or prosperity (*puṣṭi*), fire can be acquired from a householder. Then, one generates a majestic fire by pouring ghee into it.[359] In the middle of the fire, the practitioner visualizes the seed syllable (*bīja*) *paṃ*, which turns into a multicolored lotus.

Then he visualizes Agni, the fire divinity (*agnideva*), who is white (or black; see note 360) and has three faces and six arms. Agni, as described in the commentaries on the VBhT, holds a rosary (*mālā*), a water jug, and a small knife in his three right hands. With his three left hands, he displays the mudrā of fearlessness and holds a three-pronged staff (*tridaṇḍa*) and a skull. The practitioner visualizes this wrathful form (*krodha*) of Agni standing in the *pratyālīḍha* pose

357. See note 888.

358. MMK 13.9cd–11ab, p. 90: *śucau deśe parāmṛṣṭe nadīkūle tathā vare// ekasthāvaradeśe ca śmaśāne śūnyaveśmani/ kuryādd homaṃ susaṃrabdho parvatāgre tathaiva ca// śūnyadevakule nityaṃ mahāraṇye tathaiva ca/ yāni sādhanadeśāni kathitānyagrapudgalaiḥ// etāni sthānāny uktāni homakarmānī* [em. *karmiti*, ed.] *sarvataḥ/*.

359. *Kṛṣṇācārya's *pañjikā*, 459: *me'i gzi byin mar me chen pos bskyed.*

(with right foot bent forward and left foot retracted) and adorned with terrifying ornaments.[360] Agnideva abides as the sādhaka's own seed syllable at the heart. Then the practitioner should invite the *jñānadevatā* (the actual Agni) and offer him water for rinsing the mouth (*arghya*) and washing the feet (*pādya*). Afterward, the practitioner should introduce Agni into his *samaya* (which means he should remind Agni of his pledge to the Buddha that he will come to aid anyone who calls on him and worships him).[361] Then the practitioner visualizes the seed syllable of the fire divinity, *raṃ*, in his own[362] mouth and with his mouth slightly open, he recites the mantra *oṃ agnaye svāhā*.

Afterward, in his own heart, he visualizes Vajrabhairava, he performs the ritual installation (*adhiṣṭhāna*) of the eyes, he invites the knowledge being (*jñānasattva*), and then he worships him.[363] Again, he places in (his?) mouth

360. *Kṛṣṇācārya (pp. 459–60) gives a very similar sequence: "In the middle of the fire, he should visualize the seed syllable *paṃ*, [which turns into] a multicolored, eight-petal lotus. Atop that, on the seat of the sun, he should generate Agnideva transformed from the seed syllable *raṃ*. Agnideva is black with three faces, six arms, hair, head, eyes, mouth, and so on and ornamented with wrathful bone ornaments. In his right hands, he holds a knife, a rosary, and makes a mudrā of fearlessness (*abhayamudrā*). His left hands hold a skull, a three-pronged staff (*tridaṇḍa*), and a water jar. He should be generated as standing in the *pratyālīḍha* pose" (*me'i dbus su pam las sna tshogs pad ma 'dab ma brgyad pa/ de'i steng du ram las nyi ma'i gdan la ram las byung ba'i me'i lha sku mdog nag po zhal gsum phyag drug pa dbu skra dang spyan dang zhal la sogs pa khros pa rus pa'i rgyan can/ g.yas rnams su gri gug dang bgrang phreng dang mi 'jigs pa rnams so/ g.yon rnams su thod pa dang dbyu gu rtse gsum dang ril ba spyi blugs so/ g.yon brkyang ba'i stabs kyis bzhugs pa bskyed la*).

361. *Kṛṣṇācārya (p. 460) gives a parallel description: "From the seed of his heart, he summons the *deva* Agni, he offers him water for washing his feet, hands, and mouth, he gives offerings and he reminds him about the vows" (*thugs ka'i sa bon las me lha bkug la zhabs dang phyag dang zhal bsil ba dang mchod pa rnams byas la dam tshig la bcug*).

362. *Kṛṣṇācārya's commentary (p. 460) makes it clear that the seed syllable *raṃ* must be visualized in Agni's mouth and not in the sādhaka's.

363. *Kṛṣṇācārya's description (p. 460) reads: "He visualizes *raṃ* in the mouth of that Agnideva, reciting *ha ha oṃ agnaye* [this mantra seems to be corrupted; probably it was originally *svāhā oṃ agnaye* and then *svā* became corrupted to *ha*] and performs *homa* correctly with the substances (*dravya*s) and the name of the target. Then, in his heart, he generates the form of Vajrabhairava previously [taught]. Having empowered the sense fields and the *jñāna*[*sattva*], he should do the ritual sprinkling (*abhiṣeka*) and the sādhana. He should also perform worship with the sequence of ritual substances (*dravya*s), praises, and so on, whichever he knows. In the belly of that [Vajrabhairava], which is a fire of the great cremation ground, he should realize emptiness of all phenomena, and he should meditate on the seed syllable *raṃ* in the mouth [of Vajrabhairava] and on the triangular firepit stacked on the top of two human thigh bones. [The text says *rkan*, meaning "palate," but it does not make any sense; thus I have emended to *rkang* in accordance with Lalitavajra's commentary about the firepit made of human thigh bone—i.e., *mi rkang gi skyed po*; see

the seed syllable *taṃ*.[364] He visualizes himself as Vajrabhairava according to the procedure of the colors (namely, red for attracting, black for killing, and so on), and then he offers into the fire the oblations in accordance with the type of the *homa*. After this, the result will come about as it was taught.[365]

The MMK (in chapter 13) partly conforms to the procedure of summoning the fire at the beginning of the *homa* ritual, as expounded by the VBhT's commentators, but it also differs on critical points. In accord with the VBhT, the MMK starts by summoning the fire as a rite in which a sādhaka offers into it three oblations of ghee that have been empowered by a single recitation of the fire heart-mantra, which is further classified as all-purpose (*sarvakarmakara*) and bestowing all desires (*sarvakāmada*).[366] The fire heart-mantra (*agnihṛdaya*) is given as:

> *Oṃ uttiṣṭha haripiṅgala lāhitākṣa dehi dadāpaya / hūṃ phaṭ phaṭ sarvavighnāṃ vināśaya svāhā / eṣa saḥ mañjuśrīḥ paramāgnihṛdayaṃ sarvakarmakaraṃ sarvakāmadam/* (MMK chap. 13, p. 90).

> *Oṃ*, get up, O brown and yellow one [referring to the fire], O you with red eyes. Give, give. *Hūṃ phaṭ phaṭ*, destroy all obstacles, *svāhā*. This, O Mañjuśrī, is the supreme fire heart-mantra, which is all-purpose and bestows all desires.

Unlike the VBhT, however, the MMK describes only three types of *homa* that follow the earliest threefold pattern of pacifying rites (*śāntika*), rites promoting welfare or recuperation after illness (*pauṣṭika*), and fierce rites (*raudra*) given in the *Susiddhikara*.[367]

---

note 555 below]. He should burn the ritual substances (*dravyas*) together with the name of the target. Then whatever he says, will be." For the Tibetan, see *Kṛṣṇācārya's *pañjikā*, 460.

364. This is probably the corruption of *raṃ*; see the parallel sequence in *Kṛṣṇācārya's commentary above, where *raṃ* (instead of *taṃ*) should be visualized in the mouth of Vajrabhairava.

365. *Śoṇaśrī's *pañjikā*, 406.

366. MMK chap. 13, p. 90: *ādau tāvat sādhakena anenāgnihṛdayena sakṛjjaptaṃ ghṛtāhutitrayaṃ agnau hotavyam/ agnirāhvānito bhavati/*.

367. The development of *homa* rituals is believed to have taken place through a process of gradual expansion, in which the earlier set of three (Strickmann 1983) expanded into four, five, and eventually eight categories (Payne 2016). The early kriyā tantra *Susiddhikara*, dated to the sixth century, follows the threefold scheme of *homa* based on the siddhis one wishes to accomplish. Thus the *śāntika* bestows the highest siddhis, *pauṣṭika* the mid-

Expanded *homa* according to Lalitavajra

Lalitavajra provides an expanded account of the aggressive *homa* rituals (*abhicārahoma*) with regulations concerning the sequence, including the number of ghee oblations, which are performed with two sacrificial ladles—a large ritual ladle (Tib. *dgang gzar*, Skt. *pātrī*), and a small ritual ladle (Tib. *blugs gzar*, Skt. *sruvaḥ*) often used in *homa*. Moreover, Lalitavajra gives prescriptions for (1) the shape and design of the firepit, (2) the firewood in terms of its dimensions and where the fire should be acquired, (3) the two types of things that are to be offered into the fire—the articles for worship and the oblations—along with their arrangement, (4) the meditative generation of the firepit, the god Agni, and (5) Vajrabhairava, which arise from the transformation of the seed syllables, as follows:[368]

> He makes a triangular firepit measuring twenty fingers wide and ten fingers deep, in an isolated place. He anoints it with the charcoal of the cremation ground and so on. In the middle of the firepit, he draws a vajra[369] with confidence and makes a three-pointed vajra on a rim around it.
>
> Having prepared the firepit, he burns the firewood, which should be black and have thorns, like the *kovidara* and so on. The thorny wood should measure ten fingers long. He purifies the fire with the mantra and water; he takes the fire from the house of a cobbler and so on, sets up a firepit, and he builds the fire up while reciting *jvala jvala* ("flame, flame").
>
> The articles for worship are black flowers, incense of fragrant

dling, and *abhicāruka* the lowest. The *śāntika* rites are concerned with eliminating calamities that have befallen the practitioner. The *pauṣṭika* rites are concerned with restoration of health. The *abhicāruka* rites target the evildoers, people harboring wicked thoughts and those who have fallen from their pledges. In the STTS (Weinberger 2003, 213), we find a fourfold *homa*, including subjugating under's own will (*vaśīkaraṇa*). The tenth chapter of the NTGS has five *homa* categories: *śānti*, *puṣṭi*, *abhicāruka*, *vaśya*, and *utsāraṇa* (driving away). For a discussion of *homa* in tantric traditions, see Payne 2016, Payne and Witzel 2015, and Goodall and Isaacson 2016, 19–24.

368. Lalitavajra's *pañjikā*, 329–32.

369. Lalitavajra's description of firepit for the *abhicāra homa* matches the one found in the *Susiddhikara* (Giebel 2001, 186): "Dig a triangular hearth in black ground with one corner facing outward. The distance is twenty fingers breadth and ten fingers depth. Smear with crematory ashes and in the bottom of the hearth, fashion a *vajra*, eight fingers long and three fingers high."

herbs, great honey (?), butter lamps, and so on. He gathers edibles to offer the deity—many types of meat, blood, and poisonous scented water. He offers as oblations into the fire the substances such as human excrement, urine, excrement of a donkey and a camel, and pungent mustard-seed oil (*kaṭutaila*), as well as hair, nails, and a clear footprint of the target, and human bone. He arranges the substances: on the right side, the articles for worship (*mchod rdzas*), and on the left side, the fire oblations (*bsreg rdzas*). He fills the large ritual ladle and the small ritual ladle with ghee and places a vajra bell in front. Then he blesses the substances, first with the mantras that have the *oṃ* [syllable], and then he blesses the articles for worship with the mudrā.

While in meditative stabilization, the sādhaka generates a firepit on the top of the sun disc [arising] from his own syllables. From the seed syllable *ra*[*ṃ*] arises a triangular fire maṇḍala transformed from the three syllables; from their transformation arises a fierce fire: wrathful in appearance, rising upward all around and reddish-brown in color, his body is ornamented with many lights, and he has three faces: black, white, and the left one green. He has six arms, he holds a vajra and a water pot, and with the third right hand, he makes a mudrā of fearlessness (*abhaya*). His left hands hold a bell, a club, and a rosary. Having visualized him as possessing these ornaments, the sādhaka invites that deity with his own mantra: *ehi ehi mahābhūtadevarṣisattama mahāhuti asmin nihito* [corr. *nihato*, ed.] *bhavati agne mama śātruṃ māraya phaṭ*. Endowed with this mantra and while in meditative absorption, he summons the deity near the fire, and the deity enters the firepit through this ritual, and so on. To that deity who has become identical [with the firepit], he offers worship by means of water with offerings made previously together with his own mantra. Then, into the mouth of the fire, he offers with mantra a large ladle containing white mustard and poison. Then, onto the firewood (*yam shing*) [corr. *yam sang shing*, ed.], he offers all the oblations into the sacrificial fire in sequence. Having completed it, at the end, he offers a large ladle.

After that, he should visualize in his heart the great Vajrabhairava emerging from the seed syllable *hūṃ* on the top of the red [letter]. Then he also invites the circle of knowledge beings (*jñānacakra*) in front with the mantra *oṃ hrīḥ ha bho mahākrodha āgaccha asmatpūjāṃ pratigṛhṇātu prasādaṃ me kuru śātruṃ māraya phaṭ*

> and so on. He then scatters water with preliminary offerings; having made this ritual and so on, he will summon [Vajrabhairava]. To the one who has become identical with him, he worships with water and other offerings, as before. After that, he offers a large ladle of ghee, then, he kindles fuelsticks that are to be offered into the fire and offers them in sequence. Then he offers seven large ladlefuls. Then he offers worship. He should complete the ritual with black flowers, reciting the mantra *oṃ hrīḥ ṣṭrīḥ vikṛtānana mama śātruṃ māraya phaṭ.* He accomplishes *homa.* Afterward, he places water for drinking and honors the deity. Then he meditates on that deity departing. He worships fire with remaining things, as before. He visualizes the deity departing. He collects for himself the vow [substances] that were left out and completes the ritual. This is the expanded version of *homa.*

The essential difference between the *homa* procedures delineated in the MMK and the one elaborated upon in the commentarial literature of the VBhT is that the former is devoid of the inner-outer dynamics that characterize *homa* descriptions in the VBhT's commentaries. In the expositions of the VBhT's exegetical writers, we see that external *homa* rituals are accompanied by internal meditative practices. The commentaries give specific instructions on how to visualize the deities invoked during the *homa*, such as Agni and Vajrabhairava. Thus the praxis of visualization amounts to generating deities meditatively from the seed syllables. In so doing, the commentators on the VBhT adhere to the distinction of inner-outer *homa* attested for the first time in the *Mahāvairocana Sūtra* in the sixth or seventh century (Giebel 2017). In this regard, the following definition of what constitutes the inner and outer *homa* is given in chapter 27 of the *Mahāvairocana Sūtra* (Giebel 2005, 193):

> Lord of Mysteries, these are empowered by the form of fire [i.e., Agni]. With one's own shape and color confirming with theirs and the drugs and other materials the same too, one performs external *homa*, accomplishing siddhi at will. Next, in one's own heart, that which is of one nature but tripartite, three places (deity, fire, and officiant) united to form one, represents the internal *homa* of the yogin.

Buddhaguhya's commentary on the *Mahāvairocana Sūtra* (181.4–5 in Wayman 1992, 202) explains that the "outer *homa*" is linked to the preparation of firepits for accomplishing siddhis connected with *śāntika*, *pauṣṭika*, and *abhicāruka*.[370] The inner *homa*, however, is a rite of meditation, one that rests on the praxis of contemplating the identity of fire, the divinity to whom the fire oblations are made, and the sādhaka (Wayman 1992, 202). Furthermore, Buddhaguhya (184.1–2 in Wayman 1992, 201–2) clarifies that through inner *homa*, one changes into the form of a deity from one's own seed syllable. The generation of the deity as a living entity through inner meditative practice that begins with the visualization of the seed syllables located in one's own heart and the union with that deity, paired with the external performance of *homa*, is attested in the exegetical literature of the VBhT. By incorporating the inner-outer *homa* taxonomy that entered into the tantric Buddhist discourse with the *Mahāvairocana Sūtra*, the VBhT's commentators want to distance the root text from the one-sided *homa* framework propounded in the scriptures of the kriyā tantras (e.g., *Susiddhikara Sūtra*, *Mañjuśriyamūlakalpa*, and so forth), which focus predominantly on the external *homa*. For the VBhT commentators, the actual performance of *homa* is not only a means to accomplish various siddhis, it is also an instrument for reaching the goal of the yoga tantras—union with the deity.

370. The term *abhicāruka* is a common form of a more frequently used variant *abhicāra*, attested in the Buddhist kriyā tantras (i.e., *Susiddhikara Sūtra*, MMK, etc.) but rarely seen in Śaiva texts, with the exception of the Niśvāsa corpus and the Nepalese version of the *Sārdhaśatikakālottara* (150-verse recension, v. 69cd: *yajanaṃ vihitaṃ skanda anilām abhicāruke*, NAK 5-4632 ["Kālottara"], part 3, fol. 4r). I thank Prof. Alexis Sanderson for this reference.

6. The Influence of Nondual Śaiva-Śākta Traditions

THE TOPIC of Śaiva-Śākta influence upon the Buddhist tantras has been initiated and developed by pioneering work of Alexis Sanderson in a number of influential articles (1993, 1994, 1995, 2009). Sanderson has argued that the development of tantric Buddhism must be seen first and foremost as a process of adaptation and appropriation of non-Buddhist Śaiva and Śākta elements—namely, those cults belonging to the *mantrapīṭha* ("seat of mantras") and the *vidyāpīṭha* ("seat of *vidyās*") of the *mantramārga* or householder Śaivism (Sanderson 1988). According to Sanderson (2009, 128), the tendency to incorporate Śaiva elements into tantric Buddhist ritual repertoire is already attested in the earliest Buddhist tantras, such as the *Mahāvairocanābhisaṃbodhi*, later categorized as the tantra of the performance or caryā class or the *Mañjuśriyamūlakalpa*, an early kriyā tantra. Among the two, the *Mañjuśriyamūlakalpa* is the text whose dependence upon Śaivism is spelled out most clearly, insofar as three chapters of this text are dedicated to the cult of the Śaiva deity Tumburu and his four sisters, prominent in the left-current (*vāmasrota*) division of the *vidyāpīṭha* (Sanderson 2009, 129).

Not only did the trend of Śaiva appropriation linger, it was strengthened and further enhanced by additional Śākta elements in the next phase of tantric Buddhism, the emergence of the so-called yoga tantras. The *Sarvatathāgatatattvasaṃgraha*, the foundational text of the yoga tantras, provides many instances of Śaiva-Śākta influence. Among these, the notion of possession (*āveśa*) as the prerequisite of a successful initiation (*abhiṣeka*), a concept that originated from within the Śaiva-Śākta Kaula tradition, is perhaps the most profoundly accentuated (Sanderson 2009, 133). The *Sarvatathāgatatattvasaṃgraha* is also the first Buddhist tantra that puts emphasis on the antinomian issues of tantric practice, such as sexual intercourse, "as a higher form of practice" (Sanderson 2009, 140), another feature of the standard repertoire of the *vidyāpīṭha* cults. Such transgressive, antinomian practices explicitly evoking sexuality and ritual ingestion of forbidden, impure substances come to the forefront in the *Guhyasamāja Tantra*, another tantra of the eighth century.

However, the greatest influence of Śaiva material upon the Buddhist tantras is seen in what is considered the final stage of the development of Buddhist tantras—the emergence of the yoginī tantras. The yoginī tantras, although officially Buddhist, derive from the non-Buddhist Bhairava cult of *vidyāpīṭha* Śaivism (Sanderson 2009, 148). On the one hand, the yoginī tantras embody the fullest apotheosis of cult of the cremation grounds of Kāpālika Śaivism, and on the other, they are replete with terrifying, flesh-devouring yoginīs and ḍākinīs, denizens of these cremation grounds that, similar to the tantras of *vidyāpīṭha*, accompany the central male deity, Bhairava or Heruka (Sanderson 2009, 148). Sanderson (2009, 188) has also demonstrated that the earliest text of the yoginī tantras, which was most certainly composed in India in the early eighth century—namely, the *Sarvabuddhasamāyogaḍākinījālasaṃvara Tantra*—was intertextually dependent upon the two *vidyāpīṭha* scriptures, the *Sarvavīrasamāyoga* and the *Yoginījālaśaṃvara*. Another important yoginī tantra identified by Sanderson as produced under the influence of the Śaiva tantras is the passage on *abhiṣeka*, or initiation, in the *Laghuśaṃvara* (known also as the *Herukābhidhāna* or *Cakrasaṃvara Tantra*). Sanderson (2009, 203–19) has showed that at least 150 verses of the *Laghuśaṃvara* are drawn from the Śaiva *Picumata-Brahmayāmala*, the Yoginīsāṃcāra section of the *Jayadrathayāmala*, and the *Tantrasadbhāva*. This strong textual evidence of Buddhist appropriation of earlier Śaiva and Śākta models even to the point of "pious plagiarism" is further substantiated by the visual proof of iconography of "new" tantric Buddhist deities that appeared together with the emergence of the yoginī tantras (Sanderson 2009, 132). The possible influence of Śaiva iconography on the development of the image of Vajrabhairava was discussed above in chapter 2. In the next section, I will examine the two practices described in the VBhT that have been influenced by the Śaiva-Śākta tradition, (1) the consumption of the five nectars and (2) the entry into cremation ground with mad laughter.

The Five Nectars

The five nectars, or five jewels (*pañcāmṛta*, *ratnapañcaka*)—namely, semen, menstrual blood, urine, excrement, and phlegm (Sanderson 2005)—commonly feature in the Kaula rituals and are also often referred to in the *vidyāpīṭha* texts such as the *Jayadrathayāmala* and the *Picumata-Brahmayāmala*. The ritual use of the five nectars has two functions, and the VBhT and its commentators have adopted these two functions into its tantric technology.

First, these five are regarded as powerful substances that attract a certain class of wrathful deities and dangerous spirits. The supernatural beings are constantly on the lookout for these five nectars, and they procure them by extraction. For example, the *Tantrasadbhāva*, an early Śākta tantra of the *vidyāpīṭha*, refers to a certain class of dangerous female spirits called *ḍāmarī*s, whose minds are constantly focused on the repetition of the mantra and who devour the five nectars after having extracted them from their human victims.[371] Even though the extraction of the five nectars from living beings is not prescribed in the Kāpālika observance (*kāpālikavrata*), literary sources, such as the eighth-century *Mālatīmādhava*, written by Bhavabhūti, refer to it as a feature of the Kāpālika transgressive conduct (*vāmācāra*):

> [Now enters Skull Earring (Kapālakuṇḍalā), terrifyingly radiant, flying through the air]: "Victorious is the lord of powers who is surrounded by his *śākti*s, who is constantly sought by the sādhakas of unriveted attention, who bestows siddhi upon those who know him. His substance is concealed within the heart, centered on the wheel of the sixteen *nāḍi*s (5.1, ed. Grimal 1999, 157). Look at me now, here I come [. . .], dispersing the clouds in the sky before me, without becoming exhausted by my flight because of extracting the five nectars of all beings through the sequence of arising of the veins (*nāḍi*s)." (5.2, ed. Grimal 1999, 159)

Törzsök (2011, 3) says that with regard to the accuracy of the Kāpālika practices, the *Mālatīmādhava* and other nonsectarian Sanskrit texts, such as Mahendravarman's seventh-century *Mattavilāsa* or Kṛṣṇāmiśra's eleventh-twelfth–century *Prabodhacandrodaya*, should be taken with caution, for they crystalized certain "Kāpālika stereotypes" that obscured some of the more complex aspects of the Kāpālika practice. Still, they do provide some insights into the original "Kāpālika practice" if corroborated with information drawn from the early Śākta and Śaiva textual sources, such as the *Jayadrathayāmala* and the *Brahmayāmala*.

In support of the accuracy of Bhavabhūti's description of the extraction of the five nectars as belonging to the original Kāpālika praxis, we have textual evidence from the Yoginīsaṃcāra section of the *Jayadrathayāmala* (*ṣaṭka* 3), which refers to the "procedure of the nectar" (*amṛtasya prayoga*) through the veins (*nāḍī*s) as part of the left-(hand) path (*vāmācāra*)—that is, the Kāpālika path. The yogin should install the mantras of Bhairava on his body

371. Alexis Sanderson, private conversation.

along with the fierce circles (*ugracakra*), having first killed an animal victim (*paśu*, in a sense of "uninitiated person"). Then he should begin the ritual. He should extract the nectar through the subtle veins (*nāḍī*). The successive arising, which is taking place through the *nāḍī*s, takes two *ghaṭika*s (forty-eight minutes).[372] One *ghaṭika* is 360 vital breaths (*prāṇa*s). The procedure ends with the dictum "Know that it is the cycle of time, which is difficult to obtain for those of left-handed conduct."[373] What follows thereupon is an even more detailed description of how to perform this extraction: "Having visualized the victim in front of him, he should visualize the spell syllable on the victim's head. He visualizes the syllable *phaṭ* together with *oṃ* and places it upon the imagined victim, visualizing him as black and hollow and as if sucking in the nectar. As he breathes in, he extracts the blood, which is the syllable *oṃ*." Then, the sādhaka imagines his own mouth as the vessel, which is the wind of great power. He makes [the wind] to rise up through the *nāḍī*s by the yoga of breath, and imagining what has filled his mouth, he gazes upon the vessel. In this procedure he extracts all vital essences one by one through the yoga of one's own *nāḍī*s.[374]

The five nectars as power substances are also used in tantric worship. Again, the Yoginīsaṃcāra section of the *Jayadrathayāmala* refers to the five nectars

372. One *ghaṭika* is 360 *prāṇa*s, and one *prāṇa* is four seconds. Therefore one *ghaṭika* is approximately twenty-four minutes.

373. Yoginīsaṃcāra section of *Jayadrathayāmala* 5.41–42 and 5.45–5.46:
ato devi pravakṣyāmi prayogam amṛtasya/
pūrvaṃ vinyasya deveśi sakalaṃ bhairavaṃ tanum// 41
ugracakratrayopetaṃ sarvakarmapradāyakam/
paśum ālabhya yatnena tataḥ karma samārabhet// 42
...
nāḍīcakrasya udayaṃ sūryacakrodayānugam/
ghaṭikādvayaṃ bhavet sārdham udayaṃ nāḍīṣu kramāt// 45
ghaṭikāṃ prāṇa<śa>tāni syuḥ trīṇi ṣaṣṭyuttarāṇi (em. *anta*, cod.) *tu/*
kālacakraṃ tu taṃ jñeyaṃ durlabhaṃ vāmakarmaṇām// 46

374. Yoginīsaṃcāra section of *Jayadrathayāmala* 5.53cd–57:
sādhya<ṃ> hi purato dhyātvā vidyā<ṃ> mūrdhani sādhakaḥ// 53cd
phaṭkāre guṇivasthena soṅkāraṃ yojayet tataḥ/
asitaṃ chidrarūpaṃ tu karṣayantam ivāmṛtam// 54
soṅkāraṃ karṣayed rakta<ṃ> pūrakena samīritaḥ/
vicintya vadanaṃ (em. *vaca*, cod.) *pātraṃ vāyubhūto mahābalaḥ//* 55
ānaye śvāsayogena ūrdhva<ṃ> nāḍiṣu yojitam/
āpūrya vadanaṃ devi tataḥ pātraṃ nirīkṣayet// 56
anenaiva vidhānena pañcānām api tatkṣaṇāt/
svanāḍīkarmayogena kuryād ākarṣaṇam (em. *ākarṣaṇe*, ms.) *budhaḥ//* 57

in the context of preparing the sacrificial pap (*caru*) that should be offered by the tantric practitioner to the deities in anticipation of the highest siddhis. The passage reads: "O goddess, having taken the five nectars in accordance with the Kula tradition, having properly prepared these *carus*, which will give the highest siddhis, he should offer it to the gods. After that, he should leave the sacrificial enclosure and cast to the ground a propitiating offering (*bali*) to various supernatural beings: *lāmās*, *cumbikās*, *cūṣikās*, and *pūtanās*. Equipped with great human nectars, the hero should also cast, in due order, ransom to the male demons, liquor, and meat. He should [request permission from these deities] to perform repetition of his own mantra (*japa*)."[375] The mere fact that these dangerous, wrathful deities are attracted by these powerful substances means that by offering these substances to them, one is able to obtain the highest siddhis from them.

With regard to the use of powerful substances in worship, the last part of the chapter 5 of the VBhT similarly refers to the offering of the two "nectars"—excrement and blood—in front of the Vajrabhairava painting if the practitioner desires the highest siddhi. The fact that these nectars attract wrathful deities may also be the reason for smearing the practitioner's body with them. In the description of entry into the Vajrabhairava maṇḍala (VBhT, chap. 1), which should be drawn as the cremation ground, the body of the sādhaka should be anointed with feces and urine. Similarly, in the *Guhyasamāja Tantra*, the efficacy of the ritual action seems to be dependent upon the cloth drenched in feces and urine that is worn during the aggressive rites (*abhicāra*): "Having worn a garment soaked in urine and feces, disgusting because of its appalling odor, he should then repeat the mantra until it dries. As soon as it dries, the victim will die."[376]

Another related context in which the five nectars appear in tantric texts as power substances is in their consumption, a practice attested in both the GS

375. Yoginīsaṃcāra section of *Jayadrathayāmala* 4.49cd–53:
gṛhya pañcāmṛtaṃ devi kulācārakrameṇa tu// 49cd
caruṃ susaṃskṛtaṃ kṛtvā mahāsiddhipradāyakam/
tatas tu sādhayitvā tu devatānāṃ nivedayet// 50
yāgabhūmau bahir (em. *yadir*, ms.) *gatvā prakṣipe<t> tu baliṃ tataḥ/*
lāmānāṃ cumbikānāṃ ca cūṣikā<ṃ> pūtanāṃ (em. *pūtanas*, ms.) *tathā//* 51
mahāmṛtasamāyukto bhūtānāṃ ca yathākramam/
prakṣipeta baliṃ vīro madyamāṃsasamanvitam// 52
mahā[...] *sthitvā anujñāṃ prārthayet tataḥ /*
tato japet svamantraṃ tu [...] // 53

376. GS 14.51, p. 68): *viṇmūtrārdragataṃ vastraṃ pūtigandhajugupsitam/ prāvṛtya mantram āvartec chuṣyate mriyate kṣaṇāt//*.

and VBhT.[377] The role they assume in this setting is either to help the sādhaka transcend the dichotomizing thought constructs of "pure and impure," or to grant the siddhi of a long, healthy, and ageless life. In this regard, Lalitavajra, while commenting upon the final part of chapter 4 of the VBhT, discusses each of the four nectars, one by one, and provides a specific ritual procedure for each. The result one can expect from consuming each of the nectars is the same—namely, long life without old age, as well as sexual prowess. Below is the description by Lalitavajra:

> "He should always abide in the cremation ground" and so on is taught as the method of consuming the [five] nectars [as follows:] On the evening of the first day of the waxing moon, making use of a virgin woman, he engages in sexual intercourse [with her] until the break of the next day without letting his semen fall into her vagina. Then he collects [the semen] with an iron vessel[378] before the heat does not fade away [from the semen]. Having drunk it through a straw for a day, or even if he has poured it into his mouth directly, he will have a long life and he will be free from aging; he will become similar to a hot vajra.[379]

377. Chapter 4 of the VBhT discussing the Vajrabhairava sādhana describes the following practice: "The fearless one, having sat himself up in the cremation ground and so on, should consume the five nectars continuously while meditating. [In this way] he accomplishes that means of mastering (*sādhana*) and not otherwise. Alternatively, the yogin devouring human flesh and so on and wandering at night recites the mantra consisting of three hundred thousand [syllables]. The mantra master who has done the recitation of the mantra performs all the rituals [successfully]." A similar "praxis" appears also in GS 17.47, although one "nectar" seems to be missing: "Let him not be disgusted by feces, urine, semen, or blood. He should always eat them, in accordance with the ritual prescription; this is the secret born of the three vajras" (*viṇmūtraśukraraktānāṃ jugupsāṃ naiva kārayet/ bhakṣayed vidhinā nityam idaṃ guhyaṃ trivajrajam/*. GS 17.47, p. 103).

378. A simlilar procedure for collecting the semen discharged after sexual intercourse into a vessel is attested in the *Kaulāvalīnirṇaya* of Jñānānanda Paramahaṃsa (5.81a–82a, quoted in White 2003, 219). The semen is afterward offered to the goddess, who quenches her thirst by drinking it. The sādhaka who does that will obtain everything he desires. This particular practice may also be referencing the *vajrolīmudrā*, in which the semen is collected into the tube, which is inserted into the urethra (see Mallinson 2018).

379. "Hot vajra" may be the sādhaka's sexual energy or the accumulation of energy that makes the body feel hot. I have not found any textual examples of a similar usage of this term, but the *Kaulajñānanirṇaya* 3.25 refers to a *liṅga* as a vajra: "This *liṅgam* is eternally erect, a *vajraliṅgam*, and may not be destroyed by raging fire, landslide, or torrent" (trans. Bagchi 1986, 7).

Also, on the first day of the waning moon, he finds a woman in menses. He generates lust by [knowledge of the] *Kāma Sūtra* and makes intercourse with her for three days, from evening till dawn. He mixes together the two fluids[380] [semen and menstrual blood or female sexual secretion], and he drinks it until the heat does not fade away or, alternatively, he drinks it through a straw for a day. [If he does that], the benefits will be similar to [what has been described] before.

He eats the correct measure of the three white foods and the three sweets every day, he scatters half the excrement that has come out [of him]. After three days, when the filth has dried, he retrieves the human excrement left there, and he mixes the powder of the [dry feces], the measure of a cat's paw, with milk. If he drinks it, he will become like that [that is, having a long life without aging and becoming like a hot vajra].

Having sliced the flesh of a hero who has won many battles [and] whose [flesh] has been offered to Death, who has passed away to a good land, he rolls it up, and he places it in the sealed clay bowl. That also he seals well with plaster. On the top of it, he kindles a fire, and the heat produces the fluid; [then] he collects it. If he drinks it, he will be similar [to what has been described above].

By forgoing the previous habit of consuming spicy meals, in the same manner as before, at midnight on the third night, he places in the vessel, which has three compartments, the urine and feces he has retrieved. When the three days have passed, he should smear himself with the first part. The middle part, he drinks. If he discards the last part, he will become like before.

Also, if he mixes the powder of the three fruits with the previous five nectars and eats it, or moreover, if he makes actual pills [out of it] and eats each of them, there will be a siddhi, without any doubt. This is the meaning.[381]

The first two rituals that rest upon the production of sexual fluids through the sexual activity (*melāpa*) reflect the typical *imaginaire* of the Kaula world,

380. The technical term for the combined male and female sexual fluids that appears in the Kaula tradition is *kuṇḍagolakodbhava*; see, for example, chap. 29 of Abhinavagupta's *Tantrāloka*.

381. Lalitavajra's *pañjikā*, 325–26.

where the worship of the yoginīs with sexual fluids reached its prime.[382] One of the most vivid examples is the ninth–tenth-century *Kaulajñānanirṇaya* attributed to Matsyendranātha (11.8–11), where the five nectars, including menstrual blood, semen, and blood, are part of a daily ritual (*nitya*) through which one becomes equal to the yoginīs. Chapter 18 of the same text (18.21) instructs about preparing the sacrificial pap (*caru*), which consists, among other things, of semen and blood that has to be consumed by a sādhaka in the course of a worship (*pūjā*), as this is the favorite oblation that can be offered to the siddhas and the yoginīs. Jayaratha's commentary (*viveka*) on the *Tantrāloka* 29.6–166 (see White 2003, 320) clearly states that by "merely eating [the fluid deposited in one's own body through the sexual intercourse], a man becomes immortal and praised as 'Śiva.' It is said in all the teachings that non-aging and immortality are afforded through the primary mouth that is the mouth of the yoginī." What is the mouth of the yoginī? Jayaratha explains that the genital region located at the base of the carnal vault of *suṣumnā* is the triangle at the foundation of birth, also called the mouth of the yoginī. "As it is stated, 'the supreme energy (*parāśakti*) in her coiled form [called *kuṇḍalinī*] rises up from the triangular sacred seat.'"[383] According to the *Jayadrathayāmala*, *kuṇḍalinī* releases its "nectar" in two places, in the upper place (*ūrdhva*), at the crown of the head, and in the lower place, in the region of the genitals. In both places, she emits a fluid equated with a seminal discharge, which flows out. By consuming this fluid, one becomes immortal, as the *Jayadrathayāmala* says, "The nectar that is the juice of *kuṇḍalī* comes out of his body. By just eating this, (yogins) become immortal and free of old age, wrinkles, white hair, and all diseases."[384]

In appropriating the Kaula ritual framework and the five nectars—the "signature" of the Yoginīkaula sect—the VBhT as well as the commentarial tradition represented by Lalitavajra betray the influence of non-Buddhist tantric traditions on the production of the root text and the adoption of specific Kaula practices into the Vajrabhairava sādhana. The *Jayadrathayāmala* and Jayaratha's commentary on the *Tantrāloka* envelop the consumption of the sexual fluids with the yogic praxis of rising the *kuṇḍalinī*, and thus represent a

382. White 2003 discusses this topic extensively in chapters 3 and 4.

383. *Tantrāloka* 3.94: *trikoṇam ity anena yoginīvaktrāparaparyāya—janmādhārarūpatvam apy asya sūcitam/ tata eva hi parā śaktir udeti—iti bhāvaḥ/ yad uktam—"yadollasati śṛṅgāṭapīṭhāt kuṭilarūpiṇī/" iti.*

384. *Jayadrathayāmala* 4.21.79–80: *tasya dehād viniṣkrāntam amṛtaṃ kauṇḍalīrasam* [*kh: kauṇḍilī- ; k: kauṇilī-*]/ *tena prāśitamātreṇa bhavanti hy ajarāmarāṃ/ valipalitanirmuktāṃ* [*k:-tanirmuktā*] *sarvavyādhivivarjitāṃ/.*

point in time when some strands of the Śākta ritual went in a direction of sublimating some of the hardcore practices by aligning them with a more sophisticated yogic nomenclature. This sophistication is missing in Lalitavajra's commentary, for its focus is merely on the use of the five nectars in the context of attaining some non-soteriological siddhis.

A different explanation of the same practice centered upon the consumption of transgressive substances is given in the context of *paṭasādhana*, or "protecting the painting." The VBhT (§52) gives a description of the different types of food and drink that should be consumed by the mantra master at night:

> The mantra master should protect the painting with full concentration, with effort. He should not set it up near anybody. Nor should he unroll it in front of anybody. During the night, continually, he should eat food that can be licked, drinks, food that needs to be chewed, and food that can be easily swallowed, such as human meat.

*Akṣobhya clarifies in his commentary that "although he [the mantrin] is alone, in order to keep [the practice] secret, as soon as people lie down at night, he eats the vow substances in order to remove the tiredness of the body."[385] *Akṣobhya seems to imply that the ingestion of the vow substances helps the sādhaka to stay vigilant at night and prevents him from falling asleep, which would jeopardize the praxis of safeguarding the painting. *Akṣobhya, who glosses the vow substances (*dam tshig gi rdzas*) as human flesh and vajra water (urine), and so on, acknowledges that consuming these substances and offering them in the pūjā is a part of the transgressive praxis (*ngan pa'i spyod pa*).[386] However, the explanation *Akṣobhya offers in order to validate their role in the Vajrabhairava sādhana is predicated upon the usage of these substances to facilitate the sādhaka's training in the praxis of pure mind.

*Akṣobhya elaborates on this praxis as follows:

385. For the Tibetan text, see note 869.

386. The "'vow substances' [means] human flesh and vajra water [urine], etc. 'As for this' [means] this [practice] indeed must be done with a pure mind"; *dam tshig gi rdzas zhes bya ba ni sha chen po dang rdo rje chu la sogs pa ste/ 'di ni re zhig sems sbyangs pas bya'o/*. *Akṣobhya's *ṭīkā*, 382.
"'Whoever desires the highest siddhi' [means] these transgressive acts (*duṣṭācārya*) should be performed with a pure mind and not otherwise"; *gang zhig dngos grub mchog 'dod pa/ zhes bya ba ni ngan pa'i spyod pa 'di dag ni sems dag pas bya'i gzhan du ma yin la*. *Akṣobhya's *ṭīkā*, 383.

> For the highest siddhis are obtained with a pure mind, but they are not [obtained] by enjoying these filthy things like a pig and so forth.[387]

The pure mind is the capacity to maintain equanimity between the disgusting substances—feces, urine, and so on—and the desirable objects of the senses (*kāmaguṇa*s) in order to transcend the polarized superimpositions we conventionally associate with them.[388] In equating the five nectars with the vow substances, *Akṣobhya comes close to Abhayākaragupta, who also refers to them as vow substances[389] and makes a similar argument in which the use of five nectars is the means to eradicate the impurity of thought constructs. In support of the need to transcend constructed thoughts, *Akṣobhya quotes (without attribution) the last verses from the *Pañcakrama* by the tantric Nāgārjuna (ninth–tenth century), a text associated with the Ārya school of Guhyasamāja, which says:

> As is oneself, so is an enemy; as is a wife, so is a daughter. As is a mother, so is a whore; as is an outcaste, so is a twice-born [a brahman]. As is cotton, so is leather; as is a jewel, so is chaff. As is urine, so is liquor; as is food, so is excrement. As is a sweet-smelling camphor,[390] so is a stink from an impure offering. As is praise, so is disparagement. In the same way, Vajrī [Vajradhara/Vajrapāṇi] and Rudra are not different. As is day, so is night; as is dream, so are things seen while awake; as is a thing lost, so is a thing retained. As is comfort, so is pain; as is a villain, so is a son. As is heaven, so is hell. Likewise is the difference between vice and virtue. Understanding reality in this way, if the gnostic per-

387. *Akṣobhya's *ṭīkā*, 383: *dngos grub chen po rnams ni sems dag pas thob kyi/ mi gtsang longs spyod pas ni ma yin te/ phag la sogs pa bzhin no/.*

388. "As for the 'pure mind,' it means to create equanimity between the [filthy things] and the desired object of the senses (*kāmaguṇas*): wine of *śāli* rice, human meat, perfume of excrement, incense of camphor [i.e., semen]"; *sems dag pa ni 'bras sā li'i* (corr. *lu*, ed.) *chang dang/ mi'i sha dang/ bshang ba'i dri dang/ ga bur gyi dri dag la 'dod pa'i yon tan du mnyam par 'gyur te/.* *Akṣobhya's *ṭīkā*, 383.

389. See, e.g., *Āmnāyamañjarī*, 296a. The *Abhayapaddhati* also contains passages examining the praxis of using the impure substances to eradicate the same negative thought constructs.

390. In the *Cakrasaṃvara Tantra* 1.11cd (ed. Gray 2012), we find a taxonomy of the five nectars and their corresponding code words, according to which "honey" means semen, "red" means blood, "camphor" means human meat, "red" (employed again) means urine, and "sandalwood" means excrement.

> forms everything without inhibition (*nirviśaṅka*), he is capable of everything. Having assumed the vow of disguise, he accomplishes all the secret practices, and he will obtain all good things.[391]

The foregoing passage highlights the importance of nondual gnosis (*advayajñāna*), the coveted goal of tantric Buddhist yogins, which aims at perceiving all things through the prism of equanimity, the type of cognition that penetrates through the illusion of the artificial thought constructs of "pure" and "impure." The consumption of the five nectars is a tool to reach that level of equanimity. Jñānaśrī explains that:

> ambrosias such as semen, blood, feces, urine, and human flesh, considering them void [of intrinsic reality] by the appropriate method and repeatedly considering those very things as if they were the divine ambrosia, if one enjoys them without passion, gradually concepts such as "pure" and "impure" will not arise. Then will arise the certain knowledge that different concepts that arise with regard to all things are false.[392]
>
> Whichever objects are considered impure [like] meat and ambrosias, those should be consumed without passion. When one sees [with] equanimous perception, one no longer needs to consume those for his/her own sake.[393]

391. *Pañcakrama* 5.30–35, pp. 53–54: *yathātmani tathā śatrau yathā bhāryā tathātmajā/ yathā mātā tathā veśyā yathā ḍoṃbī tathā dvijā// yathā vastraṃ tathā carma yathā ratnaṃ tathā tuṣam/ yathā mūtraṃ tathā madyaṃ yathā bhaktaṃ tathā śakṛt// yathā sugandhi karpūraṃ tathā gandham amedhyajam/ yathā stutikaraṃ vākyaṃ tathā vākyaṃ jugupsitam// yathā rudras tathā vajrī yathā rātris tathā divā/ yathā svapnaṃ tathā dṛṣṭaṃ yathā naṣṭaṃ tathā sthitam// yathā saukhyaṃ tathā duḥkhaṃ yathā duṣṭas tathā sutaḥ/ yathāvīcis tathā svargas tathā tu puṇyapāpayoḥ// evaṃ jñātvā carej jñānī nirviśaṅkas tu sarvakṛt/ pracchannavratam āsādya sidhyante sarvasampadaḥ//.*

392. Prof. John Newman (in personal communication) argues that rather than "false," the concepts of purity and impurity are "unreal." On the basis of Madhyamaka's distinction of two realities, the concepts of purity and impurity are phenomenally (*saṃvṛtyā*) real, but from the ultimate perspective, they are unreal (*mṛṣā*), because they vanish when subjected to ultimate analysis.

393. **Vajrayānāntadvayanirākaraṇa* ascribed to Jñānaśrī (fol. 19a), Toh. 3714, Bstan 'gyur, rgyud grel, *tsu*, 115b2, quoted in Wedemeyer 2012, 367. For other examples of the praxis that relies upon the consumption of five impure substances in order to remove thought constructs, see *Prajñopāyaviniścayasiddhi* 5.29–30 and *Guhyasiddhi* 6.8, both quoted in Tanemura 2009, 505–6.

There is no doubt that the tantric Buddhist concept of nondual knowledge as the ultimate goal of the tantric sādhaka that is reached through the consumption of transgressive substances, which had entered into tantric Buddhist discourse from the time of the *Guhyasamāja Tantra*, bears striking similarity to the Śaiva praxis of nonduality (*advaitācāra*). As has been explained by Sanderson (1995, 17), rituals involving contact with impure persons or/and substances were characteristic of the wider practice of nonduality (*advaitācāra*), which sought to transcend the Vedic notions of purity and impurity, typical of the dualistic observance. The *advaitācāra* involves consumption of those five nectars, often called "nondual substances" (*advaitadravyāṇi*), that were regarded as impure by Brahmanical orthodoxy. The practice itself was the means of liberating consciousness from the contraction (*saṃkoca*) or inhibition (*śaṅkā*) of dualistic thought constructs (*vikalpas*) distinguishing pure from impure, which holds it in bondage (Sanderson 1985, 198). As noted above, consuming the five nectars is a huge part of the Kālīkula worship inside the Śākta tantras of the *vidyāpīṭha* and related texts, including the Kaula texts.[394] Consumption of the five nectars also plays an important role in the Krama and Trika-Kaula initiation ritual (Sanderson 2005, 113), and they are also prescribed as part of the Buddhist tantric initiation in the *Laghuśaṃvara*, which according to Sanderson is based on passages from the *Yoginīsaṃcāra*. In the *Tantrāloka* (29.198cd), the guru is instructed to give the initiand a sacrificial pap (*caru*), which, as Jayaratha explains, consists of the five "jewels": urine (*śivāmbu*, lit. "Śiva's water"), semen (*retas*), menstrual fluid (*raktam*), phlegm (*nālājyam*), and feces (*viśvanirgamaḥ*).[395] The consumption of these substances is considered a test for the initiand's aptitude for the praxis of nonduality. If his hand trembles, he requires more training in the scriptures and the guru's instructions, as he is still not ready to forsake the notion of "pure" and "impure" that belongs to those of the ordinary perception rooted in differentiating thought constructs. However, if he eats those substances without hesitation, he is ready to be bestowed a ritual of initiation for the purpose of liberation (*nirvāṇadīkṣā*), because he has proved he has gone beyond the dichotomizing tendencies of ordinary consciousness.

The Śaivas were seemingly aware of the ritual use of transgressive substances by tantric Buddhists. Differently from them, they interpreted those substances not as means for reaching the nondual gnosis but as a test, one that would determine whether the mind is fickle or fixed. We know this from the

394. For the discussion of the five nectars in the Śaiva-Śākta tantras, see Sanderson 2005, 111–14.

395. Wallis 2008, 267.

fourteenth-century Jayaratha, commentator of Abhinavagupta's *Tantrāloka*, who in his discussion on the consumption of impure substances quotes two passages from Buddhist tantras, the first from Abhayākaragupta's *Vajrāvalī* and the second from the *Hevajra Tantra*:

> The Vedic sages too were like this with the nondiscriminating mentality, "like this" [meaning] maintaining this distinction between pure and impure as being on the basis of whether something is one with consciousness or is not one with consciousness. As it has been said there [in the *Vajrāvalī*]: "The Vedic sages of ancient times ate cow flesh and human flesh as well." Had they not been aware that purity is nothing other than the identity of the substances with consciousness, then how on earth could they have eaten stinks such as beef, which are outlawed by the scriptures and opposed to ordinary conduct? That is why these substances, which are opposed to both worldly and śāstric values, have been taught as means for getting rid of dualistic constructs in accordance with such statements as "In the practice of the outsiders [the Buddhists], the truth of what should be eaten by heroes is any substance that is hateful to the world, that is prohibited by the scriptures, and that is disgusting and condemnable." It is certainly because the fact that these substances are opposed by the scriptures and so on is not their real nature of all-inclusive consciousness. So what here could be disgusting or blameworthy if each is the same in being consciousness? For that reason, the purpose of consuming these things is simply to test the firmness of one's mind, to determine whether one's mind is one-pointed. As has been said by the Buddhists in the *Hevajra Tantra* [2.2.2]: "The ascetic discipline, which has been called the 'frightening practice' (*bhīmācāra*), has not been taught for the sake of enjoyment but to determine whether one's mind is firm or fickle."[396]

For *Akṣobhya, the highest siddhi is obtained when the sādhaka consumes the transgressive substances with a pure mind—that is to say, once the notion of duality that normally underlines ordinary perception is dissolved and the state of equanimity (*samatā*) is reached. This notion of equanimity propounded by *Akṣobhya is similar to the doctrinal positions on the consumption of five nectars advocated by Jñānaśrī and Abhayākaragupta. The Śaiva hermeneutical tradition of Abhinavagupta's Trika, where the notion of purity

396. *Tantrālokaviveka* 4.243cd.

of consciousness is similarly equated with the highest form of knowledge—that is, liberation—adopts the same framework of applying transgressive substances for similar purposes. Despite the obvious differences in the metaphysical formulations of the concept of consciousness/mind[397] in the Śaiva and Buddhist tantras, the usage of the five nectars as a praxis that helps to eradicate the superimposition of dichotomizing thought constructs appears to be quite similar in both traditions.

Maṇḍala Entry and Mad Laughter

Another practice that clearly shows Śaiva influence upon the development of the Vajrabhairava cult is given in chapter 1 of the VBhT, when the mantra master, while remaining in union with Vajrabhairava, enters the maṇḍala, which is the cremation ground, where Vajrabhairava resides for the duration of the ritual. This entry, heralded by the sounding of the rattle drum (*ḍamaru*) and boisterous "ha ha" laughter, which can be done either by a sādhaka alone or when he is accompanied by one or three assistants (*uttarasādhaka*s),[398] goes

397. For the discussion of similarities and differences of various concepts in Śaiva and Buddhist tantras, see Sferra 2003, 66–71.

398. The term *uttarasādhaka* (also *sahāya*) is used for an assistant of the sādhaka during his mantra sādhana. The term occurs often in the *Niśvāsottara* (4.34). The same term is used in Buddhist tantras for an assistant of a sādhaka or *vajrācārya*. In the *Sarvavajrodaya* (1.33, p. 30, line 2–4), we find: "The yogin should then be requested by all the *uttarasādhaka*s present who are endowed with *tathāgatahaṃkāraḥ* to draw the great maṇḍala." In chapter 11 of the *Caryāmelāpakapradīpa* (Wedemeyer 2007, 317), the *uttarasādhaka* is responsible for the food provision for the great sacrifice performed on lonely mountains, by pooling streams, in charnel grounds, etc. In the Jaina tantric text *Kumārapālaprabodhaprabandha* (paragraph 24), we find a reference to a yogin who asks the king Kumārapāla to be his *uttarasādhaka* in the ritual on Citrakūṭa performed on the fourteenth day of the dark fortnight (*kṛṣnacaturdaśī*). In paragraph 61 of the same text, the *uttarasādhaka* should be a woman of *padminī* kind (*padminī* refers to her sexual characteristics). In nonsectarian literary sources, such as Śivadāsa's *Vetālapañcaviṃśatikā*, we find a similar passage where a yogin wanders through the whole world in order to find a suitable *uttarasādhaka* for his *mṛtakavidhi* "corpse-ritual." Then, he asks the king to become his *uttarasādhaka*, which should guarantee the eightfold siddhis for the yogin (see Schmidt-Madsen 2014, 128). Another synonym of *uttarasādhaka* is *uparisādhaka*. The only references to this term are found in Kalhaṇa's "Chronicle of the Kings of Kashmir," *Rājataraṅgiṇī* (3.2.8 and 3.3.17). (I thank Alexis Sanderson for these references.)

In the *Picumata-Brahmayāmala*, the term *sakha* is used for the companion of a sādhaka during his mantra sādhana. For example, in BY 46.4, we find a passage describing the beginning of a sacrifice (*yāga*), where a sādhaka is surrounded by excellent companions (*sakhāyaiḥ śobhanair vṛtaḥ*). From another passage (46.52), it is clear that companions are

back to the Pāśupata tradition of mad laughter (*aṭṭahāsa*),[399] where it features as part of the vow of madness (*unmattavrata*) and the vow of Pāśupata (*pāśupatavrata*). The same description, but with additional Kāpālika elements, is repeated in chapter 5 of the VBhT (§51), where the sādhaka is instructed to be drawn "entering that cremation ground, carrying a rattle drum, a skull, a skull staff,[400] the top of their head adorned with a skull, laughing."

---

present throughout the duration of the *yāga*: "Having taken the offering (*bali*) at the center, he should eat it along with his companions. He should then gratify the goddess and the god with *picu* and wine" (*puramadhye baliṃ gṛhya sakhāyaiḥ saha bhakṣayet/ picunā madireṇaiva devīdevāṃ sa tarpayet//*). In another passage (46.3), we find information that matches the above description of the VBhT except that companions are optional; the sādhaka can also go alone: "The one observing the great vow (*mahāvrata*) should go at night to the cremation ground, taking with him the full equipment for worship and either accompanied by excellent companions or on his own" (*gatvā niśi* [corr. *nisi*, ms.] *śmaśānan* [corr. *smasānan*, ms.] *tu yāgopaskarasaṃbhṛtaḥ/ sakhāyais śobhanair* [corr. *sobhanair*, ms.] *yukta eko vātha mahāvrataḥ//*).

399. *Aṭṭahāsa*, the practice of "mad laughter" goes back to the Pāśupata tradition, being prescribed in the *Pāśupata Sūtra* and its commentary *Pañcārthabhāṣya* attributed to Kauṇḍinya (fourth–fifth century), where it constitutes one of the conducts adopted by the Pāśupata ascetics of the Atimārga during the worship of the Lord, together with dancing, singing, sleeping and bathing in ashes, wearing the garlands offered to the gods (*nirmālya*), and imitating the conduct of the bull (*Pāśupata Sūtra* 1.8; see Acri 2018, 5). The antinomian context of these practices, regarded as inappropriate for orthodox brahmans, had as its purpose the imitation of the conduct of Śiva by enacting his deeds. For instance, in the Anuśāsanaparvan of the *Mahābhārata* (13.14.84d), Śiva enacts all the conducts associated with the vow of madness (*unmattavrata*) of the Pāśupatas mentioned in the *Pāśupata Sūtra* 1.8. These behaviors were also meant to garner the practitioner the label of a "madman" (*unmatta*) by the people, who would feel disgust at such vivid transgression of social rules. This behavior "inviting abuse" was believed to facilitate the "transfer of karma" (Ingalls 1962, 293), as a result of which people would give the Pāśupata ascetic their good karma and take his bad karma. In the NTGS (3.30–33), "mad laugther" is part of the *gaṇavrata*, where a person conducting the Pāśupata observance imitates the troupes (*gaṇas*) of Śiva: "He dances, he sings, crazy, he laughs as he speaks, smeared with ashes, and wearing rags; this is the *gaṇavrata*" (*nṛtyate gāyate caiva unmatto hasate bruvan/ bhasmāṅgī cīravāsaś ca gaṇavratam idaṃ smṛtam*). This passage follows the description of the cremation ground observance (*śmaśānavrata*) in the same text (3.28–29), where we learn: "Carrying a *khaṭvāṅga*, smeared with ashes, he should roam about in the cremation ground at night, this is said to be a cremation ground *vrata*" (*khaṭvāṅgī bhasmaguṇṭhitaḥ/ śmaśāne carate rātrau śmaśānavrata*[*ṃ*] *ucyate*). Similar association of the *aṭṭahāsa* with *gaṇavrata* is given in the *Niśvāsamukha* (1.166–1.167b) where "playing of the lute (*tantrīvādya*), bellowing (*huḍukkāra*), dancing (*nṛtya*), performing the mouth-sound (*mukhavādya*) and boisterously laughing (*aṭṭahāsa*) confer the status of *gaṇa*" (Acri 2018, 6).

400. The *khatvāṅga*, the ascetic skull-topped staff, is an attribute of Śaiva practitioners, who carry it as a penance for killing a brahman, thus imitating the conduct of Śiva or

Tantric Buddhist deities are also often associated with "mad laughter." In the *Laghuśaṃvara* (2.15–16), we find the main deity to be installed in the maṇḍala is referred to as *vīraṃ mahābhairavabhīṣaṇam*, "the Hero who is the terror of Mahābhairava" (Gray 2007a, 167), who is also the "great roar of mad laughter" (*aṭṭahāsamahāravaṃ*).[401] Mañjuśrī, in his form as Vajrabhairava, is labeled in the MNS with several appellations linked to "mad laughter" (see Wayman 1985, 83). Also, Yamāntaka is described as "the one who roars the mad laughter" (*aṭṭahāsanādine*), as reported in the Yamāntaka mantra attested in the GS (14.9–11) and MMK (52.28, p. 450). This appellation is preceded by "he causes fear to all the demons" (*sarvabhūtabhayaṅkara*).

The reason to translate *sarvabhūta* as "all demons" rather than "all beings" depends on the role that *aṭṭahāsa* assumes in tantric traditions—namely, subjugation of demonic and other dangerous beings. This is attested in the *Brahmayāmala*, where the practice of mad laughter is associated with the subjugation of *bhūta*s, *rākṣasa*s, and *śākinī*s, often residing in the cremation grounds, thus betraying an association with the early exorcistic, pre-Mantramārgic tradition that survived both in Śaiva and in Buddhist tantras.[402] The *Brahmayāmala* (87.119cd) says: "The learned one should stick his tongue out (*jihvāṃ lālayet*), wiggle it about, and make a sound 'ha ha' (*hāhākāraṃ tu kārayet*). By these sounds all *guhyaka*s, *rākṣasa*s, and so on, are destroyed. As soon as they see him, they come under his power; the

Bhairava, who is said to have cut off the head of Brahmā. For the origins of the *khatvāṅga* in the Dharmaśāstra, and its earlier connotations of a "bedpost," see Brick 2012.

401. See Sanderson 2009, 204. For the theme of laughter, see also chapter 42 of *Laghuśaṃvara* in Gray 2007a, 338–42.

402. The textual evidence of "laughter" as the conduct associated with exorcistic practices—i.e., subduing of the demons—is attested outside of the tantric tradition in the *Devīmāhātmya* (ca. fifth–sixth century; Kinsley 1978, 490), a popular Purāṇic text that is considered to be a part of the *Mārkaṇḍeya Purāṇa*. This text, which Coburn (1991) believes to have been derived from non-Āryan traditions, exerted considerable influence upon the "subjugation of the Maheśvara myth" narrated in the STTS, as argued by Iyanaga (1985) and Linrothe (1999). Minutes before the epic battle between the goddess Durgā and the demons (*asura*s) begins, the form of Caṇḍikā appears, "bellowing with laughter again and again" (*Devīmāhātmya* 2.31, Coburn 1991, 42). As a result of this, "the entire atmosphere is filled with her terrible noise," oceans and earth begin to tremble, etc. In another passage (8.37, Coburn 1991, 66), we learn that demons are shattered by the cruel laughter of Śivadūtī and fall to the ground as she gobbles them up. The function of "laughter" is to create terror—heralding, as it were, the upcoming havoc—and to destroy the demons. Similarly, when the *śakti* Caṇḍikā emerges from the body of the goddess Durgā, she is described as "gruesome and yelping like a hundred jackals" (2.31, Coburn 1991, 64). For the importance of the jackal's cry in tantric traditions, see, note 409 below.

*bhūta*s along with the *śākinī*s come under his power."[403] The fourth *ṣaṭka* of the same *Jayadrathayāmala* (4.2.588), in a passage on the mudrā of fangs (*daṃṣṭramudrā*), gives a similar description: "He should move his tongue at a speed, while uttering a 'ha ha' sound. He should issue a terrifying laughter" (*jihvaṃ sañcarayet vegāt, hāhākāraṃ samundanam/ aṭṭahāsaṃ nadet ghoram* [...]).

In accord with the *Jayadrathayāmala*, the VBhT's commentators agree that the "*hāhākāra*" the sādhaka has to utter upon entry into the cremation-ground maṇḍala denotes the eight types of laughter. In addition, *Kṛṣṇācārya says that the sādhaka should do the eight types of laughter—"ha, hi," and so on—in order to remove impediments.[404] The Tibetan tradition[405] also accounts for the eight types of laughter (four syllable pairs): threatening laughter "ha ha" (*sdigs pa'i gad mo ha ha*), gleeful laughter "he he" (*dgyes pa'i gad mo he he*), enticing laughter "hi hi" (*sgeg pa'i gad mo hi hi*), and subjugating laughter "ho ho" (*zil gyis gnon pa'i gad mo ho ho*). That the *hāhākāra* is linked to the subjugation of demons is preserved in the Tibetan tradition. In the myth section on the origins of the deity Vajrabhairava preserved in the Tibetan canon (Siklós 1996, 64), we read that Vajrabhairava "overpowered the great *māra* (*bdud*) by roaring 'Ha ha hi hi.'"[406]

According to Alexis Sanderson,[407] most of the tantric Buddhist mantras containing the characteristic string of *ha, he, hi* syllables placed in the middle derive from early exorcistic tradition that infiltrated Śaivism and later passed to tantric Buddhism. The early Śaiva text *Niśisaṃcāra*, which survives in a Nepalese palm-leaf manuscript, gives plenty examples of such combinations. For example, the mantra used for the preparation of the skull seat (*kapālāsanamantra*) has a characteristic string of "laughing" syllables embedded within the main mantra: *oṃ hrīṃ hūṃ he ha phaṭ*. Similarly, the mantra

403. BY 87.119cd–20: *jihvāṃ* [em. Sanderson, *jihvā*, ms.] *tu lālayet prajño* [em. Sanderson, *prajñā*, ms.] *hāhākāraṃ* [em. Sanderson, *hāhākāran*, ms.] *tu kārayet/ tasya śabdena naśyante guhyakā rakṣasādayaḥ/ dṛṣṭvā tu vaśam āyānti bhūtāḥ śākinibhiḥ saha/*. I thank Prof. Alexis Sanderson for this reference.

404. For the Tibetan text, see page 218 below.

405. The Rangjung Yeshe *Tibetan-English Buddhist Dictionary*, https://rywiki.tsadra.org/index.php/khro_bo%27i_bzhad_pa_brgyad quoted in Siklós 1996, 38n64, as four types of heroic laughter (*vīrahasya*).

406. The same is conveyed in the Vajrabhairava origins myth narrated by A mes zhabs when Vajrabhairava arrives to the fourteen sādhana places and, uttering "ha ha," binds under oath different beings; see page 73 above.

407. Alexis Sanderson, private conversation.

for pleasing the spirits (*toṣaṇamantra*), used universally in the exorcistic rituals, has a similar form: *Ha ha ha hā hi hi hu hu he he ha ho ḥau haṃ haḥ*. The scriptures of tantric Buddhism,[408] especially those belonging to the yoginī tantras, provide similar examples. For example, Ānandagarbha's *Vajrajvālodayā*, which is based upon the *Sarvabuddhasamāyoga*, gives the following heart mantra (*hṛdayamantra*) of Heruka: *Ha ha ha hā rulu rulu hūṃ*. The common mantra (*sāmānyamantra*) of the same deity is: *Ha ha ha hā rulu rulu hūṃ*.

The use of laughter to summon and control spirits residing in cremation grounds evident in the sādhanas described in both Śaiva and Buddhist tantras, as quoted above, and in the ritual employment of the mantras is ideologically linked to the entire range of tantric concepts and teachings predicated on the accumulation and control of transgressive power. The tantric texts also employed a number of other techniques that served similar purposes, such as the jackal's cry,[409] which reflects the same symbolism of inauspiciousness and transgression that is paramount to the success of tantric sādhana.

408. The STTS contains plenty of examples of mantras with "laughing syllables," e.g., *vajrasūkṣmakrodhamahāsakrodha ha ha ha ha hūṃ phaṭ* (STTS, p. 227, line 6), *oṃ vajrāṭṭahāsani hasa hasāṭṭāṭṭahāsena* [*māraya jiḥ*] (STTS, p. 215, line 1), and *oṃ padmāṭṭahāsaikadaśamukha haḥ haḥ haḥ haḥ huṃ* (STTS, p. 323, line 14).

409. Paralleling the praxis of laughter is the sounding of a jackal's cry performed by the sādhaka during his mantra sādhana. The jackal's cry reflects the symbolism of inauspiciousness that augurs misfortune, reference to which is found already in the *Atharva Veda* (Ohnuma 2019, 3). In the *Mānavadharmaśāstra* (4.115), it is prescribed that brahmans should not recite the Vedas when the jackal howls (Taylor 2007, 57). Jackals are distinctively associated with cremation grounds and necrophagy, and they participate in the symbolism of impurity together with crows, dogs, and vultures (Ohnuma 2019, 2). The association of the jackal with transgression and inauspiciousness is perhaps why his cry was adopted in the sādhana delineated in the *Brahmayāmalatantra*, where we find the following description (46.3–4ab): "The heroic sādhaka who has mastered the tantra, who is established in the *mahāvrata* body, should enter the great wilderness [i.e., the cremation ground] after adopting the aforesaid installation of the mantras. Letting loose the cry of a jackal, facing Bhairava [. . .], [he should begin the ritual]" *tantrajño* [em. *tantrajñānaḥ*, ed.] *sādhako* [em. *sādhakaḥ*, ed.] *vīraḥ mahāvratatanusthitaḥ/ pūrvvoktanyāsayogena praviśeta mahāvanaṃ// śivārāvaṃ pramuñcanto bhairavābhimukhasthitaḥ/*. In BY 46.38cd–39ab we come across a similar passage: "Having worshiped them [the goddesses] according to the ritual procedure, he should then rattle his *ḍamaru*, and he should make the jackal's cry" *evaṃ pūjya yathānyāyaṃ pūrvvokavidhicoditaṃ// ḍamarukaṃ vādayet paścāc chivārāvāṃ pramuñcatāṃ/*.

7. Early Tantric Magic

When we examine examples of magical procedures (*karma*s) in the VBhT, we soon realize that there is a collection of recipes presenting common areas of interest and practice with other early Śaiva and Buddhist tantras (Wenta 2024), especially with an early Buddhist kriyā tantra, the *Mañjuśriyamūlakalpa* (MMK), as well as with the Śaiva *Guhyasūtra* (NTGS) of the *Niśvāsatattvasaṃhitā*, a text that not only asserts a continuity between the Atimārga and the Mantramārga traditions of Śaivism but also provides a linkage between pretantric and tantric Śaiva soteriology and non-Śaiva, non-soteriological magic found in the Buddhist kriyā tantras (Goodall and Isaacson 2011, 125). The periods of compilation and textual layering of the MMK and *Guhyasūtra* can be traced back to the time between the sixth and the eighth centuries.

Magical procedures can be classified according to the magical techniques they employ—paralyzing (*stambhana*), driving away (*uccāṭana*), and so on—or according to the field of their application: combat magic, "love" magic, neutralization of poison, and so on. This simply means that the same technology can be applied in different contexts. For instance, *stambhana* can be used in "love" magic to paralyze a maiden but also in combat magic to stop the army from attacking the kingdom.

The capacity to execute magical recipes is regarded as siddhi, or accomplishment. The siddhis are usually classified into three categories: low, intermediate, and highest.[410] In accordance with this division, an early Śaiva Siddhāntantra, the *Kiraṇa Tantra* (in its earlier Nepalese recension) refers to lower (*adhamā*), middling (*madhyamā*), and highest (*uttamā*) siddhis (50.13ab–14cd).[411] The *adhamā* siddhis include the category of aggressive magic, such as subjecting to one's will (*vaśīkaraṇa*), creating dissent (*vidveṣa*), and paralysis (*stambhana*). The *madhyamā* siddhis are the obtainment of a magical sword (*khaḍga*), often

410. For an analysis of siddhi classification in the Śaiva tantric traditions, see Vasudeva 2012.

411. *Kiraṇa Tantra* 50.13ab: *uttamā madhyamās siddhīr* (em. *siddhir*) *adhamāś ca śṛṇuṣvataḥ*. Quoted in Vasudeva 2012, 266.

from a zombie (*vetāla*), collyrium (*āñjana*), and *bilottha*, which is the ability to enter into the underworld through caves. The highest siddhi is *lokāloke tu yāyitvaṃ*, moving freely through all the worlds.[412] The tripartite division described above also occurs, with slight variations, in a number of early Śaiva and Śākta scriptures—namely, the *Siddhayogeśvarīmata*, the *Svacchanda Tantra*, and the *Picumata-Brahmayāmala* (Vasudeva 2012, 266–67),[413] as well as in the Buddhist tantras (*Susiddhikara Sūtra*; see Giebel 2001, 191–92).

Despite containing different classifications of the highest and intermediate siddhis, the early tantras seem to agree that aggressive magic (*abhicāra*),[414] which includes subjugation under one's will (*vaśya*), paralyzing (*stambhana*), and so on, belongs to the category of low siddhis. The same understanding is attested in the commentary of *Akṣobhya, where such karmas as subduing, summoning, and so on are described as belonging to the category of *kṣudra-* or low- siddhis. *Akṣobhya states that "all siddhis refers to low ones. Such siddhis are [low] for ordinary people. For the sādhakas, such acts are called salvific activity."[415] What *Akṣobhya seems to be saying is that siddhis mean different things for different categories of adepts. For the ordinary people (that includes

412. For an explanation of *lokāloke* in the context of Śaiva and Purāṇic mythology, see Vasudeva 2012, 267.

413. The second *ṣaṭka* of the Śākta scripture *Jayadrathayāmala* (3.49–54) gives a different list of the three siddhis—namely, *sāmānya* (or low-level siddhis), which include *vaśya, ākarṣaṇa, vidveṣa, māraṇa, uccāṭana, śānti* (averting evil), *puṣṭi* (rites to restore health), finding treasures, concocting elixirs, curing poison, exorcising demons, fever, insanity, and producing rain; *madhyamā* siddhis, which include becoming invisible, having a *paṭa, rasa, yakṣiṇī-siddhi*, sword, preventing eclipses, mastery over *kṛtyās, vetāla*s, *bhūta*s, etc.; *uttamā* siddhis, which include entering into the underworld (*pātāla*), flying through the sky, clairvoyance, clairaudience, mind reading, siddhis of the yoga tradition (*aṇimā*, etc.), and union with the goddess. *Jayadrathayāmala* 2.3.49–54 (fol. 131r9–v3): *vaśyakarṣaṇavidveṣamāraṇoccāṭanādikam/ śāntiḥ puṣṭikriyā* [conj. *puṣṭiḥkriyā*, cod.] *dhātukhanyavādaṃ rasāyanam// viṣabhūtajvaronmādadhvaṃsanaṃ* [conj. *onmādaṃ*, cod.] *meghanigrahaḥ/ evamādyā siddhayaś ca sāmānyāḥ* [corr. *sāmānyā*, cod.] *sādhakātmanām// antardhānaṃ paṭaṃ khaḍgaṃ rasaṃ caiva rasāyanam/ yakṣiṇīsiddhir atulā divyagrahanivāraṇam// kṛtyāvetālabhūtānāṃ kiṃkarādiprasādhanam/ eṣā sā madhyamā siddhir vyākhyātā sādhakasya hi// uttamāḥ siddhayo* [corr. *uttamā siddhiyo*, cod.] *jñeyāḥ* [corr. *jñeyā*, cod.] *pātālākāśasādhanam/ dūrācchravaṇavijñānaṃ darśanaṃ sparśanaṃ tathā// aṇimādiguṇāvāptir devyāmelāpam uttamam/ evamādyaṃ tu saṃjñeyaṃ sādhakasya mahātmanaḥ//*. I thank Alexis Sanderson for this reference; all emendations to the text are his.

414. The *abhicāra* category further expanded into six karmas (*ākarṣaṇa, vaśīkaraṇa, stambhana, māraṇa, vidveṣaṇa*, and *uccāṭana*); these constitute the so-called six acts (*ṣaṭkarmāṇi*). Additional categories were eventually added, e.g., *jvara* or *unmādana*.

415. *Akṣobhya's *ṭīkā*, 373: *dngos grub thams cad ces bya ba ni phra mo rnams te/ de dag ni*

the non-Buddhists), siddhis bring accomplishment of worldly ends, while for the sādhakas the same siddhis are the means to effect the liberation of sentient beings.

Combat Magic

One area of interest in magical recipes is military purposes. These can be classified under the heading "combat magic." Given that much of tantric repertoire was designed for kings who engaged in warfare, the existence of such magical procedures is understandable. Different types of combat magic are found in tantric texts. One is averting evil (*śānti*) meant to bring peace to a place at war or neutralize a soldier attacking with a weapon. Despite the great emphasis placed on the apotropaic role of tantric officiating priests (*rājagurus*) engaged in rituals to protect the kingdom, early tantric texts contain very few rituals that would actually confirm their defensive purpose. For example, the VBhT (§60) gives only one *homa* procedure for the *śānti* ritual that protects the kingdom from being attacked by an enemy king (see p. 295). The early Śaiva tantra of the Vāmasrotas (Törzsök 2016, 137) the *Vīṇāśikha* also provides one *śānti* procedure to bring about the pacification of a person who is about to attack by discharging his weapons.[416] Thus, at least in the light of the content of the magical rituals themselves, there is not much evidence that tantric masters (*ācāryas*) composed the tantras having in mind the protection of kings from evil. If they had, we would surely find a greater number of *śānti* rituals reflecting that purpose, especially since, as Geslani (2018) has demonstrated, in the *Atharvavedapariśiṣṭas*, "*śānti* has matured into a central theme of Atharvan discourse."[417]

Another type of magical technique used specifically in combat magic was

dngos grub tu bzhag pa phal pa rnams kyi yin la/ grub pa rnams kyi ni phrin las bzhag pa yin pa'o. I thank John Newman for this clarification.

416. See *Vīṇāśikha Tantra* (181–82), in Goudriaan 1985, 116. An early Buddhist tantra, the *Siddhaikavīra* (1.14), also contains a recipe that prevents the discharge of an enemy's weapons through *stambhana* and not *śānti*. This is accomplished when one writes a mantra in saffron and wears it on either one's neck or one's arm.

417. Geslani (2018, 99) has demonstrated that from the time of the *Kauśika Sūtra* through the *Śāntikalpa*, there was a gradual promotion of *śānti* rituals as the primary specialization of the *purohitas* (whose function, according to Sanderson, was subsumed by the tantric *rājagurus*), which reached its peak in the *Atharvavedapariśiṣṭas*. Much earlier, the *Arthaśāstra* also acknowledges the fact that *śānti* belonged to the specific expertise of magic specialists called *siddha ascetics* (*siddhatāpasī*), who are twice referred to as those engaged in the pacification rites (*śāntika*; 4.3.13 and 4.3.25).

paralysis, or *stambhana*. An example of that is given in the NTGS (3.105cd–6cd), where an interesting recipe for a spell causing the paralysis of an army (*senāstambhana*) is given: *kālayukto yadā mantras trayodaśakalāhataḥ/ stambhayet sarvasainyāni sarvaduṣṭāni caiva hi*, "If the *mantra* is conjoined with time (*ma*) and is surmounted by the thirteenthth *kalā* (*o*), (if it's *hmoṃ*), then he can paralyze, stop any army and all wicked beings." The recipes for the *senāstambhana* were circulating also in the seventh- and the eighth-century Buddhist tantras,[418] such as the MMK, the *Amoghapāśakalparāja*, and the *Siddhaikaivīra*.[419]

In the *Siddhaikavīra*, for example, the adept writes the mantra on a rag taken from a cremation ground, customized with the names of the commanders of the opposing army in the center of a double vajra. Outside the double vajra, he writes eight *laṃ* (the *bīja* mantra of earth) and, outside of these, the maṇḍala of Indra. The mantra should then be placed in the belly of a Gaṇapati made of beeswax adorned with the double vajra. When it is buried next to the opposing army, it will stop the army.[420]

The *senāstambhana* also constitutes, for example, the main topic of chapter 8 of the Śaiva *Kakṣapuṭa Tantra* attributed to the siddha Nāgārjuna, who is usually dated somewhere between the seventh and tenth centuries. Despite its Buddhist author, the text contains no Buddhist features, and "most of the references are cited from the Hindu tantras" (Yamano 2013, 63).

Another magical technique used in combat magic is driving away (*uccāṭana*). The NTGS (3.94ab–5ab) provides us with the following recipe:

> *bhasmanā snāpayet liṅgan tad bhasma punar eva hi/*
> *liṅgasyopari dattvā tu hastaṃ dattvā tato japet //*
> *śīghram uccāṭayec chatruṃ mahāduṣṭo 'pi yo bhavet/*

He should first bathe a *liṅga* with ash, and then he should again

418. The paralysis of wicked beings through magical means, preventing a person from engaging in violent combat, is a favorite in the repertories of tantric siddhas in the Tibetan Buddhist tradition. One illustration is given in Tāranātha's *Gshin rje chos 'byung* (p. 118), which narrates the story of Amoghavajra Junior, a guru of Zhang Lo tsā ba, who took part in the transmission of Vajrabhairava-Yamāntaka cycle from India to Tibet. One day, when he was crossing the mountain in the Stong lung district, a horde of bandits appeared. When they tried to climb the mountain, he used his threatening finger, and they froze (*rengs*). Without resorting to fighting, he passed safely.

419. For a general discussion on "war magic" in Buddhism, see Sinclair 2014.

420. *Siddhaikavīramahātantrarājaḥ*, Toh. 544. See §1.16 of the translation by the Dharmachakra Translation Committee at 84000.co, last accessed April 10, 2019.

> place that ash upon the *liṅga* and put his hand on that and recite the mantra. He will quickly expel his enemy, even if he [the sādhaka] is a great sinner.

The aforesaid recipe can be interpreted in two ways: it can mean either that one causes the enemy to flee in panic or that one makes an army flee in battle. The latter meaning is also attested in chapter 9 of the *Kakṣapuṭa Tantra* (Yamano 2013, 65).

Unlike the practices linked to Yamāntaka described in the MMK, which are dedicated solely to the destruction of the king's enemy,[421] recipes for military combat do not feature in the VBhT. This fact is especially interesting considering that later adoptions of the Vajrabhairava-Yamāntaka cult, especially in China, already discussed in chapter 1, consistently associate him with the combat magic employed in the context of political warfare.

"Love" Magic

Another cluster of recipes can be classified as "love" magic. Judging from the contents of magical formularies, it becomes evident that "love" magic has nothing to do with romance or inducing feelings of love in the desired woman and rather aims at attracting a woman for the sole purpose of sexual intercourse. This gives us some indications of what men in medieval India looked for in tantric magic—namely, an instrument for satisfying their sexual desires. One of the crudest technologies for coercing a woman into sex was called *kanyāstambhana*, or "paralysis of a maiden," part of the standard repertoire of magic in Buddhist tantras (see, e.g., GS 15.19 and VBhT §34).

The following example of *kanyāstambhana* comes from the VBhT:

> Next is a procedure for paralyzing a girl. He should draw with poison and the rest the yantra of Yamāri on a rag taken from the

421. MMK 51.35–37ab, p. 433: "When the repetition of the mantra is done at midnight in the presence of the [Yamāntaka] *paṭa*, [then] the same thing will happen for the destruction of the enemies. His kingdom will be destroyed, and there will be an outbreak of plague in his army. Bad omens—the sky as if ablaze, a hurricane, or excessive rainfall—[will happen]. The whole of the army of the enemy will be lost." *ardharātre yadā jāpaḥ kriyate paṭasannidhau/ śatrūṇāṃ ca vadhārthāya tat tathaivānuvartate// 35 rāṣṭrabhaṅgaṃ bhavet tasya senāyāṃ mārisambhavam/ agnidāhaṃ mahāvātaṃ mahāvṛṣṭiś ca jāyate// 36 samastaṃ sarvataś cakraṃ paracakreṇa hanyate/ 37ab.*

> cremation ground. Having made an effigy [of the target] using charcoal from the cremation pyre, he should make [an image of] the Hideous One measuring one span. He should place [the effigy] in its heart. Having pressed down on the yantra with his left foot and while maintaining meditative union with the Buffalo-Faced One, he should then repeat the ten-syllable mantra, [formulating his purpose in these words:] "May I quickly paralyze girl X." [If he does that,] he will [indeed] paralyze her.[422]

*Akṣobhya (p. 378) comments that "to paralyze a maiden" means "through the activities of intoxication in order to experience whatever pleasure he wishes" (*bu mo rmongs par bya ba ni/*[423] *myos par bya bas ci dgar longs spyad par bya ba'i phyir ro*). *Akṣobhya's explanation clearly conveys that the ritual is meant to have an effect similar to a contemporary date-rape drug, acting as an incapacitating agent to render a woman or girl vulnerable to sexual assault. This ritual relies on the principle of sympathetic magic. A maiden is represented by an effigy, which is used for an imitative operation symbolizing a violent act—paralysis. An effigy is placed in a position subordinate to another image, representing Vajrabhairava. After establishing himself in meditative union with Vajrabhairava, the mantra master steps on the yantra device and recites the mantra, customized with the magical formula *śīghram amukāṃ kanyāṃ stambhayāmi iti*. The whole sequence is intended to inflict paralysis on the target's image (the effigy) so that a corresponding paralysis will afflict the girl as a means for raping her.

The masculine nature of tantric magic, made vivid by its focus on the sexual conquest of women, is mirrored in another recipe involving a technique of visualization to make a woman sexually excited, even if she is far away. The intensity of her sexual desire is expressed by a simile in which she (or rather her vagina) "drips wet as a sap-rich tree" (*strīyaṃ drāvayati kṣīriṇavṛkṣam iva drāvayati*). The VBhT (§83) provides the following recipe:

> Next [is given] the meditation procedure for getting a woman sexually aroused from a distance. Having visualized the target in front of him, he should visualize at her feet the bow-shaped wind maṇḍala, gray in color and empowered by the syllable *yaṃ*. Above that,

422. See the translation on page 240.

423. The Tibetan gives *rmongs par bya ba*, which suggests the Sanskrit *mohayet*, "stupefy." But *Akṣobhya clearly glosses *stambhayet*, "paralyze," which means that there is a mistake in the Tibetan transmission of the text.

> in the region of the genitals, he [should visualize] a three-cornered fire maṇḍala empowered by the syllable *ra* [fire] on top. Above that, in the heart, he should visualize the earth maṇḍala, which is yellow, square, and empowered by the syllable *laṃ*. Above that, on the forehead, he should visualize the moon maṇḍala. In the middle of that, he should visualize nectar flowing down with the letter *vaṃ* [the water syllable]. Having carefully visualized in this manner, he should fan the fire with the wind, making it blaze up. [Then,] he imagines the earth maṇḍala is heated up by this fire. He visualizes that that nectar disc is melting from the heat of the earth maṇḍala. By this mere procedure, he causes the woman to become moist, making her drip like a sap-rich tree, and not otherwise.[424]

*Akṣobhya's commentary elaborates on this technique by saying that it functions as the *vaśīkaraṇa* recipe (bringing a woman under one's own power). For him, filling a woman with sexual desire operates on two levels, mental and physical: she becomes enthralled as soon as her body drips wet with her great desire.[425] This obsessive passion gives her no respite until she yields to her yearning.

The techniques for "love" magic mentioned so far resemble the methods for magical procurement of wives prominent in the *yakṣinī* sādhanas, which play an important role in tantric magic. *Yakṣiṇīs* or *yakṣīs* are mythical beings common to Hindu, Buddhist, and Jaina traditions. In their outward appearance, *yakṣiṇīs* are meant to epitomize the ideal of feminine beauty. They are depicted as curvaceous and sexually attractive, a kind of Barbie doll with wide hips, narrow waists, and large, round breasts. Perhaps owing to their physical attractiveness, *yakṣiṇīs* are characterized in tantric magic as trophy wives of sorts, but in their actual role, they are little more than sexual playthings. Both Śaiva and Buddhist tantras (including the VBhT) regard mastery over the *yakṣiṇīs* as one of the *vidyādhara*'s coveted siddhis.

The sexual objectification of *yakṣiṇī* wives, who are valued as objects for fulfilling male sexual desire, is apparent in the NTGS (10.81ab–84ab), which provides the following rite of subjugation of a *śalabhañjikā*, which is a type of *yakṣiṇī*:

424. Siklós's translation (1996, 48) of this recipe from Tibetan and Mongolian misses the point when he says, "Merely by this practice that woman melts. Like the sacred fig tree, it will doubtless melt."

425. See note 963 below.

> Having made a doll of a *śalabhañjikā* with white mustard and silk cotton,[426] he should place it at the feet of the god and should worship the doll at the three junctures of the day. Having worshiped it, he should recite the mantra ten thousand times for three nights during the dark fortnight. Having worshiped the god with *bali* offerings, he should tap the doll's heart with a thousand *jāti* flowers. She will be mastered, and she will say, "What can I do for you?" He will say, "Be my wife." He enjoys with her for as long as the moon and the stars endure. This is the rite of the *yakṣiṇī*.[427]

This procedure is also based on the principle of sympathetic magic: a doll resembling a *śālabhañjikā yakṣiṇī* is crafted from white mustard and silk cotton, made to come "alive" through the process of worship, and then manipulated to serve the wishes of the ritual master. In its basic form, this ritual resembles the *vaśīkaraṇa* described in the VBhT (§28): to subjugate under one's will, one makes an image of a target with *siddhadravya*s—that is, saffron and yellow orpiment—and worships the image with red flowers at the three junctures of the day. Both rituals are interesting in how they combine relatively simple conceptions of image magic with deity worship at the three *sandhyā*s, derived more specifically from Hindu/Indian culture; thus they represent with particular clarity the mingling of magical and religious traditions. The formula in the NTGS in particular demonstrates an awareness of congruity of the appeal to divine powers and the pursuit of worldly ends with the technology of magic.

The treatment of a *yakṣiṇī* as a wife and lover, and also as the source of various siddhis for the man who is able to master her through the power of sādhana, finds its expression also in a passage of the *Mañjuśriyamūlakalpa*. The text classifies *yakṣiṇī*s into three categories—mother, sister, and wife—the difference between them being the type of benefit they grant to the sādhaka. The text says:

426. Alternatively, one may read *śālabhañjikasiddhārtha* [emend to °*ārthe*?] *śālmalīpratimāṃ kṛtvā*, which would yield the translation "having made [a doll] of silk cotton for the purpose of mastering a śālabhañjikā."

427. NTGS 10.81ab–84ab: *śālabhañjikasiddhārthaśālmalīpratimāṃ kṛtvā devasya pādayo sthāpya trisandhyaṃ devi pūjaye pratikṛtim. arcayitvā daśasahasrāṇi japet krṣṇe tṛrātrikām. sabali devaṃ pūjya jātipuṣpasahasreṇa pratimāṃ hṛdi tāḍayet. siddhā sā kiṃ karomīti bhāryā me bhavasveti. tayā saha ramate yāvac candratārakaṃ. yakṣiṇyā eṣa vidhiḥ.*

> First, one should recite the mantra a hundred thousand times, after which he should make a *pūrvasevā*. Then he enters a great forest, lives on fruit, and continues the recitation [of the mantra] until she appears in person. Upon her arrival, she will say, "What can I do for you?" If she is a mother, then she fulfills all his desires in a manner of a mother: she gives him a kingdom, she makes him a millionaire, she empowers him with a long life. If she is a sister, she will bring to him any woman he desires, even though she may be a thousand *yojana*s away. Every day, she will give him a hundred thousand *dinara*, which he will have to spend. If she is a wife, then she takes him home, and he enjoys with her mounted on a divine chariot for a long time, for thirty thousand years. He can travel wherever he wishes, and he becomes indistinguishable from a great *yakṣa*.[428]

Due to their association with the lord of wealth Kubera (or Vaiśravaṇa), *yakṣiṇī*s have been traditionally regarded as bestowers of prosperity and treasures. This aspect is reinforced in the above passage, where *yakṣiṇī*s assume different feminine roles and bestow on the sādhaka various boons, ranging from power and money to longevity and women. As in the passage of the NTGS above, here again the *yakṣiṇī* of the "wife" class is presented as a highly sexualized woman reduced to a sexual plaything in the household.

Examples of "love" magic that incorporate sexual violence and the procurement of *yakṣiṇī*s as sexually compliant wives suggests that the production of early tantric magic was the domain of men, who created it with a male clientele in mind. It can be assumed that men of various social standings were the owners of the grimoires and were also responsible for the dissemination of a sexually subservient image of femininity in magical rites. The perception of females undergoes a paradigm shift with the later arrival of the yoginī tantras, which incorporated the cult of the yoginī (a powerful female practitioner, an expert of yoga) from the Śaiva cults of Bhairava. The yoginīs, usually organized into clans (*kula*), are portrayed as powerful, dangerous, airborne, and often teriomorphic goddesses, who must be propitiated with offerings of meat

428. MMK chap. 52, p. 447: *ādau lakṣam ekaṃ japet. pūrvasevā kṛtā bhavati. tato mahāraṇyaṃ praviśya phalāhāraḥ tāvaj japed yāvat svarūpeṇopatiṣṭhate. āgatā ca bravīti—kiṃ karomīti. yadi mātā bhavati. mātṛvat sarvāśāṃ paripūrayate. rājyaṃ dadāti. mahādhanapatiṃ karoti. dīrghāyuṣkatām adhitiṣṭhate. atha bhaginī yathepsitaṃ strīm ānayati yojana-sahasrasthitām api. dīnāralakṣaṃ dine dine dadāti. sa ca vyayīkartavyaḥ. atha bhāryā bhavati svabhavanaṃ nayate divyavimānābhirūḍho tayā sārdhaṃ ramate. dīrghakālaṃ triṃśad varṣasahasrāṇi yatheṣṭaṃ vicarate. mahāyakṣapratirūpo bhavati.*

and liquor. In the *Cakrasaṃvara Tantra*,[429] for example, seeking the company of the yoginīs is part of the sādhana. Believed to be both the source and the guardians of powerful, esoteric teachings, yoginīs can bestow various supernatural powers.

Underworld Magic

The concept of a maiden bestowing sexual favors is also found in the descriptions of the underworlds (*pātāla*s) where Śaiva and Buddhist tāntrikas enter for the sole purpose of delighting in sensual pleasures. The *pātālasiddhi*, the ability to enter into the underworld, is one of the attainments sought by a *vidyādhara* in the VBhT. Early tantric texts explicitly portray the underworld as the domain of females; it is the place inhabited by *asurī*s, the semidivine female beings who, from the time of the *Atharva Veda*, have been associated with herb witchcraft, used to seduce Indra. In tantric texts, *asurī*s command women whose only role is to sexually please the mantra master.

Entry into the underworld is somewhat tricky. It requires specific magical skills to unlock a *bila*—a portal into the underworld.[430] The NTGS (10.86) gives the following *homa* rite for opening a sealed *bila*: "If he performs ten thousand times the offering of *bilvā* fruit into the fire, he will be allowed to enter into the underworld and not remain stuck at the *bila* entrance" (*bilvāhomayutenāpūrya praveśayati na bile tiṣṭhati*). Another passage of the NTGS (10.125) identifies the underworld as the place where the *asurī*s, upon the sādhaka's successful entry, adore him: "If he enters the *bila*, then by reciting the mantra, he will destroy all the seals. Others who have entered previously will immediately become his [. . .]. He becomes a darling of the *asurī*s" (*bilapradeśe japtaḥ sarvayantrāṃ praṇāśayet. pūrvapraviṣṭaś ca ye te tasya* [. . .] *asurīṇāṃ priyo bhavati*). The text of the procedure is too corrupted to be reconstructed with certainty, but the overall idea seems clear—the *asurī*s "take care" of the sādhaka, including services of a sexual nature. In this regard, the MMK is more explicit in the sexual motivation for entering the underworld:

> If the mantra expert wants to have sex and is blind with lust, his mind deluded, he may attract with mantras and enjoy a *yakṣī* or *rākṣasī*, a *nāgī*, a *gandharvī*, a *daitya* woman, or a *kinnarī*, or he can

429. For the portrayal of *yoginī*s and women in the *Cakrasaṃvara Tantra*, see Gray 2007a, 90–103.

430. On *bilasiddhi*, see Sanderson 2004, 280–82, Sanderson 2007, 49–50, and Vasudeva 2012, 275–78. On other reasons for entering into the underworlds, see Mayer 2007.

> enter into a splendid world beneath which is an excellent city of *asuras* where there are countless women. Having entered, he may dwell there for a whole *kalpa* constantly reciting his mantra. Then, when eventually Maitreya Sambuddha becomes a Buddha, he will hear his teachings and be released.[431]

The above passage clearly expresses the idea that women are the main reason for entering into the underworld. The text suggests that those looking for sexual adventures can either make their way to the underworld or perform the rite of *ākarṣaṇa* to attract other categories of mythical semi-divine beings, who are then bound by the spell of the mantra to act as sexual servants. In any case, one can then enjoy celestial pleasures and eventually gain liberation.

Neutralization of Poison

Neutralization of poison (*viṣavināśana*) is a large portion of the tantric repertoire. Recipes dealing with this topic are found in the GS, VBhT, NTGS, and MMK and include such techniques as the installation of seed syllables, the "clenched fist" exorcism, and mantra recitation. The existence of this type of ritual suggests that poisoning was common in medieval India and that, therefore, the demand for antidotes was considerable.

The NTGS (3.95ab–8ab) provides a technique for neutralizing poison that supplements the mantra with additional seed syllables:

> With the syllable *huṃ*, he can bind the poison; with the mere name [of the poison] he can paralyze it. By instilling *hrīṃ* into his head, he can paralyze the poison. With *haiṃ*, his fist can make the poison shift wherever he wishes. By reciting *ho*, he can always supress the poison; with *hau* he can make [the poison] dance [like a puppet]. With *huṃ*, he causes all poisons to be transferred with his fist.[432]

431. MMK 52.5.7ab–9ab, p. 446: *maithunārthī yathā mantrī rāgāndho mūḍhacetasaḥ. mantrair ākṛṣya bhuñjīta yakṣīṃ vā atha rākṣasīṃ* [em. *rākṣasī*, ed.] *nāgīṃ* [em. *nāgī*, ed.] *ca matha gandharvīṃ* [em. *gandharvīṃ*, ed.] *daityayoṣim atha kinnarīm. pātālabhavanaṃ ramya asurāṇāṃ purottamam. praviśet tatra mantrajñaḥ yatra strīṇām asaṅkhyakam. tatra gatvā vaset kalpaṃ* [em. *kalpa*, ed.] *mantrajño mantrajāpinaḥ. maitreyo nāma sambuddhaḥ yadā buddho bhaviṣyati. tadāsau śroṣyati saddharmaṃ śrutvā mukto bhaviṣyati.*

432. NTGS 3.98ab–100cd: *huṃ iti viṣaṃ badhnāti; nāmenaiva tu stambhayet. hrīṃ mūrdhni viṣastobhe* [. . .]. *haiṃ viṣaṃ saṅkrāmayati muṣṭinā yatra cecchati. ho nigrahaṃ sadā kuryāt hau nṛtyāpayate.* (*sarvapātrāṇi bhūtāni* [. . .]). *huṃ viṣāṇi tu sarvāṇi saṅkrāmayati muṣṭinā.*

Even though the passage is lacunose, it is possible to distinguish two methods to neutralize poison. One is to bind or paralyze the poison, which stops its progress through the body. The other is to transfer the poison away from the body of the afflicted to another location, as a type of exorcisim. The second method involves not only seed syllables but also a mudrā called *muṣṭi*, "clenched hand" or "fist." *Muṣṭi* is traditionally used in Sanskrit texts to indicate "beating," "forced exit," or to represent the "gripping of weapons," and these meanings align with the sense of *muṣṭi* intended in the NTGS.

One of the most common types of poisoning tantric magic addresses is snakebite (*viṣadaṣṭa*). Instances of such recipes are found already in the earliest tantric scriptures, and the demand for a snakebite cure must have grown steadily, for in the tenth century, we find an entire corpus of tantric scriptures, called the Gāruḍa Tantras, that specifically deal with this topic (Slouber 2017). The recipes for curing snakebite given in early tantric texts include a variety of methods, from the already mentioned "clenched fist" to the use of metals and visualization. Here I will examine three methods in detail, and analyze the evidence for their use in three different textual sources.

The first method for curing snakebite, given in the NTGS (10.122), uses mercury, which is seen both as exorcistic and medicinal in nature. The ritual instructs, "If he wipes with quicksilver, even the 'possessing evil spirits' (*skandagrahas*) will let go. He will cause the person bitten by a poisonous snake to be released" (*sūtakena*[433] *upamārjane skandagrahā 'pi muñcati. viṣadaṣṭe* [em. *viṣadaṣṭa*, ms.] [. . .] *mocāpayati*). Analyzing this passage, we may note that this is perhaps one of the earliest appearances of mercury in tantric literature. Mercury, or quicksilver, is the "star" of Indian alchemy and medicine, but its usage here in the tantric context is unprecedented. More significant for our purposes, quicksilver is mentioned here as the remedy that releases a person from any disease inflicted by the evil seizer (in the sense that it cures the ailment by exorcising the possessing evil spirit [*skandagraha*] from the person's body) and as a cure for snakebite.

The same understanding of poisoning as affliction caused by an evil "seizer" (*graha*) is found in the MMK where it deals with snakebite:[434]

433. The word *sūtaka* has three unrelated meanings: "a woman who has just given birth," "quicksilver," or "impurity."

434. The Śaiva *Uḍḍāmareśvara Tantra* gives a recipe for the terminal cases of snakebite as a concoction made of seven ingredients: the three *madhus* (honey, milk, and ghee; see p. 139), black pepper, long pepper, and ginger. When this mixture is administered to a person fatally bitten by a snake together with salt, he will instantly recover (Zadoo 1947, 11–12).

> Having entered the river that flows to the ocean and having performed the clenched fist with his right hand, [the sādhaka] recites [the mantra] for thirteen days. All those bitten by a snake will be revived. With the clenched fist, he destroys all the seizers.[435]

The second method given in the VBhT (§82), intended for the fatal cases of snakebites (*kāladaṣṭa*), completely departs from the material approach of exorcising poison through the clenched-fist mudrā or quickilver and instead employs visualization:

> Next is declared the meditation procedure for resurrecting a person who has been fatally bitten by a snake. Having visualized an eight-petal lotus, white in color, in his own heart, he should visualize the third vowel (*i*) above it, and on the eight petals, eight white *phaṭ*s. By this he should also visualize himself having the form of the *nāga* king Śeṣa, white in color. He should imagine him emitting a flood of nectar through the letter *i* upon his head. Having caused that nectar to go out from the eyes of that snake, he should visualize it falling down onto the body of that target. Through this meditation procedure, he makes poison free of poison, even if it is a poison that fills the universe, even were he to swallow that poison a thousand times.

Fever Magic

One of the most common magical technologies used in *abhicāra* rites is the use of specific substances believed to have an innate potency for causing harm. By analyzing various magical recipes in early tantras, it is possible to delineate four that seem to be well known and accepted by tāntrikas regardless of sectarian affiliation. These are poison (*viṣa*), blood (*rakta/rudhira*), salt (*lavaṇa*), and black mustard (*rājikā*).[436] There is no reason to think that these substances

435. MMK chap. 55, p. 552: *samudragāminīṃ nadīm avatīrya dakṣiṇahastena muṣṭiṃ kṛtvā trayodaśadivasāṃ japet. sarvaviṣadaṣṭakāni cotthāpayati. muṣṭinā sarvagrahāṃ nāśayati.*

436. In early Buddhist tantras such as the GS (15.81, p. 78), the set of five "wrathful" substances—black mustard (*rājikā*), salt (*lavaṇa*), oil (*taila*), poison (*viṣa*), and datura (*dhattūraka*)—are known collectively as the supreme destroyers of all the buddhas (*rājikaṃ lavaṇaṃ tailaṃ viṣaṃ dhattūrakaṃ tathā/ māraṇaṃ sarvabuddhānām idaṃ śreṣṭhamaṃ smṛtam//*). The VBhT (§13) repeats the same fixed group of five already mentioned in the GS but adds neem (*nimba*) to make a set of six ingredients. These are

were not also in use in nontantric sources, and there is evidence that they were. Black mustard, for example, seems to be widely popular outside the tantric corpus. The already mentioned text, the *Āsurīkalpa* of the *Atharvavedapariśiṣṭa*s (Magoun 1889), entirely dedicated to the *abhicāra* procedures, derives its name from the *āsurī* plant, which the *Aṣṭāṅgasaṃgraha* of Vāgbhaṭa (7.153cd–155), a classical text of Āyurveda, identifies as another name for black mustard (*rājikā*). As the title itself indicates, the *Āsurīkalpa*'s aggressive magical rites are based, almost exclusively, on its wide use of the *āsurī* plant.

In tantric texts, application of these four substances seems to fall into two distinct methods. The first involves smearing[437] them on the object that is being magically manipulated—for example, a doll representing the target or a *liṅga*. The second way is to employ them in the *abhicāra homa*. Below I examine each of these techniques in greater detail by analyzing their prescription in different sources.

The first context in which "wrathful" substances are smeared onto objects in tantric texts is related to so-called fever magic—magical procedures for inflicting fever on a target. The textual examples from the VBhT's exegetical literature and the MMK display remarkable parallelism on this topic and may therefore be combined for reconstructing the first method for deploying "wrathful" substances in tantric magic. The commentators of the VBhT (*Akṣobhya, *Śoṇaśrī, and *Vajrasiddha) expound the original "fever procedure" given in the root text in a similar manner: the mantrin—who is naked with disheveled hair, faces south and is anointed with pungent mustard-seed oil (*kaṭutaila*)—retrieves a human skull from the cremation ground. The procedure is epitomized by this passage from *Śoṇaśrī:

> The skull must be of a person who was either killed by a sword or hung [possibly a criminal]. Into this skull, the mantrin draws the illustration of fever, either with the juice of the *sen rtsi* plant or with chalk from white earth. There are two types of fever the target can be inflicted with. To inflict the target with hot fever, the mantrin depicts the fever as red with red hair shooting upward. If he wants

---

commonly said to comprise the ink prescribed for drawing a mantra/yantra/maṇḍala of Vajrabhairava. Thus they often occur in association with the Sanskrit verbal root √ *likh*, "to write."

437. These substances often appear with verbs that mean "smearing": *āloḍya* (VBhT, VS), *ākta* (MMK, GS, *Āsurīkalpa*, VS), *abhyakta* (GS, MMK), and *abhyajya* (MMK). As examples, we find the expressions *kaṭutailaviṣaṃ raktaṃ tenāloḍya* (VS 165–67, p. 74) and *chuchundarīcarmāloḍya saviṣādibhir dravyair* (VBhT, §17).

to inflict the target with cold fever [i.e., chills], he draws the fever as white, with white hair hanging down. Both types of fevers should be drawn as wrathful, with three legs and three arms.

Then, the mantrin obtains charcoal from the fire where the corpses have been burnt and dust from the footprint of the target and mixes them together. With this mixture, he draws an image of the target and puts this yantra [of Vajrabhairava], prepared according to the procedure stated above, at the heart of the image.[438] Having smeared the image of the target with poison (*viṣa*), salt (*lavaṇa*), black mustard (*rājikā*), and so on, he puts it into another skull bowl (*padmabhāṇḍa*).[439] Having sat down on both skulls, he then takes the skull into which he has drawn the fever and places it mouth down on the top of the other skull with the doll inside [smeared with "wrathful" substances], imagining that the target is seized by fever. Then he burns the two skulls below the hearth. Accordingly, if he performs this rite at night, in meditative union with Vajrabhairava, the target will definitely be seized by fever.[440]

This procedure requires manipulation of two skulls: one into which the image of a fever is drawn, and another containing the doll representing the target with the yantra placed on its heart. The text makes abundantly clear that the doll representing the target must be smeared with poison, salt, black mustard, and other substances (by which, possibly, blood is intended). In this case, these substances are assumed to attract fever, drawn in the first skull, which seizes the target in the second skull.

This visual image of fever given by *Śoṇaśrī conforms to the iconographical and textual representation of Śiva as fever, who is always represented with three legs and three arms and, sometimes, with three heads as well. According to the mythological narrative, fever as a *jvārāsura* (fever demon) arose either out of Śiva's anger or from a drop of sweat when he was disrespected by his father-in-law, Dakṣa. The shrines to Śiva as Jvara are most commonly found adjacent to the main Śiva temples in Tamil Nadu. But Śiva as Jvarahareśvara is also found in the Kathmandu Valley, installed inside the compound of the

438. This is supported by *Akṣobhya's commentary.

439. Literally, "lotus receptacle"; this the code word for a skull bowl.

440. *Śoṇaśrī's *pañjikā*, 397. *Akṣobhya adds interesting detail in which the yantra placed at the heart of the doll has to be customized with the formula *amukasya jvaram utpādaya*, "give rise to the fever of the target."

Pāśupatinātha temple.[441] It does not seem to be a coincidence that *Śoṇaśrī's understanding of the iconography of the fever matches the one described in Śaiva mythology that depicts Śiva as fever demon. Rather, this similarity provides evidence of points of contact between tantric Śaivism and Buddhism that were well underway even during the early stages in the development of Vajrayāna.

This is further supported by another piece of evidence of the "fever procedure" in the MMK. This version does not rely solely on the method of smearing the object that is being magically manipulated with the "wrathful" substances; it also employs an item from Śaiva culture: a *śivaliṅga*. Why would a *śivaliṅga* be used in tantric Buddhist magical procedure were it not for the pervasive belief (perhaps present also on the level of popular/folk culture) that the origins of fever in an afflicting evil spirit or demon are associated with Śaiva mythology? The text says:

> He should go to an isolated *liṅga* or a temple of Śiva, he should smear the *liṅga* with poison, blood, black mustard (*rājikā*), and sour gruel (*kañjika*), and he should worship it with the *picumarda* leaves. Having made himself a sacred thread from the strings of human intestines, holding a human skull in his right hand, having subsisted on alcoholic drink, threatening the *liṅga* [. . .] with his left hand, standing naked with disheveled hair, his left foot on the Śiva *liṅga*, he recites the wrathful mantra then by the force of the mantra, the Śiva *liṅga* will split in two. He will hear a huge roar, but he should not be afraid. The enemy, whoever he may be—whether a rogue king or even the great *yakṣa*—is in that very moment seized by a fever.[442]

This procedure can be assessed in numerous ways, but two elements are especially relevant to our purpose here. First, the use of *śivaliṅga* for magical purposes is a characteristic feature of early tantric magic, whether Śaiva

441. Diwakar Acharya, personal communication.

442. MMK chap. 52, p. 438: *ekaliṅge maheśvarasyāyatane taṃ liṅgaṃ viṣarudhirarājikākāñjikenābhyajya picumardapatrair arcayitvā mānuṣāntranālibhir ātmanā yajñopavītaṃ kṛtvā mānuṣaśirakapālena dakṣiṇahastena surāhāro* [em. *saprahāro*, ed.] *bhūtvā vāmahastena liṅgaṃ tarjayamānaḥ* [. . .] *nagnako muktaśikhaḥ maheśvaraliṅgaṃ vāmapādenākramya krodhamantraṃ tāvaj japet yāvan maheśvaraliṅgo madhye sphuṭita iti dvividalībhūtaṃ mahāṃś ca huṅkāraḥ śrūyate. tato na bhetavyam. tad ahā eva* [em. *tadeho*, ed.] *duṣṭarājñaḥ anyo vā yaḥ kaścin mahāyakṣaḥ aris tatkṣaṇād eva jvareṇa gṛhyate.*

or Buddhist.[443] Already in the NTGS, the *śivaliṅga* appears as one of the objects manipulated for different magical purposes. A neglected *śivaliṅga*—one that does not receive regular worship—is believed to become home to genie-like beings who, when activated through magical means, bring about magical results on the sādhaka's behalf.[444] The NTGS (10.47cd–48) illustrates this in the following ritual: "When there is an eclipse of the moon or the sun, he should smear the god with ghee. When the *liṅga* has been smeared with ghee, he should then assail it with a hundred mustard seeds (*sarṣapa*). All the creatures present in the *liṅga* will make the world submit to his will" (*candrasūryagrahe devaṃ ghṛtābhyaktaṃ* [em. *ghṛtābhyaṃ*, ms.] *tu kārayet. ghṛtābhyakte kṛte liṅge tāḍayec chatasarṣapaiḥ. liṅge tu saṃshitā ye tu te kurvanti jagad vaśam*). If we interpret the above passage of the MMK along these lines, it may be possible to assume that once the *śivaliṅga* is magically manipulated and splits into two, the genie-like beings inhabiting the *liṅga* come out and afflict the target with fever.

In support of the argument just mentioned, let us turn to the second interpretative context. Since it is a widespread conviction in early tantric magic that diseases are caused by evil "possessing spirits" or "seizers" (*skandagrahā*s), the cure of diseases is concomitant with a wide range of exorcistic practices to drive those *grahā*s away.[445] For example, one can exorcise the "seizers" by reciting the mantra in front of them or by wiping the afflicted person with mercury. The verb often used in the context of becoming free of disease is *muñcati*, from the verbal root *muc*, to "let go," "release," "give up," or "allow to depart." If the *grahā*s, like demons, can be exorcized, the same logic could apply to the reverse process: inflicting the target with a disease or a fever could be associated with summoning the evil spirits with the substances they

443. A *śivaliṅga* is one of the suitable places for undertaking tantric sādhana for both Śaiva and Buddhist tantric masters.

444. Alexis Sanderson, personal communication.

445. This is attested in NTGS 3.103: *ītivyādhivinirmukto hy akālamṛtyuvarjitaḥ. grahāṃś ca nāśayet śīghraṃ dhāraṇā rephasaṃyutaḥ*, "He will be free of all plagues and diseases, he will be free of untimely death, he will be able to quickly destroy any possessors [i.e., possessing spirits] if he has the *dhāraṇā* adding *ra* [the fire element] to the seed syllable." Similarly, NTGS 10.53 says: *skandagrahagṛhītānāṃ āvāhyāgrato* [conj. *bāhyāgrato*, ms.] *jāpet/ trīn vārān sarvaduṣṭagrahāś ca ye prapalāyanti*, "For those who have been possessed by Skanda or a seizer, he should recite in front of them after having summoned them. He should recite the mantra three times, and all evil *grahā*s will flee." Likewise, NTGS 10.121: *grahagṛhītasyāgrato japet, yāvat graha muñcati*, "He should recite it in front of someone who has been seized by a seizer until such time that the seizer lets go [i.e., releases the seized]."

deem impossible to resist, in this case, poison, blood, black mustard, and the less-known sour gruel. Whether fever can be categorized as a *graha* is an open question.[446] The above passage certainly supports this interpretation insofar that it describes fever (*jvara*) as seizing the target (*gṛhyate*, which is derived from the same verbal root as *graha*). The same applies to diseases, which, in a manner similar to *grahās*, are said to seize (*gṛhyante*) the enemy.

This becomes exemplified in another passage, from chapter 52 of the MMK (p. 438), which illustrates the second means for deploying "wrathful" substances—that is, *abhicāra homa*:

> There is another ritual procedure. Having lit the fire with thorns of thorn-apple wood[447] at the right side of the *liṅga* of Maheśvara, he should make eight hundred oblations using *vaikaṅkata* tree[448]—fuel sticks smeared with poison, blood, and black mustard. Then all his enemies will be seized with great disease.[449]

Like in the "fever recipe," here also poison, blood, and black mustard are deemed efficacious in making an enemy sick. In this case, however, the three "wrathful" substances are smeared on the fuel sticks, which are then sacrificed

446. The expression *jvaragraha* is found, for example, in the alchemical work *Siddhasāra* 5.117, but it is unclear whether it should be understood as a *karmadhāraya* or a *tatpuruṣa*. See Conrad and Wujastyk 2000, 65, 75.

447. The thorns of thorn-apple wood (*madanakaṇṭaka*) also appear in the early NTGS (3.88cd–90ab) in the recipe meant for attracting a person from a long distance: *kapāle bhagam ālikhya lākṣayā rudhireṇa vā,* [. . .] *madanakaṇṭakaiś ca* [. . .] *ca vahninā. āgacched yojanaśatāt kṛtakṛtyor mṛṣet bhagam. tatkṣaṇād eva mantraistu* [em. *mantrastu*, ms.] *punar eva nayet kṣaṇāt*, "Having drawn a vagina on a skull bowl with lac or blood, having [*lacuna*] with thorns of thorn-apple wood, with fire, that person will come from a hundred *yojanas*. Once he has finished his purpose, then he can rub out that vagina; instantly, he can bring her back again with the mantras."

448. The *vaikaṅkata* tree, or Indian plum, is one of the types of trees in the *abhicārahoma* mentioned in the NTGS (10.13cd–15ab): *abhicāruke badarāmrakolakhādira hutvā abhicāre ca nityaśaḥ. tathā vaikaṅkatā devi bhavate cābhicārukam* [em. *cābhicāruke*, ms.]. *tathā* [. . .] *viṣarudhirāktena ca. kaṭutailasamāyuktaḥ śatrunāśaṃ bhavet dhruvaṃ*, "In the *abhicāra*, he should always sacrifice into the fire jujube tree, mango, black pepper, catechu tree, and Indian plum, o goddess, and he should offer something smeared with poison and blood. If he includes *kaṭutaila*, there will be certain destruction of his enemies."

449. *Mahāvyādhi* could mean either a "great disease for which there is no remedy" or "black leprosy." The latter meaning is attested in Āyurvedic literature.

MMK chap. 52, p. 438: *aparam api karma bhavati. maheśvaraliṅgasya dakṣiṇāmūrttau madanakaṇṭakakaṣṭhair agniṃ prajvālya vaikaṅkatasamidhānāṃ viṣarudhirarājikābhyaktānāṃ aṣṭasahasraṃ juhuyāt. sarve śatravo mahāvyādhinā gṛhyante.*

into the fire as part of *abhicāra homa*. The use of poison, blood, and black mustard either as the substances smeared on the objects offered into the fire or as the suitable fire offerings themselves is found pervasively in tantric magic, employed in a wide range of *abhicāra* procedures. The Śaiva NTGS mentions poison and blood as ingredients that should be smeared on the items in the *abhicāra homa* (see note 448) used for the destruction of the enemies. Also, the Śaiva *Vīṇāśikha Tantra* (v. 155, ed. p. 114) refers to the same purpose in a recipe for the *abhicāra homa*, taking place in the cremation ground where a sādhaka sacrifices into the fire black mustard seeds smeared with poison and blood, with bones as fuel sticks: *athābhicārakaṃ kuryāt samidhānāṃ tathāsthibhiḥ/ rājikāviṣaraktāktaṃ śmaśāne homam ārabhet*. A similar usage associated with *homa* is attested in Buddhist tantras.[450] In addition to the MMK quoted above, we have an example from the GS (15.19), which gives the details of a fire sacrifice causing the paralysis of maidens, where the set of four substances—poison, blood, salt, and black mustard—should be offered into the fire of thorny wood.[451]

I have already pointed out that these "wrathful" substances were believed to have an innate magical power to cause harm. I have also mentioned the possibility that, at least in case of the procedures intended to inflict a target with disease or fever, these substances may have been viewed as capable of summoning/activating the evil possessing spirits (*graha*s), fever demons (*jvārāsura*), or genie-like figures imprisoned inside the *liṅga*. Even though this argument cannot be fully substantiated by textual examples, there is sufficient evidence to indicate that "wrathful" substances were used to summon demonic entities in the service of *abhicāra*-related goals. The MMK (chap. 52, pp. 438–39) provides the following example:

> On the fourteenth day of the dark fortnight, at midday, [the sādhaka,] having fasted for one night, makes a fire on a pyre in the cremation ground, and he makes an offering of black mustard

450. This is attested in the *Susiddhikara Sūtra* (Giebel 2001, 185–87), which became very influential in East Asia. The text gives a long list of various substances suitable for the *abhicāra homa*, including white mustard, mustard-seed oil, one's own blood, salt, black mustard seed, human and animal feces, fats, etc. Each of these offerings must be mixed with three substances: poison, blood, and salt. This would correspond to the sequence *viṣa, rudhira, lavaṇa* given in the GS and VBhT, with the exception of *rājikā*, which is missing. The same text instructs about the preparation of fuel sticks that should be smeared with poison and mustard seed oil.

451. GS 15.19, p. 72: *viṣarudhirasaṃyuktaṃ lavanaṃ rājikān tathā/ kaṇṭakāgnau juhet kruddhaḥ kanyānāmapadaiḥ saha//.*

> (*rājikā*) smeared with poison and blood. Then all the ghosts (*preta*s) come shouting "ha ha," rushing toward him. He should not be afraid. He should say to them, "Kill my enemy!" They say, "So be it!" (*evam astu*) and disappear. Then, in a mere *muhūrta* (2.5 hours), they can travel even up to a thousand *yojana*s and kill the enemy. They can uproot his family. And they can do other actions like this.[452]

The passage makes it explicit that the mantra master summons the spirits of the dead through an *abhicāra homa* consisting mainly of "wrathful" substances. Through this, he is able to conjure ghosts, talk to them, and send them to kill the enemy and his family.

452. MMK chap. 52, pp. 438–39: *madhyāhne śmaśānaṃ citāv ekarātroṣitaḥ kṛṣṇacaturdaśyāṃ śmaśānakāṣṭhair agniṃ prajvālya viṣarudhirāktāṃ rājikāṃ juhuyāt. tato hāhākāraṃ kurvantaḥ sarvapretā āgacchanti. na bhetavyam. tato vaktavyaṃ śatruṃ me ghātayeti. evam astv iti kṛtvāntardhīyante. tato muhūrtamātreṇa yojanasahasram api gatvā śatruṃ ghātayanti kulān utsādayanti. evamādīni karmāṇi kurvanti.*

8. Conclusion and Prospects for Future Research

THE MAIN OBJECTIVE of this book has been the cult of the tantric Buddhist deity Vajrabhairava, which was achieved through a study of the *Vajrabhairava Tantra*. The book has examined an early cult of Vajrabhairava as presented in the neglected corpus of Indian exegetical literature on the VBhT in order to cast light on the Indian origins of the Vajrabhairava practice that underpins later Tibetan, Mongolian, and Chinese traditions. The findings have shown that the VBhT represents a transitional stage in the development of esoteric Buddhism, for it was composed at the point when Buddhism tried to redefine itself against more robust tantric techniques that developed in the Śaiva fold. In this regard, the practice of borrowing specifically Śaiva practices, such as the entry into the cremation ground with mad laughter and the consumption of the five nectars, are examples of incorporating more and more non-Buddhist elements drawn from the Śaiva sources. The transitional character of the VBhT is also indicated by the fact that the scripture does not possess a clear yoga-tantra identity. On the one hand, the VBhT draws upon the concepts of the yoga tantras, as is visible, for instance, in the sādhana passage of chapter 4. One the other hand, it is rooted in the kriyā-tantric technology of the MMK, in which the sādhaka has a power to invoke and dismiss the deity. Knowing "how" to call upon the deity through the evocation of sacred spells and attractive offerings that the deity cannot resist is the core of tantric sādhana.

Second, an attempt has been made to contribute to the understanding of the origins of the deity Vajrabhairava in India and Tibet. Prior scholarship has reduced the origins of Vajrabhairava to an evolutionary model that stems from the Hindu-Buddhist god of death, Yama, and its tantric Buddhist "avatar," Yamāntaka. My findings show instead that the origins of Vajrabhairava are linked to the Śiva complex not only in the appropriation of Śaiva iconographic attributes but also in its recapitulation of an earlier myth of the subjugation of Maheśvara. The narratives have also revealed that the tradition regards the MNS as a textual antecedent to the VBhT. There, one of Mañjuśrī's "names," "Vajrabhairava who creates fear," became the impetus that prompted

Lalitavajra to establish a totally new tantric tradition dedicated solely to Mañjuśrī's wrathful form as Vajrabhairava. The textual layer of the VBhT seems to indicate that this story may in fact be true. This suggests that, rather than locating Vajrabhairava's origins in the Yama/Yamāntaka prototype, the genesis of Vajrabhairava could be located in the sādhana practice existing in early yoga tantras such as the NMAA. The scope of Vajrabhairava's origins ought to be reevaluated in light of the new evidence I have presented.

This book aimed to uncover the textual and intellectual relationship between the VBhT and Śaiva tantric traditions. Comparison of the magical procedures described in the VBhT has exposed instances of Śaiva-Buddhist intertextuality, indicating that these early tantric scriptures, Śaiva and Buddhist, shared the same magical worldview and technology, following models that may predate the earliest-known textual evidence as part of a religious "substratum." My findings reveal that magical recipes demanded a whole range of material objects—grains, chemicals, sweets, animals, items retrieved from the cremation ground, and so on. The early tantric milieu shared a very similar understanding of the categories of magic and the manipulation of objects, which further supports the argument that the "culture of magic" was widespread and crossed sectarian boundaries.

Although Vajrabhairava has been used as a daily practice by Sa skya pa and Dge lugs pa monks in pursuit of soteriological goals over the *long durée*, this book does not approach this topic directly. This book has provided a thorough overview of the Indian background of the Vajrabhairava cult based on the Indian exegetical tradition preserved in the Bstan 'gyur, but the reception of this cult in Tibet has only been touched upon. The understanding of how, why, and where such an ostensibly antinomian tradition endured as the preferred vehicle for intellectually and philosophically sophisticated versions of monastic Mahāyāna remains a desideratum. The notion of transmission often arises in concomitance with the transmission of texts and related practices. As can be easily gleaned from the various transmission lineages presented in this work, there are hundreds of texts dedicated to Vajrabhairava in the Tibetan tradition—some of which have been mentioned in this book—that have yet to be investigated by scholars. Future study of Vajrabhairava would need to involve a careful examination of several such scriptures to track changes in the doctrine and practice within given Tibetan lineages, to inquire into the causes of these variations, and to correlate them with other social and political factors. A particularly interesting category of texts that could throw new light on the Vajrabhairava cult in Tibet is crematory manuals, which were popular, for example, in the Dge lugs tradition. Systematic analysis of these manuals could expand greatly our understanding of the ritual purpose of the Vajrabhairava cult beyond the paradigm of aggressive magic.

In any event, the extensive literary output on Vajrabhairava in the post-canonical period means there are ample riches to be mined for further study of this tradition that has remained active across centuries and in diverse cultural spheres.

Part II
Annotated Translation

Notes on the Translation

The translation that follows is the first-ever English translation of the entire *Vajrabhairava Tantra* based on a critical edition of the Sanskrit text of the tantra, prepared by me, which is forthcoming in another publication. A partial edition of the Sanskrit VBhT has been published in 2007 in the *Dhīḥ* series no. 43 of the Central Institute of Higher Tibetan Studies in Sarnath, Varanasi, edited by Ngawang Samten and Shrikant Bahulkar. The "Sarnath edition," which contains only the first three chapters of VBhT, mentions two textual witnesses on which it is based—namely, ms. B (see below) and the Tibetan translation of the VBhT (Toh. 468). The "Sarnath edition" closely follows the reading of ms. B and often replicates the mistakes found in ms. B. Unlike the Sarnath edition, the critical edition that I have prepared and the translation below, which stems from it, are based on the three manuscript witnesses.

Probably the earliest manuscript of the *Vajrabhairava Tantra* is written in proto-Bengali script on palm leaves, which I refer to as the "Beijing ms." in translation annotation. The colophon does not indicate the date of its composition, but on the basis of paleographical evidence, it can be dated somewhere between the late thirteenth and early fifteenth centuries. The manuscript is currently held in the Peking University Library. Although the manuscript is incomplete, it is of great value for establishing the constituent text of the VBhT, for it contains parts that are missing in the other two manuscripts.

The second oldest textual witness of the Sanskrit VBhT is a palm-leaf manuscript written in a Newārī script ("ms. A" in the sigla I employ in the translation). On the basis of paleographical grounds, this manuscript can be dated to the early sixteenth century (Diwakar Acharya, personal communication). This incomplete manuscript, currently held in the National Archives of Kathmandu, has a number of interesting linguistic features that support the East Indian origins of the VBhT.

The last of the manuscript witnesses of the VBhT is a paper manuscript written in a Devanāgarī script (with the sigla "ms. B"). This manuscript is a kind of transcript prepared in the twentieth century by some paṇḍita working for

Hemrāj Śārman, who was the royal religious preceptor and chief librarian of the government of Nepal. This incomplete manuscript, whose available folios correspond to the ones found in ms. A, is also currently held in the National Archives of Kathmandu.

Another important source that helps to establish the constituent text of the VBhT is the *Saṃpuṭodbhava Tantra*, the text that was transmitted in Nepal in the eleventh century (Szántó 2013, 348) and that, as a number of scholars have demonstrated, is an anthology of different Vajrayāna texts (see Noguchi 1995, Skorupski 1996, Sanderson 2009, and Szántó 2013). Throughout my edition and translation, I am using three different manuscript sources of the *Saṃpuṭodbhava* to trace the parallels and differences between the VBhT and the *Saṃpuṭodbhava*. Two of the *Saṃpuṭodbhava*'s manuscripts—namely, the "Hodgson ms." (with the sigla "ms. R"), held in the Royal Asiatic Society, London, and the "Wellcome ms." (with the sigla "ms. P"), held at the Wellcome Instiute for the Study of Medicine, London—are dated to the eleventh century. However, a slightly later manuscript of the *Saṃpuṭodbhava*, the "Kolkata ms." (with the sigla "ms. K"), held in the Royal Asiatic Society, Kolkata, and dated to the twelfth century, is the best textual witness. The evidence of the *Saṃpuṭodbhava* is important for tracking the changes in the transmitted text of the VBhT. The numeration of the *Saṃpuṭodbhava* follows the Sanskrit edition prepared by Wiesiek Mical and produced by the Dharmachakra Translation Committee.

Apart from the Sanskrit sources listed above, another group of texts especially useful for translating the contents of the root text and for establishing the constituent text of the tantra are the VBhT's commentaries. In my translation, I am using all the six canonical commentaries of the tantra preserved in the Tibetan canon, and I provide the full translation of each of them. In case of emendations to the Tibetan text, the Dpe bsdur ma edition of the Tibetan canon as well as other editions of the six canonical commentaries, including the Co ne, Gser bris ma, Sde dge, Snar thang, and Beijing, have been consulted. The commentaries are very useful to understand some of the VBhT's content and to correct some errors in the Tibetan translation. The VBhT's commentaries are currently extant only in the Tibetan translation, with the exception of the *Vajrabhairavatantrapañjikā* by Kumāracandra, which is also available in Sanskrit. A critical edition of Kumāracandra's *pañjikā* based on two palm-leaf manuscripts, dated to the fourteenth century, currently held in the Peking University Library and prepared by me is forthcoming in another publication. In my translation, I am using the Sanskrit version of Kumāracandra's *pañjikā* only if it significantly differs from the Tibetan version.

Finally, my translation also compares the Sanskrit and Tibetan versions of the VBhT. The Tibetan translation of the VBhT was translated by Rwa lo tsā ba Rdo rje grags from a Sanskrit manuscript belonging to his Nepali guru, Bha ro phyag rdum (Siklós 1996). The Tibetan version edited and translated by Siklós (1996) closely follows the Sanskrit text. Significant variants between the Tibetan and the Sanskrit versions are recorded in my translation. My translation critically analyzes Siklós's translation of the VBhT from the Tibetan and corrects numerous mistakes, omissions, and misunderstandings that sometimes produced erroneous interpretation of the VBhT's contents.

In the notes to my translation, I also provide parallels from other early and late tantric works, both Buddhist and Śaiva, that contribute to the understanding of the issue of intertextuality. There are two reasons why a focus on the intertextual dimension of the VBhT is valuable. First, it highlights the fact that Buddhist tantras came into being through the reuse of textual fragments, "copy-paste" practices, and the adoption of established clichés. Second, this in turn advances the study of tantric Buddhist texts not as a culture of scriptural transmission but as a shared cultural environment in which textual (and ritual) fragments circulated across sectarian boundaries and were reused and interspersed in the ritual literature of different, and sometimes competing, religious groups.

1. Explanation of the Maṇḍala

Oṃ. Obeisance to Lord Vajrabhairava, who is called Mañjuśrī.

[§1] I will now duly explain the means of mastering (*sādhana*) [the deity] Vajrabhairava, who is very fierce and terrifying to all the gods.[453]

453. *Śoṇaśrī (pp. 393–94) and *Vajrasiddha (p. 413): "**duly explain**: the meaning of 'duly' here is recitation, yantra, *homa*, meditation, and rituals" (*yang dag rab bshad bya zhes bya ba la yang dag pa'i don ni 'dir bzlas pa dang 'khrul 'khor dang sbyin sreg dang bsam gtan dang las rnams so*).

*Kṛṣṇācārya (p. 442) glosses **means** ("*upāya*") as "the fruit—that is to say, the methods of the sādhana, which are taught to be accomplished by the yogin through this scripture" (*thabs zhes pa ni 'bras bu ste/ gzhung 'dis rnal 'byor pa la sgrub pa'i thabs su bstan pa'o*). This passage seems to correlate the double meaning of Vajrabhairava, as a deity and as a text, with two meanings of the *lyuṭ sādhana*—namely, action (*bhāva*) and instrument (*karaṇa*). The compound *vajrabhairavasādhanaṃ* is understood as a *karmadhāraya* and can be interpreted in two ways. (1) By saying that the instrument/means is the fruit, he alludes to the practice of the fruit (i.e., to the *devatāyoga*=the identification with Vajrabhairava). (2) By saying that the fruit is the method accomplished through this scripture, he refers to Vajrabhairava as the *Vajrabhairava Tantra*. The next gloss (see below) explains *sādhana* in the meaning of the *lyuṭ sādhana* as action (*bhāva*). I thank F. Sferra for clarifying these points.

Sādhana: Siklós (1996, 27) translates *bsgrub pa* as "evocation," but this is inaccurate. The meaning intended here is *sādhana*, "the means of mastering." *Akṣobhya (p. 369): ***sādhana*** [means] "as for the first chapter, it teaches only the sādhana, but all [the other] chapters also teach mainly the sādhana, because the range of rituals is also contained in the sādhana" (*sgrub pa ste zhes bya ba ni le'u dang po ni/ sgrub pa 'ba' zhig ston pa yin la rtog pa ril yang sgrub pa gtsor gyur pa ste/ las rab 'byam yang sgrub pas bsdus pa'o*). *Kṛṣṇācārya (p. 442) introduces here the standard Mahāyāna model of *svārtha* and *parārtha* and glosses ***sādhana*** as "the method, which accomplishes the benefit for oneself and for others" (*sgrub pa zhes thabs des bdag gzhan gyi don grub par byed pa'o*). *Śoṇaśrī (p. 394) and *Vajrasiddha (p. 413): "***Vajrabhairava sādhana***: it is explained as *vajra-śūnyatā-tattva*" (*rdo rje 'jigs byed sgrub thabs zhes bya ni/ rdo rje stong pa nyid rab gsungs*). "By Vajrabhairava-*prayoga* is understood that *śūnyatā* and *vajra* are not differentiated from Vajrabhairava, who has the character of Vajrasattva. **The sādhana** of that [means] by this [sādhana], one is made to accomplish the nature of the deity Vajrabhairava" (*rdo rje 'jigs byed sbyor bas so/zhes bya ba* *stong pa nyid dang rdo rje tha mi dad pa rdo rje sems dpa'i ngo bo ni rdo rje 'jigs byed do/ de'i sgrub thabs ni lha rdo rje 'jigs byed kyi ngo bor 'dis sgrub par byed pa yin te*).

Vajrabhairava: Kumāracandra (p. 287): "[Vajrabhairava is] ***vajra*** because of his quality of wisdom, and because of his quality of method he is ***bhairava***. Moreover, he frightens all wrathful gods. Furthermore, he himself is the fruit of compassion, but since he could not tame those who are wrathful toward sentient beings by using compassion, and since he could not tame them with peaceful means, he became Bhairava possessing that vajra. He is adorned with a garland of skulls, so one should meditate on a skull. He is the great reservoir of a mass of sunlight, and his body is similar to a wrathful vajra, which is cold like ice on the inside but wrathful on the outside in order to protect sentient beings. For that reason, he is called the one possessing *jñānavajra*" (*rdo rje ni shes rab nyid kyi phyir dang thabs nyid kyi phyir na 'jigs byed do/ de yang shin tu drag po'i lha thams cad 'jigs pa nyid kyi phyir ro/ de yang snying rje 'bras bu nyid de/ gang du gdug pa'i sems can rnams la snying rjes 'dul* [em. *du*, ed.] *ma yin/ gang phyir zhi ba'i yon tan gyis 'dul ba ma yin te/de phyir rdo rje can de 'jigs byed yang dag gyur/ thod pa'i phreng bas rgyan byas thod pa bsams pa'o/ nyi 'od khrod pa'i rdzing bu che/ mtshungs pa'i sku ni rdo rjes khro nang* [em. *gngas*, ed.] *kyi kha ba bzhin du bsil/ phyi rol drag pos 'gro ba skyongs/ shes rab rdo rje can gyis gsungs so*). (See also *Kṛṣṇācārya's commentary below.) The Sanskrit version of this passage differs in content: "He is ***vajra*** because of wisdom; ***bhairava*** is thought to be the means (*upāya*), because he produces fear in all fierce deities, and the fruit of that is compassion. That is what is meant by the vajra holder: "Being compassionate to all wicked beings is not a proof. They [the wicked beings] cannot be pleasant with good qualities; that is to say, he [Vajrabhairava] becomes the vajra holder, the terrorizing one, the kapālin, adorned with a garland of skulls, resembling the great lake heated by the rays of sun. There is no change in his wrath [because he is] cool as ice within. But by being hot on the outside, he protects the world."

*Kṛṣṇācārya (p. 442) divides the name **Vajrabhairava** into two units: (1) *vajra* stands for the truth body (*dharmakāya*), which is taught as emptiness (*śūnyatā*) and wisdom (*prajñā*), and (2) *bhairava* represents the form body (*rūpakāya*), which is taught to exist as both compassion (*karuṇā*) and means (*upāya*) (*rdo rje ni chos sku stong pa nyid dang shes rab ston pa yin la/ 'jigs byed gzugs sku thugs rjes thabs rnams grub par ston pa'o*). Kumāracandra (p. 287): "Vajrabhairava [means that] *bodhicitta*—the ultimate object of undifferentiated emptiness and compassion—is Bhagavān Śrī Vajradhara" (*rdo rje 'jigs byed ces pa ni stong ba nyid dang snying rje dbyer med pa'i don dam pa byang chub kyi sems te bcom ldan 'das dpal rdo rje 'chang ngo*).

Very fierce and terrifying: *Akṣobhya (p. 369): "**very fierce** on the inside and **terrifying** on the outside; moreover, he causes fear because of great anger" (*rab tu 'khrugs pa zhes bya ba ni lhag pa'i bdag nyid do/ 'jigs byed ces bya ba ni phyi rol lo/yang na rab tu 'khrugs pas 'jigs byed pa'o*). *Śoṇaśrī (p. 394) and *Vajrāsiddha (p. 413): "**very fierce** because of wrathful mind and **terrifying** because of hideous form" (*drag shul can zhes bya ba ni sems ma rungs pa'i phyir ro/ 'jigs byed ces bya ba ni gzugs mi sdug pa'i phyir ro*).

To all the gods: Standard Sanskrit grammar supports the meaning "among the gods" for the genitive plural *devānāṃ*. However, my translation follows *Kṛṣṇācārya's commentary, which understands *devānāṃ* in the sense of the dative case, meaning "to." *Kṛṣṇācārya (p. 442): "**gods** [means] Vajrabhairava [inspires terror and fear] to all the gods, such as Brahmā, who are arrogant" (*lha rnams zhes pa rdo rje 'jigs byed kyis lha rnams drag shul dang bcas tshangs pa la sogs pa*). He further explains: "Moreover, con-

[§2] In this [sādhana], the mantra master, having first sat in a place conducive to concentration,[454] is entitled to accomplish whatever ritual [he intends].

[Next,][455] I explain the places[456] that apply there. Having sat himself down

---

cerning this topic that Vajradhara impels that terrorizing one [i.e., Vajrabhairava] with compassion, that incomparably great wrathful one, who is fierce like the fire at the end of time and has the radiance of the sun, is endowed with wrathful body and heads, arms, phallus, ornaments, clothing, seat, and so on because one cannot benefit beings who are extremely wicked with only compassion. He is both the fruits of emptiness and compassion, *dharmakāya* and *rūpakāya*. This is taught by the verse 'cold as ice on the inside but wrathful on the outside in order to protect those beings'" (*de yang stong pa nyid dang snying rjes 'bras bu chos sku dang gzugs sku nyid de gang gdug pa dang ldan pa'i sems can rnams la snying rjes phan par mi 'gyur bas rdo rje 'chang des 'jigs par mdzad pa de/ sku shin tu 'jigs pa dbu dang phyag dang mtshan ma dang rgyan dang/ na bza' dang gdan dang nyi ma'i 'od zer dus mtha'i me ltar drag po mtshungs pa med pa'i khro bo chen po snying rjes bskul ba'o/ de yang nang na kha ba lta bur bsil/ phyi rol drag pos 'gro la skyob/ ces pas bstan pa'o*). Kumāracandra also supports the dative case but takes the adjective "**very fierce**" to qualify all the gods: "Those **gods** such as Svacchandabhairava, since they 'play' with the lives of others, are **very fierce** and cause all fear; **to them** [means] to all of them, who are very fierce, and cause terror to all; he [Vajrabhairava] is **terrifying** [means] he arouses fear" (*sarveṣāṃ svacchandabhairavādīnāṃ paraprāṇādibhir ddīvyantīti devāḥ. teṣām atyugrāṇām sarvabhīkārakāṇāṃ bhayānakaṃ bhayāvahaṃ*).

454. *Akṣobhya (p. 369) explains ***manonukūlasthāne***, "**in a place conducive to concentration**" simply as "a suitable place" (*gang yang rung ba'i gnas*); "those places are going to be explained" (*'chad par byed pa rnams la'o*). *Kṛṣṇācārya (p. 443) adopts the interpretation of the "places pleasing to the mind" from the *Yogācārabhūmi*: beautiful places that set the mind in a meditative mood. He says, "One should sit himself up in an isolated place that is pleasing to the mind, such as a cremation ground. Furthermore, *manonukūla* should be understood [metonymically] to include your assistant (*sahāya/uttarasādhaka*) and the substances and articles for worship" (*yid du 'ong zhes pa dur khrod la sogs pa yid dang mthun pa spro ba'i gnas gcig tu gnas par bya'o/ yang grogs dang rdzas dang ldan par byas la sdud* [em. *sdod*, ed.] *par shes par bya'o*). Lalitavajra (p. 302) follows *Kṛṣṇācārya when he says, "According to a brief explanation, **in any place conducive to concentration**" [means] that what is accomplished in the sādhana are various rituals, such as initiation, etc." (*gang yid du 'ong ba'i gnas su'o/ ci bsgrub na dbang la sogs pa'i las sna tshogs 'grub par bya zhes lus mdor bstan nas*).

455. Lalitavajra (p. 302) adds "according to the succession" (*de nas zhes bya ba ni rim gyi don to*).

456. *Akṣobhya (p. 369) glosses the word **places**: "These are definitions of the places suitable for the sādhana" (*gnas rnams zhes bya ba ni bsgrub pa'i gnas nges pa'o*).

in a cremation ground,[457] on the bank of a river,[458] at a solitary tree,[459] at a solitary *liṅga*,[460] at a crossroads,[461] on a mountain peak,[462] in an empty house,[463]

457. Lalitavajra (p. 302): "**Cremation ground** [means] the external cremation ground—that is, the grove of death" (*dur khrod ni phyi'i dur khrod de shi ba'i tshal lo*). *Kṛṣṇācārya (p. 444): "a place of execution, or a place where corpses are deposited" (*dur khrod ces pa ni bsad pa'i gnas ro skyel sa la bya'o*). *Sa la bya* corresponds to the Sanskrit *gamane*, the locative of *gamana*.

458. Lalitavajra (p. 302): "**The bank of a river** [means] [the bank] of a great river" (*chu 'gram ni chu bo chen po'i'o*). *Kṛṣṇācārya (p. 444): "It is a big river or an island; there, he should accomplish a practice of mastering a male or female *yakṣa* and a male or female *nāga* (*chu'i ngos zhes pa ni chu bo'am mtshan gling yin te/ der gnod sbyin pho mo dang klu pho mo bsgrub par bya'o*).

459. *Kṛṣṇācārya (p. 444): "**A solitary tree** [means] a tree not covered by the shadow of another tree" (*shing gcig ces pa ni shing gzhan gyi grib mas mi sleb mi reg pa'o*). The same gloss is given by *Śoṇaśrī (p. 394), *Vajrasiddha (p. 413), and Kumāracandra (p. 288). The same definition of a solitary tree is attested in the *Yogaratnamālā*'s commentary on the *Hevajra Tantra* 6.6 (Tripathi and Negi 2006, p. 46): *yasya chāyā nānyena vṛkṣeṇa ākramyate, yaś ca nānyasya ākrāmati, sa ekavṛkṣaḥ*. Lalitavajra (p. 302): "a big forest of trees such as mango trees" (*shing gcig ni ā mra* [corr. *ā smra*, ed.] *la sogs pa'i shing nags chen po'o*).

460. Lalitavajra (p. 302): "**A solitary *liṅga*** [means] the *liṅga* of Mahādeva," i.e., Śiva (*mtshan ma gcig pa ni/ ma hā de ba'i ling ga'o*). *Kṛṣṇācārya (p. 444): "an empty plain except for the *liṅga* of Maheśvara" (*mtshan ma gcig pa ni dbang phyug chen po'i mtshan ma thang stong la yod pa'o*). The *Śrīcakrasādhanāvidhāna* (f.20v4–6) describes a solitary *liṅga* as a *liṅga* within a certain radius: "*Ekaliṅga* is defined as the one with respect to which one does not see another *liṅga* within the interval of five *krośas*" (*pañcakrośāntare yatra na liṅgāntaram īkṣyate/ tadekaṃ liṅgaṃ ākhyātaṃ tatra siddhir anuttamā*). Also in Gadādharabhaṭṭācārya's *Tripurārcanamañjarī* chap. 4, fol. 9r8–10, the two definitions are attested, the other mentions the interval of four *krośas*: *teṣu ekaliṅgasthānaṃ matsyasūkte "catuḥkrośāntare yatra na liṅgaṃ dṛśyate param/ ekaliṅgaṃ vijānīyāt tatra siddhir anuttamā" // anyatrāpi "pañcakrośāntare yatra na liṅgāntaram īkṣyate/ tad ekaliṅgam ākhyātaṃ tatra siddhir anuttamā." purāṇaprasiddham ekaliṅgasthānaṃ mevāḍadeśe prasiddham iti vadanti*. I thank Alexis Sanderson for these references.

461. *Kṛṣṇācārya (p. 444): "**A crossroads** [means] crossroads; there should be an ideal place to paralyze. This place too should be understood to include your assistant, substances, and articles for worship" (*bzhi mdo zhes pa ni lam rgya gram ste/ der rengs pa'i gnas bya'o/ de yang grogs* [corr. *grong*, ed.] *dang rdzas dang ldan par byas la sdud* [em. *sdod*, ed.] *par shes par bya'o*).

462. *Kṛṣṇācārya (p. 444): "**A mountain peak** [means] at the top of the mountain; it is a place for driving away" (*ri rtse zhes pa ni ri mtho ba'i steng du ste bskrad pa'i gnas so*).

463. *Kṛṣṇācārya (p. 444): "**In an empty house** and an empty **temple** [means] there are two places for accomplishing prior service (*pūrvasevā*), sword, eye ointment, pill, alchemy, ambrosia, treasure, ghost, and zombie" (*khang stong lha khang stong pa gnyis* [em. *dngos po*,

in a temple of the mother goddesses[464] or any temple,[465] in a battlefield,[466] or in other places such as cities,[467] forests,[468] or villages,[469] the mantra master—[that

ed.] *der bsnyen sgrub dang ral gri dang/ mig sman dang/ ri lu dang/ gser 'gyur dang/ bcud kyis len dang/ gter dang 'byung po dang ro langs bsgrub pa'i gnas so*).

464. Lalitavajra (p. 302): "**Mothers** [means] the temple of the seven mothers" (*ma mo ni ma mo bdun gyi khyim mo*), possibly referring to the temple of the *saptamātṛkas*. *Kṛṣṇācārya (p. 444): "**In a temple of the mother goddesses** [means that] in the place where the wives of the eight gods reside, there is a place for accomplishing [the rituals] of subjugation and summoning and for the sādhana in general" (*ma mo'i khyim zhes pa ni lha brgyad kyi chung ma gang na yod pa'i brten sa la bya ste/ der dbang dang dgug pa dang bsgrub pa'i gnas so*). Kumāracandra (p. 288): "**Mothers** [means] the wife of Brahmā, the wife of Viṣṇu, the wife of Rudra, and so on" (*ma mo ni tshangs pa mo dang khyab 'jug mo dang drag mo la sogs pa'o*).

465. Lalitavajra (p. 302) explains: "As to the deity, even the temple dedicated to Mahādeva and so on" (*lha ni lha'i khang pa ste ma hā de ba la sogs pa yang bsngo*).

466. *Akṣobhya (p. 369): "**A battlefield** [means] a place where kings have fought" (*'thab mo'i gnas zhes bya ba ni/ rgyal po'i gyul 'gyed pa'i sa'o*). Lalitavajra (p. 302) seems to have a different reading in front of him, as he glosses "many destructions" as "the place where the battle was fought" (*mang po phung pa ni gyul 'gyed pa'i gnas so*). *Kṛṣṇācārya (p. 444): "**A battlefield** [means] a place of mutual conflict, a place of death, with many corpses; it is a place for [the ritual of] fomenting dissent" (*'thab mo'i sa zhes pa ni phan tshun 'thabs pa'i sa ro mang du shi ba'i sa ste dbye ba'i gnas so*). Kumāracandra (p. 288): "By **battlefield** [is meant] a place of battle where many soldiers have died" (*'thab mo yis ni gyul ngo gang du dmag mi mang po shi ba'o*).

467. Lalitavajra (p. 302): "**City** [means] a big city, one area where many dwellings are assembled" (*grong khyer ni grong khyer chen po ste/ mang po 'dus pa'i gnas phyogs gcig go*). *Kṛṣṇācārya (p. 444): "**Cities or forests** include one's own house or a *koṭara* [a hole in a tree]; these are ideal places to master a *piśāca* and to bring someone under one's own power" (*grong ngam nag khrod ces pa ni rang gi khyim dang shing gseb dang sha za dang/ dbang du bya ba sgrub pa'i gnas so*).

468. Lalitavajra (p. 302): "**Forest** [means] an assemblage of trees that is difficult to traverse" (*nags tshal ni bgrod par dka' ba'i shing gi khrod do*).

469. Lalitavajra (p. 302): "**Village** [means] the estate of a ruler" (*grong ni rgyal po'i phro brang ngo*).

is to say,] the yogin[470] who has received initiation (*abhiṣikto yogī*)[471] in this tan-

470. Lalitavajra (p. 302) describes the **yogin** as "one who has been duly consecrated into the maṇḍala of the *Vajrabhairava Tantra*—that is, the one who has been consecrated by purifying the three impurities through the three empowerments of the vase and so on, by serving a master endowed with the correct view. It is said, 'Such a person, by possessing wisdom and method, is a yogin.' The union of method and wisdom is said to be yoga." This is a quotation of GS 18.33ab (Matsunaga 1978: *prajñopāyasamāpattir yoga ity abhidhīyate*). I thank John Newman for this clarification. (*rdo rje 'jigs byed kyi rgyud kyi dkyil 'khor du legs par dbang thob pa ste/ bla ma mtshan nyid dang ldan pa mnyes pas bum pa'i dbang la sogs pa gsum gyis dri ma gsum dag par byas pas dbang thob pa ste/ de lta bu'i gang zag shes rab dang thabs su ldan pas na rnal 'byor pa ste/ thabs dang shes rab snyoms 'jug pa/ rnal 'byor zhes ni bshad pa yin/ zhes gsungs pa'o.*)

471. *Akṣobhya (pp. 369–70) says of ***abhiṣikto yogī***: "We have to draw out from another tantra—namely, the *Kṛṣṇayamāri Tantra*, which is a tantra concordant with this tantra (i.e., the *Vajrabhairava Tantra*)—initiation method, *bali*, rites related to yantras, hymns, and so on. Therefore the *yogin* who has received initiation in that way (***abhiṣikto yogī***) should accomplish the rites of subjugation and so on. Some say that the rites with the sword and so on must be accomplished following the explanation of this tantra. Yet others say they must be accomplished according to the tradition of another tantra. In the same way, it is said, 'For the ritual procedures that do not exist and for which there is no original rule, wise men take recourse to the procedure as taught in the compatible tantra (*sāmānyatantra*)'" (*dbang bskur thob pa zhes bya ba ni/ gshin rje dgra nag po'i rgyud ces bya ba rgyud 'di nyid dang rjes su mthun pa'i rgyud de las 'dir dbang bskur ba'i tshul dang/ gtor ma dang/ 'khrul 'khor gyi bya ba dang/ bstod pa la sogs pa drang bar bya ste/ de bas na de ltar dbang bskur ba'i rnal 'byor pa des dbang du bya ba la sogs pa bsgrub ste/ kha cig ni rgyud 'di nyid las gsungs la/ ral gri la sogs pa kha cig ni rgyud gzhan gyi lugs su bsgrub po/ de ltar yang/ gang nyid du ni rang nyid kyi/ las kyi cho ga rnams med pa// de ni spyi rgyud las grags pa'i/ cho ga mkhas pas shes par bya// zhes gsungs so*).

The quote also appears in the *Cakrasaṃvaravivṛti* 2.1: *yasmin karmāṇi na vidyante na karmavidhayaḥ svakāḥ/ tatra sāmānyatantrokto viddhir āśrīyate budhaiḥ //*.

*Kṛṣṇācārya (p. 444): "**The yogin who has received initiation in [this tantra of] the venerable Great Vajrabhairava** [means] the mantras *hrīḥ ṣṭrīḥ* of Vajrabhairava generated from the *ya-varga*, etc., have to be recited one hundred times. The [mantras] *jinajik*, etc., for the retinue of the twelve generated from [the seed syllable] *kṣem*, etc., are to be recited ten thousand for each. Combining the four yogas (*yoga*, *atiyoga*, *anuyoga*, and *mahāyoga*) with these, he is one who has completed the prior service (*pūrvasevā*). He has to master the preliminary rituals [setting up the altar, infusing the articles and the disciple], prepare the maṇḍala, [perform the] sādhana, and receive the four initiations, all correctly. The qualifications of the yogin that are included in the *abhiṣikto* are that he relies on the four yogas, performs the *pūrvasevā*, [does] the sādhana, and performs the karmas" (*dpal rdo rje 'jigs byed chen por dbang bskur ba'i rnal 'byor pas zhes pa ni/ ya las bskyed pa'i rdo rje 'jigs byed kyi hrīḥ ṣṭrīḥ ya 'bum kshem la sogs las bskyed pa/ 'khor bcu gnyis la rdzi na rdzik sogs khri khri'i bsnyen pa rnal 'byor bzhi dang ldan pas bsnyen pa byas la/ sta gon dang dkyil 'khor bsgrub pa dang dbang bzhi'am ci rigs pa thob pa'o/ rnal 'byor bzhi la brten nas bsnyen pa byas pas dbang la sogs pa bsgrub pa dang las la sbyar ba'o*).

tra of the Great Vajrabhairava—is entitled to accomplish [the rituals of] subjugation, attraction,[472] killing,[473] driving away,[474] inciting hostility between two people,[475] paralyzing, sword,[476] eye ointment,[477] underworld, pill,[478] elixir,[479]

472. Lalitavajra (p. 305): "**Attraction** [means] he summons [someone's] feet and body. Moreover, he summons the earth and the sky" (*dgug pa zhes bya ba ni/ rkang pa dgug pa dang/ lus dgug pa'o/ de yang sa dang nam kha' la dgug pa'o*).

473. Lalitavajra (p. 305) quotes from the GS (14.46, p. 68): "As for **killing**, it is said [in the GS] that he should perform the ritual, such as killing and so on, against those who harm the Three Jewels, those who revile the master and so on, those without vows, those who revile the Mahāyāna, and those who assert faults in the tantras of the Mantra[yāna]" (*gsad pa ni dkon mchog gsum la sogs pa la gnod pa byed pa la ste/ bla ma smod stsogs dam tshig med/ theg pa chen po smod pa dang/ sngags kyi rgyud la dpyas ba* [em. *dpya' ba*, ed.] *la/ gsad pa la sogs las bya'o/ zhes gsungs pa'o*).

474. Lalitavajra (p. 305): "**Driving away** [means] he should expel from one's own place" (*rang gi gnas las dbyung ba ni bskrad pa'o*).

475. Lalitavajra (p. 305): "**Inciting hostility** [means] creating mutual hostility between two friends" (*dbye ba ni mdza' bo dag phan tshun zhe sdang ba'o*).

476. Lalitavajra (p. 305): "**Sword** [means] a *vidyādhara* who has mastery over the sword siddhi and so on (*ral gri ni ral gri la sogs pa'i rig pa 'dzin pa'o*).

477. Lalitavajra (p. 305) glosses **eye ointment** as "the means to perceive the world systems" (*mig sman ni 'jig rten mthong ba'i thabs so*). *Kṛṣṇācārya (pp. 444–45): "**Sword, eye ointment,** and so on: all the substances that are caused to manifest as the special products through this deity, mantra, and tantra are to be understood as common and not different from [those mentioned in] other tantras" (*ral gri dang mig sman zhes pa la sogs pa ni lha dang sngags dang rgyud 'dis khyad par du byas pa'i bya ba rdzas thams cad rgyud gzhan las khyad par med de thun mong du go bar bya'o*).

478. Lalitavajra (p. 305): "**Underworld** [means] he enters into the netherworld" (*sa 'og ni sa 'og tu 'jug pa'o*).

Lalitavajra (p. 305): "**Pill** [means a pill that] is made of three metals (*triloha*) and accomplishes [the siddhi of] invisibility" (*ri lu ni lcags gsum dang bcas pa ste/ mi snang ba bsgrub pa'o*). Śaiva and Buddhist exegetical literature universally holds that the "three metals" (*triloha*) are "gold, silver, and copper." For example, Kṣemarāja's commentary on the *Svacchanda Tantra*, the *Svacchandoddyota* (9.107), mentions gold, silver, and copper as three metals for wrapping up the *guṭikā* (*trilohaṃ hema rājata tamraṃ*). Abhayākaragupta's *Abhayapaddhati* (*paṭala* 2, *prayoga* 7), which is a commentary on the *Buddhakapāla Tantra*, not only prescribes wrapping up the pill (*guṭikā*) in three metals of gold, silver, and copper, but it also gives the exact measurement for the gold to be used (*guṭikaṃ hematāraśullaṃ krameṇa veṣṭayitvā* [. . .] *atra suvarṇamānaṃ sārdharāthikādikamaṣatrayaṃ*) "Having wrapped the pill in gold, silver, and copper one after the other . . . here the measure of gold is one *maṣa* (0.97 grams) and three and a half *rāthikā*."

479. Lalitavajra (p. 305): "**Elixir** [means] the *rasāyana* (rejuvenating technique), which allows one to subsist without aging and so on (*bdud rtsi ni bcud kyi len te/ rgas pa la sogs pa med cing gnas pa'o*).

alchemy, treasure, ghosts,[480] zombie,[481] bloodthirsty demon,[482] *yakṣas*[483] and *yaksiṇīs*,[484] serpents,[485] and so on[486] by the following ritual procedure.

[§3] In this [sādhana], this is the ritual procedure. First of all, the man-

480. Lalitavajra (p. 305): "**Ghosts** [means] the host of sentient beings, with two legs and so on, who will be subjected to one's will" (*'byung po ni/ sems can gyi tshogs te/ rkang gnyis la sogs pa ste/ de dag dbang du byed pa'o*). *Kṛṣṇācārya (p. 445): "**Ghosts** [means] Aparājita" (*'byung po zhes pa ni a pa ra ji ta'o*). Kumāracandra (p. 288): "**Ghosts** [means] *dikpālas* such as Vijaya and so on" (*'byung po ni phyogs skyong rnam par rgyal ba la sogs pa'o*). The Sanskrit version of Kumāracandra's commentary gives a slightly different reading: "**Ghosts** [means] great magical power, Aparājita, and the like" (*mahārddhikā aparājitaprabhṛtayaḥ*).

481. Lalitavajra (p. 305): "**Zombie** [means] he will accomplish the *vetāla* [sādhana]" (*ro ni ro langs bsgrub pa'o*). *Kṛṣṇācārya (p. 445): "**Zombie** [means] it should be without wounds and he should come from a good family, be strong, be young, and so on" (*ro langs zhes pa ni ro rma med pa'i rigs dang stobs dang gzhon pa la sogs pa bya'o*).

482. Lalitavajra (p. 305): "**Bloodthirsty demon** [means] an emaciated hungry ghost" (*'dre ni yi dags phra mo'o*). *Kṛṣṇācārya (p. 445): "**Bloodthirsty demon** [means] the *rākṣasī* Caṇḍikā" (*sha za zhes pa ni srin po candi ka'o*). Kumāracandra (p. 288): "**Demon** [means] the flesh-eater who consumes the food that has been purged and so on" (*sha za ni skyugs pa zas su za ba la sogs pa'o*).

483. Lalitavajra (p. 305) glosses ***yakṣa*** as "one who is a hole dweller and so on" (*gnod sbyin ni gang bug pa* [em. *brag pa*, ed.] *brang po la sogs pa'o*). *Kṛṣṇācārya (p. 445): "***Yakṣa*** [means] Jambhala or his son" (*gnod sbyin zhes pa ni jambha la 'am bu'o*). Kumāracandra (p. 288): "***Yakṣa*** [means] Vaiśravaṇa and so on" (*gnod sbyin ni rnam thos sras la sogs pa'o*). The Sanskrit version of Kumāracandra's commentary gives Kubera instead.

484. Lalitavajra (p. 305) glosses ***yakṣiṇī*** as "a hungry ghost endowed with magical powers" (*gnod sbyin mo ni rdzu 'phrul dang ldan pa'i yi dags so*). *Kṛṣṇācārya (p. 445): "***Yakṣiṇī*** [means] Jambhala's wife or Vasudhāriṇī" (*mo ni de'i chung ma dang nor rgyun ma'o*).

485. Lalitavajra (p. 305) glosses **serpents** as "a serpent that belongs to the lineage [of the *nāgas*]" (*klu rnams ni rigs kyi khyad par gyi klu'o*). *Kṛṣṇācārya (p. 445): "**Serpents** [means] the eight great *nāgas*, or rainmakers, beginning with Apālala, (rain-related god), and the females of these classes; the eight consorts of eight *nāgarājas* and so on" (*klu ni klu chen po brgyad dang sog ma med la sogs pa'i char 'bebs pa rnams so/ mo yang klu mo brgyad la sogs pa'o*).

486. Lalitavajra (p. 305) explains: "**And so on** includes the frightening *rākṣasas* and others" (*stsogs kyis srin po 'jigs pa la sogs bsdu do*). He (p. 305) also indicates an **and so on** after the word *yakṣiṇī* that is not present in the Sanskrit version: "By **and so on** are included other [beings] such as divine musicians (*gandharvas*), *asuras*, humans, or whatever" (*stsogs kyis bsdus pa dri za dang lha ma yin dang mi 'am ci la sogs pa'o*). *Kṛṣṇācārya (p. 445): "**And so on** [means] friendly *śaktis*; he is assisted by these particular places" (*sogs zhes pa ni yul gyi khyad par gyis grogs nus pa rnams so*). It seems that Kṛṣṇācārya's explanation here is corrupted.

tra master—[that is,] the teacher (*ācārya*)—at midnight, naked, having loosened his topknot, [established] in yoga with the Buffalo-Faced One [Vajrabhairava], draws a maṇḍala[487] with the ashes of the cremation ground[488] in the cremation ground, and so on.

487. *Kṛṣṇācārya (p. 445): "**He draws a maṇḍala** [means] he should draw it at the time of the sādhana [and not during initiation]. He should draw it with a fine powder of the cremation ground. Drawing should be preceded by the ritual of taking the site and outlining, and he should also make a line with a thread taken from the corpse" (*dkyil 'khor bri bar bya zhes pa ni bsgrub pa'i dus te/ dus khrod kyi tshon gyis bri ba ste/ sa'i cho ga dang thig sngon du song bar byas la bri ba ste/ thig skud yang ro'i srad bus bya'o*). *Kṛṣṇācārya's reference to the thread taken from a corpse shows the Kāpālika influence. The same is attested in the *Yoginīsaṃcāra* (8.6), where we read, "The one holding the thread should trace the outline [of the maṇḍala] with a thread taken from a corpse (*śavasūtreṇa*) soaked in blood" (*sūtrayed rudhirāktena śavasūtreṇa sūtradhṛk*; Sanskrit text given in Sanderson 2009, 203). This description matches the passage of the *Laghuśaṃvara* (2.11) where we also find the thread of a corpse (*mṛtakasūtra*) colored in human blood. The same appears in the third *ṣaṭka* of the *Jayadrathayāmala*, where we find a reference to the cord made of hair from a human corpse (*śavamūrdhajarajju*): "Then one should draw an excellent maṇḍala using the terrifying ash [of the cremation ground]. First, having drawn an outline using a cord made from the hair of a human corpse, he should draw it [the maṇḍala], O goddess, as having three enclosing lines with colors white, red, and so on" *ālikhen maṇḍalavaraṃ tato raudreṇa bhasmanā/ prathamaṃ sūtrayitvā tu śavamūrdhajarajjunā/ trirekham ālikhed devi śuklaraktādivarṇaiḥ//*, *Jayadrathayāmala*, *ṣaṭka* 3, 4.20cd–21ab, edition by Sanderson (unpublished draft dated January 2015). What these examples indicate is that the VBhT, as one of the earliest transgressive Buddhist tantras, is seemingly given a Kāpālika "packaging" by the commentators who lived in the period when the penetration of the Śaiva-Śākta elements into yoginī tantras reached its climax.

488. The Tibetan text takes **the ashes of the cremation ground** to refer to the body of the sādhaka on which they should be smeared (*ro bsregs pa'i thal chen gyis lus byugs*; Siklós 1996, 80). This would correspond to the Sanskrit *citibhasmāliptāṅgo*, "whose body is dusted with the ashes of the cremation ground," but this interpretation is not supported by the commentaries, which unanimously take the ashes of the cremation ground to refer to the powder used for drawing the maṇḍala. In addition, the Vajrabhairava sādhaka is often mentioned in the VBhT as smearing his body with urine and feces (see VBhT §8, p. 217) and not ashes; therefore the Tibetan text must be corrupted. *Akṣobhya (p. 370) comments on **the ashes of the cremation ground**: "Here [in this tantra], because the chief activities are wrathful rites, [the Lord] teaches ashes instead of divine powders. For the same reason, [in the preparation of the maṇḍala,] one should also make only one line instead of five. It is said, 'Whatever powders are taught, all those are of one line'" (*ro bsregs pa'i thal bas zhes bya ba ni/ 'dir drag shul spyad pa gtso bor gyur pas lha'i tshon* [em. *chon*, ed.] *gyi gor thal phye bshad pa yin la/ de nyid kyis ri mo yang gcig kho na lnga'i gor sbyar ro/ thal phyer gang dag bshad pa ni/ de dag thams cad ri mo gcig/ ces gsungs pas so*). *Akṣobhya refers here to the common procedure in the preparation of the Buddhist maṇḍala where five lines are normally drawn to indicate the five buddha families. Here, however, since we are dealing with the wrathful rites (*raudra*), only one line, drawn with ashes, is included.

[He should draw] a maṇḍala square[489] with four doors[490] ornamented with four arches,[491] decorated with bells,[492] banners,[493] pennants,[494] and the like [and also] adorned with a string of flowers.[495] In all the corners and in the points where the doors meet the porticos, [the maṇḍala square] is inlaid with the vajra jewels, and similarly with the half moons. In the center of that

---

*Śoṇaśrī (p. 394) and *Vajrasiddha (p. 413) list five types of powders: "'Ashes of cremated corpses' [means] white powder; 'black' [means] with the charcoal of cremated corpses; 'yellow' [means] with orpiment; 'red' [means] with the brick of a cremation ground; 'green' [means] with petals of *neem* and *sundhara*, etc. [perhaps *sundari*, a species of mangrove]. With these powders is linked to **draws the maṇḍala**'" (*ro bsregs pa'i thal ba zhes bya ba'i tshon ni dkar ba'o/ nag po ni ro bsregs pa'i sol bas so/ ser po ni ba blas so/ dmar po ni dur khrod kyi so phag gis so/ ljang gu ni nim pa dang ni sun dha ra la sogs pa'i lo mas so/ rdul tshon de rnams kyis dkyil 'khor bri bar bya'o zhes par 'brel lo*). The explanation of the powders of four colors matches the description of the *Yogaratnamālā* (2.19, Tripathi and Negi 2006, 21): *kṛṣṇarajaḥ śmaśānāṅgāreṇa; sitarājo narāsthicūrṇena; pītarajo haritālakena; raktarajaḥ śmaśāneṣṭakena.*

489. *Kṛṣṇācārya (p. 445): "**Maṇḍala square** [means] all dharmas are not unequal but equal" (*gru bzhi zhes bya ba ni mi mnyam pa med cing mnyam pa nyid do*). *Śoṇaśrī (p. 394) and *Vajrasiddha (p. 413) give the same gloss. This is a standard description of the maṇḍala square attested in other early Buddhist tantras.

490. *Kṛṣṇācārya (p. 445) says of the **four doors** that "because of purification (*viśuddhi*), the symbolism of the four doors is emptiness, singlessness, wishlessness, and uncompoundness" (*sgo bzhi zhes pa ni stong pa nyid dang mtshan ma med pa dang smon pa med pa dang/ mngon par 'dus ma byas pa nyid rnam par dag pa'o*). *Śoṇaśrī (p. 394) and *Vajrasiddha (p. 413) give the same gloss.

491. *Kṛṣṇācārya (p. 445): "**Four arches** [means] the nature of the four meditations (*dhyāna*)" (*rta babs bzhi zhes pa ni bsam gtan bzhi'i rang bzhin no*). *Śoṇaśrī (p. 394) and *Vajrasiddha (pp. 413–14) give the same gloss.

492. *Kṛṣṇācārya (p. 445): "**Bells** [means] to understand emptiness of all the phenomena" (*dril bu zhes pa ni chos thams cad stong par rtogs pa'o*). *Śoṇaśrī (pp. 394–95) and *Vajrasiddha (p. 414) give the same gloss.

493. *Kṛṣṇācārya (p. 445): "**Banners** [means] purification of the eight consciousnesses" (*dar gyi* [em. *ral gri*, ed.] *'phan zhes pa ni rnam par shes pa brgyad dag pa'o*).

494. The Tibetan text lists pennants (Skt. *pātaka*; Tib. *dar*) (Siklós 1996, 80), but Siklós (*ibid*., 28) takes it to refer to silk. *Kṛṣṇācārya (p. 445): "**Pennants** [means] purification of the nine branches of the scriptures" (*pravācana*—that is, *sūtra*, *udāna*, *jātaka*, etc.) (*ba dan zhes pa ni gsung rab yan lag dgu rnam par dag pa'o*). *Śoṇaśrī (p. 395) and *Vajrasiddha (p. 414) give the same gloss.

495. *Kṛṣṇācārya (p. 445): "**Adorned with a string of flowers** [means] purification of the five sense objects" (*me tog phreng ba zhes pa ni 'dod pa'i yon tan lnga rnam par dag par ro*). *Śoṇaśrī (p. 395) and *Vajrasiddha (p. 414) give the same gloss.

[maṇḍala square], he draws a circle, which is round[496] and divided into nine segments.[497] He should keep one door[498] open [and] keep the others closed.

496. The Sanskrit and Tibetan texts take *vajraratnais* as a *karmadhāraya* meaning "vajra jewels," but *Kṛṣṇācārya (p. 445) seems to understand it as a *dvandva*, because he glosses *vajra* and *ratna* separately: "***Vajra*** [means] indivisible" (*rdo rje zhes pa ni mi phyed pa'o*), and "**jewels** [means] the great compassion, which increases unsurpassed joy" (*rin po che zhes pa ni bla na med pa'i dga' ba rgyas pa'i snying rje chen po'o*). For *Śoṇaśrī (p. 395) and *Vajrasiddha (p. 414), "***vajra* jewels** [means] emptiness" (*rdo rje rin chen zhes bya ba ni rdo rje ni stong pa nyid do*), and **jewels** has a gloss identical to that of *Kṛṣṇācārya.

*Kṛṣṇācārya (p. 445): "**The half moons** [means] the growth of the *bodhicitta*" (*zla ba phyed pa zhes pa ni byang chub kyi sems 'phel ba'o*). *Śoṇaśrī (p. 395) and *Vajrasiddha (p. 414) have the same gloss.

*Akṣobhya (p. 370): "**Round** [means] surrounded by the inner vajra garland" (*zlum po zhes bya ba ni nang gi rdo rje phreng bas bskor ba'o*).

497. *Kṛṣṇācārya (pp. 445–46): "**Nine segments** [means] the places for the nine deities: a double vajra (*viśvavajra*) [in the middle] and four *viśvapadma*s in the four intermediate directions. One should also draw the inner circle of the deity (*devapaṭikā*), the vajra fence, and the doors, and one should install the symbols (*cihna*s) of the deity [there]" (*re'u mig dgu zhes pa ni lha dgu'i gnas te sna tshogs rdo rje dang mtshams bzhir sna tshogs pad ma bzhi'o / lha'i snam bu dang rdo rje ra ba dang sgo rnams kyang bri zhing lha'i mtshan ma dgod pa'o*).

498. *Kṛṣṇācārya (p. 446): "**Door** [means] the sādhaka should shut all but one. For aggressive *abhicāra* rituals, the southern door is left open. The southern door is also [left open] for subjugation (*vaśya*) and pacification (*śānti*). These doors symbolize the four gateways of liberation (*vimkoṣa*) of the completion stage (*utpannakrama*). This gateway is called a *door* (*dvāra*) because one exits and enters. Through the door of emptiness (*śūnyatādvāra*), one enters in the form of four kinds of yoga and exits through the perfectly realized maṇḍala. One does not enter nor exit through other doors. Through the door of signlessness (*animitadvāra*), one introduces the four mantras and four kinds of repetitions (*japa*s)—that is, one arrives at the four maṇḍalas through the door of the wind corner. In the door of wishlessness (*apraṇihittadvāra*), one places the four dharmas, and the *cakra* with sixteen petals, *kṣe* and so on, in the navel. By joining wind and fire, it blazes. In the heart, one [places] the eight-petal *cakra*, *hi*, and so on. In the navel, [one places] *oṃ hūṃ* and so on; it blazes. In the throat, one [places] the eight-petal *cakra*, and in the navel [one places] *ya* on *oṃ* and so on, and the essences flow from that door. On the head, one [places] the four-petal *cakra*, *dhaiḥ* on *oṃ*, *hūṃ*, *haṃ*. When one enters through the navel in the door of flow, the great bliss arises. In the uncompounded door (*anabhisaṃskṛtadvāra*), one should meditate that the shape of the deity, mantra, and attributes are one, indivisible, and that they neither exist nor not exist. And each of these enters and exits through their respective doors and not through other doors; that's why they need to remain closed. The one door through which one enters is a liberation door, and it is open" (*sgo gcig ces pa ni sgrub pa po gcig las med na gzhan bcad pa'o / drag po dang 'di nyid kyi* [em. *kyis*, ed.] *lho'i sgo gcig kho nas bya'o / dbang dang zhi ba 'ang lho'i sgo kho na'o / yang rdzogs rim gyi sgo rnam par thar pa'i sgo bzhi ste / sgo ni 'gro dang 'ong bas sgo ste / stong pa nyid kyi sgor rnal 'byor bzhi dbyibs su 'jug pa mngon par rtogs pa'i dkyil 'khor gyi sgor 'gro ba'o / gzhan du mi 'jug mi 'gro ba'o /*

[§4] In the center of that [circle], he draws a corpse;[499] in the east, a head;[500] in

---

mtshan ma med pa'i sgor sngags bzhi gzhug cing bzlas thabs bzhi rlung gi sgor dkyil 'khor bzhir 'ong ba'o/ smon pa med pa'i sgor [em. *sgo*, ed.] *chos bzhi lte bar yang/ rtsa 'dab bcu drug la kshe la sogs dang rlung dang me'i sbyor bas 'bar ba'i rnam pa dang snying gar rtsa 'dab brgyad la hi la sogs pa lte bar oṃ dang hūṃ la sogs pa 'bar ba'i rnam pa dang/ mgrin par rtsa 'dab brgyad la lte bar oṃ la ya la sogs pa'i snying po rnams 'bab pa'i sgo nas/ spyi bor rtsa 'dab bzhi la oṃ la dhaiḥ hūṃ haṃ lte bar 'bab pa'i sgor 'jug bde ba chen por 'ong ba'o/ mngon par 'dus ma byas pa'i sgo de gsum mi phyed par gcig tu dbyibs dang sngags dang chos rnams yod pa ma yin med pa ma yin gnyis ka med pa ma yin par bsgom pa'o/ de yang rang rang sgor 'gro 'ong la/ gzhan dang gzhan du mi 'gro mi 'ong bas bcad pa'o/ 'jug pa'i sgo la gcig la grol ba'i sgo 'ong ba 'ang gcig kho nas so*).

499. *Akṣobhya (p. 370) specifies: "**He should keep the others closed** [means] the other three doors should be closed except for the door in the southern direction. As it is said: 'one has to construct a big door with a platform, but [with] one [portion] that is more distinguished.' As for 'blocking other doorways,' it is said, 'With white powder in the middle portion of a doorway, one should draw a subtle line'" (*sgo rnams gzhan ni gcad par bya/ zhes bya ba ni lho phyogs las gzhan pa gsum gcad pa ste/ ji skad du/ chab sgo chen po stegs bur bcas/ cung zad gcig ni lhag par bya// chab sgo gzhan rnams bcad pa ni/ phye ma dkar po dag gis su/ sgo yi dbus kyi cha dag tu// ri mo phra mo bri bar bya/ zhes gsungs pa'o*). This passage, quoted from an unidentified source, is also found in Kāmadhenu's *Mahākalparājasyaṭīkā* commentary on the *Sarvadurgatipariśodhana*, p. 1560.

*Akṣobhya (p. 370): "**He draws a corpse**—that is to say, as a seat (*āsana*)" (*ro bri'o zhes bya ba ni gdan te*). What *Akṣobhya means is that the corpse is the seat of the deity Vajrabhairava. He then outlines the three general rules for depicting divine beings in the maṇḍala drawing. He says, "First, one draws the shape [of the deity]; second, one draws the form of the mudrā; and third, one draws their places and seats. These [three rules] are known as the ways to draw" (*dang por gzugs su bri bar bya/ gnyis pa phyag rgya'i gzugs su bri/ gsum pa gnas dang stan dag tu/ bri ba'i cho ga yongs su bsgrags zhes so*). *Kṛṣṇācārya (pp. 446–47): "**In the center of that [circle], he draws a corpse** [means] the sacred seat (*pīṭha*)—i.e., the throne of the deity. It [the corpse] has one head, two arms, red eyes, yellow hair flowing upward. It is naked and black in color, has barred fangs, and in the right hand, [holds] a sword and in the left hand, carries a skull. The eight [corpses should be put] in the corners [of the maṇḍala] and another one in the actual center. He should draw Śiva and Umā. In the four corners, he should draw a skull filled with nectar (*amṛta*) standing on the lip of the four vases" (*dbus su ro langs bri zhes pa ni lha'i gdan mgo bo gcig lag pa gnyis mig dmar ba skra ser ba g.yen du brdzes pa gcer bu mdog nag pa/ so dang mche ba gtsigs pa/ g.yas ral gri/ g.yon thod pa thogs pa brgyad dang/ dbus ngos su ma ha de ba dang/ u ma de ba bri'o/ grwa bzhir thod pa bdud rtsis gang ba bzhi bum pa'i khar bri'o*). *Śoṇaśrī (p. 395) and *Vajrasiddha (p. 414) give an almost identical description of the corpses, the only difference being that they have three red eyes (*mig dmar ba gsum yod pa*) and hold in their left hand a skull filled with blood (*g.yon na khrag gis bkang ba'i thod pa 'dzin pa rnams so*).

500. *Akṣobhya (p. 370) specifies, referring to the maṇḍala of Solitary Hero Vajrabhairava in the VBhT: "Moreover, in the maṇḍala of Solitary Hero (*ekavīra*) one has to fix many symbols, as it is stated (in the root text)—**in the east, a head,** and so on." (*'on kyang dpa' bo gcig pa'i dkyil 'khor du ni/ phyag mtshan ji snyed pa dgod par bya ba yang yin pas na/ shar*

the south, an arm; in the west, entrails; in the north, a leg. In the eastern corner, [he draws] a skull;[501] in the southern corner, a [skull] cup; in the western corner, a rag of the cremation ground; in the northern corner, a man impaled on a stake. These are the symbols he should position in the center of the circle.

[§5] Next, there are the symbols outside the circle:[502] on the strip in the eastern direction, he draws a dagger, a spear,[503] a pestle, a knife, a single-pointed vajra,[504] a hook, and so on.[505] On the southern strip, he draws an axe, an arrow,

---

du ni mgo bo zhes bya ba la sogs pa smos te). *Kṛṣṇācārya (p. 447): "**In the east, a head,** and so on [means] at the fourth [eastern] door, he should draw the head of a corpse, an arm, intestines, and a leg" (*shar du mgo bo zhes pa ni sgo bzhir ro'i mgo dang lag pa dang rgyu ma dang rkang pa bri'o*).

501. *Kṛṣṇācārya (p. 447) has instead "**In the northern corner, a skull** [means] in the northeastern corner, and then one has to proceed clockwise" (*byang gi grwar thod pa zhes bya ba ni byang shar gyi grwa la sogs pa g.yas skor ro*).

502. *Kṛṣṇācārya (p. 447): "**Next, outside the circle,** [means] beginning with the Īśāna corner (i.e., the northeastern direction), installation [of the symbols] must be done clockwise" (*de nas dkyil 'khor phyi rol zhes pa ni lha snam de dbang ldan gyi gnas nas dgod pa g.yas skor du dgod pa'o*). Kumāracandra (p. 289): "**Next** [means] as for the supplementary signs and symbols outside the wheel, these symbols, a knife and so on, should be fixed beginning with the direction of Īśāna. One should draw them sequentially, proceeding clockwise, fixing them there at each corner" (*de nas zhes bya ba la sogs pa la 'khor lo'i phyi rol gyi 'phar ma phyag rgya dang rtags ni gri gug la sogs pa'i mtshan ma ni dbang ldan gyi mtshams nas bzung ste/ g.yon skor du mtshams de nyid du thug par bri bar bya'o*).

503. Tibetan text (Siklós 1996, 81) has "a single-pointed spear" (*mtshon rtse gcig pa*). *Kṛṣṇācārya (p. 447) also has this reading in front of him, and he glosses "a single-pointed **spear** that is an iron lance ornamented with peacock feathers (*mayūrapiccha*)" (*mtshon rtse gcig pa zhes pa ni lcags mdung rma bya'i sgro'i chun po dang ldan pa'o*). Kumāracandra (p. 289) has an identical gloss. This could also refer to a *mayūrapiñcchaka*, a fan made of peacock feathers that is often in the possession of the sādhaka in the Bhūta tantras, according to which he must either possess it or ornament himself with it. In BY 47.10cd, one should wave the *piñcchaka* during the sādhana while observing the great vow (*piñcchakaṃ bhrāmayet paścān mahāvratatanusthitaḥ*). The *piñcchaka* is also used for sweeping up the maṇḍala after its completion. In the *Cakrasaṃvara* (35.5), we find the expression "let him wave his *piñcchaka*." I thank Alexis Sanderson for this explanation.

504. *Kṛṣṇācārya (p. 447): "**A single-pointed vajra** [means] a half spear" (*rdo rje rtse gcig pa zhes pa phyed mdung ngo*). Kumāracandra (p. 289) gives an identical gloss.

505. *Kṛṣṇācārya (p. 447): "**And so on** [means] others, which are easy to deduce" (*gzhan rnams ni go sla'o*).

a club,[506] a skull staff, a wheel, and a noose.[507] On the western strip, he draws a vajra, a drum,[508] a shield, a bow, a bell, a banner blowing in the wind, and so on. On the northern strip, he draws a threatening finger, a triple-ribbon banner, an elephant hood, a vajra hammer, a spear, a firepit, and so on.[509] In the four doors and in the corners of the doors, he should position the great zombies.[510]

506. In comparison with the Sanskrit text, the Tibetan text (Siklós 1996, 81) lists those two weapons in reverse order—that is, the skull staff comes before *dbyig to*, which Siklós (1996, 29) translates as "staff." Actually, *dbyig to* is a corruption of *dbyug to*, meaning "a stick" or "a club." This is supported by Kumāracandra's commentary (p. 289), which glosses *dbyug to* as "club" (*dbyug pa*).

507. The Tibetan text (Siklós 1996, 81) has "a vajra noose" (*rdo rje zhags pa*).

508. The Tibetan text (Siklós 1996, 81) has *rde'u chung*, which Siklós (29) translates as a "sword." Actually, *rde'u chung* is a corruption of *rnga chung*, "a small drum." Further, his translation has an additional weapon, "knife," that does not feature in the Tibetan text. Thus his translation has seven weapons, while the Tibetan and Sanskrit texts have six.

509. If one counts all the symbols deposited inside and outside the center, the total is thirty-two. This number corresponds to the thirty-two weapons held by Vajrabhairava's thirty-two hands. However, *Akṣobhya (p. 371) disagrees with that iconography and claims that Vajrabhairava has thirty-four arms, with two extra hands holding an elephant hide, which stands for wisdom (*prajñā*) and means (*upāya*). He comments on it by glossing **and so on**: "As for the other [weapons], they are explained by drawing suitable weapons encapsulated by the word *ādi*, "and so on." As for that which constitutes the method of excellent and nondual means and wisdom, it [is portrayed iconographically as Vajrabhairava] holding an elephant hide in both hands. Moreover, as for the thirty-two symbols of the tathāgata's great compassion, those are displayed by the other (thirty-two arms) holding various weapons; because of this, it is not permissible to draw any other weapons" (*gzhan dag ni sogs pa zhes bya ba'i sgras mtshon cha gang yang rung ba bri bar 'chad do/ thabs dang shes rab phul du byung ba dbyer med pa'i tshul du 'gyur ba ni/ phyag gnyis glang po che'i pags pa dang bcas pa yin la/ de bzhin gshegs pa'i thugs rje chen po'i sum cu gnyis nyid ni/ phyag gi mtshon cha dang bcas pa lhag mas ston pas na/ mtshon cha gzhan gang yang rung/ bri ba ni mi 'thad pa nyid do*).

510. *Akṣobhya's commentary (p. 371) glosses: "**The great zombies** [the number "eight" is missing in the Sanskrit version] [means] naked, with relaxed hair, sharp teeth, black like the *rākṣasas*, and holding a crooked knife and a skull. These zombies become assistants of the sādhaka and achieve his desired magical karma" (*ro langs chen po brgyad ces bya ba ni gcer bu skra grol ba so rno ba nag po srin po lta bu gri gug dang/ thod pa thogs pa rnams so/ 'di dag ni sgrub pa po'i grogs su gyur pa 'dod pa'i las 'grub pa'o*). Kumāracandra (p. 289): "**Zombie** [means] a corpse" (*ro langs ni ro'o*). *Śoṇaśrī (p. 395) and *Vajrasiddha (p. 414): "**The great zombies** [means] they have two hands, one face, and three red eyes; they are yellowish, with spiked hair, naked, mouths baring fangs, and black in color. In their right hands, the zombies brazenly hold a crooked knife; in their left hands, they hold a skull filled with blood" (*ro langs chen po zhes bya ba ni ro langs te/ lag pa gnyis pa/ gdong gcig pa mig dmar ba gsum yod pa skra ser skya g.yen du phyogs pa gcer bu kha mche ba gtsigs pa/ kha*

[§6] He should offer a lamp with human oil.[511] If he desires the highest siddhi,[512] he should offer the meat of a human, a donkey, a camel, a dog, a jackal, a buffalo, an elephant, a horse,[513] a cow, a sheep, a deer, a pig, and so on.

[§7] Among others, he should offer the meat of a vulture, an owl, a crow, an eagle, a crane, a water hen, a stork, a peacock, a big rooster, a big myna, and so

dog nag po lag pa g.yas na gri gug gdengs pas [em. *pa*, ed.]/ *g.yon na khrag gis bkang ba'i thod pa 'dzin pa rnams so*).

511. *Kṛṣṇācārya (p. 447): "**Human oil** [means] a butter lamp containing melted human fat" (*mar khu chen po zhes pa ni mi'i tshil bzhu ba'i mar me'o*). This corresponds to the instructions for worshiping the goddess Kālī in the Śākta tantra *Kramasadbhāva* (4.53cd), where we read: "One has to offer the lamps with human oil" (*mahātailena dīpāni dāpayed*).

512. Syntactically, it makes better sense to connect *mahātailena pradīpaṃ dadyāt* with the meat offerings. The Tibetan text (Siklós 1996, 81), however, connects it with the highest siddhi (*gal te mchog gi dngos grub 'dod na mar khu chen po'i mar me dbul lo*, "If he desires the highest siddhi, he should offer lamps of human oil"). This is also supported by Lalitavajra's commentary (p. 307), who offers the following explanation: "Otherwise, **if he desires the highest siddhi**, when a hero has died in a battle or has been struck down, [the mantra master] takes a hair of a[nother] deceased man and a cloth of *arga* and makes him lay down on the wool. He offers a butter lamp made of that [person's] fat. He binds the skull of the former [hero who died in a battle?] with the hair of the man and covers it up. The yogin meditates on himself as possessing the true nature of Yama with a consort in the cremation ground. He offers to him human flesh and so on. Then, through meditative absorption, he will 'accomplish the highest siddhi,' it is said" (*gzhan dag gal te/ dngos grub mchog 'dod bya ba la/ dpa' bo g.yul du shi ba 'am 'gags te shi ba'i thong par de'i skra dang arga'i ras bal la sdod* [em. *sdod bu*, ed.] *byas la/ de'i zhag gi mar me btang ste/ snga ma'i thod pa mi'i skra'i skud pas btags pas kha bcad pas dur khrod du gnas la bdag nyid rnal 'byor dang ldan pas de nyid ya ma* [em. *ya ba*, ed.] *yum du bsams la/ de la mi'i sha la sogs pas mchod la/ de nas snyoms par 'jug pas mchog gi dngos grub bsgrub par bya'o zhes zer ro*). The last sentence resembles a verse from the STTS, p. 346, line 15: *ātmānam uttāmāṃ siddhiṃ prapnoti susamāhitaḥ*.

513. Tibetan (Siklós 1996, 81) has *ba lang* (ox) instead of horse, which is found in the Sanskrit.

on.[514] With a most concentrated mind,[515] he should do the rituals of *homa*[516] and *bali*[517] with food that is chewed (*bhakṣa*) and that is stirred by a tongue and swallowed (*bhojya*).[518] [Then], he drenches the maṇḍala with blood on

514. The Tibetan text (Siklós 1996, 81) has eleven types of birds, the last three being *khyim bya*, *ri skegs*, and *khyung chen po*. *Khyim bya*, or "chicken," is missing in the Sanskrit text. Siklós (21) translates *khyung chen* as "eagle." In the *Tibetan Rangjung Yeshe Dictionary*, *khyung chen* is translated as "great *garuḍa*." The Sanskrit text lists only ten types of birds, ending with *mahāmantrī*, which seems to be a corruption, but *Kṛṣṇācārya (p. 447) and Kumāracandra (p. 289) gloss *mahāmantrī* as "domestic fowl" (*sngags chen po zhes pa ni khyim bya'o*). Perhaps *mahāmantrī*, "the great one who recites the mantra," is an epithet of a rooster.

515. *Kṛṣṇācārya (p. 447): "Established **with a most concentrated mind** [means] one should abandon other thought constructs (*vikalpas*) and establish [one's own] mind on the deity and emptiness" (*shin tu mnyam par gzhag ces pa ni lha dang stong pa nyid du sems bzhag pa rtog pa gzhan spangs pa'o*).

516. *Kṛṣṇācārya (p. 447) offers a more esoteric interpretation of *homa* and *bali*: "**The rituals of *homa* and *bali*** [means that] in the belly of oneself as Vajrabhairava, in the blazing fire, one should generate Agnideva Vajrabhairava in the heart of the fire maṇḍala; one should invite the wisdom deity (*jñānadevatā*) of the fire, who dissolves [there]. Then the noose of Agnideva and one's own tongue is made into a vajra [drinking] straw [. . .]" (*sbyin sreg dang gtor ma la sogs zhes pa ni bdag rdo rje 'jigs byed kyi lto bar me 'bar ba la me'i dkyil snying gar me lha rdo rje 'jigs byed bskyed la ye shes pa me lha spyan drangs bstim la/ me lha'i ljags dang rang gi lce rdo rje'i sbu gur byas la . . .*). The second part of the passage is corrupted and beyond reconstruction, but generally speaking, *Kṛṣṇācārya seems to be giving an exposition of the internal *homa*, *bali*, and the yogic way of eating.

517. *Akṣobhya (p. 371) specifies that "**the rituals of *bali*** are to be offered at dusk by a practitioner [who is engaged in a sādhana practice], but during the formal maṇḍala initiation of a disciple, these should be offered after he has constructed the maṇḍala. Moreover, in both cases [i.e., during the maṇḍala initiation and the sādhana], these should be offered at midnight" (*gtor ma'i las ni zhes bya ba sgrub pa pos srod la sbyin te/ slob ma dbang bskur ba la ni dkyil 'khor bsgrub par byas la'o/ yang na gnyis kar nam phyed na'o*).

518. ***Bhakṣa*** and ***bhojya*** are technical terms for two types of food that should be offered to the deity during worship. According to Hemādri (thirteenth century), *bhakṣa* denotes any food that "is ingested after having been broken into pieces," while *bhojya* denotes a type of food that "is not too hard and does not depend on being broken into pieces, but which is swallowed after merely having been stirred by a tongue" (Ikari 1994, 379). *Akṣobhya (p. 371) specifies that *bhakṣabhojya* "should be offered in the *gaṇacakra* (*pūjā*) when the mantra master has entered the maṇḍala" (*bza' ston ni dkyil 'khor du 'jug pa na tshogs kyi 'khor lo bya ba'o*).

all sides.[519] He should offer all the offerings[520] while remaining in meditative union with the Buffalo-Faced One, Lord Vajrabhairava.

[§8] Then the mantra master, who has completed the purification rites [of the mantra] (*kṛtapuraścaraṇa*), either with three people, with a good companion,[521] or alone, with his body anointed with feces and urine, naked,

519. *Kṛṣṇācārya (p. 447) interprets **blood** as "human blood" and says that one should sprinkle it "at the time of drawing the above maṇḍala" (*khrag chen pos gdab ces pa ni gong gi dkyil 'khor bri ba'i tshe'o*).

520. *Kṛṣṇācārya (p. 447): "**He should offer all the offerings** [means] that what has been taught at the time when one is eating [implies] that during all the ritual procedures—namely, at the time when one is Vajrabhairava, at the time when one is purifying the seven (?), at the time when one dissolves into the knowledge being (*jñānasattva*), at the time of the maṇḍala initiation, and at the time when one is putting rituals into practice—one should give these offerings to Śrī Vajrabhairava by assuming a divine pride of oneself as Vajrabhairava" (*lha bshos thams cad dbul bar bya zhes pa ni bdag gi bza' ba'i dus gsungs pa de 'jigs byed yin pa dang bdun dag pa'i dus dang ye shes sems dpa' bstim pa'i dus dang dbang bskur ba dang/ las 'chol ba'i dus thams cad la bdag lha'i nga rgyal gyis dpal rdo rje 'jigs byed la dbul ba'o*).

521. The whole passage is corrupted in Tibetan (Siklós 1996, 81–82), where it reads *bdag zhi bar gyur ba'i shin tu mthun pa'i grogs sam bdag gcig pu rnam par snang mdzad kyis lus byugs te*, which Siklós (30) translates as "a close friend who has calmed his own ego should anoint him with *vairocana* or he should do it himself." Actually, the Sanskrit has *ātmacaturthaḥ*, "he himself as the fourth," and it is easy to decipher that the corruption in Tibetan has arisen by dropping the letter *b* in *bdag (b)zhi par gyur ba*. The term *ātmacaturthaḥ* in reference to oneself as the fourth person occurs also in the NTGS (10.33). Similarly, *shin tu mthun pa'i grogs* is an equivalent of the Sanskrit *susamāyin*, "a close friend," which reflects the concept of a good companion or an assistant of the sādhaka, as conveyed also by other terms, such as *susahāya* or *uttarasādhaka*. The appearance of this term in the VBhT is an example of the "early tantric ritual syntax" that has been borrowed from tantric Śaiva literature (see page 166 and note 398 above).

his hair disheveled, beats a *ḍamaru* at midnight. With calm mind,[522] having howled the mad laughter,[523] he enters the maṇḍala of Great Vajrabhairava.[524]

If he desires siddhi, he should offer a flavorful drink[525] of wine and delicious food.

[§9] After that, having visualized[526] [that he has achieved] the success over the target[527] in the center,[528] he should visualize the Buffalo-Faced Lord Vajra-

522. *Kṛṣṇācārya (p. 448): "**With calm mind** [means] his mind should not be distracted from the process of the rite" (*mnyam par gzhag ces pa ni cho ga'i rim pa las sems gzhan du ma yengs pa'o*).

523. Entry into cremation ground with mad laughter emulates the analogous Śaiva practice; see discussion above on page 166. *Kṛṣṇācārya (pp. 447–48): "**Having howled the mad laughter** [means] he should do the eight types of laughter—ha, hi, and so on—in order to remove impediments" (*ha ha zhes pa ni ha hi la sogs pa brgyad de lta ba'i gad mo brgyad bya'o/ bar chad sel ba'i phyir dgod pa'o*). As noted in the discussion above, later Tibetan tradition accounts for eight types (i.e., four syllable pairs) of laughter of the wrathful deities. These are (1) threatening laughter "ha ha" (*sdigs pa'i gad mo ha ha*), (2) gleeful laughter "he he" (*dgyes pa'i gad mo he he*), (3) enticing laughter "hi hi" (*sgeg pa'i gad mo hi hi*), and (4) subjugating laughter "ho ho" (*zil gyis gnon pa'i gad mo ho ho*). *Śoṇaśrī (p. 395) and *Vajrasiddha (p. 414) similarly gloss this expression as "eight types of laughter" (*ha ha zhes sgrogs byed ces pa ni gad mo brgyad kyis rnam par byed pa'o*).

524. *Kṛṣṇācārya (p. 448) understands the syntax of this passage differently, i.e., "he enters the maṇḍala if he desires siddhi," which he glosses as "One must cultivate the four yogas with whatever one's mind desires, beginning with pacification (*śānti*), and this applies also to the time of initiation" (*dkyil 'khor dngos grub 'dod pas 'jug par bya zhes pa ni zhi ba la sogs pa gang 'dod pas rnal 'byor bzhi sgom pa dang dbang bskur ba'i dus dang 'brel to*).

525. *Kṛṣṇācārya (p. 448): "**A flavorful drink** [means] he accomplishes the siddhis he desires after a tantric feast (*gaṇacakra*), a gathering of heroes (*vīramelāpa*)" (*zhim pa'i chang zhes pa ni tshogs kyi 'khor lo dang dpa' bo'i ston mo de nas 'dod pa'i dngos grub la*). For the explanation of the *vīramelāpa* in Śākta-Śaiva sources, see Sanderson 2007, 284–87.

526. *Kṛṣṇācārya (p. 448): "**Having visualized** [means] if he has faith, [then] a disciple at the time when he has received intiation, or the best *ācārya*, or [the practitioner] himself will receive [the siddhis] from Śrī Vajrabhairava" (*dmigs zhes pa ni dbang nod pa'i slob ma'i dus dang slob dpon mchog gam rang la mos pa yod la dpal rdo rje 'jigs byed las blang ba'o*).

527. The Tibetan text (Siklós 1996, 82) has *phyi nas dngos grub dang dngos grub ma yin pa la dmigs la,* which Siklós (30) translates "then, he considers whether he will succeed or fail." The Sanskrit text has a different reading—namely, *sādhyasiddhiṃ vicintya,* "having visualized [that he has achieved] the success over the target," which indicates that the Tibetan text has been corrupted. *Śoṇaśrī (p. 395) and *Vajrasiddha (p. 414): "**The target in the center** [means] the siddhi that is desired" (*de dbus bsgrub bya zhes bya ba ni mngon par 'dod pa'i dngos grub bo*).

528. *Kṛṣṇācārya (p. 448): "**In the center** [means] at the time of initiation, he visualizes the deity, and at the time of sādhana, he will obtain siddhi. When he is initi-

bhairava on the top of that [target].[529] He should then [begin to] repeat the ten-syllable mantra[530] with one-pointed mind while maintaining the sense of identity [with the deity] and standing in front[531] [of the maṇḍala] in the archer pose.[532]

---

ating somebody into becoming a disciple, the *ācārya* should be wrathful and confer secret initiation (*guhyābhiṣeka*), and at the time of the wisdom-knowledge initiation (*prajñājñānābhiṣeka*), he should pile up the powders [of the maṇḍala] or make them into a lump; throughout this time, he should remain in union with Vajrabhairava" (*de'i dbus su zhes pa dbang bskur ba'i dus su lha bsgom pa dang sgrub pa'i dus su dngos grub nod pa'o/ slob ma la dbang bskur ba'i dus su slob dpon gyis dbang la khro bcas pa dang/ gsang ba'i dbang nod pa dang shes rab ye shes la rdul tshon steng ngam bsdus la rdo rje 'jigs byed dang ldan pas bsdad pa'o*). *Akṣobhya (p. 372): "**Having visualized the target in the center** [means] he should visualize the target as the seat of whosoever has been harboring ill will toward the Buddha's teaching. Moreover, on the image of the target in the center, one places a yantra and a doll (*puttalikā*) together with meat of *yamaputra* [perhaps, *yamaputrī*, an effigy of Yama made of meat]. Here, in case of pacification (*śānti*) and recuperation (*puṣṭi*), one puts [the target] in front. Other commentators say that, except for the disciplined ritual procedure (*saṃvarakrama*) stated before, because there is no instruction that [the practitioner] should perform in this way, the person to be killed [that is, the target in the center] is to be imagined as a seat, if [the practitioner] wants to perform repetition of the mantra (*japa*). Except for the supreme siddhi, there is no maṇḍala-drawing instruction; therefore this view that the target has to be made into the seat (*āsana*) is not right. According to the previous teaching, it is appropriate to do it through meditative stabilization" (*dbus su bsgrub bya dmigs la zhes bya ba ni sangs rgyas kyi bstan pa la 'khu ba gang su yang rung ba zhig gdan du dmigs par bya'o/ gzhan yang dbus su bsgrub bya'i gzugs su 'khrul 'khor dang pu ta linga dang bcas pa'i ya ma pu tra sha bzhag la'o/ 'dir zhi ba dang/ rgyas pa la ni mdun du'o/ gzhan dag ni sngar gsungs pa'i sdom gyi las ma lus pa la 'di ltar bsgrub par bya ba min pas na/ gsad par bya ba gdan du brtags te bzlas pa bya bar 'dod de/ dngos grub mchog sgrub pa dag ma yin pa la dkyil 'khor bri ba ni gang du yang mi 'gyur bas na de ni mi rigs te/ sngar bstan pa ltar ting nge 'dzin gyis ni rung ngo*).

529. The Tibetan text (Siklós 1996, 82) reflects the Sanskrit correctly as *de'i steng du dpal rdo rje 'jigs byed chen po ma he'i gdong can bsam par bya'o*, but Siklós (30) translates *de'i steng du* as "begins." *Śoṇaśrī (p. 395) and *Vajrasiddha (p. 414): "**On the top of that** [means] mounted on that" (*de'i steng du zhes bya ba ni de la zhon pa'o*).

530. *Akṣobhya (p. 372): "**The ten-syllable mantra** [means] it is established as suitable for all the rituals (*karmas*). The root mantra is only established for yantra rituals. Even the heart mantra is only for inviting the deity. This is what is mainly implied" (*yi ge bcu pa'i gsang sngags zhes bya ba ni bya ba thams cad la de nye bar gnas pa ste/ rtsa ba'i sngags ni 'khrul 'khor gyi bya ba tsam la gnas la/ snying po'i sngags kyang lha nye bar gyur pa tsam la gtso bor 'gyur bas so*).

531. Kumāracandra (p. 289): "**In front** [means] in front of the maṇḍala" (*de'i mdun ni/ dkyil 'khor gyi mdun no*).

532. Lalitavajra (p.309) explains **archer pose** as "in front of the southern door" (*brkyang bskus gnas zhes pa ni/ lho'i sgor de'i mdun du'o*).

[§10] Then the most frightening things will arise.[533] The mantra master should not be afraid of them. If he is afraid, then those great impeders will create a weak point. If there is a weak point, the sādhana will not succeed. Therefore the mantra master must not be afraid.

Then Great Vajrabhairava is delighted, and being delighted, he says, "What boon should I bestow on you?"

The *vidyā* holder[534] should say,[535] "Give me the sword, the underworld, the elixir, the rejuvenating technique." Or he receives any other siddhi that his mind desires;[536] that is beyond doubt. If it should happen that the mantra mas-

533. The Tibetan text (Siklós 1996, 82) has *de nas 'jigs byed chen po byung na*, which Siklós (30) translates as "then should the great Bhairava arise [. . .]." The Sanskrit text does not agree with the Tibetan version, for it has *tato mahābhayāny utpadyante*, but *Kṛṣṇācārya's commentary (p. 448) supports both interpretations when it states: "**Then, the most frightening things** [means] the Bhagavān will arrive, or there will manifest disgusting forms, sounds, smells, tastes, and tactile sensations. The **impeders** are the things that hurt the sādhaka and block the sādhaka from obtaining siddhis. If he does not succumb to fear, whatever siddhi he wishes for will be granted" (*de nas 'jigs pa chen po zhes pa ni bcom ldan 'das byon pa'am gzugs dang sgra dang dri dang ro dang reg mi sdug pa 'byung ba'o/ bar chod ni sgrub pa po la gnod pa dngos grub kyi gegs byed pa'o/ 'jigs pa ma byas na de'i rjes la dngos grub gang 'dod ster ba'o*). The disgusting things that appear to the sādhaka are considered signs (*nimitta*) of approaching siddhis, and mentions of them are common in the early kriyā tantras and in the Śākta tantras as well. For example, BY 15.39–42 gives the following list of impediments (*vighnas*) that the sādhaka may expect during the practice of resurrecting the zombie (*vetālasādhana*): "Terrible impediments to his practice arise around him. There occurs the hideous howling of jackals and confused sounds. In the morning he sees everything clearly. He hears the bellowing of cows, bulls (?) and the cawing of crows. He sees people flying in the air. [But] he must not stop the *homa*, O goddess. When he has made the *arghya* offering, the mantra master sees a garden there. When he hears the sound of a military camp, the neighing of horses, the barking of dogs, and the trumpeting of elephants, he must not be afraid; nor should he neglect the *homa*" (*vighnāny asyopajāyante raudrāṇi ca tato bahiḥ/ śivārāvaṃ mahāghoraṃ kalakalaṃ ca prajāyate// prabhātaṃ paśyate sarvāṃ gorambhāṃ śrūyate tathā/ kākaśabdaṃ prajāyeta lokaṃ paśyati utthitam// homaṃ devi na moktavyaṃ arghaṃ dattvā tu/ mantriṇā ārāmaṃ paśyate tatra skandhāvāradhvanis tathā// heṣāravo* [em. Acharya; *hemāravo*, mss.] *tathāśvānāṃ gajagarjadhvanis tathā/ tan* [em. *tāṃ*, mss.] *śrutvā tu na bhetavyaṃ na ca homaṃ pramādayet*).

534. *Kṛṣṇācārya (p. 448): "***Vidyā* holder** [means] the sādhaka" (*rig pa 'dzin pa zhes pa ni sgrub pa po'o*). Kumāracandra (p. 289) has an identical gloss.

535. *Akṣobhya (p. 372): "**The *vidyā* holder should say** [means] he honors the deity after having offered him *arghya* of human blood to drink" (*rig sngags 'chang gis gsol ba btab pa zhes bya ba ni khrag chen po'i yon chab phul nas gus par byas te'o*).

536. *Akṣobhya (p. 372): "**Any other siddhi that his mind desires** [means] whatever he desires that is compatible with his talent. After having joined in praises [of Vajrabhairava] and having offered a stream of offerings with one-pointed mind, he should bow his head in obeisance. According to what has been stated, 'One obtains the boon concordant with

ter does not achieve the siddhi,[537] then, inevitably, all the minor rituals[538] will succeed.

Completed is the first[539] chapter,[540] Explanation of the Maṇḍala, in the yoga tantra[541] of the venerable Great Vajrabhairava, [which is a part of the tantra] called the *Śrīmañjuśriya* [*Tantra*].

---

one's own faith and effort. If one has obtained the boon, one should bow down in obeisance with joy, one should offer praises and give offerings with faith, one should recite the mantra and ask the deity to leave'" (*gzhan yang yid la gang 'dod pa/ zhes bya ba ni rang gi sbyangs pa dang mthun pa tsam las gang 'dod pa ste/ bstod dang bcas nas mchod yon rgyun sbrengs nas/ rtse gcig sems kyis gdong btud phyag byas te/ dad dang 'bad pa'i rjes mthun dam pa blang/ dam pa thob na dga' bas phyag byas te/ dad pas bstod nas mchod yon phul nas su/ gsang sngags brjod cing slar yang gshegs su gsol/ zhes ji skad gsungs pa lta bu'o*). This unidentified verse quote is also found in Kāmadhenu's *Mahākalparājasyaṭīkā* commentary on the *Sarvadurgatipariśodhana*, p. 1645.

537. *Śoṇaśrī (pp. 395–96) and *Vajrasiddha (pp. 414–15): "**If it should happen that the mantra master does not achieve the siddhi** [means] if he propitiates Bhagavān, he will be bestowed even the *mahāmudrā*. If it does happen that the yogin does not achieve [the siddhi] on account of not having merit, 'at that time, inevitably, all the minor rituals will succeed,' it is said. This happens so that his faith is made to grow" (*de nam zhig sngags pas ma grub na zhes bya ba ni bcom ldan 'das mnyes na phyag rgya chen po'ang ster bar byed do/ nam zhig rnal 'byor pa bsod nams ma yin pa'i dbang gis ma grub na/ de'i tshe las phran tshegs rnams nges par 'grub par 'gyur ro zhes dad pa nye bar 'phel bar bya ba'i don du'o*).

538. *Kṛṣṇācārya (p. 448): "**Minor rituals** [means] accomplishments linked to [the use of] yantras, which are going to be explained" (*phra mo las thams cad ces pa ni 'khrul 'khor dang 'brel pa'i las ston pa rnams grub pa'o*). The same meaning is attested in the commentary by *Akṣobhya (p. 372), who glosses "**minor rituals** to be done" as "yantra, *homa*, and those things accomplished by meditation that will be explained" (*las phra mo bya ba ni 'khrul 'khor dang/ sbyin sreg dang/ bsam gtan gyis bsgrub par bya ba 'chad par 'gyur ba rnams so*).

539. *Kṛṣṇācārya (pp. 448–49): "**First** [means] the first of seven [chapters]; **completed** [means] it teaches without exception the rituals of the maṇḍala. It is the first chapter of the *Śrī Vajrabhairava*[*tantra*] to be examined" (*dang po ni bdun pa'i sngon du dang po* [em. *bdun pa*, ed.] *rdzogs pa ni dkyil 'khor gyi cho ga ma lus par bstan pa'o/ dpal rdo rje 'jigs byed kyi rtog pa dang po'i bshad pa'o*).

540. *Kṛṣṇācārya (p. 448): "**Completed is the first chapter** [means] each chapter is examined individually" (*rtog pa dang po rdzogs so zhes pa ni las so so la rtog dpyod pa'o*).

541. *Kṛṣṇācārya (p. 448): "**Yoga tantra** [means] this is the maṇḍala explanation accomplished from the [tantra] of Vajramahābhairava in seven chapters [belonging to the collection] of rituals [that feature] among the five groups of father tantras. Moreover [the maṇḍala] is accomplished by completing the previous *pūrvasevā* and initiation" (*rnal 'byor gyi rgyud ces pa ni pha'i rgyud sde lnga las phrin las kyi rdo rje 'jigs byed chen po'i le'u bdun las sgrub pa'i dkyil 'khor bstan pa'o/ de yang bsnyen pa dang dbang sngon du song bas sgrub pa'o*).

2. Accomplishment of All Magical Recipes

[§11] I will now tell you the procedures for the repertoire of magical rituals (*karmaprasara*), according to the correct method, in due order. A very wrathful mantra master performs [rites] such as killing, driving away, and so forth while remaining in union with the venerable Great Vajrabhairava.

[§12] First of all, indeed, the mantra master should perform[542] the [preliminary] rite of protection (*niśumbhana*[543]). Why is that?[544] This is done at the outset because yoga tantra and deity yoga have, as their chief method, the yoga [of meditative absorption].[545]

542. *Akṣobhya (pp. 373–74): "**He should perform** [means] he should recite [the *niśumbhana* mantra (see below)] when he draws the yantra in order to achieve protection; [it should be recited] seven times, etc. Others say, 'If you wish to protect [yourself], utter [the mantra] *oṃ phu phu phu hi hi hi*.' But whatever is permissible [is allowed], because [the *niśumbhana* mantra] is established for protecting the tathāgata family" (*bzlas te zhes bya ba ni 'khrul 'khor 'bri ba na bsrung ba'i phyir lan bdun la sogs par ro/ gzhan dag ni/ oṃ phu phu phu hi hi hi/ zhes bya bas bsrung bar 'dod do/ gang yang rung ste de bzhin gshegs pa'i rigs kyi bsrung ba la 'di nye bar gnas pas so*).

543. Siklós (1996, 31) translates *niśumbhana* (Tib. *gnod mdzes su bya*) as "he should cleanse himself from all impurities," which is inaccurate. *Niśumbhana* is associated with the preliminary *krodha* rites that have to be performed at the beginning of all wrathful rites. By means of *niśumbhana*, the sādhaka merges with *krodharāja*—i.e., takes on the wrathful nature of the deity—while protecting himself at the same time. The *niśumbhana* mantra, *oṃ śumbha niśumbha hūṃ hūṃ phaṭ phaṭ*, goes back to the earliest scripture of "mature" tantric Buddhism, the STTS. The *niśumbhana* mantra also appears as a preliminary protective rite in Candrakīrti's *Vajrasattvasādhana*, and in the thirtieth chapter of the *Herukābhidhāna*. *Akṣobhya (p. 373) glosses "the mantra of *niśumbhana*" [but the root text omits the word *mantra*] as "the mantra with four *hūṃ* syllables" (*gnod mdzes kyi gsang sngags zhes bya ba ni yi ge hūṃ bzhi pa'i sngags so*).

544. The Tibetan text has *de ci'i phyir zhe na,* which corresponds to the Skt. *kathaṃ tat*; Siklós (1996, 31), however, omits the translation.

545. The Tibetan text reads *rnal 'byor gtso bo yin pa'i phyir ro/ rnal 'byor gyi rgyud la lha'i sbyor ba dang ldan pas/ thog mar ni de bya ste* (Siklós 1996, 83): "Because the chief thing is yoga, in yoga tantra, the one endowed with deity yoga should do it at the outset."

[§13] In this [sādhana], this is the rite: If he wishes to accomplish the ritual [of killing], then facing south, naked, with his hair disheveled,[546] while in the meditative union with the Buffalo-Faced One, he should draw with the feather of a big crow or with a pen[547] a sixteen-segmented wheel of Great

Siklós's translation (31) is inaccurate: "This is because he is the lord of yoga. In the *yoga-tantras*, the one in union with the deity should do this since he is himself the lord of yoga." *Akṣobhya's commentary (p. 374) seems to be corrupted, for he glosses: "**The chief method** of this yoga tantra [is yoga] [means] the way in which the *niśumbhana* yoga is taught in this tantra is not extant in other yoga tantras" (*sbyor ba'i rgyud kyi gtso bo zhes bya ba ni/ ji ltar rgyud 'di nas tshar bcad pa'i sbyor ba bstan pa ltar/ sbyor ba rgyud gzhan las de ltar lhur ma mdzad pas na'o*). *Akṣobhya (p. 374) glosses "the one endowed with **the deity yoga**" by quoting an unidentified source: "There will be a siddhi if the yogin has attention (*manasikāra*) to visualize the form of deity according to the prescription. However, if he wavers, then the procedure will not be achieved. As it is said, 'Although they may be performed at the outset, all repetitions of the mantra (*japa*) and austerities (*tapas*) will be worthless if they are performed with a mind somewhere else and through some other [means]'" (*lha'i gzugs tshul bzhin yid la byed pas thob par bya'o/ gal te rnam par g.yengs na sbyor ba mi 'grub ste/ bzlas brjod dang ni dka' thub kun/ dus ni dang por byas gyur kyang/ gzhan sems pa dang gzhan pas ni/ de dag thams cad don med 'gyur/ zhes gsungs pas so*). The Sanskrit version of this quotation has been identified by P. D. Szántó (private conversation) in Mañjukīrti's *Ādikarmāvatāra* (fol. 12v, ms. Göttingen Xc 14.50) as:

> *japās tapāṃsi sarvāṇi dīrghakālakṛtāny api |*
> *anyacittena mandena vṛthaivety āha sarvavid iti ||*
>
> All mantra recitation and asceticism, even if you have done them for a long time, will become worthless if the mind is elsewhere or is slow; so taught the omniscient one.

A comparison between the verse and the above passage in Tibetan suggests that *dang por* is a corruption of *ring por*, which is a typical error in Tibetan transmitted texts; *gzhan pas* is also a corruption for *zhan pas*. There is another version of this passage in the *Ādikarmapradīpa* by Anupamavajra (ed. La Vallée Poussin 1898, 203), where it is referred to as a passage coming from the *Vidyādharapiṭaka* (*tathā cokta[ṃ] vidyādharapiṭake: japās tapāṃsi sarvāṇi dīrghakālakṛtāny api/ anyacittena mandena sarvaṃ bhavati niṣphalam// iti*).

546. Lalitavajra (p. 311) provides the additional information that his body should be smeared with excrement (*rnal 'byor lhor bltas pas gcer bu skra grol zhes pa ni lus la dri chen byug pas so*).

547. Lalitavajra (p. 311): "**A pen** [means] the tip of a feather or [anything] suitable for that activity" (*smyu gu ni sgro rtse 'am rung ba* [em. *pa*, ed.] *las so*). The Tibetan text (Siklós 1996, 83) has a pen made of human bone (*mi'i rus pa'i smyu gu*).

Vajrabhairava[548] on a rag of the cremation ground[549] [drenched] with poison, blood,[550] salt, black mustard, neem, and juice of datura. There [on the rag of the cremation ground], in the middle of the two fires[551] [i.e., in between the

548. Lalitavajra (p. 311): "'He should make the Great Vajrabhairava' is connected with '**he should draw the sixteen-segmented wheel** of that tantra.' To divide the wheel into sixteen parts, he first makes two lines with the thread from the corpse; again, he makes two [lines] as borderlines; and again, he makes four [lines] in [four] directions. In the same way, regarding the outer parts, he makes the same [division], and they become sixteen. Then, just past halfway in, going clockwise, he makes nine [compartments]. Outside of halfway in, going clockwise, he makes twelve [compartments]. Then, outside that, going clockwise, he makes twelve [compartments]. Then, outside that, going clockwise, he makes sixteen [compartments]. This is the meaning of 'setting up the lines'" (*rdo rje 'jigs byed chen po'i bya ba ni de'i rgyud kyi 'khor lo bcu drug pa bri zhes bya bar 'brel to/ bcu drug cha bgo ba'i phyir/ ro'i skud pas dang por thig gnyis so/ yang gnyis mtshams* [em.; *'tshams* ed.] *su'o/ yang bzhi ni phyogs su'o/ de bzhin du phyi'i cha ni de bzhin du bgros pas bcu drug tu 'gyur ro/ de nas phyed las nang du bskor bas cha dgu'i ling tshe'o/ phyi'i phyed las bskor bas cha bcu gnyis pa'o/ de nas phyi bskor bas cha bcu gnyis pa'o/ de nas phyi bskor bas cha bcu drug pa ste/ la zhes bya ba ni de ltar thig btab la zhes pa'i don to*). The second part of Lalitavajra's commentary seems corrupted, for it contains unneccesary repetition regarding the making of the twelve compartments. *Kṛṣṇācārya (p. 449): "He draws a circle with twelve spokes, which is the dependent-origination wheel endowed with the body of Yama" (probably resembling the image of the wheel of time with Yama, instead of Kāla, holding a wheel in his hands); "in the center, he draws the eighth box" (*gshin rje'i lus dang ldan pa'i 'khor lo rten 'brel 'khor lo bcu gnyis bri bar bya zhing dbus su re'u mig brgyad pa bri'o*).

549. Lalitavajra (p. 311): "**A rag of the cremation ground** [means] a crematory shroud of a [dead] person" (*dur khrod kyi ras ni skyes bu'i ro shun no*). *Kṛṣṇācārya (p. 449): "**A rag of the cremation ground** [means:] one should take a shroud on the twenty-second day of the lunar month, which falls in the dark fortnight, from a corpse killed in an accident that is being transported to the cremation ground" (*dur khrod kyi ras zhes pa 'di grir shi ba'i ro dur khrod du bskyal ba mar gyi ngo'i nyi shu gnyis la blangs la*). *Kṛṣṇācārya is referring here to the corpse of a person who died a sudden death (*akālana-maraṇa*). The usual time period for taking the shroud is from the second up to the twelfth day of the dark fortnight of the moon. According to Bhavabhaṭṭa, one has to remove the shroud before the corpse is put into the fire. I thank P. D. Szántó for this explanation.

550. *Kṛṣṇācārya (p. 449): "Human ashes, white ashes, five nectars (*amṛtas*), blood of a human, a dog, etc., and various types of poison, etc., mixed with the five pigments" (*thal chen dang/ sa dkar dang/ bdud rtsi lnga dang mi dang khyi la sogs pa'i khrag dang/ dug gi rigs sna tshogs dang/ tshon rtsi lnga dang sbyar*).

551. *Śoṇaśrī (p. 396) and *Vajrasiddha (p. 415): "**In the middle of the two fires** [means] fire is the letter *ra*. If someone were to ask what is the logic [behind this], it is because [*ra*] is the seed of fire. This is obtained only because of metaphorical designation of cause as effect" (*me gnyis kyi dbus su zhes bya ba ni me ni ra yig go/ gang la rtog ce na me'i sa bon yin pa'i phyir te/ rgyu la 'bras bu btags pa'i phyir ro zhes bya ba kho nar thob bo*). Kumāracandra (p. 290) gives a different explanation, for he glosses **two fires** as "a triangle, two storeys"

letters *phaṭ*], he writes the customized name of the target surrounded by the ten-syllable mantra at the center of the platform [and] eight *hūṃs*.[552] Having drawn a letter *phaṭ* in the corners and having anointed himself with a pungent mustard-seed oil (*kaṭutaila*),[553] he places the yantra [i.e., the sixteen-segmented wheel of Vajrabhairava] between the two skulls.[554] Having placed

(*me gnyis ni gru gsum nyis brtsegs go*). The Sanskrit version of Kumāracandra's commentary reads: "a double triangle" (*agnidvayaṃ trikoṇadvayaṃ*). Lalitavajra (pp. 311–12) says, "**He should write the name of the target in the middle of the two fires** [means] he should put a small [inscription of the target's] name in between the wind *bīja* in the center and the fire [letter] in the compartments of the intermediate directions; that is, he puts [the name of the target] in between the two [letters] *ra* [as well as] in the four directions and in the twelve [compartments of the intermediate segments of the diagram]. 'He should surround [the name] with the ten-syllable mantra' [means] customizing the name of the target with the ten-syllable mantra" (*me gnyis bar du bsgrub* [corr. *sgrub*, ed.] *bya'i ming zhes bya ba la/ dbus su rlung gi sa bon gyi dbus su chung ba'i ming dang/ mtshams* [corr. *'tshams*, ed.] *kyi ling tshe la me ste ra gnyis kyi bar du chud pa dang/ phyogs kyi bzhi dang bcu gnyis pa la yi ge bcu ba'i sngags kyis bskor zhes pa ste/ yi ge bcu bsgrub bya'i ming dang bcas pas so*).

552. Lalitavajra (p. 312) seems to have a different reading in front of him, which also provides us with an explanation of the subduing nature of the syllable *hūṃ*, when he says: "'He overcomes [the target] with the eight *hūṃ* syllables' [means] he draws eight *hūṃs* in the eight compartments of the diagram; he puts each one in an empty [compartment] and draws as stated before. Others say, 'He draws the name [of the target] in the central eighth compartment, in the twelfth [compartment], and in the center of the syllable *raṃ*. He draws surrounding [the name of the target] with the ten-syllable [mantra] at the edges of the yantra. In the sixteen compartments, he subjugates with eight *hūṃs*, which means drawing eight *hūṃs*. In the empty [compartments], he draws [the eight *hūṃs*], customizing them with the name of the target'" (*hūṃ yig brgyad pas mnan zhes pa ni ling tshe brgyad la hūṃ brgyad bris la/ re re bzhag pa'i stong pa la snga ma bzhin bri'o/ gzhan dag ni nang gi brgyad pa dang/ bcu gnyis pa la ram gyi dbus su ming bris la/ de'i mtha' yi ge bcu pas bskor 'bar bris la/ bcu drug pa la brgyad bas* [om. *la*, ed.] *mnan la hūṃ brgyad bris la stong pa la bskul tshig ming dang bcas pa bri ro zhes zer*).

553. *Akṣobhya (p. 375): "**Pungent mustard-seed oil** [means] oil from the black mustard, or mustard oil" (*tsha ba'i mar khu zhes bya ba ni/ ske tshe'i mar khu'am yungs mar ro*).

554. Lalitavajra (p. 312): "**He places the *cakra* between the two** [means] he places the object [*cakra*] while in the state of meditative absorption, and then he affixes the *cakra* to the skull of a barren woman; this is the meaning of 'he ties the *cakra* up [to the skull] with human hair'" (*'khor lo can dang gnyis su gzhug ces bya ba/ ting nge 'dzin gyis don bcug la de nas rabs chad kyi thod pa kha sbyar du gzhug ste mi'i skra'i skud pas bcing zhes bya ba'i don to*). *Akṣobhya (p. 375) glosses the two skulls in the context of the "characteristics of the skulls" (*kapālalakṣaṇa*): "**Two skulls** [means] four pieces, three, or many" (*thod pa gnyis zhes bya ba ni dum bu bzhi pa ste/ gsum pa yang mang ngo*). The word *mang* could be a corruption of *rung*, in which case the translation would be: "Two skulls [means] four pieces, but if there are three, that is also suitable." I thank P. D. Szántó for this explanation.

[the skulls with the yantra] on the top of the hearth[555] made of three bones, having lit up[556] the fire with the cremation-pyre wood,[557] and pressing down on it with his left foot,[558] he should repeat the ten-syllable mantra.[559] In an instant, the target will die; there is no doubt about this.

[§14] Alternatively, if he wants the target to be seized with a fever, he puts the same wheel in between two human bones,[560] and he digs out a half cubit below the hearth; then the target will be seized by a fever.[561]

555. Lalitavajra (p. 312) glosses **hearth** as "He puts [the yantra] on the top of the three-storey hearth made of human thigh bone. Others also say, 'He makes a hearth of skulls'" (*sgyed po zhes bya ba la/ mi rkang gi skyed po gsum gyi thog tu bzhag pa'o/ gzhan dag thod pa'i sgyed po byed zhes kyang zer*). Lalitavajra refers to the hearth, called the "three-skull hearth" (*trimuṇḍacūlikā*), which has three skulls (*kapāla*s) as the foundation, with a fourth skull placed on top. Siklós (1996, 31) translates "when he has placed this [diagram] above the three hearths," which does not make much sense, as the meaning intended here is the hearth made of three thigh bones or skulls.

556. *Akṣobhya (p. 375) elaborates on the karma procedure that makes use of an effigy and glosses **lit up** as "One should place the yantra in the heart of an effigy and merely heat it up. By doing this, the enemy will be struck by an acute fever and die" (*bsros la zhes bya ba ni pu ta ling ga'i snying ga'i 'khrul 'khor dros pa tsam du ste/ 'dis dgra bo tsha ba'i rims kyis btab nas 'chi bar 'gyur te*).

557. *Akṣobhya (p. 375): "**Having lit up the fire with the cremation-pyre wood** [means] merely fueling it" (*dur khrod kyi me la bsros na zhes bya ba ni dro ba tsam ste*).

558. Lalitavajra (p. 312): "**Pressing down on it with his left foot** [means] he himself steps down on it without being distracted and in a playful stance" (*rkang pa g.yon pas mnan zhes pa ni bdag nyid ma yengs pas rol pa'i stangs kyis mnan pa'o*).

559. *Akṣobhya (p. 375): "**He should repeat the ten-syllable mantra** [means] this is taught in order to block the recitation of the thirty-two-syllable mantra. The ten-syllable mantra has to be recited at the time of drawing the yantra but only after one has performed the preliminary service (*puraścaraṇa*) and not otherwise" (*yi ge bcu pa'i gsang sngags bzlas na zhes bya ba ni/ yi ge sum cu rtsa gnyis zlos pa dgag pa'i phyir smos pa ste/ de ni bsnyen pa byas la 'khrul 'khor 'dri ba'i tshe bzlas par bya'i gzhan du ma yin pas so*).

560. The Tibetan text (Siklós 1996, 84) has *mi'i nya phyis gnyis kyi dbu bu*, which Siklós (31) translates as "within the two crania." This meaning is confirmed by the exegetical explanation; see page 184 above.

561. *Akṣobhya (p. 375): "By doing this, the enemy will be struck by an acute fever and die. [Why does it work?] Because of the special kind of power, that of dependent origination, which is unfathomable to the mind" (*'dis dgra bo tsha ba'i rims kyis btab nas 'chi bar 'gyur te/ rten cing 'brel par 'byung ba'i mthu'i khyad par bsam gyis mi khyab pa'i phyir ro*). For a discussion on the fever ritual in the context of tantric magic, see page 183 above.

[§15] [Next,] I will explain another procedure using the same sixteen-segmented wheel, but there is this difference. Having enclosed the mantra, which has thirty-two syllables,[562] [and] also the ten-syllable mantra together with the name of the target,[563] he should install the mantra syllables. With the same aforesaid substances,[564] with the leftovers [picked up] by a crow, with feces (*vairocana*), he draws a wheel on the rag of the cremation ground that has been trampled upon,[565] according to the procedure already stated. If he

562. The Tibetan text (Siklós 1996, 84) has *'on kyang 'di'i khyad par ni yi ge sum bcu rtsa gnyis pa'i sngags dang ldan pa yi ge bcu pa'i sngags bsgrub bya'i ming dang lhan cig tu yi ge dang sngags spel lo.* Siklós (31) not only translates the sentence wrongly, when he says "a particular feature here is that the syllables of the subject's name and of the spell are to be written alternately," but he also omits the information about the thirty-two-syllable mantra. The Sanskrit text has the "twenty-one-syllable mantra" and not the one of thirty-two syllables; this appears to be a corruption insofar as all the commentators refer to the thirty-two-syllable mantra, which is the root mantra of the VBhT (see page 107 above). Lalitavajra (p. 313) talks about the mantra that has thirty-two syllables (*yi ge sum cu rtsa gnyis kyi bskor bya ba la*). He says that this other procedure uses the thirty-two-syllable mantra of Yama (*gshin rje'i sngags sum cu rtsa gnyis pa bzhin te*), and moreover, this other ritual has one special aspect—namely, one has to smear [the yantra or the body] with excrement (*dri chen gyis byug pa'i khyad par ni 'di'i khyad par ro*). *Akṣobhya (p. 376): "**Having enclosed the mantra, which has thirty-two syllables** [means] previously in relation to yantra [the VBhT] did not teach the installation (*nyāsa*) of the thirty-two-syllable root mantra, but now it does" (*yi ge sum cu rtsa gnyis pa'i sngags smos shing zhes bya ba ni sngar 'khrul 'khor la rtsa ba'i sngags bkod pa ma gsungs pas de bstan pa'o*). Kumāracandra (p. 290) seems to have a thirty-one-syllable mantra as his root mantra, for he says, "Having put together the two *ya* letters, and counting them together, we will have 'the thirty-one-syllable mantra'" (*ya gnyis gcig tu byas nas brtsis pas yi ge sum cu rtsa gcig gi sngags dang ldan pa zhes gsungs so*).

563. *Akṣobhya (p. 376): "**Having enclosed the ten-syllable mantra together with the name of the target** [means] together with the customization that was taught before, [the thirty-two-syllable mantra] that was blocked from the chapter is permissible [here]. [The ten-syllable mantra together with the name of the target] should also be written in between the letters *hūṃ* and *phaṭ*. For that reason, there is a small distinctive feature of the ritual that is different from what was taught before" (*yi ge bcu pa'i gsang sngags dang yang bsgrub bya'i ming lhan cig smos te zhes bya ba ni sngar ji skad bstan pa'i bskul ba smos pas chog par rtog pa las dgag ste/ hūṃ dang phaṭ kyi dbus su yang de bri'o/ de bas na sngar bstan pa las khyad par cung zad ni de yin no*).

564. *Kṛṣṇācārya (p. 450): "**With the same aforesaid substances** [means] human ashes, white earth, and so on, leftovers (*bali*) left by a crow, human feces, the cloth of a corpse before it touches the ground (*sngon tu bstan pa'i rdzas zhes pa thal chen dang sa dkar la sogs pa dang/ bya rog gis zos pa'i 'phro'i gtor ma dang/ dri chen gyi ro ras* [add. *sa*] *la ma spangs pa yang*).

565. The Tibetan text has *dur khrod kyi ras la byugs,* while both the Sanskrit manuscripts (A and B) before emendation have *stambhayitvā*, which clearly is a corruption.

buries[566] [the wheel] in the cremation ground, [the target] will die; if he buries it under a solitary tree, he will be driven away; if he buries it under a solitary *liṅga*, he will cause dissension; if he puts it in water,[567] [the target] will be paralyzed; if he puts it in a house, [the target] will be pacified; if he takes it out and washes[568] it, [the target] is released.[569]

[§16] Furthermore,[570] there is another procedure. Having drawn the wheel of the mantra of Yama on the rag of the cremation ground [that has been buried] in the cremation ground, at a crossroads, under a solitary tree, under an anthill, at the bank of a river, under a solitary *liṅga*, and near the royal gate, he makes an eight-inch effigy representing the target[571] with feces (*vairocana*), urine

566. *Akṣobhya (p. 376): "**If he buries it** [means] in the hole, which is four cubits deep" (*sbas na zhes bya ba ni dong khru bzhi pa'i gting du'o*).

567. *Kṛṣṇācārya (pp. 450–51): "**Water** [means] water that is not flowing quickly will cause paralysis of speech" (*chu zhes pa ni drag tu mi 'bab par ngag rengs pa'o*). *Kṛṣṇācārya (p. 451) further expands the ritual by giving details that do not feature in the root text. He says, "For subjugation (*vaśya*), hide [the *cakra*] in the vagina of the woman. For creating dissent (*vidveṣaṇa*), do it on the back of the horse and the buffalo" (*dbang la ni bud med kyi bha gar sba'o/ dbye bar rta dang ma he'i rgyab tu bya'o*).

568. Lalitavajra (p. 313) specifies that it is a water of sandalwood and milk: "If he takes the *cakra* out and washes it with water of sandalwood and milk, the target will be released [from the spell]" (*'khor lo phyung ste 'o ma dang tsan dan gyi chus bkrus na grol bar 'gyur ro*).

569. *Akṣobhya (p. 376): "**Is released** [means] [this applies] for all the rituals" (*'grol* [em. *gol*, ed.] *bar 'gyur ro zhes bya ba ni thams cad do*). In other words, for reversing the effect of a magical ritual, there is one procedure for all of them.

570. *Kumāracandra (p. 290): "**Furthermore** [means] *oṃ ya ma rā ja/ sa do me ya/ ya me do ru/ na* [Skt. ms., *ṇa*] *yo da ya/ ya da yo ni/ ra ya kṣe* [Skt. ms., *kṣa*] *ya/ ya kṣe* [Skt. ms., *kṣa*] *ya cca/ ṇi rā ma ya/ phaṭ phaṭ*." This is explained as *yamarājaśloka*; see page 108 above.

571. Lalitavajra (pp. 313–14) explains: "**He makes an eight-inch effigy** of a target from the substances [already mentioned]. '**Heart**' [means] in its heart, he places a *cakra* of the thirty-two-syllable mantra. As for '**he pierces the effigy** with a dagger at five joints,' [it means] he stabs it with a best dagger [i.e., a dagger made of human bone] at the throat, at the heart, at the navel, at the genitals, between the eyes. 'He pierces it with **sharp thorns**' [means] he stabs it all with thorns, literally. As for 'he puts the skull,' [it means] he puts it inside the mouth of the skull of a barren woman and ties it up with the string made of a human corpse" (*rdzas rnams las bsgrub bya'i gzugs sor/ brgyad pa byas la/ snying kha ste de'i snying khar sngags te sum cu rtsa gnyis pa'i 'khor lo gzhug pa'o/ yan lag lnga la phur bus gdab bya ba ni lkog ma dang snying kha dang lte ba dang gsang ba dang smin mtshams* [corr. *'tshams*, ed.] *ltar mchog gi phur bus gdab pa'o/ tshig rnams rnon pos dgang bar bya zhes pa ni/ tshig thams cad tsher mas dgang ba'o/ thod par gzhag pa ni rabs chad kyi thod pa kha sbyar gyi nang du bcug ste mi shi ba'i skra'i skud pas btags* [em. *bkri'o*, ed.]).

(*vajrodaka*), and charcoal of the cremation ground.[572] Having placed the mantra at its heart, he then pierces [the effigy] with a human bone at five points,[573] beginning with the head.[574] [Then] he should fill [the effigy] with sharp thorns at every joint. Having placed that [effigy] within the two skull bowls [one on top of the other],[575] [he should fashion] a representation of Yama with soil from seven anthills.[576] [The representation of Yama is] one cubit long, with

572. The Tibetan text has a different reading, where the places refer to actual places the soil for making the effigy must be taken from (Siklós 1996, 84). The same is supported by Kumāracandra's commentary, which says, "Having taken the earth of the places beginning with the cremation ground and ending with the royal gate" (*śmaśānādīnāṃ rājadvāraparyantānāṃ sthānānāṃ mṛttikā grahyā*) and adds "earth from both sides of a river that flows to the ocean" (*samudragāminyo nadyaḥ pārāvārobhayatatayormṛttikā*). In the Sanskrit text, however, only feces, urine, and charcoal of the cremation ground constitute the material substances for making an effigy, while the places indicate the different locations wherein the rag of the cremation ground was previously buried. Thus the Sanskrit version forms a logical unit with the previous ritual.

573. *Akṣobhya (p. 376): "**At five points** [means] the five points of the image that he [stabs] with a vajra dagger (*vajrakīla*). As it is said: 'He stabs at the forehead, throat, heart, and in the same way, at the two arms'" (*gnas lngar zhes bya ba ni/ rdo rje yi ni phur bu yis/ gzugs brnyan gyi ni gnas lnga po/ dpral ba mgrin pa snying ga dang/ de bzhin dpung pa gnyis su gdab/ ces gsungs pa'o*). Kumāracandra (p. 290): "**The five points** [means] head, forehead, throat, heart, and genitals he should stab with a dagger made of human bone according to the procedure stated earlier" (*gnas lnga ni spyi bo dang dbral ba dang mgrin pa dang snying ga dang gsang ba'i gnas su mi'i rus pa'i phur bus gdab par bya ste/ gong du gsungs pa de nyid kyis so*).

574. The Tibetan omits *mūrdhādau*, "beginning with the head" (see Siklós 1996, 84). *Kṛṣṇācārya (p. 451): "From the **head** [means] forehead, mouth, heart, genitals, and the head again" (*spyi bo las zhes pa ni dpral ba dang/ kha dang snying ga dang gsang gnas dang spyi bo sngon po*).

575. The Tibetan text states that the image of Yama has to be made out of an anthill and the earth from the seven places (*de grog mkhar dang gnas bdun gyi sas gshin rje'i gzugs*, Siklós 1996, 84), while the Skt. has *saptavalmīkena yamarūpaṃ*). The Tibetan translation is incorrect, as it takes *saptavalmīkena* as a *dvandva*, but it is actually a *tatpuruṣa* (*karmadhāraya*). Kumāracandra (p. 290) makes it clear when he glosses **seven anthills** as "earth substances of seven anthill piles" (*grog mkhar gyis bdun zhes pa ni grog mkhar gyi sa bdun gyi sa'i rdzas*). The Sanskrit version of Kumāracandra's commentary provides an additional bit of information: "The seven earths [means] beginning with the cremation ground and ending with the royal gate" (*śmāśanādirājadvārāntāḥ sapta mṛdaḥ*).

576. *Akṣobhya (p. 376): "**Representation of Yama** [means it applies] to all aggressive rituals" (*gshin rje'i gzugs zhes bya ba ni tshar bcad pa thams cad la'o*). *Kṛṣṇācārya (p. 451): "**Representation of Yama** [means] after having performed the ritual installation (*pratiṣṭhā*) [of the deity], the sign [of siddhi?] appears, and then it hides again" (*gshin rje'i gzugs zhes pa ni rab tu gnas pa byas nas rtags byung ba dang sba'o*).

distorted face, fat belly, two arms, one face, holding a sword.[577] [The sādhaka] naked, with disheveled hair,[578] having placed in [Yama's] heart those two skulls bowls, should bury (*nikhane*) it at midday or at midnight in the cremation ground, near the place where the fire has burned. He should bury it at a good distance [from human habitation],[579] face down and with the head pointing south. Having returned home,[580] he should recite the ten-syllable mantra with determination, having customized it with the name of the target, [while] in meditative union with the Buffalo-Faced One. [The target] dies in three days. If he lifts it out and washes it, [the target] is released.[581]

[§17] Next, I will explain the procedure for paralysis. He [the mantra master], having smeared the skin of a shrew[582] with the substances beginning with poison, and so on, and having written the ten-syllable mantra on that skin, he takes earth from the footprint of the target and earth from the place where he

577. The description of Yama in the Tibetan text differs slightly from that given in the Sanskrit. In the former, Yama is described as *zhal gtsigs pa*, probably a corruption for *brtsigs pa*, corresponding to the Sanskrit *vikṛtānana*, which is an appellation of Yamāntaka. For a discussion, see page 63 above. In his hands, he holds a sword and a noose, but the latter is omitted in the Sanskrit. The noose is a characteristic weapon of Yama; therefore it probably featured in the original version of the text.

578. Siklós (1996, 32) takes "naked, with disheveled hair" to refer to Yama, but Yama is never referred to in that way. On the other hand, the sādhaka in the VBhT is often described by these two adjectives; therefore it is more probable that *nagno muktaśikho* qualifies the sādhaka.

579. The Skt. *sudūraṃ* is never used for time but only for place; however, the Tibetan equivalent, *shin tu ring por*, is ambiguous and can be used for both time and space. Siklós (1996, 32) translates it as "he keeps [the image of Yama] facing south for a long time."

580. *Akṣobhya (p. 376): "**Having returned home** [means] the yogin who has done this and other rituals incorrectly" (*khyim du yang ni 'ongs nas zhes bya ba la sogs pas ni legs par ma byas pa'i rnal 'byor pa yis so*). It also indicates that the yogin is a householder and not a monastic.

581. Lalitavajra (p. 314) expands on the annulment procedure, saying, "If he washes it with sandalwood and milk, [the target] will be released [from the spell]" (*tsan dan dang 'o mas bkrus na sos par 'gyur ro*).

582. *Akṣobhya (p. 376): "**Having smeared the skin of a shrew** [means] he strips off the skin" (*tshu tshun da ra'i pags pa zhes bya ba ni gsob bshus pa'o*). *Kṛṣṇācārya (p. 451): "**Skin** [means] he fills the inside of the skinned pouch with excrement, urine, and the earth from the target's footprint. He recites the mantra for seven nights, fills [the pouch] with mustard seed, and tramples on it" (*pags pa zhes pa car mar* [em. *kha na mar*, ed.] *bshus pa'i nang du dri dang chu dang rkang rjes kyi sa blugs/ nub bdun du sngags dang yungs kar blugs la mnan pa bya'o*).

has urinated,[583] then fills[584] that [skin] with it and binds it with [the target's] hair.[585] Having mixed together the urine of a donkey and feces (*vairocana*),[586] he fills up the interior of a clay bowl[587] with it. Having placed the yantra[588] in it and having placed it on a piece of wood from the cremation ground, having then trampled on it with his left foot and in union with Yama, he should recite the ten-syllable mantra.[589] After one day, [the target] will be paralyzed. This is the procedure for which there is no antidote.[590] This procedure should be done by a very wrathful mantra master. If he does not do this [correctly, the ritual] will not succeed.[591]

[§18] Next is the procedure for causing dissension. Having written the

583. *Akṣobhya (p. 376): "With the **earth** that has been taken, **he fills with it** [means] he fills up the effigy (*puttalikā*) [i.e., the shrew skin] with the earth" (*sa blangs pas dgang zhing bya ba ni pu ta lin ga dang/ sas dgang ba'o*). This comment is redundant, as the root text provides this information as well.

584. Kumāracandra (p. 290): "He should fill it up with earth from the footprint [of the target] and urine" (*pādaṃśumūtramṛttikābhyāṃ pūrayet*).

585. Lalitavajra (p. 315) explains the procedure for sealing the shrew skin: "He binds the opening [of a shrew-skin pouch] with the hair of that [target]" (*de'i skra'i skud pas kha bcings la*). *Akṣobhya (p. 376): "**He binds it with the target's hair** [means] many types of hair, such as skin hair, *grul ba* (?), or genital hair" (*de'i skras bcing ngo zhes bya ba ni/ pags pa grul ba dang/ yan lag dang ro smad kyi cha'o*).

586. *Akṣobhya (p. 376): "**Having mixed together the urine of a donkey and feces** [means that] in accordance with the prescription, the yantra for apprehending the object is just like butter and honey; cut it into small pills (Tib. *ri lu*, Skt. *guṭikā*)" (*de nas bong bu'i chu ngan dang/ dri chen du sbyar te zhes bya ba ni/ ji ltar rjes su gzung ba'i 'khrul 'khor la mar dang sbrang rtsi lta bu ste/ tshar gcad pa'i ri lu'o*).

587. *Akṣobhya (p. 376): "He places **a clay bowl** [means] on the two skulls, and he covers it up with that [effigy]. He fills the effigy up in such a way that it is not modified" (*kham phor bzhag la zhes bya ba ni thod pa gnyis ka la des glan te/ pu ta ling ga mi 'gyur bar dgang ngo*).

588. *Akṣobhya (p. 376): "**Having placed** that yoga [which must be a corruption of *'khor lo*, or *yantra*] **in it** [means] that skin" (*der sbyor ba de* [corr. *da*, ed.] *bzhag nas zhes bya ba ni pags pa de'o*).

589. *Akṣobhya (p. 376): "**The ten-syllable mantra** is a synecdoche (*upalakṣaṇa*) for the yantra" (*yi ge bcu pa'i gsang sngags zhes pa ni 'khrul 'khor nye bar mtshon pa'o*). I thank P. D. Szántó for this explanation.

590. The Tibetan text (Siklós 1996, 85) has *'di ni phyis rjes su bzung ba mi 'grub pa'i rab tu sbyor ba'o*, which Siklós (32) translates as "this is the practice for those who in the end are unable to attain skill in magic."

591. The Tibetan text omits this sentence (Siklós 1996, 85).

mantra of Yama with the procedure stated before,[592] he makes [an image of] a buffalo and a horse with the earth from the seven anthills.[593] Having put the mantra[594] in the heart of those two [images],[595] he places them one atop the other in mutual hostility, and he puts them at the foot of the neem tree. He should write the mantra[596] with the blood of a buffalo and a horse. This is a characteristic feature of this mantra. If he performs it with a fully concentrated mind, he will cause dissension in three days.

[§19] Next, if he wishes to drive away, the mantra master should make [an image of a] camel with soil from the seven anthills.[597] Having visualized on its back a wind maṇḍala in the shape of a crescent moon generated from the syllable *yaṃ*, he should visualize the target on the top of it. Having visualized the form of Yama[598] holding a club in his hand on the top of that [target], he should think [of him] being struck by a club and being sent to the south. He places the same wheel in his heart having customized it with the name of the

592. Lalitavajra (p. 315) explains that just "like in the case of prior procedure, this method [also] makes use of the thirty-two-syllable *cakra*" (*sngon gyi thabs ni sum cu rtsa gnyis ba'i 'khor lo'o*).

593. The Tibetan text has *gnas bdun gyi sas* (Siklós 1996, 85).

594. The Tibetan text has *'khor lo*—i.e., a *cakra*, or yantra, and not a mantra.

595. *Akṣobhya (pp. 376–77): "**Having put the mantra in the heart of those two**—that is to say, having put the effigy together with the yantra [i.e., mantra] in such a way that one is on the top of the other, [means that] he puts one on the top, whichever way round. Or else [referring to the buffalo and the horse] he lets one emerge on the top of the other in such a way as if they were fighting" (*de gnyis kyi snying gar gsang sngags bcug nas zhes bya ba ni/ 'khrul 'khor can gyi pu ta ling ga gcig gi steng du gcig bzhag nas zhes bya ba ni gang yang rung ba'i steng du gzhag go/ yang na 'thab pa ltar gcig gi steng du gcig 'gro bar spro bar bya'o*). A similar recipe for creating dissent (*vidveṣaṇa*) in the context of Vajrayoginī, involving visualization of a horse and a buffalo as if they were fighting, is given in *Yogaratnamālā* 2.34 (Tripathi and Negi 2006, 27): *sādhyau aśvamahiṣārudhau dhyātvā anyonyaṃ yudhyamānau japaṃ kuryāt* [...] *niyataṃ vidveṣayati.*

596. The Tibetan text has *'khor lo*, i.e., a *cakra*, and not a mantra.

597. Lalitavajra (p. 315) gives a slightly different procedure that also makes use of the previous thirty-two-syllable *cakra*: "He places the previous *cakra* in the heart of the camel fashioned with [the earth] of seven places" (*gong gi 'khor lo gnas bdun gyis las byas ba'i rnga mong gi snying khar bcug ste*). Again, Siklós's translation (1996, 86) takes the anthill and the earth of seven places separately; see note 575 above.

598. *Akṣobhya (p. 377) reads *yamapuruṣa*, "the servants of Yama" (*gshin rje'i skyes bu*), and not *yamarūpa*, "the form of Yama." He says, "Other [commentators] gloss *yamapuruṣa* as 'arising from the letter *ya*'" (*gzhan gshin rje'i skyes bu zhes bya ba ni yi ge ya las 'byung ngo*).

target in accordance with the prior procedure, [after which the target] will be driven away in seven days; there is no doubt about this.[599]

[§20] Next is another[600] procedure.[601] Having smeared the body of an outcaste[602] with pungent mustard-seed oil[603] (*kaṭutaila*) on a Sunday and having made him climb the neem tree, he should be made to stay there. While [the outcaste] remains there, he [the sādhaka] removes the oil from his [the outcaste's] body with a mother-of-pearl shell, and he gathers the oil. Having gathered the oil, he obtains a rag from the black flag of Śiva and burns it in a smoky fire.[604] He should mix the soot that remains [from burning the flag] with the oil, and he should smear the sandals of whomever he wishes to drive away. Or he can rub [the target's] hands and feet. In the absence of those, [he should rub the target's] head or his towel.[605] [The target] will be driven away in an instant.

599. For the discussion of "camel magic" in other tantras, see Wenta 2024.

600. *Akṣobhya (p. 377): "**Another procedure** [means] a procedure other than the yantra. Since it is not the main [ritual], it is an addendum to the teaching" (*sbyor ba gzhan yang zhes bya ba ni 'khrul 'khor las gzhan pa'i sbyor ba ste/ zhar la bstan pa tsam yin gyi 'di gtsor ma gyur pas so*).

601. Lalitavajra (pp. 315–16) gives a different procedure: "There is also another explanation. On a Sunday of the Rudra constellation (*gtum po*)—that is, on the asterism of the waning moon—he anoints an outcaste (*caṇḍāla*) with hot butter, and he makes him stay on the neem tree. Then, with a mother-of-pearl shell, he scrapes the previous oil [from the body of the *caṇḍāla*], he takes the flag of Mahādeva (i.e., Śiva), and he mixes the two. Then he burns them in a fire without smoke. He mixes the charcoal [from the fire] with the butter that has been scraped with the mother-of-pearl shell. In accordance with what has been taught on the basis of the instruction, if he anoints [the body with the mixture], [the target] will stay" (*yang gzhan bshad de/ gtum po'i nyi ma ste mar ngo'i skar ma* [add: *la*] *gtum po la tsha ba'i mar khus byugs te/ nim ba'i* [corr. *pa'i*, ed.] *shing kar gnas nas/ nya phyis kyis snga ma'i mar bzhar la/ ma hā de ba'i ras dang bslang* [om. *nga*, ed.] *gnyis kha sbyar bar du du ba med par bsregs pa'i thal ba nya phyis bzhar ba'i mar dang bsres te/ man ngag dang ldan pas gsungs pa ltar byugs na sdod par 'gyur ro*). Unlike the root text preserved in the Tibetan version (see Siklós 1996, 86), Lalitavajra interprets this ritual as causing a person to remain (*sdod par 'gyur*), but it is possible that *sdod* (remain) is a corruption of *skrod* (drive away).

602. Kumāracandra (p. 290): "**An outcaste** [means] a woman of low caste" (*can da la ni g.yung mo'o*). The Sanskrit version of Kumāracandra's commentary has a low-caste man.

603. Siklós (1996, 33) translates it as "clarified butter," which is wrong. *Kaṭutaila* is a pungent mustard oil often used in aggressive magic.

604. Skt. *taddhūmena* is omitted in the Tibetan (see Siklós 1996, 86).

605. The Tibetan text omits the last sentence.

[§21] Next there is another procedure. He should draw [the wind maṇḍala][606] with the charcoal of the cremation pyre[607] and the blood of a crow on a sheet of birch bark[608] with a pen made of bone.[609] Having customized the middle of the wind maṇḍala with the name of the target, he should tie it on the neck of a crow. He should take hold of a crow, and while remaining in the meditative union with the Buffalo-Faced One,[610] facing south, he should set the crow free. In that very moment, [the target] wanders the world [aimlessly] like a crow.[611]

[§22] Next is another procedure for driving away. [The mantra master,] having anointed himself with pungent mustard-seed oil (*kaṭutaila*),[612] and having

606. The Tibetan text takes the wind maṇḍala to be the object of the sentence, but that is absent in the Sanskrit.

607. The Tibetan text does not mention the charcoal of the cremation ground as ink, referring only to the crow's blood (*bya rog gi khrag*).

608. The Tibetan text (Siklós 1996, 86) has *dur khrod kyi ras sam gro ga'i lo ma la*, "on a crematory cloth or birch bark," but the Sanskrit omits the crematory cloth. *Akṣobhya (p. 377) comments: "The passage containing the words 'on the birch bark,' and so on [means] the ritual [that makes use] of yantra. Other [commentators] understand this to be a different ritual (not involving the yantra). Regarding this, the words 'another procedure' have the meaning that the yantra is not excluded. If the others [say], 'Here were the rituals without the yantra,' and yet later, having suppressed the yantra, [the text again] introduces the yantra, then those subsequent rituals (*prayogas*) are companions [to the yantra]. Otherwise, how could it be that there is no opportunity to use the yantra elsewhere?'" (*gro ga'i shun pa la zhes bya ba la sogs pa ni 'khrul 'khor gyi sbyor ba ste/ kha cig ni 'di yang sbyor ba gzhan du rtog go/ 'dir sbyor ba gzhan ni zhes pa'i sgras ni 'khrul 'khor mi 'gegs kyi don las so/ gzhan dag 'dir 'khrul 'khor dang bral ba'i sbyor ba dag las/ yang rjes la 'khrul 'khor mnan la de'i grogs su de dag gi sbyor gyi/ gzhan du na skabs ma yin par ga la 'byung zhes 'dod do*).

609. The Tibetan text omits "a pen made of bone" as a stylus and has, instead, "a crow's feather" (*bya rog gi smyu gus*).

610. Lalitavajra (p. 316): "**The Buffalo-Faced One** [means that the sādhaka,] being himself in the deity yoga, summons [the target] and visualizes [the target] being driven away with light" (*ma he'i zhal ni bdag nyid lha'i sbyor ba dang ldan pas bkug ste/ 'od kyis bskrad par bsam mo*).

611. Skt. *tatkṣaṇād eva kākavat paryaṭati mahīm* corresponds to Tib. *de'i skad cig gis bya rog bzhin sa kun tu 'khor ro*, which Siklós (1996, 33) translates wrongly as "instantly he will journey to whatever place the crow does." *Kākavat paryaṭati* is a common phrase indicating "aimless wandering" as the outcome of driving away (*uccāṭana*). See also VS verses 171–73, p. 74; *Tantrasārasaṃgraha* of Nārāyaṇa 17.56cd–57ab (Goudriaan 1978, 364); *Svacchanda Tantra* 6.76; and *Phetkāriṇī Tantra* 13.35–38. For the discussion of this expression in the tantras, see Wenta 2024.

612. Siklós (1996, 33) incorrectly translates as "hot clarified butter."

taken hold of the nest of a crow in the neem tree, burns that nest with wood taken from the fire of the cremation ground and collects the ashes. The person on whose head [the ashes] are placed is driven away.[613]

[§23] There is also another procedure for causing dissension. [The mantra master,] having combined the wings of a crow and an owl, hairs from a brahman and an outcaste, lights up the fire with thorn-apple wood, making a fire free of smoke.[614] Having gathered the ashes[615] of that fire, and having empowered [the ashes] by the recitation of the ten-syllable mantra, he should place the ashes in between a man and a woman. They will fall out with each other instantaneously.[616]

[§24] Next [the mantra master writes the ten-letter mantra] on a rag from the cremation ground with the substances beginning with poison and encloses it with the name of the target. Having customized the *smaraṇa* [mantra][617] and

613. The same recipe is given in *Saṃpuṭodbhava* 7.1.58: *kaṭutailenābhyaṅgayitvā picumardakavṛkṣād balibhugāvāsaṃ* [ms. R; *balibhukāvāsaṃ* ed., p. 321] *gṛhya tena hastenaiva pitṛvanakāṣṭhena dagdhvā bhasma gṛhītvā yasya śirasi dīyate tam uccāṭayati.*

614. In the MMK, chapter 13 (on *homa*), the fire without smoke (*nirdhūmāgni*) features only in the case of *pauṣṭika* rites. In the case of *abhicāra* rites, one should offer oblations into a smoky fire. But there are other recipes in the MMK that feature smokeless fire. For example, MMK chap. 55, p. 524, says, "If he wants to subject a king or simply a chieftain to his will: having made an effigy of him with the leftovers from honey, if [the mantra master] throws the effigy into the smokeless embers, that [king] will be subject to his will within a week" (*rājānaṃ rājamātraṃ vā vaśīkartukāmaḥ tasya madhūcchiṣṭakena pratikṛtiṃ kṛtvā nirdhūmāṅgāreṣu kṣipet saptarātraṃ sa vaśo bhavati*).

615. With regard to the translation of *chāraṃ* as "ashes," we have the testimony of the *Buddhakapāla Tantra*, which says, "Having gathered the ashes, he should then place them in the unbaked clay bowl" (*tasya chāraṃ saṃgṛhya śarāve sthāpayet*). The *Abhayapaddhati* of Abhayākaragupta, 7r.4, glosses it as *chāraṃ iti bhasma*. The *Saṃpuṭodbhava* (7.1.59) also has *chāraṃ*: *kākolūkapakṣayor brāhmaṇanigranthayoś ca keśān ekīkṛtya dhutturakakāṣṭhenāgniṃ prajvālya nirdhūmaṃ dagdhvā tacchāraṃ* [mss. R, P, K; *taṃ kṣāram*, ed., p. 321] *gṛhya yayoḥ puruṣayoḥ striyor vā śayyāśayane gupte prakṣipet. tatkṣaṇād vidveṣo bhavati.* See also MMK chap. 41, p. 463, and NTGS 3.90cd–92ab.

616. The same recipe is given in *Saṃpuṭodbhava* 7.1.59.

617. The Tibetan text omits the part on the *smaraṇa* mantra and has *bran pa'i bar du* instead, which Siklós (1996, 33) translates as "moistening." The term *smaraṇa* is a signature of the *Picumata-Brahmayāmala*, where it is used in a technical sense as the seed syllable *hūṃ* that animates the mantra of this system: *oṃ hūṃ caṇḍakapālinī*. The sense is that a true sādhaka accomplishes siddhi simply by maintaining the awareness of Śiva that this seed syllable is said to embody. It is praised in the text as the source of all mantras and all language. The *Picumata-Brahmayāmala* (5.10cd–11ab, quoted in Kiss 2014, 208) defines

having acquired the hair of a mongoose and a slough of a snake, he should put it [on the rag] and fashion a wick. In whatever house he lights it,[618] the inhabitants will fight among each other.[619]

[§25] Then, if he wishes to kill, [the mantra master] makes an image [of the target] in feces and urine, smears the top of it[620] with powdered bone,[621] and then chops it repeatedly. Then, naked, with hair disheveled, facing south, while in the meditative union with the Buffalo-Faced One, he should offer that into a fire taken from the cremation pyre at midnight. The person in whose name he offers that into the fire will die instantly. This procedure has been taught by Vajrabhairava himself.

---

smaraṇa as: *na japeṇa na homeṇa na ca yantra na pūjāya/ sarvadā smaraṇenaiva tena siddhir na saṃśayaḥ//*. Following the authority of the *Picumata*, this meaning of *smaraṇa* is also retained in the *Tantrāloka* (50.156): "The supreme god has declared in such scriptures as the *Picumata* that there is no need for the ceremony and the process of worship and that the desired siddhi may be accomplished simply through the power of the seed syllable called awareness." Further, the *Tantrāloka* (29.65cd) says: *siddhayet sarvadā smaraṇena hi*. The seed syllable *hūṃ* constitutes one of the seed syllables in the ten-syllable mantra of Vajrabhairava. Kumāracandra's gloss misses the point: "***smaraṇa*** [means] purpose" (*smaraṇaṃ prayojanaṃ*).

618. For the same ritual, see NTGS 3.90cd–92ab, and MMK chap. 41, p. 463.

619. Lalitavajra (p. 316) gives the following recipe: "Also with regard to poison and so on—[that is,] with the [substances such as] salt explained before, [which are used as ink] on the rag of the cremation ground—[these are employed] again to customize [the rag of the cremation ground] with the name of the target in the middle [of the rag]. He writes the [name of the] other [person he wants the target to fight] in the same way. As for that [rag with the names of the two persons], he rolls it up together with the skin of a mongoose and a snake, and a cotton wool. Having done it first, he scatters the pungeant mustard oil [Tib. "butter"] and recites the mantra. Others also say, you have to write a *cakra* on the flag of Mahādeva [i.e., Śiva], like before. When it is to be done, the instruction [should be followed] exactly" (*yang dug la sogs pa ste/ sngon du gsungs pa'i snga* [em. *snag*, ed.] *tshas dur khrod kyi ras la bgrub* [corr. *sgrub*, ed.] *bya'i ming dbus su yang spel ba gzhan sngon ltar bris pa de ni ne'u le dang sprul gyi lpags pa ras bal dang ldan par dril te/ sngon bu byas te mar me btang la sngags bzlas pa'o/ gzhan yang ma hā de ba'i ras la 'khor lo sngon ltar bris te/ man ngag ji lta bas byas na'o*).

620. This is reflected in the Tibetan *de'i steng du rus pa phye mas*; however, Siklós (1996, 33) leaves *de'i steng du* untranslated.

621. The Sanskrit manuscripts have *ahicūrṇena*, "with a powdered snake," instead of *asthicūrṇena*, "with a powdered bone." The emendation to *asthicurṇena* is supported by the Tibetan *rus pa phye mas* (Siklós 1996, 87).

[§26] Then, if he wishes to drive away, [the mantra master,] having drawn a sixteen-segmented wheel on the banner cloth[622] with the aforesaid substances together with some charcoal of the cremation pyre and having customized it with the name of a person, should place it on the sheet of a neem [tree]. He drives away that person [whose he inscribed].

[§27] Next, if he wants to paralyze [the target], he should draw a *cakra* of Yama on a stone slab or on a strip of cloth with yellow orpiment or turmeric and place it together with the name of the target, who will become paralyzed.

[§28] Alternatively, should the mantra master wish to subject another to his will: having made an effigy[623] of the target with soil from an anthill, saffron, and yellow orpiment and measuring sixteen fingerbreadths tall, whether of a man or a woman, he should draw a *yamayantra* on birch bark with yellow orpiment and blood from a ring finger. Having placed [the yantra] on [the effigy's] heart and having offered *pūjā* to it with red flowers[624] at the three times of the day, that person in whose house he places it †. . . † [will be drawn under his will].[625] Facing west, he recites the ten-syllable mantra. After seven days, he will draw even Indra into his power, how much more so a mere human being.

622. *Akṣobhya (p. 377): "As for the ritual (*prayoga*) that says **on the banner cloth**, [it means] it is a *prayoga* of driving away by inducing madness" (*rgyal mtshan gyi ras la zhes bya ba la sogs pa'i sbyor ba 'di ni smyo bar 'gyur ba'i bskrad pa'i sbyor ba'o*).

623. Lalitavajra (p. 316) gives the following procedure: "Also, the ritual of subjugating under one's own will is explained. Having made an effigy with the earth of the seven places and so on, he draws the *cakra* like before. Having worshiped that *cakra*, he places it at the heart of the former [effigy] and recites the mantra" (*yang dbang gi las bshad pa/ gnas bdun gyi sas* [em. *sa*, ed.] [om. *la*, ed.] *sogs pa la gzugs brnyan byas pa la 'khor lo ji lta ba bzhin bris te/ 'khor lo de mchod nas gong gi snying khar bcug nas sngags bzlas pas so*).

624. *Akṣobhya (p. 377): "**Having offered *pūjā* to it with red flowers** [means] to this Śrī Vajrabhairava himself. Because a flower is a synecdoche (*upalakṣaṇa*), you should offer various kinds of offerings, provided they are red, together with a guest offering (*arghya*). Some people say this means offering the yantra, but this is wrong, because by doing that, the aim is not achieved. If somebody were to ask, is the goal achieved if you worship only the mantra? Alas, that's like making offerings to the ministers and so on while the king is sitting there. How could it be? This is not what is said in the text" (*me tog dmar pos mchod cing zhes bya ba 'di dpal rdo rje 'jigs byed nyid la ste/ me tog ni nye bar mtshon pa yin pas mchod pa kha dog dmar po yon chab dang bcas pa dbul lo/ kha cig ni 'khrul 'khor mchod par 'dod de de ni mi 'thad de/ des don du mi 'gyur ro/ gsang sngags nyid la mchod pas don du 'gyur ba'o zhe na/ kye ma rgyal po bzhugs bzhin du sna chen po la sogs* [em. *gtogs*, ed.] *pa mchod pa lta ga la rigs/ de ni mi brjod do*).

625. The Sanskrit *yasya gṛhe sthāpayitvā* corresponds to the Tibetan *rang gi khyim du bzhag la*, but this detail is missing in Siklós's translation (1996, 34).

[§29] Or, if he wishes to attract, [the mantra master,] having drawn the yantra on the skull with yellow orpiment and blood of the ring finger, should then heat it in a fire made from *khadira* wood.[626] In whoever's name [he does that],[627] that person comes to him with the speed of the wind.

[§30] If the mantra master wants to drive someone mad, he takes a thorn apple and mixes it with human flesh and the sawdust of a bookworm. The person in whose food or drink he places it and recites the mantra over becomes instantly crazed.[628] He dies within seven days.[629]

[§31] Here is another procedure. The mantra master, having inscribed the mantra of Yamāri (*yamārimantra*) on the rag from the cremation ground with the substances beginning with the poison and having made an effigy out of human flesh[630] and feces (*vairocana*), places the mantra in its heart. He should then go to the cremation ground and cut [the effigy] with a sharp knife while in meditative union with the Hideous-Faced One[631] (Vajrabhairava). He should

626. *Akṣobhya (p. 377): "**He should heat it in a fire made from *khadira* wood** [means that] if the effect [of the magical ritual] does not come to pass within seven days, he should take the effigy from the skull and burn it, because it did not work the first time around" (*seng ldeng gi me la bsros na zhes bya ba ni gal te zhag bdun gyis ma byung na/ pu ta ling ga thod pa nas phyung ste/ bsro'i dang po nas ni ma yin no*). It appears that here, "the effigy" means the yantra.

627. The verb that follows the ten-syllable mantra is missing in the Sanskrit, while the Tibetan text has "he recites [the spell] with the name of a person" (Siklós 1996, 34).

628. *Kumāracandra (p. 290): "**Crazed** [means] the one who is made distressed" (*smyon pa ni gnod pa byas pa'o*).

629. *Akṣobhya (p. 377): "**He dies within seven days** [means], in the same way, he will become deranged within seven days through these substances. Others say, 'unless you have freed him first.' The effects of magic are overturned by mixing datura and sulphur" (*zhag bdun gyis 'chi bar 'gyur ro zhes bya ba ni zhag bdun du rdzas* [add. *gyis*] *smyo ba bzhin na'o/ gzhan kha cig ni gal te slar ma dkrol na'o zhes 'dod de/ 'di ni thang phrom dang sbyar ba'i mu zis dril lo*).

630. The Tibetan text (Siklós 1996, 88) has *mar me chen po*, which corresponds to the Sanskrit *mahāpradīpa*. Siklós (34) translates it as "human oil," but actually, *mahāpradīpa* also means "human flesh"; thus it is a synonym of *mahāmāṃsa*, literally, "great meat." I thank Alexis Sanderson for this information.

631. The Tibetan text has *rnam par brtsegs pa'i sbyor bas rnal 'byor pa gnas la*, which Siklós's translation omits entirely (Siklós 1996, 35). It is possible that *brtsegs pa* is a corruption of *brtsigs pa* (literally, "a hideous-looking face"), and that *rnam par* corresponds to the Sanskrit prefix *vi*, which reflects the prefix of the word *vi-kṛtānana* in the Sanskrit. We have already seen before (in note 577) that *zhal gtsigs pa* / *brtsigs pa* is used in the VBhT as an appellation of Vajrabhairava and Yamāntaka.

smear the body with feces, and facing south, he should cast [the effigy's pieces] into the fire of the cremation pyre.[632] [The target] immediately dies.

[§32] Alternatively, there is this procedure for causing dissent. [The mantra master,] having got hold of bone from a crow and an owl,[633] traces with a metal pin the ten-syllable mantra on them together with the name of the target.[634] That person in whose name he recites [the mantra] in an isolated place will become hated.

[§33] Next [is another procedure]. [The mantra master,] having drawn a *cakra* of Yama on a piece of birch bark, and having placed the names of a man and a woman on the stomach of a frog,[635] should slip it beneath the threshold [of their house]. He in whose name [he does it] will have his arm dismembered by a sword.

[§34] Next is a procedure for paralyzing a girl. He should draw with poison and the rest the yantra of Yamāri on a rag taken from the cremation ground. Having made an effigy [of the target] using charcoal from the cremation pyre, he should make [an image of] the Hideous One (*vikṛtaṃ*)[636] measuring one span. He should place [the effigy] in its heart. Having pressed down on the yantra with his left foot and while maintaining meditative union with the Buffalo-Faced One, he should then repeat the ten-syllable mantra, [formulat-

632. Siklós (1996, 35) translates, "He burns it in a cremation fire having placed the pieces across each other." However, the Tibetan edition only says *ro bsregs pa'i me la* (Siklós 1996, 88–89). *Akṣobhya (pp. 377–78): "**If he casts [the effigy's pieces] into the fire** [means] [he offers *homa*] to the Bhagavān seated in the middle of the fire of wind" (*sbyin sreg byas na zhes bya ba ni rlung gi me'i dbus su bzhugs pa'i bcom ldan 'das la'o*).

633. *Akṣobhya (p. 378): "**Bone from a crow and an owl** [means] marrow from a thigh or the lower part of a leg" (*bya rog dang 'ug pa'i rus pa zhes bya ba ni brla'am rje ngar gyi rkang ngo*).

634. The Tibetan text has, in addition, *de cig la gcig drud na*, which Siklós (1996, 35) translates as "if he rubs one against the other." It is omitted in the Sanskrit.

635. *Akṣobhya (p. 378): "**Of a frog** [means one that has been] made from boiled rice/ beeswax (*sbal pa'i zhes bya ba ni spra tshil la bzo byas pa'o*).

636. The Tibetan text has *ro bsregs pa'i sol bas gzugs brnyan mtho gang tsam gyi tshad brtsigs la* (Siklós 1996, 89), but Siklós (35) leaves out the translation of *brtsigs la*, which corresponds to the Sanskrit *vikṛtam* (see note 631). The Sanskrit actually gives the procedure for making two effigies: the first is made with the ashes of a cremated corpse (*cityaṅgāreṇa pratikṛtiṃ kṛtvā*), and the second is the image of the Hideous One measuring one span (*vitastipramāṇaṃ vikṛtaṃ kārayet*). However, Siklós's translation (1996, 35) mentions only one effigy measuring one span, made from the ashes of the cremated corpse.

ing his purpose in these words:] "May I quickly paralyze girl X." [If he does that,] he will [indeed] paralyze her.[637]

[§35] These procedures should not be told to anyone.[638] If the mantra master, being full of delusion, does so, he will fall into a terrible hell. They should be done to anyone who harms the Three Jewels, who harms his teacher, who does not follow the rules, who mocks the mantras and the tantras, and who harms living beings. Having taken [a mental belief that he is doing] them a service,[639] the mantra master does this procedure of the mantras[640] with a mind that is moist with compassion,[641] and it is for their benefit; otherwise, he will be an

637. *Akṣobhya (p. 378): "**He will paralyze a woman** [means] through the activities of intoxication, in order to experience whatever pleasure he wishes" (*bu mo rmongs par bya ba ni/ myos par bya bas ci dgar longs spyad par bya ba'i phyir ro*). For a discussion in the wider context of "love" magic, see pages 175 above.

638. *Akṣobhya (p. 378): "**These procedures should not be told to anyone** [means] if those foolish people come to know [these rituals] without understanding the Buddha Śākyamuni's intention and disseminate them, they will fall to the hells. It is said: 'Just like sweet juice, sweet ghee, honey, and sugar when digested are like ambrosia but when undigested turn into poison, in the same way, the spread of ambrosia-like Dharma, when unwise people [teach] the intention [behind] those words to those foolish people, [the ambrosia-like Dharma] turns into terrifying poison.' Well then, if someone asks, what is, then, the purpose of this teaching? For that, the text says: 'It is for those who cause harm to the Three Jewels,' and this has been taught extensively" (*smra bar mi bya ste zhes bya ba la sogs pa ni byis pa'i rang bzhin can de dag gis shes nas thub pa chen po'i dgongs pa ci yin pa mi shes par ldang ba las de dag byed par 'gyur ba de dmyal bar ltung ste/ zhu ba'i rtsi* [em. *rting*, ed.] *la za ba ni/ mar gyi snying khu sbrang rtsi dang/ kha ra rnams ni bdud rtsi'i bzhin/ ma zhu zas ni dug 'gyur ro/ de bzhin rab rgyas bdud rtsi'i chos/ dgongs pa'i tshig la mi mkhas shing/ byis pa'i blo dang ldan rnams la/ mi bzad pa yi dug tu 'gyur/ zhes gsungs so/ 'o na 'di las dgongs pa gang zhe na/ de'i phyir/ dkon mchog gsum la gnod* [em. *gnas*, ed.] *byed dang/ zhes bya ba la sogs pa rgyas par gsungs so*). The quotation appears frequently in the Prajñāpāramitā literature, e.g., in the *Mahāyāna Mahāparinirvāṇa Sūtra*, chapter 12 (on the *tathāgatadhātu*): "And such Mahāyāna-sūtras are what also contain poison. It is like butter, *sarprimaṇḍa*, or rock candy, which when taken and digested, act as medicine. If not digested, then they are nothing but poison. It is the same with the *vaipulya-sūtras*. The wise make of them *amṛta*, and the ignorant, not knowing the value of the Buddha-Nature, make of them poison" (trans. Yamamoto 1973).

639. The Skt. *teṣām upakāram ādāya mantrī* does not feature in the Tibetan text.

640. The Tibetan text has *gnod pa rab tu sbyor bar bya'o* (Siklós 1996, 89), which Siklós (35) translates as "a devotee takes up their evil upon himself." The Sanskrit has, instead, *prayogaṃ karoti*, "he does the procedure."

641. The Tibetan text is corrupted, for it reads: *snying rjes gdungs pa'i sems kyis* (Siklós 1996, 89) "with a mind that is overcome with compassion," but the Sanskrit reads *karuṇārdreṇa cetasā*; therefore it should be *snying rjes brlon pa'i sems kyis*.

inhabitant of a great hell, and he will be one who has broken his vows. If he does otherwise, as it is said elsewhere:

> [§36] Strive to kill or otherwise displace those who defame the masters, who defile the Mahāyāna, and who ridicule mantras, tantras, and skill in the procedures.[642]

[§37] If the yogin does otherwise, acting out of cruelty toward anyone, then the magical procedure enacted by him will rebound on him. Why? Because the yogin is a harmer of living beings.

This is the second chapter, Accomplishment of All Magical Recipes, in this yoga tantra of the venerable Great Vajrabhairava, [which is a part of the tantra] called the *Mañjuśriya* [*Tantra*].

642. The first part of this quotation is from GS 14.47, p. 67: *ācāryanindanaparā mahāyānāgranindakāḥ/ māraṇīyāḥ prayatnena athavā sthānacālanam//*.

3. Extraction of the Mantra

[§38] Next,[643] I will explain extraction of the mantra (*mantroddhāraṇa*) as it is, in due order. Having sat down in a clean place,[644] the mantra master should extract the mantra.[645]

643. *Śoṇaśrī (p. 398): "**Next** [means] the intended meaning, which was explained in chapter 2, will not be achieved without the mantra. Because of this, in order to act without a doubt with respect to the mantra, the chapter on the extraction of the mantra beginning with the word 'next' is taught" (*rtog pa gnyis pa gsungs pa'i dgongs pa de nyid sngags med par 'grub par mi 'gyur bas sngags la the tshom med par bya ba'i don du/ de nas zhes bya ba la sogs pa sngags btu ba'i rtog pa gsungs pa*). *Kṛṣṇācārya (p. 451): "**Next** [means] the purpose (*prayojana*) of the mantra is meant for the *cakra*/yantra and for the sādhana, and the extraction of the mantra is taught in case there is a mantra error and one does not achieve [the ritual]. Moreover, one draws a smooth foundation on the ground, anoints it with nice fragrance, and writes the letters of the alphabet, the vowels and the consonants, and offers *pūjā*, offerings, oblation, and then erases it" (*de nas zhes pa ni 'khor lo dang sgrub pa la sngags dgos shing sngags nor na mi grub pas sngags btu ba bstan te/ de yang sa gzhi dri zhim pos byugs pa la A li dang ka li bri zhing mchod pas mchod pa dang/ gtor ma yang gtang bar bya'o*).

644. *Akṣobhya (p. 378): "**Clean place** [means] a solitary place; what is also meant by 'a solitary place' is definitely a greatly purified place" (*gtsang ma'i gnas zhes bya ba ni dben pa ste/ cis kyang dben pa ni nges par ches gtsang bas so*).

645. *Akṣobhya (p. 378): "**He extracts the mantra** [means] on a solid mud floor, with a piece of chalk (*khaṭikā*), he first writes the letters of the alphabet [i.e., gutturals, palatals, cerebrals, dentals, labials] and puts them in order in two lines; when that is clear, he adds the vowels. Then, when that is clear, he should write down [the mantra] or recite it" (*gsang sngags btu ba zhes bya ba ni sa 'thas pa skyang nul byas la kha ti khas las dang por gzhi'i yi ge go gnyis par bris la dag pa na dbyangs rnams sbyin zhing/ de nas dag pa na bri ba'am bzlas pa bya'o*).

[§39] The first of the sixth class (*ya*),[646] the fifth of the fifth class (*ma*).[647]

The second of the sixth class[648] (*ra*) connected with the second vowel[649] (*ā*): *rā*. (1)

The third of the second[650] class (*ja*), connected with the second vowel[651] (*ā*) again: *jā*. The third[652] of the seventh[653] class (*sa*), the third[654] of the fourth class[655] (*da*) connected with the thirteenth vowel[656] (*o*): *do*. (2)

646. *Kṛṣṇācārya (p. 451): "**The first of the sixth** [means] he should know the division into seven [classes (*vargas*)]. These are differentiated so that the [five in the] class of *ka* [velars], the [five in the] class of *ca* [palatals], the [five in the] class of *ṭa* [retroflexes], the [five in the] class of *ta* [dentals], the [five in the] class of *pa* [labials], together with the [four in the] class of *ya* [semivowels] make six [classes], and seven with the [four in the] class of *śa* [three sibilants plus *ha*]" (*drug pa'i dang po zhes pa ya yin te/ de yang ka'i sde tshan dang/ tsa'i sde tshan dang/ ṭa'i sde tshan dang/ ta'i sde tshan dang/ pa'i sde tshan dang/ ya'i sde tshan dang drug/ sha'i sde tshan dang bdun du phye bas shes pa'o*). Lalitavajra (p. 318) and Kumāracandra (p. 290): "**The first of the sixth** is *ya*, which is the first" (*drug pa'i dang po ni ya ste dang po'o*).

647. *Kṛṣṇācārya (p. 451): "**The fifth** [means] *ma*" (*lnga pa zhes pa ma'o*). Lalitavajra (p. 318) and Kumāracandra (p. 290) give the same gloss.

648. *Kṛṣṇācārya (p. 451): "**The second of the sixth** [means:] *ra*" (*drug pa'i gnyis pa zhes pa ni ra'o*). Lalitavajra (p. 318) gives the same gloss. Kumāracandra (p. 290): "**The second of the sixth** [means] *ma*" (*drug pa'i gnyis pa ni ma'o*). The Sanskrit version of Kumāracandra's commentary gives *ra*.

649. *Kṛṣṇācārya (p. 451): "**With the second vowel** [means] it is a long *ā* connected with *ra*, which gives *rā*" (*dbyangs yig gnyis pa zhes pa ni ā ring po ste ra dang sbyar bar ra ring por 'bod pa'o*). Lalitavajra (p. 318) and Kumāracandra (p. 290) give the same gloss.

650. *Kṛṣṇācārya (p. 451): "**The third of the second** [means] *ja*" (*gnyis pa'i gsum pa zhes pa ja*). Lalitavajra (p. 318) and Kumāracandra (pp. 290–91) give the same gloss.

651. *Kṛṣṇācārya (p. 451): "**With the second vowel** [means] a long *ā* connected with *ja*, which gives *jā*" (*dbyangs yig gnyis pa zhes pa ni ā ring po ja dang sbyar bas ja ring po'o*). Lalitavajra (p. 318) and Kumāracandra (p. 291) give the same gloss.

652. *Kṛṣṇācārya (p. 451): "**The third [of the seventh]** [means] *sa*" (*gsum pa zhes pa ni sa*). Lalitavajra (p. 318) and Kumāracandra (p. 291) give the same gloss.

653. *Kṛṣṇācārya (p. 451): "**The seventh** [means] the *śa varga*" (*bdun pa zhes pa sha'i sde tshan*).

654. *Kṛṣṇācārya (p. 451): "**The third** [**of the fourth**] [means] *da*" (*gsum pa zhes pa ni da*). Lalitavajra (p. 318) and Kumāracandra (p. 291) give the same gloss.

655. *Kṛṣṇācārya (p. 451): "**The fourth** [*varga*] [means] the *ta varga*" (*bzhi pa zhes pa ni ta'i sde tshan*).

656. *Kṛṣṇācārya (p. 452): "**With the thirteenth vowel** [means] *o*; he should join a short *o* so it becomes a metrically short *o*. As for the rest, it should be recognized in the same way. I have not written it out in fear that the text becomes too long" (*dbyangs yig bcu gsum zhes pa ni o/ thung ngu dang sbyar bas do thung ngur 'gyur ba'o/ gzhan rnams kyang de ltar*

The fifth of the fifth class[657] (*ma*) connected with the eleventh vowel[658] (*e*): *me*. The first of the sixth class[659] doubled: *ya ya*.[660] (3)

The fifth of the fifth class (*ma*) topped by the eleventh vowel (*e*): *me*.[661] The third of the fourth class (*da*) topped by the thirteenth vowel (*o*): *do*.[662] (4)

The second of the sixth class (*ra*) connected with the fifth vowel[663] (*u*): *ru*. The fifth of the third class[664] (*ṇa*), then he should give the seed syllable of the wind (*ya*) connected with the thirteenth vowel (*o*): *yo*.[665] (5)

---

shes par 'gyur bas gzhung mangs pas 'jigs pas ma bris pa'o). *Kṛṣṇācārya refers here to the fact that *o* is always long in Sanskrit, but for the sake of the meter, one should add here a short *o*. Lalitavajra (p. 318) simply states, "Adorned with the thirteenth vowel, i.e., *o*, it becomes *do*" (*de bcu gsum pa os brgyan pas dor 'gyur ro*). Kumāracandra (p. 291) has *o* as well (*dbyangs yig bcu gsum pa ni o'o*).

657. Lalitavajra (p. 318): "**The fifth of the fifth** [means] also *ma*" (*lnga pa'i lnga pa'i yang ma'o*)

658. Lalitavajra (p. 318) says: "By adorning it with the eleventh, i.e., *e*, gives *me*" (*bcu gcig pa es brgyan pas me'o*).

659. Lalitavajra (p. 318): "**The first of the sixth** [means] *ya*; by this, the sun of the first mantra [is taught]; the first of the sixth is *ya* again" (*drug pa'i dang po ya'o/ des nyi ma dang po'i sngags so/ yang ni drug pa'i dang po ya'o*). Kumāracandra (p. 291) also gives *ya* and adds that it should be doubled (*drug pa'i dang po ni ya'o/ gnyis 'gyur ni ya'o*).

660. The Tibetan text (Siklós 1996, 91) has a different reading: *drug pa yi ni dang po dang yang ni rlung gi sa bon sbyin*, which Siklós (36) translates as "the first of the sixth and then the seed syllable of wind," which gives the same double *ya*.

661. Lalitavajra (p. 318): "**The fifth of the fifth** is *ma*, [which joined] with the eleventh [vowel] gives *me*" (*lnga pa'i lnga pa ma ste de la bcu gcig pas mer ro*). Kumāracandra (p. 291) gives the same gloss.

662. Lalitavajra (p. 318): "**The third of the fourth** [means] *da*, [which joined] with the thirteenth vowel is *do*" (*bzhi pa'i gsum pa da ste/ bcu gsum pas do'o*). Kumāracandra (p. 291) gives the same gloss.

663. Lalitavajra (p. 318): "**The second of the sixth** is *ra*; because it is adorned with the fifth vowel, i.e., *u*, it becomes *ru*" (*drug pa'i gnyis pa ra la/ dbyangs yig lnga pa us brgyan pas rur 'gyur ro*). Kumāracandra (p. 291) gives the same gloss.

664. Lalitavajra (p. 318): "**The fifth of the third** [means] *ṇa*" (*gsum pa'i lnga pa ṇa'o*). Kumāracandra (p. 291) gives the same gloss.

665. Lalitavajra (p. 318): "He should place the seed syllable of the wind *ya*, following that [*ṇa*], and because it is adorned with the thirteenth [vowel], i.e., *o*, it becomes *yo*" (*rlung gi sa bon ya de'i 'og tu bzhag pa la/ bcu gsum pa os brgyan pas yo'o*). Kumāracandra (p. 291) gives the same gloss.

The third of the fourth class (*da*)[666] with the wind syllable again (*ya*).[667] The first of the sixth class (*ya*),[668] then the third of the fourth class (*da*).[669] (6)

Then the wind syllable again (*ya*) connected with the thirteenth vowel (*o*): *yo*.[670] The fifth of the fourth (*na*), [connected with the third vowel, *ni*].[671] (7)

Then he should give the fire syllable (*ra*), and in the same manner, the wind syllable (*ya*).[672] Then he should give [the syllable] at the end of the letters (*kṣa*) connected with the eleventh vowel (*e*): *kṣe*.[673] (8)

The first of the sixth class (*ya*), and then the wind syllable (*ya*).[674]

666. The Tibetan text (Ṣiklós 1996, 91) exactly matches the order given in the Sanskrit text, but Siklós's translation omits the whole verse *bzhi pa yi ni gsum pa dang de nas rlung gi sa bon sbyin* and jumps to the next line, *drug pa yi dang* [. . .]. Kumāracandra (p. 291): "**The third of the fourth** [means] *da*" (*bzhi pa'i gsum pa da'o*).

667. Lalitavajra (p. 318) says: "As for the seed syllable of the wind, and so on, it is just like before, so that is easy to understand. For that reason, the sun becomes the mantra, which is recited as the second, third, and fourth [in the verse]" (*rlung gi sa bon la sogs pa snga ma bzhin de go sla'o/ des na nyi ma gnyis pa gsum pa dang bzhi pa'i bzlas pa'i sngags su 'gyur te*). It is difficult to interpret this passage. It seems that Lalitavajra understands *ya* to be also the syllable of the sun. He seems to refer to the number of times that the *ya* syllable appears in the root mantra. *Ya* is the *bīja* of Vajrabhairava; see page 101 above. Kumāracandra (p. 291) confirms that the *bīja* of the wind is *ya* (*rlung gi sa bon ni ya'o*).

668. Kumāracandra (p. 291): "**The first of the sixth** [means] *ya*" (*drug pa'i dang po ni ya'o*).

669. Kumāracandra (p. 291): "**The third of the fourth** [means] *da*" (*bzhi pa'i gsum pa ni da'o*).

670. Kumāracandra (p. 291): "**The *bīja* of the wind** [means] *ya*, **the thirteenth vowel** [means] *o*" (*rlung gi sa bon ni ya'o/ dbyangs yig bcu gsum pa ni o'o*).

671. The Tibetan text (Siklós 1996, 38) has here "connecting it with the third vowel," which would give *ni*. This indeed seems to be the correct reading, insofar that it is also attested in other examples of the same mantra (see p. 107 above). This is confirmed by Kumāracandra (p. 291): "**The fifth of the fourth** [means] *na*, **the third vowel** [means] *i*" (*bzhi pa'i lnga pa ni na'o/ dbyangs yig gsum pa ni i'o*).

672. Kumāracandra (p. 291): "**The *bīja* of the fire** [means] *ra*; **the *bīja* of the wind** [means] *ya*" (*me'i sa bon ni ra'o/ rlung gi sa bon ni ya'o*).

673. Kumāracandra (p. 291): "**The final letter** [means] *kṣa*; **the eleventh vowel** [means] *e*" (*yi ge'i mtha' ni kṣa'o/ dbyangs yig bcu gcig pa ni e'o*).

674. Kumāracandra (p. 291) gives the reversed order: "**The *bīja* of the wind** [means] *ya*; **the first of the sixth** [also means] *ya*" (*de nyid kyi rlung gi sa bon ni ya'o/ drug pa'i dang po'i dang po ni ya'o*).

Then he should give [the syllable] at the end of the letters (*kṣa*) connected with the eleventh vowel (*e*): *kṣe*.[675] (9)

Then he should give the wind syllable (*ya*).[676] The first of the second class (*ca*) he should double (*cc*).[677] (10)

The fifth of the fourth class (*na*) connected with the third vowel (*i*): *ni*.[678] Then he should give the fire syllable (*ra*) connected with the second vowel (*ā*): *rā*.[679] (11)

The fifth of the fifth class (*ma*), then he should give the wind syllable (*ya*).[680] Then he should, at first, give *vairocana*[681] connected with the supreme lord.[682] (12)

675. Kumāracandra (p. 291): "That which abides as the last letter [means] *kṣa*; **the eleventh vowel** [means] *e*" (*yi ge'i mthar gnas pa ni ksa'o/ dbyangs yig bcu gcig pa ni e'o*).

676. Kumāracandra (p. 291): "**The *bīja* of the wind** [means] *ya*" (*rlung gi sa bon ni ya'o*).

677. Kumāracandra (p. 291): "**The first of the second** [means] *ca*; **counted twice** [means] *ca* [again, making *cca*]" (*gnyis pa'i dang po ni ca'o/ gnyis bgrang ba ni ca'o*). This gloss is missing in the Sanskrit version of Kumāracandra's commentary.

678. Kumāracandra (p. 291): "**The fifth of the fourth** [means] *na*; **the thirteenth vowel** [means] *i*" (*bzhi pa'i lnga pa ni na'o/ dbyangs yig gsum pa i'o*). This gloss is missing in the Sanskrit version of Kumāracandra's commentary.

679. Again, the Tibetan text (Siklós 1996, 92) is correct and matches with the Sanskrit when it says "*de nas me yi sa bon la dbyangs yig gnyis pa ldan pa dang*," but Siklós's translation (36) omits information on the second vowel. Kumāracandra (p. 291): "**The *bīja* of the fire** [means] *ra*; **the second vowel** [means] *ā*" (*me'i sa bon ni ra'o/ dbyangs yig gnyis pa ni ā'o*). This gloss is missing in the Sanskrit version of Kumāracandra's commentary.

680. Kumāracandra (p. 291): "**The fifth of the fifth** [means] *ma*; **the *bīja* of the wind** [means] *ya*" (*lnga pa'i lnga pa ni ma'o/ rlung gi sa bon ni ya'o*). This gloss is missing in the Sanskrit version of Kumāracandra's commentary.

681. Siklós (1996, 36n51) explains that the Tibetan blockprints of the VBhT he consulted have the variants *thog mar* or *dang por* qualifying *vairocana*. Although in his translation he seems to prefer the *thog mar* variant, he gives *dang por* in his edition, where we read: *dang por rnam par snang mdzad sbyin* (Siklós 1996, 92), translated as "at the end he puts *vairocana*" (36). Actually, the Sanskrit supports the *dang por* reading. Therefore we have "he should, at first, give *vairocana*," which is a code word for the seed syllable *oṃ*. The same reading is supported by Lalitavajra (p. 318), who glosses "at first, *vairocana*" as "he should put *oṃ*" (*sngon du rnam par snang mdzad de oṃ bzhag pa la*). Kumāracandra (p. 291) gives a slighty different explanation, for he glosses "at first, *vairocana*" as the letter *o* (*dang po rnam par snang mdzad ni o'o*). The Sanskrit version of Kumāracandra's commentary gives *hū* (*ādau vairocanaṃ hū*). Siklós (1996, 36) also thinks that *vairocana* means the seed syllable *hūṃ*, although he acknowledges that "at first, *vairocana*" means *oṃ*.

682. Siklós (1996, 36) translates *mchog gi dbang phyug dang sbyar ba*, which is a Tibetan translation of *parameśvarayojitaṃ*, as "with the highest power added." Kumāracandra (p. 291) glosses **the supreme lord** as "the two: the crescent moon and the *bindu*," meaning *uṃ*

The second of the fifth class (*pha*) and the first of the third class (*ṭ*): *phaṭ*;[683] the wise should say it twice, *phaṭ phaṭ*. (13)

This is the root mantra of the Buffalo-Faced One in the tantra of the Great Vajrabhairava in [the text called] *Śrīmañjuśriya* [*Tantra*]. As a result of reciting [this root mantra,] the accomplisher of all purposes,[684] one hundred thousand times,[685] he then accomplishes all magical recipes.[686] This is the king among mantras. There never has been [one like this,] nor will there ever be [another].

[§40] The fourth of the seventh class[687] (*ha*) connected with the fourth vowel[688] (*ī*): *hī*. Then he should give the syllable of fire[689] (*ra*). Then the wise [knows it as] the end of the sixteenth (*ḥ*).[690] (14)

(*dam pa'i dbang phyug ni zla tshes dang thig le gnyis so*). Thus, together with the initial *vairocana*, which is *o*, "it gives *oṃ*" (*des ni oṃ mo*). The Sanskrit version of Kumāracandra's commentary gives the same gloss as the Tibetan version but concludes that *parameśvara* means *hūṃ* (*tena hūṃ*).

683. Lalitavajra (p. 318): "**The second of the fifth** is *pha*, and **the first of the third** is *ṭa*; [connected] with the fifth [*pha*], it becomes *phaṭ*. It is doubled, and it should be recited fixed at the end" (*lnga pa'i gnyis pa pha dang/ gsum pa'i dang po ṭar lnga pas phaṭ tu 'gyur la/ de gnyis 'gyur du mjug tu btags te/ bzlas par bya'o*). Kumāracandra gives the same gloss.

684. *Akṣobhya (p. 378) glosses "**accomplisher of all purposes**" (*karmakāramantraḥ*): "[It is called the *all-purpose mantra*] in order to praise karma rituals and because it perfects them by means of yantra" (*las kyi sngags zhes bya bas ni las rab 'byam la rab tu bsngags pa'i phyir dang/ 'khrul 'khor yang 'dis rdzogs par byed pas so*).

685. *Akṣobhya (p. 378): "**One hundred thousand times** [means] by being established in supremely equipoised mind" (*'bum phrag gcig ces bya ba ni shin tu mnyam par gzhag pas so*).

686. *Kṛṣṇācārya (p. 452): "[Accomplisher] of **all purposes** [means] by knowing in that way that [the mantra recitation] is preceded by *pūrvasevā* and sādhana, he achieves the supreme siddhi and all other karmas like *śānti* and so on" (*las thams cad ces pa ni de ltar shes pas bsnyen sgrub* [add. *gong du*] *song bas mchog* [add. *dngos*] *dang zhi ba la sogs pa'i las thams cad byed pa'o*).

687. Lalitavajra (p. 320): "**The fourth of the seventh** [means] *ha*" (*bdun pa'i bzhi pa ni ha'o*). Kumāracandra gives the same gloss.

688. Lalitavajra (p. 320): "**Connected with the fourth vowel** gives *i*" (*dbyangs yig bzhi pa ldan pa ni i'o*). Kumāracandra gives *ī*.

689. Lalitavajra (p. 320): "**The syllable of fire** is *ra*" (*me'i sa bon ni ra ste*). Kumāracandra gives the same gloss.

690. Lalitavajra (p. 320): "Below *ha* is the letter *ra*. As for the *visarga*, these are the two dots that cut vehemently; thus it is pronounced as *hrīḥ*" (*ha'i 'og tu ra ldan pa'o/ tsheg drag*

The third of the seventh class (*sa*)[691] connected with the fourth vowel[692] (*ī*): *sī*. The first of the third class[693] (*ṭa*), he should place the form of the fire (*ra*) below it.[694] (15)

After that, the wise [knows it as] the end of the sixteenth (*ḥ*). The fourth of the sixth class[695] (*va*) connected with the third vowel[696] (*i*): *vi*. The first of the first class[697] (*ka*) connected with the seventh vowel (*ṛ*): *kṛ*.[698] (16)

The first of the fourth class (*ta*) connected with the second vowel[699] (*ā*): *tā*. The wise should then double the fifth of the fourth class, *na na*.[700] (17)

---

ni drag par gcad pa'i tsheg gnyis ste hrīḥ zhes bya bar 'gyur ro). *Kumāracandra: "**The end of the sixteenth** [means] two dots" (*bcu drug mtha' ni thig le gnyis so*).

691. The Tibetan text (Siklós 1996, 93) has *bdun pa yi na gnyis pa la*, which Siklós (37) translates as "the second of the seventh." This translation would reflect the syllable *ṣa*; however, the Sanskrit texts gives *sa* instead—namely, "the third of the seventh." The *ṣa* variant is also supported by Lalitavajra (p. 320) and Kumāracandra, who gloss *bdun pa'i gnyis pa* as *ṣa* (p. 292). Note that the mantra at the end of the Sanskrit mss. gives the *ṣa* variant instead (see p. 316 below).

692. Lalitavajra (p. 320): "**Connected with the fourth** [means] *ī*" (*bzhi pa ī ldan pa'o*). Kumāracandra gives the same gloss.

693. Lalitavajra (p. 320): "**The first of the third** [means] *ṭa*; it is below *ṣa*" (*gsum pa'i dang po ṭa ste/ sha'i 'og tu'o*). Kumāracandra gives the same gloss.

694. Lalitavajra (p. 320): "**The *bīja* of the fire** [means] *ra*; by putting that there, it gives *ṣṭrīḥ*; it is endowed with *visarga*, as before" (*me'i sa bon ra te de der bcug pas ṣṭrīḥ te/ tsheg drag dang ldan pa snga ma bzhin no*). Kumāracandra gives the same gloss.

695. Lalitavajra (p. 320): "**The fourth of the sixth** [means] *va*" (*drug pa'i bzhi pa ni va'o*). Kumāracandra gives the same gloss.

696. Lalitavajra (p. 320): "**The third vowel** [means] *i*; by uniting with [*v*], it is *vi*" (*dbyangs yig gsum pa ni i'o/ de ldan pas vi'o*). Kumāracandra gives the same gloss.

697. Lalitavajra (p. 320): "**The first of the first** [means] *ka*; the *bīja* of the fire is *ra*; by putting it below *ka*, it becomes *kṛ*" (*dang po'i dang po ni ka'o/ me'i sa bon ni ra te 'og tu ldan pas krir 'gyur ro*). Kumāracandra gives the same gloss.

698. The Tibetan text (Siklós 1996, 93) has an additional sentence: *'og tu me yi sa bon sbyin*, which Siklós (37) omits, explaining in the footnote that it would result in a tautological syllable. This conforms to the Sanskrit text, where this sentence is missing.

699. Lalitavajra (p. 320): "**The first of the fourth** [means] *ta*; the second vowel [means] *ā*; by connecting [*ta*] with that [vowel], it becomes *tā*" (*bzhi pa'i dang po ni ta'o/ dbyangs yig gnyis pa ni ā ste/ de dang ldan pas tā ring por 'gyur ro*). Kumāracandra gives the same gloss.

700. Lalitavajra (p. 320): "**The fifth of the fourth** [means] *na*; that itself is spoken again [means] twice" (*bzhi pa'i lnga pa ni na'o/ de kho na zhes pa yang na ste gnyis so*). Kumāracandra gives the same gloss.

He should, at first, add *vairocana*[701] (*oṃ*),[702] the eighth letter of the *ya* class (*ha*) conjoined with the sixth vowel (*ū*): *hū*,[703] its head adorned with the *bindu*: *hūṃ*. (18)

The second of the fifth class (*pha*), the first of the third class (*ṭ*): *phaṭ*.[704] (19ab)

This is the king among mantras, famed as the action mantra that accomplishes any procedure[705] [meant] for the union with the Buffalo-Faced One. If he recites it three hundred thousand times,[706] he accomplishes any magical procedure.

701. Lalitavajra (p. 320): "**At first, *vairocana*** on the head [means] he should put *oṃ*" (*glad du rnam par snang mdzad de oṃ bzhag go*). Kumāracandra: "**At first, *vairocana*** [means] *oṃ*" (*rnam par snang mdzad ni oṃ'mo*). The Sanskrit version of Kumāracandra's commentary: *vairocana* [means] *oṃ* (*vairocanaṃ oṃ*).

702. Siklós (1996, 37) translates *dang por rnam par snang mdzad sbyin* as "at the beginning he adds *vairocana*."

703. Kumāracandra: "**The eighth letter** [means] *ha*; **the sixth vowel** [means:] *ū*" (*brgyad pa ni ha'o/ dbyangs yig drug pa ni ū'o*).

704. Kumāracandra: "**The second of the fifth** [means] *pha*; **the first of the third** [means] *ṭa*" (*lnga pa'i gnyis pa ni pha'o/ gsum pa'i dang po ṭa'o*).

705. Siklós (1996, 37) translates *las kyi sngags su grags pa* as "it is known as the spell of rites," but this translation is inaccurate, for the Tibetan text reads "it is known as the action mantra." The Sanskrit text has *sarvakarmakarakarmamantraḥ*, which means "action mantra that accomplishes any procedure."

706. *Akṣobhya (pp. 378–79): "**Three hundred thousand times** [means] it is taught for the sake of intermediate practitioners" (*'bum phrag gsum zhes bya ba ni sngags pa bar ma'i phyir bstan pa'o*). *Kṛṣṇācārya (p. 452) refers to the number of mantra recitations as being one hundred thousand, three hundred thousand, and seven hundred thousand (but the Sanskrit text mentions only one and three hundred thousand). *Kṛṣṇācārya further comments on these numbers as follows: "A hundred thousand, three hundred thousand, and seven hundred thousand [mantra recitations] should be applied to *pūrvasevā*, sādhana, and karmas. To achieve [the desired goal], they should be recited within a span of two or six months. Later, one should do it every day and every night with the mind endowed with compassion" (*'bum dang sum 'bum dang bdun 'bum zhes pa ni bsnyen pa dang sgrub pa dang las sbyor gyi sgrub pa zla gnyis dang drug gis 'grub par 'gyur zhing/ phyis snying rje dang ldan pa'i sems kyis zhag re dang nyin res bya'o*).

[§41] The first of the sixth class (*ya*). The fifth of the fifth class (*ma*) connected with the second vowel (*ā*): *mā*.[707] The first of the fourth class (*ta*).[708] (20)

Before that the last of the fifth class (*anusvāra*);[709] he should place it on its head.[710] The first of the first class (*ka*), then he should, at first, add *vairocana* (*oṃ*).[711] (21)

[He should place] the *smaraṇa* topped by the ° [symbol, [i.e., a *bindu*] at the end of it.[712] (22ab)

Then the second of the fifth class (*pha*) and the first of the third class (*ṭ*), *phaṭ*.[713] (23ab)

707. Kumāracandra: "**The first of the sixth** [means] *ya*; **the fifth of the fifth** [means] *ma*; **the second vowel** [means] *ā*" (*drug pa'i dang po ya'o/ lnga pa'i lnga pa ma'o/ dbyangs yig gnyis pa ā'o*).

708. Kumāracandra: "**The first of the fourth** [means] *na*" (*bzhi ba'i dang po na'o*), which is incorrect. The Sanskrit version of Kumāracandra's commentary correctly glosses "The first [means] *ta*" (*prathamaṃ ta*).

709. Siklós (1996, 37) translates *de yi lnga pa glad du* as "the fifth of that group before it," which would give the letter *ṇa*. But what the Sanskrit says is that before the letter *ta* one has to put the last of the fifth class, which is *ma*, or *anusvāra*. In addition, the Sanskrit says that one puts it on the "head" of the letter *ta*, which indicates *ānta* (in *yamānta*). This detail is reflected in the Tibetan *glad du*, meaning "on the head."

710. Kumāracandra: "**The last [letter] of the fifth class** [means] *ta*" (*lnga pa'i tha ma ta'o*), which is incorrect. The Sanskrit version of Kumāracandra's commentary mistakenly glosses "The last [letter] of the fifth class [means] *na* (*pañcamāntikaṃ na*).

711. See note 681 above. Kumāracandra: "**The first of the first** [means] *ka*; **at first, *vairocana*** [means] *oṃ*" (*dang po'i dang po ka'o/ rnam par snang mdzad oṃ'o*). The Sanskrit version of Kumāracandra's commentary: "*Vairocana* [means] *oṃ* (*vairocanam oṃ*)."

712. The Tibetan text (Siklós 1996, 94) has *ya tshogs brgyad pa'i sa bon la/ dbyangs yig drug pa dang ldan la/ spyi bo ru ni thig les brgyan*, which Siklós (37) translates "[He] adds the seed syllable which is the eighth of the YA group with the sixth vowel adorned with the drop on top"; this would give *h* and the vowel *ū* with *bindu* on top, i.e., *hūṃ*. Lalitavajra (p. 320) explains: "The eighth of the ya *varga* and so on [means] *ha*; the sixth [means] *ū*; because it is adorned there, it gives *hū*. On the top it is adorned with the *bindu* [hence *hūṃ*]" (*ya la sogs pa'i brgyad pa ha'o/ drug pa u ste der brgyan pas hu'o/ steng du thig les brgyan pa'o*). The Sanskrit gives a totally different reading, i.e., *smaraṇa*, which in the *Picumata-Brahmayāmala* represents the seed syllable *hūṃ* (see note 617 above). Kumāracandra glosses *smaraṇa* as "the crescent moon" (*dran pa'i mtha' ni zla tshes so*; *smaraṇam ardhenduḥ*). Kumāracandra then gives another gloss that does not feature in the Sanskrit version of the VBhT, namely "emptiness deity, [meaning] *bindu*" (*stong pa lha ni thig le'o*). The Sanskrit version of Kumāracandra's commentary reads "Indeed from emptiness [means] *bindu*" (*śūnyad eva binduḥ*).

713. Lalitavajra (p. 320): "**The second of the fifth** [means] *pha*, and **the first of the third**

This is the famous heart mantra[714] of the Buffalo-Faced One. He who is engaged in the rite of extracting the mantras and is fully concentrated,[715] if he

---

is *ṭa*; with that, it is *phaṭ*" (*lnga pa'i gnyis pa pha dang gsum pa'i dang po ta ste des phaṭ do*). Kumāracandra gives the same gloss.

714. *Akṣobhya (p. 379): "**Heart mantra** [means] it is prescribed for those yogins who, for the most part, find it difficult to visualize [the mantra]. This is called *heart* because the reciter is to definitely meditate upon it in his heart. Although it is possible for mantras generally to achieve their effect merely by recitation, when it comes to heart mantras, they surely achieve their effects through visualization. Therefore it is said, 'What is known as *samādhi* is the heart; it is there where the mind is endowed with equipoise'" (*snying po'i gsang sngags zhes bya ba ni phal cher bsgom pa la dka'* [em. *dga'*, ed.] *ba'i rnal 'byor pa la bstan pa yin pas na/ 'di ni zlos pa pos ni nges par snying gar bsgom par bya bas na snying po zhes bya ste/ gsang sngags rnams ni bzlas pas kyang bya ba de byed srid kyi/ snying po rnams ni nges par bsgom pas don de rdzogs par bya ba yin te/ de nas snying po shes par ting nge 'dzin/ gang du mtshungs par ldan pa'i sems/ zhes bshad do*).

715. *Akṣobhya (p. 379): "**Fully concentrated** [means] 'Just like people who hold a sword, if they do not hold it properly, their hand will be cut off, in the same way, if one does not recite the mantra properly, there will be no [desired] result, and indeed, the outcome will be misfortune.' In order to eliminate the situation taught in this verse, when one performs the extraction of the mantra, at that time, it is very bad to have the mind on something else, just like it is forbidden to defecate and urinate while bathing" (*legs par mnyam par gzhag pa zhes bya ba la sogs pa ni/ ji ltar ral gri 'dzin pa'i mi dag gis/ legs par ma bzung lag pa 'chad par 'gyur/ de bzhin sngags kyang legs par ma bzlas na/ 'bras bu med dam yang na ma rungs 'gyur/ zhes gsungs pa'i gnas skabs spang ba'i phyir/ yi ge btu ba rtsom na/ de'i tshe sems gzhan du byed pa ni/ rab tu smad de/ khrus byed pa de yang bshang gci byed pa bzhin du de dgag pa'i phyir ro*).

recites the syllable[716] one hundred thousand times,[717] he accomplishes the rituals in all aspects[718] present in the three realms.[719]

This is the third chapter, Extraction of the Mantra, in this [yoga] tantra of the venerable Great Vajrabhairava, [which is a part of the tantra] called the *Śrīmañjuśriya* [*Tantra*].

716. The Tibetan text (Siklós 1996, 94) has *yi ge re re 'bum bzla,* but *Akṣobhya's commentary (see below) understands it as *yi ge 'bum bzla,* which connotes only one syllable of the *hṛdaya* mantra and not all of them. The same is supported by the Sanskrit reading *akṣaralakṣajāpena.*

717. *Akṣobhya (p. 379): "[If he recites] **the syllable one hundred thousand times** [means that] as for this syllable, it is the syllable of the heart" (*yi ge 'bum zhes bya ba la yi ge ni snying po'i yi ge'o*). *Akṣobhya further glosses "one hundred thousand": "[This is taught] to introduce lazy people; alternatively, as many syllables as there are [in the mantra], that many times [one should recite] a hundred thousand. It is said that 'When it comes to the syllables of the mantra under fifteen, a wise person has to recite it as many as one hundred thousand times as there are syllables, but this rule holds only [for the mantras] under fifteen.' Others say, 'This means one should recite it as per the numbers of the syllables, provided one has achieved clarity in meditation'" (*'bum zhes bya ba ni le lo can rnams gzhug pa'i phyir ro/ yang na yi ge 'bru ji snyed pa de snyed kyi 'bum phrag ste/ mkhas pas gsang sngags yi ge ni/ bco lnga man chad grangs rnams la/ yi ge'i sdom ni ji snyed pa/ de snyed 'bum phrag bzlas brjod bya/ zhes gsungs pas so/ gzhan kha cig ni 'di ni bsgom pa byang bar byas pas/ sgra ji bzhin pa'i bzlas par brjod do*). *Akṣobhya's explanation corresponds to the injunctions given in the *Susiddhikara* (Giebel 2001, 212): "If [the mantra] has fifteen syllables, you should recite it fifteen *lakṣa* times (1 *lakṣa* = 100,000), and if it has thirty-two syllables, you should recite it three *lakṣa* [times]. Those with more than this number [of syllables] should be recited ten thousand times or more."

718. *Akṣobhya (p. 379): "**He accomplishes the rituals in all aspects** [means] this is the teaching that is appropriately connected with those rituals that use the action mantra (*karmamantra*) as their chief thing but not with those that use yantra" (*las de dang de dag ces bya ba la sogs pa ni 'di ni las kyi sngags kyi gtsor* [em. *gor,* ed.] *sbyar du rung bar ston pa'o/ 'on kyang 'khrul 'khor ni ma yin no*).

719. The Tibetan text (Siklós 1996, 94) ends with an additional sentence not in the Sanskrit: *sngags btu ba'i cho ga'i dus 'dir mchod par bya'o,* which Siklós (37) translates "When the ritual of assembling the spells is performed, offerings should be made."

4. Visualization

[§42] Next,[720] I will duly explain[721] the means of mastering[722] [the deity] Vajra-

720. *Śoṇaśrī (p. 399) and *Vajrasiddha (p. 418): "Because the objectives of the things taught in those [previous chapters] cannot be achieved without visualization of the deity, the sādhana chapter is taught via 'next,' etc., for the visualization of the deity." "**Next** [means] immediately after the [chapter on the] extraction of the mantra" (*de dag bstan pa'i dgos pa ni lha'i dmigs pa med par 'grub par mi 'gyur bas lha'i dmigs pa'i don du de nas zhes bya ba la sogs pa sgrub thabs kyi rtog pa gsungs pa/ de nas zhes bya ba ni sngags btu ba'i de ma thag tu'o*). *Kṛṣṇācārya (p. 453): "Regarding the sādhana with the use of the mantra, if it is done without visualizing the deity, it will not be successful. For the purpose of a clear understanding, the means of mastering, beginning with the word 'next,' is taught. **Next** [means] after the extraction of the mantra, connecting it with the necessity of meditation on the deity" (*sngags kyis 'grub pa la lha la dmigs pa med na mi 'grub pas mngon par rtogs pa'i don du/ de nas zhes bya ba la sogs pa sgrub pa'i thabs gsungs pa nyid do/ de nas zhes pa ni sngags btus pa song ba dang lha bsgom dgos pa 'brel to*). Kumāracandra (p. 292): "**Next** [means] having performed the supreme worship with its seven aspects (*anuttarapūjā*), one should meditate on the four *brahmavihāras* [love, compassion, etc.,] and expel obstacles using the rays of light of the seed syllable situated in the center of the sun disc in one's own heart, as will be explained" (*de nas zhes bya ba la sogs pa la rnam pa bdun gyis bla na med pa'i mchod pa byas nas/ tshangs pa'i gnas bsgoms te/ rang gi snying gar nyi ma'i dkyil 'khor la gnas pa'i sa bon gyi 'od zer gyis bgegs rnams bskrad de/ ji skad gsungs bzhin du bya'o*).

721. *Śoṇaśrī (p. 399) and *Vajrasiddha (p. 418): "**I will duly explain** [means] the correct meaning here will be explained through the oral instruction of the guru; concerning this, the instruction is as follows" (*yang dag rab bshad bya zhes bya ba la yang dag pa'i don ni 'dir bla ma'i man ngag gis bshad par bya'o/ de la man ngag ni 'di yin te*). *Kṛṣṇācārya (p. 453): "**I will duly explain** [means] the method" (*yang dag rab bshad bya zhes ba ni thabs so*).

722. Siklós (1996, 37) translates *bsgrub pa* as "evocation," which fails to convey the meaning intended here, i.e., *sādhana*, "the means of mastering." Chapter 4 of the VBhT may be one of the earliest expositions of the sādhana of the yoga-tantra class extant in Sanskrit; see page 88 above. *Śoṇaśrī (p. 399) and *Vajrasiddha (p. 418) give a linguistic analysis of "the method of Vajrabhairava sādhana" as "the method by which one accomplishes Vajrabhairava" (*rdo rje 'jigs byed sgrub pa'i thabs zhes bya ba ni rdo rje 'jigs byed du thabs gang gis sgrub par byed*). This is followed by the semantic gloss: "That which causes one to become [Vajrabhairava] himself is his sādhana" (*bdag nyid du 'gyur bar byed pa ni de'i sgrub thabs so*).

bhairava.[723] After first having [meditated on] the selfless nature of all dharmas, he should take the deity as his object [of meditation]. So, first of all,[724]

723. *Kṛṣṇācārya (p. 453): "**Vajrabhairava** [means] that what is to be achieved—namely, the target (*sādhya*)—and the explanation of the method is that which achieves, the sādhana. Moreover, the method of the sādhana will be correctly explained. With the instruction of the guru, the yogin should understand that all the dharmas are empty, and by clearly visualizing the deity, he achieves the mantra. As for the instruction: in the places previously taught, with the substances and [the help of the] assistant (*uttarasādhaka*), he should outline the maṇḍala, arrange the shape [of the deity], and offer *pūjā*, *bali*, and so on" (*rdo rje 'jigs byed ces pa ni bsgrub par bya ba yin la/ thabs yang dag par bshad pa ni sgrub byed yin no/ de yang sgrub thabs yang dag par 'chad pa ste/ bla ma'i man ngag gis rnal 'byor pas chos thams cad stong par rtogs shing lha la dmigs pa gsal bas sngags 'grub po/ man ngag ni sngar gyi gnas bstan par rdzas dang grogs dang bcas pas dkyil 'khor bri ba dang sku gzugs* [em. *gzug*, ed.] *dgram pa dang mchod gtor dbul ba la sogs pa bya'o*).

The Sanskrit text has *sarvakarmanairātmyapūrvakaṃ*, which has been emended to *sarvadharmanairātmyapūrvakaṃ*, as supported by the Tibetan edition of the VBhT (Siklós 1996, 95): *sngon du chos thams cad la bdag med pa*, and by the VBhT commentaries. *Akṣobhya (p. 380): "**All dharmas** [means] aggregates (*skandhas*), elements (*dhātus*), and sense fields (*āyatanas*)" (*chos thams cad ces bya ba ni/ phung po dang/ khams dang skye mched do*). Lalitavajra (p. 322): "Then, in order to meditate on emptiness, he establishes with conviction that all things, such as *skandhas* and so on, are selfless in their inherent nature; this is meaning of 'he should generate the deity'" (*de'i rjes su stong pa nyid bsgom pa'i phyir/ dngos po thams cad de phung po la sogs pa rang bzhin med par mos pa la sogs pa byas las lha bskyed ces bya ba'i don to*).

724. *Śoṇaśrī (pp. 399–400) and *Vajrasiddha (pp. 418–19): "**First of all** [means] the mantra master, relying on some special person, should sit on a comfortable seat. He should place in his mouth a pellet (*guṭikā*) made of five nectars. The yogin should be naked, with hair disheveled, and facing south. Then, he visualizes that from his heart, rays of light of the seed syllables abiding in the sun, pervade the ten directions. He invites the buddhas, bodhisattvas, and the deities, starting with furies (*krodha*). He asks them to hover in the air in front of him, and he propitiates them with [the help of] the four goddesses—Vajracarcikā and so on—who arise from the light of the seed at [his] heart. They [the four offering goddesses=*pūjādevīs*] present offerings in front of the buddhas, holding sacrificial implements for worship, such as a lotus, in their hand. He confesses his sins and so on and dismisses them" (*dang por re zhig sngags pas skye bo 'ga' zhig la brten nas stan bde ba la 'dug ste/ bdud rtsi lnga la sogs pa'i ri lu khar bcug la rnal 'byor pa gcer bu gtsug phud bshig pa/ kha lhor mngon par phyogs pa ste/ de nas rang gi snying gar nyi ma la gnas pa'i sa bon gyi 'od rnams kyis phyogs bcu'i 'jig rten gyi khams mngon par khyab ste/ sangs rgyas dang byang chub sems dpa' dang/ khro bo la sogs pa'i lha tshogs spyan drangs te/ mdun gyi nam mkha'i phyogs su bzhugs su gsol la/ de nas snying ga'i sa bon gyi 'od zer las byung ba'i rdo rje carci ka la sogs pa'i lha mo bzhis mchod pa'i yo byad sna tshogs lag pa'i pad ma lta bu gzung ba rnams kyis legs par mchod do/ sdig pa bshags pa la sogs pa dang/ gshegs su gsol ba byas nas*). *Kṛṣṇācārya (pp. 453–54): "**First of all** [means] first, at that time, in those places [i.e., the suitable places previously described; see page 204], he should take a comfortable seat, and he should purify his mouth with the five nectars (*amṛtas*). Naked, his

he utters the mantra of intrinsic purity (*svabhāvaśuddha*).[725] Having brought about the selfless nature of all dharmas,[726] he should visualize a wind disc, gray

---

hair disheveled, facing south, with the letter *ma* in the heart and the seed syllable, he performs the protection of the lattice tent (**jālapañjara*), both the sides and the top. He protects the place and the deity with compassion, and with the meditation on emptiness, he protects himself, the yogin. With that light endowed with five rays in the seed syllable of his heart, pervading all the world systems in the ten directions, he impels all the five lineages of the buddhas. Having purified the five classes of beings, he visualizes in the space in front of him all the buddhas, bodhisattvas, wrathful ones, and [his] gurus. From the seed syllable in his heart, he emits the *pūjādevīs* and, with Vajracarcikā and so on, he correctly offers the outer (*bahya*), inner (*antara*), and real (*tattva*) forms of worship (*pūjā*)" (*dang po kho nar zhes pa ni de'i tshe dang po ste gnas der stan bde ba la 'dug ste/ bdud rtsi lnga yis kha dag par byas la/ gcer bu skra grol ba lhor mngon par phyogs par bya ste/ snying ga'i ma dang sa bon gyis dr[w]a gur gyi bsrung bas/ gnas dang snying rje chen pos* [em. *po*, ed.] *dang lha dang stong pa nyid kyi ting nge 'dzin bsrung bas rnal 'byor pa yang bsrung bar 'gyur ro/ snying ga'i sa bon gyi 'od zer lnga dang ldan pa'i 'od de nyid kyis phyogs bcu'i 'jig rten gyi khams thams cad du khyab pas sangs rgyas thams cad rigs lnga bskul/ 'gro ba'i rgyud lnga sbyangs nas/ sangs rgyas dang byang chub sems dpa' dang khro bo dang bla ma thams cad mdun gyi nam mkha' la dmigs la/ rang gi snying ga'i sa bon las mchod pa'i lha mo spros la rdo rje carci ka la sogs kyis phyi dang nang dang de kho na nyid kyi mchod pas yang dag par mchod pa dang*). Lalitavajra (p. 322): Then, '**first of all** he utters *sarva*': as for 'the first,' it [means] *oṃ śūnyatājñānavajra*; then, with the mantra *svabhāvātmako 'ham*, he meditates on the meaning of that" (*des na dang por sar ba zhes pa la/ dang por zhes bya ba ni/ oṃ shu nya ta dznya na badz ra ste/ de nas sva bha va a tma* [corr. *dma*, ed.] *ko 'ham zhes bya ba'i sngags pas de'i don bsgom zhes pa'o*).

725. The root text seems to refer here to the mantra *oṃ svabhāvaśuddhāḥ sarvadharmāḥ svabhāvaśuddho 'ham*, which treats the selfless nature of all dharmas (*dharmanairātmya*). The commentaries by *Śoṇaśrī, *Akṣobhya, and *Kṛṣṇācārya understand this mantra to be the first mantra to be applied in the visualization process. According to the commentators, this is followed by the second mantra, *oṃ śūnyatājñānavajrasvabhāvātmako 'ham*, which treats the selflessness of the individual (*pudgalanairātmya*). I thank John Newman for this clarification.

726. *Akṣobhya (p. 380): "**Having brought about the selfless nature of all dharmas** [means] they become natural luminosity, empty in nature, free of perceived object-perceiving subject [duality]" (*de dag bdag med pa'i bdag nyid du byas nas zhes bya ba ni/ gzung ba dang 'dzin pas dben pa rang bzhin gyis 'od gsal bar 'gyur ba'o*). For *Śoṇaśrī, *Vajrasiddha, and *Kṛṣṇācārya, this is contextualized as the meditation on the four *brahmavihāras*, the four alternatives (*catuṣkoṭi*), dependent origination, and so on. *Śoṇaśrī (p. 400) and *Vajrasiddha (p. 419): "What is expressed by the phrase **selfless nature of all dharmas** (***sarvadharmanairātmya***) is the meditation on the four sublime states (*brahmavihāras*). In this regard, love (*maitrī*) has the characteristic of love for all sentient beings as though they were your own son; compassion (*karuṇā*) is the desire to completely liberate [sentient beings] from the suffering and the cause of suffering; joy [means] stabilizing contentment by means of firm bliss; and equanimity (*upekṣā*) is to be even-minded, disregarding all thought constructs related to perception (*grāhyaṃ*) and

in form,[727] produced from the syllable *yaṃ* in the center of space. Then, having

perceiver (*grāhakaḥ*). Then, he [should contemplate the emptiness by] perceiving the dependent origination of all and by being devoid of the four alternatives (*catuṣkoṭi*), and he should both recite and realize the meaning of the mantra '*Oṃ* I have as my nature the nondual [lit. "admantine"] gnosis of emptiness' (*oṃ śūnyatājñānavajrasvabhāvātmako 'ham*); he should strip the appearance ([*an*]*ābhāsa*) of both himself and the three realms" (*chos thams cad bdag med pa zhes bya ba'i tshig gis tshangs pa'i gnas bzhi bsgoms pa mtshon pa'o/ de la sems can thams cad la bu gcig pa ltar sdug pa'i mtshan nyid ni byams pa'o/ sdug bsngal dang sdug bsngal gyi rgyu las yang dag par 'dod pa'i* [corr. *'don*, ed.] *snying rje dang/ bde ba brtan pa nyid kyis dga' ba dang/ gzung ba dang 'dzin pa'i rnam par rtog pa thams cad la btang snyoms su byed pa'i phyir btang snyoms so/ de nas thams cad rten cing 'brel bar 'byung ba dang/ mu bzhi dang bral bar rnam par bltas la/ oṃ shū nya tā dznyā na badz ra swa bhā va atma ko 'ham/ zhes bya ba'i sngags brjod la sngags kyi don mngon du byed cing bdag nyid khams gsum la snang ba med par byas nas*). *Kṛṣṇācārya (p. 454) has a corresponding passage: "He confesses his sins and so on, and he meditates on the four *brahmavihāras*; one knows them [as follows]: (1) *maitrī-lakṣaṇa*, 'love,' is defined as that which is never forsaken and graciously extends to all beings; (2) *karuṇā-lakṣaṇa*, 'compassion,' is defined as that which desires to protect all sentient beings from suffering; (3) *muditā-lakṣaṇa*, 'joy,' is defined as a desire to rescue the beings from *saṃsāra* [this normally features in the *karuṇā-lakṣaṇa*] and place them in contentment and a desire to not to be dissociated from them; (4) *upekṣā* is defined as that which understands 'equanimity,' freedom from the divisiveness of a biased mind and freedom from the eight worldly dharmas. Then, realizing that nothing is established as existing innately (*svabhāva*) [and that they are instead] empty of one and many, free of the four points or *koṭis* [i.e., existence, nonexistence, both existence and nonexistence, and neither existence nor nonexistence], and arise in dependent origination (*pratītyasamutpāda*), [in order to seal this realization] he recites the mantra *oṃ śūnyatājñānavajrasvabhāvātmako 'ham*. The purpose of that mantra is to place his mind in a 'no focus on anything state,' pervading the entirety of space, having the nature of the immutable gnosis of emptiness" (*sdig pa bshags pa la sogs pa rnams byas la tshangs pa'i gnas bzhi bsgoms te/ sems can thams cad la brtse bas khyab pa mi gtong ba byams pa'i mtshan nyid/ sdug bsngal las skyob par 'dod pa'i snying rje'i mtshan nyid de/ 'khor ba las bsgral bar 'dod pa'i bde bar 'dod pa dang/ mi 'bral bar 'dod pa dga' ba'i mtshan nyid do/ nye ring gis mi 'byed cing chos brgyad spangs pa btang snyoms su shes pa'o/ de'i rjes su chos gcig dang du mas stong pa mu bzhi dang bral ba rten cing 'brel bar 'byung ba'i rang bzhin ma grub par rtogs nas/ oṃ shū nya tā dznyā na badz ra swa bhā wa atma ko 'ham zhes brjod la/ sngags de'i don stong pa nyid kyi ye shes mi 'gyur ba'i rang bzhin du nam mkha' khyab pa rang gi blo mi dmigs par bzhag go*).

727. Syntactically, this is a difficult passage to translate. The Sanskrit text supports *dhūmravarṇākāraṃ* as qualifying the color of the initial letter *a* and not the color of the wind disc, but such a reading is supported neither by the commentaries nor by parallel passages in the Tibetan and Sanskrit. In this regard, the Tibetan text (Siklós 1996, 95) reads *nam mkha'i dkyil du yaṃ gi rnam pa las grub pa'i rlung gi dkyil 'khor mdog du ba'i rnam pa bsam mo*, which Siklós (1996, 37) translates as "one thinks of the smoke-colored wind-*maṇḍala* arisen from the syllable YAṂ in the middle of space." Similarly, in the *Saṃpuṭodbhava* (7.4.54), we find the reading "In the center of space, he should visualize

visualized a moon disc[728] upon it, arising from the initial letter *a*,[729] and then, having mentally generated Mañjuśrī[730] in a form of a youth from the syllable

the wind disc of a gray color [coming] from the letter *yaṃ*" (*bhagamadhye tu yaṃkāreṇa vāyumaṇḍalaṃ dhūmrākāraṃ vicintayet*). *Akṣobhya's commentary (p. 380) also supports the gray color as describing the wind disc: "After that, one meditates on the gray wind disc formed from the blue letter *yaṃ* in the middle of space" (*de'i 'og tu de nyid la nam mkha'i dkyil du yi ge yaṃ sngon po las grub pa'i rlung gi dkyil 'khor du ba'i mdog can du bsams te*). The Tibetan *de'i 'og tu* seems to be a mistake of *de'i steng du*, which reflects the Sanskrit *tasyopari*, which however does not feature in the Sanskrit manuscripts available to me. A more correct reading would be *de nyid la*, "in the same place"—i.e., in the expanse of space. *Akṣobhya (p. 380) further says that **the wind disc, gray in form,** is "the seat of Mahākrodha" (*'di ni khro bo chen po'i gdan te*). Quoting from the early (probably pre-ninth century) unidentified source, he explains the reason for Mahākrodha occupying the wind disc: "Because this [*Vajrabhairava*]*tantra* has as its chief topic *abhicāra*, it is that which scatters all malevolent entities. For that reason, it is said, "All those deities designated by the name 'wrathful' (*krodha*), such as servants starting with emissaries: their activity is unhindered everywhere. For that reason, the maṇḍala [suitable] for them is either fire or wind" (*rgyud 'di ni mngon spyod gtso bor byas pa yin pas na/ gdug pa rnams rab tu 'thor bar byed pa yin te/ pho nya la sogs bran rnams dang/ khro bo'i ming du gang 'dogs pa/ kun du thog med spyod pa rnams/ kun gyi dkyil 'khor me* [em. *ma*, ed.] *dang rlung/ zhes gsungs pas so/*). *Akṣobhya's *ṭīkā*, 380.

728. *Akṣobhya (p. 380): "**Moon disc** [means that] it is the seat of the noble Mañjughoṣa and that it is a transformation from [the letter *a*]" (*zla ba'i dkyil 'khor zhes bya ba ni/ 'phags pa 'jam pa'i dbyangs kyi gdan te/ de ni yongs su bsgyur bar bya ba yin na*). Lalitavajra (p. 322): "As for the initial letter *a*, it is a moon generated from the letter *a*" (*dang po ni a las byung ba'i zla ba'o*).

729. The NMAA has a corresponding passage in which one visualizes one's own consciousness in the form of the syllable *a* in the middle of empty space. Interestingly, the commentators of the VBhT pass over in silence any exegetical explanation on the syllable *a*, but from other textual sources it can be inferred that this concept was influential in contemporaneous tantric circles. In both the yoga and caryā tantras, the symbolism of the letter *a* seated on a moon disc typically connotes the selfless nature of all the dharmas (*sarvadharmanairātmya*). In the NMAA, *a* is the letter from which the Mañjuśrī *jñānasattva* is "born," insomuch as he is referred to as *akārasaṃbhavaḥ, akārajanitāḥ* on the basis of MNS 5.1, the introductory verse of the Vajradhātu maṇḍala chapter. The letter *a* seated on a moon disc is located in *jñānasattva* Mañjuśrī's heart, and "it symbolizes its nature or the source of identity" (Tribe 1994, 33). In Vilāsavajra's understanding, *a* is a synonym of emptiness, so *jñānasattva* Mañjuśrī stands for awareness of the ultimate emptiness of all things. The letter *a* also represents the *dharmadhātu* and the essence of the perfection of wisdom, which is understood, in Madhyamaka and Vijñānavāda terms, as nondual awareness (Tribe 1994, 34).

730. *Śoṇaśrī (pp. 400–401) and *Vajrasiddha (pp. 419–20): "**Mañjuvajra** [means] the protector with one face, two arms, holding a sword and a book [in his hand]. [Mañjuvajra should be visualized] sitting in the cross-legged vajra posture and as being of the

dhīḥ[731] above that, he visualizes a sun disc[732] whose form has been produced from an *āḥ* syllable in Mañjuśrī's heart.[733] Then, having caused a mass of rays

nature of the causal vajra-holder (*hetuvajradhara*). Then he [Mañjuvajra] should be generated as adorned with the eight cremation grounds [around him], which symbolize that he has the nature of the resultant vajra-holder (*phalavajradhara*), as taught in various tantras. That means that he is free of egoism (*nirahaṃkāra*), nondual with regard to existence (*bhāva*) and cessation (*nirvāṇa*). At this point, he [the yogin] should recite the mantra: '*Oṃ svabhāvaśūnyatāḥ sarvadharmāḥ svabhāvaśūnyo 'ham*' (*'jam pa'i rdo rje zhes bya ba ni mgon po zhal gcig phyag gnyis pa phyag na ral gri dang glegs bam can/ rdo rje'i skyil mo krung gi sbyor bas rgyu'i rdo rje 'dzin pa'i bdag nyid can no/ rgyud dang rgyud du gsungs pa'i rim pas 'bras bu rdo rje 'chang gi ngo bor bdag nyid dur khrod brgyad kyis brgyan par bskyed la srid pa dang zhi ba gnyis su med pa'i nga rgyal med cing/ oṃ swa bhā wa shū nya tā sar wa dhar ma swa bhā wa shū nya 'ham/ zhes bya ba'i sngags brjod par bya'o*). For the explanation of this mantra, see note 725 above. Note that commentaries substitute the word "śuddha" in the standard form of this mantra, with the word "śūnya."

731. *Śoṇaśrī (p. 400) and *Vajrasiddha (p. 419): "**From the syllable *dhīḥ*** [means] from the yellow *dhīḥ*" (*dhīḥ las zhes bya ba ni dhīḥ ser po las so*). *Kṛṣṇācārya (pp. 454–55): "**from the syllable *dhīḥ* above that** [means] he should meditate on the primordial Buddha (*ādibuddha*) [through the stages of] yoga, anuyoga, atiyoga, mahāyoga. [*Dhīḥ* means] at the time of ritual action, one should visualize [Mañjuśrī] as a solitary hero (*ekavīra*) manifesting in the center. The appearance of the maṇḍala is the same otherwise except that *dhīḥ*, the sword, and the deities are yellow. One should meditate on [Mañjuśrī] holding a book in his left hand. He sits on the lotus and the moon disc in the cross-legged vajra posture." (*de'i steng du* [em. *nang du*, ed.] *dhīḥ yig las zhes pa ni dang po'i sangs rgyas rnal 'byor dang rjes su rnal 'byor dang shin tu rnal 'byor dang/ rnal 'byor chen po rnams bsgom pa'o/ las sbyor gyi dus su dpa' bo gcig pa ni dkyil* [em. *dkyus*, ed.] *kyi gsal ba de nyid do/ khyad par ni dhīḥ dang ral gri lha rnams ser ba'o/ g.yon po ti bsnams pa nyid bsgom pa'o/ pad ma dang zla ba la rdo rje skyil mo krung du bzhugs pa'o*). This depiction corresponds to the passage of the NMAA where one has to visualize the *ādibuddha* (Mañjuśrī) transformed from the syllable *dhīḥ*: "He should visualise a moon-disc in his [Mahāvairocana's] heart; [and] above that, transformed out of the syllable DHĪḤ [he should visualise] the Fortunate One, the Ādibuddha, having five faces, having five crests (*pañcacīraka*) [. . .]" (Tribe 1994, 106). He is portrayed as tranquil, with the ornaments of a youth (*kumārābharaṇopeta*), and has eight arms, four of them holding "the one hundred thousand [verse] Perfection of Wisdom [scripture]," the other four hands holding a "sword of wisdom in a gesture of striking" (Tribe 1994, 106).

732. About the sun disc as Vairocana, see below.

733. The parallel passage of the *Saṃpuṭodbhava* (7.4.54) reads: "Above that, in the middle of the moon having visualized oneself in the form of Mañju[śrī], who is a transformation of the syllable *dhīḥ*, he meditates upon the sun disc [produced] from the syllable *āḥ* in Mañju[śrī]'s heart" (*tasyoparīndumadhye dhīḥkārapariṇataṃ mañjurūpam ātmānaṃ vicintya taddhṛdi āḥkāreṇa sūryamaṇḍalaṃ dhyātvā*, ed., p. 345). The Tibetan text (Siklós 1996, 95) and Siklós's translation (37) have the syllable *a* instead of *āḥ*, but this is not supported by the VBhT commentaries, which uniformily give the syllable *āḥ* and not *a*.

to exit from that sun disc, he arouses to action the tathāgatas, the bodhisattvas, the wisdom deities, and the wrathful deities,[734] which fill the limits of space in all ten directions.[735] Then he should visualize the mass of rays returning again into the same sun disc. Then he should meditate upon that sun disc as fused into oneness with Mañjuśrī and those tathāgatas and so on. He should visualize that sun disc as having a form radiant like fire and as pervading a hundred thousand *yojanas*.[736] Above that [sun disc], [he should visualize] a black syllable *hūṃ* endowed with five rays.[737] Then, emitting and withdrawing the rays of

---

*Śoṇaśrī (p. 400) and *Vajrasiddha (p. 419) say: "Atop the sun disc, which has arisen from the red syllable *āḥ*, is a syllable *hūṃ*, which emits five rays of light" (*yi ge āḥ dmar po las byung ba'i nyi ma'i steng du hūṃ yig* [em. Newman, *gi*, ed.] *'od zer lnga 'phro ba can no*). The syllable *āḥ* stands for Mahāvairocana, *vairocana* meaning "belonging to the sun," or "solar" (Tajima 1992, 248). The imagery of light that penetrates the universe and its link with Vairocana goes back to the *Gaṇḍavyūhasūtra*, which "describes reality as a universe of infinitely reflected light" (Orzech 1987, 5607). The symbolism of luminous interpenetration is preserved in the VBhT, stating that the sun disc (or Mahāvairocana) causes the mass of rays of light to exit and entice the tathāgatas, the bodhisattvas, the wisdom deities, and the wrathful deities in all directions of space. The rays of light return back to the sun disc, and then the sun disc fuses in oneness with Mañjuśrī and those tathāgatas and the rest.

In the NMAA, Mahāvairocana as the central deity of the Vajradhātu maṇḍala is also generated from the syllable *āḥ* (Tribe 1994, 105). He is depicted as four-faced "since the four faces are the freedoms (*vimokṣa*) of emptiness and the rest" [...] (105) and displays the *bodhyāgri* mudrā "because he has both wisdom and means as his nature" (105). He emits the luminous rays of light from his [four] faces that illuminate the world as well as the tathāgatas, buddhas, and bodhisattvas and then reenter Mahāvairocana's mouths (111). Those rays are "conceived as identical with the essencelessness of all *dharmas*, [and] become united with the mantra-syllable [*a*] on the moon[-disc] in one's own heart" (111). Both texts refer to the same function of Mahāvairocana, who emits the rays of light in order to illuminate/entice the deities stationed in various directions of space. Those rays go back and forth, reenter Mahāvairocana, and finally fuse in oneness with Mañjuśrī or the syllable *a* that represents its source.

734. The parallel passage of the *Saṃpuṭodbhava* (7.4.54, ed., p. 345) gives a much shorter description: "Thereafter, having caused the rays to exit from the sun disc [and] having performed *pūjā* according to the ritual prescriptions" (*tataḥ sūryamaṇḍalād raśmiṃ niścārya vidhivat pūjāṃ kṛtvā*).

735. The Tibetan text (Siklós 1996, 95) omits the phrase *anantaparyantāvasthitān* and simply mentions the ten directions as the location of the tathāgatas, bodhisattvas, wisdom goddesses, and the wrathful ones.

736. The parallel passage of the *Saṃpuṭodbhava* (7.4.54, ed., p. 345) omits the passage beginning with "arouses to action" and ending with "one hundred thousand *yojanas*."

737. The parallel passage of the *Saṃpuṭodbhava* (7.4.54, ed., p. 345) reads: "Above that [sun disc], having meditated upon the syllable *hūṃ* endowed with five rays, [one should visualize] Vajrabhairava surrounding that [syllable *hūṃ* with five rays]" (*tadupari*

the syllable *hūṃ* as explained before [. . .].[738] Having fixed [them], he should

hūṁkāraṃ pañcaraśmisaṃyuktaṃ dhyātvā tatparāvṛtaṃ vajrabhairavaṃ). What follows is a description of Vajrabhairava.

738. The passage on the black vajra endowed with five rays arising from the syllable *hūṃ* and the transformation of the vajra into Vajrabhairava (see Siklós 1996, 38) is missing in the VBhT, and does not feature in the parallel passage found in the *Saṃpuṭodbhava*.

The last stage of the sādhana in the VBhT is the generation of the vajra from the syllable *hūṃ*. The sun disc of the previous phase (i.e., *vairocana*) becomes fire, and above it one visualizes the black syllable *hūṃ* endowed with five rays, which, in the same manner as the rays of Mahāvairocana before, go forth and return back to the *hūṃ* that is their source. The visualization of the vajra, preserved only in Tibetan translation, contains the following instructions:

> One thinks that from that *vajra*, minute *buddhas*, *bodhisattvas*, wrathful ones, and wisdom goddesses seated on solar discs fill the sphere of space like a mass of sesame seeds and are in the solar disc. By means of these *buddhas* and so on, one brings sentient beings to maturation and places them in the state of enlightenment. One then thinks that these gather together and reenter the *vajra*. One thinks that the *vajra* itself becomes the glorious Buffalo-headed Vajramahābhairava (trans. Siklós 1996, 38).

The NMAA (4.34) has a corresponding passage in which a practitioner should visualize himself as "the great syllable HŪṂ, dark blue in colour, endowed with masses of flames of wrath, surrounded by many hundreds thousands of rays of light" (Tribe 1994, 102). The syllable *hūṃ* emits many rays, and one should visualize that all the tathāgatas manifest "from the ends of the rays, and that they [that is, the light-rays, together] with all those Tathāgatas, go to all the Buddha-fields [and] purify all the mass of beings in all the world-spheres without reminder. Having generated the thought of enlightenment and so forth [in those beings] [. . .], they return back again [and] enter that syllable HŪṂ" (Tribe 1994, 102–3). Then, one visualizes a knowledge vajra (*jñānavajra*), transformed out of that syllable *hūṃ*.

In this case too, both texts share striking similarities with regard to the generation of the vajra out of the syllable *hūṃ*. The noticeable difference, however, is that in the case of the VBhT, the vajra transforms itself into Vajrabhairava himself, while in the NMAA, the function of the knowledge vajra is to protect the space for the sādhana in order to make it "unapproachable by the Māras" (Tribe 1994, 103). The reference to the vajra as *jñānavajra* is important. In Kumāracandra's commentary, *jñānavajra* is a name for Vajrabhairava's *liṅga* as an iconographic appropriation of the Śiva *liṅga*, through the use of which Vajrabhairava protects beings. In the mythic stories narrating the origins of Vajrabhairava in the Tibetan tradition, *jñānavajra* is the name of Vajrabhairava's *liṅga*, which he uses to convert all the evil ones. The reference to *jñānavajra* is also found in chapter 1 (11–12) of the STTS, in connection with the emanation of Vajrasattva, when it denotes multiple *jñānavajras* that come together into one *jñānavajra* that pervades the whole of space. This *jñānavajra* emits rays of light with tathāgatas abiding at the edges and performs the actions similar to the ones described in the sādhana's emanation of light rays from the syllable *hūṃ* of chapter 4 of the NMAA (Tribe 1994, 103). On the *jñānavajra* understood as

visualize [them] coming together again in the same way and entering the vajra orb.

[§43] That vajra orb is the great Vajrabhairava who has a form of the buffalo[739] with nine faces.[740] He is the fire of time of the great destruction, the

advayajñāna ("nondual wisdom"), see Candrakīrti's *Pradīpoddyotana* commentary on the GS, chapter 13.

739. The Tibetan text (Siklós 1996, 96) has *ma he'i gdong can* (*mahiṣamukham*) instead of *mahiṣarūpam*. *Śoṇaśrī (p. 404) and *Vajrasiddha (p. 423) gloss ***mahiṣamukham***—namely, **has a face of the buffalo**—as "because he is the lord over the triple worlds" (*khams gsum pa rnams la bdag nyid yin pa'i phyir ma he'i zhal lo*). *Kṛṣṇācārya (p. 455): "**Buffalo** [means] in order to tame those to be tamed with wrathful buffalo-faced deity" (*ma he ni lha drag po ma he'i gdong 'dul ba'i phyir ro*).

740. *Śoṇaśrī (p. 404) and *Vajrasiddha (p. 423): "**Nine faces** [means] because he brings about the ripening of all beings by teaching nine branches of the dharma [*sūtra*, *udāna*, *adbhūta*, *jātaka*, etc.]" (*zhal dgu ni yan lag dgu'i chos ston pas sems can yongs su smin par byed pas na'o*). *Akṣobhya (p. 381): "**Nine faces** [means] three to the left and three to the right, connected with the first [face] in the middle; there is one [face] above and one further above that, in due order. In that way, these nine [faces] are progressive meditative absorbtions (*nirodha-samāpattis*) culminating in buddhahood" (*zhal dgu pa zhes bya ba ni/ dbus dang de 'brel pa nas brtsams pa'i g.yas pa gsum dang/ de bzhin du g.yon pa gsum dang/ steng dang de'i steng rnams rim pa bzhin du sangs rgyas kyi mthar gyis gnas pa'i snyoms par 'jug pa dgu'o*). *Kṛṣṇācārya (p. 455): "**Nine faces** of *vajratattva* [means] at the time of accomplishing [the deity] Vajrabhairava, who is the resultant vajra-holder (*phalavajradhara*), one should do the empowerment of the innate nature (*svabhāva*) of *vajradhātu*, which is saṃsāra and nirvāṇa without any distinction, and one has to imagine the pride of the deity. One should recite *oṃ vajradharmadhātusvabhāvātmako 'ham*. Then there is an introduction of the knowledge being (*jñānasattva*), the empowerment of the senses, the achievement of the body, speech, and mind, the *abhiṣeka*, worship, praise, and the savoring of the nectar, and so on. This should also be done from the oral instruction" (*rdo rje de nyid zhal dgu pa zhes pa ni 'bras bu rdo rje 'chang rdo rje 'jigs byed du grub pa'i dus der/ srid pa dang zhi ba dbyer med pa chos kyi dbyings kyi rang bzhin du byin gyis brlab cing nga rgyal du bya ba/ oṃ badz ra dhar ma dhā tu swa bhā wa atma ko 'ham zhes* [em. *rdzogs pa'o*, ed.] *brjod pa'o/ der yang ye shes sems dpa' gzhug pa dang/ skye mched byin gyis brlab pa dang/ sku gsung thugs sgrub pa dang/ dbang bskur ba dang/ mchod pa dang/ bstod pa dang bdud rtsi myang ba la sogs pa yang man ngag las bya'o*). The above sādhana instruction is followed by a gloss on the symbolism of the **nine faces**, which *Kṛṣṇācārya (p. 455) understands as "nine progressive meditative absorptions that cause the maturation of the sentient beings" (*zhal dgu zhes pa ni mthar gyis snyoms par 'jug pa dgu ste sems can smin par byed pa'o*).

great brilliance,[741] devouring the three worlds.[742] He is hideous looking[743] as he lets out the mad laughter,[744] rolling his tongue[745] [and] furrowing his terrifying eyebrows. Knitting his brows and similarily his eye, he is roaring like the time of the great destruction. He should be visualized as devouring human blood, flesh marrow, blood, meat, fat, and bone marrow.[746] He points a threatening finger[747] toward the gods, [those] mundane, [those] supermundane, and others. He devours Indra,[748] Brahmā, Īśvara (i.e., Śiva), Viṣṇu, Kumāra,[749] and other [gods], who, looking downward, have fallen to [their] knees. He has

741. *Kṛṣṇācārya (p. 455): "Fire like **brilliance** is to tame *māras*, which is the fruit of generating a mind with compassion" (*me ltar 'bar ba ni thugs rjes thugs bskyed pa'i 'bras bu bdud 'dul ba'o*).

742. *Akṣobhya (p. 381): "**Three worlds** [means] he is the lord of these [three worlds]: Jayakāra, Madhukāra, and Sarvārthasiddhikāra" (*'jig rten gsum zhes bya ba ni de'i bdag po ste/ rgyal bar byed pa dang/ sbrang rtsir byed pa dang/ don kun 'grub pa'o*). The same gloss appears in NMAA (Tribe 2016, 104), who glosses *trailokya* [with *loka* meaning "people" rather than "worlds"] as the three brothers, i.e., Jayakāra, Madhukāra, and Sarvārthasiddhikāra: "He whose way is to conquer these [brothers] is [also] called 'the conqueror of the three worlds.' For this very reason the fortunate one Vajradhara is a 'hero,' not to be overcome by the enemies." *Kṛṣṇācārya (p. 455): "**Devouring the three worlds** should be understood as the emptiness of all dharmas. It should be understood as the emptiness of all dharmas" (*khams gsum za ba ni chos thams cad stong pa nyid du rtogs pa'o*).

743. *Kṛṣṇācārya (p. 455) has *zhal brtsegs pa*, "stacked up faces," which he glosses as "to frighten the four *māras*" (*zhal brtsegs pa ni bdud bzhi spa bkong ba'o*). Most probably *brtsegs pa* is a mistake for *brtsigs pa*, "hideous"; see note 631 above.

744. *Kṛṣṇācārya (p. 455): "**He lets out the mad laughter** [means] because he possesses *āśvāsa* (breath, cheering up, etc.), he delights the mind" (*ha ha ni sems brtas* [em. *rtas*, ed.] *par byed de dbugs 'byin pa'o*).

745. *Kṛṣṇācārya (p. 455): "**Rolling his tongue** [means] he causes subjugation under one's will" (*ljags 'dril ba ni dbang du byed pa'o*).

746. The Tibetan text (Siklós 1996, 96) has only four items: *mi'i khrag dang tshil dang zhag dang rkang za ba* "He devours human blood, oil, fat, and marrow." *Kṛṣṇācārya (p. 455): "**Human meat** [means] he accomplishes great bliss" (*mi sha zhes pa bde ba chen por 'grub pa'o*).

747. *Kṛṣṇācārya (p. 455) glosses **threatening finger** as "He works for the benefit of all beings, without being distracted" (*sdigs mdzub ces pa ni mi yengs* [em. *yangs*, ed.] *par 'gro don mdzad pa'o*).

748. *Kṛṣṇācārya (p. 455): "**Indra** [means] in order to show the sign that he makes them servants" (*brgya byin zhes pa bka' nyan byed pa'i rtags su bstan pa'o*).

749. The Tibetan text (Siklós 1996, 96) adds the *yakṣa* (*gnod spyin*), which Siklós (38) translates as "a spirit" featuring in the Tibetan text as the fifth being to be eaten by Vajrabhairava. The parallel passage of the *Saṃpuṭodbhava* (7.4.54, ed., p. 346) mentions only Brahmā, Indra, Upendra (Viṣṇu), Rudra, etc.

a crest made of skull ornaments[750] and causes a great fear.[751] He utters a *phet̩* sound[752] and has a topknot on his head. He is adorned with a sacred thread

750. The Tibetan text (Siklós 1996, 96) has *thod pa gtsigs pa'i rtse mo 'jig su rung ba'i thod pas thod byas pa,* which Siklós (38–39) translates as "the top of his head with bared teeth is ornamented with frightful skulls." The passage in Tibetan seems to be corrupted; both *Śoṇaśrī's (pp. 401–2) and *Vajrasiddha's commentaries (p. 421), read *thod pas* perhaps an error for *tog thod du byas pa,* which corresponds to the Sanskrit *kapālakṛtaśekharaṃ,* "**He has a crest made of skull ornaments** because he possesses the nature of the five knowledges (*jñānas*)" (*tog* [em. *thod pas,* ed.] *thod du byas pa zhes pa ni ye shes lnga'i rang bzhin yin pa'i phyir ro*). *Kṛṣṇācārya (p. 455): "The **skull** garland on the head [means] he is the chief of the five families" (*mgo bo'i phreng ba'i thod de ni rigs lnga'i bdag po'o*). *Kṛṣṇācārya (p. 455): "**Skull** garland [means] *viśuddhi* of vowels and consonants" (*thod pa'i phreng ba ni dbyangs dang gsal byed kyi yi ge dag pa'o*). *Śoṇaśrī (p. 402) and *Vajrasiddha (p. 421) additionally have "adorned with the skull ornament," which they gloss as "because he emerges from the *dharmadhātu*" (*thod pa'i rgyan gyis brgyan pa zhes bya ba ni chos kyi dbyings nas bzhengs pa yin pa'i phyir ro*).

751. *Śoṇaśrī (p. 402) and *Vajrasiddha (p. 421): "**He causes a great fear** because he makes *māras* terrified" (*'jigs su rung ba chen po zhes bya ba ni bdud rnams sngangs par byed pa'i phyir ro*).

752. *Śoṇaśrī (p. 402) and *Vajrasiddha (p. 421): "**He utters a *phet̩* sound** because he causes fear to those who are hateful and so forth" (*phet'i sgra brjod pa ni sdang ba la sogs pa rnams skrag par byed pa'i phyir ro*); *Kṛṣṇācārya (p. 455) says: "***Phaṭkāra*** [means] he threatens all" (*phaṭ kyi sgra ni thams cad bsdigs pa'o*).

and skull ornaments. He has sixteen feet[753] and is naked,[754] ithyphallic,[755] and standing with right leg bent and left leg extended.[756] He has a big belly,[757]

753. *Śoṇaśrī (p. 402), *Vajrasiddha (p. 421) and *Kṛṣṇācārya (p. 455): "**Sixteen feet** [means] the sixteen emptinesses because [he is] purified by the sixteen emptinesses" (*zhabs bcu drug ni stong pa nyid bcu drug rnam par dag pas so*). *Akṣobhya (p. 381): "**Sixteen feet** is a purification (*viśuddhi*) of sixteen emptinesses. For the same reason, the sixteen [beings] beginning with human corpse are made to be the symbols of sixteen perceptions as real existences (*vastu*), whether outer or inner, etc. And because these [sixteen perceptions] are overcome by the sixteen types of emptiness, these sixteen feet are said to trample upon them" (*zhabs bcu drug pa zhes bya ba ni stong pa nyid bcu drug rnam par dag pa'o/ de nyid kyi phyir mi ro la sogs pa bcu drug ni phyi rol dang nang la sogs pa'i dngos por 'dzin pa bcu drug gi mtshan mar mdzad pa yin la/ de dag stong pa nyid bcu drug gis bcom pa yin pa'i phyir zhabs bcu drug gis brdzis pa'o*).

754. *Śoṇaśrī (p. 402) and *Vajrasiddha (p. 421): "**Naked** because he frees one from the obscurations of the dharmas" (*gcer bu ni chos rnams kyi sgrib pa nyid grol bar byed pa'i phyir ro*). *Akṣobhya (p. 381): "**Naked** [means] because he has given up the thought constructs (*vikalpas*). Clothes are worn because there is shame and embarrassment, but covering oneself with cloth is taught for the foolish people since it is said, 'Although foolish people wear cloth, they are always naked, unlike a wise man, who, even though he lives naked, is wearing clothes'" (*gcer bu'i sku la zhes bya ba ni rnam par rtog pa spangs pa dang/ ngo tsha shes pa dang/ khrel yod pa'i phyir gos yin gyi/ ras la sogs pas bkab pa ni byis pa'i gos yin par bstan pa'i phyir te/ byis pa gos rnams gyon yang rtag par gcer/ mkhas pa gcer bur 'dug kyang gos dang bcas zhes bshad pas so*). *Kṛṣṇācārya (p. 456): "It is a truth body (*dharmakāya*), free from mental elaboration (*niṣprapañca*)" (*gcer bu ni chos kyi sku spros pa dang bral ba'o*).

755. *Śoṇaśrī (p. 402) and *Vajrasiddha (p. 421): "**Ithyphallic**, because he is of the nature of great bliss" (*mtshan ma 'greng ba ni bde ba chen po'i* [em. *por*, ed.] *rang bzhin gyis so*). *Kṛṣṇācārya (p. 456): "The body of great bliss" (*mtshan ma gyen du 'greng ba ni bde ba chen po'i sku'o*). *Akṣobhya (pp. 381–82): "**Ithyphallic** [means] it shows that he [Vajrabhairava] is similar to Mahādeva because [Vajrabhairava] has tamed him. It is said that 'because that [Mahādeva] was extremely full of passion after ceasing three years of asceticism, he was not sated with the pleasure of sexual union with Umā, and his *liṅgam* was constantly ready for action.' For that reason it is said, 'By overcoming passion (*rāga*), [wrong] view, and hatred, one tames Mahādeva, Brahmā, and Viṣṇu'" (*mtshan 'greng zhes bya ba ni 'di lha chen po dang 'dra bar bstan pas de 'dul ba'i phyir te/ de ni lhag par chags pa can yin pas/ lo gsum du dka' thub bzlog pa* [em. *ma*, ed.] *dang gnyis kyi gnyis su bde bas bde ba u ma* (em. Newman *ma*, om., ed.) *tshim zhing rtag tu mtshan ma las su rung ba'o zhes grag go/ de bas na chags dang lta ba zhe sdang bsngo/ lha chen tshangs pa khyab 'jug 'dul zhes bshad do*).

756. *Śoṇaśrī (p. 402) and *Vajrasiddha (p. 421): "**Left leg extended**, because he arranges everything in its own place and puts all dharmas into emptiness" (*chos thams cad stong pa nyid so sor bzhag pa'i phyir g.yon brkyang ba'i gom pa'o*). *Kṛṣṇācārya (pp. 455–56): "because he serves other beings" (*g.yon brkyang ba ni 'gro don mdzad pa'o*).

757. *Śoṇaśrī (p. 402) and *Vajrasiddha (p. 421): "**A big belly**, because he is fierce and

raised hair,[758] and roars a howling sound. One should imagine the buffalo-headed great Śrī Vajrabhairava as having thirty-four arms[759] and holding an elephant skin. Having correctly visualized[760] [Vajrabhairava] in that way and having made [this visualization] firm, the mantra master with perfectly concentrated mind[761] should always[762] meditate [on him] in that manner, with reality yoga.[763]

[§44] Then, in the first of his right hands, [Vajrabhairava holds] a chopper,[764]

---

wrathful" (*gtum pa khro bo yin pa'i phyir gsus pa che ba'o*).

758. *Śoṇaśrī (p. 402) and *Vajrasiddha (p. 421): "**Raised hair**, because he shows the state of nirvāṇa" (*skra gyen du brdzes pa ni mya ngan las 'das pa'i go 'phang ston pa'i phyir ro*). *Kṛṣṇācārya (p. 456): "On the inside blazing with knowledge, on the outside threatening to demons" (*skra gyen du brdzes pa ni nang na ye shes 'bar zhing phyi rol du bdud bsdigs par mdzad pa'o*).

759. *Śoṇaśrī (p. 402), *Vajrasiddha (p. 421), and *Kṛṣṇācārya (p. 456): "**Thirty-four arms** [means] it is a purification (*viśuddhi*) of the thirty-four doctrines conducive to enlightenment (*bodhipākṣikadharma*)" (*phyag sum cu rtsa bzhi ni byang chub kyi phyogs kyi chos sum cu rtsa bzhi rnam par dag pa'o*).

760. *Śoṇaśrī (p. 402) and *Vajrasiddha (p. 421) comment: "'Right effort, correct mindfulness, and correct meditative stabilization' are included in Bhagavān's body, speech, and mind" (*yang dag pa'i rtsol ba dang/ yang dag pa'i dran pa dang/ yang dag pa'i ting nge 'dzin dang/ bcom ldan 'das nyid kyi sku gsung thugs kyi ngo bor bsdus pa'o*).

761. *Śoṇaśrī (p. 402) and *Vajrasiddha (p. 421): "He is established in **perfectly concentrated mind** because his body, speech, and mind do not waver" (*shin tu mnyam par bzhag pas lus dang ngag dang yid ma yengs pas so*). *Kṛṣṇācārya (p. 456): "**Perfectly concentrated mind** in *tattvayoga* [means] the last stage of *mahāyoga*" (*de nyid kyi rnal 'byor la mnyam par gzhag ces pa ni rnal 'byor chen po'i rim pa'o*).

762. *Śoṇaśrī (p. 402) and *Vajrasiddha (p. 421) gloss *rag tu*, "always," as "at the three times" (*rtag tu zhes bya ba ni dus gsum du'o*).

763. *Śoṇaśrī (p. 402) and *Vajrasiddha (p. 421) gloss **reality yoga** (*tattvayoga*) as "He has no observation of that which is to be meditated on, meditator, or meditation" (*de kho na nyid kyi sbyor ba zhes bya ba ni bsgom bya dang sgom pa po dang sgom pa rnams dmigs su med pa'o*). This probably references the famous verse of the *Guhyasamāja* (2.3):

> *abhāve bhāvanābhāvo bhāvanā naiva bhāvanā* |
> *iti bhāvo na bhāvaḥ syād bhāvanā nopalabhyate* ||3||

I thank John Newman for this clarification.

764. *Śoṇaśrī (p. 402) and *Vajrasiddha (p. 421): "**Chopper** cuts ignorance" (*gri gug ni ma rig pa gcod pa'o*). *Kṛṣṇācārya (p. 456): "It cuts away the six faults—pride and so on" (*gri gug ni skyon drug nga rgyal la sogs pa gcod pa'o*).

in the second a javelin,[765] in the third a pestle,[766] in the fourth a knife,[767] in the fifth a single-pointed vajra[768], in the sixth an axe,[769] in the seventh a spear,[770] in the eighth an arrow,[771] in the ninth an elephant goad,[772] in the tenth a club,[773]

765. *Śoṇaśrī (p. 402) and *Vajrasiddha (p. 421): "The **javelin** puts to an end the thought constructs (*vikalpa*) of object-subject [duality]" (*bhi ndi pha la* [a Tib. transliteration of the Skt. *bhiṇḍipāla*] *ni gzung ba dang 'dzin pa'i rnam par rtog pa 'byed pa'o*). The Tibetan text (Siklós 1996, 97) has *mtshon rtse gcig pa*, which Siklós (39) translates as "a one-pointed javelin." *Kṛṣṇācārya (p. 456) has *tho ba*, "hammer," instead, which he glosses as "He is endowed with power and fearlessness" (*tho ba ni stobs dang mi 'jigs pa dang ldan pa'o*).

766. *Śoṇaśrī (p. 402), *Vajrasiddha (p. 421), and *Kṛṣṇācārya (p. 456): "The **pestle** overcomes the loss of recollections" (*gtun shing ni dran pa nyams pa 'joms pa'o*).

767. *Śoṇaśrī (p. 402) and *Vajrasiddha (p. 421): "The **knife** cuts evil deeds" (*chu gri ni sdig pa gcod pa'o*). *Kṛṣṇācārya (p. 456): "cuts attachment" (*chu gri ni sred pa gcod pa'o*).

768. *Śoṇaśrī (p. 402): The **single-pointed vajra** destroys faults of body and speech" (*rdo rje rtse gcig pa ni lus ngag gi nyes pa 'joms pa'o*). *Vajrasiddha (p. 421): "destroys faults of body, speech, and mind" (*rdo rje gcig pa ni lus ngag yid gsum gyi nyes pa 'joms pa'o*). A passage of the *Saṃpuṭodbhava* (7.4.56, ed., p. 346), as well as both manuscripts of the VBhT, read *kaṇaya/kanaya*, which has been emended to *kaṇapa*. This reading is supported by the Tibetan, for *rdo rje rtse gcig pa* is a translation of the Sanskrit *kaṇapa*; see Chandra 1976, 1265. This reading is also attested in the Tibetan text (Siklós 1996, 97) and in the commentaries by *Śoṇaśrī and *Vajrasiddha. *Kṛṣṇācārya (p. 456): "**Single-pointed** [means] cutting through the three groups" (*rtse gcig pa ni phung po gsum 'bigs pa'o*). *Phung po gsum* is a technical term that corresponds to the Skt. *triskandhaka*.

769. *Śoṇaśrī (p. 402): "The **axe** cuts the mind's stiffness" (*sta re ni sems kyi mkhregs pa gcod pa'o*). *Vajrasiddha (p. 421): "The **axe** destroys the thick latent traces of the mind" (*sta re ni sems gyi sra ba'i bag chags 'joms pa'o*). *Kṛṣṇācārya (p. 456): "**Axe** [means] the axe with which he cuts off birth and aging related to saṃsāra" (*sta res 'khor ba'i skye rga gcod pa'o*).

770. All the Sanskrit recensions have *kunta*, meaning "spear," but the Tibetan text seems to have based its translation on the Sanskrit *śakti*, which is *mdung thung* in Tibetan, meaning both "spear" and "lance." Siklós (1996, 39) translates "lance." *Śoṇaśrī (p. 402) and *Vajrasiddha (pp. 421–22): "The **spear** pierces perverted views" (*mdung ni lta ba ngan pa 'bigs pa'o*). *Kṛṣṇācārya (p. 456): "It is the understanding of the profound meaning, which is realization of the emptiness of all dharmas" (*mdung ni zab pa'i don chos thams cad stong pa nyid du rtogs pa'o*).

771. *Śoṇaśrī (p. 402) and *Vajrasiddha (p. 422): "The **arrow** serves to destroy the thorn of all concepts/stupidity" (*mda' ni kun du rtog pa'i* [*shin tu rmongs pa'i*, *Vajrasiddha] *zug rngu 'bigs par byed pa'o*). *Kṛṣṇācārya (p. 456): "It pierces ignorance" (*mda' ni ma rig pa 'bigs pa'o*).

772. *Śoṇaśrī (pp. 402–3) and *Vajrasiddha (p. 422): "**An elephant goad**, because it causes to summon" (*lcags kyu ni 'gugs par byed pa'i phyir ro*). *Kṛṣṇācārya (p. 456): "It attracts beings" (*lcags kyu ni 'gro ba 'dren par byed pa'o*).

773. *Śoṇaśrī (p. 403) and *Vajrasiddha (p. 422): "The **club** serves to destroy the impurity

in the eleventh a skull staff,[774] in the twelfth a wheel,[775] in the thirteenth a vajra,[776] in the fourteenth a vajra hammer,[777] in the fifteenth a sword,[778] in the sixteenth a rattle drum.[779]

In the first of his left hands [Vajrabhairava holds] a skull,[780] in the second a

of action" (*mtshon ka ta* [*ka ta* is a Tib. transliteration of the Skt. *gadā*] *ni las kyi sgrib pa 'joms par byed pa'o*). *Kṛṣṇācārya (p. 456): "He renders the *asuras* defeated" (*dbyug pa ni lha ma yin pham par byed pa'o*).

774. *Śoṇaśrī (p. 403) and *Vajrasiddha (p. 422): "The **skull staff** has the nature of *bodhicitta*" (*kha tvam ga ni byang chub sems kyi ngo bo'o*). *Kṛṣṇācārya (p.456): "It manifests the deities" (*kha tvan ga ni lha rnams gsal ba'o*).

775. *Śoṇaśrī (p. 403) and *Vajrasiddha (p. 422): "**A wheel**, because he puts in motion the wheel of dharma" (*'khor lo ni chos kyi 'khor lo bskor ba'i phyir ro*). *Kṛṣṇācārya (p. 456): "It removes the obstacles that are the four *māras*" (*'khor lo ni bar chad kyi bdud bzhi sel ba'o*).

776. *Śoṇaśrī (p. 403) and *Vajrasiddha (p. 422): "The **vajra** has the nature of the five knowledges (*jñānas*) that come to have a single taste" (*rdo rje ni ro nyam par 'gyur ba ye shes lnga'i bdag nyid do*). *Kṛṣṇācārya (p. 456): "It symbolizes the purification of the five kinds of opposing poisons, such as the five types of knowledges (*jñānas*)" (*rdo rje ni ye shes lnga'i ngo bos phas kyi dug lnga sbyong ba'o*).

777. *Śoṇaśrī (p. 403) and *Vajrasiddha (p. 422): "The **vajra hammer** causes separation from jealousy" (*rdo rje tho ba ni ser sna 'byed par byed pa'o*). The Sanskrit manuscripts of the VBhT read only *mudgara*. The vajra hammer is also supported by the *Saṃpuṭodbhava* (7.4.56, ed., p. 346) and Tibetan translation (Siklós 1996, 97). *Kṛṣṇācārya (p. 456) has *triśūla*, which he glosses as "cutting through the faults of the body, speech, and mind" (*rtse gsum ni lus ngag yid gsum gyi nyes pa 'bigs pa'o*).

778. *Śoṇaśrī (p. 403), *Vajrasiddha (p. 422), and *Kṛṣṇācārya (p. 456): "The **sword**, because it bestows the siddhi of a sword and so on" (*ral gri ni ral gri la sogs pa'i dngos grub ster ba'i phyir ro*).

779. *Śoṇaśrī (p. 403) and *Vajrasiddha (p. 422): "The **rattle drum** excites all the buddhas with supreme joy" (*mchog tu dga' bas sangs rgyas thams cad skul bar byed pa ni da ma ru'o*). *Kṛṣṇācārya (p. 456): "It proclaims the sound of dharma" (*da ma ru ni chos kyi sgra sgrogs par byed pa'o*).

780. *Śoṇaśrī (p. 403) and *Vajrasiddha (p. 422): "**Skull** filled with blood [means] he protects the vows (*samayas*)" (*khrag gis bkang ba'i thod pa ni dam tshig skyong bar byed pa'o*). *Kṛṣṇācārya (p. 456): "He sports great bliss" (*thod pa khrag gis bkang ba ni bde ba chen por rol pa'o*).

head,[781] in the third a shield,[782] in the fourth a leg,[783] in the fifth a noose,[784] in the sixth a bow,[785] in the seventh entrails,[786] in the eighth a bell,[787] in the ninth a hand,[788] in the tenth a rag of the cremation ground,[789] in the eleventh a man

781. *Śoṇaśrī (p. 403) and *Vajrasiddha (p. 422): "The **head** of Brahmā, because out of compassion he fulfills the aims of sentient beings" (*tshangs pa'i mgo bo ni snying rjes 'gro ba'i don mdzad pa'i phyir ro*). *Kṛṣṇācārya (p. 456): "He removes eternalism" (*bram ze'i mgo bo ni rtag lta sel ba'o*).

782. *Śoṇaśrī (p. 403) and *Vajrasiddha (p. 422): "**A shield**, because he overcomes the demons" (*phub ni bdud las rgyal ba'i phyir ro*). *Kṛṣṇācārya (p. 456): "He protects sentient beings" (*phub ni 'gro ba rnams skyob pa'o*).

783. *Śoṇaśrī (p. 403) and *Vajrasiddha (p. 422): "**A leg**, because he bestows the state of a buddha on the one who meditates" (*rkang pa ni sgom pa po la sangs rgyas kyi go 'phang ster ba'i phyir ro*). *Kṛṣṇācārya (p. 456): "He is endowed with four bases of miraculous powers (*ṛddhipādas*)" (*rkang pa ni rdzu 'phrul gyi rkang pa bzhi dang ldan pa'o*).

784. *Śoṇaśrī (p. 403) and *Vajrasiddha (p. 422): "**A noose**, because he causes to bind with true wisdom" (*zhags pa ni yang dag pa'i ye shes bcing bar byed pa'o*). *Kṛṣṇācārya (p. 456): "he pulls people out from damnation with his great compassion" (*zhags pa ni thugs rje chen pos ngan 'gro rnams 'dren pa'o*).

785. *Śoṇaśrī (p. 403) and *Vajrasiddha (p. 422): "**A bow**, because he overcomes the three worlds" (*gzhu ni 'jig rten gsum las rgyal ba'i phyir ro*). *Kṛṣṇācārya (p. 456): "He has control over wisdom of emptiness that is victorious over the three worlds" (*gzhu ni 'jig rten gsum las rgyal ba'i stong pa nyid kyi shes rab mnga' ba'o*).

786. Śoṇaśrī (p. 403) and *Vajrasiddha (p. 422): "**Entrails**, because he renders emptiness intelligible" (*rgyu ma ni stong pa nyid du go bar byed pa'i phyir ro*). *Kṛṣṇācārya (pp. 456–57): "wisdom of equality" (*rgyu ma ni mnyam pa nyid kyi ye shes so*).

787. *Śoṇaśrī (p. 403) and Vajrasiddha (p. 422): "**A bell**, because he has the nature of Prajñāpāramitā" (*dril bu ni shes rab kyi pha rol tu phyin pa'i rang bzhin no*). Kṛṣṇācārya (p. 457): "investigative gnosis (*pratyavekṣaṇā*)" (*dril bu ni so sor rtog pa'i ye shes so*). I thank John Newman for the explanation of this gloss.

788. *Śoṇaśrī (p. 403) and *Vajrasiddha (p. 422): "**A hand**, because he performs all ritual actions" (*lag pa ni las thams cad byed pa'i phyir ro*). *Kṛṣṇācārya (p. 457): "wisdom of diligent actions" (*lag pa ni bya ba nan tan gyi ye shes so*).

789. *Śoṇaśrī (p. 403) and *Vajrasiddha (p. 422): "**A rag of the cremation ground** [means] he destroys the obscuring cover of ignorance with regard to the selfless nature of all dharmas" (*dur khrod kyi ras ni chos thams cad bdag med pa la ma rig pa'i sgrib g.yogs 'joms par byed pa'o*). *Kṛṣṇācārya (p. 457): "mirror-like wisdom" (*dur khrod ras ni me long lta bu'i ye shes so*).

impaled on a stake,[790] in the twelfth a hearth,[791] in the thirteenth a cup,[792] in the fourteenth a threatening finger,[793] in the fifteenth a flag with three strips of cloth,[794] and in the sixteenth a cloth blown by the wind.[795] In two [additional] hands, he holds an elephant skin.[796]

790. *Śoṇaśrī (p. 403) and *Vajrasiddha (p. 422): "**A man impaled on a stake**, in order to understand the phrase 'pierce the emptiness of all things'" (*gsal shing gis phug pa zhes bya ba ni dngos po thams cad stong pa nyid du phug pa yin no zhes rtogs par bya ba'i phyir ro*). *Kṛṣṇācārya (p. 457): "All dharmas are of the same essence" (*gsal shing gis phug pa'i ro ni chos thams cad ngo bo gcig pa'o*).

791. *Śoṇaśrī (p. 403) and *Vajrasiddha (p. 422): "**A hearth** [means] he illustrates the nature of clear light of all dharmas" (*me thab ces bya ba ni chos thams cad 'od gsal ba nyid mtshon par byed pa'o*). *Kṛṣṇācārya (p. 457): "because he burns demons after having protected the people with three *ālokas*" (*me thab ni snang ba gsum gyis 'gro ba la skyob cing bdud sreg par byed pa'o*). The three *ālokas* are (1) *āloka* (light), (2) *ālokābhāsa* (the appearance of light), and (3) *ālokopalabdhi* (the perception of light).

792. The Sanskrit recensions have *caṣaka*, meaning "cup," and this reading is also attested in *Śoṇaśrī's and *Vajrasiddha's commentaries, which give the Tibetan transliteration as *tsa sha ka*; however, the Tibetan text has *thod tshal* (Siklós 1996, 97), meaning "skull fragments," which Siklós (40) translates as "a skull-cup with hair." *Śoṇaśrī (p. 403) and *Vajrasiddha (p. 422) gloss **a cup** as "He is filled with the nectar of compassion" (*tsa sha ka ni snying rje bdud rtsis bkang ba'o*). *Kṛṣṇācārya (p. 457) has "skull fragments" (*thod tshal*): "because he possesses the compassion of suchness (*dharmatā*)" (*thod tshal ni chos nyid kyi snying rje mnga' bas so*).

793. *Śoṇaśrī (p. 403), *Vajrasiddha (p. 422), and *Kṛṣṇācārya (p. 457): "**A threatening finger**, because he scorns the demons" (*sdigs mdzub ni bdud rnams la tho 'tsham par byed pa'i phyir ro*).

794. *Śoṇaśrī (p. 403), *Vajrasiddha (p. 422), and *Kṛṣṇācārya (p. 457): "**A flag with three strips of cloth** [means] he causes to show the unity of the body, speech, and mind" (*'phan rtse gsum pa ni lus dang ngag dang yid rnams kyi ngo bo gcig tu rtogs par byed pa'o*).

795. The Tibetan text (Siklós 1996, 97) has *rlung gis 'phyar ba'i dur khrod kyi ras*, which Siklós (40–41) translates as "a cemetery cloth billowing in the wind." The commentaries only gloss *rlung gi ras*, which corresponds to the Skt. *vaṭakarpaṭaka*, where *karpaṭaka* means "a patch of cloth." *Śoṇaśrī (p. 403) and *Vajrasiddha (p. 422) gloss **a cloth blown by a wind** as "He illustrates the illusion of all the dharmas" (*rlung gi ras ni chos thams cad sgyu mar mtshon par byed pa'o*). *Kṛṣṇācārya (p. 457): "**A cloth blown by a wind** [means] freedom from eternalism and nihilism" (*rlung ras ni rtag chad las grol ba'o*).

796. *Śoṇaśrī (p. 403) and *Vajrasiddha (p. 422): "**An elephant skin**: the elephant represents delusion (*moha*)" (*glang po che'i pags pa zhes bya ba ni gti mug glang po che'o*). *Kṛṣṇācārya (p. 456): "**He holds an elephant skin in two [additional] hands** [means] having purified delusion (*moha*), which is inseparable from the *dharmadhātu*, he also connects others to the *dharmadhātu* by means of method and wisdom" (*gnyis glang po che'i pags pa bzung ba ni gti mug dag nas chos kyi dbyings dang mi 'bral ba dang/ thabs dang shes rab kyis gzhan yang chos kyi dbyings la sbyor ba'o*).

[§45] Under the first of his right feet,[797] [Vajrabhairava tramples] a man, under the second a buffalo, under the third a bull, under the fourth a donkey, under the fifth a camel, under the sixth a dog, under the seventh a sheep, and under the eighth a jackal. These are the vehicles of the right feet.[798] Under the first of his left feet[799] [he tramples] a vulture, under the second an owl, under the third a crow, under the fourth a parrot,[800] under the fifth an eagle,[801] under the sixth a rooster,[802] under the seventh a big bird,[803] under the eighth a crane.

[§46] The first [head of Vajrabhairava] is the buffalo face of the great Vajrabhairava, which is very dark and very wrathful. There are three faces to the [side of the] right horn: the first is blue, the right [one] is red, and the left is

797. The *Saṃpuṭodbhava* (7.4.58, ed., p. 346) gives a locative singular, *pāde*, while it should be the locative plural, *pādeṣu*, as attested in the Sanskrit manuscripts of the VBhT, since the intended meaning here is many feet each trampling upon a different thing. *Śoṇaśrī (pp. 403–4) and *Vajrasiddha (pp. 422–23): "**Under his right feet** [he tramples] 'the eight [things]—a man and so on' is a purification (*viśuddhi*) of the eight great siddhis" (*zhabs g.yas pa rnams su mi la sogs pa brgyad ni dngos grub chen po brgyad rnam par dag pa'o*). *Kṛṣṇācārya (p. 457): "The seats of his **right feet** [means] he accomplishes the eight siddhis" (*zhabs g.yas kyi gdan rnams ni dngos grub brgyad bsgrub pa'o*). It seems that Kṛṣṇācārya reads *āsanas* here, and not *vāhanas*.

798. The Tibetan text (Siklós 1996, 97) has *zhabs g.yas pas 'di dag la zhon pa'o*, which agrees with the Skt. *dakṣinapādavāhanāni etāni*, but Siklós (41) omits the translation of this sentence.

799. *Śoṇaśrī (p. 404) and *Vajrasiddha (p. 423): "**With his left feet** [he tramples] the eight [things]—a vulture and so on—is a *viśuddhi* of the eight great lordships (*aṣṭaiśvarya*) [e.g., he multiplies his body, speaks all the languages, knows the mind of all beings, sees all the worlds, etc.]" (*zhabs g.yon pa rnams su bya rgod la sogs pa brgyad ni dbang phyug chen po brgyad rnam par dag pa'o*). *Kṛṣṇācārya (p. 457): "He is the protector of beings of the *khecara* type [i.e., those who move in space]" (*g.yon pa'i bya rgod la sogs pas ni mkha' spyod kyi 'gro ba skyob pa'o*).

800. The *Saṃpuṭodbhava* (7.4.58, ed., p. 346) has "lion" *singha* (ms. K) or *siṃha* (ms. R), the latter shared with the Beijing ms. of the VBhT, both of which seem to be corruptions. The Sanskrit manuscripts A and B have *śuka*, "parrot," which is also supported by the Tibetan text (Siklós 1996, 97), which has *ne tsho*. These words do not receive any exegesis in the commentaries.

801. *Śyena* has been reconstructed based on the Tib. *khra* (Siklós 1996, 97).

802. The Sanskrit recensions have *mantra,* whereas the Tibetan text (Siklós 1996, 97) has *khyung chen po*, which Siklós (41) translated as "an eagle." For a justification of the translation of *mantrī* as "rooster," see note 514 above.

803. The Sanskrit recensions have *mahāśakuna*, which seems to indicate "any big bird of unspecified species," but the Tibetan text (Siklós 1996, 97) has *ri skegs*, which is an equivalent of the Skt. *śārikā*, "myna," and indeed Siklós (41) translates *ri skegs* as "myna."

yellow. These are wrathfully open-mouthed. There are three faces to [the side of] the left horn: white, gray, and black.[804] They should be imagined as exceptionally wrathful and hideous. In the middle of the two horns,[805] one should imagine a very red[806] and a very terrifying face, blood [dripping] from [its] throat.[807] Above it, one should visualize the face of Mañjuśrī,[808] slightly yellow and slightly wrathful,[809] wearing the ornaments of a youth[810] and the crown of the head made of five locks of hair.[811] One should imagine that all his faces

804. *Kṛṣṇācārya (p. 457) comments on the colors of the faces, saying that "it is in order to show the nature of the six classes of beings" (*zhal gyi mdog ni rigs drug gi ngo bo'o*).

805. *Śoṇaśrī (p. 404), *Vajrasiddha (p. 423), and *Kṛṣṇācārya (p. 457): "**Two horns** [means] *viśuddhi* of two truths" [i.e., conventional truth (*saṃvṛtisatya*) and ultimate truth (*paramārthasatya*)] (*bden pa gnyis rnam par dag pas rwa gnyis so*).

806. *Kṛṣṇācārya (p. 457): "**Red** [**face** means] intense attachment for sentient beings" (*dmar ba ni 'gro ba la shin tu chags pa'o*).

807. *Śoṇaśrī (p. 404) and *Vajrasiddha (p. 423): "Upper **red face, blood dripping from its throat**, because he impassions all sentient beings with the Buddhadharma" (*sangs rgyas kyi chos kyis sems can rnams 'tshed par byed pas steng gi zhal dmar po khrag 'dzag pa'o*).

808. *Śoṇaśrī (p. 404) and *Vajrasiddha (p. 423): "The ninth face, which symbolizes that he is an emanation of Mañjuśrī, is yellow" (*'jam dpal gyi sprul pa mtshon pa'i zhal dgu pa ser po'o*). *Kṛṣṇācārya (p. 457): "**The Mañjuśrī face** [shows his] immutable nature" (*'jam dpal gyi zhal ni ngo bo mi 'gyur ba'o*).

809. *Kṛṣṇācārya (p. 457): "**Wrathful** [means] he is the protector" (*khros pa ni skyob pa'o*). The *Saṃpuṭodbhāva* (7.4.55, ed., p. 346) ends with *kumāra* ("a boy"), which is missing in the Tibetan text (Siklós 1996, 98) and the Beijing manuscript, but it features in *Kṛṣṇācārya's commentary (p. 457), which glosses a "boy as he resides in the body of a bodhisattva" (*gzhon pa ni byang chub sems dpa'i skur bzhugs pa'o*).

810. *Śoṇaśrī (p. 404) and *Vajrasiddha (p. 423): "**Wearing the ornaments of a youth**, because of his youthful nature" (*gzhon nu'i rgyan gyis brgyan pa ni gzhon nu'i ngo bo'i phyir ro*).

811. *Śoṇaśrī (p. 404) and *Vajrasiddha (p. 423) seem to have a different reading in front of them—i.e., the one that reads *pañcamudrā* (*phyag rgya lnga*) before the description of the hair—for they gloss *phyag rgya lnga* as "having the nature of the five tathāgatas" (*phyag rgya lnga zhes bya ba ni de bzhin gshegs pa lnga'i rang bzhin no*). *Pañcamudrā* (also known as *pañcamātrā*) is a term for the attire of the Kāpālika ascetic, which consists of five bone ornaments; see Sanderson 1985. This is followed by a gloss on the hairstyle of the face of Mañjuśrī, which reads: "Endowed with five braided skulls" (*Śoṇaśrī) and "Endowed with five locks on the crown" (*Vajrasiddha), "it is a purification (*viśuddhi*) of the five forms of perfect awakening" (*zur phud lnga'i thod can ni rnam pa lnga rnam par dag pas so*, *Śoṇaśrī, p. 404) and (*spyi bor ral pa lnga dang ldan pa ni/ mngon par byang chub pa lnga'i dag pa'o*, *Vajrasiddha, p. 423). The gloss refers to the old yoga-tantra concept of the perfect awakening with five aspects (*pañcākārābhisaṃbodhi*). *Akṣobhya (p. 382) and *Kṛṣṇācārya (p. 457): "The tuft **made of five locks of hair** is taught as endowed

have three eyes.[812] Thus one should visualize oneself as the buffalo-headed venerable Vajrabhairava.

[§47] The mantra master who is perfectly concentrated continously abides in the heroic state; then the yogin recites the mantra. During the course of the recitation, he should imagine the sun disc[813] in his own heart, and he should install the letters of his own mantra[814] [on it]. After it starts blazing,[815] he

with five wisdoms" (*zur phud* [em. *rol pa*, ed.] *lnga pa zhes bya ba ni ye shes lnga dang bcas par ston pa'o*).

812. *Śoṇaśrī (p. 404) and *Vajrasiddha (p. 423) gloss the **three eyes** as "He sees the three times" (*dus gsum du gzigs par byed pa'i phyir spyan gsum mo*). *Akṣobhya (p. 382): "**All his faces have** also **three eyes** [means] it is because whatever way he displays himself for sentient beings arises from the three gateways to liberation" (*zhal thams cad kyang spyan gsum dang ldan pa'o zhes bya ba ni sems can gyi phyir snang ba ston pa'i sgo ji snyed pa la* [em. *las*, ed.] *yang rnam par thar pa gsum gsum las byung ba'i phyir ro*). *Kṛṣṇācārya (p. 457): "He perceives through three types of compassion" (*spyan gsum ni snying rje gsum gyis gzigs pa'o*).

813. *Akṣobhya (p. 382): "**Sun disc** [means] emerging from the red letter *āḥ*" (*nyi ma'i dkyil 'khor zhes bya ba ni yi ge āḥ* [em. *ā*, ed.] *dmar po las byung ba'o*).

814. *Akṣobhya (p. 382): "**He should focus on his own mantra** refers to the syllable of the dark blue *yaṃ* or the dark blue *hūṃ* in the center; he should meditate upon the three strings of mantras around the edges surrounding them in a clockwise fashion" (*de la rang gi gsang sngags dmigs la zhes bya ba ni dbus su yaṃ sngon po'am hūṃ sngon po'i yi ge ste/ mtha' mar sngags gsum gyi phreng ba g.yas skor du bsgom mo*). Lalitavajra (pp. 324–25): "**He should recite his own heart mantra** [means] if someone asks, 'How to recite?' [the answer given is] at the time of recitation, **in one's own heart**; [this means] in the sun of the heart of knowledge being (*jñānasattva*). **His own mantra** [means] the root mantra, or he meditates on the subordinate heart mantra (*upahṛdaya*) and deposits [the letters of the mantra]" (*rang gi snying po'i sngags bzlas so bya ba la/ ji ltar bzla zhe na/ bzlas pa'i dus su rang gi snying la ste ye shes sems dpa'i thugs ka'i* [corr.; *kha* ed.] *nyi ma la rang sngags zhes bya ba/ rtsa ba'i sngags sam nye ba'i snying po bsams te dgod pa'o*).

815. Lalitavajra (pp. 324–25): **After it starts blazing** [means] "he recites endowed with light or mental stillness, which means he should recite undisturbed. At that time, the mantrin, in union with Vajrabhairava, should not be afraid and should be free of thought constructs (*vikalpas*)" (*'bar ba ste 'od dang bcas par bzlas pa 'am/ sems gnas te ma yengs pas bzlas pa'o/ de'i tshe sngags pa 'jigs byed kyi rnal 'byor pas 'jigs med de rtog pa dang bral bas*).

should do the recitation [of the mantra][816] with one-pointed mind.[817] The

816. *Śoṇaśrī comments (p. 404): "This is how [the yogin] should perceive himself through the deity yoga and so on. As long as he does not get weary of it, the yogin should recite the mantra. Whichever mantra syllables (*mantrākṣaras*) he recites, those have to be visualized in his own heart on top of the sun disc, going around in the circle, clockwise. Then, with the rays of light, he has to visualize that he performs the welfare of all sentient beings with *spharaṇa* yoga as he breathes out through his nostril. Then [he performs] the reabsorbtion by drawing [the mantra] in through his nostrils while inhaling, and causes them to remain [on the sun disc]. It is said that he should continuously repeat [the mantra] with this ritual alone, as long as he is without fatigue. Then, when he is weary, he makes sacrificial offerings according to the prescription, exactly as it is in the ritual. Then he should respectfully dismiss the knowledge being (*jñānasattva*) and abide in the yoga with the deity" (*lha'i rnal 'byor la sogs pas de ltar bdag nyid rnam par bltas la/ ji srid yid ni mi skyo bar/ de srid rnal 'byor pas sngags bzla/ sngags kyi yi ge gang dag bzlas pa de dag rang gi snying gar nyi ma'i dkyil 'khor gyi steng du g.yas phyogs su bskor bas zlum po byas pa 'od zer dang bcas pa rnams blta zhing/ dbugs byung ba sna'i* [em. *sgo'i*, ed.] *bu ga nas byung ba spro ba'i sbyor bas 'gro ba'i don byas nas/ yang bsdus la dbugs rngub pa'i sna'i bu ga nas bcug la gnas pa'o zhes yang dang yang du ji srid mi skyo ba'i mthar thug par cho ga 'di nyid kyis bzlas par bya'o/ de nas skyo na cho ga ji lta ba bzhin du gtor ma byin la ye shes sems dpa' gshegs su gsol la lha'i rnal 'byor gyis gnas par bya'o*).

817. *Akṣobhya (p. 382): "**With undistracted mind** [means], ultimately, he should not contemplate even emptiness. As it has been said, 'The reciter, when doing the mantra recitation, even if an exquisite sign (*nimitta*) appears, should not resort to thought constructs (*vikalpa*), except in the case of *vidyā* deities'" (*g.yeng ba med pa'i yid kyis zhes bya ba ni tha na stong pa nyid kyang mi bsam ste/ rig sngags lha ni ma gtogs par/ mtshan* [em. *bsgom pa*, ed.] *mchog tu gyur pa yang/ zlos pas bzlas brjod byed pa'i tshe/ kun rtog bzung nas mi bsam mo/ zhes gsungs so*). This passage also appears at the end of the *Rahasyānandatilaka* (p. 724) attributed to Mahāmati, the guru of Bodhibhadra of Somapuravihāra as the quotation from the *Sarvakalpasamuccaya*'s chapter on the mantra recitation, the earliest explanatory tantra of the *Sarvabuddhasamāyoga*. In Ānandagarbha's commentary, the *Sarvakalpasamuccaya*, we find the following passage: "Do not be angry at the time of reciting [the mantra] and do not find pleasure in the objects (*viṣayas*). Give up whatever depression, fear, and self-loathing you have. Do not think of anything at the time of reciting. Do not make it into a category (*aṅga*). After you have been shaken by the wind of thought constructs (*vikalpa*), do not think of anything." Though this passage is cited as a quote from the *Sarvakalpasamuccaya*, it is not found in the Bstan 'gyur text of that title, perhaps because there were many texts bearing the same title.

The passage quoted by *Akṣobhya is also found in the *Susiddhikara Sūtra*, the only surviving text of the Susiddhi cycle, preserved in two Chinese translations and in a Tibetan translation with various recensions. The corresponding passage in Chinese (Giebel 2001, 214) is different: "He does not forsake his own deity; and even if he sees a strange sign, he should not be surprised by it. At times of recitation he also does not discriminate between various signs." The key difference is the appearance of the word *mtshan*, "sign," instead of *bsgom pa*, the latter being seemingly a corruption. The same goes with the word "except for," *ma gtogs par*, which, in the light of the Chinese translation, should be *ma rtog pa*, "he

yogin who abides in this yoga should perform all the rituals. The fearless one, having sat himself up in the cremation ground and so on, should consume the five nectars continuously while meditating. [In this way] he accomplishes that means of mastering and not otherwise. Alternatively, the yogin devouring human flesh and so on and wandering at night recites the mantra consisting of three hundred thousand [syllables]. The mantra master who has done the recitation of the mantra performs all the rituals [successfully].

This is the fourth chapter, Visualization (*dhyāna*), in the [yoga] tantra of the venerable Great Vajrabhairava, which is a part of [the tantra] called the *Śrīmañjuśriya* [*Tantra*].

---

should not discriminate." If these emendations are introduced, we can reconstruct the hypothetical original available to *Akṣobhya, which reads: "The reciter, when doing the mantra recitation, should not forsake his *vidyā* deity if he sees an exquisite sign, and he should not entertain it [i.e., the sign] with a thought construct (*vikalpa*)."

*Kṛṣṇācārya (p. 457) comments on the passage describing the recitation in which one beholds the deity **with unwavering mind** as follows: "'Having understood that in that way—i.e., with an undistracted mind—he visualizes the deity and recites the mantra' [means] whatever you like [this seems to be a corruption, for the phrase should read 'when he is tired of viṣualization'], he arranges the seed syllables [of the mantra], in a clockwise fashion, on the lotus in his heart and in the sun [disc]. Then the mantra syllables are emitted through the exhaled breath of the nostrils to the outside, and this excites the hearts of all the buddhas, who then clear away the obscurations of all sentient beings. Then the mantra syllables come back inside via the inhaled breath, and they dissolve into the mantra. He recites the mantra unperturbed and obtains whatever he wishes" (*de ltar shes par byas nas ma yengs pa'i sems kyis lha la dmigs la sngags bzlas pa ni/ gang yang rung bar* [em. *rung ba*, ed.] *snying gar pad ma dang nyi ma la sa bon gyi yi ge la g.yas skor du bkod pa la/ sna bug gi rlung 'byung ba las spros pas sangs rgyas thams cad kyi thugs kar* [em. *dam*, ed.] *bskul/ sems can thams cad kyi sgrib pa sbyangs la 'jug pa'i rlung gis tshur bsdus la sngags la bstim mo/ mi skyo'i bar du bzlas shing rang gang 'dod bsgrub pa'o*).

5. The Ritual of Painting the *Paṭa*

[§48] Next, I will describe the ritual of drawing the painting (*paṭavidhāna*) revealed by the venerable Vajrabhairava. An excellent sādhaka should draw [the painting] on a hero's cloth,[818] on a cloth covering the corpse,[819] on a cloth with menstrual discharge,[820] or on a cloth on which a child was born;[821] absent any of those [he may draw] on any cloth.[822]

818. Lalitavajra (p. 326) glosses **a hero's [cloth]** as "a loincloth of a hero who has died in a battle" (*dpa' bo zhes bya ba la/ dpa' bo'i shun pa ste g.yul du shi ba'o*). Kumāracandra: "A hero's cloth is that garment [worn by] the one who has fallen in battle confronting [his foe]" (*yat paridhāya yuddhe 'abhimukhaṃ patitaḥ tad vīrakarpaṭaṃ*).

819. Lalitavajra (pp. 326–27) has *'dril ba*, **a cover**, which he glosses as "a cloth of a corpse" (*'dril ba ni ro'i gos so*).

820. The Sanskrit version has "woman's flower" (*strīpuṣpa*), a common way of referring to menstrual blood. Lalitavajra (p. 327) glosses *flower cloth* as "the cloth of a maiden" (*me tog ras ni bu mo'i gos so*), perhaps indicating the cloth of a girl who had her first menses.

821. Lalitavajra (p. 327) glosses "[**a cloth on which**] **a child was born** as 'a woman's cloth'" (*bu btsas pa ni bud med kyi gos so*). Kumāracandra: "**A cloth on which a child was born** is that garment [worn by] a woman who has recently delivered a child" (*yat paridhāya prasūtā strī tat prasūtakarpaṭaṃ*).

822. The *Saṃpuṭodbhava* (9.3.6, ed., p. 371) also lists a cloth tinted with human blood (*mahārudhirarañjitakarpaṭa*) as one of suitable canvases, but this type of cloth is missing in the Beijing ms. and in the Tibetan text (see Siklós 1996, 100).

[§49] A painter is like[823] this:[824] free from thought constructs,[825] a good painter,[826] free from anger,[827] skillful,[828] pure,[829] clever,[830] endowed with

823. The parallel passage of the *Saṃpuṭodbhava* (9.3.5, ed., p. 371) enumerates eleven adjectives describing the qualities of a good painter, while Beijing ms. and Tibetan version give nine: (1) Tib. *bzang po*, "good," without a Sanskrit equivalent. (2) Tib. *rnam rtog pa med pa* = Skt. *nirvikalpaḥ*, (3) Tib. *mi khro ba* = Skt. *akrodhanaḥ*, (4) Tib. *gtsang ba* = Skt. *śuci*, (5) Tib. *mkhas pa* = Skt. *dakṣaḥ*, (6) Tib. *yid gzhungs pa* = Skt. *aśaṭho* (absent in Beijing ms.), (7) Tib. *brtse ba can* = Skt. *dayāluḥ*, (8) Tib. *sred pa dang bral ba* = Skt. *vitṛṣṇaḥ*, (9) Tib. *dad pa dang ldan pa* = Skt. *śrāddho*. The additional adjectives corresponding to the English *young* (*yuvā*) and *steady* (*dhīro*) listed in the *Saṃpuṭodbhava* (9.3.5) are missing in the Beijing ms. and the Tibetan version.

The Tibetan text also has "good" (*bzang po*) as the first adjective, while the Beijing ms. has "good painter" instead as the second adjective.

824. Lalitavajra (p. 327) glosses **like this** as "a painter who has the above qualities and who has been initiated; [or else it can be painted] by a sādhaka—that is, a hero who makes an effort to attain siddhis" (*'di lta bu zhes pa gong gi mtshan nyid dang/ dbang dang ldan pa'i ri mo mkhan la/ dngos grub lhur len pa'i dpa' bo ste sgrub pa pos so*). This passage should be understood as referring to two types of people qualified to draw the painting.

825. *Kṛṣṇācārya (p. 458) glosses **free from thought constructs** as "He understands the emptiness of all dharmas" (*rtog pa med pa zhes pa ni chos thams cad stong par rtogs pa'o*), and *Śoṇaśrī (p. 405): "He understands suchness" (*rnam par rtog pa med pa zhes bya ba ni de kho na nyid shes pa'o*). Kumāracandra: "**Free from thought constructs** [means] free from thought constructs about what is to be eaten and what is not to be eaten" (*rtog pa zhes bya ba ni bza' bar bya ba dang/ bza' bar bya ba ma yin pa'i rnam par rtog pa dang bral ba'o*).

826. Kumāracandra: "**Good painter** [means] initiated" (*sucitrakaro abhiṣikto*). *Kṛṣṇācārya (p. 458), *Śoṇaśrī (p. 405), and *Vajrasiddha (p. 424) gloss **good painter** as "a someone who has been initiated" (*ri mo mkhan bzang zhes pa ni dbang thob pa'o*). Lalitavajra (p. 327), however, seems to have a different reading in front of him that mentions Buddhist affiliation as the first quality of a suitable painter: "In order to teach the qualities of a painter, [the passage] beginning with 'Buddhist' and ending with 'painter' is taught. Since it is easy to understand, there is no need to specify [the meaning]" (*ri mo mkhan gyi mtshan nyid bstan pa'i phyir/ sangs rgyas pa zhes pa nas 'bri* [corr. *'dri*, ed.] *mkhan gyi bar du gsungs te go sla bas ma phye'o*).

827. Kumāracandra (p. 293): "**Free from anger** [means] having a kind mind" (*maitryacittaḥ*).

828. *Śoṇaśrī (p. 405) glosses **skillful** as "skilled in the [art of] painting" (*byang ba zhes bya ba ni ri mo'i las la'o*).

829. *Kṛṣṇācārya (p. 458) glosses **pure** as "endowed with vows" (*gtsang zhes pa ni dam tshig dang ldan pa'o*). *Śoṇaśrī (p. 405) has *gsang ba*, "secret," which is probably a corruption of *gtsang ba*, "pure," which he glosses as "infallible in meditative stabilization" (*gsang ba zhes bya ba ni ting nge 'dzin ma 'khrul pa'o*). Kumāracandra: **pure** [means] "one who does not have the impurity of sin" (*śucir anāpattikalmaṣaḥ*).

830. Kumāracandra: "**Clever** [means] enthusiastic" (*dakṣo udyuktaḥ*).

faith,[831] compassionate,[832] and free from sense desires.[833] If he wishes the siddhi, he should offer a[834] hero's fee[835] with his hand.[836] This is the ritual procedure for this: having established himself in a secret place,[837] in meditative

831. Kumāracandra: "**Endowed with faith** [means] one who has faith in the Three Jewels, etc." (*śrāddhas triratnādyabhisampratyayitaḥ*).

832. *Kṛṣṇācārya (p. 458) glosses **compassionate** as "a sādhaka who has no [other] reason [for doing this practice] than benefiting others" (*brtse ba dang ldan zhes pa ni rgyu med sgrub pa po de la phan gdags snyam pa'o*). Kumāracandra: "desiring the siddhi of a sādhaka" (*dayāluḥ sādhakasiddhikāṃkṣī*).

833. Kumāracandra: "**Free from sense desires** [means] desiring less" (*viṭṛṣṇo 'lpecchuḥ*).

834. *Śoṇaśrī (p. 405) glosses **hero's fee** as referring to the attitude of the sādhaka, who has "a mind pleased from enjoying wine and meat" (*dpa' bo'i rim pa zhes bya ba ni chang dang sha la nye bar rol cing dga' ba'i sems so*). *Vajrasiddha (p. 424) gives also another explanation: "In some scriptures the word for this is 'hero's fee,' and it [means] that he gives to the painter [the fee] he desires" (*glegs bam la lar ni/ dpa' bo'i tshong zhes pa'i tshig/ de la ri mo mkhan 'dod pa de byin la*). The explanation given by *Vajrasiddha corresponds to the regular meaning of the "hero's fee" (see p. 133 above). *Akṣobhya (p. 382) has a "special fee" (*lhag pa'i yon*) instead, which he glosses as "a price that is superior to the normal price of a painter" (*lhag pa'i yon ni zhes bya ba ni 'dri mkhan gyi tshad las rgal ba'o*). Kumāracandra has "**hero's fee**" which he glosses as "as much as the painter says" (*vīrakrayaṃ yathoktaś citrakareṇa*).

835. Siklós (1996, 42) translates this sentence as "If accomplishments are desired, offerings to the heroes should be made" (*gal te dngos grub 'dod pas dpa' bo'i yon sbyin no*). This is incorrect, as *dpa' bo'i yon* is a technical term corresponding to the Sanskrit *vīrakraya* or *vīramūlya*, "a hero's fee."

836. The Tibetan text (Siklós 1996, 100) has a corresponding line that says, "He should draw on the hero's cloth with the hand of the painter like this" (*de lta bu'i ri mo mkhan gyi lag pas dpa' bo'i ras la bri bar bya'o*); however, Siklós's translation (42) does not seem to follow the text printed in the edition: "Or, if these are not available, on any suitable cloth."

837. Lalitavajra (p. 327) glosses **secret place** as "The text says, 'He should draw [the painting] being seated in an isolated place such as cremation ground and so on.' If you ask 'Why?' [the answer] is, in order to not show it to people who are without fortune and without initiation" (*gsang ba'i gnas ni dur khrod la sogs pa dben pa'i gnas su 'dug nas bri zhes pa'i don to/ ci'i phyir zhe na/ sems can gzhan te skal pa med cing dbang bskur ba med cing la mi bstan pa'i phyir zhes pa'i don to*).

equipoise, he[838] should draw[839] [the painting].[840] One should not show [the painting] to other people, but the practitioner and the painter can see it.[841]

[§50] He should draw [Vajrabhairava as having] sixteen legs, thirty-four arms, nine heads. He is naked, black in color, standing in a *pratyālīḍha* pose [with a left leg extended]. He is frightening, and he also takes the form of the one who causes fear [i.e., Bhairava], and he has an upraised phallus (*liṅga*). He should be painted with a buffalo as his main head and with the three very wrathful heads on the right side: blue, red, and yellow. On the left side [of the main buffalo head], he has [three more heads]: white, gray, and black. Between them, he should draw [a head] in deep red [color]. Above that, he should paint a

838. The *Saṃpuṭodbhava* (9.3.6, ed., p. 371) has an additional sentence: "Otherwise, an initiate should have a painter draw it" (*athavā samayī* [mss. K, R; *samayi*, ed., p. 371] *citrakareṇāpi lekhayet*). This information is not given in the Beijing ms. and in the Tibetan version of the VBhT.

839. The *Saṃpuṭodbhava* (9.3.7, ed., p. 371) has a passage on the brushes, which is missing in the Sanskrit and Tibetan version of the VBhT: "He should draw the painting with a [stylus] made of a human bone, with five pigments as described above, scented with camphor of olibanum tree and so on. He should draw [the painting] with a brush of a human hair" (*likhāpayet narakasthair yathoktaiḥ pañcavarṇakaiḥ sihlakarpūrādibhāvitaiḥ. śavakeśasya* [corr., *śrāyakeśasya* R, K, P, ed.] *kuñcyā lekhanīyaṃ*). The passage in the *Saṃpuṭodbhava* has been identified as *Hevajra Tantra* 2.6.7 (in Tripathi and Negi 2006, 178).

840. *Kṛṣṇācārya (p. 458) has an additional gloss that is missing in the root text: "'He should draw in accordance with the procedure of the hero (*vīra*)' [means] he should worship in an isolated place and offer *bali* three times a day. While in yoga with Śrī Vajrabhairava, he should consecrate the [body] maṇḍala [of Vajrabhairava] on the cloth. At the heart [of the Vajrabhairava image] he should draw the heart mantras; in the mouth, he should draw a mantra; in the navel, he should deposit the root mantra; and in the sense organs such as the eyes, he should place *oṃ sarvatathāgatavajracakṣusvabhāvātmako 'ham*; and in the three places [forehead, throat, and heart], he should also deposit the heart mantra of the three bodies [*oṃ āḥ hūṃ*]. At the crown of the head, he should place the heart mantra for *abhiṣeka*" (*dpa' bo'i cho gas bri zhes pa ni gnas dben par mchod pa dang gtor ma dus gsum du dbul zhing/ dpal rdo rje 'jigs byed kyi rnal 'byor pas ras la dkyil 'khor du byin gyis brlab pa dang/ sngags rnams snying po thugs kar bri ba dang/ sngags zhal du bri ba dang/ rtsa sngags lte bar dgod pa dang/ mig la sogs pa'i skye mched la oṃ sar wa ta thā ga ta badz ra tsa kshu swa bhā wa ātma ko 'haṃ zhes bya ba la sogs pa dgod pa dang/ sku gsum gyi snying po'ang gnas gsum du dgod do/ dbang bskur ba'i snying po spyi bor dgod par bya'o*).

841. The Tibetan text (Siklós 1996, 100) reflects the Sanskrit almost perfectly, with the exception of the last verb, which is "draw" in Tibetan, but "see" in Sanskrit: *ri mo mkhan dang sgrub pa pos mthong ba las 'jig rten pa gzhan gyis mi mthong bar bri bar bya ste.* Siklós (1996, 42) translates the sentence, slightly inaccurately, as "the painter or the practitioner should paint the painting so that the layman does not see it."

Mañjuśrī's face, yellow [in color] and slightly wrathful. In his right hand, [Vajrabhairava holds] a chopper, a javelin, a pestle, a knife, a single-pointed vajra, an axe, a spear, an arrow, an elephant goad, a club, a skull staff, a wheel, a vajra, a vajra hammer, a sword, and a rattle drum. With his left hand, [he holds] a skull, a head, a shield, a leg, a noose, a bow, entrails, a bell, a hand, a rag of the cremation ground, a man impaled on a stake, a hearth, a cup, a threatening finger, a flag with three strips of cloth, and a cloth blown by the wind.[842] With two of his hands, he holds an elephant skin. Under his right feet, he [tramples] a man, a buffalo, a bull, a donkey, a camel, a dog, a deer[843], and a jackal.[844] Under his left feet [he tramples] a vulture, an owl, a crow, a parrot, an eagle, a rooster, a big bird, and a crane.[845] He should paint Great Vajrabhairava[846] like this.[847]

[§51] Beneath him,[848] he should paint the great cremation ground,[849] very

842. For the discrepancy between the Sanskrit and the Tibetan lists of weapons, see note 509 above.

843. Tibetan text (Siklós 1996, 101) has *lug*, "sheep," which corresponds to the Sanskrit *meṣa* instead of *mṛga*, "deer," attested in the mss.

844. The Sanskrit mss. have *śṛgāla*, which means either "fox" or "jackal." The Tibetan translation favored the first meaning, translating it as *wa*, "fox."

845. For the discrepancy between the list of birds trampled upon by Vajrabhairava in the Sanskrit and Tibetan recensions, see note 514.

846. Lalitavajra (p. 327) comments: "The image of **the Great Vajrabhairava** [means] he teaches the way to draw and so on. In one box, mix the pigments and the five nectars (*amṛtas*), using human hair from the crown of the head [to mix them]. Being cognizant of the faults of using wrong pigments, [paint] Vajrabhairava as he is taught, in the proper dimensions" (*'jigs byed chen po'i gzugs zhes bya ba la sogs pa'i bri ba bstan te/ ga'u gcig par tshon bdud rtsi lnga dang sbyar te/ mi'i skra'i spyi por* [corr. *spir*, ed.] *gyis tshon gyis* [corr. *gyi*, ed.] *skyon shes par byas la tshad dang ldan par ji skad gsungs pa'i rdo rje 'jigs byed*). I thank John Newman for clarifying this gloss.

847. The Tibetan text (Siklós 1996, 101) reflects the Sanskrit perfectly when it says "He should paint such a Great Vajrabhairava" (*'di lta bur 'dug pa'i rdo rje 'jigs byed chen po bri bar bya'o*), but Siklós's translation (42) reads "Vajramahābhairava should be drawn standing like this."

848. The Tibetan text (Siklós 1996, 101) reflects the Sanskrit perfectly, for it also has "beneath" (*'og tu*); however, Siklós (42) translates it as "around" while explaining in his note 121 that *'og tu* means "after that."

849. *Kṛṣṇācārya (p. 458) glosses "cremation ground outside of him [Vajrabhairava]" (instead of the **great cremation ground beneath him** given in the root text) as "He should draw the eight cremation grounds populated with eight guardians of the directions (*dikpālas*), eight gods, eight *nāgas*, trees, and a stūpa, a sādhaka, and spirits of dead

scary. He should paint it equipped with[850] *yakṣas*, demons,[851] site guardians, and zombies.[852] He should illustrate there such frightening things as a man impaled on a stake. He should also portray a man being burned. He should depict a man hung high up on a banyan (*vaṭa*) tree.[853] He should also draw a man run through with a spear.[854] He should draw different birds: vulture,

people (*pretas*), birds and carnivorous animals, and serpents. He should draw them surrounded by many corpses that are greatly terrifying" (*de'i phyi rol dur khrod ces pa ni dur khrod brgyad bri bar ste/ phyogs skyong brgyad lha brgyad dang/ klu brgyad dang/ shing dang/ mchod rten dang/ sgrub pa po dang/ yi dwags dang/ bya dang/ gcan gzan dang/ sbrul dang/ ro sna tshogs shin tu 'jigs pas bskor ba bri'o*).

850. In *Akṣobhya's commentary (p. 382), the Skt. *samanvitam* is translated as "He should draw a wheel" (*'khor lo bri bar bya'o zhes bya ni*), which *Akṣobhya (p. 382) glosses, "As for this [cremation ground], it should be surrounded by the host of nonhumans. Or if the basis is not drawn in the style of the maṇḍala, install the vajra ground, and so on" (*'khor lo bri bar bya'o zhes bya ba ni 'di ni mi ma yin pa'i tshogs kyis bskor ba'am/ dkyil 'khor gyi tshul las/ 'gram gzhi* [conj. *phyag rgya* Szántó, ed.] *mi bri bar rdo rje ra ba la sogs* [em. *sgo*, ed.] *bkod* [em. *gdod*, ed.] *pa'o*). The passage refers to the old and new ways of drawing the cremation grounds—i.e., either populating them with nonhumans (the old way) or installing the vajra ground (*vajrabhūmi*), vajra fence (*vajraprākāra*) and vajra tent (*vajrapañjara*), which is a later invention popular in yoga-tantra commentaries.

851. *Akṣobhya (p. 383) glosses **demons and so on** as "It is said, 'He should draw them within the cremation ground area itself'" (*srin po zhes bya ba la sogs pa ni/ dur khrod kyi de kho na zhes par 'gyur ro*).

852. The parallel passage describing the cremation grounds beneath Vajrabhairava is also found in the *Saṃpuṭodbhava* (7.4.59, ed., p. 346): *tasyādho mahāśmaśānaṃ rākṣasakṣetrapālavetālānvitaṃ*. This list omits *yakṣa*, which features in the Sanskrit manuscripts of the VBhT available to me. The list without *yakṣa* conforms to the reading given in the Tibetan recension (Siklós 1996, 101), which similarly omits *yakṣa*.

853. The Tibetan text (Siklós 1996, 101) has *n.ya gro dha'i shing*, which Siklós (43) translates as "a fig tree."

854. The parallel passage describing the four types of criminals illustrated in the cremation ground beneath Vajrabhairava is also found in the *Saṃpuṭodbhava* (7.4.59, ed., p. 346): *śūlabhinnapuruṣaṃ* [*vaṭa*]*vṛkṣasyodbaddhapuruṣaṃ dahyamānapuruṣaṃ kuntabhinnaṃ ca*. For the explanation of their function in other Buddhist and Śākta tantras, see pages 136–37.

crow, dog, jackal, and a flock of cranes.[855] He should also draw the sādhaka[856] gazing up at the lord[857] naked,[858] his hair untied, and adorned with the five insignia and so on.[859] He should paint [the sādhaka] entering that cremation ground[860] carrying a rattle drum, a skull, and a skull staff, the top of his head adorned with a skull, laughing.

855. The Tibetan text (Siklós 1996, 101) has a slightly different reading: *bya sna tshogs dang bya rgod dang bya rog dang khyi dang lce spyang dang ha ha 'byin pa bri*, which Siklós (43) translates as, "One should also draw various birds, vultures, crows, dogs, and jackals uttering 'ha ha.'" When compared to the Sanskrit recension, we can see that the "flock of cranes" is missing in the Tibetan text. Also, in the Sanskrit, jackals are not portrayed laughing. The parallel passage is also preserved in the *Saṃpuṭodbhava* (7.4.59, ed., p. 346), which reads: *anekakākapakṣiśvānayutaṃ hāhākārasamākulam*, "[He should draw the cremation grounds] filled with various birds like crows, dogs, full of 'ha ha' sound." The reading *sārasakulam*, "flock of cranes," seems to be better than *samākulam*. The parallel passage in the *Saṃpuṭodbhava* (7.4.59, ed., p. 346) ends *evaṃ vibhāvayed yogī sarvakrūrakarmaprasiddhikaraṃ nāma mahābhairavam / ity āha bhagavān*, "In this way indeed, the yogin should visualize Mahābhairava, who causes the success of all wrathful rites. The Bhagavān said thus."

856. *Akṣobhya (p. 383) says that the painter draws the sādhaka himself into the painting: "As for the sādhaka, from what has been taught, one should draw the exact likeness of the shape of the body and so on" (*sgrub pa po zhes bya ba ni ji ltar bstan pa las sha tshugs la sogs pa rab tu 'dra bar bri'o*).

857. The Tibetan text (Siklós 1996, 101) reads slightly differently: *bcom ldan 'das la rtse gcig tu lta ba*, which Siklós (43) translates as "single-pointedly looking at the lord." The Sanskrit version omits "single-pointedly."

858. *Kṛṣṇācārya (p. 458) glosses **naked** as "He should draw himself as a sādhaka" (*gcer bu zhes pa ni sgrub pa po rang nyid bri ba'o*). This adjective (*gcer bu*) qualifying the sādhaka(s) also features in the Tibetan text (Siklós 1996, 101), but Siklós (43) fails to translate it.

859. The Tibetan text (Siklós 1996, 101–2) has *phyag rgya lngas brgyan pa*, which Siklós (43) translates as "adorned with five symbols," explaining in his note 123 that *mudrā* "refers to the five bone ornaments of the *yogin*," by which he means the Kāpālika ascetic. While this interpretation fits well with the typical Kāpālika territory we encounter in this passage, one could also suggest that the Sanskrit manuscripts of the VBhT available to me read *pañcaṃcūḍādyalaṃkṛtaṃ* and not *pañcamudrādyalaṃkṛtaṃ*. The words *mudrā* and *cūḍā* look almost identical in Newārī script. In that case, the sādhakas could be styled upon the image of the young Mañjuśrī adorned with five tufts of hair.

860. Lalitavajra (p. 327) says: "**Entering** in the middle of the eight **cremation grounds** refers to the sādhaka and so on in the eight cremation grounds; this is the meaning of 'He should paint a place'" (*dur khrod brgyad kyi dbus su chud pa / dur khrod brgyad na sgrub pa po la sogs pa gnas pa bri zhes pa'i don to*).

[§52] Having put the painting[861] down in an isolated place,[862] he should fumigate [the painting] with human flesh.[863] In front of it,[864] he should repeat the mantra at the three times [of the day] using a rosary made of human bone. The mantra master should protect the painting with full concentration,[865] with effort.[866] He should not set it up near anybody. Nor should he unroll it in front

861. The Tibetan text (Siklós 1996, 101) reads: *'di ni gsang ba'i bris sku te*. This sentence is missing in the Sanskrit version.

862. *Kṛṣṇācārya (p. 458) glosses **in an isolated place** as "In a single place [means] it is inappropriate to change locations while drawing [the painting] or performing the service (*sevāsādhana*)" (*gnas gcig tu zhes pa bri ba dang bsnyen sgrub kyi gnas spor mi rung ba'o*). Lalitavajra (pp. 327–28), however, glosses it as "in any suitable, isolated place, such as a cremation ground and so on" (*gcig tu gzhag ces pa ni/ dur khrod la sogs pa gang yang rung ba dben pa'i phyogs gcig tu'o*).

863. *Akṣobhya (p. 383) glosses **he should fumigate with human flesh** as "at first—i.e., in the beginning of the eye-opening ceremony" (*sha chen po'i bdug spos phul te zhes bya ni dang por spyan phye la'o*).

864. The Tibetan text (Siklós 1996, 101) reflects the Sanskrit correctly when it says *de'i mdun du dung chen gyi 'phreng bas bzlas pa bya*, but for some reason Siklós (43) translates *de'i mdun du* as "over that [i.e., painting]," while the Tibetan text clearly says "in front of that [i.e., painting]."

865. *Kṛṣṇācārya (p. 458) glosses **full concentration** as "He completes the four preparatory practices through the former *gaṇapūjā* at the three times [of the day] and recites the action mantra using the rosary made of human skulls, undisturbed. He counts the beads on the rosary without mixing them up, and he [utters] the word *hūṃ* while counting the beads on the rosary, as stated before, with the wrathful emanation [of Vajrabhairava] as his focal object" (*shin tu mnyam par zhes pa ni dus gsum du tshogs sngon du song ba can gyis sbyor ba bzhi rdzogs par byas shing/ dung chen po'i phreng bas/ las sngags la ma yengs par bzla ba'o/ phreng ba hūṃ gi gong du khro bo sprul pa'i* [em. *spro ba'i*, ed.] *dmigs pas tshig dang ma 'dres par bgrangs pa'o*).

866. The expression *rakṣitavyaṃ prayatnataḥ*, "ones should protect with effort," in the sense of concealing oneself against those who are uninitiated, is an idiomatic expression also found in Śaiva-Śākta sources. For example, in the *Picumata-Brahmayāmala* (45.130) it occurs in the context of guarding the tantra: *rakṣitavyaṃ prayatnena gūḍhe* [em. *gūḍhaṃ*, ed.] *saṃyānti* [em. *saṃrakti*, ed.] *raśmayaḥ* [corr. *rasmayaḥ*, ed.]/ *gopitavyaṃ prayatnena yadicchej jīvituṃ naraḥ*, "He should guard [the tantra] carefully. If it is concealed, the rays [i.e., the yoginīs] will assemble. [This] should be concealed carefully if a person wishes to live." The aforementioned passage refers to the concept of the Kaula concealment, which resembles the famous line from the *Kulapañcaśatikā*, fol. 4v5: *avyaktaliṅginaṃ dṛṣṭvā saṃbhāṣanti* [corr. *sambhāsanti*, cod.] *marīcayaḥ*, "when the *yoginīs* (lit. the rays) see a person who does not show his sectarian affiliation, they address him." This has been quoted by Kṣemarāja in his *Śivasūtravimarśinī* 3.26 (Chatterji 1910, 112). On the other hand, if a person does show his sectarian affiliation, the yoginīs run away. For a discussion on the tantric initiate who should be secretly a Kaula but should

of anybody.[867] During the night, continually,[868] he should eat food[869] that can be licked, drinks, food that needs to be chewed, and food that can be easily swallowed,[870] such as human meat. At the three times of the day, he should

act in the outside world as a Śaiva and the follower of the Vedic orthopraxy (as per *Tantrālokaviveka* 3.27), see Sanderson 1985, 205. The praxis of concealing the painting described in the VBhT may have been influenced by the Kaula tradition. This argument does not seem to be too far-fetched, especially since the praxis accompanying the protection of the painting is based on the consumption of the five transgressive Kaula substances—namely, the five nectars (*amṛtas*); see page 154 above.

867. *Akṣobhya (p. 383) quotes the following verse from an unidentified source: "'He should not reveal it to others': it is said in the scriptures, 'If the scriptures and images are taught to the ignorant ones, there will be no siddhi in this lifetime, and there will be no siddhi even in other rebirths'" (*gzhan la bstan par mi bya'o zhes bya ba ni/ glegs bam dang ni bris sku dag/ rmongs pa dag la bstan byas na/ tshe 'dir dngos grub mi 'byung ste/ tshe rabs gzhan du'ang dngos grub med/ ces gsungs pas so*).

868. The Tibetan text (Siklós 1996, 102) reflects the Sanskrit when it says *rtag tu mtshan mo*, "always at night," but Siklós (43) translates *mtshan mo* as "at midnight." In this instance, the Tibetan *rtag tu* could render the Sanskrit *nitya* in the sense of "daily," "quotidianly"; see, e.g., *nityakarma*, "quotidian (or 'obligatory') rituals."

869. *Kṛṣṇācārya (p. 459) comments: "He eats and drinks everything at night, and in the afternoon, he engages in pleasures and does a lot of [sādhana] practice" (*bza' btung thams cad mtshan mo dang phyi dro longs spyod cing mang bar spyod pa'o*). *Akṣobhya (p. 383) gives a different explanation: "As for **he continually eats at night**, [it means] although he is alone, in order to keep [the practice] secret, as soon as people lie down at night, he eats the vow substances in order to remove the tiredness of the body" (*rtag tu nub mo za bar bya'o/ zhes bya ba ni gcig tu 'ang gsang bar bya ba'i phyir mtshan mo mi nyal tsam na dam tshig rdzas dag lus dub pa bsal ba la sogs pa'i phyir bza'o*). *Akṣobhya (p. 383) also comments on the dietary regime to be followed by the sādhaka during the day, which is not part of the root text: "As for the consumption of human meat during the day, this is to bring to an end those who attack and slander the perfectly enlightened Buddha and also to introduce oneself among the jackals and ghosts (*bhūtas*)" (*nyin par mi'i sha la sogs pa bza' ba ni/ yang dag par rdzogs pa'i sangs rgyas la 'gro ba skur pa smra ba'i mtha' la thug par 'gyur zhing bdag nyid kyang ce spyang gi dang 'byung po'i khongs su 'jug pa'i phyir ro*).

870. For the definition of the various types of food indicated by the words *bhojya* and *bhakṣya/bhakṣa*, see note 518 above. The technical terms *klog pa*, *bza' ba*, and *ston mo* have been inaccurately translated by Siklós (1996, 43) as "tasting," "eating," and "feast," respectively.

offer incense [871] along with feces and blood in front of the painting if he desires

871. The reading *dhūpo deya(ḥ)* (probably the outcome of irregular *sandhi* for *dhūpo deyo* [*yadīcchet*]) is not only supported by the Tibetan translation but also attested in a number of magical rituals found in the MMK (see below). Furthermore, a similar expression is attested in VBhT §50: *ekānte saṃsthāpya mahāmāṃsena dhūpaṃ dattvā*. For this reason, I have preserved it, although there are reasons to believe that it constitutes the outcome of a Buddhist redaction of the originally Śaiva expression *dhūmodaye*, "when it begins to smoke," as an allusion to the three signs of the obtainment of siddhis: first, when the object begins to heat up (*uṣme*); second, when smoke arises (*dhūme*); third, when it bursts into flames (*jvalite*). These three types of siddhis belong to the "ritual syntax" of the early tantric milieu, commonly found in the MMK and the *Niśvāsa* corpus (Goodall and Isaacson 2016). These are also found in the *Susiddhikara Sūtra* (Giebel 2001, 192), which says, "If you wish to effectuate drugs or other articles, there are three signs of accomplishments: the arising of bright flames is the highest siddhi, smoke is middling, and warmth constitutes the lower siddhi." One reason is that *dhūmodaye* is associated with the Śaiva cliché *yadīcchet siddhim uttamām*, which also occurs in the aforementioned passage of the VBhT. Since the author of the text was already drawing upon an established Śaiva phraseology, it is plausible to assume he could have also borrowed the way of referring to the three signs of siddhis that was common in the early tantric milieu. The reading could have become subsequently corrupted in the text, once the "early tantric syntax" lost its momentum, or it could even reflect a conscious Buddhist redaction.

Contextually related passages containg both readings are found in the MMK. For instance, in the MMK chap. 55, p. 548, we find a recipe involving the *paṭa* where a similar Śaiva context is clearly alluded to. Similar to the VBhT, in this passage only one of the three siddhis—i.e., *jvalite*—is referred to. The passage reads:

> *ekavṛkṣe pratītyasamutpādagarbhacaityaṃ* [em. *caitya*, ed.] *pratiṣṭhāpya lakṣam ekaṃ japet. lakṣaparisamāptau poṣadhikena rūpakāreṇāśvatthakāṣṭhamayaṃ triśūlaṃ lakṣaṇopetaṃ kṛtvā saṃpātābhihūtaṃ* [em. *sapātābhihūtaṃ*, ed.] *kṛtvā paurṇamāsyāṃ sugandhagandhaiḥ samupalipya yathā vibhavataḥ paṭasyāgrataḥ pūjāṃ kṛtvā dakṣiṇahaste kṛtvā sakalāṃ rātriṃ sādhayet. yāvaj jvalatīti. jvalite mahādevo bhavati.*
>
> Having set up a *caitya* containing the dependent origination [i.e., the mantra *ye dharmā* . . .] near the solitary tree, he should recite [the mantra] one hundred thousand times. Having completed one hundred thousand recitations, the maker of images, who has fasted, should endow the *caitya* with the landmark of a trident made of *aśvattha* wood. Having poured oblations of the *saṃpāta* type on the day of the full moon, and having anointed the *paṭa* with a fragrant incense, he should perform *pūjā* in front of it according to his means. Having done it with his right hand, he should accomplish all at night, "until [the *paṭa*] bursts into flames." When it bursts into flames, he will become Śiva.

The Sanskrit grammar does not make it clear whether the object that should burst into flames is a trident or a painting (*paṭa*); grammatically, both options are possible. What is clear, however, is that once the item bursts into flames, the siddhi of becoming Śiva follows. Thus this description is comparable to the passage of the VBhT referred to above, when the sign of the smoke coming from the painting (*paṭa*) indicates the highest siddhi.

the highest siddhi.[872]

The foregoing passage of the MMK clearly exposes the Śaiva context of the ritual on two different occasions, and it does so also with regard to the *aśvattha* wood, which has been identified by Goodall and Isaacson (2016) as the feature of the "early tantric syntax." It is interesting to notice that, in this specific ritual, the *caitya* has to be endowed with the *tṛśūla* (Skt. *triśūla*), an emblem of Śiva that marks it specifically as a Śaiva place. Of course, this should not come as a surprise, since the coveted siddhi for the Buddhist practitioner carrying out this ritual is, oddly, to become Śiva himself.

A second instance of the Śaiva context is visible in the adoption of the Śaiva terminology of *saṃpāta-homa*, present also in the magical ritual of the NTGS (10.30). The *saṃpāta-homa* is a type of "split" oblation, when one pours a half of an oblation onto one thing and the other half of it onto something else. This *homa* is popular in the Śaiva ritual of initiation, when one splits the mantra *svāhā*, meaning "oblation," into *svā* and *hā*. This ritual is described in the *Svacchandatantra* (3.153) as follows: *svā ity agnau prapātayet hā iti śiṣyasya śirasi saṃpātaḥ*, "*Saṃpāta* is when one gives *svā* into the fire and *hā* onto the head of the disciple." Kṣemarāja's commentary on that text, the *Svacchandoddyota* (vol. 1. chap. 3, p. 223), defines it as *saṃpāto yugapat sarvatrāgnīṣomātmakasvarūponmīla nātmā saṃskāra ityarthaḥ*, "It is a *saṃskāra* consisting of awakening through this splitting simultaneously of the Agni and Soma nature of everything." For another instance of the *saṃpāta-homa* in the *Susiddhikara*, see Giebel 2001, 282–84.

A passage of the MMK attesting the reading *dhūpo deyaḥ*, which suggests a Buddhist redaction, is found in chapter 55 (p. 538): *arthakāmaḥ, śucinā śucivastraprāvṛtenāhorātroṣitaḥ paṭasyāgrataḥ kunduruka***dhūpo deyaḥ***; svapne kathayati śubhaṃ vāśubhaṃ vā, saptasahasrāṇi rūpakaṃ labhati*, "The one who wants wealth, who is pure, who is covered with white cloths, who has fasted for a day and night, who offers frankincense in front of the painting, if he recites [the mantra] during sleep, auspicious or inauspicious, he will obtain seven hundred coins."

The topic of fumigations seems to occupy an important place in the description of magical karmas in the MMK. In this regard, fumigations may be unspecified or specified. For example, we find magical rituals where fumigations are simply referred to without specifying the ingredients that should be used, e.g., *mahāmāṃsaṃ ghṛtena saha dhūpaḥ puṣṭikaraṇam* (MMK chap. 41, p. 359): "Human flesh and incense together with ghee, causes prosperity"; *mānuṣāsthicūrṇaṃ kākolūkapakṣāṇi ca dhūpaḥ māraṇam* (MMK chap. 41, p. 359): "The feathers of a crow and an owl, the powder of human bones, and incense cause death." On other occasions, ingredients such as incense are clearly specified, e.g., *sarṣaparājikādhūpaṃ jvarakaraṇaṃ* (MMK chap. 41, p. 359), "Incense of mustard seed and black mustard causes fever." Based on these passages in the MMK, it is plausible to argue that by stating *dhūpo deyaḥ*, the VBhT refers to some unspecified incense that should be offered in front of the painting, together with feces and blood, if a person wishes for the highest siddhi.

872. *Kṛṣṇācārya (p. 459) glosses **if he desires the highest siddhi** as "With the sequence of generation (*utpatti*) and completion (*utpanna*), he offers worship to the painting and meditates. [The practice of] meditation is related to [the exposition given] in the first and last chapters. It also relates in part to the oral instruction of the guru" (*mchog 'dod na zhes pa ni bskyed pa dang rdzogs pa'i rim gyis bris sku la mchod cing bsgom par bya'o/ de*

This is the fifth chapter, The Ritual of Painting the *Paṭa*, in this yoga tantra of the venerable Great Vajrabhairava, which is a part of [the tantra] called the *Śrīmañjuśriya* [*Tantra*].

---

dang po'i le'u dang tha ma'i le'u 'brel par byas la bsgom pa'o/ la la bla ma'i ngag la yang ngo).

*Akṣobhya's gloss (p. 383) interprets it differently: "Whoever **desires the highest siddhi** [means] these transgressive acts (*duṣṭācārya*) should be performed with a pure mind and not otherwise, for the highest siddhis are obtained with a pure mind, but they are not [obtained] by enjoying these filthy things like a pig and so forth. As for the 'pure mind,' it means to create equanimity between the [filthy things] and the desired object of the senses (*kāmaguṇas*): wine of *śalī* rice, human meat, perfume of excrement, incense of camphor [i.e., semen]. For that reason, it is explained, 'Whatever he offers with a pure [mind], for such a person, wine is just like smell; in the same way, excrement is just like food, and good incense is just like camphor [i.e., semen]. In the same way, whatever comes with excrement is perfume'" (*gang zhig dngos grub mchog 'dod pa/ zhes bya ba ni ngan pa'i spyod pa 'di dag ni sems dag pas bya'i gzhan du ma yin la/ dngos grub chen po rnams ni sems dag pas thob kyi/ mi gtsang ba longs spyod pas ni ma yin te/ phag la sogs pa bzhin no/ sems dag pa ni 'bras śā li'i* [em. *lu*, ed.] *chang dang/ mi'i sha dang/ bshang ba'i dri dang/ ga bur gyi dri dag la 'dod pa'i yon tan du mnyam par 'gyur te/ de bas na/ gang dag pas* [em. *dga' ba*, ed.] *dbul te/ 'di ltar chang dang de bzhin dri/ ji ltar bza' ba de bzhin bshang* [em. *bshad*, ed.]*/ ji ltar dri bzang* [em. *bzangs*, ed.] *ga pur dag/ de bzhin bshang* [em. *bshad*, ed.] *pa las byung dri/ zhes gsungs pa lta bu'o*). For the explanation of this quotation, see page 162 above.

6. Prescriptions for the Rule of *Homa*

[§53] Now, I will explain the rule of fire offerings (*homavidhi*),[873] correctly and in due order. First, the mantra master should go to the cremation ground[874] and commence the fire-offering ritual at night.[875] He should perform all ritual actions while remaining in the previously explained deity yoga.

[§54] In this [sādhana], the ritual procedure is [as follows]. If he wishes to kill,[876] then he should put together[877] human bone, feces[878] (*vairocana*),

873. *Akṣobhya (p. 384): "**Rule of fire offerings** [means] I will explain the *homa* in an abbreviated form; as for the extensive explanation, know it from tantras that are compatible with this [tantra]" (*sbyin sreg gi cho ga zhes bya ba ni/ rab tu bsdus pa bshad par bya/ rgyas par 'di dang cha mthun pa'i rgyud las shes par bya*).

874. The Tibetan text (Siklós 1996, 103) has *dben pa'i gnas*, "an isolated place."

875. The Tibetan text (Siklós 1996, 103) has *mtshan phyed*, "midnight."

876. *Kṛṣṇācārya (p. 459): "**If he wishes to kill** [means] for those humans and nonhumans who are difficult to tame through peaceful means, with great compassion and having [performed] the service of Bhagavān Vajrabhairava, he causes them to pass away in this lifetime via the ritual process of this *homa* rite and so forth. He should make a wish that they achieve Akṣobhya's pure land in their future bodies, and prior to that he should purify them through meditative stabilization as before" (*bsad par 'dod pa zhes pa ni zhi bas mi 'dul ba'i mi dang mi ma yin pa de la snying rje chen pos/ bcom ldan 'das rdo rje 'jigs byed kyi bsnyen pa nas sbyin sreg la sogs pa'i rim pas tshe 'dir 'phor bcug la/ ma 'ongs pa'i lus mi bskyod pa'i zhing khams dag der sgrub snyam pa dang/ sngon ltar ting nge 'dzin sbyang bar bya'o*).

877. Lalitavajra (p. 328): "**He should put together** [means] he mixes them all together and burns them, or else he burns them individually (one by one)" (*bsres nas zhes pa ni gcig tu bsres te bsreg pa 'am yang na so sor bsreg pa'o*).

878. Lalitavajra (p. 328) glosses [human] **feces** and so on as "The substances to be offered into the fire; it is easy to understand" (*dri chen zhes bya ba la sogs pa ni bsreg rdzas te go sla'o*).

excrement of a donkey,[879] thorns, hair, and fingernail clippings.[880] Having smeared all those things with a pungent mustard-seed oil (*kaṭutaila*),[881] he should sacrifice them into cremation-ground fire[882] 108 times[883] while facing south[884] and established in the meditative equipoise.[885] [That person] in whose name [he does that] while in union with the Buffalo-Faced One will die

879. The Sanskrit *laṇḍa* can also mean "penis," but this meaning is neither supported by the Tibetan text, which says *bong bu'i spangs pa*, nor by Lalitavajra's commentary (p. 330), which has *bong bu rtug pa*.

880. The Tibetan text (Siklós 1996, 103) also has "dog's dung," which the Sanskrit omits; however, this reading is supported by the parallel passage in the *Saṃpuṭodbhava* (7.2.16, ed., p. 329), which also mentions *śvānalaṇḍa*.

881. *Akṣobhya (p. 384): "**Oil** [means] with black mustard seed or red mustard seed" (*'bru mar gyi zhes bya ba ni/ ske tshe'am yungs [d]mar gyis so*). The parallel passage of the *Saṃpuṭodbhava* (7.2.16, ed., p. 329) reads *tailenāloḍya*, but it probably means *kaṭutailena*, as supported by *Akṣobhya's commentary. Siklós (1996, 43) has "melted butter," which does not seem accurate.

882. Lalitavajra (p. 328): "If you ask 'where' [to burn them], [I reply:] in the fire of the cremation ground. [That means] he does not construct a firepit; this is the meaning" (*gang du zhe na dur khrod me ste thab mi bca' zhes pa'i don do*). *Kṛṣṇācārya (p. 459): "He should kindle the fire [means] in the fire of the cremation ground, or in the fire taken from a blacksmith, or in the fire taken from the outcaste woman (*caṇḍālī*), with the wood of the cremation ground" (*dur khrod kyi me'am lcags las byung ba'am candali'i me la dur khrod shing gis me sbar la*).

883. Lalitavajra (p. 329): "**108 times** [refers to the] mantra. He burns the items 108 times while uttering [the mantra] customized with the name of the target" (*brgya rtsa ba brgyad zhes pa sngags la bsgrub bya'i ming bskul tshig dang bcas pas brgya rtsa brgyad bsregs*).

884. Lalitavajra (p. 329): "**Facing south** [means] in order to kill, he meditates on the Buffalo-Faced One inside the fire. The mantra of Yama [means] the root mantra or that, through the subordinate heart mantra (*upahṛdaya*), he does *homa* rituals for the sake of worship" (*lho phyogs su blta ba ni gsod pa'i phyir ro/ me'i nang du ma he'i zhal bsams la gshin rje'i sngags te rtsa ba'i sngags sam nye ba'i snying pos mchod pa'i sbyin bsreg byas la*).

885. Lalitavajra (pp. 328–29) glosses very steady instead of "established in the meditative equipoise" as "steady by being established in the deity yoga" (*shin tu mi g.yo zhes pa ni lha'i rnal 'byor las mi g.yo ba'o*). Lalitavajra (p. 330) says further that one generates the deity by uttering *oṃ hūṃ phaṭ phaṭ* (*lhar bskyed la/ oṃ dang hūṃ phaṭ gnyis ldan pas*).

in three days.[886] Or else,[887] having sat himself in an isolated place[888] and having

886. The *abhicārahoma* given in the *Saṃpuṭodbhava* (7.2.16, ed., p. 329) has a longer version that includes a whole set of ingredients prior to the "human bone" that are missing in the VBhT. It starts with the standard opening *atha abhicāraṃ kartukāmena*, followed by the list of ingredients and their measurements: "If he wishes to perform *abhicāra*, he takes a portion of black sesame and so on and dark blue *bhalāttaka* fruit. Having smeared them with black, pungent oil, he mixes them with blood. Having gathered thorns of vetches (*kālavṛkṣa*) and marking nut (*kubja* = achryanthes aspera), three bitter juices, and so on, and ten *aṅgula*s from the roots of all trees, human bone, excrement (*vairocana*), dung of a donkey, hair, dung of a dog, hair again, fingernail clippings, [and having] smeared with oil all those things, he should sacrifice them into the cremation fire 108 times facing south while in meditative equipoise. He in whose name he does that will die in three days" (*atha abhicāraṃ kartukāmena tilakṛṣṇamāṣādi bhallātakaphalaṃ* [corr. *phala*, ms. R, ed.] *kālakatīkṣṇatailenālodya rudhiramiśrakaiḥ saha/ kālavṛkṣasya kubjasya kaṇṭakaṃ* [corr. *kaṇṭaka*, ms. R, ed.] *kaṭukatiktādīni sarvavṛkṣajāni daśāṅgulāni/ narāsthivairocanagard abhalaṇḍakeśaśvānalaṇḍakeśanakhaṃ sametya* [em. *samet*, ms. R, ed.]/ *tatsarvaṃ tailena samālodya cityagnau samāhitena dakṣiṇābhimukham aṣṭottaraśataṃ juhuyād yasya nāmnā dinatrayeṇa mriyate*).

The version from the *Saṃpuṭodbhava* corresponds more closely to the Tibetan text insofar as both texts have *śvānalaṇḍa*, "dung of a dog" (translated into Tibetan as *khyi'i spangs pa*), which is missing in the Sanskrit manuscripts of the VBhT. Lalitavajra's commentary (p. 330) additionally mentions the dung of a donkey and a camel (*bong bu rnga mo rtug pa dang*) as suitable offerings for the *abhicārahoma*.

887. Lalitavajra (p. 329): "**Or else** is a conjunctive adverb that indicates 'another place'—that is, a place for setting up the firepit" (*yang na zhes pa ni phyogs gzhan ston pa'i tshig gi phrad do/ thab khung bca' ba'i phyogs so*).

888. The Tibetan text reads *yang na phyogs gcig tu gnas la me thab gru gsum byas nas*, which clearly indicates a location of the firepit, but Siklós (1996, 44) takes it adverbially as referring to the sādhaka who makes the firepit single-pointedly. This interpretation is not supported by Lalitavajra's commentary (p. 329), which says "**As for an isolated place**, that is a place of firepit rituals" (*dben pa'i gnas ni thab bya ba'i gnas so*). *Śoṇaśrī and *Vajrasiddha understand an isolated place to be one's own home. *Śoṇaśrī (pp. 405–6): "**Or else**, dwelling at home in an isolated place, on the fourteenth day of the dark fortnight, he makes a red triangular firepit measuring twenty fingerbreadths on each side" (*yang na khyim du gnas la dben par byas la bcu bzhi la zur gsum dmar po/ sor nyi shu'i tshad*). *Akṣobhya (p. 384) glosses the outskirts of the city (missing in the root text) as probably another example of an isolated place: "**The outskirts of the city** [means] wherefrom the great sound of the city is not heard" (*bas mtha' zhes bya ba ni gang nas grong gi sgra* [corr. *dgra*, ed.] *chen po yang mi thos pa'o*). *Kṛṣṇācārya (p. 460): "**Or else, having sat himself in an isolated place** [means] in his own house, facing south, he makes *homa* according to the teaching; whatever he says will come about. Moreover, as for the direction of the house (?), having performed the ritual on the fourteenth day of the waning moon, he will achieve that [karma]" (*yang na phyogs gcig ces pa ni rang gi khyim gyi lhor phyogs par bstan pa ltar bsregs nas yang gsungs pa ltar 'gyur ro/ yang na khyim gyi phyogs ni mar tshes zla ba bri ba'i bcu bzhi nas las de 'grub pa'o*).

made a triangular firepit,[889] he makes an offering into the fire taken from an outcaste[890] with the same substances mentioned above.[891] By that yoga, [the target] is led to the world of Yama.[892] There is no doubt about it.[893]

[§55] Next, if he wishes to create dissent, [he collects] a crow, an owl, a peacock, [the slough] of a snake, a hair, an unhusked rice, and flesh from a buffalo and a horse. In whosoever's name he sacrifices that [into the fire], [the target] will be rendered an enemy. Alternatively, if he sacrifices [these items] having [first] kindled the fire with the wood of the cremation ground while sitting in [his own] house, [then] in seven days, even Vajradhara [that is, Indra] will be rendered an enemy.

[§56] Alternatively, if he wishes to drive away,[894] [the mantra master], who is naked, his hair disheveled, having [first] sat down facing south,[895] kindles the

889. Lalitavajra (p. 329) comments on the measurement of the firepit: "It has the length of twenty fingerbreadths and the depth of ten fingerbreadths (*me thab sor nyi shu pa'i thab zabs su sor bcu pa byas la zhes pa'i don to*). For different types of firepits for each *homa*, see page 141.

890. Siklós (1996, 44) translates *gtum po'i me* as a "fierce fire," which is wrong, as Lalitavajra's commentary (p. 329) clearly specifies the type of a person who is regarded as an outcaste when he says, "**The fire of an outcaste** [means] a fire from the house of a cobbler or a butcher" (*gtum po'i me ni mi rdol pa 'am sme sha can gyi khyim gyi me la'o*). *Akṣobhya (pp. 384–85) glosses "a butcher," not given in the root text, as "a fire sought from a butcher" (*sme sha can zhes bya ba yang sme sha can las btsal ba'i me ste*).

891. Lalitavajra (p. 329): "**The same substances mentioned above** [means] *homa* substances such as human feces and so on" (*sngon du gsungs pa'i rdzas zhes pa ni bsreg rdzas te dri chen la sogs pa'o*).

892. *Kṛtānta* is an appellation of the god of death (Yama).

893. The Tibetan text gives a different meaning: *sbyor ba des ni las de nyid 'grub bo*, "That procedure accomplishes that specific action (i.e., killing)." *Akṣobhya (p. 385) comments: "If that is not [done properly], how could these two [alternative] procedures not incur the fault of rebounding upon oneself?" (*de lta ma yin na sbyor ba 'di gnyis rang bzlog pa'i nyes par ji ste mi 'gyur*). I thank John Newman for clarifying this translation.

894. *Kṛṣṇācārya (p. 460): "**Alternatively, if he wishes to drive away** [means] he should make a firepit one cubit long and one cubit high, blue in color, shaped like a bow, and surrounded by a series of hammers and vajra-sticks. He does *pūjā* and offers *homa* oblations, and he does all that with the mind focused on driving away" (*de nas yang bskrad par 'dod na zhes pa ni thab khung khru gang rgya dang dpangs su bya zhing kha dog sngon po gzhu'i dbyibs can du tho ba dang rdo rje dbyug pa'i phreng bas bskor ba'o/ mchod pa dang rdzas bsregs pa yang bskrad pa'i sems gtsor bya ba'o*).

895. Lalitavajra glosses as "He is **facing south** with the buffalo face" (*ma he zhal gyis lhor*

cremation-ground fire[896] in the middle of the [firepit featuring a drawing of a] wind maṇḍala. [He then], with his left hand, sacrifices into [that firepit] a hundred thousand oblations of crow's flesh and the excrement of a camel in the target's name,[897] together with wine. [By this the target] is driven away and not otherwise.

[§57] Alternatively, if he wants to cause paralysis, [the mantra master], having sat down facing north,[898] should make a square maṇḍala[899] [while being] in union [with a deity] in accordance with the ritual. If into the fire he sacrifices

---

bltas te), which indicates the sādhaka who has generated himself as Vajrabhairava. See the next footnote.

896. The Tibetan text (Siklós 1996, 104) has *rlung gi dkyil 'khor gyi dbus su/ dur khrod kyi shing la me rab tu sbar la*, which Siklós (44) translates as "He kindles a fire in the cremation wood in the center of a wind maṇḍala," which does not make much sense. Based on Lalitavajra's commentary (p. 333), one realizes that the above passage should actually read "On the top of the wind maṇḍala, he should generate [himself as] a deity, it is said" (*rlung gi dkyil 'khor thog tu lha bskyed ces pa'o*). Thus it seems that the root text has been corrupted. *Akṣobhya (p. 385) takes it to mean the drawing inside the hearth: "**In the middle of the wind maṇḍala** [means] he should draw [the wind maṇḍala] in the center of the firepit in such a way that it is either a crescent or triangular" (*rlung gi dkyil 'khor gyi dbus su zhes bya ba ni/ thab* [em. *tha ba*, ed.] *zla ba phyed pa lta bu'am/ gru gsum pa'i dbus su de ltar bri ba'o*). Kumāracandra: "**Wind maṇḍala** [means] a firepit in the shape of a half moon" (*vāyumaṇḍalam ardhacandrākāraṃ kuṇḍam*).

897. Lalitavajra (p. 333): "He customizes [means] by inserting *uccāṭaya* ["drive away"] so and so in the mantra" (*ming bcug pa ni sngags la che ge mo utsa ta ya bcug pas so*). The Tibetan text (Siklós 1996, 104) has additional information about the customization of the name of a person with the Yama mantra.

898. The Tibetan text has "and visualizes the yoga which accords with this rite" (Siklós 1996, 44), which *Akṣobhya (p. 385) glosses, "He visualizes yoga in harmony with this rite [means] as it has been formerly said, the deities together with the god Agni" (*las dang mthun pa'i rnal 'byor zhes dmigs te zhes bya ba ni/ sngar brjod pa dang me lha dang lhan cig pa'i lha rnams so*).

899. Lalitavajra (p. 333) glosses a **square maṇḍala** as a special type of firepit, which in reality is a wide hearth (*dkyil 'khor gru bzhi pa thab kyi khyad par te rgyas ba'i thab ji lta ba bzhin te*). He (p. 333) also glosses **realgar and so on** as the substances offered into the fire (*ldong ros zhes bya ba la sogs pa ni bsreg rdzas so*). *Akṣobhya (p. 385) also comments on the **square maṇḍala** as "in the firepit, which is yellow and similar to the earth (lit. Mahendra) maṇḍala" (*gru bzhi dkyil 'khor zhes bya ba ni/ thab khung ser po dbang chen gyi dkyil 'khor lta bu'o*).

yellow orpiment, turmeric, and realgar together with bovine concretion in whosoever's name,[900] that person is paralyzed.[901]

[§58] Alternatively, if he wants to drive the town away, [the mantra master], having established himself in union with Yama, kindles the fire with the wood of the neem tree. Having smeared the excrement of a dog with the blood of a cat[902] on the flesh of a dog and a hen, if he sacrifices in the town's name ten thousand oblations [of the above things] in the middle of the wind maṇḍala[903] [using] the ten-syllable mantra, the town is driven away.[904] These rituals should be done with perfectly concentrated mind. Otherwise, the mantra master himself will fall down, and therefore, he should not tell it to anyone.

[§59] Next, if he wants to cause the paralysis of a girl, he offers into the fire one thousand oblations of thorns, venom, and mustard seed, smeared with human blood;[905] certainly, that girl will be paralyzed. If he recites the ten-syllable mantra, he will cause the paralysis, and not otherwise.

900. Lalitavajra (p. 333): "By inserting the word 'Paralyze!' (*stambhaya*) with the name of [the target] and by making fire oblations to the yellow god of fire using a wide hearth, he paralyzes [the target]" (*de'i ming dang stam bha ya zhes pa btags te/ me lha ser po la thab* [corr. *thabs*, ed.] *rgyas pas bsregs na rengs pa'o*).

901. The Tibetan text adds "in seven days" (Siklós 1996, 104).

902. *Akṣobhya (p. 385) has "cat urine" instead of "blood," which he glosses: "He mixes with cat's urine [means] he burns the substances one by one and then fills them up [with cat urine?]" (*byi la'i mu tra dang sbyar la/ zhes bya ba ni rdzas de dag re re nas bsregs pa bkang ba'o*). This corruption could have easily arisen by misreading *rudhi*[*reṇa*] for *mūt*[*reṇa*]. Tibetan text has one extra item, "frog's flesh (*sbal ba'i sha*)" (see Siklós 1996, 104), which the Sanskrit omits.

903. Here "the wind maṇḍala" could refer either to the painting inside the firepit or to the generation of the deity (see note 896).

904. The *homa* ends with a warning that urges the sādhaka to perform this *homa* with full meditative concentration; otherwise, dire consequences will follow (see Siklós 1996, 44). *Akṣobhya (p. 385) glosses it: "Established in **perfectly concentrated mind** [means] he should be moistened with compassion" (*legs par mnyam par gzhag par bya'o zhes bya ba ni snying rjes rab tu brlan par bya'o*).

905. *Akṣobhya (p. 385) explains: "He mixes the substances [i.e., thorns, venom, and mustard seed] with **blood** [means] with whatever blood, provided it is not sinful [i.e., not obtained from killing], he mixes the given substances, and with that he makes an image of a girl. In the heart [of that image] he places the customized mantra, chops the image, and burns it" (*khrag gis brdzis te zhes bya ba ni khrag sdig med pa gang yang rung bas brdzis la bu mo'i gzugs brnyan snying gar sngags bskul ba smos la bzhag pa byas na de bcad cing bsregs pa'o*). The Tibetan text (Siklós 1996, 104) has "his own blood" (*rang gi khrag*) instead.

[§60] Alternatively, if he wants to bring peace[906] [to a country at war], [he offers] ghee, honey, and milk together with Bermuda grass into the fire that was kindled with a *palāśa* wood. If he, having sat down facing east,[907] makes [these] oblations into the fire 108 times with the mind [focused on] bringing peace,[908] then he brings peace[909] even to a country [at war].

906. Lalitavajra (p. 334) says, "A person who **wants to bring peace** [means] a person who wants to protect from the eight types of dangers" (*zhi bar 'dod pas ni 'jigs pa brgyad las skyob par 'dod pas so*). Lalitavajra (p. 334) then gives instructions for the maṇḍala preparation, for he glosses *maṇḍala*, which is missing in the root text, as "measuring one cubit in length, round, half a cubit deep, and having a raised platform of four fingerbreadths. It should be smeared with incense and white earth" (*dkyil 'khor zhes pa khru gang gi tshad la zlum po thur du khru phyed pa sor bzhi pa'i kha khyer can/ dri dang sa dkar pos byugs te*). *Kṛṣṇācārya (p. 461): "**If he wants to bring peace** [means] the firepit is round, with the measurement the same like in other cases, the fire of monks and so on [possibly meaning that it has to be taken from the monastery], and white. Agnideva has one face, two arms, and holds a rosary and a small waterpot" (*zhi bar 'dod na zhes pa ni thab khung zlum po tshad la sogs pa gzhan ltar ro/ dge 'dun gyi me la sogs pa dkar po'o/ me lha zhal gcig phyag gnyis pa phreng ba dang ril ba 'dzin pa'o*).

907. Lalitavajra (p. 334): "**Facing east** [means] the yogin is facing east toward the white-bodied Agnideva. Since the substances, such as offering articles are also white, and so forth [i.e., auspicious], the presentation of the substances reverses [the war situation]." (*me lha sku mdog dkar po la rnal 'byor pa shar du bltas mchod rdzas yang dkar po la sogs pa dang ldan pas rdzas bzhag pa go zlog ste*).

908. *Akṣobhya (p. 385): "**He who concentrates on bringing peace** [means] he visualizes the deities, Agnideva, and the substances as white in color. It is said, 'The form of fire is just like Guhyapati, who gives blessings. One must understand that even the material substances are my form'" (*zhi bar dmigs pa'i bdag nyid kyis/ zhes bya ba ni lha dang me'i lha dang rdzas rnams kha dog dkar por bsams te/ gsang ba'i bdag por de ltar me yi gzugs ni byin rlabs te/ bdag gi rang gi gzugs dang ni/ rdzas kyang de yi ngo bor bya zhes gsungs pas so*). Lalitavajra (p. 334): "**Bring peace** [means] with the mind set on helping [others]" (*zhi ba ste phan gdags pa'i sems kyis*).

909. A longer version of the same *homa* is given in the *Sampuṭodbhava* (7.2.13, ed., p. 328): *śālitaṇḍuladhānyāni tilaś ca/ tantuṃ* [em. *taṃ tu*, mss. R, K, P, ed.] *yavaphalaṃ ca dūrvā kṣīrabhaktaṃ ghṛtamadhunā saha pañcāmṛtaṃ ca havyam/ pañcakṣīravṛkṣajāḥ sārdrāḥ saparṇavāḥ/ etā agrabhāgasthā* [em. *atra°*, mss. R, K, P, ed.] *madhurakṣīraghṛtāktobhayāgrā hotavyāḥ/ udumbarapalāśotpāditāgniṃ prajvālya śāntikāmena triṣkālaṃ pūrvābhimukhe sthitvā aṣṭottaraśataṃ juhuyāt/ tato maṇḍalasyāpi śāntir bhavati*, "He should make oblations of black cumin, unhusked rice, grain, sesame, cotton thread, barley, Bermuda grass, a portion of milk, and the five nectars together with ghee and honey. He should offer into the fire five sappy kindlings taken from the front part of the twig, together with leaves, which are green. The front tips should be smeared with honey, milk, and ghee [. . .]." The rest of the recipe is identical to the one translated above.

[§61] Alternatively, if he wants to cause prosperity,[910] [the mantra master takes] sesame, unhusked rice, and barley, together with ghee. Having kindled a fire with *udumbara* wood while being sustained in yoga with a deity in accordance with the ritual, and having sat down facing north, if he sacrifices into the fire a thousand oblations at the three times of the day[911] with full concentration,[912] there will be prosperity.[913]

[§62] Alternatively, if he wishes to attract, [the mantra master] makes an effigy with mustard seed and cuts it in the center. If he sacrifices [its parts] 108 times into a *khadira* fire, his purpose will be achieved. Within seven days he will attract whatever he wants, and not otherwise.

[§63] Alternatively, if he wishes to induce insanity, then in whosoever's name he sacrifices into the fire human flesh and bird flesh,[914] [the target] will become mad. If he sacrifices rice chaff into the fire, [the target] will become healthy [again].[915]

910. *Kṛṣṇācārya (p. 461): "**If he wants to cause prosperity** [means] if the yogin himself wants longevity, merit, sons, and many attendants, [then] he should make a firepit one cubit long and two cubits deep, just like in other cases. [He should use] the fire of a householder and [visualize] a yellow deity and so on" (*rgyas par 'dod na zhes pa rnal 'byor nyid tshe dang bsod nams bu dang 'khor mang bar 'dod na bya ba ste/ thab khung khru do khru gang gzhan ltar ro/ khyim bdag gi me dang lha ser po la sogs pa'o*).

911. The Tibetan text has "using a ten-syllable mantra" (*yi ge bcu pa'i sngags kyis*), Siklós 1996, 105.

912. *Akṣobhya (p. 385) glosses **with full concentration** as "in the meditative equipoise, which pours down the rain of great jewels and many riches" (*mnyam par gzhag pa'i yid kyis zhes bya ba ni rin po che dang/ nor sna tshogs kyi char dbab pa'i ting nge 'dzin la'o*).

913. The enlarged version of this *homa* is included in the *Saṃpuṭodbhava* 7.2.14. See Wenta 2024.

914. Sanskrit *śakuna* means "any bird," but sometimes also a "vulture" (see Monier-Williams 1899, 1042). The Tibetan text has *bya rgod chen po'i tshang*, "a nest of a big vulture," which does not feature in the Sanskrit. *Akṣobhya (p. 385) glosses "the nest of a big vulture" as "One should not divide the nest that was collected into separate parts" (*bya rgod chen po'i tshang* [corr. *tshad*, ed.] *zhes bya ba de ni ci bsags pa'i tshang* [corr. *tshad*, ed.] *bye brag mi bya bar ro*).

915. *Svastho bhavati* corresponds to the Tibetan *bde legs 'gyur*, which Siklós (1996, 105) translates incorrectly as "He will be blessed with good fortune"; this is clearly not the meaning intended here. Lalitavajra (p. 334): "**If he sacrifices rice chaff into the fire**, he frees [the target] of ritual invocation and makes him recover" (*'bras phub* [add. *ma*] *bsregs te las kyi bskul ba dang bral bas bya bas sos so*).

[§64] Alternatively, if he wants to turn wealth into poverty,[916] [the mantra master takes] the datura fruit; if he sacrifices it into a fire of cottonwood 108 times, [the target's wealth] will perish. If he sacrifices yellow myrobalan into the fire, there will be restoration [of wealth, lit., "he will be made whole"].

[§65] [Next], if he does a fire sacrifice[917] of human flesh [together] with wine in front of the Lord[918] 108 times at the three junctures of the day[919] for six months, he will become a ruler of the entire country.

[§66] [Next], if he sacrifices into the fire a thousand oblations of beef[920] mixed with blood,[921] [the target] remains as a slave as long as he lives, there is no doubt.

[§67] [Next], if he sacrifices into the fire 108 oblations of dog flesh together with vajra water[922] in whosoever's name, that person by himself[923] or with his wealth comes under his power.

916. *Akṣobhya (pp. 385–86) comments on the *homa* as follows: "**Turn wealth into poverty** [means] by uttering the mantra with the following customization [*bskul pa smos pa* = *vidarbhaṇa*]: *amukasya nāma* (of someone with this name) *dravya adravyaṃ kuru* (make this property into non-property)" (*nor ma yin par 'gyur te zhes bya ba ni a mu ka na ma tra bya a tra bya ku ru zhes bskul ba smos pas so*).

917. The Tibetan text specifies the time of the sacrifice through the expression "at night" (*mtshan mo sbyin bsreg*).

918. Lalitavajra (p. 334) understands as "**in front of** [Vajrabhairava's] painting" (*bris sku'i mdun du bya zhes pa yang go sla'o*). *Akṣobhya (p. 386): "In front **of the Lord** [means] in front of the place where he [the Bhagavān] stands," which probably means in front of Vajrabhairava's statue (*bcom ldan 'das kyi spyan snga nyid du zhes bya ba ni de bzhugs pa'i gnas su de'i spyan sngar te*). None of these details feature in the Sanskrit text.

919. The Tibetan text omits *trisaṃdhya*.

920. Lalitavajra (p. 334): "**Beef** and so on are the five special features of the ritual of subjugation under one's power. Individually, they are easy to understand; no explanation is needed" (*ba lang sha dang zhes bya ba la sogs pa'i dbang gi las lnga'i khyad par ni so sor go sla ste ma phye*). Indeed, what follows are the five different *vaśyahomas*, each of which requires an oblation consisting of a different type of meat.

921. *Akṣobhya (p. 386): "**Blood** [means] even that of a bull" (*khrag ces bya ba yang ba lang nyid kyi'o*). Tibetan has "together with whosoever's name" (*gang gi ming bcas par*); Siklós 1996, 105.

922. *Akṣobhya (p. 386): "**Vajra water** (*vajrodaka*) [means] one's urine" (*rdo rje chu ni rang gi mu ta'o*).

923. The Tibetan text mentions *skyes pa'i bdag nyid kyis*, which Siklós (1996, 45) translates literally as "with his self as it came into being."

[§68] [Next], if he, having visualized the king, makes 108 oblations of horse flesh together with excrement (*vairocana*)[924] at night, having sat himself down in one place,[925] then within seven days, the king together with his army [926] comes under his power.

[§69] [Next], if he sacrifices into the fire the flesh of an elephant together with its semen, then within seven days, he subjects all humankind under his power.[927]

[§70] [Next], if he makes 108 oblations of the flesh of a fish[928] together with wine[929] without hesitation, then as soon as [he does that], all women fall under his power.

[§71] Alternatively, say he wants to drive [someone] away. If he sacrifices only crow's flesh into the fire a thousand times[930] in whosoever's name, then within

924. The Tibetan text additionally has "with the Yamāntaka mantra" (*gshin rje gshed kyi sngags kyis*); Siklós 1996, 106.

925. Siklós (1996, 45), however, takes *gnas gcig tu gnas la* as referring to a practitioner who is "visualizing at night a king with a single-pointed concentration." This seems to be inaccurate, as *gnas gcig tu gnas la* most likely reflects the Sanskrit *ekānte sthitvā*, "having sat down in one place."

926. The Tibetan text has "along with his retinue" (*'khor dang bcas pa*); Siklós 1996, 106. However, the Monier-Williams dictionary gives "an army, troops" or "royal camp" for the Sanskrit word *kaṭaka*. *Akṣobhya (p. 386): "King and his retinue: why even mention other things? This is the real meaning" (*rgyal po'i pho brang 'khor zhes bya ba ni gzhan gyi tshogs lta ci smos zhes bya ba'i tha tshig go*).

927. Tibetan: "If he performs a thousand sacrifices at night with the flesh and semen of an elephant using the ten-syllable mantra, visualizing all human worlds, within seven days they will come into his power" (Siklós 1996, 45).

928. The Tibetan text treats *matsyamāṃsa* as a *dvandva* (*nya dang sha*), but it seems to be a *tatpuruṣa*, "flesh of a fish." The latter is supported by Lalitavajra's commentary (see note 920 above), which mentions the five types of meat as a special feature of the five *vaśyahomas*.

929. The Tibetan text has "using the ten-syllable mantra" (*yi ge bcu pa'i sngags kyis*); Siklós 1996, 106.

930. The Tibetan text has "using the ten-syllable mantra" (*yi ge bcu pa'i sngags kyis*); Siklós 1996, 106.

three days,[931] even Vajradhara [that is, Indra][932] will run away, to say nothing of an ordinary person.

[§72] Alternatively, if he sacrifices into the fire a crow's nest together with unhusked rice [while reciting] the ten-syllable mantra, having [first] kindled the fire in thorn-apple wood at midnight, then in whosoever's name he does that, [that person] will be driven away within seven days.

[§73] Next, if he wishes to subject under his will,[933] [he should mix] sesame and rice together with menstrual blood and vajra water [i.e., urine]; if the mantra master sacrifices them into an acacia-wood fire in whosoever's name, facing west and having meditatively sustained the red form [of Vajrabhairava],[934] then within seven days, [the target] will come under his will and will not be released [from the spell] as long as he lives.[935]

931. The Tibetan text omits the time period.

932. Vajradhara here should be understood as an epithet of the Hindu god Indra, who is often referred to as such, and not as Vajradhara the Buddha (*rigs kun khyab bdag*). I thank John Newman for this explanation.

933. The parallel passage given in the *Saṃpuṭodbhava* (7.2.15, ed., p. 328) has a number of ingredients and measurements missing in the Sanskrit and Tibetan: *atha vaśīkartukāmaḥ/ tilaraktakṛṣṇasya vā priyaṅgunāgakeśaraṃ campakāśokabakulabāṇaśatapuṣpaṃ ca gandhaṃ ca ghṛtamadhuyojitam/ devadāruvaṭaṃ caiva pippalodumbarādipādapabhavāny aṣṭāṅgulāni śallakīguggulavṛkṣayoḥ kṣīram evaṃ sugandhādīn/ tataḥ strīpuṣpeṇa saha vajrodakasaṃmiśreṇa raktarūpam ālambya paścimābhimukho yasya nāmnā juhoti/* [*taṃ*, om. ed.] *saptāhād vaśam ānayati/ yāvajjīvaṃ na muñcati//*, "If he wants to subject under his will, he takes red and black sesame, *priyaṅgu*, rose chestnut (*nāgakeśara*), *campaka* flower, *aśoka* flower, *bakula* flower, crested Philippine violet (*bāṇa*), dill (*śatapuṣpa*), and incense mixed with ghee and honey. [Fuel sticks] should be from a cedar tree, a banyan tree, *pippal*, *udumbara*, etc., eight *aṅgula*s long, with *śallakī* and *gugullu* trees, [adding] milk, perfumes, etc."

The rest of the *homa*, from *raktarūpam* to *muñcati*, identical to the one translated above, is clearly drawn from some other text. The use of *priyaṅgu* and *nāgakeśara* for *vaśyahoma* is also given in the MMK chap. 55, p. 533: *priyaṅgunāgakesarasamidhānāṃ yasya nāmnā juhoti; sa vaśyo bhavati*, "In whosoever's name he sacrifices fuel sticks of *priyaṅgu* and *nāgakeśara* tree into the fire, that person will come under his will."

934. The Tibetan text has *rnal 'byor gyi gzugs dmar po dmigs nas*, which appears to be a corruption. The Sanskrit text only has *raktarūpam ālambya*, which corresponds to *gzugs dmar po dmigs nas*. The *rnal 'byor* could be originally *rnal 'byor pa(s)*, the yogin being the subject of the sentence.

935. The Tibetan text has *ji srid 'tsho'i bar du mi 'bral lo*, corresponding to the Skt. *yāvajjīvaṃ na muñcati*, which Siklós (1996, 46) incorrectly translates as "She will not be

[§74] Alternatively, if he wishes to attract, he should make oblations of five nectars together with ghee in a fire of acacia wood 108 times in whosoever's name; as soon as [he does that, that person] will come to him instantly.

[§75] These rituals should be performed by a mantra master who has done the prior service (*kṛtapuraścaraṇa*). Otherwise, he will be everybody's object of ridicule, there is no doubt. He should not speak about the specifics of the tantra. He should not give the specific details [of the rituals] to anybody. If he does disclose the details, that person will achieve neither siddhi nor benefit. [The secrecy] is explained in other tantras. Just as the details ought to be performed, likewise they should not be recounted [to anybody]. Even the Buddha will not succeed if he discloses the details. That mantra master should not perform this repertoire of rituals[936] in front of anybody. He should not do them with anybody. If the mantra master wants to perform the ritual, he should do it only by himself.[937] In that event, all the rituals performed by the mantra masters will be accomplished.

This is the sixth chapter, Prescriptions for the Rule of *Homa*, in this [yoga] tantra of the venerable Great Vajrabhairava, [which is a part of the tantra] called the *Śrīmañjuśriya* [*Tantra*].

---

parted from him as long as she lives." The verb *muñcati* typically refers to the release from the magical karma.

936. *Akṣobhya (p. 386): "**Repertoire** (*prasara*) [means] various kinds of ritual methods. As for other [rituals], because here I have explained everything in a condensed manner, you should look to the affiliated tantras [for details]" (*rgya chen po zhes bya ba ni las kyi rnam grangs mang po ste/ gzhan ni 'dir ni rab tu bsdus pas/ rgyud gzhan la ltos pa'i phyir ro*).

937. *Akṣobhya (p. 386): "**He should do** [the *homa*] **only by himself** [means] because it is difficult to find a friend who is concordant with a sādhaka and because one should not associate with ignorant people, it is easier to do the practice by oneself. As it is said, 'Just like a lonely chief elephant who protects against fears and acts by himself'" (*bdag nyid gcig pu bya ba yin/ zhes bya ba ni rjes su mthun pa'i grogs rnyed par dka' ba'i phyir te/ byis pas grogs su mi 'gyur phyir/ gcig pu spyod pa byed sla bas/ ma tang dgon pa'i glang po bzhin/ sems khral bskyangs te gcig pur spyad/ ces gsungs pa lta bu'o*). Here, a comparison is established between a lonely sādhaka and a *nirviśaṅkasiṃha*—normally a lion, but here assuming the form of an elephant.

7. Accomplishing Siddhi through Visualization and "Testing the Disciple"[938]

Now, I will explain, according to the precepts, the ritual of visualization. Through visualization and mantra, he accomplishes all rituals.

[§76] This is the ritual procedure. First [of all], having established himself in union with the Buffalo-Faced One, the yogin who has done the purification of the mantra can perform all the rituals. Having [first] visualized a fire maṇḍala transformed from the syllable *raṃ*, blazing brightly, he should visualize above that a target who is naked, with disheveled hair, and confused. Many wrathful forms emerge from his own body in the space in front. He should imagine [the target] is stabbed[939] by the wrathful ones, [and he should visualize them] drinking the [target's] blood. He should imagine [them] eating the target's flesh and pulling out [the target's] entrails. He should also imagine the wrathful ones like this.[940] "Strike, strike, kill, kill [anyone] who harms the Three Jewels, who harms the teacher." By this meditation procedure alone, within seven days, even Vajradhara [that is, Indra] will die, to say nothing of an ordinary person.[941]

938. *Śoṇaśrī (p. 407) and *Vajrasiddha (pp. 426–27) give a brief rationale for the appearance of the seventh chapter: "When the mantrin becomes fatigued with meditation and recitation of the mantra, for the benefit of the mantrin, the seventh chapter was taught by the Omniscient One" (*gang gi tshe sngags pas bsam gtan sngags bzlas byas pas dub pa na/ de la phan phyir kun mkhyen gyis/ rtog pa bdun pa bstan pa'o*). A similar explanation is given by *Kṛṣṇācārya (p. 461).

939. The Tibetan text (Siklós 1996, 108) mentions the knife (*ral gri*), but that is missing in Sanskrit.

940. The Tibetan text (Siklós 1996, 46) reads, "One should say this" (*'di skad smra bar bya ste*).

941. *Śoṇaśrī (p. 408) and *Vajrasiddha (p. 427) give the following exegesis on this procedure, which describes the practice of taking over another person's body (*parakāyapraveśa*). This technique is also taught in the last chapter of the *Raktayamāri Tantra* and in Śrīdhara's *Sahajālokapañjikā*. I thank P. D. Szántó for this information. "The passage

[§77] Then another procedure of visualization is set forth. [The mantra master], who through entering [into meditative equipoise] remains in union[942] with the Buffalo-Faced One, can accomplish all rituals. Having visualized the target, crying in the middle of the fire maṇḍala, he should imagine many demons in front of him. The demons howl. [The mantra master] should visualize [them] violently breaking [the target's body], devouring [it],[943] and drinking [the target's] blood. He should imagine that different birds, [like] vultures, crows, and owls, [as well as] dogs and jackals devour [the target] and drink [his] blood. Through this procedure [the target] will die, there is no doubt about it.

[Alternatively], he can attract [a person] who is a hundred *yojana*s away.[944]

---

beginning with 'next' is easy to understand. The distinction is this: if the mantrin wishes to kill, having visualized himself in union with Vajrabhairava, he should visualize the emanation body (*nirmāṇakāya*) of himself surrounded by many *krodha* beings that have arisen from the seed syllable located in the sun of his own heart. This [entity, i.e., the *nirmāṇakāya* of himself] goes out to the heart of the target and sets up residence in the heart of the target. [As] the deities preside over him, he should offer a proper deity worship and make a request. As for this aspect, it should be performed exactly like this: '[This person I have possessed] would certainly go to the hells maintaining these evil deeds, and I will make him renounce it and you [*krodha* deities] go away!' For that reason, with [the ritual of] protection, he attracts the deities back to his own place, and he offers worship and so on. Those deities who enter via the mouth and are joined with the seed of the heart, once they have been properly worshiped should be made to leave. Then those protective deities are taken by the *krodha*s, and they go to the sky" (*de la zhes bya ba la sogs pa go sla'o/ bye brag ni 'di kho na ste/ gal te sngags pas gsod par byed na/ rang nyid rdo rje 'jigs byed rnal 'byor du dmigs nas/ rang gi snying gar nyi ma la gnas pa'i sa bon las nges par 'byung ba'i khro bo'i tshogs du mas bskor ba'i sprul pa'i gzugs kyis song nas/ bsgrub bya'i snying gar song ste/ bsgrub bya'i snying gar bzhugs nas/ de byin gyis rlob par byed pa'o/ lha legs par mchod de gsol ba gdab par bya'o/ 'di ni rnam pa 'di lta bu'i las bgyid pa/ nges pa kho nar dmyal bar 'chi ba lags kyis/ de bas 'di yongs su bor la khyed cag gshegs shig/ des na de dag bsrung ba dang bcas pa rang gi gnas su bkug nas mchod yon la sogs pa phul la/ rang gi zhal gyi lam nas bcug la snying ga'i sa bon gyis sbyar ba dang legs par mnyes par byas la gzhag par bya'o/ bsrung ba'i lha rnams ni khro bo rnams kyis khyer te nam mkha' la gshegs so*, *Vajrasiddha (*Śoṇaśrī is less precise: *bsrung ba'i lha bzung nas nam mkha' la dong ngo*).

942. The Tibetan text (Siklós 1996, 108) reads instead "established in divine pride by means of union with the Buffalo-Faced One" (*ma he'i gdong pa'i sbyor bas nga rgyal la gnas te*).

943. The Tibetan text (Siklós 1996, 108) reads, "devouring the flesh [of the target] violently" (*shin tu gtum par sha za ba*).

944. *Akṣobhya glosses (p. 386) "**a hundred *yojana*s**" as follows: "Child-like practitioners [i.e., beginners] are discouraged with respect to something that lies far away, when they think 'It is difficult to obtain'" (*dpag tshad brgya zhes bya ba ni byis pa lta bu'i sgrub pa po rnams ring bar gnas pa la re ba chad pas sgrub par dka' mod kyi zhes pa'o*). *Śoṇaśrī (p.

[The mantra master] should begin this visualization procedure, after having taken [a desired person] as the object [of the visualization]. [This procedure] should be done by a mantra master with his visualization stabilized.

[§78] Now, if he wishes to incite hostility, [the mantra master] should think of one target in the heart of the buffalo, and he should think of the other target in the heart of the horse. He should contemplate the fight [ensuing] between the two, the buffalo and the horse, until the buffalo and horse are reduced to powder. Then he should meditate those fearless targets[945] are picking a fight. By this mere visualization, within seven days, he will inevitably cause a fight, and not otherwise.

[§79] Or else, if he wishes to drive away, he should think about a camel generated from the syllable *yaṃ*. Having visualized on its back a wind maṇḍala in the shape of a crescent moon generated from the syllable *yaṃ*, he should visualize the target standing on top of it. Having established himself in union with the Buffalo[-Faced One], the mantra master sends off the camel, which is facing the southern direction. On the camel's back, he should visualize the form of Yama with disheveled hair and holding a stick. He should visualize the mantra being recited by Yama together with [the target's] name. By this mere visualization, the yogin will drive away even Vajradhara [that is, Indra] within seven days.[946]

[§80] Or else, there is [this] visualization procedure. [The mantra master] thinks of the target standing on the back of a crow or a vulture. Imagining the target with his hair disheveled and naked, he visualizes Yama on the target's back. He imagines him [Yama] as being commanded by the Buffalo-Faced One, as holding a hammer, as grasping the target's hair, as facing south, and as

408) and *Vajrasiddha (p. 427) give the following exegesis: "Then he sees the target's body empty, and he should do the following—that is, 'even if a person were at a distance of one hundred *yojanas*, he is also seized.' 'He becomes acquainted with his age, complexion, features, bodily form, name' is connected with '**He should begin this visualization procedure** [of the target]'" (*de nas bsgrub bya'i lus stong par bltas la las de dag bya'o/ dpag tshad brgyar gnas pa'i skyes bu yang bzung ste zhes pa ni/ na tshod dang mdog dang mtshan ma dang/ gzugs dang ming rnams shes par byas la/ bsam gtan brtsam mo zhes bya bar 'brel to*).

945. The Tibetan text (Siklós 1996, 109) mentions *bsgrub bya*, but Siklós (47) omits the translation. This changes the meaning of the sentence: "He thinks that the two hate each other."

946. For the parallel "camel recipes," see *Yogaratnamālā* I.11.34, *Kakṣapuṭa* 9.23, *Saṃvarodaya* 10.54–55, and Wenta 2024.

going away. The yogin, with concentrated mind, will drive away [the target] within seven days.

[§81] Next, if he wishes to attract, he should visualize a wind disc transformed from the syllable *yaṃ* and, above that, a moon disc arisen from the letter *a*.[947] Above that he visualizes the form of Yama[948] that holds a hook[949] in his hand.[950] While remaining in the state of union with the Buffalo-Faced One,[951] by his command he should give the [following] order: "Go, you whose form is death, to such and such place and summon such and such female [target] quickly." Having thus commanded, having sent him, he should visualize [Yama] dispatched by the syllable *jaḥ*.[952] Remaining in this meditation, the mantra master, having lured any woman anywhere in the three worlds,[953] should enjoy her. This procedure is to be done for as long as the mantra master

947. *Akṣobhya (p. 386): "**A moon disc arisen from the letter *a*** [means a disc] that is similar to the color of a coral" (*a las sgrub pa'i zla ba'i dkyil 'khor zhes bya ba ni byi ru'i mdog 'dra bar ro*).

948. *Śoṇaśrī (p. 408) and *Vajrasiddha (p. 427): "**The form of Yama** [means] having the form of Lotus Yamāntaka with one face and two arms" (*gshin rje gzugs can zhes bya ba ni pad ma gshin rje gshed kyi gzugs zhal gcig pa phyag gnyis pa'o*).

949. The Tibetan text (Siklós 1996, 110) mentions a form of Yama holding a hook and a noose in his hands (*gshin rje'i gzugs lcags kyu dang zhags pa lag tu thogs pa*). The same is supported by the Beijing ms. and commentaries of *Śoṇaśrī and *Vajrasiddha (see below). A thematically similar visualization of Yamāntaka endowed only with a vajra hook (*vajrankuśa*) is found in GS 14.37–38 (Fremantle 1971, 308), and it is connected to the Mañjuvajra: *sarvākāravaropetaṃ mañjuvajraṃ vibhāvayet/ yamāntakaṃ mahākrodhaṃ vajrāṅkuśaṃ vicintayet/ kalpoddāhamahācakraṃ dhyātvā yakṣīṃs tu bhuñjayet* [*sādhayet*, Matsunaga 1978, 66]//, "One should visualize Mañjuvajra, having all divine aspects, and visualize the great wrathful one, Yamāntaka, the vajra hook. Then, having visualized the great circle of blazing fire [at the end] of the eon, one should enjoy a *yakṣa* maiden."

950. *Śoṇaśrī (p. 408) and *Vajrasiddha (p. 427): "**Holds a hook** and a noose **in his hands** [means] he holds a hook and a noose" (*lag na lcags kyu dang zhags pa 'dzin pa zhes bya ba ni lcags kyu zhags pa 'dzin pa'o*).

951. *Śoṇaśrī (p. 408) and *Vajrasiddha (p. 427): "**In union with the Buffalo-Faced One** [means] because the yogin has the face of the buffalo" (*ma he'i gdong gi sbyor ba zhes pa ni ma he'i zhal gyi rnal 'byor dang ldan pas so*).

952. The Tibetan text (Siklós 1996, 110) reads, "He should visualize [Yama] setting off in the form of syllable *yaṃ*" (*yaṃ gyi rnam par bskyod de song bar rnam par bsam par bya'o*).

953. *Akṣobhya (p. 386): "**Three worlds** [means] underworld (*pātāla*), earth, and heaven" (*sa gsum zhes bya ba ni sa 'og dang sa yul dang sa bla'o*).

remains firm in his meditation; otherwise, it should not be done under any circumstances.[954] [So] it is said.

[§82] Next is declared the meditation procedure for resurrecting a person who has been fatally bitten by a snake.[955] Having visualized an eight-petal lotus,[956] white in color, in his own heart,[957] he should visualize the third vowel[958] (*i*) above it, and on the eight petals, eight white *phaṭ*s. By this he should also

954. The Tibetan text (Siklós 1996, 110) reads *ji ltar bsam pa brtan par gyur na 'di'i rab tu sbyor bas de dag bya'i gzhan gyis mi bya'o*, "In this way, if his thoughts are firm, this ritual can be executed. In other circumstances, it should not be done." Siklós's translation (47) reads, "If his thoughts are firm, through these practices he can do these things."

955. Mss. A and B contain another sentence: "First is declared a wind disc presided over the syllable *yaṃ*," which appears to be there mistakenly, for it features neither in the parallel passage found in the Beijing ms., in the *Saṃpuṭodbhava*, nor in the Tibetan version of the tantra. This passage belongs to the procedure described in §79.

956. *Śoṇaśrī (pp. 408–9) and *Vajrasiddha (pp. 427–28): "**Eight-petal lotus** [means] white" (*pad ma 'dab ma brgyad pa zhes bya ba ni dkar po'o*). Then, a further exegetical portion follows: "On the calyx, he visualizes the seed syllable *hrīḥ* trickling the nectar. On the eight petals [he should visualize] eight white *i* [syllables]. 'On the head, from [the letter] *a*,' is connected with 'from the letter *a*, which abides in the moon disc transformed from the letter *a*'" (*de'i ze 'bru hrīḥ yi sa bon bdud rtsi 'dzag pa'o/ de'i 'dab ma brgyad la i dkar po brgyad do/ spyi bor a las bya ba ni yi ge a yongs su gyur pa las zla ba'i dkyil 'khor la gnas pa'i yi ge a las bya bar 'brel to*). *Kṛṣṇācārya (p. 463): "On the **eight-petal lotus** [means] eight *a* [letters]" (*pad ma'i 'dab ma brgyad la a brgyad*). Lalitavajra (p. 336): "He visualizes an **eight-petal** [**lotus**] **in his heart** [means] a white lotus arising from the seed syllable *paṃ*" (*snying khar 'dab brgyad bsam zhes pa paṃ las byung ba'i chu skyes dkar po*)

957. *Kṛṣṇācārya (pp. 462–63): "**His own heart** [means] in the heart of Vajrabhairava, on the lotus arisen from [the seed syllable] *paṃ*, he should generate a *nāga* in the heart of the moon arisen from the letter *a*" (*rang gi snying ga zhes pa rdo rje 'jigs byed kyi snying gar paṃ las pad ma* [add. *la*] *a las zla ba'i khar klu bskyed la*). Lalitavajra (p. 336): "**His own heart** [means] even Yama is visualized as white" (*rang snying zhes pa 'ang gshin rje de dkar pos bsams pa*).

958. Lalitavajra (p. 336): "**The third vowel** [means] *i*" (*dbyangs yig gsum pa ni i ste*).

visualize himself having the form of the *nāga* king Śeṣa, white[959] in color.[960]

959. *Akṣobhya (pp. 386–87): "**The white form of a *nāga* king Śeṣa** [means] this is the mudrā of the great *nāga* king Sāgara, who removes all poisons. Having visualized himself as white and peaceful, [the sādhaka] should generate in his heart a white lotus with eight petals that has arisen from a white seed syllable *vaṃ*. From the calyx [of that lotus] arises a white letter *i*, and from that [letter arises] a white emerald. All this transforms, and from that [transformation] arise two white snakes whose tails are intertwined. They rise upward, their mouths open wide. They rear up threateningly, each focused intently on the other's eye. On the top of their tails, he should visualize a vajra with three prongs on each end, and in both of their mouths abides [something] similar to the fruit of an egg-born. The snakes glare at one another, flicking their tongues. On their heads, he should visualize a flaming jewel that looks like the letter *hi*; he should visualize it dripping [nectar]. Then he should place the heads of those two snakes on the top of the target's head; the jewel of the letter *i* and the tears-like nectar [from the snake's eyes] sprinkle water (*abhiṣeka*) from the crown [of the target's head]. Whatever is stated in the text will happen to the target.

Moreover, he should interlace [the fingers of] his two hands and join the thumbs to the little fingers of the opposing hand, while fashioning the remaining fingers into the sign of a vajra, making each look like the hood of a snake; this is purification. *Namo vajrapāṇi oṃ hūṃ phaṭ svāhā*: with these words, he does the *adhiṣṭhāna* empowerment. If he shows it to a snake, he will overcome its poison without hindrance, even in the case of invisible poisonous snakes. He also makes *bali* offerings made of the three sweets to the deity with the mudrā. This is my own excursory explanation, and it is not something that is done for the ritual [of the VBhT discussed] here" (*des klu lhag ma can gyi gzugs dkar po zhes bya ba ni 'di klu'i rgyal po rgya mtsho chen po'i phyag rgya/ dug thams cad sel ba ste/ bdag nyid kha dog dkar po zhi bar bsams pa'i snying gar vaṃ gyi yi ge dkar po las 'byung ba'i pad ma dkar po 'dab ma brgyad pa bskyed la de'i lte bar yi ge i dkar po'o/ de las nor bu mrka ta dkar po ste/ de yongs su gyur pa las ni/ sbrul dkar po gnyis phan tshun mjug ma 'brel cing langs pa bsgyings te/ mig rtsa bsgrims nas gcig la gcig bsdigs pa ltar 'dug pa'i bar mjug ma'i steng nas rtse mo gsum gsum pa'i rdo rje kha gnyis la* [em. *pa*, ed.] *sgong skyes nas 'bras 'dra ba gnas pa/ gcig la gcig blta zhing lce 'byin pa/ gnyis ka'i mgo la yi ge hi lta bu'i nor bu 'od 'bar ba 'dzag par bsams te/ de nas de gnyis kyi mgo bsgrub bya'i mgo'i steng du gnas par bya ste/ nor bu'i yi ge i dang/ mchi ma'i bdud rtsis spyi bo nas dbang bskur nas ji skad gsung ba der 'gyur ro/ gzhan lag ngar gnyis phan tshun bsnol te/ dkris la lag pa gnyis kyi mthe bong mthe'u chung rnams lu gu rgyud du sbrel nas/ sor mo lhag ma rnams rdo rje'i mtshan nyid las sprul mgo gdengs ka ltar byas te/ nas re re tsam du bar dag byas pa 'di/ na mo badz ra pa ni/ oṃ hūṃ phaṭ swā hā/ zhes bya bas byin gyis brlabs te/ sbrul can la bstan na thogs pa med par de'i dug 'joms te/ mi snang ba'i klu dug can rnams kyang ngo/ mngar sna gsum gyi gtor ma yang phyag rgyas* [em. *phyag rgya'i*, ed.] *lha la dbul lo/ 'di ni bdag gi zhar la bshad pa yin gyi/ gnas skabs kyi bya ba ni ma yin no*).

960. The Tibetan text (Siklós 1996, 110) has a slightly different reading: *de yis i 'og gi klu'i gzugs rnam par bsam par bya ste*, "By this, one should visualize the form of a snake beneath." The Sanskrit versions, both in the *Saṃpuṭodbhava* (7.4.126, ed., p. 352) and the VBhT, mention that the mantra master should imagine himself as a snake (*ātmānaṃ ca śeṣanāgarūpaṃ* [. . .] *cintayet*), but this is missing in the Tibetan version, which has the word "beneath" instead.

He should imagine him emitting a flood of nectar through the letter *i* upon his head.[961] Having caused that nectar to go out from the eyes of that snake, he should visualize it falling down onto the body of that target. Through this meditation procedure, he makes poison free of poison, even if it is a poison that fills the universe,[962] even were he to swallow that poison a thousand times.

[§83] Next [is given] the meditation procedure for getting a woman sexually aroused from a distance.[963] Having visualized the target in front of him, he

961. *Kṛṣṇācārya (p. 463): "**The letter *i* upon his head** [means] with the light of that [letter *i*], he [the snake-practitioner] absorbs the nectar of all the buddhas, and it descends into the heart. Having merged into the snake, it also descends into the body of the target, and he imagines that the disease becomes pacified" (*klu'i mgo bo la i/ de'i 'od zer gyis sangs rgyas thams cad kyi bdud rtsi blangs la snying gar dbab/ klu la thim nas yang bsgrub bya'i lus la dbab cing nad zhi bar bsam mo*).

962. The parallel passage in the *Saṃpuṭodbhava* (7.4.126, ed., p. 352) reads *atha kāladaṣṭotthāpane hṛdaye padmam aṣṭadalaṃ cintayet/ tadupari tṛtīyasvaraṃ pattrāṣṭake sitavarṇaṃ vicintayet/ ātmānaṃ ca śeṣanāgarūpaṃ sitavarṇam ikārāmṛtasravantaṃ cintayet/ tasya nāgākṣibhyām amṛtaṃ niścārya tasmin sādhyaśarīre nipatantaṃ cintayet/ anena dhyānayogena traidhātukaparipūrṇaṃ viṣaṃ nirviṣaṃ karoti/*, "Next, in reviving one fatally bitten by a snake, he should visualize an eight-petal lotus in his heart. Above that, he should visualize the third vowel, white in color, on eight petals. He should meditate on himself as having the form of the *nāga* Śeṣa, white in color, emitting a flood of nectar from the letter *i*. Having caused the nectar to issue from the snake's eyes, he should imagine it falling down onto the body of the target. By this meditation procedure, he makes poison become free of poison, even if it is a poison that fills the three worlds." In comparing this passage to the one preserved in the VBhT, we notice that the eight *phaṭ* letters are missing in the *Saṃpuṭodbhava*, as is the mention of the head after "emitting the flood of nectar from the letter *i*."

963. Siklós (1996, 48) translates *de nas zhu ba'i bsam gtan gyi rab tu sbyor ba 'byung ste* as "Now the practice of the meditation of melting will be told," and he further explains in footnote 141 that this is a practice dealing with the activation of the crown *cakra*. However, this interpretation is incorrect, insofar as this meditation procedure is part of "love magic," intended to make a woman sexually excited; see page 175 above. *Kṛṣṇācārya (p. 463): "**Next, getting a woman sexually aroused** [means] it is a meditation on a target who becomes subject to one's power; this is easy to understand" (*de nas bzhu ba zhes pa dbang du gyur pa'i bsgrub bya la bsgom pa go sla'o*). *Kṛṣṇācārya proceeds to describe a different ritual to relieve physical fatigue. "This is the ritual that refreshes the fatigued body of the yogin. He assembles all the *cakra* deities. Having set them up in sequence, he then assembles Mañjuvajra having a face and body at [the yogin's] head. He visualizes the syllables in the abodes exactly as explained: at the navel, he visualizes a disc [transformed] from the [seed syllable] *vaṃ*, and at the head, [a disc] from [the seed syllable] *haṃ*. He should visualize that he has assembled [the deities] in the lower [parts of the body]. With wind, he kindles fire; with fire the water rises, and the earth becomes moist with warm steam. From [the seed syllable] *haṃ*, nectar trickles down and spreads throughout [his] body. He will

should visualize at her feet the bow-shaped[964] wind maṇḍala, gray in color and empowered by the syllable *yaṃ*.[965] Above that, in the region of the genitals,[966] he [should visualize] a three-cornered fire maṇḍala empowered by the syllable *ra* [fire] on top. Above that, in the heart, he should visualize the earth maṇḍala, which is yellow, square, and empowered by the syllable *laṃ*. Above that, on the forehead, he should visualize the moon maṇḍala. In the middle of that, he should visualize nectar flowing down with the letter *vaṃ*[967] [the water syllable]. Having carefully visualized in this manner, he should fan the fire with the wind, making it blaze up. [Then,] he imagines the earth maṇḍala is heated up by this fire. He visualizes that that nectar disc is melting from the heat of the earth maṇḍala. By this mere procedure, he causes the woman to become moist, making her drip like a sap-rich tree, and not otherwise.[968]

---

live for thousands of years. Moreover, he should know the instruction (*upadeśa*) that the seed syllable *dhīḥ* attracts the nectar of wisdom" *rnal 'byor pa'i* [em. *pas*, ed.] *lus dub gso ba'i cho ga ni 'khor lo'i lha thams cad bsdus la rim pas 'dus nas spyi bor 'jam pa'i rdo rje'i zhal dang lus su bsdus la/ gnas rnams su yi ge'i bshad pa ltar bsgom ste/ lte bar ni vaṃ las dkyil 'khor spyi bor haṃ las thur du 'dus pa can bsgoms la/ rlung gis me sbar/ mes chu bskol chus sa dros pa'i rlangs kyis haṃ las bdud rtsi babs pas lus rgyas par gyur nas lo stong 'tsho bar 'gyur ro/ de yang sa bon dhīḥ* [*sa* omit.] *ye shes kyi bdud rtsi dgug pa man ngag tu shes par bya'o*).
*Akṣobhya (p. 387): "**Getting a woman sexually aroused** [means] this is a practice of subjecting under one's own will. That woman will become enthralled as soon as her body drips wet with great desire. This happens in a manifest way as well" (*bzhu ba ni/ zhes bya ba ni chags pa chen pos lus bzhu ba tsam du gdungs par 'gyur ba'i dbang du bya ba'i sbyor ba'o/ de yang dngos su ni 'dzag pa nyid zhu'o*).

964. The representation of *dhanvākāra* as the letter *ya* belong to the early Gupta period. In the seventh century, the letter *ya* loses its bow shape. See, for example, Vasudeva 2007, 532.

965. The Tibetan text (Siklós 1996, 111) has a slightly different reading: *de'i rkang pa gnyis la yi ge yaṃ las gyur ba'i rlung gi dkyil 'khor bsam par bya*, "He should visualize the wind disc transformed from the seed syllable *yaṃ* at her feet."

966. Siklós (1996, 111) translates *gsang ba'i gnas su*, an equivalent of the Skt. *guhyapradeśe*, rather literally as "in a secret place," but it does not convey the meaning intended here—i.e., in the region of the genitals.

967. The Tibetan text (Siklós 1996, 111) reads: *de'i dbus su yi ge baṃ mgo thur du gnas pa* [. . .]. Although the syllable *vaṃ* is clearly stated in the above passage, Siklós (1996, 48) translates it as the syllable *paṃ*. The syllable *vaṃ* makes more sense here insofar as it is commonly regarded as a water syllable, from which nectar drops.

968. The *Saṃpuṭodbhava* (7.4.81, ed., p. 348) gives an abbreviated description of the same meditation procedure: *sādhyaṃ yāvad pādam ārabhya vidhinā dhūmraraktapītasitaṃ* [em. °*sita*, mss. R, K, P, ed.] *vāyavyādi yathākramam/ anena dhyānadṛṣṭamātreṇa striyaṃ drāvayati kṣīravṛkṣa iva nānyathā*, "[One should visualize] the target, beginning with the feet, in accordance with the ritual procedure: as gray, red, yellow, and white, according to the sequence of the sub-directions starting with northwest and so on. By this mere medi-

[§84] Next, to subject a king to his will and a royal minister to his will, the mantra master who desires that remains in meditative absorption with the Buffalo-Faced One. Having visualized himself as red in color, he enters the middle of the area where the target is.[969] Then, he should emit from his own body a form of Mañjuśrī, which is red and holds a goad and a noose.[970] With that Mañjuśrī, he visualizes that Mañjuśrī is bringing the target back, after having lassoed the target at his heart or neck. Then he should cause [the target] to enter Mañjuśrī. He should imagine that, having entered the body of Mañjuśrī, the target becomes confused.[971] Using this meditation procedure, he should imagine the ten-syllable mantra[972] in his [the target's] heart, red in color.[973] The *sādhaka*, further, taking on the form of knowledge [letters],[974] should enter those

---

tation that is practiced, a woman will melt like a sap-rich tree and not otherwise." The colors gray, red, yellow, and white correspond to the gross elements: gray is wind (*ya-bīja*), red is fire (*ra-bīja*), yellow is earth (*la-bīja*), and white is water (*va-bīja*). Since they occur just prior to the mention of the intermediate points of the compass (*vāyavyādi*), it is also possible that they stand for the main directions (i.e., north, south, west, and east based on the color or, based on the element, east, south, north, and west). These seed syllables with their corresponding colors are to be visualized on the target's body beginning with the feet (= wind, *ya-bīja*, gray), followed, in ascending sequence, by the genitals (= fire, *ra-bīja*, red), heart (= earth, *la-bīja*, yellow, according to the Tib. text) and lastly, forehead (= water, *va-bīja*, white).

969. The Tibetan text (Siklós 1996, 111) reads: *de nyid mdog dmar por bsams te/ bsgrub bya gang du gnas pa de'i steng du gnas la*, which Siklós (48) translates as "One thinks of himself as red. He should be above where the subject is [...]."

970. Tibetan text (Siklós 1996, 111) reads *phyi nas rang gi lus 'jam dpal mdog dmar po phyag na lcags kyu dang zhags pa can phyung ste*, which reflects the Skt. *paścāt svaśarīrād aṅkuśapāśahastaṃ raktavarṇaṃ mañjuśrīrūpaṃ niścārayet*, but Siklós (48) translates this sentence as "He arises as Mañjuśrī red in color holding a hook and a noose in his hands." Thus, Siklós's translation is inaccurate, for the passage mentions Mañjuśrī as an entity emitted from the mantrin's body and not, as Siklós thinks, arising as the mantrin.

971. *Akṣobhya (pp. 387–88): "**Confused** [means] the mind [of the target] becomes agitated by desire" (*myos pa zhes bya ba ni chags pas sems 'khrugs par gyur pa'o*).

972. *Akṣobhya (p. 388): "**The ten-syllable mantra** [means] it should be of red color" (*yi ge bcu pa'i gsang sngags zhes bya ba ni mdog dmar ba'o*). *Akṣobhya's explanation aligns with that of *Saṃpuṭodbhava* (7.4.119, ed., p. 351), which also refers to the ten-syllable mantra as being red in color; see note 977 below.

973. *Akṣobhya (p. 388): "**In his heart** [means] beginning with this, another practice is taught" (*de'i snying gar zhes bya ba la sogs pa ni sbyor ba gzhan ston te*).

974. *Akṣobhya (p. 388): "**The form of knowledge [letters]** [means] the mind of the target becomes the red letters" (*ye shes kyi yi ge'i gzugs zhes bya ba bsgrub bya'i sems yi ge dmar por* [em. *po*, ed.] *gyur pa'o*). Thus *Akṣobhya's commentary aligns with the

syllables.[975] He should [then] visualize the target being fused in oneness with them. By this meditation procedure, within seven days,[976] he brings under his power even a universal emperor as long as he lives, without doubt.[977]

Saṃpuṭodbhava's version, where it is a *sādhya*, and not a sādhaka, who assumes the form of knowledge and enters those letters: see note 977 below.

975. *Akṣobhya (p. 388): "**Should enter those syllables** [means] this has been elaborated by me [further below]; for that reason it is said 'He visualizes [the target] being fused in oneness'" (*yi ge de la gzhug ste zhes bya ba ni bdag gis spros pa la ste/ de'i phyir gcig tu 'dres par bsam mo zhes gsungs so*). *Akṣobhya (p. 388) then provides a further explanation: "What is taught here is that the yogin thinks of himself as being in union with the deity, and he visualizes himself as red in color. In the heart of that deity, he introduces the syllables and visualizes the red moon with red syllables surrounding it. Then he visualizes that he impels the mantra, and with *vajrajapa* [i.e., a special type of *japa* recitation coupled with breath regulation (*prāṇāyāma*), which is one of the *pañcakrama*s], he expels those syllables from the heart, and they shoot into the heart of the target. Moreover, the ten syllables become red in color and of the nature of the mind of that [target]. After that, those two become mixed [the mantra that he shoots out of his own heart and the consciousness of the target as the mantra], and then those two lines [the red-syllable mantras] in the heart melt into the red syllable, which is on the red moon. Because this yoga is the best there is, this procedure 'will within seven days bring the ruler under his power who will be subjugated as long as he lives'" (*di skad du bshad par 'gyur te/ bdag nyid kha dog dmar po lha nyid du 'ong ba'i rnal 'byor gsal bar bsams la/ de'i snying gar yi ge bcug par dmar po zla ba dmar pos bskor bar bsams la/ de nas sngags bskul bar mos pas rdo rje'i bzlas pa brjod pas/ yi ge de dag snying ga nas byung ste/ bsgrub bya'i snying gar gnas shing/ de yang de yi sems kyi rang bzhin yi ge bcu dmar po'i mdog tu gyur te/ yang de dag 'dres te/ slar thig de dag gi snying gar zla ba dmar po'i yi ge yang dmar po la bstim mo/ 'di lta bu'i rnal 'byor ni mchog yin pas na/ rnal 'byor 'di ni nyi ma bdun na 'khor los sgyur ba yang dbang du 'gyur te/ ji srid 'tsho'i bar du dbang du 'gyur ro zhes gsungs so*).

976. Tibetan text (Siklós 1996, 112) reads *bsam gtan 'di'i rab tu sbyor bas nyi ma bdun gyis*, but the mention of the seven-day time period is missing in Siklós's translation (48).

977. *Saṃpuṭodbhava* (7.4.119, ed., p. 351) has a parallel visualization procedure: *atha vaśīkartukāmenāśokāṣṭamyām aśokatalaṃ gatvā raktavastraṃ paridhāya sarvālaṅkārabhūṣito mantraṃ japet/ trimukhayoge sthitvā ātmānaṃ raktavarṇaṃ dhyātvā paścāt svaśarīrād dvibhujāṃ raktām aṅkuśapāśagṛhītahastāṃ niścārayet/ tena sādhyaṃ hṛdi viddhvā āniyantaṃ cintayet/ svaśarīre tāṃ devīṃ praveśayet/ sādhyaṃ vihvalībhūtam/ tasya hṛdaye daśākṣaramantraṃ nyased raktavarṇam/ punaḥ sādhyena jñānarūpeṇa teṣv akṣareṣu praveṣṭavyaṃ taiḥ sārdham ekalolībhūtaṃ cintayet/ anena dhyānayogena saptāhāc cakravartinam api vaśam ānayati yāvajjīvaṃ na saṃśayaḥ/*, "Next, if he wants to subject under his will, the one adorned with all the ornaments, having gone to the *aśoka* grove on the eighth *aśoka* asterism, puts on a red cloth and recites the mantra. While remaining in union with the three-faced one, having imagined himself as red in color, he then emits from his own body the two-armed [goddess], red in color, holding a goad and a noose in her hands. With that [goad], having hooked the target at his heart, he thinks that she brings the target back. He causes the goddess to enter back into his own body. The tar-

[§85] The ritual procedure [of the VBhT] should be carried out by a mantra master with perfectly concentrated mind and with his visualization steady.[978] The mantra[979] must never be given to anyone. The visualization for identification with the venerable Great Vajrabhairava [too] should not be given to anyone, nor should it be spoken of. The mantra should not be revealed. He should not unroll the painting in front of anybody. He should always keep the painting concealed. Let him neither recite the procedure for this mantra in the presence of anybody[980] nor perform a fire offering.[981] If he does tell, then by the command of Vajrabhairava, he will be devoured by the yoginīs or by the

---

get becomes confused. He ritually places the ten-syllable mantra, red in color, in his heart. Further, the target (*sādhya*), taking on the form of knowledge, should enter those syllables. He should imagine [the target] being fused in oneness with them. By this meditation procedure, within seven days, he brings under his power even the universal emperor as long as he lives, without doubt."

When compared with the passage in the VBhT, we notice important divergences. First, the beginning of the meditation procedure has some preliminaries that are missing in the VBhT. Second, the deity emitted from the practitioner's body that catches the target is referred to as the goddess, although her description matches the one of Mañjuśrī. Third, the ten-syllable mantra is referred to as red in color, while in the VBhT this description defines the form of knowledge. Fourth, the passage of the *Saṃpuṭodbhava* has a target (*sādhya*) after *paścāt*, while the VBhT (both in Skt. and Tib. recensions) has a practitioner (*sādhaka*). This completely changes the meaning of a person who assumes the form of knowledge. Fifth, the *Saṃpuṭodbhava* has *taiḥ sārdhaṃ ekalolībhūtaṃ cintayet*, while the VBhT, in both Skt. and Tib. recensions, has *taiḥ sādhyaṃ ekalolībhūtaṃ vicintayet*. A parallel recipe is also found in the *Yogaratnamālā* 2.34 (Tripathi and Negi 2006, 26).

978. *Akṣobhya (p. 388): "Because these procedures do not succeed if one is not in *dhyāna*, the root text says, 'The mantra master should be in a perfectly concentrated state and with his visualization steady'" (*las de dag ni bsam gtan ma yin pas 'grub par mi 'gyur bas na/ sngags pa shin tu mnyam gzhag cing/ bsam gtan la ni brtan par bya/ zhes gsungs so*).

979. The Tibetan text (Siklós 1996, 112) has *tantra* instead of *mantra* and one additional sentence missing in the Sanskrit: "He must not show the spell either" (Siklós 1996, 48). This reading is supported by *Akṣobhya's commentary (p. 388), which glosses *tantra* as: "The entire *kalpa* [i.e., *Saptakalpa*, the VBhT in seven chapters] is secret. Ultimately, even giving out parts of it is forbidden" (*rgyud ces bya ba ni rtog pa rdzogs pa gsang ba'o/ lhag ma rnams ni phyogs 'ga' zhig sbyin pa yang dgag pa'o*). *Akṣobhya (p. 388) glosses "He should not show even the mantra" and "This applies even to the written mantra" (*sngags kyang mi* [add. *mi*] *bstan par bya'o zhes bya ba ni yi ger bris pa tsam yang ngo*).

980. The Tibetan text (Siklós 1996, 112) has a slightly different reading: *rgyud 'di'i rab tu sbyor ba dang/ blzas pa dang smra ba gzhan su la 'ga' tsam yang mi smra*, which Siklós (48) translates as, "He must not speak of the practices nor the recitations, nor must he read this *tantra* aloud, even to a few people."

981. This phrase is missing in the Tibetan edition by Siklós.

[ḍākinīs][982] as the one who has broken the vows.[983] Therefore the mantra master should not give it to anybody.

[§86] Rather, [the person to whom] it may be given[984] is one who does not transgress the pledges, who is free of doubt, who is firm in his vow, who is brave, who is devoted to his teacher,[985] who knows how to behave properly,[986] who is completely committed to the teaching of the Tathāgata, who conceals his mantra,[987] who is not given to anger, who is compassionate, who is intent on recitation (*japa*) and visualization (*dhyāna*), and who is not overly timid.[988] To the disciple who is distinguished by such qualities, who has been shown the

982. The Tibetan text (Siklós 1996, 112) has a different reading: *gal te smras na dpal rdo rje 'jigs byed dang/ gzhan yang rnal 'byor ma rnams dang mkha' 'gro ma rnams kyis za'o.* The Sanskrit text before emendation has *yadi brūyāt śrīmahāvajrabhairavādyābhiḥ yoginībhir vā bhakṣayet*, "If he does tell, he will be devoured by Vajrabhairava as the first or by the yoginīs," which does not make much sense insofar as the yoginīs and the ḍākinīs commonly appear in tantric texts in the context of a punishment that awaits the sādhaka for the transgression of the vows. In this regard, it is very unusual to find the main deity devouring the sādhaka, and for that reason, it is likely that a corruption has occurred here (I thank Alexis Sanderson for this explanation). Further, the appearance of *vā* connecting two nouns suggests that ḍākinīs did originally feature in the Sanskrit recension. This reading is supported by *Akṣobhya's commentary (p. 388), which glosses both yoginīs and ḍākinīs: "**Devoured by the yoginīs** [means] these are *sahaja* yoginīs who number twenty-five thousand" (*rnal 'byor mas bza'o* [em. *rnal 'byor ma bzang*, ed.] *zhes bya ba ni lhan cig skyes pa'i rnal 'byor ma stong phrag nyi shu rtsa lnga'o*); (p. 388): "**Ḍākinīs** [means] *kṣetrapālas* and so on" (*mkha' 'gro ma zhes bya ba ni zhing srung ba la sogs pa'o*).

983. The Tibetan text (Siklós 1996, 112) reads *dam tshig nyams par 'gyur bas*, which Siklós (48) translates as "since the pledges become spoilt," but this phrase actually reflects the Skt. *samayadrohīn*, "the one who has broken the vows," and forms a logical unit with the previous sentence (and not with the next sentence, as Siklós suggests), where the dire consequences for those who have transgressed the vows of secrecy are spelled out.

984. This sentence, which introduces the description of an ideal recipient—i.e., a disciple—is missing in the Tibetan edition by Siklós (1996, 112).

985. The Tibetan text (Siklós 1996, 112) reads *dpa' bo bla ma*, "heroic master," but the Sanskrit recension only has "guru."

986. The qualification of an ideal disciple as *vinītas*, "disciplined," features also in the Tibetan text (Siklós 1996, 112) as *dul ba can*, but Siklós (48–49) leaves it untranslated.

987. The Tibetan text (Siklós 1996, 112) has *rgyud sbas pa*—i.e., "He conceals the *tantra*" instead of *mantra*.

988. The Tibetan text (Siklós 1996, 113) reads *rnam par smin pa la 'dzem pa*, which Siklós (49) translates as "who shrinks from actions leading to rebirth." The Sanskrit recension only has *abhīruḥ*, which does not connote such a technical meaning.

maṇḍala,[989] who is firmly devoted to Great Vajrabhairava and whose mind is moist with great compassion,[990] free of distinction, and devoted to his guru, one whose qualities have been thoroughly tested[991] and who is well regarded by [his] teacher—to such a pupil the tantra of Great Vajrabhairava may be given. If the mantra master gives it otherwise, then he will go to hell along with his disciple. There is no doubt [about it. The one who breaks this rule] also experiences great disasters in this world, and after death, he goes straight to hell, because he is the one who has broken the pledges.[992]

989. The Tibetan text (Siklós 1996, 113) reads *dkyil 'khor dam pa dpal rdo rje 'jigs byed chen po la mchog tu gus pa*, which partially reflects the Skt. *dṛṣṭamaṇḍalāya śrīmahāvajrabhairavasya dṛḍhabhaktāya*.

990. "Mind moist with compassion" is a common phrase in Buddhist tantras: see, e.g., MMK 51.58cd; p. 556.

991. The Tibetan text (Siklós 1996, 113) reads *rab tu brtag pa la*, which Siklós (49) translates "the teachings"; this, however, reflects the Skt. *suparīkṣita*. "Testing the disciple" (*parīkṣā*) appears to be a common feature of the final sections of tantric texts, found also in Śaiva-Śākta tantras. See, for example, *Yoginīsaṃcāra* of the *Jayadrathayāmala* (*ṣaṭka* 3), 5.26cd–5.28cd: "This is the highest secret; it has to be concealed carefully. I have taught it to no one else in this world, especially to anyone who has any defects. It should be given to one who is completely devoted to the guru, who is in peace, who has been tested thoroughly. The sādhaka too should guard it, O empress of gods, with utmost care. If he does so, the siddhis will come about; otherwise he risks dying" *etad guhyaṃ paraṃ devi gopanīyaṃ* [em. *yopanīyaṃ*, ms.] *prayatnataḥ// na kasyacid ihākhyātaṃ dṛṣṭadoṣaviśeṣataḥ/ gurubhaktāya śāntāya* [corr. *śāntāyaṃ*, ms.] *samyakparīkṣitāya ca* [em. *te cod*, ed.]// *sādhākenāpi deveśi gopanīyaṃ prayatnataḥ/ pravartate siddhir eva anyathā prāṇasaṃśayaḥ//*. A similar example illustrating the relevance of *parīkṣā* in the tantric milieu is also attested in the Kaula text *Kaulajñānanirṇaya* attributed to Matsyendranātha, already referred to above, which describes both the type of pupils to whom one should never reveal the tantra and the characteristics of those who are suitable to receive the teachings (14.4cd–11; trans. by M. Magee in Bagchi 1986, 63–64).

992. The Tibetan text (Siklós 1996, 113) reads *dam tshig kyang nyams par 'gyur ro*, which Siklós (49) translates as "Even the pledges will be damaged"; however, the Sanskrit text has *samayabhedin*, "a person who has broken the vows." In the *Vīṇāśikha Tantra* (Goudriaan 1985, 318), the term *bhraṣṭa* appears in the context of a person who has given the tantra to the unqualified. The list includes those who obtained their mantras without initiation, atheists (*nāstikā*), revilers of the Vedas (*vedanindakāḥ*), those who have fallen from their vows and who spoil the tantras, those who are intent upon harming their gurus, and those who disturb the essence of the tantras. The gurus who give the tantra to such people are said by the yoginīs to be *bhraṣṭāḥ*, "those who have fallen [from the vows]" and the destroyers of the dharma. The term *vidhibhraṣṭa*, "one who has fallen from the rules," is known already in the Abhidharma literature for the one who has transgressed monastic instructions (see Vasubandhu's *Abhidharmakośabhāṣya* 4.94, in Pradhan 1975, 258). The MMK (4.17, p. 41, and 33.19, p. 264) says that those who

Here ends the seventh chapter, Accomplishing Siddhi through Visualization and "Testing [the Disciple]," in this yoga tantra of the Wheel of Great Vajrabhairava,[993] [which is a part of the tantra] called the [*Śrī*]*mañjuśriya* [*Tantra*].[994]

This completes the chapter on the means of achieving the siddhi of the Buffalo-Faced Venerable Great Vajrabhairava, the partial[995] chapter[996] that bestows siddhi merely by being recited (*paṭhitasiddhaḥ*),[997] which was extracted from the 100,000-line tantra of the Venerable Wheel of Great Vajrabhairava,[998]

---

fall from the rules will not succeed [in their practice] (*vidhibhraṣṭā na sidhyeyuḥ*), while in the *Guhyasiddhi* (8.47, p. 57), punishment awaits a person antagonistic toward the vows (*samayavidveṣacetasya*).

993. *Akṣobhya (pp. 388–89) glosses ***cakra*** as "maṇḍala and yantra, because here [in this tantra], they are the chief topic" (*'khor lo zhes bya ba ni dkyil 'khor dang 'khrul 'khor dag 'dir gtso bor gyur pas so*).

994. The Tibetan text (Siklós 1996, 113) reads *'di ni 'jam dpal 'jam dpa'i mchog/ dpal rdo rje 'jigs byed chen po'i rnal 'byor gyi rgyud las bsam gtan gyi las sgrub pa'i brtag pa'i rtog pa ste bdun pa'o*, which Siklós (49) translates as "This is the seventh chapter, on success in the rites of meditation, from the *yoga-tantra* of the glorious Mahābhairava, the highest manifestation of Mañjuśrī." In his translation, Siklós fails to translate *brtag pa*, which reflects the Skt. *parīkṣā*, "testing" [the disciple].

995. *Akṣobhya (p. 389): "**Partial** (*ekadeśa*) [means] a fragment of *upadeśa* extracted from the entire [teachings]" (*phyogs gcig pa zhes bya ba ni kun las btus pa'i man ngag gi phyogs gcig tu byas pa'o*).

996. *Akṣobhya (p. 389): "**Chapter** [means] collection of rituals" (*rtog pa zhes bya ba ni cho ga'i tshogs so*).

997. *Akṣobhya (p. 389): "**Bestows siddhi merely by being recited**: by *satpuruṣas*—i.e., holy beings" (*bklags pas 'grub pa zhes bya ba ni skyes bu dam pa rnams kyis so*). *Akṣobhya's commentary (p. 389) ends with the motivation for composing the work: "Ignorant fools say, 'This surely is the best,' but they do that without relying on the explanation of the guru. In doing so, they interpret the meaning of the tantra in a contrary way, and they delude childish people. I have written this, which clarifies this misinterpretation, for my students. This work contains extensive *prayoga*s, which are in concordance with the instructions (*upadeśa*) taught by my guru. Now, by this virtue, may the world become the Munīndra [the Buddha as Lord of Sages]. This is the *pañjikā* of the *Śrī Vajrabhairava Tantra* written by the *vajrācārya* *Akṣobhya, and it finishes now" (*bla ma mi bsten man ngag gtam bral bar/ mi mkhas dag ni nges par mchog yin zhes/ rgyud don log par 'chad cing byis pa bslu/ de dag bslu ba shes byed 'di byas slob ma'i phyir/ sbyor ba rgya chen ji skad bla mas smras pa bzhin/ 'on kyang dge 'dis 'gro ba thub pa'i dbang por gyur/ dpal rdo rje 'jigs byed kyi rgyud kyi dka' 'grel/ rdo rje slob dpon mi bskyod pas mdzad pa rdzogs so*).

998. The Tibetan text (Siklós 1996, 113) reflects the Sanskrit almost perfectly when it says *dpal rdo rje 'jigs byed chen po'i 'khor lo rgyud 'bum pa nas btus nas phyung ba rtog pa'i phyogs*

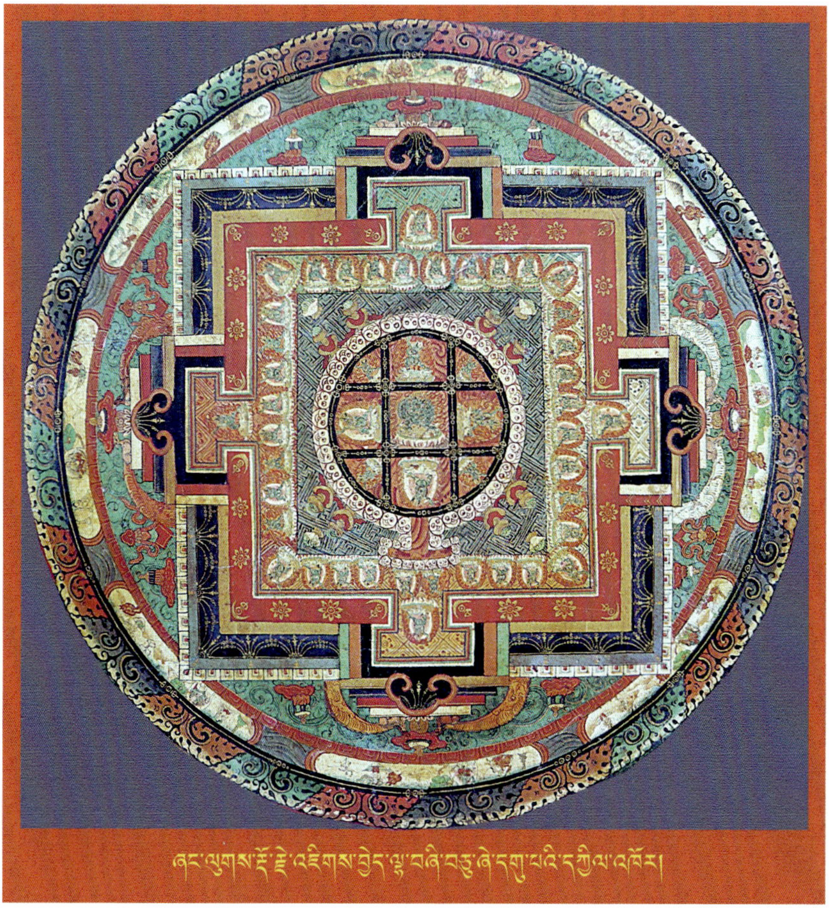

Plate 1. The maṇḍala of Forty-Nine Deity Vajrabhairava of the Zhang tradition.
See description in the appendix.

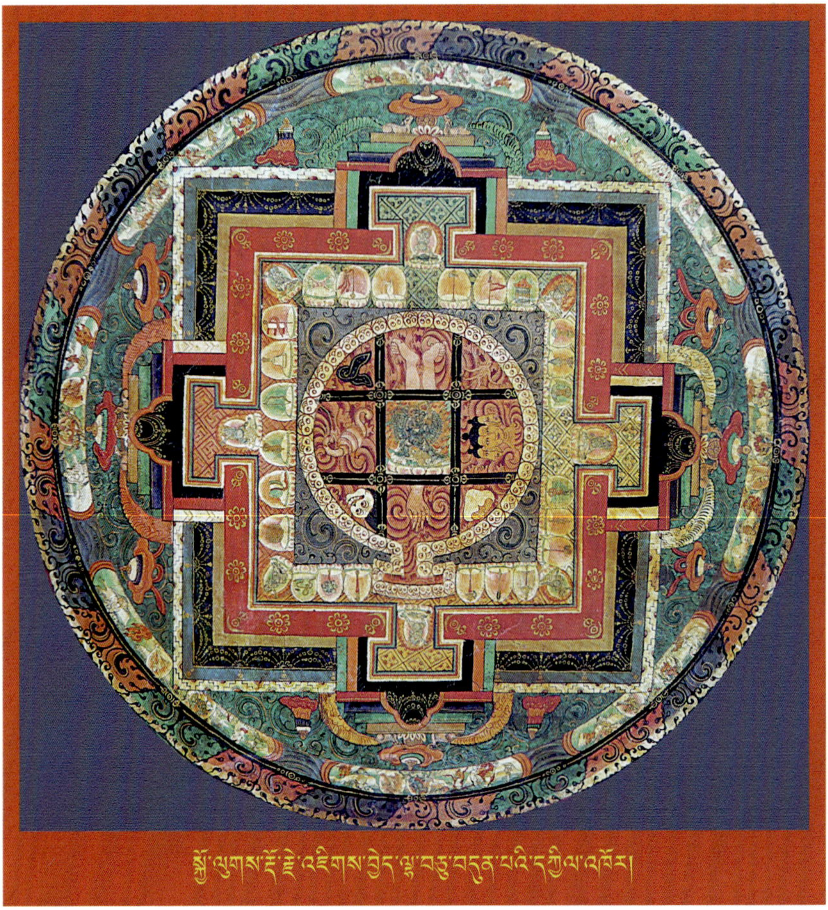

Plate 2. The maṇḍala of the Nine- or Seventeen-Deity Vajrabhairava of the Skyo tradition. See description in the appendix.

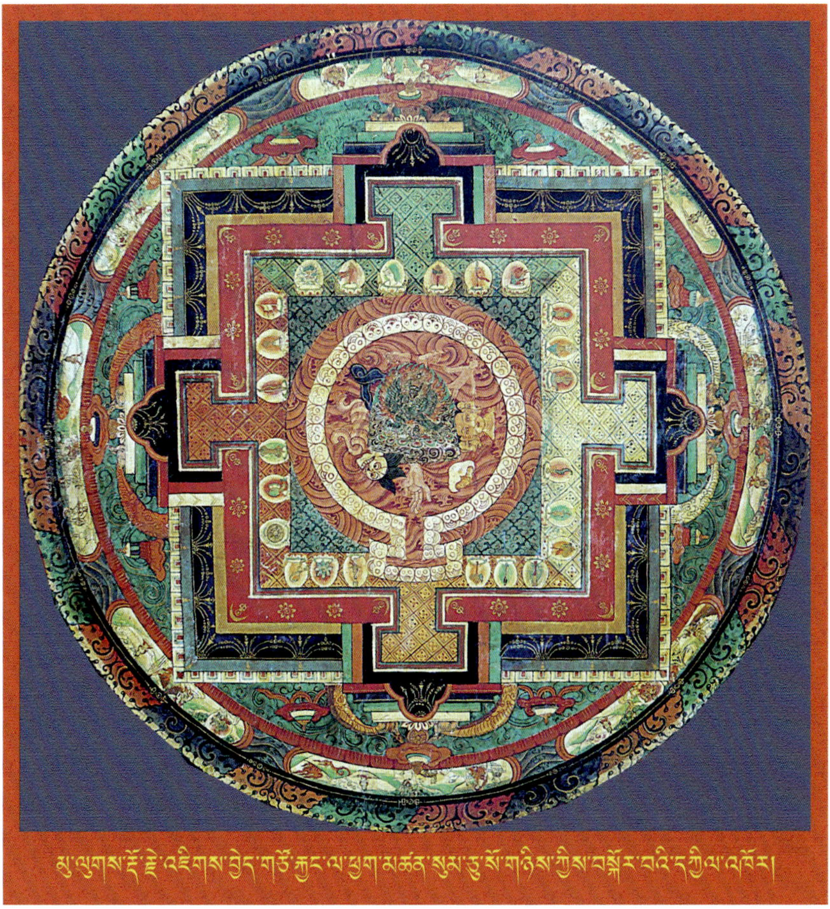

Plate 3. The maṇḍala of Vajrabhairava surrounded by eight zombies and thirty-two symbols according to the Rwa Tradition, transmitted to the Sa skya by Mal Lo tsā ba. See description in the appendix.

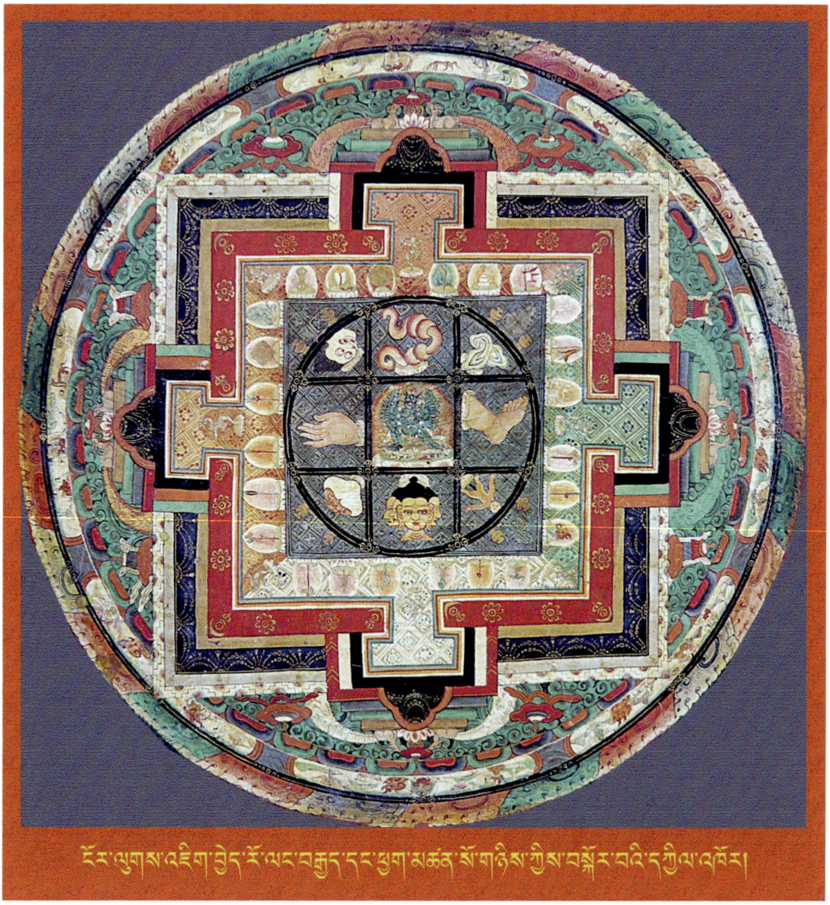

Plate 4. The maṇḍala of Vajrabhairava surrounded by eight zombies and thirty-two symbols according to the Sa skya Ngor tradition. See description in the appendix.

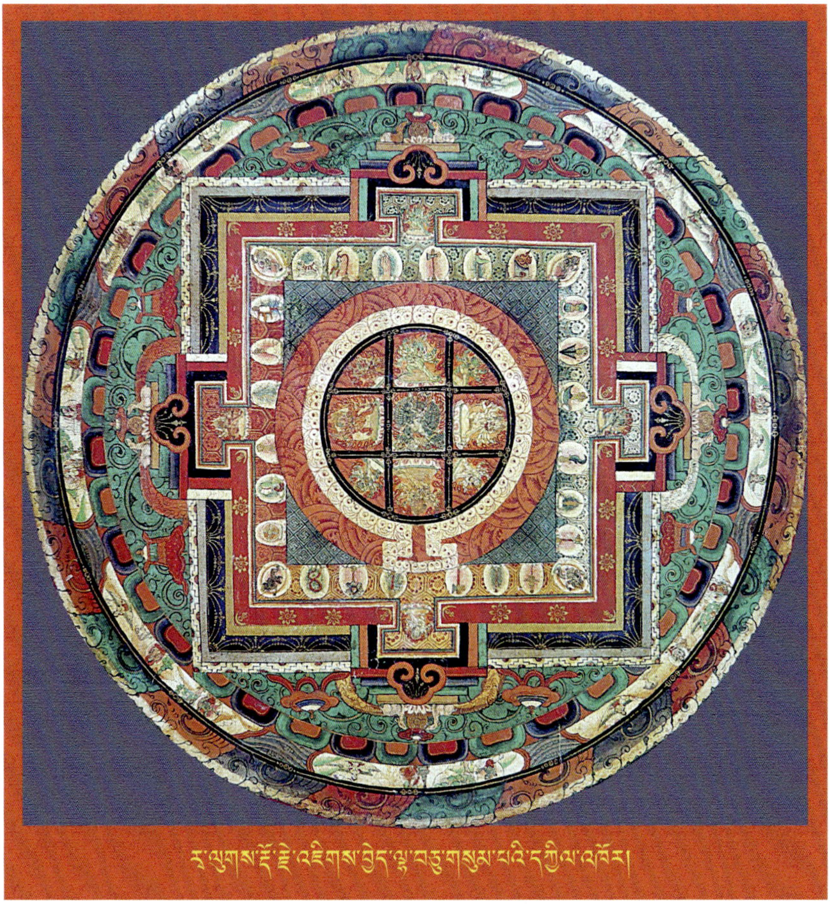

Plate 5. The maṇḍala of the Thirteen-Deity Vajrabhairava unique to the Rwa tradition.
See description in the appendix.

Plate 6. Forty-Nine-Deity Vajrabhairava *kesi*, Yuan dynasty, China, fourteenth century. Image provided by the Metropolitan Museum of Art, New York, Lila Acheson Wallace Gift, 1992.

Plate 7. Solitary Hero Vajrabhairava, mid-fifteenth century, Sa skya Monastery, Tibet.
From the Nasli and Alice Heeramaneck Collection,
Los Angeles County Museum of Art.

Plate 8. Vajrabhairava with a consort, seventeenth century, Dge lugs tradition. Gift of Christian Humann, Los Angeles County Museum of Art.

Plate 9. Solitary Hero Vajrabhairava, Ming dynasty (1368–1644), China. In the upper right corner is almost certainly the Dge lugs pa bla ma Byams chen chos rje Shākya Ye shes (1355–1435), who visited the Ming court and conducted tantric rituals. Image provided by the Metropolitan Museum of Art, New York, Lila Acheson Wallace Gift, 1993.

Plate 10. Vajrabhairava with a consort; statue originally held in the Lama Temple in Beijing. The inscription at the back of the statue identifies the name of the donor to be the Qing dynasty emperor Jiaqing (r. 1796–1820).
© The Trustees of the British Museum, London.

Plate 11. Vajrabhairava, stylistically resembling the fifteenth-century style of the Ming dynasty Yongle and Xuande emperors, but possibly produced during the reign of the Qing dynasty Qianlong emperor, who ruled 1736–95. © Virginia Museum of Fine Arts, Richmond.

Plate 12. Daiitoku myōō commissioned for To-ji by Kūkai, Heian period (eleventh century), Japan. Gift of the Clark Center for Japanese Art & Culture, Minneapolis Institute of Art.

bklags pas 'grub pa, but Siklós (49) inaccurately translates it "obtained by reading those sections which appeared after the selection from the *One Hundred Thousand Chapter Tantra* of the cycle of the glorious Vajrabhairava." Siklós mistranslates both *rtog pa'i phyogs*, which reflects the Skt. *kalpaikadeśaḥ*, and *bklags pas 'grub pa*, which reflects the Skt. *paṭhitasiddhaḥ*; the latter is a technical term (see below). Siklós's translation of *btus* is also inaccurate, as it reflects the Skt. *uddhṛtaḥ*, "extracted," i.e., from the *One Hundred Thousand Chapter Tantra*—that is, the *Śrīmahāvajrabhairavacakra*.

The concept of *paṭhitasiddhaḥ*, as the way of referring to a particularly powerful mantra, is a common feature of the proto-tantric material of the Mahāyāna sūtras. For example, the *Amoghapāśahṛdaya-dhāraṇī* (Meisezahl 1962), a text dedicated to magic spells recited by the bodhisattva Avalokiteśvara that was popular in Khotan, China, and Japan, states, "The following are the ritual procedures for this mantra over which you have mastery just by reciting it" (*paṭhitasiddhasyāsya mantrasya karmmāṇi bhavanti*; Meisezahl 1962, 324). A similar reference is given in the *Hayagrīvavidyā* found among the Gilgit manuscripts (for a study and translation of which, see Kakas 2011). The text begins with a number of verses to the Three Jewels and Avalokiteśvara, after which the reciter, Avalokiteśvara himself, repeats the *paramahṛdaya-* mantra, a.k.a. *hayagrīva*, which is described as "the king among the mantras, which is mastered just by being recited" (*ayaṃ hayagrīvavidyārāja paṭhitasiddhaḥ*; Dutt et al. 1939, 44). The text elaborates on the extraordinary efficacy of this mantra: "The charm with which you can break any spells, the fruit, flower, water, or the like you can subject to your will. However, this [*vidyārāja*] needs only to be recited to have its effect (*paṭhitasiddhaḥ*); it will bring about anything you desire without having first mastered it through sādhana" (*sarvamudrāmokṣanāṃ udakena vaśīkaraṇaṃ phalapuṣpaiḥ/ ayaṃ paṭhitasiddhaḥ/ asādhita eva sarvakarmāṇi kurute*; Dutt et al. 1939, 45). In other words, a mantra classified as *paṭhitasiddhaḥ* does not need to be mastered through a long process of *puraścaraṇa/pūrvasevā*. The end of the *paramahṛdaya* mantra of Hayagrīva reads:

> Subject all *graha*s and *piśāca*s to my will. Cut off with your horse face all those who wish me harm, *phaṭ*. Homage to Ārya Avalokiteśvara, the bodhisattva mahāsattva! May these mantra utterances (*mantrapada*s) bring me success. Lord Hayagrīva commands, *svāhā*. (*sarvagrahapiśācān me vaśamānaya/ yāvanto mama* [*ye kecit*] *ahitaiṣiṇastān sarvān vaḍvāmukhena chindayet phaṭ/ namo nama āryāvalokiteśvarāya bodhisattvāya mahāsattvāya/ sidhyantu mama mantrapadā hayagrīvo bhagavān ājñā[pa]yati svāhā*; Dutt et al. 1939, 44).

The concept of *paṭhitasiddhaḥ* permeated also the Buddhist tantras. It is found, for example, in an early kriyā tantra, the MMK. In chapter 52 (p. 438) of this tantra, one of the two of the so-called Yamāntaka chapters, the mantra of Yamāntaka, known as *krodharāja*, "wrathful king," is described like this: "This is the Krodharāja, which is successful just by being recited; it bestows the supreme siddhi" (*paṭhitasiddhā eṣa krodharājā uttamāṃ siddhim anuprayacchati*). The same description is repeated in the last verse before the chapter's final colophon (p. 450): "This Krodharāja Yamāntaka, which is successful just by being recited, ends here" (*paṭhitasiddhā eṣa krodharājā yamāntako nāma parisamāpta iti*). The placement of this description at the end of the chapter seems to indicate that the notion of *paṭhitasiddhaḥ* applies here not only to the mantra but, just as in the case of the *Vajrabhairava Tantra*, to the entire text. A similar placement is also found in the conclud-

which came from Oḍḍiyāna,[999] the sacred site of the yoginīs. May the people of the world become equal to the venerable Great Vajrabhairava through this merit. *Oṃ hrīḥ ṣṭrīḥ vikṛtānana hūṃ phaṭ. Oṃ yamāntaka hūṃ phaṭ.*

Of those dharmas that arise from a cause,
the Tathāgata taught their cause
and also their cessation.
Thus spoke the Great Śramaṇa.

Auspicious.[1000]

---

ing verse of the last chapter of a yoginī tantra, the *Herukābhidāna* (*Cakrasaṃvara*; see Gray 2007a, 382); in the *Saṃvarodaya Tantra* (see Tsuda 1970, 36 and 312), which stylistically closely resembles the final colophon of the *Vajrabhairava Tantra*; and in the *Hevajra Tantra* (2.9.6: *asmin tantre na hotavyaṃ mudrābandhakriyā na ca/ paṭhitasiddhaṃ mahātantraṃ dhyānamātreṇa sidhyati*; Tripathi and Negi 2006, 196).

999. This sentence does not feature in the Tibetan edition (Siklós 1996, 113). The mention of Oḍḍiyāna, referred to as *dpal u rgyan*, appears in the context of the mythical Ur text, the *Mañjuśrī Tantra*, the king among the tantras that has come down from the great *pīṭha* of the venerable Oḍḍiyāna, wherefrom the VBhT has been extracted.

1000. The passage beginning "May the people" and ending with "Auspicious" does not feature in the Tibetan edition (Siklós 1996, 113–14).

Appendix. Keys to the Maṇḍalas in Plates 1–5

Plates 1–5 in this volume are drawn from a collection of initiation-card (*tsag li* or *tsaka li*) images published in 2007 by Rdzong gsar Monastery (*Rgyud sde kun btus dkyil tsaka*, BDRC W2PD17497), and the Tibetan captions under the images are from that publication. The descriptions below, except where specified otherwise, are based on those in the *Rgyud sde kun btus*, the compendium of tantras compiled by the Ngor Monastery master 'Jam byang blo gter dbang po (1847–1914), whose collection contains paintings of 139 maṇḍalas. References to the *Rgyud sde kun btus* here are to the thirty-two-volume edition made available digitally in 2004 by Sachen International in Kathmandu (BDRC W27883).

Plate 1

The maṇḍala of Forty-Nine-Deity Vajrabhairava of the Zhang tradition
Dpal rdo rje 'jigs byed zhang lugs lha zhe dgu ma'i dkyil 'khor, *Rgyud sde kun btus* 10:45–70

Center: Solitary Vajrabhairava, with nine heads, thirty-four arms, and sixteen legs

Deities inside the central circle of the maṇḍala

East: (1) Vajra Head
South: (2) Vajra Arm
West: (3) Vajra Entrails
North: (4) Vajra Leg
Southeast: (5) Vajra Skull
Southwest: (6) Vajra Skull Fragments
Northwest: (7) Vajra Rag of the Cremation Ground
Northeast: (8) Vajra Man Impaled on a Stake

Deities in the maṇḍala square outside the circle

Eastern strip: (9) Vajra Chopper, (10) Vajra One-Pointed Spear, (11) Vajra Pestle, (12) Vajra Knife, (13) One-Pointed Vajra, (14) Vajra Hook, (15) Vajra Buffalo, (16) Vajra Ox

Southern strip: (17) Vajra Axe, (18) Vajra Arrow, (19) Vajra Club, (20) Vajra Skull Staff, (21) Vajra Wheel, (22) Vajra Noose, (23) Vajra Swine, (24) Vajra Donkey

Western strip: (25) Vajra Vajra, (26) Vajra Drum, (27) Vajra Shield, (28) Vajra Bow, (29) Vajra Bell, (30) Vajra Fluttering Banner, (31) Vajra Camel, (32) Vajra Dog

Northern strip: (33) Vajra Threatening Finger, (34) Vajra Banner with three Ribbons, (35) Vajra Elephant Hood, (36) Vajra Hammer, (37) Vajra Spear, (38) Vajra Firepit, (39) Vajra Sheep, (40) Vajra Wolf

Deities at the doors and corners of the maṇḍala square

Eastern door: (41) Vajra Vulture
Southern door: (42) Vajra Owl
Western door: (43) Vajra Crow
Northern door: (44) Vajra Parrot
Southeastern corner: (45) Vajra Eagle
Southwestern corner: (46) Vajra Raven
Northwestern corner: (47) Vajra Myna
Northeastern corner: (48) Vajra Swan

All forty-eight Vajra deities share the following iconographic features: they have a blue body, a single face like a buffalo, and two arms. Their right hand holds a symbol concordant with their name, and their left hand holds a skull filled with *amṛta* nectar; their *liṅga* is erect in victory; their right leg is bent, and their left leg, outstretched, stands on the back of a buffalo; they have three eyes, gaping fangs, and their hair is dark yellowish and stands on end like flames (*Rgyud sde kun btus*, 10:58–59).

Plate 2

The maṇḍala of the Nine- or Seventeen-Deity Vajrabhairava of the Skyo tradition
Skyo 'od 'byung nas brgyud pa'i dpal rdo rje 'jigs byed lha dgu 'am lha bcu bdun gyi dkyil 'khor, Rgyud sde kun btus 10:1–44.

Center: Solitary Vajrabhairava, with nine heads, thirty-four arms, and sixteen legs

Symbols inside the central circle of the maṇḍala

East: head of Brahmā
South: arm
West: entrails
North: leg
Southeast: skull
Southwest: skull fragments
Northwest: rag of the cremation ground
Northeast: man impaled on a stake

Symbols in the maṇḍala square outside the circle

Eastern strip: knife, spear, pestle, chopper, one-pointed vajra, hook
Southern strip: axe, arrow, club, skull staff, wheel, noose
Western strip: vajra, a drum, shield, bow, bell, fluttering banner
Northern strip: threatening gesture, banner with three ribbons, elephant hood, hammer, spear, firepit.

Deities located at the doors and corners of the maṇḍala square

Eastern door: (1) Yama Iron Hook–Vulture
Southern door: (2) Yama Noose-Owl
Western door: (3) Yama Iron Chain–Falcon
Northern door: (4) Yama Thunderbolt-Crow
Southeast corner: (5) Yama Consort-Goose
Southwest corner: (6) Yama Fangs-Duck
Northwest corner: (7) Yama Club-Crane
Northeast corner: (8) Kālarātrī-Peacock

All eight Yama (Gshin rje) deities have a tail, they are gasping and angry, and they have an extremely wrathful and evil appearance. They are young and exuberant, naked, with prominent nipples and gaping fangs. Fiercely laughing, they have three round, red eyes, and the reddish-yellow hair on their head hangs loose. Their right hand wields a knife, and their left hand holds a skull filled with human blood, which they drink (*Rgyud sde kun btus*, 10:9–14).

This maṇḍala appears also in Sagaster 1991, 173.

Plate 3

The maṇḍala of Vajrabhairava surrounded by eight zombies and thirty-two symbols according to the Rwa tradition, transmitted to the Sa skya by Mal Lo tsā ba.
Rdo rje 'jigs byed ro langs brgyad dang phyag mtshan so gnyis kyis bskor ba (*Mal lugs*), *Rgyud sde kun btus*, 9:135–230.

Center: Solitary Vajrabhairava, with nine heads, thirty-four arms, and sixteen legs

Symbols inside the central circle of the maṇḍala

East: (1) head
South: (2) arm
West: (3) entrails
North: (4) leg
Southeast: (5) skull
Southwest: (6) skull fragments
Northwest: (7) rag of the cremation ground
Northeast: (8) man impaled on a stake

Symbols in the maṇḍala square outside the circle

Eastern strip:
  To the right of the door: (9) chopper, (10) spear, (11) pestle
  To the left of the door: (12) knife, (13) single-pointed vajra, (14) hook
Southern strip:
  To the right of the door: (15) axe, (16) arrow, (17) club
  To the left of the door: (18) skull staff, (19) wheel, (20) vajra noose
Northern strip:
  To the right of the door: (21) five-pronged vajra, (22) drum, (23) shield
  To the left of the door: (24) bow, (25) bell, (26) wind-blown cloth
Western strip:
  To the right of the door: (27) threatening gesture, (28) banner with three ribbons, (29) elephant hood
  To the left of the door: (30) hammer, (31) spear, (32) firepit

Eight zombies

The eight great zombies, black in color and visualized as transformed from the seed syllable *phaiṃ*, should be placed at the doors of the cardinal and intermediate directions in the maṇḍala square.

The Tibetan caption to this plate erroneously ascribes it to the "Mu lugs." The image follows the description of maṇḍala in the *Rgyud sde kun btus* (9:135) with regard to the placement of the eight symbols inside the wheel (which matches the description in the VBhT, see pages 212–13). The symbols outside the wheel do not correspond to the description in the *Rgyud sde kun btus* or the VBhT, and the eight zombies, mentioned in both texts, are nowhere to be seen.

Plate 4

The maṇḍala of Vajrabhairava surrounded by eight zombies and thirty-two symbols according to the Sa skya Ngor tradition. *Rdo rje 'jigs byed ro langs brgyad dang phyag mtshan so gnyis kyis bskor ba.* The description below is based on the plate rather than the *Rgyud sde kun btus.*

Center: Solitary Vajrabhairava, with nine heads, thirty-four arms, and sixteen legs

Symbols inside the circle

East: (1) leg
South: (2) head
West: (3) arm
North: (4) entrails
Southeast: (5) man impaled on a stake
Southwest: (6) skull
Northwest: (7) skull fragments
Northeast: (8) rag of the cremation ground

Symbols in the maṇḍala square

Eastern strip: (9) threatening gesture, (10) banner with three ribbons, (11) elephant hood, (12) vajra hammer, (13) spear, (14) firepit

Southern strip: 15) dagger, (16) iron lance ornamented with peacock's feathers, (17) pestle, (18) knife, (19) single-pointed vajra, (20) hook
Northern strip: (21) vajra, (22) drum, (23) shield, (24) bow, (25) bell, (26) fluttering banner
Western strip: (27) axe, (28) arrow, (29) club, (30) skull staff, (31) wheel, (32) noose

Eight zombies

These are substituted in the drawing by the eight dancing female figures located at the doors of the cardinal and intermediate directions outside the wheel.

The first symbols on the right side inside the circle do not correspond to the sequence given in the VBhT or in the *Rgyud sde kun btus*, but the symbols outside the circle match the order delineated in the VBhT, except for the directions. This maṇḍala has been also reproduced in Sagaster 1991, 167–69.

Plate 5

The maṇḍala of the Thirteen-Deity Vajrabhairava unique to the Rwa tradition
Rwa tshar gnyis kyi thun mong ma yin pa'i bzhed pa rdo rje 'jigs byed lha bcu gsum pa'i dkyil 'khor, Rgyud sde kun btus 9:375–578

Center: Vajrabhairava, with nine heads, thirty-four arms, and sixteen legs, with consort Lha mo rdo rje bde ba ma, who has one face and two arms and holds a knife and a skull (*Rgyud sde kun btus*, 9:426)

Thirteen deities

Center: (emanating from the center of the palace is) (1) Yamāntaka Miserliness (*ser sna*)
East: (emanating from the head symbol is) (2) Yamāntaka Ignorance (*gti mug*)
South: (emanating from the hand symbol is) (3) Yamāntaka Desire (*'dod chags*)
West: (emanating from the entrails symbol is) (4) Yamāntaka Jealousy (*phrag dog*)
North: (emanating from the leg symbol is) (5) Cārcikā
Southeast: (emanating from the skull symbol is) (6) Varāhī

Southwest: (emanating from the skull fragments symbol is) (7) Sarasvatī
Northwest: (emanating from the fluttering banner symbol is) (8) Gaurī
Northeast: (emanating from the man impaled on a stake symbol is) (9)
Yamāntaka Hammer
Eastern door (in the maṇḍala square): (10) Yamāntaka Club
Southern door (in the maṇḍala square): (11) Yamāntaka Lotus
Western door (in the maṇḍala square): (12) Yamāntaka Sword
Northern door (in the maṇḍala square): (13) absent

All twelve deities above are white with three faces and six arms. Their main face is white, the face on the right is blue, and the face on the left is red. In their left hands, they hold a skull filled with blood, a jewel, and a lotus. In their right hands, they hold a skull filled with blood, a wheel, and a knife (*Rgyud sde kun btus*, 9:432–35).

Symbols in the maṇḍala square

Eastern strip:
To the right of the door: chopper, spear, pestle
To the left of the door: knife, single-pointed vajra, hook
Southern strip:
To the right of the door: axe, arrow, club
To the left of the door: club, wheel, vajra noose
Northern strip:
To the right of the door: five-pronged vajra, drum, shield
To the left of the door: bow, bell, wind-blown cloth
Western strip:
To the right of the door: threatening gesture, banner with three ribbons, elephant hood
To the left of the door: vajra hammer, spear, firepit (*Rgyud sde kun btus*, 9:417)

This maṇḍala depicts the eight guardians of the directions (*phyogs skyong ba brgyad*) as the deities of the Hindu pantheon:

Indra (east, yellow, riding a large elephant and holding a vajra)
Yama (south, blue, riding a buffalo and holding a skull staff)
Varuṇa (west, white, riding a crocodile and holding a snake lasso)
Yakṣa (north, yellow, riding a horse and holding a mongoose)
Agni (southeast, red, riding a goat and holding a rosary)

Rākṣasa (southwest, blue, riding a *vetāla* and holding a sword)
Vāyu (northwest, gray, riding a deer and holding a banner)
Bhūta (northeast, white, riding a bull and holding a trident)

All of them hold an attribute in their right hand that identifies them, and with the left hand, they pay respect to Bhagavān Vajrabhairava. See Stag tshang lo tsā ba, *Gsang 'dus 'jam pa'i rdo rje mngon par rtogs pa*, 1:549.

Bibliography

Sanskrit Sources and Tibetan Translations of Sanskrit Texts

Abhayapaddhati of Abhayākaragupta. *Śrībuddhakapālamahātantrarājaṭīkā Abhayapaddhatiḥ = Dpal Sangs rgyas thod pa'i rgyud kyi rgyal po chen po'i rgya cher 'grel pa 'jigs pa med pa'i gzhung 'grel zhes bya ba bzhugs so.* See Chog Dorje 2009.

Abhidharmakośabhāṣyam of Vasubandhu. See Pradhan 1975.

Abhisamayamañjarī. See Samdhong and Dwivedi 1993.

Ādikarmāvatāra of Mañjukīrti. Niedersächisische Universitäts und Staatsbibliothek, Göttingen Xc 14.50

Ādikarmapradīpa of Anupamavajra. In La Vallée Poussin 1898.

Āmnāyamañjarī of Abhayākaragupta. Tibetan translation: *Man ngag gi snye ma*, Toh. 1198. Sde dge Bstan 'gyur, Rgyud 'grel, *cha*, 1b–316a.

Amoghapāśahṛdayadhāraṇī. See Meisezahl 1962.

Amṛtakaṇikoddyotanibandha of Vibhūticandra. See Lal 1994.

Arthaśāstra of Kauṭilya. See Kangle 1969.

Aṣṭāṅgasaṃgraha of Vāgbhaṭa. See Vaidya 1999.

Āsurīkalpa of the *Atharvavedapariśiṣṭas*. See Magoun 1889.

Bhramaharanāma Hevajrasādhana of Ratnākaraśānti. See Isaacson 2002.

Cakrasaṃvaratantra. See Gray 2012.

Cakrasaṃvaravivṛti of Bhavabhaṭṭa. See Pandey Shastri 2002.

Caryāmelāpakapradīpa. See Wedemeyer 2007.

Dhātupāṭha of Pāṇini. See Vasu 2019.

Devīmahātmya. See Coburn 1991.

Devīpañcaśatika (*Kālīkulapañcaśataka*). NAK 5-358. NGMPP B30/26.

Gaṇḍīsūtra. Tibetan translation: *Gaṇ ḍī'i mdo*, Toh. 298. Sde dge Bka' 'gyur, Mdo sde, *sha*, 301b–303b. Translated by Annie Bien at https://read.84000.co/translation/toh298.html (accessed February 25, 2020).

Garuḍa Purāṇa. Bombay: Venkateshwara Steam Press, n.d. (Pothi or Oblong).

Gūḍhapadā. Royal Asiatic Society, London, ms. Hodgson no. 34. Palm leaf, 180 folios, Old-Newar.

Guhyasamājatantra (GS). See Matsunaga 1978. See also Fremantle 1971.

Guhyasamājatantrapradīpoddyotananāmaṭīkāṣaṭkoṭīvyākhyā of Candrakīrti. Tibetan translation: *Gsang 'dus sgron gsal.* 1 vols. Chengdu: Si khron bod yig dpe rnying bsdu sgrig khang, 2016.

Guhyasiddhi. See Samdhong and Dwivedi 1987a.

Guhyasūtra of the *Niśvāsatattvasaṃhitā* (NTGS). NAK 1–227, NGMPP A41/14; palm-leaf ms.; devanāgarī transcript by D. Goodall. The chapter and verse numeration used in this paper is based on D. Goodall's transcript. I thank Prof. Alexis Sanderson for sharing this transcript with me.

Hayagrīvavidyā. See Dutt et al. 1939 (edition) and Kakas 2011 (study and translation).

Hevajratantra. See Snellgrove 1959.

Hevajratantram with *Yogaratnamālāpañjikā* of Mahāpaṇḍitācārya Kṛṣṇapāda. See Tripathi and Negi 2006.

Jayadrathayāmala (JY), *Ṣaṭka* 2. A draft edition based on six manuscript sources provided by Alexis Sanderson (unpublished), January 2015.

Jayadrathayāmala, Ṣaṭka 3. A draft edition based on five manuscript sources provided by Alexis Sanderson (unpublished), January 2015.

Jayadrathayāmala, Ṣaṭka 4. A draft edition based on two manuscript sources provided by Alexis Sanderson (unpublished), March 2016.

Kakṣapuṭatantra. See Yamano 2013.

Kaulajñānanirṇaya. See Bagchi 1986.

Kaulāvalīnirṇaya of Jñānānanda Paramahaṃsa. See Avalon 1928.

Khacakrapañcakastotra. See Dyczkowski 2018.

Kiraṇatantra. NAK 5-893, NGMPP A40/23; palm-leaf; Licchavi script; incomplete; copied in 924 AD.

Kramasadbhāva. NAK 1-76 Śaivatantra 144; NGMPP A 209/23; paper; Newari script.

Kṛṣṇayamāritantrapañjikā of Kumāracandra. See Samdhong and Dwivedi 1991.

Kulapañcāśikā. NAK 1-1078, NGMPP A14/13: palm-leaf; Newari script; probably twelfth century.

Kulārṇavatantra. See Vidyāratna 1965.

Mahābhārata: Anuśāsanaparvan. Electronic text © Bhandarkar Oriental Research Institute, Pune, India, 1999. E-texts entered by Muneo Tokunaga et al., revised by John Smith, Cambridge, et al. https://gretil.sub.uni-goettingen.de/gretil/1_sanskr/2_epic/mbh/mbh_13_u.htm (accessed July 21, 2024).

Mahābhārata: Śāntiparvan. Electronic text © Bhandarkar Oriental Research Institute, Pune, India, 1999. Text entered by Muneo Tokunaga et al., revised by John Smith, Cambridge, et al. https://gretil.sub.uni-goettingen.de/gretil/1_sanskr/2_epic/mbh/mbh_12_u.htm (accessed January 18, 2020).

Mahākalparājasyaṭīkā of Kāmadhenu on the *Sarvadurgatipariśodhana*. Tibetan translation: *Cho ga zhib mo'i rgyal po chen po'i rgya cher 'grel pa*, Toh. 2625. In Bstan 'gyur Dpe bsdur ma, 33:1467–1761. Beijing: Krung go'i bod rig pa'i dpe skrun khang, 1994–2008.

Mahāmāyātantra with *Guṇavatī* by Ratnākaraśānti. See Samdhong and Dwivedi 1992.

Mahānayaprakāśa of Śitikaṇṭha. See Ram Shastri 1918.

Mahāvyutpatti. See Sakaki 1916–25.

Mahāyāna Mahāparinirvāṇasūtra. See Yamamoto 1973.

Mālatīmādhava of Bhavabhūti. See Grimal 1999.

Mālinīvijayottaratantra. See Vasudeva 2004.

Mānavadharmaśāstra. See Olivelle 2005.

Mañjuśrīnāmasaṃgīti (MNS) See Wayman 1985; Davidson 1995b.

Mañjuśriyamūlakalpa (MMK). See Vaidya 1964.

Mārkaṇḍeya Purāṇa. See Śarma Ācārya 1967.

Muktāvalī of Ratnākaraśānti. See Tripathi and Negi 2001.

Mūlamadhyamakakārikā of Nāgārjuna. See Siderits and Katsura 2013.

Nāmamantrārthāvalokinī of Vilāsavajra (NMAA). See Tribe 1994 and Tribe 2016.
Netratantra with the commentary (*Netroddyota*) of Rājānaka Kṣemarāja. See Kaul Śāstrī 1926 and 1939.
Niśvāsamukha. See Kafle 2015.
Niśvāsamūla. See *Niśvāsatattvasaṃhitā*.
Niśvāsatattvasaṃhitā. See Goodall et al. 2015.
Niśvāsottara of the *Niśvāsatattvasaṃhitā* (NTGS). NAK 1–227, NGMPP A41/14; palm-leaf ms.; Devanāgarī transcript by D. Goodall. The chapter and verse numeration used in this paper is based on D. Goodall's transcript. I thank Prof. Alexis Sanderson for sharing this transcript with me.
Nityādisaṃgrahapaddhati by Rājānaka Takṣakavarta. A copy of a single manuscript of this text originally from Pune is kept at the Bodleian Library, University of Oxford (Acc. Nr. MS Stein Or. d. 43).
Pañcakrama. See Mimaki and Tomabechi 1994.
Pāśupata Sūtras with Pañcārthabhāṣya of Kauṇḍinya (PS) (editor unknown). Varanasi: Sarv adarśanācāryaśrīkṛṣṇānandasāgaraḥ (n.d).
Phetkāriṇītantra. See Gopinatha Kaviraja 1970.
Picumata-Brahmayāmala. NAK 1-363, NGMPP A42/6; palm-leaf; Newar script; AD 1052. Transcript by S. Hatley.
Pradīpoddyotana of Candrakīrti. Tibetan translation: *Sgron ma gsal bar byed pa zhes bya ba'i rgya cher bshad pa*, Toh. D 1785. Sde dge Bstan 'gyur, Rgyud, *ha*, 1b–201b.
Prajñāpāramitāśāstra. See Lamotte 2001.
Prajñopāyaviniścayasiddhi. See Samdhong and Dwivedi 1987b.
Rahasyānandatilaka of Mahāmati. Tibetan translation: *Gsang chen dga' ba'i thig le*, Toh. 1342. Sde dge Bstan 'gyur, 10:722–35. Delhi: Delhi Karmapae Choedhey, Gyalwae Sungrab Partun Khang, 1982–85.
Rājataraṅgiṇī. See Stein 1960.
Rāmāyaṇa of Vālmīki. See Rao 1998.
Sādhanamālā. See Bhattacharya 1928.
Sahajālokapañjikā of Śrīdhara. IASWR MBB-II-150-153, palm-leaf, 5 fols., Bhujimola script, undated, incomplete = Tucci collection, 15/LVIII (Box Tucci sscr 7), paper, 24 sheets, Devanāgarī, incomplete.
Saṃpuṭodbhava:
a) Royal Asiatic Society no. 4854; palm-leaf manuscript; Proto Bengali-cum-Maithili.
b) ("Hodgson ms."), London, Royal Asiatic Society, no. 37.
c) London, Wellcome Institute for the Study of Medicine, ser. no. 630, shelved at epsilon 2.
d) *Emergence from Sampuṭa*. Edited and translated by the Dharmachakra Translation Committee, 84000: Translating the Words of the Buddha, 2020.
Saṃvarodayatantra. See Tsuda 1970.
Śāradātilakam of Lakṣmaṇadeśika. See Avalon 1982.
Śāradātilakapadārthādarśa of Rāghavabhaṭṭa. See Avalon 1982.
Sārdhaśatika-Kālottara, NAK 5-4632 ["Kālottara"], part 3; palm-leaf; Newari script.
Sarvabuddhasamāyogaḍākinījālasaṃvarakalpa. See Negī 2018.
Sarvadurgatipariśodhana. See Skorupski 1983.
Sarvakalpasamuccaya of Ānandagarbha. Tibetan translation: *Rtog pa thams cad 'dus pa*, Toh. 1662. Bstan 'gyur Dpe bsdur ma, 14:49–151. Beijing: Krung go'i bod rig pa'i dpe skrun khang, 1994–2008.

Sarvatathāgatatattvasaṃgraha (STTS). See Snellgrove and Chandra 1981.
Sarvatathāgatatattvasaṃgrahanāmamahāyānasūtra. See Yamada 1981.
Sarvavajrodaya. See Mikkyo Seiten Kenkyukai 1986.
Sekanirdeśapañjikā of Rāmapāla. See Isaacson, Sferra, and Mathes 2014.
Siddhaikavīra (*Siddhaikavīramahātantrarājaḥ*). Tibetan translation: *Dpa' bo gcig pu grub pa zhes bya ba'i rgyud kyi rgyal po chen po*, Toh. 544, Sde dge Bka' 'gyur, Rgyud 'bum, *pa*, 1b–13a. Trans. by the Dharmachakra Translation Committee, at 84000: Translating the Words of the Buddha, https://read.84000.co/translation/toh544.html.
Śivasūtravimarśinī of Kṣemarāja. See Chatterji 1910.
Śrīcakrasādhanāvidhāna, Fogg ms. (photocopy made by Prof. Alexis Sanderson in 1995 of a paper manuscript in the Devanāgarī script then in the possession of Sam Fogg Rare Books & Manuscripts, London).
Śrīvajrabhairavatantraṭīkā of *Akṣobhya. Tibetan translation: *Dpal rdo rje 'jigs byed kyi rgyud kyi dka' 'grel*, Toh. 1970. Bstan 'gyur Dpe bsdur ma, 24:364–92. Beijing: Krung go'i bod rig pa'i dpe skrun khang, 1994–2008. Bstan 'gyur Gser bris ma 45: 342-72. Snar thang: 1600-1699. Bstan 'gyur Sde dge 47: 220-40. Delhi: Karmapae Choedhey, Gyalwae Sungrab Partun Khang, 1982–85. Bstan 'gyur Pe cing 45:271-300. Pe cing pho brang, 1724. Bstan 'gyur Snar thang 45: 238-58. Snar thang dgon, 1800.
Śrīvajrabhairavatantrasūtraṭippaṇīnāma of *Śoṇaśrī. Tibetan translation: *Dpal rdo rje 'jigs byed kyi rgyud kyi mdor bshad pa zhes bya ba*, Toh. 1971. Bstan 'gyur Dpe bsdur ma, 24:393–411. Beijing: Krung go'i bod rig pa'i dpe skrun khang, 1994–2008. Bstan 'gyur Sde dge 47: 240-52. Delhi: Karmapae Choedhey, Gyalwae Sungrab Partun Khang, 1982–85. Bstan 'gyur Snar thang 45: 258-73. Snar thang dgon, 1800.
Śrīvajrabhairavatantrasūtraṭippaṇīnāma of *Vajrasiddha. Tibetan translation: *Dpal rdo rje 'jigs byed kyi rgyud kyi mdor bshad pa zhes bya ba*, Toh. 1972. Bstan 'gyur Dpe bsdur ma, 24:412–30 Beijing: Krung go'i bod rig pa'i dpe skrun khang, 1994–2008. Bstan 'gyur Gser bris ma 45: 396-415. Snar thang: 1600-1699. Bstan 'gyur Pe cing 45: 316-32. Pe cing pho brang, 1724. Bstan 'gyur Sde dge 47: 252-64. Delhi: Karmapae Choedhey, Gyalwae Sungrab Partun Khang, 1982–85. Bstan 'gyur Snar thang 45: 275-90. Snar thang dgon, 1800.
Śrīvidyārṇavatantra. See Kak and Śāstrī 1932–37.
Susiddhikarasūtra. See Giebel 2001.
Svacchandatantra with the *Svacchandoddyota* of Kṣemarāja. See Kaul Śāstrī 1921–35.
Tantrāloka of Abhinavagupta. See Kaul Śāstrī 1918–38.
Tantrasārasaṃgraha of Nārāyaṇa. See Unithiri 2002.
Tripurārcanamañjarī of Gadādharabhaṭṭācārya, Fogg ms. (photocopy made by Prof. Alexis Sanderson in 1995 of a paper manuscript in the Devanāgarī script then in the possession of Sam Fogg Rare Books & Manuscripts, London).
Uḍḍāmareśvaratantra. See Zadoo 1947.
Vajrabhairavatantra (eds).
a) Sanskrit edition of chapters 1–3: Ngawang Samten and S. S. Bahulkar, eds. "Śrīvajrabhairavamahāyogatantram" In *Dhīḥ: Journal of Rare Buddhist Texts Research Unit* 43 (2007): 165–76. (Sarnath and Varanasi: Central Institute of Higher Tibetan Studies).
b) Tibetan and Mongolian editions; See Siklós 1996.
Vajrabhairavatantra (mss.):

1) NAK A994/3 (photographed second time as NAK A1306/32); palm-leaf manuscript; Newari script.
2) NAK B112/16; paper manuscript; Devanāgarī script.
3) Beijing ms. 107; palm-leaf manuscript; proto-Bengali script.

Vajrabhairavatantrapañjikā of Kumāracandra.
a) Tibetan translation: *Rdo rje 'jigs byed kyi rgyud kyi dka' 'grel*, Toh. 1973. Bstan 'gyur Dpe bsdur ma, 24:431–40. Beijing: Krung go'i bod rig pa'i dpe skrun khang, 1994–2008. Bstan 'gyur Pe cing, 45: 332-40. Pe cing pho brang, 1724. Bstan 'gyur Gser bris ma, 45: 415-24. Snar thang: 1600-1699. Bstan 'gyur Sde dge 47: 264-70. Delhi: Karmapae Choedhey, Gyalwae Sungrab Partun Khang, 1982–85. Bstan 'gyur Snar thang 45: 288-95. Snar thang dgon, 1800.
b) Beijing ms. 106; ms. 86; palm-leaf manuscripts; proto-Bengali script.

Vajrabhairavatantrapañjikāratnamālā of *Kṛṣṇācārya. Tibetan translation: *Rdo rje 'jigs byed kyi rgyud kyi 'grel pa rin po che'i phreng ba zhes bya ba*), Toh. 1974. Bstan 'gyur Dpe bsdur ma, 24:441–64. Beijing: Krung go'i bod rig pa'i dpe skrun khang, 1994–2008. Bstan 'gyur Sde dge 47: 270-89. Delhi: Karmapae Choedhey, Gyalwae Sungrab Partun Khang, 1982–85.

Vajrabhairavatantravṛttyalaṃkāropadeśa of Lalitavajra. Tibetan translation: *Rdo rje 'jigs byed kyi rgyud kyi 'grel pa man ngag dang ldan pa'i rgyan.* Bstan 'gyur Gser bris ma no. 2806, 83:299–338 (fols. 149r–168v). Snar thang (n.d.). Bstan 'gyur Dpe bsdur ma, 46: 1011-44. Beijing: Krung go'i bod rig pa'i dpe skrun khang, 1994–2008. Bstan 'gyur Pe cing, 83:222-54. Pe cing pho brang, 1724. Bstan 'gyur Snar thang, 83: 210-38. Snar thang dgon, 1800.

Vajrajvālodayā of Ānandagarbha. Niedersächsische Staats- und Universitätsbibliothek, Göttingen, ms. Xc 14/39 (fols. 170r–186r5). Palm-leaf, Newari script.

Vajrasattvasādhana of Candrakīrti. See Hong and Tomabechi 2010.

Vajraśekhara. See Nihom 1998.

**Vajrayānāntadvayanirākaraṇa* ascribed to Jñānaśrī. Tibetan translation: *Rdo rje theg pa'i mtha' gnyis sel ba*, Toh. 3714. Sde dge Bstan 'gyur, Rgyud, *tsu*, 115r7–120r2.

Vetālapañcaviṃśatikā of Śivadāsa. See Schmidt-Madsen 2014.

Vīṇāśikhatantra. See Goudriaan 1985.

Yogaratnamālā. See under *Hevajratantram.*

Sources in Tibetan

A khu ching Shes rab rgya mtsho. *'Jigs byed dpa' bo gcig pa la brten pa'i sku gdung sreg chog.* In *Gsung 'bum Shes rab rgya mtsho*, 3:179–84. Lhasa: Zhol par khang, 1998–99. BDRC MW21505.

A mes zhabs Ngag dbang kun dga' bsod nams. *Gsung 'bum*, 29 vols. Kathmandu: Sa skya rgyal yongs gsung rab slob gnyer khang, 2000.

———. *Gshin rje chos 'byung.*
a) *Gshin rje gshed skor gyi dam pa'i chos 'byung ba'i tshul legs par bshad pa 'jam dpal chos kun gsal ba'i nyin byed*, Sde dge 1633, 76 fols. This was published as a modern edition as:
b) *Gshin rje chos 'byung: Religious History of the Circle of Yamāri: Correct Explanation of the Excellent Religious History of the Circle of Yamāri: The Sun That Clarifies All*

Dharmas of Mañju[ghoṣa]. In: *A History of the Yamāntaka Cycles of Esoteric Practice In India and Tibet*. Dehradun: Sakya Centre 1985.

———. *Sa gsum gyi bla ma chos kyi rgyal po 'phags pa rin po che'i gsung rab rgyal bu 'ji 'big de mur la gtam du bya ba nor bu'i 'phreng ba'i rnam par bshad pa dgyes pa'i lha'i rol mo dpyod ldan yid 'phrog 'phrin las kun khyab*. In *Rare and Precious Buddhist Scriptures*, vol. AMAI033. Baudha, Kathmandu: Chodung Karmo Translation Group, 2012.

———. *Sa skya'i gdung rabs ngo mtshar bang mdzod*. Beijing: Mi rigs dpe skrun khang, 1986.

'Bri gung pa Dpal 'dzin. *Rdo rje 'jigs byed kyi man ngag phyogs sdeb*. Scanned from dbu med manuscript. BDRC W3CN2615.

Bsod nams 'od zer. *Grub chen u rgyan pa'i rnam par thar pa byin brlabs kyi chu rgyun*. Gangtok: Sherab Gyaltsen Lama, 1976.

Byams chen chos rje'i rnam thar. 23 fols. scanned from photocopy of unknown origin. BDRC W25577.

Dpal rdo rje 'jigs byed rwa lugs kyi sgrub thabs bdud 'joms snang ba. A sādhana practice focusing upon Vajrabhairava according to the Rwa tradition transmitted among the Ngor pa by Ngor chen Dkon mchog lhun grub. New Delhi: T. G. Dhongthog Rimpoche, 1978.

Dpal rdo rje 'jigs byed zhang lugs lha zhe dgu ma'i dkyil 'khor (57). In *Rgyud sde kun btus* (digital edition), 10:51–258. Kathmandu: Sachen International, 2004.

Dzaya paṇḍita. *Thob yig "the Bright Mirror."* Peking ed. See Wayman 1959b.

Gangs ljongs skad gnyis smra ba du ma'i 'gyur byang bla gsal dga' skyed. Mtsho sngon: Kan lho bod rigs rang skyong khul rtsom sgyur cu'u, 1983. BDRC W24697.

'Gos lo Gzhon nu dpal. *Deb ther sngon po*. Chengdu: Si khron mi rigs dpe skrun khang, 1984. See also Roerich 1949–53 (repr. 1996).

'Jam dbyangs blo gter dbang po. See *Rgyud sde kun btus* below.

Kun dga' bzang po. *'Jigs byed kyi rwa rtse sems 'dzin skyo lugs kyi brgyud 'debs*. In *Gsung 'bum*, 1:45–46. Dehradun: Sakya Centre, 199?.

Mdzad pa po mi gsal. *Byams chen chos rje'i rnam thar*, 23 fols., scanned from a photocopy of unknown origin. BDRC W25577.

Mkhas grub rje. *Rgyud sde spyi'i rnam par gzhag pa rgyas par brjod*. See Lessing and Wayman 1978.

Mkhas grub rje Dge legs dpal bzang. *Rje btsun bla ma tsong kha pa chen po'i ngo mtshar rmad du byung ba'i rnam par thar pa dad pa'i 'jug ngogs*. In *The Collected Works of Rje Tsong-kha pa bla bzang grags pa*, 1:1–143. Delhi: Ngawang Gelek Demo.

Ngor chen Kun dga' bzang po. *Thob yig rgya mtsho*. In *E waṃ bka' 'bum*, 1:165–386. Beijing: Krung go'i bod rig pa dpe skrun khang, 2009–10.

'Phags pa Blo gros rgyal mtshan. *Zhe dgu ma'i sgrub thabs zhi khro rnam rol*. In *Sa skya bka' 'bum*, 14:564–77. Dehradun: Sakya Center, 1992–93.

Rgyud sde kun btus of 'Jam dbyangs blo gter dbang po:

a) *Rgyud sde kun btus* (digital edition), 32 volumes (Sde dge blockprints). Kathmandu: Sachen International, 2004.

b) See also Tachikawa 1989.

c) See also Chandra et al. 2006.

Rgyud sde kun btus dkyil tsaka. Rdzong gsar Monastery, 2007. BDRC holds digitally scanned images (BDRC W2PD17497).

Rwa Ye shes seng ge. *Rwa lo tsā ba rnam thar* (*Mthu stobs dbang phyug rje btsun rwa lo tsā ba'i rnam thar pa kun khyab snyan pa'i rnga sgra*). Xining: Mtsho sngon mi rigs dpe skrun khang, 1997. For translation, see Ra Yeshé Sengé 2015.

Seventh Dalai Lama. *The Self-Initiation Portion of the Ekavīra Vajrabhairava Maṇḍalavidhi*

Called "Triumph Over Māra" (Rgyal ba bskal bzang rgya mtsho'i gsung rdo rje 'jigs byed dpa bo gcig pa bdud las rnam rgyal gyi dkyil chog la bdag 'jug bya tshul 'don sgrigs nag po), edited by Gling Rin po che [Blo bzang lung rtogs bstan 'dzin 'phrin las]. Bodh Gaya: privately published, 1977.

Sgra sbyor bam po gnyis pa. A Critical Edition of the sGra sbyor bam po gnyis pa: An Old and Basic Commentary on the Mahāvyutpatti. Edited by Ishikawa Mie. Studia Tibetica 18. Materials for Tibetan-Mongolian Dictionaries, vol. 2. Tokyo: The Toyo Bunko, 1990.

Sher chen Ye shes rgyal mtshan. *Lam 'bras bla ma brgyud pa'i rnam thar.* In 'Jam dbyangs blo gter dbang po's *Gsung ngag rin po che lam 'bras bla ma brgyud pa'i rnam thar kun 'dus me long*, 1:315–19. Beijing: Mi rigs dpe skrun khang, 2002.

Stag tshang lo tsā ba Shes rab rin chen. *Dpal ldan sa skya'i gdung rabs 'dod dgu'i rgya mtsho.* Composed in 1467. Unpublished *dbu med* ms. BDRC W1CZ1883.

———. *Gsang 'dus 'jam pa'i rdo rje mngon par rtogs pa bzhugs so.* In *Gsung 'bum*, 1:541–601. Kathmandu: Sa skya rgyal yongs gsung rab slob gnyer khang, 2007.

Tāranātha. *Buddha gupta'i rnam thar (Grub chen Buddha gupta'i rnam thar rje btsun nyid kyi zhal lung las gzhan du rang rtog gi dri mas ma sbags pa'i yi ge yang dag pa'o).* In the *Collected Works (gsung 'bum) of Jonang rJe btsun Kun dga' snying po*, 17:531–75. Leh: C. Namgyal & Tsewang Taru, 1985. Text translated in Templeman 2009.

———. *Rgya gar chos 'byung.* See Chattopadhyaya 1990.

———. *Gshin rje chos 'byung. Rgyud rgyal gshin rje gshed skor gyi chos 'byung rgyas pa yid ches ngo mtshar.* In *Gsung 'bum*, 10:13–160. Leh: C. Namgyal & Tsewang Taru, 1982–87.

Tsong kha pa. *Rdo rje 'jigs byed lha bcu gsum ma'i sgrub thabs rin po che'i za ma tog bkod pa.* In Tsong kha pa's *Gsung 'bum*, 10:475–510. Bla brang bkra shis 'khyil, 199?. BDRC W22273 P. This text has been partly translated into English as *A Casket of Jewels: Meditation on the Thirteen Deity Glorious Vajrabhairava by Je Tsongkhapa* (San Jose: Gyuto Vajrayana Center, 2009).

———. *'Jigs byed kyi sgrub thabs bdud las rnam rgyal.* In Tsong kha pa's *Gsung 'bum*), 10:511–42. Bla brang bkra shis 'khyil, 199?. BDRC W22273 P.

Zhang G.yu Brag pa Brtson 'grus grags pa. *Dpal chen rgwa lo'i rnam thar.* In *Gsung 'bum*, 1: 195–236. Kathmandu: Gam po pa Library, 2004. BDRC MW26673_CA4E6F.

Secondary Sources (Including Translations of Primary Sources)

Acharya, Diwakar. 2006. "The Role of Caṇḍa in the Early History of the Pāśupata Cult and the Image on the Mathurā Pillar Dated Gupta Year 61." *Indo-Iranian Journal* 48: 207–22

Acri, Andrea. 2014. "Pañcakuśika and Kanda Mpat: From a Pāśupata Śaiva Myth to Balinese Folklore." *Journal of Hindu Studies* 7.2: 146–78.

———. 2016a. "Introduction: Esoteric Buddhist Networks along the Maritime Silk Routes, 7th–13th Century AD." In *Esoteric Buddhism in Mediaeval Maritime Asia: Networds of Masters, Texts, Icons*, edited by A. Acri, 1–28. Singapore: Institute of Southeast Asian Studies, Yusof Ishak Institute.

———. 2016b. "Once More on the 'Ratu Boko Mantra': Magic, Realpolitik, and Bauddha-Śaiva Dynamics in Ancient Nusantara." In *Esoteric Buddhism in Mediaeval Maritime Asia: Networds of Masters, Texts, Icons*, edited by A. Acri, 323–48. Singapore: Institute of Southeast Asian Studies, Yusof Ishak Institute.

———. 2018. "Performance as Religious Observance in Some Śaiva Ascetic Traditions from

South and Southeast Asia." In *Theatrical and Ritual Boundaries in South Asia. Part II*, edited by Elisa Ganser and Ewa Debicka-Borek. *Cracow Indological Studies* 20.1: 1–30.

Aditia Gunawan. 2019. *Bhīma Svarga: Teks Jawa Kuno Abade ke-15 dan penurunan naskahnya*. Jakarta: Perpustakaan Nasional Republik Indonesia.

Anderl, Christoph, and Jessie Pons. Forthcoming. *Dynamics of Text Corpora and Image Programs: Representations of Buddhist Narratives along the Silk Route*. Leiden: Brill.

Ary, Elijah S. 2015. *Authorized Lives: Biography and the Early Formation of Geluk Identity*, Somerville, MA: Wisdom Publications.

Avalon, Arthur (John Woodroofe), ed. 1928. *Kaulāvalīnirṇaya of Jñānānanda Paramahaṃsa*. Calcutta: Sanskrit Press Depository.

———. 1982. *Śāradātilakam of Lakṣmaṇadeśika with the Commentary (-padārthādarśa) of Rāghavabhaṭṭa*. Delhi: Motilal Banarsidass (reprint).

Bagchi, P. C., ed. 1986. *Kaulajñānanirṇaya of the School of Matsyendranātha*. Translated by Michael Magee. Tantra Granthamala 12. Varanasi: Prachya Prakashan.

Beane, Wendell Charles. 1977. *Myth, Cult and Symbols in Śākta Hinduism: A Study of the Indian Mother Goddess*. Leiden: Brill. [Rpt. New Delhi: Munshiram Manoharlal, 2001.]

Bentor, Yael. 1996. *Consecration of Images and Stūpas in Indo-Tibetan Tantric Buddhism*. Leiden: Brill.

Berger, Patricia. 1994. "Preserving the Nation: The Political Uses of Tantric Art in China." In *Latter Days of the Law: Images of Chinese Buddhism 850–1850*, edited by Marsha Weidner, 89–123. Honolulu: University of Hawai'i Press.

Bharati, Swami Agehananda. 1993. *Tantric Traditions*. Delhi: Hindustan Publishing Corporation.

Bhattacharji, Sukumari. 1970. *The Indian Theogony*. Cambridge: Cambridge University Press.

Bhattacharyya, Benoytosh, ed. 1928. *Sādhanamālā*, 2 vols. Baroda: Oriental Institute.

———. 1958. *The Indian Buddhist Iconography, Mainly Based on the Sādhanamālā and Cognate Tāntric Texts of Rituals*. 2nd ed., rev. and enlarged. Calcutta: Firma Mukhopadhyay.

Bhattacharyya, N. N. 1999. *History of the Tantric Religion*. Delhi: Munshiram Manoharlal.

Bianchi, Ester. 2005. "Sādhana della divinità solitaria Yamāntaka-Vajrabhairava: Traduzione e glossario della versione cinese di Nenghai (Parte 1)." *Revue d'Etudes Tibétaines* 8: 4–39.

———. 2006. "Sādhana della divinità solitaria Yamāntaka-Vajrabhairava - Traduzione e glossario della versione cinese di Nenghai (Parte 2)." *Revue d'Etudes Tibétaines* 10: 4–42.

———. 2008. "Protecting Beijing: The Tibetan Image of Yamāntaka-Vajrabhairava in Late Imperial and Republican China." In M. Esposito (ed.) *Images of Tibet in the 19th and 20th centuries*. Paris: EFEO, 329–56.

Bisschop, C. Peter. 2018. "Buddhist and Śaiva Interactions in Kali Age: the Śivadharmaśāstra as a Source of the Kāraṇḍavyūhasūtra." *Indo-Iranian Journal* 6.4: 396–410.

Bloomfield, M. 1899. *The Atharvaveda*. Strassburg: Verlag von Karl J. Trübner.

Böhtlingk von Otto, Roth Rudolph. 1855–75. *St Petersburg's Sanskrit Dictionary* (*Grosses Sanskrit Wörterbuch*). Saint Petersburg: Eggers.

Boyd, James W. 1971. "Symbols of Evil in Buddhism." *Journal of Asian Studies* 31.1: 63–75.

Brick, David. 2012. "The Origin of the *Khaṭvāṅga* Staff." *Journal of the American Oriental Society* 132.1: 31–39.

Brockington, John. 1998. *The Sanskrit Epics*. Leiden: Brill.

Broido, Michael M. 1983. "A Note on dGos 'brel." *Journal of the Tibet Society* 3: 5–19.

Brunner, Hélène. 2003. "Maṇḍala and Yantra in the Siddhānta School of Śaivism: Definitions, Description and Ritual Use." In Bühnemann et al. 2003, 153–77.

Bühnemann, Gudrun. 1991. "Buddhist Deities and Mantras in the Hindu Tantras: I The Tantrasārasaṃgraha and the Īśānaśivagurudevapaddhati." *Indo-Iranian Journal* 42: 303–34.

Bühnemann, Gudrun, et al. 2003. *Maṇḍalas and Yantras in the Hindu Traditions*. Brill's Indological Library 18. Leiden: Brill.

Buswell, Robert E., Jr., and Donald S. Lopez Jr., eds. 2014. *The Princeton Dictionary of Buddhism*. Princeton, NJ: Princeton University Press.

Cabezón, José I. 1991. "Vasubandhu's *Vyākhyāyukti* on the Authenticity of the Mahāyāna Sūtras." In *Texts in Contexts: Traditional Hermeneutics in South Asia*, edited by Jeffrey Timm, 221–43. Albany: State University of New York Press.

Cecil, A. Elizabeth. 2014. "Seeking the 'Lord with a Club': Locating Lakulīśa in the Early History of Pāśupata Śaivism (sixth to ninth century CE)." *South Asian Studies* 30.2: 142–58.

Chandra, Lokesh. 1976. *Tibetan-Sanskrit Dictionary*. Kyoto: Rinsen Book Company.

———. 1980. "Oḍḍiyāna: A New Interpretation." In *Tibetan Studies in Honour of Hugh Richardson*, edited by Michael Aris and Aung San Suu Kyi, 73–78. Warminster: Aris and Phillips.

Chandra, Lokesh, M. Tachikawa, and S. Watanabe. 2006. *A Ngor Maṇḍala Collection*. Kathmandu: Vajra Publications.

Chappell, D. 1980. "Early Forebodings of the Death of Buddhism." *Numen* 27: 122–54.

Charleux, Isabelle. 2011. "Mongol Pilgrimages to Wutai Shan in the Late Qing Dynasty." *JIABS* 6: 275–326.

Chatterji, J. C., ed. 1910. *The Shiva Sūtra Vimarshinī: Being the Sūtras of Vasu Gupta with the Commentary called Vimarshinī by Kshemarāja*. Kashmir Series of Texts and Studies 1. Srinagar.

Chattopadhyaya, L. and C. A. 1990. *Tāranātha's History of Buddhism in India*. Delhi: Motilal Banarsidass.

Chen, Qingying, and Lianlong Ma. 2007. *Zhangjia guoshi*. Beijing: Zhongguo Zangxue Chubanshe.

Chiodo, Elisabetta. 2000. *The Mongolian Manuscripts on Birch Bark from Xarbuxyn Balgas in the Collection of the Mongolian Academy of Sciences, part 1*. Wiesbaden: Harrassowitz Verlag.

Chog Dorje, ed. 2009. *Abhayapaddhati of Abhayākaragupta: Commentary on the Buddhakapālamahātantra*. Text in Sanskrit with rendering in Tibetan and Hindi preface. Bibliotheca Indo-Tibetica 68. Sarnath: Central Institute for Higher Tibetan Studies.

Chou, Yi-Liang. 1945. "Tantrism in China." *Harvard Journal of Asiatic Studies* 8: 241–342.

Clark, Walter E. 1965. *Two Lamaistic Pantheons*. New York: Paragon Book Reprint Corp.

Coburn, B. Thomas. 1991. *Encountering the Goddess: A Translation of the Devī-Mahātmya and a Study of Its Interpretation*. Albany: State University of New York Press.

———. 1998. "Devī: The Great Goddess." In *Devī-Goddesses of India*, edited by John S. Hawley and Donna M. Wulff, 31–49. Delhi: Motilal Banarsidass.

Conrad, Lawrence I., and Dominik Wujastyk, eds. 2000. *Contagion: Perspectives from Pre-Modern Societies*. London and New York: Routledge.

Coulter, Charles Russell, and Patricia Turner, eds. 2000. *Encyclopedia of Ancient Deities*. New York: Routledge.

Covaci, Ive, ed. 2016. *Kamakura: Realism and Spirituality in the Scultpure of Japan*. New Haven, CT: Asia Society Museum & Yale University Press.

Cuevas, Bryan J. 2015. "Rva lo tsā ba and His Biographies." In *The Illuminating Mirror: Tibetan Studies in Honour of Per K. Sørensen on the Occasion of his 65th Birthday*, edited by Olaf Czaja and Guntram Hazod, 57–79. Wiesbaden: Dr. Ludwig Reichert Verlag.

———. 2021. *The Rwa Pod and Other "Lost" Works of Rwa Lo Tsā Ba's Vajrabhairava Tradition*. Vienna: Arbeitskreis für Tibetische und Buddhistische Studien Universität Wien.

Dalton, Catherine, and Péter-Dániel Szántó. 2019. "Jñānapāda." In *Brill's Encyclopedia of Buddhism, Vol. II: Lives*, edited by J. A. Silk et al., 264–68. Leiden: Brill.

Dalton, Jacob. 2004. "The Early Development of the Padmasambhava Legend in Tibet: A Study of IOL Tib J 644 and Pelliot tibétain 307." *Journal of the American Oriental Society* 124.4: 759–72.

———. 2005. "A Crisis of Doxography: How Tibetans Organized Tantra during the 8th–12th Centuries." *JIABS* 28.1: 115–81.

Davidson, Ronald M. 1981. "The *Litany of Names of Mañjuśrī*: Text and Translation of the *Mañjuśrīnāmasaṃgīti*." In Strickmann 1981, 1–69.

———. 1991. "Reflections on the Maheśvara Subjugation Myth: Indic Materials, Sa-skya-pa Apologetics, and the Birth of Heruka." *JIABS* 14.2: 197–235.

———. 1995a. "The Bodhisattva Vajrapāṇi's Subjugation of Śiva." In *Buddhism in Practice*, edited by Donald S. Lopez Jr., 547–55. Princeton, NJ: Princeton University Press.

———. 1995b. "The Litany of Names of Mañjuśrī: Text and Translation of the Mañjuśrīnāmasaṃgīti." In *Religions of India in Practice*, edited by Donlad S. Lopez Jr., 104–25. Princeton, NJ: Princeton University Press.

———. 2002. *Indian Esoteric Buddhism: A Social History of the Tantric Movement*. New York: Columbia University Press.

Debreczeny, Karl. 2011. "Wutai shan: Pilgrimage to Five-Peak Mountain." *JIATS* 6:1–133.

Decleer, Hubert. 1998. "Review of Bulscu Siklós, The Vajrabhairava Tantras, Tibetan and Mongolian Version, English Translation and Annotations. Tring: The Institute of Buddhist Studies (Buddhica Britannica, Series Continua VII), 1996." *Indo-Iranian Journal* 41: 290–301.

Dhongthog Rinpoche. 2016. *The Sakya School of Tibetan Buddhism: A History*. Trans. Sam van Schaik. Somerville, MA: Wisdom Publications.

Doctor, Andreas. 2005. *Tibetan Treasure Literature: Revelation, Tradition, and Accomplishment in Visionary Buddhism*. Ithaca, NY: Snow Lion Publications.

Donaldson, Thomas E. 2001. *Iconography of the Buddhist Sculpture of Orissa*. 2 vols. Delhi: Indira Gandhi National Centre for the Arts, Abhinav Publications.

Douglas, William B. 1998. "Literary Sources of the Guṇakāraṇḍavyūha. Paper presented at Nepal Mandala Seminar, Kathmandu, 1998." Online resource https://lrcnepal.org.np/article-Research (accessed January 16, 2020).

Duquenne, Robert. 1983. "Daiitoku myōō." In *Hōbōgirin: Dictionnaire encyclopédique du bouddhisme d'après les sources chinoises et japonaises*, vol. 6, edited by Sylvain Lévi and J. Takakusu, 652–70. Paris and Tokyo: Maison Franco-Japonaise.

Dutt N., D. M. Bhattacharya, and V. S. Sharma, eds. 1939. *Gilgit Manuscripts, Vol. I*. Srinagar-Kashmir.

Dyczkowski, Mark. 2018. "The Khacakrapañcakastotra, Hymn to the Five Spheres of Emptiness." In *Tantrapuspāñjali: Tantric Traditions and Philosophy of Kashmir*, edited by B. S. Bäumer and H. Stainton, 67–131. Delhi: IGNCA and Arya Books International.

Edgerton, Franklin. 1953. *Buddhist Hybrid Sanskrit Grammar and Dictionary, Volume II: Dictionary*. New Haven, CT: Yale University Press. [Rpt. Delhi: Motilal Banarsidass, 1985.]

Eltschinger, Vincent. 2013. *Buddhist Epistemology as Apologetics: Studies on the History, Self-Understanding and Dogmatic Foundations of Late Indian Buddhist Philosophy*. Vienna: Verlag der Österreichischen Akademie der Wissenschaften.

English, Elizabeth. 2002. *Vajrayoginī: Her Visualizations, Rituals, and Forms*. Boston: Wisdom Publications.

Ferrari, Alfonsa. 1958. *Mkhyen Brtse's Guide to the Holy Places of Central Tibet. Completed and edited by Luciano Petech, with the collaboration of Hugh Richardson*. Serie Orientale Roma 16. Rome: Istituto Italiano Per il Medio ed Estremo Oriente.

Flores, Ralph. 2008. *Buddhist Scriptures as Literature: Sacred Rhetoric and the Uses of Theory*. Albany: State University of New York Press.

Fowler, Sherry D. 2016. *Accounts and Images of Six Kannon in Japan*. Honolulu: University of Hawai'i Press.

Fozu lidai tongzai 佛祖歷代通載 [General Records of Buddha]. Taipei: Xinwenfeng chuban gongsi, 1972.

Franke, H. 1978. *From the Tribal Chieftain to Universal Emperor and God: The Legitimation of the Yüan Dynasty*. Munich: Bayerische Akademie der Wissenschaften.

———. 1981. "Tibetans in Yüan China." In *China Under Mongol Rule*, edited by John D. Langlois Jr., 296–328. Princeton, NJ: Princeton University Press.

Fremantle, Francesca. 1971. *A Critical Study of the Guhyasamāja Tantra*. PhD dissertation, SOAS, University of London.

Geslani, M.A. 2018. *Rites of the God-King: Śānti and Ritual Change in Early Hinduism*. Oxford: Oxford University Press.

Giebel, Rolf W. 1995. "The Chin-kang-ting ching yü-ch'ieh shih-pa-hui chih-kuei: An Annotated Translation." *Journal of Naritasan Institute for Buddhist Studies* 18:107–201.

———. 2001. *Two Esoteric Sutras*. Berkeley, CA: Numata Center for Buddhist Translation and Research.

———. 2005. *The Vairocanābhisaṃbhodhi Sutra*. Berkeley, CA: Numata Center for Buddhist Translation and Research.

———. 2017. *Mahāvairocana Sūtra/Tantra*. Oxford Bibliographies Online. https://www.oxfordbibliographies.com/view/document/obo-9780195393521/obo-9780195393521-0236.xml.

Goodall, Dominic, et al. 2015. *The Niśvāsatattvasaṃhitā: The Earliest Surviving Śaiva Tantra. Vol. 1. A Critical Edition and Annotated Translation of the Mūlasūtra, Uttarasūtra, and Nayasūtra*. Pondicherry: École Française d'Extrême-Orient / Institut Français de Pondichéry, and Asien-Afrika-Institut, Universität Hamburg.

Goodall, Dominic, and Harunaga Isaacson. 2011. "Tantric Traditions." In *The Continuum Companion to Hindu Studies*, edited by Jessica Frazer, 122–91. London: Continnum International Publishing Group.

———. 2016. "On the Shared 'Ritual Syntax' of the Early Tantric Traditions." In *Tantric Studies: Fruits of a Franco-German Project on Early Tantra*, edited by D. Goodall and H. Isaacson, 1–76. Pondicherry: École Française d'Extrême-Orient / Institut Français de Pondichéry, and Asien-Afrika Institut, Universität Hamburg.

Gombrich, Richard. F. 1996. *How Buddhism Began: The Conditioned Genesis of the Early Teachings*. London and Atlantic Highlands, NJ: Athlone.

———. 2006. *Theravāda Buddhism: A Social History from Ancient Benares to Modern Colombo*. London and New York: Routledge.

Gonsalez, David, trans. 2021. *The Roar of Thunder: Yamantaka Practice and Commentary*. Dechen Ling Practice Series. Somerville, MA: Wisdom Publications, 2021.

Gopinatha Kaviraja, ed. 1970. *Phetkāriṇītantra*. In *Tantrasaṅgraha*, part 2, 161–306. Yogatantragranthamālā 4. Varanasi: Vārāṇaseyasaṃskṛtaviśvavidyālaya, 1970.

Goudriaan, Teun. 1978. *Māyā Divine and Human*. Delhi: Motilal Banarsidass.

———, ed. and tran. 1985. *The Vīṇāśikhatantra: A Śaiva Tantra of the Left Current*. Delhi: Motilal Banarsidass.

Goudriaan, Teun, and Christiaan Hooykaas. 1971. *Stuti and Stava (Bauddha, Śaiva and Vaiṣṇava Brahman Priests)*. Amsterdam: North-Holland Publishing Company.

Gray, David. B. 2005. "Guhyasamāja." In *Encyclopedia of Religion*, edited by Lindsay Jones, 6:3708–9. Detroit: Macmillan Reference USA, Thomson Gale.

———. 2007a. *The Cakrasamvara-Tantra: The Discourse of Śrī Heruka: A Study and Annotated Translation*. New York: The American Institute of Buddhist Studies at Columbia University and Columbia's University Center for Buddhist Studies and Tibet House US.

———. 2007b. "Compassionate Violence? On the Ethical Implications of Tantric Buddhist Ritual." *Journal of Buddhist Ethics* 14: 240–71.

———. 2012. *The Cakrasamvara-Tantra: Editions of the Sanskrit and Tibetan Texts*. New York: The American Institute of Buddhist Studies at Columbia University and Columbia's University Center for Buddhist Studies and Tibet House US.

Greenwood, Kevin R. E. 2013. *Yonghegong: Imperial Universalism and the Art and Architecture of Beijing's "Lama Temple."* PhD dissertation, University of Kansas.

Grimal, François, ed. 1999. *Hariharaviracitā Mālatīmādhavaṭīkā: Le Commentaire de Harihara sur le Mālatīmādhava de Bhavabhūti*. Pondicherry: Institut Français de Pondichéry / École Française d'Extrême-Orient.

Guenther, Herbert. 1996. *The Teachings of Padmasambhava*. Leiden: E. J. Brill.

Gyatso, Janet. 1991. "Genre, Authorship, and Transmission in Visionary Buddhism: The Literary Traditions of Thang-stong rGyal-po." In *Tibetan Buddhism: Reason and Revelation*, edited by Ronald M. Davidson and Steven D. Goodman, 95–106. Albany: State University of New York Press.

———. 1993. "The Logic of Legitimation in the Tibetan Treasure Tradition." *History of Religions* 33.2: 97–134.

———. 1998. *Apparitions of the Self: The Secret Autobiography of a Tibetan Visionary*. Princeton, NJ: Princeton University Press.

Harvey, Peter. 2013. *An Introduction to Buddhism: Teachings, History, and Practices*. Cambridge: Cambridge University Press.

Hatley, Shaman. 2012. "From Mātṛ to Yoginī: Continuity and Transformation in the South Asian Cults of the Mother Goddesses." In *Transformations and Transfer of Tantra in Asia and Beyond*, edited by István Keul, 99–129. Berlin: Walter de Gruyter.

Hazod, Guntram 2004. "The Ruins of lDan: Ancient Places in the Eastern Zone of the Lhasa Maṇḍala." *The Tibet Journal* 29.3: 25–54.

Heilijgers-Seelen, Dory. 1994. *The System of Five Cakras in Kubjikāmatatantra 14–16*. Groningen: Egbert Forsten.

Heissig, Walther. 2010. "A Mongolian Source to the Lamaist Suppression of Shamanism in the 17th Century." In *History of Mongolia*, edited by David Sneath, 2:569–608. Kent: Global Oriental LTD.

Heller, Amy. n.d. "Homage by an Emperor: a Yung-lo Embroidery Thangka." Online resource: https://www.thefreelibrary.com/Homage+by+an+emperor%3a+a+Yung-lo+embroidery+Thangka%3a+Amy+Heller...-a0189597193 (accessed March 2, 2020).

Hevia, James. 1993. "Lamas, Emperors, and Rituals: Political Implications in Qing Imperial Ceremonies." *JIABS* 16.2: 243–78.

Hiltebeitel, Alf. 1978. "The Indus Valley 'Proto-Śiva,' Reexamined through Reflections on the Goddess, the Buffalo, and the Symbolism of the Vāhanas." *Anthropos* 73: 767–97.

———, ed. 1989. *Criminal Gods and Demon Devotees: Essays on the Guardians of Popular Hinduism.* Albany: State University of New York Press.

Hong, Luo and Toru Tomabechi, ed. 2010. *Candrakīrti's Vajrasattvaniṣpādanasūtra (Vajrasattvasādhana): Sanskrit and Tibetan Texts.* Vienna: China Tibetology Publishing House / Austrian Academy of Sciences Press.

Hooykaas, C. 1964. *Āgama Tīrtha: Five Studies in Hindu-Balinese Religion.* Amsterdam: North-Holland Publishing Company.

———. 1973. *Balinese Bauddha Brahmans.* Amsterdam: North-Holland Publishing Company.

Ikari, Yasuke, ed. 1994. *A Study of the Nīlamata: Aspects of Hinduism in Ancient Kashmir.* Kyoto: Institute for Research in Humanities, Kyoto University.

Illich, Marina. 2006. *Selections from the Life of a Tibetan Buddhist Polymath: Chankya Rolpai Dorje (Lcang skya rol pa'i rdo rje), 1717–1786.* PhD dissertation, Columbia University.

Ingalls, Daniel H. H. 1962. "Cynics and Pāśupatas: The Seeking of Dishonor." *Harvard Theological Review* 55: 281–98.

Isaacson, Harunaga. 1998. "Tantric Buddhism in India (from ca. A.D. 800 to ca. A.D. 1200)." *Buddhismus in Geschichte und Gegenwart: Band II*, 24–49. Universität Hamburg.

———. 1999. "The Classification of Practice into Utpattikrama and Utpannakrama in the Higher Buddhist Tantric Systems." Paper presented in Hilary Term at Oriental Institute, University of Oxford (unpublished).

———. 2002. "Ratnākaraśānti's Bhramaharanāma Hevajrasādhana: Critical Edition (Studies in Ratnākaraśānti's Tantric Works III)." *Journal of the International College for Advanced Studies* 5: 151–76.

Isaacson, Harunaga, and Francesco Sferra. 2015. "Tantric Literature: Overview South Asia." In *Brill's Encyclopedia of Buddhism: Literature and Languages*, edited by Jonathan Silk, 1:307–19. Leiden: Brill.

Isaacson, Harunaga, Francesco Sferra, and Klaus-Dieter Mathes, ed. 2014. *Sekanirdeśa of Maitreyanātha (Advayavajra) with the Sekanirdeśapañjikā of Rāmapāla.* Critical edition of the Sanskrit and Tibetan texts with translation and reproduction of the mss. Naples: Universitá degli studi di Napoli L'Orientale.

Iyanaga, Nobumi. 1985. "Rècits de la soumission de Maheśvara par Trailokyavijaya d'aprés les sources chinoises et japonaises (Notes autour de Maheśvara-Śiva dans le Bouddhisme I)." In *Tantric and Taoist Studies in Honour of R. A. Stein*, edited by M. Strickmann, 1:633–745. Brussels: Institut Belge des Hautes Études Chinoises.

Jinpa, Thupten. 2019. *Tsongkhapa: A Buddha in the Land of Snows.* Boulder: Shambhala Publications.

———. 2022. *Stages of the Path and the Oral Transmission: Selected Teachings of the Geluk School.* Library of Tibetan Classics 6. Somerville, MA: Wisdom Publications.

Jones, C. V. 2021. "Translating the Tīrthika: An Enduring 'Heresy' in Buddhist Studies." In *Translating Buddhism: Historical and Contextual Perspectives,* edited by Alice Collett, 195–225. Albany: State University of New York Press.

Kafle, Nirajan. 2015. *The Niśvāsamukha, the Introductory Book of the Niśvāsatattvasaṃhitā Critical Edition, with an Introduction and Annotated Translation Appended by Śivadharmasaṅgraha 5–9.* PhD dissertation, Leiden University.

Kak, Ram Chandra, and Harabhatta Shastri, eds. 1932–37. *Shrividyarnava Tantra,* 2 vols. Srinagar: Kashmir Mercantile Electric Press.

Kakas, Beata. 2011. "Hayagrīvavidyā: Spell to the Horse-Necked One." *Acta Orientalia Academiae Scientiarum Hungaricae* 64.4: 427–35.

Kangle, R. P., ed. 1969. *Arthaśāstra of Kauṭilya.* 2nd ed. Bombay: University of Bombay.

Kapstein, Matthew. 1995. "Weaving the World: The Ritual Art of the 'Paṭa' in Pāla Buddhism and Its Legacy in Tibet." *History of Religions* 34.3: 241–62.

Kaul Śāstrī, Madhusūdan, ed. 1918–38. *The Tantrāloka of Abhinava Gupta with the Commentary by Rājānaka Jayaratha,* 5 vols. Kashmir Series of Texts and Studies 23, 28–30, 35, 36, 41, 47, 52, 57–59. Srinagar.

———. 1921–35. *Svacchandatantra with the Commentary (Svacchandoddyota) of Rājānaka Kṣemarāja.* Kashmir Series of Texts and Studies 31, 38, 44, 48, 51, 53, 56. Bombay.

———. 1926 and 1939. *Netratantra with the Commentary (Netroddyota) of Rājānaka Kṣemarāja.* Kashmir Series of Texts and Studies 46 and 59. Bombay.

Keith, A. B. 1925. *The Religion and Philosophy of the Veda and Upanishads, II.* Cambridge, MA: Harvard University Press.

Kinsley, R. David. 1978. "The Portrait of the Goddess in the Devī-mahātmya." *Journal of the American Academy of Religion* 46: 489–506.

Kiss, Csaba. 2014. "On Yantras in Early Śaiva Tantras." *Cracow Indological Studies* 16: 203–33.

Kollmar-Paulenz, Karenina. 2012. "Embodying the Dharma: The Buddhist Way into Mongolia." In *Transformations and Transfer of Tantra in Asia and Beyond,* I. Keul, 239–62. Berlin: De Gruyter.

van der Kuijp, Leonard. 1986. "Ldon ston Shes rab dpal and a Version of the Tshad ma rigs pa'i gter in Thirteen Chapters." *Berliner Indologische Studien* 4: 51–64.

———. 2010. "The Tibetan Expression 'bod wooden door' (bod shing sgo) and Its Probable Mongol Antecedent." In *Historical and Philological Studies of China's Western Regions 3,* edited by S. Weirong, 89–134. Beijing: Science Press.

Kuranishi, Kenichi. 2013. "Yantras in the Buddhist Tantras-Yamāritantras and Related Literature." In *Puṣpikā: Tracing Ancient India Through Texts and Traditions,* edited by N. Mirnig, P. D. Szántó, and M. Williams, 265–81. Oxford: Oxbow Books

Kuwayama, Shoshin 1991. "L'inscription du Gaṇeśa de Gardez et la chronologie des Turki-Ṣāhis." *Journal asiatique* 279: 267–87.

Kwon, D. K. 2002. *Sarva Tathāgata Tattva Saṃgraha: Compendium of All the Tathāgatas: A Study of Its Origin, Structure and Teachings.* PhD dissertation, SOAS, University of London.

La Vallée Poussin, Louis de, ed. 1898 *Bouddhisme: Ètudes et Matèriaux.* London: Luzac & Co. Publishers to the India Office.

Lal, Banarsi, ed. 1994. *Āryamañjuśrīnāmasaṃgīti with Amṛtakaṇikā-ṭippaṇī by Bhikṣu Raviśrījñāna and Amṛtakaṇikoddyota-nibandha by Vibhūticandra.* Bibliotheca Indo-Tibetica 30. Sarnath: Central Institute of Higher Tibetan Studies.

Lamotte, Etienne. 2001. *The Treatise on the Great Virtue of Nāgārjuna (Mahāprajñāpāramitāśāstra).* 5 vols. Translated from French by Gelongma Karma Migme Chodron. Pleasant Bay, NS: Gampo Abbey.

———. trans. 2003. *Śūraṃgamasamādhisūtra: The Concentration of Heroic Progress. An Early Mahāyāna Buddhist Scripture.* Delhi: Motilal Banarsidass.

Lessing, Ferdinand D. 1942. *Yung-Ho-Kung: An Iconography of the Lamaist Cathedral in Peking with Notes on Lamaist Mythology and Cult,* vol. 1. Stockholm: Elanders Boktryckeri Aktiebolag.

———. 1976. "The Topographical Identification of Peking with Yamāntaka." In *Ritual and Symbol: Collected Essays on Lamaism and Chinese Symbolism,* 89–90. Taipei: Orient Cultural Service.

Lessing, Ferdinand D., and Alex Wayman. 1978. *Introduction to the Buddhist Tantric Systems.* Delhi: Motilal Banarsidass.

Linrothe, Robert N. 1990. "Beyond Sectarianism: Towards Reinterpreting the Iconography of Esoteric Buddhist Deities Trampling Hindu Gods." *Indian Journal of Buddhist Studies* 2.2: 16–25.

———. 1999. *Ruthless Compassion: Wrathful Deities in Early Indo-Tibetan Esoteric Buddhist Art.* Delhi: Serindia Publications, Inc.

Magoun, H. W. 1889. "The Āsurī-kalpa: A Witchcraft of the Atharva-Veda." *The American Journal of Philology* 10.2: 165–97.

Mallinson, James. 2018. "Yoga and Sex: What Is the Purpose of Vajrolīmudrā?" In *Yoga in Transformation: Historical and Contemporary Perspectives,* edited by Karl Baier, Philipp A. Maas, and Karin Preisendanz, 181–222. Vienna: Vienna University Press.

Mallinson, James, and Mark Singleton. 2017. *Roots of Yoga.* London: Penguin Random House UK.

Mann, Richard D. 2012. *The Rise of Mahāsena: The Transformation of Skanda-Kārttikeya in North India from the Kuṣāṇa to the Gupta Empires.* Leiden: E. J. Brill.

Mar pa Chos kyi blo gros. 2003. *The Life of the Mahāsiddha Tilopa.* Trans. F. Torricelli and Āchārya Sangye T. Naga. Dharamsala: Library of Tibetan Works and Archives.

Matsunaga, Yukei, ed. 1978. *Guhyasamājatantra* (GS). Osaka: Toho Shuppan, Inc.

———. 1987. "From Indian Tantric Buddhism to Japanese Buddhism." In *Japanese Buddhism: Its Tradition, New Religions and Interaction with Christianity,* edited by Minoru Kiyota, 47–54. Tokyo: Buddhist Books International.

Mayer, Robert. 1996. *A Scripture of the Ancient Tantra Collection. The Phur-pa bcu-gnyis.* Oxford and Gartmore: Kiscadale Publications.

———. 1998. "The Figure of Maheśvara/Rudra in the rÑiṅ-ma-pa Tantric Tradition." *JIABS* 21(2): 271–310.

———. 2007. "The Importance of the Underworlds: Asuras' Caves in Buddhism, and Some Other Themes in Early Buddhist Tantras Reminiscent of the Later Padmasambhava Legends." *JIATS* 3: 1–31.

McKay, Alex, ed. 2003. *The History of Tibet.* 3 vols. London: RoutledgeCurzon.

Meisezahl, Richard O. 1962. "Amoghapāśahṛdaya-dhāraṇī: The Early Sanskrit Manuscript of the Reiunji Critically Edited and Translated." *Monumenta Nipponica* 17(1/4): 265–328.

———. 1980. *Geist und Ikonographie des Vajrayāna Buddhismus*. Sankt Augustin: VGH Wissenschaftsverlag.

Mie, Ishikawa, ed. 1990. *A Critical Edition of the sGra sbyor bam po gnyis pa: An Old and Basic Commentary on the Mahāvyutpatti*. Studia Tibetica 18. Materials for Tibetan-Mongolian Dictionaries, vol. 2. Tokyo: The Toyo Bunko.

Migmar Tseten, Lama, trans. 2018. *Sri Vajrabhairava Sadhana*. Cambridge, MA: Mangalamkosha Publications.

Mikkyo Seiten Kenkyukai, ed. 1986. "*Vajradhātumahāmaṇḍalopāyikā-sarvavajrodaya*." *Daigaku sougou-bukkyou-kenkyūjo kiyou* 8: 253–25.

Mimaki, Katsumi, and Toru Tomabechi, eds. 1994. *Pañcakrama: Sanskrit and Tibetan Texts Critically Edited with Verse Index and Facsimile Edition of the Sanskrit Manuscripts*. Tokyo: The Centre for East Asian Cultural Studies for Unesco.

Monier-Williams, Monier. 1899. *A Sanskrit-English Dictionary: Etymologically and Philologically Arranged with Special Reference to Cognate Indo-European Languages*. Delhi: Motilal Banarsidass.

Nattier, J. 1991. *Once Upon a Future Time: Studies in a Buddhist Prophecy of Decline*. Berkeley, CA: Asian Humanities Press.

Negī, Ṭhākurasena, ed. 2018. *Sarvabuddhasamāyogaḍākinījalasaṃvarakalpa* 1–8. *Dhīḥ: Journal of Rare Buddhist Texts Research Project* 58: 141–201.

Newman, John. 1987. *The Outer Wheel of Time: Vajrayāna Buddhist Cosmology in the Kālacakra Tantra*. PhD dissertation, University of Wisconsin–Madison.

———. 1990. "Vajrayāna Deities in an Illustrated Indian Manuscript of the Aṣṭasāhasrikāprajñāpāramitā." *JIABS* 13.2: 117–32.

———. 2021. "On the Origin of the Kālacakra Tantra and the Paramādibuddha." *JIABS* 44: 311–53.

Nichols, Michael D. 2019. *Malleable Māra: Transformations of a Buddhist Symbol of Evil*. Albany: State University of New York Press.

Nihom, Max. 1998. "The Maṇḍala of Caṇḍi Gumpung (Sumatra) and the Indo-Tibetan Vajraśekharatantra." *Indo-Iranian Journal* 41: 245–54.

Nishioka, Soshū. 1983. "Index to the Catalogue Section of Bu-ston's History of Buddhism." *Annual Report of the Institute for the Study of Cultural Exchange, Tokyo University* 6: 47–201.

Niu Song, ed. 2001. *Yonghegong: Zhongguo zangchuan fojiao zhuming gusi* [Yonghegong: The celebrated ancient Tibetan Buddhist monastery of China]. Beijing: Dangdai Zhongguo.

Noguchi, Keiya. 1995. "On the Inserted Verses among the Citation from the Prajñopāyaviniścaya-siddhi IV in the Saṃpuṭodbhavatantra II-ii." *Studies on the Buddhist Sanskrit Literature*, edited by the Śrāvakabhūmi Study Group and The Buddhist Tantric Texts Study Group, 141–45. Tokyo: Institute for Comprehensive Studies of Buddhism, Taisho University.

O'Flaherty, Wendy Doniger. 1976. *The Origins of Evil in Hindu Mythology*. Los Angeles: University of California Press.

Ohnuma, Reiko. 2019. "The Heretical, Heterodox Howl: Jackals in Pāli Buddhist Literature." *Religions* 10.221: 1–16.

Olivelle, Patrick. 2005. *Manu's Code of Law: A Critical Edition and Translation of the Mānava-Dharmaśāstra*. New York: Oxford University Press.

Orzech, Charles D. 1987. "Mahāvairocana." In *Encyclopedia of Religion*, edited by L. Jones 8, 5607–9. Detroit: Thomson Gale.

Padoux, André. 1992. *Vāc: The Concept of the Word in Selected Hindu Tantras*. Delhi: Motilal Banarsidass.

Pagel, Ulrich. 1995. *Bodhisattvapiṭaka: Its Doctrines, Practices and Their Position in Mahāyāna Literature*. Buddhica Britannica, Series Continua 5. Tring: The Institute of Buddhist Studies.

Paine, Robert Treat, and Alexander Soper. 1981. *The Art and Architecture of Japan*. New Haven: Yale University Press.

Pal, Pratapaditya. 1984. *Tibetan Paintings*. Basel: Ravi Kumar.

Pandey Shastri, Janardan, ed. 2002. *Śrīherukābhidhānam Cakrasaṃvatantram with the Vivṛti Commentary of Bhavabhaṭṭa*. Rare Buddhist Texts Series 26. Sarnath, Varanasi: Central Institute of Higher Tibetan Studies.

Payne Richard K. 2016. "Homa: Tantric Fire Ritual." In *Oxford Research Encyclopedia*: https://oxfordre.com/religion/view/10.1093/acrefore/9780199340378.001.0001/acrefore-9780199340378-e-82?rskey=1gIWHM&result=6 (accessed May 18, 2017).

Payne, Richard K., and Michael Witzel, eds. 2015. *Homa Variations: Ritual Change across the Longue Durée*. New York: Oxford University Press.

Petech, Luciano. 1990. *Central Tibet and the Mongols: The Yüan-Sa-skya Period of Tibetan History*. Rome: Istituto Italiano per il Medio ed Estremo Oriente.

———. 1993. 'Phags-pa (1235–1280)." In *In the Service of the Khan*, edited by I. Rachewiltz et al., 646–54. Wiesbaden: Harrassowitz Verlag.

Pha bong kha pa Bde chen snying po. 2021. *The Sādhana of the Bhagavan Glorious Solitary-Hero Vajrabhairava entitled "Victory over Demons."* In Gonsalez 2021, 249–94.

Pradhan, P., ed. 1975. *Abhidharmakośabhāṣyam* of Vasubandhu. Patna: K. P. Jayaswal Research Center.

Ra Yeshé Sengé. 2015. *The All-Pervading Melodious Drumbeat: The Life of Ra Lotsawa*. Translated by Bryan J. Cuevas. New York: Penguin Books.

Raghavan, V. 1952. *Yantras or Mechanical Contrivances In Ancient India*. Bangalore: The Indian Institute of Culture.

Ram Shastri, Mukund, ed. 1918. *Mahānayaprakāśa of Śitikaṇṭha with Commentary*. Śrīnagar: Kashmir Śaivism Texts Studies.

Rao, Desiraju Hanumanta. 1998. *Vālmīki's Rāmāyaṇa, Bālakāṇḍa*. Sanskrit text and translation. Online resource: https://www.valmikiramayan.net/utf8/baala/sarga25/bala_5F25_frame.htm (accessed March 13, 2019).

Rastelli, Marion. 2003. "Maṇḍalas and Yantras in the Pāñcarātra." In Bühnemann et al. 2003, 119–51.

Repo, Joona. 2011. "Tsong kha pa blo bzang grags pa." *The Treasury of Lives*, online resource: https://treasuryoflives.org/biographies/view/Tsongkhapa-Lobzang-Drakpa/8986 (accessed January 20, 2020).

Rintchen. 1959. *Les matériaux pour l'étude du chamanisme mongol I. Sources littéraires*. Wiesdbaden: Otto Harrassowitz.

Samdhong Rinpoche and Vrajvallabha Dwivedi, eds. 1987a. *Guhyasiddhi* [included in] *Guhyādi-aṣṭasiddhisaṅgraha / gSang pa grub pa la sogs pa'i grub pa sde brgyad bzhugs*.

Two parts: Sanskrit text and the Tibetan translation. Rare Buddhist Texts Series 1. Varanasi: Central Institute of Higher Tibetan Studies.

———. 1987b. *Prajñopāyaviniścayasiddhi* [included in] *Guhyādi-aṣṭasiddhisaṅgraha / gSang pa grub pa la sogs pa'i grub pa sde brgyad bzhugs*. Two parts: Sanskrit text and the Tibetan translation. Rare Buddhist Texts Series 1. Varanasi: Central Institute of Higher Tibetan Studies.

———. 1991. *Kṛṣṇayamāritantra with Ratnāvalīpañjikā's Commentary* by Kumāracandra. Rare Buddhist Text Series 9. Sarnath: Durlabha Bauddha Grantha Sodha Yojana, Kendriya Ucca Tibbati Siksa.

———. 1992. *Mahāmāyātantra* with *Guṇavatī* by Ratnakāraśānti. Rare Buddhist Text Series 10. Varanasi: Central Institute of Higher Tibetan Studies.

———. 1993. *Abhisamayamañjarī*. Rare Buddhist Text Series 11. Sarnath, Varanasi: Central Institute of Higher Tibetan Studies.

Roberts, Alan Peter. 2012. "Translating Translation: An Encounter with the Ninth-Century Tibetan Version of the Kāraṇḍavyūha-sūtra." *Journal of Oxford Centre for Buddhist Studies* 2: 224–42.

Rodrigues, H. P. 2009. "Durgā." In *Brill's Encyclopedia of Hinduism*, edited by K.A. Jacobsen, H. Basu, A. Malinar, and V. Narayanan, 1:535–50. Leiden: Brill.

Roerich, George N., trans. 1949 (repr. 1995). *The Blue Annals* [by 'Gos lo tsā ba]. Delhi: Motilal Banarsidass.

Sagaster, Klaus. 1991. *Ikonographie und Symbolik des Tibetischen Buddhismus: Die Sadhanas der Sammlung Rgyud-sde Kun-btus*. Wiesbaden: Otto Harrassowitz.

Sakaki, Ryōzaburō, ed. 1916–25. *Mahāvyutpatti* [= *Sgra sbyor bam po gnyis pa*]: *A Sanskrit-Tibetan-Chinese-Japanese Quadrilingual Collation*. 2 vols. Kyoto: Shingonshū Kyōto Daigaku.

Sakurai, Munenobu. 1987. "A Study of the ḥJam dpal-gsaṅ-ldan School Mainly Based upon the Nāmamantrārthāvalokinī (1)." *Mikkyogaku Kenkyū* (*Journal of Esoteric Buddhist Study*) 19: 87–109.

———. 1998. "Cakrasaṃvarābhisamaya no genten kenkyū." *Chizan Gakuho* 47: 1–32.

Samuel, Geoffrey. 1993. *Civilized Shamans: Buddhism in Tibetan Societies*. Washington and London: Smithsonian Institute Press.

Sanderson, Alexis. 1985. "Purity and Power among the Brahmans of Kashmir." In *The Category of the Person: Anthropology, Philosophy, History*, edited by Michael Carrithers, Steven Collins, and Steven Lukes, 190–216. Cambridge: Cambridge University Press.

———. 1988. "Śaivism and the Tantric Traditions." In *The World's Religions*, edited by Steward Sutherland, Leslie Houlden, Peter Clarke, and Friedhelm Hardy, 660–704. New York and London: Routledge.

———. 1993. "The Dependence of the Herukatantras on the Śaiva Tantras of the Vidyāpīṭha." Lecture Series in Trinity Term, All Souls College, University of Oxford. Unpublished.

———. 1994. "Vajrayāna: Origin and Function." In *Buddhism into the Year 2000: International Conference Proceedings*, 89–102. Bangkok and Los Angeles: Dhammakaya Foundation.

———. 1995. "Meaning in Tantric Ritual." In *Essais sur le Rituel III*, edited by A. M. Blondeau and K. Shipper, 15–95. Paris: École Pratique des Hautes Études.

———. 2004. "Religion and the State: Śaiva Officiants in the Territory of the King's Brahmanical Chaplain." *Indo-Iranian Journal* 47: 229–300.

———. 2005. "A Commentary on the Opening Verses of the Tantrasāra of Abhinavagupta." In *Sāmarasya: Studies in Indian Arts, Philosophy, and Interreligious Dialogue in Honour of Bettina Bäumer*, edited by Sadananda Das and Ernst Fürlinger, 89–148. New Delhi: D. K. Printworld.

———. 2007. "The Śaiva Exegesis of Kashmir." In *Mélanges tantriques à la mémoire d'Hélène Brunner*, edited by Dominic Goodall and André Padoux, 231–444. Publications du département d'Indologie 106. Pondicherry: Institut Français de Pondichéry / École Française d'Extrême-Orient.

———. 2009. "The Śaiva Age: The Rise and Dominance of Śaivism during the Early Medieval Period." In *Genesis and Development of Tantrism*, edited by S. Einoo, 41–350. Institute of Oriental Culture Special Series 23. Tokyo: Institute of Oriental Culture, University of Tokyo.

———. 2010. "The Influence of Śaivism on Pāla Buddhism. An outline of the lecture delivered at the University of Chicago, 1 March 2010." Available at academia.edu.

———. 2015. "Tolerance, Exclusivity, Inclusivity, and Persecution in Indian Religion During the Early Mediaeval Period." In *Honoris Causa: Essays in Honour of Aveek Sarkar*, 155–224. London: Allen Lane.

Sarbacker, Stuart R. 2005. *Samādhi: The Numinous and Cessative in Indo-Tibetan Yoga*. Albany: State University of New York Press.

Śarma Ācārya, Śrīrāma, ed. 1967. *Mārkaṇḍeya Purāṇa: Prathama Khaṇḍa*. Barelī: Saṃskṛti-Saṃsthan.

Scherrer-Schaub, Cristina. 1999. "Translation, Transmission, Tradition: Suggestions from Ninth-Century Tibet." *Journal of Indian Philosophy* 27.1–2: 67–77.

Schmidt-Leukel, Perry. 2022. "The Demonization of the Other through the Narrative of Māra's Defeat (*māravijaya*)." In *Buddhism and Its Religious Others*, edited by Christopher V. Jones, 155–75. Oxford: Oxford University Press.

Schmidt-Madsen, Jacob. 2014. *Repossessing the Past: Authorial Tradition and Scribal Innovation in Śivadāsa's Vetālapañcaviṃśatikā*. MA thesis, University of Copenhagen.

Schoening, Jeffrey D. 1995. *The Śālistamba Sūtra and Its Indian Commentaries*, 2 vols. Vienna: Wiener Studien zur Tibetologie und Buddhismuskunde.

Seyfort Ruegg, D. 1977. "The Uses of the Four Positions of the *Catuṣkoṭi* and the Problem of the Description of Reality in Mahāyāna Buddhism." *Journal of Indian Philosophy* 5.1–2: 1–71.

———. 1997. "The Preceptor-Donor (yon mchod) Relation in Thirteenth-Century Tibetan Society and Polity, Its Inner Asian Precursors and Indian Models." In *Proceedings of the Seventh Seminar of the International Association for Tibetan Studies, Graz, 1995*, edited by H. Krasser, M. T. Much, and E. Steinkellner, 2:857–72. Vienna: Verlag der Österreichischen Akademie der Wissenschaften.

———. 2003. "Mchod yon, Yon mchod and Mchod gnas / Yon gnas: On the Historiography and Semantics of a Tibetan Religio-Social and Religio-Political Concept." In McKay 2003, 2:362–72.

———. 2004. "Introductory Remarks on the Spiritual and Temporal Orders." In *The Relationship between Religion and State (Chos srid zung 'brel) in Traditional Tibet*, edited by C. Cüppers, 9–14. Lumbini, Nepal: Lumbini International Research Institute.

———. 2008. *The Symbiosis of Buddhism with Brahmanism/Hinduism in South Asia and of Buddhism with "Local Cults" in Tibet and the Himalayan Region*. Vienna: Österreichische Akademie der Wissenschaften.

Sferra, Francesco. 1999. "The Concept of Purification in Some Texts of Late Indian Buddhism." *Journal of Indian Philosophy* 27.1–2: 83–103.

———. 2003. "Some Considerations on the Relationship between Hindu and Buddhist Tantras." In *Buddhist Asia 1: Papers from the First Conference of Buddhist Studies Held in Naples in May 2001*, edited by G. Verardi and S. Vita, 57–84. Naples: Università degli Studi di Napoli "L'Orientale"; Centro di Studi sul Buddhismo.

———. 2017. "A Fragment of the Vajrāmṛtatantra: A Critical Edition of the Leaves Contained in Cambridge University Library Or.158.1." In *Indic Manuscript Cultures Through the Ages: Material, Textual, and Historical Perspectives*, edited by V. Vergiani, D. Cuneo, and C. A. Formigatti, 409–48. Berlin: DeGruyter.

———. 2019. "CUL Add.1708.2: Frammento di un commento inedito alla Mañjuśrīnāmasaṅgīti." In *Iranian Studies in Honour of Adriano V. Rossi*, edited by S. Badalkhan, G.P. Basello, and M. De Chiara, 883–99. Naples: Università degli Studi di Napoli "L'Orientale."

Shaw, Miranda. 1998. *Passionate Enlightenment: Women in Tantric Buddhism*. Princeton, NJ: Princeton University Press.

Shen Weirong. 2004. "Magic, Power, Sorcery and Evil Spirits: The Image of Tibetan Monks in Chinese Literature during the Yuan Dynasty." In *The Relationship between Religion and State (Chos srid zung 'brel) In Traditional Tibet*, edited by Christoph Cüppers, 189–227. Lumbini, Nepal: Lumbini International Research Institute.

Shulman, David. 1980. *Tamil Temple Myths: Sacrifice and Divine Marriage in the South Indian Śaiva Tradition*. Princeton, NJ: Princeton Legacy Library.

Siderits, Mark, and Shōryū Katsura. 2013. *Nāgārjuna's Middle Way: Mūlamadhyamakakārikā*. Boston: Wisdom Publications.

Siklós, Bulcsu. 1996. *The Vajrabhairava Tantras: Tibetan and Mongolian Versions, English Translation and Annotations*. Tring: The Institute of Buddhist Studies.

———. 2012. "The Evolution of the Buddhist Yama." *The Buddhist Forum*, 4:165–89.

Simmer-Brown, Judith A. 2001. *Dakini's Warm Breath: The Feminine Principle in Tibetan Buddhism*. Boston: Shambhala.

Sinclair, Iain. 2014. "War Magic and Just War in Indian Tantric Buddhism." *Social Analysis: The International Journal of Social and Cultural Practice* 58.1: 149–66.

———. 2015. "Creation of Theism Personified: A Conceptual History of the God-Maker Avalokiteśvara." In *Asian Horizons: Giuseppe Tucci's Buddhist, Indian, Himalayan and Central Asian Studies*, edited by David Templeman and Angelo Andrea Di Castro, 431–78. Melbourne: Monash University Publishing.

Sircar, Dineshchandra. 1948. *The Śākta-Pīṭhas*. Delhi: Motilal Banarsidass.

Skorupski, Tadeusz, ed. and trans. 1983. The *Sarvadurgatipariśodhana Tantra: Elimination of All Evil Destinies: Sanskrit and Tibetan Texts with Introduction, English Translation, and Notes*. Delhi: Motilal Banarsidass.

———. 1996. "The Saṃpuṭa-tantra: Sanskrit and Tibetan Versions of Chapter One." *The Buddhist Forum*, 4:191–244. London: SOAS.

Slouber, Michael. 2017. *Early Tantric Medicine: Snakebite, Mantras, and Healing in the Gāruḍa Tantras*. Oxford: Oxford University Press.

Smith, Warren. 2009. *Tibetan Nation*. New Delhi: Rupa Publications.

Snellgrove, David L., ed. and trans. 1959. *The Hevajra Tantra: A Critical Study. 2 vols. Part I, Introduction and Translation; Part II, Sanskrit and Tibetan Texts*. London Oriental Series 6. London: Oxford University Press.

———. 1987. *Indo-Tibetan Buddhism: Indian Buddhists and Their Tibetan Successors.* Boston: Shambhala.

Snellgrove, David L., and Lokesh Chandra, eds. 1981. *Sarva-tathāgata-tattva-saṅgraha*: Facsimile Reproduction of a Tenth Century Sanskrit Manuscript from Nepal. Śataka-Piṭaka Series, Indo-Asian Literatures, 269. New Delhi: Sharada Rani.

Sopa, Lhundub, with David Patt. 2004. *Steps on the Path of Enlightenment: A Commentary on Tsongkhapa's Lamrim Chenmo, Volume 1, The Foundation Practices.* Boston: Wisdom Publications.

Sørensen, Per, and Hazod Guntram. 2007. *Rulers on the Celestial Plain: Ecclesiastic and Secular Hegemony in Medieval Tibet: A Study of Tshal Gung-thang*, 2 vols. Vienna: Verlag der Österreichischen Akademie der Wissenschaften.

Staal, Frits. 1997. "Indian Theories of Meaning." In *Concise Encyclopedia of Philosophy of Language*, edited by Peter V. Lamarque, 120–26. Oxford: Pergamon.

Stearns, Cyrus. 1996. "The Life and Tibetan Legacy of the Indian Mahāpaṇḍita Vibhūticandra." *JIABS* 19.1: 127–72.

Stein, M. A., ed. 1960. *Rājataraṅgiṇī or Chronicle of the Kings of Kashmir.* Delhi: Munshi Ram Manohar Lal.

Stein, R. A. 1995. "La soumission de Rudra et autres contes tantriques." *Journal Asiatique* 283: 121–60.

Strickmann, Michael, ed. 1981. *Tantric and Taoist Studies in Honour of R. A. Stein*, vol. 1. Mélanges chinois et bouddhiques 20. Brussels: Institut Belge des Hautes Études Chinoises.

———. 1983. "Homa in East Asia." In *Agni: The Vedic Ritual of the Fire Altar*, edited by Frits Staal, 2:418–55. Berkeley, CA: Asian Humanities Press.

Szántó, Péter-Dániel. 2013. "Before a Critical Edition of the Sampuṭa." In *Tibet after Empire: Culture, Society and Religion between 850–1000*, edited by C. Cüppers, R. Mayer, and M. Walter, 397–422.Lumbini, Nepal: Lumbini International Research Institute.

Tachikawa, Musashi. 1989. *The Ngor Maṇḍalas of Tibet: Plates.* Tokyo: Centre for East Asian Cultural Studies.

Tajima, R. 1992. "The Study of the Mahāvairocana-sūtra (dainichikyo)." In *The Enlightenment of Vairocana*, edited by A. Wayman and R. Tajima, 209–372. Delhi: Motilal Banarsidass.

Tanaka, Kimiaki. 2018. *An Illustrated History of the Mandala: From Its Genesis to the Kālacakratantra.* Somerville, MA: Wisdom Publications.

Tanemura, Ryugen. 2004. *Kuladatta's Kriyāsaṃgrahapañjikā: A Critical Edition and Annotated Translation of Selected Sections.* Groningen Oriental Studies 19. Groningen: Egbert Forsten.

———. 2009. "Superiority of Vajrayāna—Part II: Superiority of the Tantric Practice Taught in the *Vajrayānāntadvayanirākaraṇa (rDo rje theg pa'i mtha' gñis sel ba)." In *Genesis and Development of Tantrism*, edited by Shingo Einoo, 487–514. Tokyo: Institute of Oriental Culture, University of Tokyo.

———. 2015. "Guhyasamāja." In *Brill's Encyclopedia of Buddhism*, edited by J. A. Silk et al. 1:326–33. Leiden: Brill.

Taylor, McComas. 2007. *The Fall of the Indigo Jackal: The Discourse of Division and Pūrṇabhadra's Pañcatantra.* Albany: State University of New York Press.

Teeuw, Andries, et al. 1969. *Śiwarātrikalpa of Mpu Tanakuṅ: An Old Javanese Poem, Its*

Indian Source and Balinese Illustrations. Bibliotheca Indonesia. The Hague: Martinus Nijhoff.

Templeman, David. 1981. "Tāranātha the Historian." *Tibet Journal* 17.1: 41–46.

———. 1989. *Tāranātha's Life of Kṛṣṇācārya/Kāṇha*. Dharamsala: Library of Tibetan Works and Archives.

———. 2009. *Becoming Indian: A Study of the Life of the 16–17th Century Tibetan Lama Tāranātha*. PhD dissertation, Monash University.

Thomas, Lynn. 1994. "The Identity of the Destroyer in the Mahābhārata." *Numen* 41.3: 255–72.

Tomabechi, Toru. 2007. "The Extraction of Mantra (mantroddhāra) in the Sarvabuddhasamāyogatantra." In *Pramāṇakīrtiḥ: Papers Dedicated to Ernst Steinkellner on the Occasion of His 70th Birthday*, edited by Birgit Kellner et al., 903–23. Wiener Studien zur Tibetologie und Buddhismuskunde 70.1–2. Vienna: Arbeitskreis für Tibetische und Buddhistische Studien, Universität Wien.

Törzsök, Judit. 2011. "Kāpālikas." In *Brill's Encyclopedia of Hinduism*, edited by Knut A. Jacobsen, Helene Basu, Angelika Malinar, and Vasudha Narayanan, 3:355–61. Leiden: Brill.

———. 2016. "The Emergence of the Alphabet Goddess Mātṛkā in Early Śaiva Tantras." In *Tantric Studies: Fruits of a Franco-German Collaboration on Early Tantra*, edited by D. Goodall and H. Isaacson, 135–56. Pondicherry: École Française d'Extrême-Orient / Institut Français de Pondichéry, and Asien-Afrika-Institut, Universität Hamburg.

Tribe, Anthony. 1994. *The Names of Wisdom: A Critical Edition and Annotated Translation of Chapters 1–5 of Vilāsavajra's Commentary on the Nāmasaṃgīti, with Introduction and Textual Notes*. PhD dissertation, University of Oxford.

———. 2016. *Tantric Buddhist Practice in India: Vilāsavajra's Commentary on the Mañjuśrī-nāmasaṃgīti*. London and New York: Routledge.

Tripathi, Ram Shankar, and Thakur Sain Negi, eds. 2001. *Muktāvalī of Ratnākaraśānti: A Commentary (pañjikā) on the Hevajra*. Bibliotheca Indo-Tibetica Series 48. Sarnath, Varanasi: Central Institute of Higher Tibetan Studies.

———. 2006. *Hevajratantram with Yogaratnamālāpañjikā of Mahāpaṇḍitācārya Kṛṣṇapāda*. Sanskrit and Hindi. Sarnath, Varanasi: Central Institute of Higher Tibetan Studies.

Tsuda, Shinichi. 1970. *The Saṃvarodaya-tantra: Selected Chapters*. PhD dissertation, Australian National University.

Tucci, Giuseppe. 1940. *Travels of Tibetan Pilgrims in the Swat Valley*. Calcutta: The Greater India Society.

Tuttle, Gray. 2011. "Tibetan Buddhism at Wutai Shan in the Qing: The Chinese-Language Register." *JIATS* 6: 163–214.

Ujeed, Uranchimeg Borjigin. 2009. *Indigenous Efforts and Dimensions of Mongolian Buddhism-Exemplified by the Mergen Tradition*. PhD dissertation, SOAS, University of London.

Unithiri, N. V. P., ed. 2002. *Tantrasārasaṃgraha of Nārāyaṇa with Mantravimarśinī Commentary by Svarṇagrāma Vāsudeva*, Parts 1 and 2. Calicut: University of Calicut.

Vaidya, Ash Ram. 1999. *Vāgbhaṭa's Aṣṭāṅgasaṃgraha: The Compendium of Eight Branches of Āyurveda, Text and English Translation with Illustrations*. Delhi: Sri Satguru Publications.

Vaidya, P. L., ed. 1964. *Āryamañjuśrīmūlakalpa*. Buddhist Sanskrit Texts 18. Darbhanga: Mithila Institute. Essentially a reprint of the edition of T. Ganapati Śāstrī 1920, 1922, and 1925 (Trivandrum Sanskrit Series 70, 76, and 84).

Vasu, Śrīśa Candra, ed. and trans. 2019. *The Aṣṭādhyāyī of Pāṇini (A Treatise on Sanskrit Grammar* (2 vols). Delhi: Parimal Publications.

Vasudeva, Somadeva, ed. and trans. 2004. *The Yoga of Mālinīvijayottaratantra, Chapters 1–4, 7, 11-17*. Pondicherry: Institut Français de Pondichéry / École Française d'Extrême-Orient.

———. 2007. "The Synaesthetic Iconography: 1. The Nādiphāntakrama." In *Mélanges tantriques à la mémorie d'Hélène Brunner: Tantric Studies in Memory of Hélène Brunner*, edited by Dominic Goodall and André Padoux, 517–50. Publications du département d'Indologie 106. Pondicherry: Institut Français de Pondichéry / École Française d'Extrême-Orient.

———. 2012. "Powers and Identities: Yoga Powers and the Tantric Śaiva Traditions." In *Yoga Powers: Extraordinary Capacities Attained through Meditation and Concentration*, edited by A. Jacobsen, 265–302. Leiden and Boston: Brill.

Verardi, Giovanni. 2011. *Hardships and Downfall of Buddhism in India*. Singapore: Institute of Southeast Asian Studies, and Delhi: Manohar.

———. 2018. *The Gods and the Heretics: Crisis and Ruin of Indian Buddhism*. Delhi: Aditya Prakashan.

Vidyāratna, T. 1965. *Kulārṇavatantra*, rev. ed. Introduction by A. Avalon and M. P. Pandit. New Delhi: Motilal Banarsidass.

Wallis, Christopher. 2008. "The Descent of Power: Possession, Mysticism, and Initiation in the Śaiva Theology of Abhinavagupta." *Journal of Indian Philosophy* 36: 247–95.

Wallis, Glenn. 2002. *Meditating the Power of Buddhas: Ritual in the Mañjuśrīmūlakalpa*. Albany: State University of New York Press.

Wang Jiapeng. 1991. "Gugong Yuhuage tanyuan" [Investigating the origin of the Yuhua pavilion at the imperial palace]. In *Qingdai gongshi tanwei* [Explorations into Qing dynasty palace history]. Beijing: Zijincheng.

Wang, Xiangyun. 1995. *Tibetan Buddhism at the Court of Qing: The Life and Work of lCang-Skya Rol-Pa'i-Rdo-Rje, 1717–86*. PhD dissertation, Harvard University.

———. 2000. "The Qing Court's Tibet Connection: Lcang skya Rol pa'i rdo rje and the Qianlong Emperor." *Harvard Journal of Asiatic Studies* 60.1: 125–63.

Watt, James C. Y., and Anne E. Wardwell. 1997. *When Silk Was Gold: Central Asian and Chinese Textiles*. New York: Metropolitan Museum of Art.

Wayman, Alex. 1959a. "Studies in Yama and Māra." *Indo-Iranian Journal* 3.1: 44–73.

———. 1959b. "Studies in Yama and Māra." *Indo-Iranian Journal* 3.2: 112–31.

———. 1973. *Buddhist Tantras: Light on Indo-Tibetan Esotericism*. New York: Samuel Weiser.

———. 1974. "The Ritual in Tantric Buddhism of the Disciple's Entrance into the Mandala." In *Worship and Ritual in Christianity and Other Religions*, 41–57. Studia Missionalia 23. Rome: Gregorian University Press.

———. 1985. *Chanting the Names of Mañjuśrī: The Mañjuśrī-Nāma-Saṃgīti, Sanskrit and Tibetan Texts*. Boston and London: Shambhala.

———. 1992. "Study of the Vairocanābhisaṃbodhitantra." In *The Enlightenment of Vairocana*, by A. Wayman and R. Tajima, 1–207. Delhi: Motilal Banarsidass.

Wedemeyer, Christian K. 2007. *Āryadeva's Lamp That Integrates the Practices (Caryāmelāpapradīpa): The Gradual Path of Vajrayāna Buddhism According to the Esoteric Community Noble Tradition*. New York: American Institute of Buddhist Studies at Columbia University.

———. 2012. "Locating Tantric Antinomianism: An Essay toward an Intellectual History of the 'Practices/Practice Observance' (caryā/caryāvrata)." *JIABS* 34.1–2: 349–420.

Weinberger, Steven Neal. 2003. *The Significance of Yoga Tantra and the Compendium of Principles (Tattvasaṃgraha Tantra) within Tantric Buddhism in India and Tibet*. PhD dissertation, University of Virginia.

Wenta, Aleksandra. 2021. "Tāranātha on the Emergence of the Tantric Cycle of Vajrabhairava-Yamāntaka: Writing a Tibetan Buddhist Historiography in Seventeenth-Century Tibet." *Revue d'Etudes Tibétaines* 61: 5–52.

———. 2022. "The Transmission Lineages of the *Raktayamāri* Tantric Cycles in the Sa skya Tradition of Tibetan Buddhism: The *Gshin rje chos 'byung* of A mes zhabs Ngag dbang kun dga' bsod nams (1597–1659)." *Revue d'Etudes Tibétaines* 65: 26–69.

———. 2024. "The Vajrabhairavatantra: Materia Magica and Circulation of Tantric Magical Recipes." In *Tibetan Magic: Past and Present*, edited by C. Bailey and A. Wenta, 61–84. London: Bloomsbury Academic.

White, David Gordon, ed. 2000. *Tantra in Practice*. Princeton and Oxford: Princeton University Press.

———. 2003. *The Kiss of the Yoginī: "Tantric Sex" in Its South Asian Contexts*. Chicago: University of Chicago Press.

Williams, Paul, and Anthony Tribe. 2000. *Buddhist Thought: A Complete Introduction to the Indian Tradition*. London and New York: Routledge.

Wylie, T. V. 1977. "The First Mongol Conquest of Tibet Reinterpreted." *The Harvard Journal of Asiatic Studies* 37.1: 103–33. (Also in McKay 2003, 2:317–61.)

Yamada, Isshi, ed. 1981. *Sarva-tathāgata-tattva-saṅgraha nāma Mahāyāna-sūtra*. A critical edition based on a Sanskrit manuscript and Chinese and Tibetan translations. Śatakapiṭaka Series 262. New Delhi: Sharada Rani.

Yamamoto, Kosho, trans. 1973. The *Mahāyāna Mahāparinirvāṇasūtra* from Dharmakshema's Chinese version. Taisho Tripitaka vol. 12, no. 374. Edited and revised by Tony Page, 2007. Online resource: https://web.archive.org/web/20131019072030/http://webzoom.freewebs.com/nirvana-sutra/convenient/Mahaparinirvana_Sutra_Yamamoto_Page_2007.pdf (accessed March 14, 2018).

Yamano, Chieko. 2013. "The Yakṣiṇī-sādhana in the Kakṣapuṭa-tantra: Introduction, Critical Edition, and Translation." *Journal of the International College for Postgraduate Buddhist Studies* 17: 61–99.

Yamasaki, Taiko. 1988. *Shingon: Japanese Esoteric Buddhism*. Boston: Shambhala.

Yang Xin, Wang Jiapeng, Liu Lu, and Hu Jianzhong, eds. 1998. *Qinggong zangchuan fojiao wenwu* [Cultural relics of Tibetan Buddhism collected in the Qing palace] Beijing: Zijincheng.

Yeshe Tsogyal. 2004. *The Lotus-Born: The Life Story of Padmasambhava*. Revealed by Nyang Ral Nyima Öser. Kathmandu: Rangjung Yeshe Publications.

Yongzhang, Qin. 2008. *Qianlong huang di yu Zhangjia guo shi*. Xining: Qinghai renmin chubanshe.

Zadoo, J. D., ed. 1947. *The Uḍḍāmareśvara Tantram: A Book on Magical Rites*. Srinagar: Research Department.

Index

Abhidharma, 32n48, 128–29, 313n992
action (*karma*)
and intention, 5–6
and rebirth, 70–71, 75
ritual, 98, 111, 214n510, 227n556, 248n684, 300n935
six, 172n414
transfer of, 167n399
afflictive emotions (*kleśa*), 17, 20, 37, 40, 61–62, 62n152, 75, 113, 275n817. *See also individual afflictions*
aggregates (*skandhas*), 61, 256n723
aggressive rites (*abhicāra*), 107–8, 138–39, 142, 149, 172, 183–84, 188–90, 211n498, 236n614, 259n727, 291n886, 296–97
Agni (*agnideva*), 146–47
Agrabodhi, 24–25, 24nn28–29
Akaniṣṭha, 70
Akṣobhya, 49, 87n218
anger, 6, 73, 185, 278n827. *See also* hatred (*dveṣa*)
asceticism, 65n159, 67–68, 82, 91, 165, 224n545, 266n755, 273n811, 283n859
Āsurīkalpa, 184
Atharva Veda, 4
Altan Khan, 55–56n136
attachment (*rāga*), 101, 273n806
attainment, means of (*sādhana*), 1, 20, 95, 96, 180, 201n453
Avalokiteśvara, 76, 76n185, 91, 130n323, 315n997
awakening, 18, 19, 20, 37–38, 40, 131n324, 273–74n811, 287n871
awareness, 64, 237n617, 259n729

B

Bari lineage, 23–24
Beijing, 52–53
Bhairava Maheśvara, 2, 72–73, 75–76. *See also* Maheśvara
bliss. *See* great bliss (*mahāsukham*)
Blue Annals, 48n102
bodhicitta, 73, 202n453
bodhisattvas, 75, 121, 129n322, 261n733, 262n738. *See also individual bodhisattvas*
Brahmā, 62, 62n152, 75, 119, 119n294, 128n321, 168n400, 266n755
Brahmanism, 115
Brahmayāmala (BY), 6, 64–66, 98, 136, 166n398, 168–69, 236–37n617, 284n866. *See also Picumata-Brahmayāmala*
'Bras spungs monastery, 51, 55–56n136
Buddha Śākyamuni, 61, 241n638
Buddhaguptanātha, 83
Buddhajñānapāda, 23, 26–28, 27n39
buddhas, 75, 121, 129n322, 261n733, 262n738. *See also* form body (*rūpakāya*); primordial buddha (*ādibuddha*); truth body (*dharmakāya*); *individual buddhas*
Buddhist cosmology, 71, 75
Buddhist "encoding," 7, 34
Buddhist ethics, 5–6
Byams chen chos rje Shākya ye shes, 52

C

Cakrasaṃvara, 4, 57, 67, 74, 76, 115
Cakrasaṃvara Tantra, 21, 49n107, 96n240, 154, 162n390, 180

Caṇḍāla (demon), 80
Caṇḍikā (goddess), 79, 79n193, 80, 168n402, 208n482
Carcikā (Durgā), 115, 205n464
caryā tantras, 13, 17, 153, 259n729
Caturmudrāviniścaya (Nāgārjuna), 90n228
Central Institute of Higher Tibetan Studies, 197
cessation (*nirvāṇa*), 9, 123, 123n305, 260n730, 263n740
cognitive obscurations, 20, 37, 40. *See also* obstacles
compassion (*karuṇā*), 5–6, 52n122, 75, 121, 121n299, 121n301, 202n453, 242, 257–58n726, 271n792
  and rūpakāya, 203n453
completion stage (*utpannakrama*), 39, 85, 211n498, 287n872
concentration, 14–16, 216n515, 252n715, 267n761, 274, 284n865
  places conducive to, 203n454
connections (*anubandhas*), 36–38, 40, 40n70
consciousness, 164, 165–66. *See also* mind
cremation grounds, 9, 129, 204n457, 279n837, 281–82
  in paṭas, 136–37

D
Daiitoku myōō, 56–57
ḍākinīs, 81, 83, 85, 86, 89–90, 91, 125n310, 154, 312n982
Dalai Lama, Fifth, 55n133
Dalai Lama, First, 55–56n136
Dalai Lama, Fourteenth, 50–51
Dalai Lama, Seventh, 50n113
ḍāmarīs (female spirits), 155
death, 9, 45, 60–61, 62, 98, 136, 159, 191, 225n549. *See also* cremation grounds; rebirth; Yama
defilements (*kleśas*). *See* afflictive emotions (*kleśa*)
deity yoga, 3, 9, 13, 39, 126–31, 129n322, 223–24n545, 275n816–276n817. *See also* completion stage (*utpannakrama*); generation stage (*utpattikrama*); union (*yoga*); visualization (*dhyāna*)
demonic entities, 2–3, 5, 64, 72n178, 78–80, 136, 208. *See also individual demons*
dependent origination, 15, 121–22, 127–28, 225n548, 258n726
desire (*rāga*), 17, 73, 75, 121, 121n301, 177
  eliminating, 15–16, 62n152, 67
Devākaracandra, 32
Devīmāhātmya, 78–79, 168n402
Dge lugs tradition, 49–55, 192
Dīpaṅkarabhadra, 26n37, 27, 27n39
doubt, 14
duality, 9, 128, 164, 165, 257n726, 268n765
Dza ya Paṇḍita, 62

E
elements (*dhātus*), 256n723
emanation body (*nirmāṇakāya*), 302n941. *See also* form body (*rūpakāya*)
emptiness (*śūnyatā*), 9, 15–16, 20n12, 121–22, 122n302, 127–28, 202n453, 256n723, 259n729, 264n742
  and dharmakāya, 203n453
  gnosis of, 258n726
energetic centers (*cakras*), 39
equanimity (*upekṣā*), 121, 121n301, 127n315, 162–63, 162n388, 165–66, 257–58n726, 288n872

F
Festival of Vajrabhairava's Maṇḍala, 54–55
fire offerings (*homa*), 1, 35, 138–45, 149–52, 216n516, 236n614, 289–300
  sequence of, 146–48
five nectars (*pañcāmṛta*), 3, 16–17, 16n6, 120n297, 154–66. *See also* impure substances
food, 28, 161–62, 216, 216n518, 218, 285, 288n872. *See also* impure substances
form body (*rūpakāya*), 202n453, 203n453. *See also* emanation body (*nirmāṇakāya*)

four Kapālabhairavas, 113, 115
four sublime states (*brahmavihāras*), 121, 121n301, 127, 127n315, 257–58n726. *See also individual brahmavihāras*

G
Gaṇḍī Sūtra, 94
Garuḍa Purāṇa, 60n145
Gaurī (Parvatī), 115, 205n464
generation stage (*utpattikrama*), 39, 85, 88, 89n226, 122n303, 287n872
Genghis Khan, 56
Gnyos lo tsā ba Yon tan grags, 41
goddesses, 124n308, 179–80, 205n464
  four, 115–16, 121, 124, 256n724
  See also ḍāmarīs (female spirits); yoginīs; *individual goddesses*
gods, 71–72, 72n178, 75, 78–79, 119, 119n294, 202–3n453. *See also individual gods*
great bliss (*mahāsukham*), 39, 211n498, 257n726, 266n755
Great Perfection (*rdzogs chen*), 82
Gshin rje chos 'byung (Tāranātha), 26, 84
Guanyu, 54, 54n131
Guhyāpanna (*Mañjuśrīnāmasaṅgītisādhana*), 24
Guhyasamāja Tantra (GS), 16, 17, 21, 21n15, 27n39, 49n107, 154
  Jñānapāda school of, 23, 120n298
Guhyasūtra (NTGS), 4, 6
  mad laughter in, 167n399
  tantric magic in, 171, 174–75, 177–79, 180, 187
Guide to Oḍḍiyāna (U rgyan pa Rin chen dpal), 83
Guṇakāraṇḍavyūha Sūtra, 94

H
hatred (*dveṣa*), 17, 62n152, 67, 73, 101, 113, 266n755. *See also* anger
Hayagrīvavidyā, 315n997
heavens, 74, 162, 304n953
  of the Four Great Kings, 71–72n177
  of the Thirty-Three, 71, 71n176
  See also Akaniṣṭha
hell, 5, 162, 241, 242, 313
hero's fee (*vīramūlya*), 133–34, 279n834
Heruka, 67, 74, 76. *See also* Cakrasaṃvara
Hevajra, 52n121
Hevajra Tantra, 36, 39, 46n95, 165
highest yoga (*yogottara*), 16, 16n5, 17, 87n218
History of Buddhism in India (Tāranātha), 22
History of the Yamāntaka Tradition (Tāranātha), 18
"Hymn to Yamāntaka," 56, 56n138

I
ignorance (*moha*), 17, 67, 73, 101, 116, 131n324, 270n789
  eliminating, 15
illusory body, 17
impure substances, 3, 164
  wrathful (*abhicāra homa*), 183–90
  See also five nectars (*pañcāmṛta*); poisons, neutralization of
Index of the Vajraśekhara Yoga Sūtra in Eighteen Sections (Amoghavajra), 21–22
Indra, 62n152, 119, 119n294, 301
insight (*vipaśyanā*), 15–16, 120n297
intention (*cetanā*), 5–6, 75, 241n638
Īśānaśivagurudevapaddhati, 117

J
Jayadrathayāmala (JY), 6, 155–56, 160–61, 172n413
joy (*muditā*), 121, 121n301, 257–58n726

K
Kakṣapuṭa Tantra, 174
Kāla, 60n145, 73, 75, 109, 225n548
Kāpālika practices, 129, 155–56
Kāraṇḍavyūha, 76
Kārttikeya, 73
Kaulajñānanirṇaya (Matsyendranātha), 160, 313n991
Khacakrapañcakastotra (Jñānanetra), 83
Kiraṇa Tantra, 171
kriyā tantras, 3, 13–14, 17, 152, 152n370, 220n553
Kṛṣṇācārya, 36–39

Kṛṣṇayamāri Tantra, 39n68, 89n225, 103, 108, 137, 206n471
Kublai Khan, 46–47nn94–96, 52
Kumāracandra, 39–40, 72, 77, 79, 119, 119n294

L

Lalitavajra, 1, 7, 8, 22–28, 34–35
 and *Vajrabhairava Tantra*, 81–94
Lcang skya Rol pa'i rdo rje, 53
liberation, 18, 39, 164, 166, 173, 181
 gateways of, 211n498, 274n812
love (*maitrī*), 121, 121n301, 257–58n726
luminosity, 17, 257–58n726, 261n733

M

mad laughter (*aṭṭahāsa*), 3, 9, 166–71, 218n523, 264n744
Madhyamaka, 36, 122n302, 127–28, 127n316, 259n729. *See also* Yogācāra tradition
Mahābhārata, 60–61
Mahādeva, 62n152, 67, 234n601, 266n755
 See also Śiva (Īśvara)
Mahākāla, 49, 60, 73, 75
Mahāparinirvāṇa Mahāsūtra, 93
Mahāvairocana, 8, 88, 261n733
Mahāvairocana Sūtra, 151–52
Mahāvajrabhairavamaṇḍala, 54
Mahāvastu, 61
Mahāvyutpatti, 15
Mahāyāna Mahāparinirvāṇa Sūtra, 241n638
Mahāyāna tradition, 9, 20, 37–38, 93, 119, 126–27, 131, 192, 201n453, 207n473, 241n638, 315n998
mahāyoga, 16, 16n5, 90, 267n761
Maheśvara, 62, 75, 76, 76n186, 77–78, 92n233. *See also* Bhairava Maheśvara
Mahiṣa (demon), 8, 80
Mahiṣāsuramardinī (goddess), 78n190, 79, 79n194
Maitrāyanīsaṃhitā, 60
Mal lo tsā ba Blo gros grags pa, 41
Mālatīmādhava, 155
Mañjughoṣa. *See* Mañjuśrī
Mañjuśrī, 2, 8, 26, 34, 35, 46–47n96, 62, 77, 84–85, 118–19, 123n303, 133, 309
 cult of, 9
 enjoyment body of, 70
 Jñānasattva, 129, 130–31n323, 259n729
 wrathful form of, 87–88 (see also Vajrabhairava)
 See also Mañjuvajra
Mañjuśrīmitra, 25
Mañjuśrīnāmasaṅgīti (MNS), 8, 24, 85, 86
Mañjuśriyamūlakalpa (MMK), 4, 6, 132, 178–79
 on tantric magic, 180–81
Mañjuvajra, 12, 129, 259–60n730, 304n949
mantra master, 119–20, 241–42, 274, 311
Māra, 19, 75, 92, 93
 four aspects of, 61–62
material body, 17
Māyājāla Tantra, 16, 21, 87, 89
meditation, 13–16, 64–65n158, 82n201, 118, 257–58n726, 302
 on four alternatives, 122n302
 on four sublime states, 127, 127n315
 See also insight (*vipaśyanā*); tranquility (*śamatha*)
merit, 20, 127, 221n537, 296n910
Metropolitan Museum of Art, 48, 52
mind
 and compassion, 5
 enlightened (*bodhicitta*), 73
 and Māra, 62
 purity of, 9, 162n388, 288n872
 undistracted, 275–76n817 (*See also* concentration)
 wrathful, 2, 72, 119
 See also awareness; consciousness
Mount Meru, 70, 70n172, 123n303
Mūlamadhyamakakārikā (Nāgārjuna), 107

N

Nāgārjuna, 127–28. *See also individual works*

nāgas, 72n177, 208n485
Śeṣa (nāga king), 306n959, 307n962
Nālandā Monastery, 9, 25, 84
Nāmamantrārthāvalokinī (NMAA), 8
Ngor evaṃ chos ldan Monastery, 45
Ngor maṇḍalas, 41–42, 45
Niśisaṃcāra, 169
Nityādisaṃgrahapaddhati (Takṣakavarta), 137
non-Buddhists (*tīrthikas*), 91–94, 92n231
nonduality, 9, 26, 123, 123n303, 164, 258n726, 259n729

O

obstacles, 18, 19, 20, 83, 90n227
eliminating, 16, 62, 130n323, 255n720
See also afflictive emotions (*kleśa*); cognitive obscurations
Oḍḍiyāna, 8, 22, 59n143, 81–84, 82n200, 316
offerings (*bali*), 16n6, 157, 206n471, 216n516–17, 217n520. *See also* fire offerings (*homa*); food; impure substances

P

Padmasambhava, 72n178, 82
painters (*citrakara*), 133–35, 278–80
Pañcakrama (Nāgārjuna), 162–63
passion (*rāga*), 266n755
paṭa. *See* sacred paintings (*paṭavidhānas*)
Pātañjalayogaśāstra, 14–15
Peking University Library, 197
perception, 121, 127n315, 163, 164, 165, 257–58n726, 271n791. *See also* sense fields (*āyatanas*)
Phag gru sne'u rdzong pa Drung chen Nam mkha' bzang po, 52
'Phags pa Blo gros rgyal mtshan, 7, 45–48, 46n94
Picumata-Brahmayāmala, 98, 236–37n617. *See also Brahmayāmala* (BY)
poisons, neutralization of, 181–83, 241n638
Prajñopāyaviniścayasiddhi, 9
primordial buddha (*ādibuddha*), 86
protective deities (*dharmapālas*), 49, 72nn177–78, 117
Purāṇic traditions, 8, 69, 78–80, 168n402
purification (*viśuddhi*), 130–31, 131n324, 273–74n811
purity, 9, 163n392, 164, 257
of mind, 9, 162n388, 165–66, 288n872
purpose (*prayojana*), 37–38, 39–40n65, 40n70, 243n643

Q

Qianlong, 52, 53

R

Rāmāyaṇa, 64
rebirth, 5, 70–71, 285n867, 313. *See also* heavens; hell
Ṛg Veda, 60, 71n176
ritual device (*yantra*), 97–100
drawing of, 100–105
and root mantra, 110
and Thirteen-Deity maṇḍala, 112
Rudra, 115n287, 129n321, 162, 205n464
Rwa lo tsā ba Rdo rje grags, 1–2, 6, 41, 51, 77–80

S

Sa skya tradition, 43–49, 192
sacred diagram (*maṇḍala*), 1, 95–97n240, 97n241, 114–15
entering, 166–71
Thirteen-Deity, 116
threefold Vajrabhairava, 52–53
Vajrabhairava, drawing of, 209–14
wind, 293n896
sacred paintings (*paṭavidhānas*), 132–37, 277–88
sacred spells (*mantras*), 1, 106–7, 125n309, 224n545, 311–12
extraction of (*mantroddhāraṇa*), 243–53
fire heart (*agnihṛdaya*), 148
heart, 118, 252n714
hūṃ syllable, 226n552, 236n617, 262n738
niśumbhana, 223n542
ten-syllable action, 117, 219n530, 227–28
thirty-two-syllable, 107–16, 228n562
Sādhanamālā, 35, 124n307, 131n323

Śaiva-Buddhist hostility, 92–93, 92n233, 93n235
Śaiva-Śākta traditions, 9, 64, 82, 136, 153–70, 172, 284–85n866
Śaivism, 3–4, 8, 10, 59–60, 59n143, 66–68, 76–77, 96n240, 115, 164–65, 166–71, 179, 186–87, 286–87n871. *See also Guhyasūtra* (NTGS); Śaiva-Buddhist hostility; Śaiva-Śākta traditions
Samantabhadra, 130n323
samayasattva, 129–30, 129n322
Saṃpuṭodbhava Tantra, 198, 260n733
saṃsāra, 5, 9, 121n301, 258n726, 263n740
Sanderson, Alexis, 153
Sarasvatī, 115, 205n464
Sarvabuddhasamāyogaḍākinījālasaṃvara Tantra, 115, 124n307, 154
Sarvakalpasamuccaya (Ānandagarbha), 275n817
Sarvatathāgatatattvasaṃgraha (STTS), 2–3, 153
selflessness, 92n232, 121, 257–58nn725–26
sense fields (*āyatanas*), 127n314, 162, 256n723
sexual practices, 16, 68, 124n307, 127n314, 159–60, 175–80, 307–8
  semen retention, 7, 67–68
Siddhaikavīra, 4
siddhas, 25, 81, 160, 174n418
  See also yogins
Siklós, Bulcsu, 10
Śiva (Īśvara), 61n150, 62n152, 80, 90, 109, 119, 119n294, 129n321, 185–86. *See also* Bhairava Maheśvara; Mahādeva; Śaivism
śivaliṅga, 186–87
six classes of beings, 273n804
skillful means (*upāya*), 16, 17, 18–19, 20, 201n453, 202n453
Skyo lineage, 41
Skyo ston 'Od 'byung gnas, 41
Śoṇaśrī, 35–36
Śrīmañjuśriya Tantra, 242, 248
Śrīvajrabhairavatantraṭīkā (Akṣobhya), 31, 32–34
Śrīvajrabhairavatantraṭippaṇīnāma (Vajrasiddha), 31, 35–36
Srong btsan sgam po, 41n72
subtle veins (*nāḍī*), 155–56
supernatural powers (*siddhi*), 82n201, 83, 96, 148–49n367, 152, 157, 162, 171–73, 177, 178, 218, 220n533, 237n617, 313n991
  accomplishing, through visualization, 301–11
  highest, 287–88n872
  of Lalitavajra, 25
  three types of, 286n871
supreme reality, 62n152
Susiddhikara Sūtra, 148, 149n369, 189n450, 275n817

T

taming, 71n176, 72n178, 74, 75, 90, 119
Tantrāloka (Abhinavagupta), 164, 165, 237n617
tantras, 9, 10, 13, 16
  fourfold classification of, 17
  resultant and method, 40
  three Black cycles, 90
  threefold division of, 36, 36nn57–58
  See also individual tantras
tantric Buddhism, 5, 9, 10, 13–20, 126, 199
  development of, 1, 2
  See also deity yoga; tantric rituals; *individual tantras*
tantric initiation (*dīkṣā, abhiṣeka*), 96, 96n240, 154
tantric magic, 10
  aggressive, 5–6
  attraction, 239
  combat, 173–75
  fever, 183–90, 227
  love, 175–80
  paralysis, 231–32, 238, 240–41, 293–94
  powers (*siddhi*), 13, 171–73
  resurrection, 305–6
  underworld, 180–81
  See also aggressive rites (*abhicāra*); tantric rituals
tantric rituals, 1, 4, 7, 95, 138, 301–11
  early, magical, 171–90

magical, 35
for peace and prosperity, 295–96
possession (*parakāyapraveśa*), 301–2n941
sacrifices in, 298–99
See also tantric magic; *individual practices*
Tāranātha, 8, 18–20, 31
on Lalitavajra, 22–23, 25–26, 26nn36–37, 27n40
thought constructs (*vikalpa*), 164, 216n515, 266n754, 268n765, 274n815, 275n817, 278n825
three ālokas, 271n791
three "sweets," 139n351
Tibetan Buddhism, 2, 7, 41–43. *See also* tantric Buddhism; *individual traditions*
Tibetan Script Edict (*'Ja sa bod yig ma*), 46
Tibetan treasure tradition (gter ma), 81–84, 81n198, 83
tranquility (*śamatha*), 15–16, 165
Triple Cycle of the Black One, 43
truth body (*dharmakāya*), 17, 202–3n453
Tsong kha pa, 49–52, 54, 55
Tugh Temür, 48
two accumulations, 20. *See also* merit; wisdom (*prajñā*)
two obscurations, 37–38. *See also* afflictive emotions (*kleśa*); cognitive obscurations
two truths, 273n805

U
Uddyota (Kṣemarāja), 139n351
union (*yoga*), 3, 4, 14–16, 36n57, 67, 90, 95, 118, 206n471, 274n815, 302n941, 304n951, 310n975. *See also* deity yoga
Ūrdhvaliṅga, 66–68

V
Vairocanamāyājāla, 17
Vaiṣṇavism, 115. *See also* Viṣṇu
Vajrabhairava, 2–3, 130
etymology of, 202n453
Forty-Nine-Deity, 32, 41, 52
iconography of, 7–8, 52–54, 74, 263–67, 272–74
ithyphallic feature, 66–68, 262n738
origins of, 62–63, 69–80
ornaments of, 267–71
Thirteen-Deity, 1
variations of, 41–42
See also Vikṛtānana; Yamāntaka
Vajrabhairava Tantra
commentaries on, 7, 28, 31–40
dates of, 21–22
lineage diagrams, 29–30
origin of, 81–94
overview of, 1–2, 6, 8–10, 191–93
practicing, 4–5
transmission of, 3–4, 7–8, 40–57
See also Vajrabhairava-Yamāntaka cycle
Vajrabhairavatantrapañjikā (Kumāracandra), 31, 36–40
Vajrabhairavatantravṛttyalaṃkāropadeśanāma (Lalitavajra), 31, 34–35
Vajrabhairava-Yamāntaka cycle, 26–28, 59–63, 81, 84–91, 108
in Dge lugs tradition, 49–55
in India, 59–63
in Japan, 56–57
in Mongolia, 55–56, 55n136
in Nepal, 57
in Sa skya tradition, 43–49
in Tibet, 17, 26–27, 32, 40–43, 44–45n87, 174n418
See also *Vajrabhairava Tantra*
Vajradhara, 37, 130n323, 301
Vajrajvālodayā (Ānandagarbha), 170
Vajrakāla, 60–61
Vajramāyājāla Tantra, 8–9
Vajrāmṛtatantra, 62n152
Vajrapāṇi, 74n182, 76, 90, 162
Vajrasiddha, 35–36
Vajrayoginī, 4, 25, 233n595
Vārāhī, 115, 205n464
Verardi, Giovanni, 92–93
views (*dṛṣṭi*), 62n152, 268n770
wrong, 266n755
Vikramaśīla Monastery, 28
Vikṛtānana, 63–66
Vilāsavajra (Sgeg pa'i rdo rje), 7, 9, 16, 22–25
Vīṇāśikha Tantra, 313n992

Virūpa, 48, 48n102
Viṣṇu, 62, 62n152, 75, 129n321, 266n755. *See also* Vaiṣṇavism
visualization (*dhyāna*), 35, 36, 88, 118–33, 146–48, 219n528, 255–76
  and siddhis, 301–11

W

wisdom (*prajñā*), 17, 19–20, 20n12, 52n122, 120n297, 202n453, 214n508
  perfection of (*prajñāpāramitā*), 86
  transcendental, 19, 20
worship (*pūjā*), 119, 127, 216n518, 237n617, 238n624, 257n724, 280n840, 302n941. *See also* offerings (*bali*)

Y

yakṣiṇīs, 177–79
Yama, 2, 8, 19, 57, 59–63, 60n145, 70–71, 304n949
  representation of, 230–31, 231n577
  Sadomeya (Yama's dog), 108
Yama Dharmarāja (Kālarūpa), 49
Yamāntaka, 17, 56–57, 56n138, 59–63, 133. *See also* Daiitoku myōō; Vajrabhairava
Yamarāja
  mantra of, 34, 35–36
  myth of, 8, 69–77
Yama-Yamāntaka cycle, 7–8, 26–27, 59–63
Yesün Temür, 48
yoga. *See* meditation; union (*yoga*)
yoga tantras, 3, 13–14, 153, 221n541, 223–24n545, 259n729
Yogācāra tradition, 36, 127n315
yoganiruttara (unexcelled) tantras, 1, 17, 17n7, 18–20
Yogaratnamālā, 36
Yogasūtrabhāṣya, 14–15
yoginīs, 179–80, 284n866, 312n982
yogins, 82n201, 118, 160, 163, 206n470–71, 252n714. *See also* siddhas
Yonghegong (Lama Temple), 54
Yongle emperor, 52

Z

Zhang Cog gru lo tsā ba Shes rab, 31–32, 41
Zhang lineage (*zhang lugs*), 31–32, 41, 41n73

About the Author

Aleksandra Wenta is an associate professor in Indology and Tibetology at the University of Florence, Italy. She holds an MPhil and a PhD from the University of Oxford and a Vidyāvāridhi (PhD) degree from Banaras Hindu University. She was an assistant professor and a member of the founding faculty of Buddhist studies at Nālandā University (2016–20) and a fellow-in-residence at the Indian Institute of Advanced Study, Shimla (2012–14). Her research focuses on the history, ritual, and literature of tantric Buddhism and Śaivism and Indo-Tibetan Buddhism, and she recently coedited the volume *Tibetan Magic: Past and Present* (Bloomsbury, 2024).

Studies in Indian and Tibetan Buddhism
Titles Previously Published

Among Tibetan Texts
History and Literature of the Himalayan Plateau
E. Gene Smith

Approaching the Great Perfection
Simultaneous and Gradual Methods of Dzogchen Practice in the Longchen Nyingtig
Sam van Schaik

Authorized Lives
Biography and the Early Formation of Geluk Identity
Elijah S. Ary

The Buddha's Single Intention
Drigung Kyobpa Jikten Sumgön's Vajra Statements of the Early Kagyü Tradition
Jan-Ulrich Sobisch

Buddhism Between Tibet and China
Edited by Matthew T. Kapstein

The Buddhist Philosophy of the Middle
Essays on Indian and Tibetan Madhyamaka
David Seyfort Ruegg

Buddhist Teaching in India
Johannes Bronkhorst

A Direct Path to the Buddha Within
Gö Lotsāwa's Mahāmudrā Interpretation of the Ratnagotravibhāga
Klaus-Dieter Mathes

The Essence of the Ocean of Attainments
The Creation Stage of the Guhyasamaja Tantra according to Panchen Losang Chökyi Gyaltsen
Translated by Yael Bentor and Penpa Dorjee

Foundations of Dharmakīrti's Philosophy
John D. Dunne

Freedom from Extremes
Gorampa's "Distinguishing the Views" and the Polemics of Emptiness
José Ignacio Cabezón and Geshe Lobsang Dargyay

Himalayan Passages
Tibetan and Newar Studies in Honor of Hubert Decleer
Benjamin Bogin and Andrew Quintman

Histories of Tibet
Essays in Honor of Leonard W. J. van der Kuijp
Edited by Kurtis R. Schaeffer, Jue Liang, and William A. McGrath

How Do Mādhyamikas Think?
And Other Essays on the Buddhist Philosophy of the Middle
Tom J. F. Tillemans

Jewels of the Middle Way
The Madhyamaka Legacy of Atiśa and His Early Tibetan Followers
James B. Apple

Living Treasure
Tibetan and Buddhist Studies in Honor of Janet Gyatso
Edited by Holly Gayley and Andrew Quintman

Luminous Lives
The Story of the Early Masters of the Lam 'bras Tradition in Tibet
Cyrus Stearns

Mind Seeing Mind
Mahamudra and the Geluk Tradition of Tibetan Buddhism
Roger R. Jackson

Minding the Buddha's Business
Essays in Honor of Gregory Schopen
Edited by Daniel Boucher and Shayne Clarke

Mipham's Beacon of Certainty
Illuminating the View of Dzogchen, the Great Perfection
John Whitney Pettit

Ocean of Attainments
The Creation Stage of the Guhyasamāja Tantra according to Khedrup Jé
Translated by Yael Bentor and Penpa Dorjee

Omniscience and the Rhetoric of Reason
Śāntarakṣita and Kamalaśīla on Rationality, Argumentation, and Religious Authority
Sara L. McClintock

Reason's Traces
Identity and Interpretation in Indian and Tibetan Buddhist Thought
Matthew T. Kapstein

Reasons and Lives in Buddhist Traditions
Studies in Honor of Matthew Kapstein
Edited by Dan Arnold, Cécile Ducher, and Pierre-Julien Harter

Remembering the Lotus-Born
Padmasambhava in the History of Tibet's Golden Age
Daniel A. Hirshberg

Resurrecting Candrakīrti
Disputes in the Tibetan Creation of Prāsaṅgika
Kevin A. Vose

Saraha's Spontaneous Songs
With the Commentaries by Advayavajra and Mokṣākaragupta
Klaus-Dieter Mathes and Péter-Dániel Szántó

Scripture, Logic, Language
Essays on Dharmakīrti and His Tibetan Successors
Tom J. F. Tillemans

Sexuality in Classical South Asian Buddhism
José I. Cabezón

The Svātantrika-Prāsaṅgika Distinction
What Difference Does a Difference Make?
Edited by Georges Dreyfus and Sara McClintock

Vajrayoginī
Her Visualizations, Rituals, and Forms
Elizabeth English

About Wisdom Publications

Wisdom Publications is the leading publisher of classic and contemporary Buddhist books and practical works on mindfulness. To learn more about us or to explore our other books, please visit our website at wisdom.org or contact us at the address below.

Wisdom Publications
132 Perry Street
New York, NY 10014 USA

We are a 501(c)(3) organization, and donations in support of our mission are tax deductible.

Wisdom Publications is affiliated with the Foundation for the Preservation of the Mahayana Tradition (FPMT).